ZION'S TRUMPET

1856 and 1857
Welsh Mormon Periodical

Volume 9: 1856
Volume 10: 1857

ZION'S TRUMPET

1856 and 1857
Welsh Mormon Periodical

Volume 9: 1856
Volume 10: 1857

Translated and Edited by
Ronald D. Dennis

RSC

RELIGIOUS STUDIES CENTER
BRIGHAM YOUNG UNIVERSITY

DESERET
BOOK

RELIGIOUS STUDIES CENTER
BRIGHAM YOUNG UNIVERSITY

DESERET BOOK

Published by the Religious Studies Center, Brigham Young University, Provo, Utah, in cooperation with Deseret Book Company, Salt Lake City.

http://rsc.byu.edu

© 2017 by Brigham Young University. All rights reserved.

Printed in the United States of America by Sheridan Books.

Any uses of this material beyond those allowed by the exemptions in US copyright law, such as section 107, "Fair Use," and section 108, "Library Copying," require the written permission of the publisher, Religious Studies Center, 185 HGB, Brigham Young University, Provo, Utah 84602. The views expressed herein are the responsibility of the authors and do not necessarily represent the position of Brigham Young University or the Religious Studies Center.

DESERET BOOK is a registered trademark of Deseret Book Company.

ISBN: 978-1-9443-9411-0
Retail US $35.99
Jacket art courtesy of Wikimedia Commons. Jacket design by Jacob F. Frandsen.

Library of Congress Cataloging-in-Publication Data

Names: Dennis, Ronald D., 1940- translator, editor.
Title: Zion's trumpet : 1856 and 1857 : Welsh Mormon periodical / translated and edited by Ronald D. Dennis.
Other titles: Udgorn Seion. Cyfrol IX-X. English.
Description: Provo : Religious Studies Center at BYU, 2017. | "Published by the Religious Studies Center, Brigham Young University, Provo, Utah, in cooperation with Deseret Book Company, Salt Lake City." | "Volume 9: 1856; Volume 10: 1857." | Includes index.
Identifiers: LCCN 2016036693 | ISBN 9781944394110 (alk. paper)
Subjects: LCSH: Church of Jesus Christ of Latter-day Saints--Periodicals. | Mormon Church--Wales--Periodicals. | Church of Jesus Christ of Latter-day Saints--Wales--History--19th century--Sources. | Mormon Church--Wales--History--19th century--Sources.
Classification: LCC BX8601 .U359 2017 | DDC 289.3/42909034--dc23 LC record available at https://lccn.loc.gov/2016036693

Dedicated to Daniel Daniels
The Reluctant Editor

Udgorn Seion, vols. 9 and 10 (1856 and 1857). Photo courtesy of L. Tom Perry Special Collections, Harold B. Lee Library, Brigham Young University. (The binder omitted "X" on the spine.)

Contents

List of Illustrations xi
Foreword. xvii
Introduction xix
Facsimile Translation Considerations xxxiii
Acknowledgments xxxvii
Annotated Contents. xxxix

Translations

Volume 9: *Zion's Trumpet*, 1856 . . . . 408 pages
Index cxli

Volume 10: *Zion's Trumpet*, 1857 . . . . 408 pages
Index cliii

Illustrations

Daniel Daniels. v
Udgorn Seion, vols. 9 and 10. vii
Udgorn Seion, vol. 9, no. 1 xii
Udgorn Seion, vol. 10, no. 1 xiii
Dan Jones. xiv
John S. Davis. xiv
Daniel Daniels. xv
Benjamin P. Evans xv
William Ajax. xv
Udgorn Seion, vol. 14, no. 31 xxxi
Udgorn Seion, vol. 9 title page . . . . . . facing translation
Udgorn Seion, vol. 10 title page . . . . . facing translation

UDGORN SEION,

NEU

Seren y Saint.

RHIF. 1.]   IONAWR 5, 1856.   [CYF. IX.

YR IAITH SAESONAEG.

(O'r "Star.")

Y MAE yn naturiol i ddynion garu y wlad yn mha un eu ganwyd ac eu dysgwyd, i lynu wrth ddulliau ac arferiadau eu tadau, ac i gredu mai yr iaith yn mha un y dysgasant gyntaf i floesg-ddweyd eu hanghenion plentynaidd yw y perffeithiaf o bob iaith arall. Y mae yn dda y fod hyn felly, a thuedda i wneuthur dynion yn foddlonach i'w sefyllfa, ac ni chwennychem ei gael fel arall er mwyn cyfnewidiad yn unig.

Saint y Dyddiau Diweddaf ydynt bobl neillduol yr Arglwydd, a gyfodwyd er cyflawni ei ddybenion yn y byd, i'r hyn y mae yr ufydd dod perffeithiaf yn anhebgorol. Mewn trefn i bobl ddyfod yn berffaith mewn undeb rhaid iddynt fod yn un yn mhob peth a ddichon ddylanwadu ar eu gweithredoedd, pa un a fyddant o natur grefyddol, wladol, cymdeithasol, neu gartrefol. Ni ellir byth wneuthur hyn yn effeithiol heb gyfrwng neu iaith gyffredinol, drwy yr hon y gall y naill berson drosglwyddo meddylddrychau neu egwyddorion i'r llall, yn yr un goleuni yn mha un eu derbyniwyd.

Bydd y Saint rhyw ddiwrnod yn feddiannol ar iaith bur, o darddiad Nefol, gyffelyb i'r hon a lefarodd Adda yn Ngardd Eden pan y llefarodd yr Arglwydd wrtho ef gydag awel y dydd, a'r hon etto a fydd yn gyfrwng cyfrinach pan y daw dynion yn ddigon perffaith i ymddyddan â'r Duwiau.

[PRIS 1g.

UDGORN SEION,

NEU:

Seren y Saint.

RHIF. 1.]   IONAWR 10, 1857.   [CYF. X.

CRYNODEB O DDYSGEIDIAETH Y LLYWYDD EZRA T. BENSON, YN NEUADD Y SAINT, ABERTAWY, TACHWEDD, 11, 1856.

[*A gofnodwyd gan William Lewis.*]

GYDA eich sylw caredig, frodyr a chwiorydd, gwnaf ychydig sylwadau, ac ni wn yn amgen nag y cymmeraf destun i ddechreu, yr hwn a fydd yn eiriau o ddoethineb i'r Saint, ac i bawb eraill a ewyllysiant wrando.

Ystyriaf yr egyr faes eang o fy mlaen. Saint, edrychwch yma, a rheddwch eich sylw i mi tra y llefarwyf. Pe byddech chwi wedi dilyn cyhyd ag ydwyf fi wedi dilyn ar bregethu, chwithau hefyd a ddymunech gael sylw. Nid wyf yn dysgwyl, wrth gwrs, y gallaf reoli cymmaint ar sylw eraill a ddichon fod yn bresennol. Wel, yn nadguddiadau Iesu Grist, trefn yw cyfraith gyntaf y nefoedd, ac heb drefn, annichonadwy ydyw i adeiladu y gynnulleidfa hon.

Daethom yma gyda yr amcan o addoli Duw: yr ydwyf fi wedi dyfod i lefaru wrthych yn enw yr Arglwydd, ac nid yn fy enw i fy hun, nac yn fy ngallu i fy hun, nac i lefaru wrthych eiriau o ddoethineb o fy eiddo fy hun, ond y cyfryw ag ydwyt wedi cael profiad o'u gwirionedd a'u hangenrheidrwydd, a'r cyfryw a ddymuna yr Arglwydd ddadguddio i'w bobl—am y rhai hyn y dymunwyf lefaru heno.

1   PRIS 1½C.

Dan Jones (1810–62).
Editor of *Prophwyd y Jubili* 1846–48 and of
Udgorn Seion 1854–56. Pioneer of Welsh Mormon
publishing. Author of many Mormon pamphlets,
poems, and hymns in Welsh.

John S. Davis (1822–82).
Editor of *Udgorn Seion* 1849–53.
Translator of the LDS standard works from
English to Welsh. Author of numerous Mormon
pamphets, poems, and hymns in Welsh.

Daniel Daniels (1807–79).
Editor of *Udgorn Seion* 1856–57.

Benjamin P. Evans (1818–93).
Editor of *Udgorn Seion* 1858–61.

William Ajax (1832–99).
Assistant to George Q. Cannon, who was
editor of *Udgorn Seion* 1861–62.

Foreword

"It is a compulsory fact that editors must have something interesting or disturbing always at hand, or they will not satisfy the corrupt appetite of their numerous readers. . . . A lie flies to the ends of the earth before truth can put on her shoes." So wrote *Zion's Trumpet* editor Daniel Daniels in his 4 July 1857 issue regarding Judge William W. Drummond's accusations about Governor Brigham Young of Utah Territory. This current compilation of *Zion's Trumpet* reveals the gathering of storm clouds leading to a federal excursion to replace Young in what later became known as the Utah War.

These translations of *Zion's Trumpet* matter deeply because they record vital historical details. They also turn readers' hearts to their fathers and mothers, allowing us to read the stories of our Welsh Mormon forebears and to personally feel their triumphs and tragedies. As readers, we smile at the very quotable lines as the authors employ a more flamboyant and fiery style than most today—unless you count Internet posts! But we appreciate that they recorded Welsh membership statistics, details of the handcart travels, and news of the impending Utah War. And we admire them for writing with the fire of faith.

Zion's Trumpet has personal meaning to me as an editor. When I began copyediting the series in 2002, I learned that Dan Jones was the second-great-grandfather of Ronald D. Dennis, the editor and translator of this series. Only later did I learn that Jones's successor as editor was Daniel Daniels, my third-great-grandfather. Jones left Wales in April 1856, and Daniels took his place not only as president of the mission but also as editor of *Zion's Trumpet*.

Daniels did not want to go into publishing, but he inherited the duties of preaching the gospel of Christ and also defending the kingdom in written form. Beginning with the 3 April 1856 issue, the pen passed from "Renowned Editor" Dan Jones (as Daniels called him) to the "Reluctant Editor" (as Daniels was nicknamed by Ron Dennis). Daniels humbly acknowledged his predecessor in these words, "We are far from being so conceited as to claim the same skill in a war as an old soldier who has been in the battle fighting with the family of the devil as if for life, and having done so from the first time the banner of Jesus waved over the hills of Gwalia until now, except for the time he was escorting a host of the Lord's Saints to their sure place of refuge."

In that light, another vital part of Daniels's duties as mission president involved raising funds and helping families prepare to gather to "Zion" in Utah. He served in both positions until December 1857, and his mission lasted well over five years. This reluctant editor passed the pen to another and returned home to his beloved family in Salt Lake City. He later moved to Brigham City and finally to Malad, Idaho. In 1865, Daniels was appointed president of the Malad Branch, then as bishop when it became a ward in 1866, serving in that capacity until 1877.

As a final note, with this last installment of *Zion's Trumpet*, Ron Dennis and I are grateful that the translation project brought together descendants of two fast friends, fellow editors, and committed Church members. We aspire to the same qualities.

R. Devan Jensen
Executive Editor at the
Religious Studies Center

Introduction

Volumes 9 and 10 of *Zion's Trumpet* are the last extant volumes of this Welsh Mormon periodical. A decade earlier in 1846, Dan Jones became the founding editor of *Prophet of the Jubilee*, the forerunner of *Zion's Trumpet*. The name change was effected in January 1849 when Jones was about to emigrate, leaving young John Davis as his replacement. Four years later Jones was back in Wales on his second mission. During all of 1853, the first year of this mission, Jones served in a support role to both William Phillips, his replacement as mission president four years earlier, and to John Davis in the publication of the periodical. At the outset of 1854 Jones began his second term as both president of the Welsh mission and as editor of the periodical.

During 1854 *Zion's Trumpet* appeared weekly until August when Jones elected to assume a less pressure-filled biweekly schedule. And in September 1854 the headquarters of the mission and the press were moved from Merthyr Tydfil to Swansea. Jones was released in January 1856 as mission president but continued as editor of the periodical for its first seven issues of that year.

Dan Jones chose as his lead article for the 5 January 1856 issue of *Zion's Trumpet* the Welsh translation of "The English Language," President Orson Pratt's encouragement for all foreign-language converts to Mormonism to learn the lingua franca of their new religion. This was timely advice to Welsh converts since the instruction given by Church leaders to all Mormon converts in Britain was to relocate to Utah where the Welsh language was known only by the relatively small number of Welsh Mormons who had settled there over the past seven years. The article no doubt provided motivation for some of the Welsh to study English, but there is little evidence that more than a small percentage of them could ever understand Brigham Young without the benefit of an interpreter.

Bilingual Captain Dan Jones had served his compatriots and fellow Mormon converts during the previous three years in Wales as a missionary. As his mission ended he was to serve over five hundred of them during the 34-day voyage on the *S. Curling* from Liverpool to Boston (19 April to 23 May 1856) and again during the 8-day train journey from Boston to Iowa City. There he helped them get ready for their handcart trek to Salt Lake City. Jones, however, would cross the plains in the small "carriage company" with Franklin D. Richards and a few others.

A goal far more important to Jones than having Welsh Mormons learn English was to locate the "Welsh-speaking Indians," the supposed descendants of a group of Welsh led to America by one Prince Madoc in about 1170. Following the conclusion of his first mission to Wales seven years earlier, Jones had gone with Parley P. Pratt on his "Southern Expedition" in hopes of finding the "Maddocians." Although unsuccessful in this quest he continued hopeful as evidenced by his brief article in the 15 March 1856 issue of *Zion's Trumpet*.[1] His ultimate objective continued to be to find this elusive group, convert them to Mormonism and take some of them back to Wales to preach the gospel to their distant compatriots. Lamentably, Jones died at the age of 51 in 1862 in Provo, Utah, his dream unfulfilled.

Jones achieved considerable success, however, in gaining adepts to Mormonism during his two missions to Wales. He started off on the first of these from Nauvoo just a few weeks following the Martyrdom of Joseph Smith, a man whom he greatly admired and one who had prophesied that Jones would survive the events at Carthage and return to his native Wales as a missionary. A fortnight prior to the Martyrdom, Brother Joseph told his Welsh friend that he had over a thousand dollars to give him as payment for Jones's half of the *Maid of Iowa*, a steamboat they owned jointly. Speaking of a $1,200 check he had recently received, Joseph told Dan: "As soon as I can get it cashed you shall have $1,100 of it, and the start for Wales, not with your fingers in your mouth but prepared to buy a Press, and do business aright."[2] More than a decade later Dan Jones explained in a letter to Thomas Bullock that he did not ever receive the promised money; however, he remained philosophical: "Thrilled with the prospects of my mission I left all, rejoicing in the exchange of a steamboat for an Eldership on the deck of the never sinking ship of life."[3]

Although he was unable to have his own press during his first mission (from 1845 to 1849) Dan Jones published the following:

- fourteen pamphlets with a combined total of 224 pages
- a 102-page history of the Church
- a 288-page scriptural commentary
- a 56-page hymnal
- 580 pages (30 full numbers) of *Prophet of the Jubilee*, a monthly periodical

All of these items were printed in Welsh and had as their express purpose that of converting the entire principality of Wales to Mormonism. Without the promised money to purchase a press of his own, Dan Jones ended up using the one owned by his older brother John, a Congregationalist minister in Carmarthenshire. On this press he printed all but 80 of the 1,250 total pages that came from his pen during this four-year period. During Jones's first mission over 3,000 of his compatriots heeded his message and converted to Mormonism, an effort that earned him the praise of President Gordon B. Hinckley many years later when he included Dan Jones among the "half dozen or so most productive missionaries in the history of the Church."[4]

At the close of his first mission in December 1848 Dan Jones selected his protégé, 26-year-old John Davis, to oversee all Church publications in Wales. Three years earlier Davis had been the typesetter for the Reverend John Jones when Elder Dan Jones printed his Welsh translation of *Proclamation of the Twelve Apostles* on his brother's press, widely labeled the "prostitute press" for compromising its principles to publish the Mormon message. The message of the *Proclamation* resonated with Davis and resulted in his baptism four months later.

During the five years that John Davis was the Church printer (1849–1853) he published numerous pamphlets, a hymnal, and six volumes of *Zion's Trumpet*, the successor to *Prophet of the Jubilee*. He also translated and published the standard works of Mormonism in an 18-month period. During 1853, Davis's last year as editor of *Zion's Trumpet*, his most frequent contributor to the publication was Dan Jones, then back on his second mission to Wales. And when Davis sailed to America in 1854, Jones resumed the editorial reins of the periodical.

In addition to his responsibilities associated with *Zion's Trumpet* over the next two years Jones also served as the president of the Church in Wales. Daniel Daniels, first counselor to Dan Jones in the presidency, was called to replace him as the presiding officer in Wales at the beginning of 1856 and as the editor of *Zion's Trumpet* beginning with issue 8 (April 12) of that year. In his first editorial Daniels verbally bowed to the "former Renowned Editor" by expressing his feelings of inadequacy: "We trust the Saints will sympathize in the most sincere way with our inability to function in such a responsible and important stewardship, and to fill it as did our more able Predecessor."[5]

There was yet another reason for Daniels's reluctance to be the substitute for his friend and mentor—after nearly a four-year absence from his wife and family in Utah he fully expected to be on the same ship home as Dan Jones. After all, they had traveled together back to Wales after receiving their mission calls from Brigham Young in August 1852. Mary Daniels expressed her feelings in a letter at learning of her husband's extension: "This news was not sweet to me at first, but, as you said in your letter, 'that the will of the Lord be done, and his counsel be respected,' is my wish, although it may not always be in accordance with the feelings of human nature."[6] She apparently was led to understand that the added time would be for just a year, as in her 30 March 1857 letter she wrote, "I was thinking you would be released to return to the bosom of the Church, and to your dear family, this year."[7] But again she expressed her support and her prayers for his well being as he extended his service for yet another year.

Daniels sounds overwhelmed as he praises the "remarkable sound of the *Trumpet*" under "the skillful editorship of its former

Editor." And there is a tone of discouragement as he laments: "Not only did our President and Editor leave our midst, but many of the old faithful, mighty, and experienced soldiers have also gone, yes, some of the bravest."[8] Daniels's apprehension and trepidation were ill-founded, however, as he revealed his own leadership skills and editorial abilities over the following two years.

Those who were selected to sail on the *S. Curling* with Dan Jones were from among the most faithful Church members in Wales, some having converted a decade or more previously. Thus many of the branch and conference presidents who were left to serve under Daniels were less experienced and often less committed leaders. Perhaps because of the loss of so many strong leaders in Wales, President Franklin D. Richards assigned Israel Evans and Benjamin Ashby, two seasoned American elders, to serve as counselors to Daniel Daniels in the presidency of the Welsh mission. Neither Evans nor Ashby spoke Welsh, although Wales was the land of Evans's forebears. In a letter to Daniel Daniels published in *Zion's Trumpet* under the title of "Greeting of Elder Israel Evans to the Welsh Saints" Evans tells of his excitement to be assigned to labor in Wales. He quotes President Franklin D. Richards as telling him, "Brother Israel—I want you and Brother Ashby to go to Wales to labor, and to learn the Welsh language, which will be an eternal blessing to you."[9] There is no evidence that either of the two learned Welsh. In fact, to the present day there is no record of any non-Welsh-speaking person's ever managing to learn Welsh to do missionary work in Wales.

There were, however, several from among the Welsh members who were of enormous help to Daniels in his responsibilities as editor of *Zion's Trumpet*. One of these who exhibited a high level of dedication and an equally high level of education was young David John from Pembrokeshire. David had converted to Mormonism at age sixteen, but his father forbade him at that time from having any further association with the Mormons. The missionaries who baptized him counseled David to obey his father until he came of age at which time he was to come back to the true religion. He ended up studying at an academy in Haverfordwest and began preaching in the Baptist chapels, one of which was the chapel in his home town of Little Newcastle. His father shed tears of joy at seeing his son at the pulpit; however, these became tears of sorrow in early 1856 when David's father learned of his son's return to Mormonism, a reversal that was prompted by a dream the night of 28 January 1856 in which 23-year-old David was instructed by an angel to be true to his Mormon beliefs. Thereupon, David composed a poem which he entitled "Feeling of a Young Saint" in which he declared that if his return to Mormonism was a "loss" to his father it was a "great gain" to him. This poem was published in *Zion's Trumpet*, as were several others of his poems and letters.[10] Despite the outrage of his mother, the bitter disappointment of his father, and the shouting of friends and neighbors David would not be dissuaded. On 31 March 1856 his father died; at the funeral David John was accused of causing his father's death. This "prodigal son" transformed his Baptist sermons into the Mormon message of the Restoration and served as a missionary for the next five years before emigrating.

Another "prodigal son" who provided active and avid support to Daniels with the production of *Zion's Trumpet* was Dewi Elfed Jones, the former Baptist minister who after four years of faithful membership in the Welsh Mormon community was excommunicated for "moving pounds into his pocket" that rightfully belonged to the Church.[11] In his 3 May 1856 letter of reconciliation Dewi Elfed Jones offers up his "sincere repentance" for the "awful offences" he was guilty of just a year earlier.[12] Daniel Daniels announces publicly in the same issue of *Zion's Trumpet* that Dewi Elfed had been forgiven and was received back into the fold with open arms.[13] Dewi Elfed proved to be of great assistance to Daniel Daniels by translating materials from English into Welsh for the periodical and also carrying out an assignment to "travel throughout the conferences of the South."

Thomas Harris, a convert of long standing, was also a faithful supporter of Daniel Daniels with the production of *Zion's Trumpet*. In addition to serving as President of the West Glamorgan Conference, Harris was also the printer of the periodical and contributor of several articles and poems during 1856.

In his opening editorial for the first issue of the 1857 *Zion's Trumpet* Daniel Daniels echoes his feelings of nine months earlier: "Your humble and inexperienced trumpeter acknowledges his lack of skill to occupy such an honorable and high office, especially when he remembers his worthy predecessor." Despite his inadequacies, however, he declares that with the "energetic assistance" of his close supporters he is willing to "make the attempt for yet another year, and to trumpet from the heart."[14]

Daniels places as the opening article for volume 10 (1857) of *Zion's Trumpet* a summary of the teaching of President Ezra T. Benson given on 11 November 1856 in Swansea to the Welsh Saints. Benson would return to Wales on 12 March 1857 with an assignment from his fellow apostle Orson Pratt, President of the Church in the British Isles, to preach the Reformation to Church members in Wales. A few weeks earlier Orson Pratt had received instructions from Brigham Young to begin the Reformation in Britain, the purpose of which was to aggressively encourage all baptized members of the Church to recommit to the teachings of the gospel and rise to a higher level of obedience to its principles. This included answering a number of interview questions designed to measure their willingness to live the gospel at a much higher level than was currently the general practice. Also required was a manifestation of their commitment by being re-baptized.

During the first part of 1857 two non-Welsh-speaking American elders, William Miller and James Taylor, arrived in Wales to replace Daniels's outgoing counselors Israel Evans and Benjamin Ashby. The major theme for the remainder of Daniels's presidency was the Restoration. Much reference is made to this topic in *Zion's Trumpet*, and the missionaries' letters printed in the periodical customarily included a progress report of their preaching of the Reformation.

The most frequent letter writer during the second half of 1857 was Pastor John E. Jones who was assigned to travel throughout the Conferences of North Wales. Daniels jokingly referred to Jones's conference reports of the North as being "From the *Weekly Gazette* of Pastor Jones."[15] Daniels's counselor James Taylor was with Pastor John E. Jones in North Wales and wrote: "I am managing splendidly among my adopted compatriots; for I feel myself as much a Welshman as anyone in the kingdom of God."[16]

The title page for volume 10 of *Zion's Trumpet*, along with a foreword and a list of contents, was printed with the 26 December issue for 1857. In the foreword Daniels expresses his feelings for his fellow Welsh converts to the gospel: "During the five years of our mission in Wales we have perceived examples of the faithfulness and devotion of the Welsh Saints with the work of our God that will never be deleted from our memory."[17]

Daniels's replacement as president of the Church in Wales and as editor of *Zion's Trumpet* was Benjamin Pearce Evans, a thirty-nine-year-old convert of 1846 from Cardiganshire. Prior to this new assignment Evans had served as president of the Monmouth Conference and had contributed but three conference reports to the periodical. Over the next three years and three months, however, he published more than any other editor of a Welsh Mormon periodical. The following table shows the comparison:

	Time as Editor	# of issues	# of pages
Dan Jones	4 years, 9 months	102	1,162
John Davis	5 years	129	2,352
Daniel Daniels	1 year, 9 months	45	710
Benjamin Evans	3 years, 3 months	170	2,704

The totals for Dan Jones include the 2 years and 6 months he served as editor of *Prophet of the Jubilee* and the 30 issues and 580 pages he published.

Lamentably, none of the three complete volumes of *Zion's Trumpet* produced by Benjamin Evans is extant in its entirety. But the fifteen surviving issues—3 from 1858, 5 from 1859, 6 from 1860, and 1 from 1861—provide ample evidence that the other 155 were, in fact, published.

Benjamin Evans's replacement in early 1861 as president of the Church in Wales was Thomas Evans Jeremy, a 45-year-old convert of 1846 from Carmarthenshire. But Evans's replacement as editor of *Zion's Trumpet* was George Q. Cannon, the president of the Church in Great Britain and editor of the *Millennial Star*. Bilingual William Ajax, a 29-year-old convert of 1853 from Glamorganshire who over the past while had helped with the publication of *Zion's Trumpet*, was called to move to Liverpool to help publish the Welsh periodical as well as the *Millennial Star*. In his journal Ajax wrote that the press that had been used for printing *Zion's Trumpet* was loaded onto the steamer *Sovereign* 24 March 1861 at Swansea and transported to Liverpool.[18] The move, apparently, was effected in order to cut costs and increase efficiency.

The last issue of *Zion's Trumpet* to be printed, according to William Ajax's journal entry for 9 April 1862, was the fourteenth for that year, most likely one dated 5 April 1862. About a month before, Cannon had purchased "a fine Ulnerstonian printing-machine," and the first item which it processed was an issue of *Zion's Trumpet*.[19] Thus it appears that John Davis's press, which had printed over 460 numbers of *Zion's Trumpet* during a thirteen-year period, was denied the honor of producing the last few issues.

Circulation for *Zion's Trumpet* peaked at about 2,000 during Davis's time and was at about 500 for the three years prior to its demise in 1862. Its readership was continually diminished by emigration. Because the rate of conversion had suffered a dramatic decrease, coupled with the fact that no one was available to replace Ajax, Church leaders in Liverpool decided to "let them read English," as it were. Ajax lamented the prospect of leaving his compatriots without a periodical in their own language:

> It would be a great loss to the Welsh Saints to lose it. . . . He [the Welshman] may manage to converse freely in the English language and to transact any business in it; but there is no language that can reach his heart as well as the Welsh.[20]

The last complete volume now extant is the one for 1857. Only seventeen isolated numbers—fifteen by Benjamin Evans and two by William Ajax—have been located for the years 1858-1861, and none for 1862. The pagination of these extant issues indicates that the periodical continued to be published on a weekly basis until the end, with 16 pages each. By combining calculated figures with known figures, it appears that approximately 7,792 pages of *Zion's Trumpet* were produced during thirteen years and three months, a truly prodigious effort in view of its limited audience and the small number of qualified persons who could assist in its publication.

The following table shows the year-by-year details of *Zion's Trumpet*:

UDGORN SEION

Vol	Year		# of Issues	Frequency	Price/ Cents	Pages/ Issue	Total Pages	Place of Publication	Editor
1.	1849	Jan–Dec	12	Monthly	2	20+4*	288	Carmarthen/ Merthyr Tydfil	John Davis
2.	1850	Jan–Dec	12	Monthly	2.5	28+4*	384**	Merthyr Tydfil	John Davis
3.	1851	Jan–Dec	26	Biweekly	1	16	416	Merthyr Tydfil	John Davis
4.	1852	Jan–Dec	26	Biweekly	[1]	16	416	Merthyr Tydfil	John Davis
5.	1853	Jan–Jun	26	Weekly	[1]	16	416	Merthyr Tydfil	John Davis
6.	1853	July–Dec	27	Weekly	1	16	432	Merthyr Tydfil	John Davis
7.	1854	Jan–Dec	39	Weekly till August and then Biweekly	1	16	624	Merthyr Tydfil till September, then Swansea	Dan Jones
8.	1855	Jan–Dec	26	Biweekly	1	16	416	Swansea	Dan Jones
9.	1856	Jan–Dec	26	Biweekly	1	16	416	Swansea	Dan Jones/ Daniel Daniels
10.	1857	Jan–Dec	26	Biweekly	1.5	16	416	Swansea	Daniel Daniels
11.	1858°	Jan–Dec	[52]	Weekly	1.5	16	[832]	Swansea	Benjamin Evans

12.	1859°	Jan–Dec	[52]	Weekly	1.5	16	[832]	Swansea	Benjamin Evans
13.	1860°	Jan–Dec	53	Weekly	1.5	16	848	Swansea	Benjamin Evans
14.	1861°	Jan–Dec	[52]	Weekly	1.5	16	[832]	Swansea/Liverpool	Geo. Q. Cannon
15.	1862†	Jan–Apr	14	Weekly	[1.5]	[16]	[224]	Liverpool	Geo. Q. Cannon

* 4-page printed wrapper
** Mispagination—numbered 149, 160, 161, etc.

° No complete volume is extant
† No issue is extant

ISOLATED EXTANT ISSUES

1858:	(1)	9 Jan	1859:	(36)	3 Sep	1860:	(5)	28 Jan	1861:	(6)	9 Feb
	(2)	16 Jan		(48)	26 Nov		(13)	24 Mar		(19)	18 May
	(40)	9 Oct		(49)	3 Dec		(18)	28 Apr		(31)	3 Aug
				(50)	10 Dec		(38)	15 Sep			
				(51)	17 Dec		(46)	10 Nov			
							(53)	29 Dec			

Notes

1. *Zion's Trumpet* 9 (15 March 1856): 95–96.
2. 20 December 1855 letter to Thomas Bullock.
3. Ibid.
4. *Ensign*, September 1993, 7.
5. *Zion's Trumpet* 9 (12 April 1856): 121.
6. *Zion's Trumpet* 9 (30 August 1856): 283–86.
7. *Zion's Trumpet* 10 (27 June 1857): 209–11.
8. *Zion's Trumpet* 9 (12 April 1856): 122.
9. *Zion's Trumpet* 9 (26 April 1856): 138–41.
10. *Zion's Trumpet* 9 (30 February [sic] 1856): 79–80.
11. *Zion's Trumpet* 8 (21 July 1855): 235–38.
12. *Zion's Trumpet* 9 (10 May 1856): 156–57.
13. Ibid., 160.
14. *Zion's Trumpet* 10 (10 January 1857): 15.
15. *Zion's Trumpet* 10 (13 June 1857): 206.
16. Ibid., 207.
17. *Zion's Trumpet* 10, foreword, [iv].
18. William Ajax Journal, entry for 24 March 1862.
19. William Ajax Journal, entry for 13 March 1862.
20. William Ajax Journal, entry for 15 March 1862.

Ronald D. Dennis

Deuwch allan o honi hi, fy mhobl i, fel na byddoch gyd-gyfrannogion o'i phechodau hi, ac na dderbynioch o'i phlaau hi.

| Rhif. 31. Cyf. XIV. | AWST 3, 1861. | Pris 1½c. |

NODIADAU GAN Y LLYWYDD HEBER C. KIMBALL, DINAS Y LLYN HALLT MAWR, EBRILL 7FED, 1861.

Y mae nodiadau y brawd Snow yn dda a dysglaer iawn i gyd i bob meddwl gwybodus. Mae genym i gynnyddu yr un fath a phlentyn sy'n myned i'r ysgol ac yn dechreu gyda'i A B C. Ar ol i'r plentyn hwnw adnabod llythyrenau y iaith Saesnaeg, y mae'n medru eu gosod yn nghyd a gwneud geiriau a brawddegau o honynt. Yna y mae arno eisiau "Ail Lyfr," ac yn mhen enyd, bydd am gael Trydydd a Phedwerydd Lyfr. Gellwch chwi a minau ymwellhau yn raddol ar yr un tir, ac nid oes un ffordd i ddyn wellhau neu gynnyddu ond trwy brofiad. Nid oes un dyn yn yr Eglwys hon ag sydd wedi byw ei grefydd ac wedi rhodio yn ngoleuni gwirionedd am yr 28 mlynedd diweddaf, nad yw yn gwybod mwy ganwaith nag y gwyddai ar ddechreu ei yrfa, a thrwy brofiad y daeth y wybodaeth hono.

Dylem werthfawrogi ein bendithion a'r doniau y mae Duw wedi gynnysgaethu arnom ni, a dylai ein serchiadau fod yn gryfach tuagat Rhoddwr y doniau nag y maent tuagat y doniau. Ai fy nyledswydd i yw meddwl mwy am Iesu, Mab y Duw byw, nag am ei Dad ef, yr hwn a'i rhoddodd megys aberth dros bechodau y byd? Pa un yw y mwyaf, Rhoddwr y ddawn neu y ddawn? Gwn am gannoedd o enghreifftiau yn y rhai y cymerwyd y doniau hyny oddiwrth y derbyn-

Facsimile Translation Considerations

1. **Size**. The size of the page and the print of the original have been enlarged by about 30 percent to facilitate reading.
2. **Leading and point size**. Whatever variations occur in the space between lines and print size in the original are imitated in the translation.
3. **Pagination**. The content of each translated page may vary by as much as four or five lines from the content of the Welsh original; all major and minor headings are on the same page as the original.
4. **Paragraphs and sentences**. The tendency of nineteenth-century writers was to use fewer paragraph breaks and much longer sentences than might seem appropriate today. However, for the sake of flavor the inordinate paragraph size and the seemingly interminable sentence length are imitated in the translation.
5. **Brackets and parentheses**. The only editorial comments in the translation are those of John Davis from the original; consequently, all brackets and parentheses are his.
6. **Italicized words**. Italics in the original are retained in the translation. Besides the normal practice of italicizing the names of periodicals, books, ships, etc., the editor used italics either to provide emphasis or to indicate the use of a borrowed word or phrase from English.

7. **Poetry**. The primary focus in translating the poetry of *Udgorn Seion* has been its content; thus, poetry translations are "informational" rather than poetic.

8. **Titles of foreign-language publications**. To facilitate reading, I have used the English translations for all foreign-language titles that appear in the text. The following is a list of these translated titles and their corresponding Welsh titles. For the items authored by John Davis or Dan Jones, I have indicated the page reference in Welsh Mormon Writings where further information is available.

Book of Hymns	*Llyfr Hymnau*	*WMW*, 159
Book of Mormon	*Llyfr Mormon*	*WMW*, 149
Book of the Church	*Llyfr yr Eglwys*	*WMW*, 97
Conversations	*Ymddyddanion*	*WMW*, 115
Doctrine and Covenants	*Llyfr Athrawiaeth a'r Cyfammodau*	*WMW*, 142
First General Epistle	*Epistol Cyffredinol Cyntaf*	*WMW*, 94
Go and Teach	*Ewch a Dysgwch*	*WMW*, 105
Great God of the Sectarians	*Duw Mawr y Sectariaid*	*WMW*, 123
The Guide to Zion	*Yr Arweinydd i Seion*	*WMW*, 190
The Hero	*Y Gwron*	
The Leader	*Yr Arweinydd*	
Marriage and Morals in Utah	*Priodas a Moesau yn Utah*	*WMW*, 207
The Old Religion Anew	*Yr Hen Grefydd Newydd*	*WMW*, 176
Pearl of Great Price	*Perl o Fawr Bris*	*WMW*, 157
Preaching to the Spirits in Prison	*Pregethu i'r Ysbrydion yn Ngharchar*	*WMW*, 103
Proclamation	*Annerchiad*	*WMW*, 177
Prophet of the Jubilee	*Prophwyd y Jubili*	*WMW*, 27
Prove All Things	*Profwch Bob Peth*	*WMW*, 83
Refutations to the Spaulding Story about the Book of Mormon	*Gwrthbrofion i'r Spaulding Story am Lyfr Mormon*	*WMW*, 185
The Scriptural Treasury	*Yr Eurgrawn Ysgrythyrol*	*WMW*, 65
That Which is in Part	*Yr Hyn Sydd o Ran*	*WMW*, 100
The Times	*Yr Amserau*	
Treatise on Miracles	*Traethawd ar Wyrthiau*	*WMW*, 130
Treatises on Miracles	*Traethodau ar Wyrthiau*	*WMW*, 154
The True Faith	*Y Wir Ffydd*	*WMW*, 209
True Repentance	*Gwir Edifeirwch*	*WMW*, 211
Unpopularity of Mormonism	*Anmhoblogrwydd Mormoniaeth*	*WMW*, 195
The Welsh Heald	*Herald Cymraeg*	
The Welshman	*Y Cymro*	
What is Mormonism?	*Pa Beth yw Mormoniaeth?*	*WMW*, 184
What is Saving Grace?	*Pa Beth yw Grâs Cadwedigol?*	*WMW*, 187
Who is the God of the Saints?	*Pwy Yw Duw y Saint?*	*WMW*, 171
Zion's Trumpet	*Udgorn Seion*	*WMW*, 72

9. **Punctuation**. Some changes in punctuation and capitalization have been made to facilitate reading.

10. **Typesetting errors**. The typesetters of the original sometimes inverted letters, cited verses that did not match the accompanying scriptural quotation, left incomplete sentences, misspelled words, or committed other typesetting errors. Lacking an unobtrusive method of indicating such aspects of the original in the translation and fearing that confusion would result for today's reader if such flaws were duplicated, I decided to "correct" these kinds of imperfections in the translation.

11. **Place names**. The modern spelling is used for all place names. The name in English is used for places that have both an English name and a Welsh name (e.g., Swansea for Abertawe, Cardiff for Caerdydd, and Blackwood for Coed-duon).

12. **Proper names**. I have corrected the spelling of Biblical and historical names; however, I have preserved the spelling used for all other proper names even when the same individual's name has variant spellings.

13. **Annotated contents**. Instead of detracting from the facsimile appearance of the translation by inserting numbers and notes, I have prepared an article-by-article commentary of all fifty-three issues. In many instances I simply give a brief statement of the article's contents, together with an indication of a source if the article is borrowed. I provide more detailed observations for those articles that contain historical information pertinent to the nineteenth-century movement of the Latter-day Saints in Wales.

Acknowledgments

For her invaluable assistance in clarifying a myriad of my trouble spots in these final two extant volumes of *Zion's Trumpet*, I express my final note of gratitude to Marilyn Davies of Prestatyn, North Wales. I am also greatly indebted to Glenys Goetinck of Tucson, Arizona, and to D. L. Davies of Aberdare, South Wales, for their translations of the writings of the Reverend Dewi Elfed Jones, the Baptist minister who after converting to Mormonism gave his chapel to the leader of his new religion.

My thanks also to Kaitlyn Adams, BrookeAnn Henriksen, Tiana Moe, Catia Shattuck, Hannah Waller, and Leah Welker, all editorial interns under the supervision of Mel Thorne of the Humanities Publications Center, Brigham Young University, for their proofreading and typesetting skills.

I am very grateful to R. Devan Jensen, Brent Nordgren, Madison Swapp, and Carmen Cole of the Religious Studies Center and student assistants Austin Ballard, Rebecca Hamson Bird, Shanna Clayson D'Avila, Leah Emal, Kimball Gardner, Hadley Griggs, Rebekah Weaver, and Lauren Whitby for reading the final proofs and making the final preparations. And a special thanks to Alex Masterson for his expertise in finalizing numerous details associated with the idiosyncrasies of the facsimile translation format.

ANNOTATED CONTENTS

VOLUME 9: 1856

Title page

> Identical in every respect to the title page for volume 8 (1855) of *Zion's Trumpet* except for two—the volume number and the year. The volume 9 (1856) title page was printed and distributed at the same time as the 27 December issue, along with the foreword and the contents.

Foreword

> Daniel Daniels states that the "Trumpet" in this volume calls thousands "to enlist under the banner of Jesus" and "to journey toward the strongholds of Israel in the tops of the Everlasting Mountains." He also declares that the "present campaign" of the Saints is "the preparatory work for the coming of our Great King in his glory, with his majestic host on high, to place vengeance on those who have refused the conditions of peace which we offer in His name." The constant message of the periodical, he says, will be "the destruction of Babylon, and the rise and increase of Zion."

Contents

> An alphabetical listing of 76 major headings in the original Welsh. The English translation is also arranged alphabetically, making the order different from that of the original. There are 5 indented headings under "Conferences," 31 under "Editorial,"

and 14 under "Letters." Nineteen incorrect page references in the original are corrected in the translation of "Contents."

JANUARY 5

The English Language 1
   The Welsh translation of this article by Franklin D. Richards as printed in *Millennial Star* 17 (29 December 1855): 821–23. President Richards encourages all Saints to learn English if they do not already know it.

Letter from the Valley. 5
   This letter by Thomas Job is dated 27 August 1855 from Salt Lake City and addressed to Daniel Daniels, the uncle of Thomas's wife Hannah. Just over one year earlier, Thomas had spirited away his two-year-old daughter Elizabeth and left Wales with her to come to Utah. At that time his wife was unwilling to make the journey, but she later changed her mind. Thomas indicated in his letter that he would gladly pay her way as well as the way for various other relatives. When he met Hannah in Salt Lake City a year later he revealed that he had a second wife. Hannah divorced Thomas and a few months later married Albert Miles. Years later she told a granddaughter that she wished she had stayed with Thomas. Eventually Thomas converted to the Reorganized Church of Jesus Christ of Latter-day Saints and became their most effective missionary in Utah. In 1988 Bliss J. Brimley, a great-granddaughter of Thomas and Hannah through their daughter Elizabeth, published *The Book of Thomas Job*, a book that is available in its entirety at http://welshmormon.byu.edu/.

Word of Wisdom 7
   A poem of twenty 4-line stanzas by John Richards of Glan Teifi about the evils of drinking alcohol and chewing tobacco.

(Editorial). 9
   In the first part of this editorial, Jones reflects back over the previous year and the opposition the Mormons dealt with during that time. In the second part, he explains that many more Welsh

Saints will be able to emigrate by pushing handcarts across the plains than by waiting for teams and wagons to be made available to them, and he quotes extensively from the *Millennial Star* to support his argument. The third part is Jones's appeal to Church members to reach out to the poor among them. In the fourth part, Jones tells of the departure of the *John J. Boyd* and encourages future emigrants to send in their deposits to secure their reservations for future departures. In the fifth part, Jones asks those who intend to cross the plains by wagons and ox teams to send their payments immediately. The sixth part is the announcement of the arrival of new missionaries in Britain. And the seventh part is a notice that bags can be obtained by contacting the office in Swansea.

Payments 16
  Payments from fourteen individuals toward the debt of the West Glamorgan Conference are shown.

Receipts for Books from December 18 to January 1 16
  Book payments from eleven book distributors are shown.

(No title) 16
  Jones compares the efforts of the conference presidents to pay their book debts to the movement of the grass on the prairies.

(No title) 16
  Jones's address in Swansea.

Contents 16
  A list of this issue's contents and their respective page numbers.

JANUARY 19

Thirteenth General Epistle of the Presidency of the
Church of Jesus Christ of Latter-day Saints 17
  Welsh translation of this epistle from the *Deseret News* for 31 October 1855, p. 4.

(Editorial). 25
> At a recent council of the conference presidents, the majority voted in favor of keeping the circulation of *Zion's Trumpet* at the current level. In this first part of the editorial, Jones presents nine reasons for doing so. In the second part, Jones presents three possible ways for the handcart emigrants to deal with their books. In the third part, he presents several news items from Utah.

Thirteenth General Epistle of the Presidency of the Church of Jesus Christ of Latter-day Saints 28
> Continued from p. 25.

Payments 32
> Payments from seven individuals toward the debt of the West Glamorgan Conference are shown.

Receipts for Books from January 1 to January 15 32
> Book payments from three book distributors are shown.

(No title). 32
> Jones's address in Swansea.

Contents. 32
> A list of this issue's contents and their respective page numbers.

FEBRUARY 2

Minutes of the General Conference of the Church of Jesus Christ of Latter-day Saints, convened in Great Salt Lake City, commencing Saturday, October 6, 1855. 33
> Welsh translation of these minutes from the *Deseret News* for 10 October 1855, p. 4. Translated by Thomas Harris.

(Editorial). 40
> In light of the many conference presidents released to emigrate in the spring Jones uses this editorial to encourage them to leave

everything in their conferences in good order. He also urges the incoming presidents to "seize the task" of their new assignments "quickly and energetically."

Minutes of the General Conference of the Church of Jesus Christ of Latter-day Saints, convened in Great Salt Lake City, commencing Saturday, October 6, 1855. 43
    Continued from p. 40.

News from the United States 45
    Several disputes between England and the United States prompt Jones to encourage the Saints to "go as far to the west as they can see" before the situation worsens.

Statistical Report of the Church of Jesus Christ of Latter-day Saints in Wales for the year ending December 31, 1855. 47
    A listing of the thirteen conferences in Wales with the names of the presidents, scribes, and the statistics.

Notice to the Emigrants to the States 47
    The *Caravan* will set sail on February 14 from Liverpool. Jones gives details as to how emigrants from South Wales can make their way to Liverpool.

Book Debts for the Different Conferences for the Quarter Ending December 31, 1855. 48
    Shown are the outstanding balance of debts owed by the fourteen Welsh conferences, Herefordshire, the Liverpool Welsh Branch, and the Office of the *Millennial Star* in Liverpool.

Receipts for Books from January 15 to January 30 48
    Book payments from five book distributors are shown.

(No title). 48
    Jones explains that several items were not included in this issue because of lack of space.

(No title). 48
    Jones's address in Swansea.

Contents. 48
    A list of this issue's contents and their respective page numbers.

FEBRUARY 16

The Gathering of the Poor. 49
    Welsh translation of Franklin D. Richards's general instructions as to how the poor members of the Church in Britain were to be assisted to emigrate. See *Millennial Star* 18 (2 February 1856): 72–76.

Sermon by President B. Young, which was delivered at the October Conference in Great Salt Lake City, 1855 55
    Welsh translation of Brigham Young's sermon at the October 1855 Conference.

(Editorial). 57
    Jones invites all conference presidents in Wales to be attendance at a conference in Merthyr Tydfil on 23 February.

Instructions on the Emigration 58
    Welsh translation of these instructions from Franklin D. Richards and his counselors. See *Millennial Star* 18 (23 February 1856): 121–23.

Peace 61
    Jones comments on several trouble spots in the world and declares that the Welsh Saints should flee towards Zion as soon as possible.

Gathering of the Saints 62
> A poem of eight 4-lines stanzas by Gwilym Ddu, the nom de plume of William Lewis (1807–75). Lewis had gone to America in 1849 on board the *Buena Vista* and had apparently sent this poem from Utah.

The Temple 63
> Jones compares the number of stones used for the foundation of the temple being built in Salt Lake City with the number used for building the Nauvoo Temple.

(No title)...................................... 63
> A state official sent to Utah by the American government already has two wives.

(No title)...................................... 63
> Jones expresses concern about the trouble brewing between the Southern and the Northern States in America.

(No title)...................................... 63
> Catholic priests in Ireland are burning Bibles.

(No title)...................................... 63
> Jones expresses concern about the trouble between the United States and Britain.

(No title)...................................... 64
> A man by the name of James Brott was fined £50 in Dover for disrupting a Latter-day Saint service. Jones hopes this will serve as a deterrent for other such men.

Payments toward the debt of the West Glamorgan Conference from January 16 to February 13 64
> Payments from eleven individuals toward the debt of the West Glamorgan Conference are shown.

Receipts for Books from January 30 to February 8 64
    Payments from two book distributors are shown.

(No title). 64
    The details of four conferences to be held during March are given.

(No title). 64
    Jones laments having to leave out things in this issue for lack of space.

Addresses 64
    The addresses for Daniel Daniels and Abednego Williams are given.

(No title). 64
    Jones's address in Swansea.

Contents. 64
    A list of this issue's contents and their respective page numbers.

FEBRUARY 30 [sic]

Sermon by President B. Young, which was delivered at the October Conference in Great Salt Lake City, 1855 65
    Continued from page 57.

(Editorial). 73
    In the first part of this editorial, Jones provides details for those who intend to emigrate this year. President Richards had given permission for the Welsh Saints to be on the same ship whether they go with a wagon company or a handcart company. Jones declares that he will have the privilege of going with them. Over five hundred Welsh were together on the *S. Curling* that left Liverpool about six weeks later. Most of these crossed the plains in the Bunker handcart company. The second part of the editorial is a

lament from Jones that the book distributors are remiss in sending in the book money.

Minutes of the Council and the General Conference 74

The presidency of the Church in Great Britain—Franklin D. Richards, Daniel Spencer, and Cyrus H. Wheelock—were in attendance for most of the four-day conference held in Merthyr Tydfil 23–26 February. Dan Jones and his only counselor, Daniel Daniels, were in attendance, as well as all except for three of the conference presidents from North Wales. Many topics were addressed by a number of speakers during what the scribes called a "never-to-be-forgotten council." Daniel Daniels was set apart as Dan Jones's replacement. American elders Israel Evans and Benjamin Ashby were also set apart as his counselors.

Feeling of a Young Saint. 79

A poem of twelve 4-line stanzas by David John, a young convert from Pembrokeshire who had studied at the Haverfordwest College to become a Baptist minister. Without a doubt, he had the greatest amount of formal education of any of the Welsh converts to Mormonism. For more information and a link to his journals see his page on the website at http://welshmormon.byu.edu.

Contents. 80

A list of this issue's contents and their respective page numbers.

MARCH 15

Summary of the Address of President Franklin D. Richards, in a Council with the majority of the outgoing and incoming Presidents of the Welsh Conferences, which was held in the "White Lion" Inn, Merthyr Tydfil, Tuesday, February 26, 1856 81

Richards tells the gathering that he was there "at the request of Brother Jones to assist him to leave his departing blessing." Richards gives a number of instructions to the new conference presidents telling them to now give their allegiance to President Daniel Daniels as their new leader. He also gives extensive encouragement for all to learn English in order to be effective in their callings and to encourage all the Saints in Wales to do likewise. These remarks were transcribed and translated by William Lewis, Swansea.

(Editorial) 88
In the first part of this editorial, Jones urges his readers to pay careful attention to the instructions about emigration contained in a notice printed elsewhere in this issue of *Zion's Trumpet*. The notice is from Franklin D. Richards and his counselors to the Saints in England, Scotland, and Ireland who have been members of the Church for ten years or more and to those in Wales who have been members for six years or more. Because of the lack of funds in the Perpetual Emigration Fund, it had become necessary to focus on "the most worthy and the most needy" Saints to be the recipients of financial assistance for emigration purposes. The notice was to be read in all Church meetings throughout the British Isles. Jones then gives some lengthy instructions specifically to the Welsh members of the Church.

In the second part of the editorial, Jones states that the emigrants should leave for Liverpool at the end of March.

In the third part, Jones reports on the departure of 120 Welsh Saints on board the *Caravan*.

In the fourth part, Jones encourages conference presidents and book distributors to send in the money for books that was owed to Jones personally and to the *Zion's Trumpet* accounts.

The Emigration 91
The message, dated 5 March 1856, to which Dan Jones refers in the first part of his editorial in this issue. Franklin D. Richards, Daniel Spencer, and Cyrus Wheelock present details as to how Church members, in light of inadequate available funding, could still be able to leave Britain for America during the next few weeks.

Sermon by President B. Young, which was delivered in the October Conference in Great Salt Lake City, 1855 92
Continued from page 57.

Address of President Daniel Daniels to the Conference
Presidents..94
> This is Daniels's first missive to his fellow leaders of the Church in Wales as their new president. He declares his "chief objective" to be that of getting as many Welsh Church members on their way to Zion as possible, and he details the manner to be used by the conference presidents in making this happen. He also encourages them to motivate their book distributors to collect the outstanding debts and submit the money to the office in Swansea. Finally, he reminds them that they are to be diligent in all their responsibilities.

The Maddocians 95
> Jones expresses his determination to continue the search for the Maddocians—the American Indians thought to be the descendants of Prince Madoc and the members of the group which, according to Welsh tradition, sailed with him in 1170 to North America. He makes an appeal to his readers and even to editors of other periodicals in Wales for any information they may have that would aid him in his quest. Six years earlier, Jones had joined the Parley P. Pratt "Southern Expedition" to search for the "Welsh Indians." See *Zion's Trumpet*, vol. 3 (1851): 256–58. Also see *Dialogue: A Journal of Mormon Thought* 18, no. 4 (Winter 1985): 112–17, for my article entitled "Captain Dan Jones and the Welsh Indians."

(No title)..96
> Jones announces the beginning of a new weekly publication, the "Western Standard," in San Francisco, California, under the editorship of George Q. Cannon.

Receipts for Books from February 9 to March 13 96
> Payments from five book distributors are shown.

Contents...96
> A list of this issue's contents and their respective page numbers.

MARCH 29

Summary of the Teaching of President Dan Jones, in the
Merthyr Tydfil General Council, February 23, 1856 97

> By arrangement with the leadership in Liverpool, Dan Jones, his counselor Daniel Daniels, and the majority of the conference presidents throughout Wales had come together in Merthyr Tydfil in a special conference at the White Lion Inn. The purpose of the meeting was to effect the release of Dan Jones as the president of the Church in Wales and the setting apart of Daniel Daniels in his place. But the leaders from Liverpool had not arrived by the appointed starting time. Six years earlier, also in the White Lion Inn, Jones had experienced a similar disappointment in a similar kind of gathering as he was about to leave Wales after presiding over the missionary work in Wales. The leaders from Liverpool failed to attend the conference as previously arranged. And on that occasion Jones essentially released himself and set apart his replacement. For Jones's account of the 1849 conference, see *Millennial Star* 11 (1 February 1849): 38–42. At the gathering in 1856, however, Jones did not act on his own; rather he elected to offer instruction to those gathered while awaiting the arrival of Franklin D. Richards and his counselors Daniel Spencer and Cyrus Wheelock. He postponed the afternoon meeting until 6:00 o'clock "in the hopeful expectation of the arrival" of the visiting brethren. Spencer and Wheelock arrived before the evening meeting began, and Richards arrived as it was nearing a close. On Tuesday, the fourth day of this special conference, Daniel Daniels, Israel Evans, and Benjamin Ashby were set apart as the new presidency of the Church in Wales. During the four-day conference, Dan Jones gave several talks touching on numerous aspects of the responsibilities of the conference presidents throughout Wales.

(Editorial) 105

> In the first part of this editorial, Jones expresses his gratitude for having been able to serve his compatriots over the past three years during this, his second mission to Wales. He then commends Daniel Daniels and his counselors to Church members throughout Wales and urges all to give their support and love to this new presidency. The second part is the announcement that

Daniel Daniels is the new editor of *Zion's Trumpet* and that all correspondence be directed to him. In the third part, Jones reminds the conference presidents of their responsibility to make sure that their treasurers send money collected for the Perpetual Emigrating Fund and the Temple Fund to the main office in Swansea.

Notice to Emigrants. Excerpt from the Letter of President
F. D. Richards. 108

Dated 5 March 1856 from Liverpool, this letter is from Franklin D. Richards directly to Dan Jones. Richards first tells of getting 530 "souls of Saints" on board the *Enoch Train* and then asks for Jones's opinion regarding the possibility of securing the *S. Curling* for the transport of the large group of Welsh emigrants on about the 19th of April. The owners of the *S. Curling* had said many good things about the large group of Mormon emigrants they had taken to New York the previous year, and Richards stated that he was inclined toward the idea of using the ship again this year. In a lengthy bracketed response directed to the readers of *Zion's Trumpet*, Jones explains why he agrees with Richards that the *S. Curling* is no doubt the best option for the Welsh emigrants.

Summary of the Teaching of President Dan Jones, in the
Merthyr Council. 110

Continued from page 105. In this final part of the "Summary," Jones encourages the conference presidents to promote the emigration with all their might. He is eager to get all of the old-time members of the Church in Wales on their way to America. Doing so, he explains, would clear the way for hundreds, even thousands, of new converts to come into the Church.

Man Surprised 111

A poem of five 4-line stanzas by Pencrych from Aberdare.

Let the Emigrants Take Notice 112

Jones is able now to confirm the April 19th departure from Liverpool of the ship for all the Welsh emigrants. He gives instructions for those going to Liverpool by steamer and also for those going by train. And he proudly states that the price for all passengers except for the Saints has risen to £6 10 shillings.

Receipts for Books from March 14 to 27 112
    Payments from four book distributors are shown.

(No title). 112
    The 20th of April is the date for the East Glamorgan Conference. Others will be announced later.

Contents. 112
    A list of this issue's contents and their respective page numbers.

APRIL 12

Speech of President Brigham Young to the Territorial Senate of Utah. 113
    The Welsh translation of Brigham Young's 11 December 1855 speech delivered in Fillmore, Utah. See *Deseret News* for 19 December 1855, 4.

Letter from the Valley. 116
    A letter from Rice Williams, a member of the 1849 crossing on the *Buena Vista*. The letter is dated 9 December 1855 from Fort Ephraim and contains assurance that Jones's wife and children are doing well. Williams also mentions that he had seen Edward Jones, Dan Jones's only sibling to convert to Mormonism, in Ephraim.

Letter of John Jones, Merthyr, to Captain Dan Jones 117
    A letter from John Jones, also a member of the 1849 crossing on the *Buena Vista*. He is now back in Wales, and the letter is dated 22 March 1856 from Merthyr Tydfil. The contrite John Jones apologizes to Dan Jones for his bad behavior of seven years earlier and recognizes that his excommunication was justified. Together with his signature he includes the name of William Sims, who had also been excommunicated.

Response of Captain Dan Jones to the Foregoing Letter . . . 118

> Dan Jones's letter of response is dated 8 April 1856 from Swansea. He addresses his response to Daniel Daniels, the leader of the Church in Wales as of 26 February 1856. Dan Jones extends his forgiveness and requests that Daniels publish John Jones's letter in *Zion's Trumpet* so that other Church members who were possibly offended by John Jones would be enabled to better understand the situation. Dan Jones indicates that he is "deprived of the pleasure of reconciling" with William Sims until such time as he receives a personal request from him. Jones, who would be sailing for America in a matter of days, leaves the matter to be resolved by Daniel Daniels.

Prayer Verses of the Troubled Saint in Babylon 119

> A poem of eleven 4-line stanzas and a 3-line chorus by Thomas Conway of Flint. He pleads for God to deliver him "from Babylon" and laments that he is being left behind by the hundreds of Welsh converts then about to sail off to Zion.

(Editorial) 121

> In this, his first editorial for *Zion's Trumpet*, Daniel Daniels laments the departure of his mentor Dan Jones and readily admits his feelings of inferiority. He pleads with his "fellow soldiers" to join with him in combining their efforts to move the work forward the best they can.

The "Spaulding Story" or the Worst Bugbear to Prevent a Host from becoming Saints 122

> Thomas Harris expresses gratitude that he had converted to Mormonism before the story began circulating throughout Wales that the Book of Mormon had its origins in the "Spaulding Romance." He recommends that "every lover of the truth" obtain copies of Dan Jones's *Irrefutable Proofs that the Book of Mormon was not obtained from the "Spaulding Romance"* to give to "every Vicar, Curate, and Sexton who are ringing the clapper of this old bell daily," for if they would read the pamphlet "it would have a better effect on their bowels to improve the colic which churns inside their insides than a tub of drugs and a whole lot of quacks." The English translation for this pamphlet is in my

Defending the Faith: Early Welsh Missionary Publications (Provo, UT: Religious Studies Center, Brigham Young University, 2003), item J24.

Farewell to Captain Jones! 125
    A poem of fourteen 4-line stanzas by Thomas Harris in praise of Dan Jones's tireless efforts to preach the restored gospel to his Welsh compatriots. The poem is dated 10 April 1856 and was most likely read aloud to Dan Jones as he was about to board the steamer in Swansea that would take him and other Welsh Mormon emigrants to Liverpool to sail away to America.

Stanzas on the Same Topic. 127
    A poem of four 4-line stanzas by John Davies, previously from Merioneth, again in praise of Dan Jones's missionary work in Wales and wishing him well. This poem is dated 4 April 1856.

Slave Trading of America. 127
    In a recent proclamation the governor of Mississippi had threatened to "rise in its might for its rights" should the government of the United States interfere in any way with slave trading.

The Emigrants 128
    "T. H." gives a brief description of the emigrating Saints in Swansea as they prepared to board the steamer for Liverpool.

Conferences 128
    An announcement of the places and dates for upcoming conferences.

(No title) 128
    Daniels's address in Swansea.

Contents 128
    A list of this issue's contents and their respective page numbers.

APRIL 26

The Millennium..................................129
    A doctrinal treatise on the Millennium by Thomas Harris, who had replaced Dan Jones as the President of the West Glamorgan Conference. Thomas Harris is among the earliest converts to Mormonism in South Wales and is mentioned several times in the three volumes of *Prophet of the Jubilee* as a missionary. His poetry and essays are sprinkled throughout all the volumes of *Zion's Trumpet* from 1849 through 1855. On page 134 is the following statement: "Peter foretold that Jesus should come in flaming fire." Here Harris has confused Paul with Peter, as the quote is from 1 Thessalonians 1:8.

Letter of the Editor to His Printer 135
    The letter is dated 20 April 1856, Liverpool, and is addressed to Thomas Harris. The author, Daniel Daniels, had accompanied Dan Jones and the large group of Welsh Mormon emigrants on board the steamer *Troubadour* from Swansea to Liverpool. Daniels requests that Harris include a brief account in *Zion's Trumpet*.

Verse 136
    An eight-line poem by D. W. from Alltwen.

(Editorial)......................................137
    In the first part of this editorial, Daniels instructs the Saints still in Wales to focus on gathering to Zion and not to worry about the impact their absence will have on those who remain behind. He reminds everyone of the assurance they received from Dan Jones and other leaders at the "unforgettable Merthyr Council" a few weeks earlier that baptisms in Wales would increase in direct proportion to the increase in emigration. In the second part, Daniels encourages conference presidents to make sure their book distributors are diligent in collecting the subscription money for *Zion's Trumpet* and submitting it to the central office. He explains that the lower number of subscribers resulting from the recent emigration makes it difficult to keep the cost per issue at just one penny unless the collection process is handled properly and promptly. In the third part of the editorial, the new editor

lvi   CONTENTS

    extols the virtue of the captain and the mate of the *Troubador*, the steamer that took about 150 Saints from Swansea to Liverpool to board the *S. Curling*. Seven years earlier it was also the *Troubador* that took Dan Jones and a large number of Welsh Mormon converts from Swansea to Liverpool to board the *Buena Vista*.

Greeting of Elder Israel Evans to the Welsh Saints 138
    Recently installed as a counselor to Daniel Daniels, Israel Evans writes this open letter to all the Welsh Saints to introduce himself to them and to explain his excitement at receiving this assignment. Evans was an American elder whose ancestors had left Wales in the eighteenth century.

Triumph of the Saints over the World. 141
    A poem of seven 12-line stanzas by John Davies, formerly of Merionethshire. It is dated 10 April 1856, Swansea, and is to be sung to the tune "The Delight of the Men of Harlech."

The East Glamorgan Conference 143
    As scribe of the East Glamorgan Conference John Price reports the proceedings of the meeting held 20 April 1856 in Merthyr Tydfil. Daniel Daniels was not present as he was yet to return from Liverpool where he had gone to accompany Dan Jones and the hundreds of emigrating Welsh Saints.

Receipts for Books from March 31 to April 24 144
    Payments from four book distributors are shown.

(No title).. 144
    Daniels encourages all in the West Glamorgan Conference who have not as yet paid their "Promises" to do so. These "Promises" were made at the request of Dan Jones several months earlier to make up for funds that had been embezzled by Dewi Elfed Jones, the former president of the West Glamorgan Conference. Brother James Tuckfield is recognized for paying his commitment of 10 shillings.

Contents. 144
    A list of this issue's contents and their respective page numbers.

MAY 10

Speech of President Brigham Young to the Territorial
Senate of Utah. 145
    Continued from page 113.

Commemorative Certificate 147
    A transcription of a lengthy certificate that was presented to Dan
    Jones prior to his departure from Swansea on April 9. The cer-
    tificate was signed by the new presidency of the Church in Wales
    and the various conference presidents who expressed their appre-
    ciation to Dan Jones for serving two missions to Wales and for
    bringing the gospel to thousands of his compatriots. Mentioned
    also are his close association with Joseph Smith, his numerous
    publications in defense of Mormonism, and his tireless efforts in
    taking two large groups of Welsh converts to America.

Summary of the Teaching of President F. D. Richards, in a
General Conference Held in Merthyr Tydfil, on the 24th of
February, 1856 150
    The summary that begins on page 81 of the 15 March issue is of
    Richards's sermon on Tuesday, the last day of the four-day con-
    ference. This summary, however, is of his teaching on Sunday,
    the second day of the conference. At the outset of his Sunday
    sermon Richards verifies that the majority of his audience—the
    outgoing presidency of the Church in Wales as well as the new
    presidency and most of the conference presidents—could under-
    stand English. He promises to speak to them "in a manner easy
    for them to understand." He then tells them of some things they
    should consider in preparing to emigrate. At the top of the list, he
    explains, is for them to learn English in order to be able to com-
    municate with the Saints in Zion. At the end of this three-page
    segment of Richards's remarks is an indication that the summary
    would continue in future issues of *Zion's Trumpet*, but this turns
    out to be the final part of the summary published.

(Editorial) 153

In the first part of this editorial, Daniels outlines what the Saints still in Wales must do to qualify for emigration. First he encourages all to focus carefully in completing the instructions given by Dan Jones in the 13 October 1855 of *Zion's Trumpet*. Then he emphasizes that all Saints should also be diligently preaching the gospel to their neighbors and making sure that all book debts are paid. In the second part, Daniels tells of the feast hosted by the First Presidency in Zion to honor returning missionaries and their wives for their sacrifices in spreading the gospel. And the third part consists of instructions as to how Church members can purchase a copy of the Commemorative Certificate that was presented to Dan Jones a few weeks earlier. Only eighty of these "splendid" copies made on blue silk in golden letters were still on hand for the price of one shilling.

Letter of Reconciliation to President Daniel Daniels 156

The author of this letter is David Bevan Jones, better known by his nom de plume Dewi Elfed Jones. Prior to his conversion to Mormonism, Jones was an ordained Baptist minister. Following his baptism in the Cynon River on 27 April 1851, he was confirmed in the Gwawr Baptist Chapel in Aberaman, near Aberdare, Glamorganshire. And after his confirmation, he handed the chapel keys to William Phillips, then president of the LDS Church in Wales, and declared the chapel to be a Mormon chapel from that time on. While presiding over the West Glamorganshire Conference in mid-1855, Jones was excommunicated for "moving pounds into his pocket" that rightfully belong to the Church. (See *Zion's Trumpet* 8:235–38.) In this 3 May 1856 letter, Jones tells of a "loving and reconciling conversation" a few weeks before that he had had with Dan Jones. Present also were Daniel Daniels, Thomas Harris, and others. The letter is to confirm the contrite feelings he now has with respect to his transgressions and the earnest desire he has to be received back into the Church in full fellowship. Included as part of the letter is a poem entitled "Hymn of Tribulation." For further information about this very colorful figure in the history of the Church in Wales, see the page for David Bevan Jones at http://welshmormon.byu.edu.

Hymn of Tribulation 157
   A poem of eight 8-line stanzas by Dewi Elfed Jones in which he expresses the great anguish he suffered after being excommunicated from the Church a little less than a year earlier.

To President Daniels............................. 159
   Thomas Harris, President of the West Glamorgan Conference, writes this 8 May 1856 letter to Daniel Daniels in support of Dewi Elfed Jones and his desire to be accepted back into the Church.

Response of President Daniels...................... 160
   In this response Daniels endorses wholeheartedly the acceptance of Dewi Elfed Jones back into the Church.

Contents.. 160
   A list of this issue's contents and their respective page numbers.

MAY 24

The Millennium................................. 161
   Continued from page 135.

West Glamorgan Conference 165
   This conference was held on 11 May 1856 at the Saints' Hall in Swansea. According to John Davies, the scribe, reports were given of the various districts within the West Glamorgan Conference by their presidents during the morning session. Following the hymn and prayer of the two o'clock meeting, President Thomas Harris announced that "since a great many gentlemen there had come to the meeting to listen" that the greater part of the meeting would be in English. He encouraged the Welsh to be patient. The American elders Israel Evans and Benjamin Ashby, counselors to President Daniel Daniels, spoke only English.

(Editorial) 169
> The first of the six items that comprise this editorial is Daniels's call for more missionaries to go out and preach the gospel. The second item is entitled "Notice of the British Presidency" and is the Welsh translation of Franklin D. Richards's plea for all the leaders throughout the British Mission to resolve all money matters prior to 30 June 1856. See *Millennial Star* 18 (24 May 1856): 330. The third item is a notice that the *Thornton* had sailed toward New York on 4 May 1856 with "764 souls on board." The fourth item is entitled "New Deseret Alphabet" and contains an announcement that "a number of books will be printed at the Liverpool Office in the New Alphabet." The fifth item is a brief report from Israel Evans of the Brecon Conference held on the 27th of April. And in the sixth item Daniels gives a brief report of the Monmouthshire Conference held in Tredegar on the 4th of May.

The Indian War 172
> Reports that the Indians have begun to retaliate for the atrocities brought upon them by the whites. In the Territory of Utah, however, the Indians are peaceful because of the good treatment given them by the Mormons. See *Millennial Star* 18 (24 May 1856): 335–36.

"Hymn of Tribulation."—the Second Part 173
> In the previous issue of *Zion's Trumpet*, Dewi Elfed Jones expressed his discouragement at being out of the Church for nearly a year with a poem entitled "Hymn of Tribulation." In a brief introduction to this second part of his hymn, he asks permission of the reader to sing "Welcome Rejoicing." Dated 22 May 1856, this second poem consists of fourteen 8-line stanzas.

Book Debts for the Various Conferences for the Quarter Ending, March 31, 1856 176
> A total debt of over £326 owed by 10 conferences plus the Liverpool Branch, the Liverpool Office, Hereford and Brecon is shown.

Receipts for Books from April 25 to May 23 176
    Payments from ten book distributors are shown.

Contents. 176
    A list of this issue's contents and their respective page numbers.

JUNE 7

Marriage and Morals in Utah. 177
    The practice of plural marriage in The Church of Jesus Christ of Latter-day Saints was recognized and officially announced at a special conference in Salt Lake City on 28 August 1852. But its practice was not announced in Great Britain until 1 January 1853 in the simultaneous publication of the issues of the *Millennial Star* and *Zion's Trumpet* for that date. On 21 December 1855, Parley P. Pratt delivered his "address on the laws of marriage and morals" to the Council of the Utah legislature. Ten days later it was read by Thomas Bullock to the full joint session, which ordered it published in the *Deseret News*. It was reprinted in the *Millennial Star* of 31 May 1856. Dewi Elfed Jones prepared a Welsh translation of the address which ran in two issues of *Zion's Trumpet*—the one for June 7 and the next one for June 21.

Opening of the "Saints' Chapel," Aberafan 184
    Emrys Davies gleefully reports to Daniel Daniels that "through the blessing of God and the instrumentality of President Thomas Harris" the Saints in Aberafan, near Port Talbot, had secured "a convenient place" to hold their meetings. The place was a chapel formerly used by the Wesleyans. The owner, John Richards, had been approached unsuccessfully by the "enemies of the truth" to dissuade him for leasing the building to the Mormons. In his letter Davies gives an account of the opening of the chapel on 18 May 1856.

(Editorial). 185
    In very strong terms Daniels tells the Saints in Wales that it is not sufficient for them to receive the gospel and do nothing further. He reminds them that recipients of the word of God had a sacred

obligation to share that with others, for "he who disregards the word of God will have his knees knocking, and every joint of his body shaking, when the golden ligature of his knees breaks from the intensity of his agonies, for refusing to listen to the voice of God through his servants, and bend his ear to their teaching."

Letter from the Valley 186
In this 30 November 1855 letter, Daniel Francis Thomas tells his relatives in glowing terms of his journey across the plains and his arrival in Salt Lake City. He encourages all to join with him and enjoy the "riches of Zion." Traveling with him the entire journey from Wales was his former missionary companion David Jeremy. For a detailed account of the savage attack on the two of them by a mob in October 1854, see Thomas's page at http://welshmormon.byu.edu.

Carmarthen Conference 189
William Jones reports on the conference that was held in the town of Carmarthen on 25 May 1856.

Longing for Zion 190
A poem of twelve 4-line stanzas and a 2-line chorus following each stanza by Joseph Proser.

The Volunteers 192
Daniel Daniels reports that "several of the brethren have gone out into the field." He rewards Noah Roberts for failing to "feel at peace without returning to the field again" by printing his poem of three 4-line stanzas.

Conferences of the North 192
The dates and places of four conferences are shown.

Conferences of the South 192
The dates and places of eight conferences are shown.

Receipts for Books from May 24 to June 5 192
> Payments from four book distributors are shown.

(No title). 192
> Daniels laments that the account of the Llanelli Conference reached him too late to be included in this issue.

(No title). 192
> Daniels states that the article of Elder Wm. F. Williams, Alltwen, will appear in the next issue.

Contents. 192
> A list of this issue's contents and their respective page numbers.

JUNE 21

Marriage and Morals in Utah. 193
> Continued from page 183.

(Editorial). 201
> In the first part of this editorial, Daniel Daniels reports the success that several missionaries are having in a number of places. In the second part he quotes from a letter written by Thomas Harris about his travels and success in preaching the gospel with several others in the towns of Pontardawe and Neath.

Fulfillment of Prophecies about Ancient Babylon 203
> This is the first of three installments by this title to be published in *Zion's Trumpet*. Mormons in Wales often referred to their homeland as "Babylon" and looked forward to fleeing to their "real home" in Zion. The author, William F. Williams, takes the Old Testament prophecies about Babylon and describes their fulfillment with a Mormon twist. His reference to the Greek historians Herodotus and Xenophon suggests that much of his information about the history of Babylon comes from their works. One of the most oft quoted scriptures to encourage Mormon converts in Britain to leave their home land and gather to Zion is Revelation

18:4, "Come out of her my people, that ye be not partakers of her sins, and that ye receive not of her plagues."

Letter from President Jones. 205
> Dan Jones writes from Boston, May 1856, in a very positive tone about the crossing of the *S. Curling* with over five hundred Welsh Saints on board. Seven years earlier after reaching New Orleans on the *Buena Vista* with about half the number Jones had a much more somber tone in his letter. The difference may well have been the Church maturity of the Saints on board the *S. Curling*. Their presence on board this later ship had been determined by their faithfulness and their service, whereas many of those on the earlier ship were very recent converts. And because of their lack of experience in the Church some parted company with the others in New Orleans and St. Louis, an indication that they had probably used the Church only as a means of getting to America. In this letter from Boston, Jones reports the cooperative conduct of the passengers during the voyage: "I don't believe that so many people have ever before lived so happily united, gentle and devout for so long under such circumstances." He had high praise for the captain and the crew and invited all the Saints in Wales to sail to America as soon as they were able.

(No title). 208
> Daniels informs his readers that a "likeness" of President Orson Spencer was available through the *Zion's Trumpet* office.

(No title). 208
> Daniels reminds the conference presidents to remember the collections for the various funds, and he reports payments received from five book distributors.

Contents. 208
> A list of this issue's contents and their respective page numbers.

JULY 5

The Millennium 209
>Continued from page 165.

The East Glamorgan Conference 214
>The scribe, T. Stephens, reports the proceedings of this conference held in Merthyr Tydfil on 29 June 1856. Israel Evans, first counselor to Daniel Daniels, warned that being selective in leaders to obey was "inconsistency and hypocrisy." There was a "Tea Party" the following afternoon, and in the evening a concert was held. Choirs from Merthyr Tydfil, Cwmbach, and Aberaman participated.

(Editorial) 216
>Daniels laments the mockery and persecution heaped upon the Saints because of the practice of plural marriage among the Mormons in America. In an effort to educate the public concerning this practice, Franklin D. Richards was encouraging all the Saints in Britain to purchase a copy of the newly published pamphlet *Marriage and Morals in Utah*. The Welsh Saints had received the text of Parley P. Pratt's pamphlet in the two previous issues of *Zion's Trumpet*; nevertheless, Richards wished for "the new English pamphlet . . . to have a place on *every hearth and family of Saints in Wales*." Daniels endorsed the idea and said that since all Welsh Mormons were encouraged to learn English the day would come when they would be "happy to have secured a copy of this valuable treatise."

Fulfillment of Prophecies about Ancient Babylon 218
>Continued from page 205.

The Hand of Providence 221
>A poem of forty-eight lines by Dark Nathan of Llywel in praise of God's handiwork in his creation of plants, animals, the world, and especially man. Dark Nathan is the nom de plume of Jonathan J. Thomas.

Another Witness for Mormonism 222
> This letter by David John is dated 7 June 1856, Pembrokeshire. Its author had been baptized into the Mormon church seven years earlier at age fifteen and had received a powerful witness of the truthfulness of the restored gospel. His father, however, forbade him from associating with the Mormons. David sought counsel from the Mormon elders and was told that because of his age he was to follow his father's instruction until age twenty-one at which time he should return to Mormonism. He eventually was able to study for the ministry at the Baptist Academy at Haverfordwest, Pembrokeshire. But on the night of 29 January 1856, the eve of his twenty-third birthday, it was made known to David in a dream that he should return to the Mormon faith. When David's father learned the news, the shock was so great to him that he fell ill, an illness that led to his death two months later. People in the neighborhood called David a murderer and accused him of having caused his father's death. In his letter to Daniel Daniels, David says that although his friends and family predicted that he would not last more than a few days with the Saints he is happy to report that he is "staying safe in the most holy faith." He closes his letter with a poem of seven 8-line stanzas, a strong affirmation of his testimony. For more information and a link to his journals see his page on the website at http://welshmormon.byu.edu.

Contents. 224
> A list of this issue's contents and their respective page numbers.

JULY 19

Tithing. 225
> The Welsh translation of an article on tithing as printed in the *Millennial Star* 18 (12 July 1856): 440–43.

Letter of Reconciliation to President Daniel Daniels. 231
> In this 12 July 1856 letter, William Sims requests forgiveness for all his transgressions as well as a place back in the Church. His name was included in John Jones's letter dated 22 March 1856 sent to Dan Jones. But the latter indicated in his response that he

was "deprived of the pleasure of reconciling" with William Sims until he received a personal request directly from him. And since Dan Jones left for America soon after extending forgiveness to John Jones only, William Sims addresses his 12 July letter to Daniel Daniels. Daniels generously responds to Sims and assures him that were Dan Jones still in Wales he would be happy to forgive Sims and welcome him back into the Church.

Religious Freedom 231
> The Welsh translation of a brief notice that appeared in the *Millennial Star* to the effect that religious freedom had recently been granted in Turkey.

(Editorial) 232
> In the first part of this editorial, Daniels lends his support to Franklin D. Richards's reflections on tithing in the first article of this issue. The second part is entitled "State of Deseret" and contains Daniels's observations on the growth of the Church from a membership of six persons to a consequential group that has become the Territory of Utah on the verge of becoming a state.

Constitution of the State of Deseret 234
> The Welsh translation by Dewi Elfed Jones of the proposed constitution for the proposed State of Deseret. See *Deseret News* (2 April 1856): 6.

(No title) 240
> An urgent invitation for all Conference Presidents in Wales who understand English to attend a special council meeting in Birmingham with newly arrived Presidents Orson Pratt and Ezra T. Benson.

(No title) 240
> An announcement that Elders John Jones and Dewi Elfed Jones have been appointed as traveling elders.

Receipts for Books from June 20 to July 16 240
> Payments received from eight book distributors are shown.

(No title). 240
 Daniels indicates that the accounting of the book debts is not included with this issue for lack of space. Also the biannual report is not included because the conference presidents failed to send a copy to Daniels of the report they sent to Liverpool.

Contents. 240
 A list of this issue's contents and their respective page numbers.

AUGUST 2

Letter of President Brigham Young 241
 The Welsh translation of Brigham Young's 11 April 1856 letter from Salt Lake City to Franklin D. Richards. See *Millennial Star* 18 (26 July 1856): 465–67.

The Merionethshire Conference. 245
 A report of the conference held in Machynlleth on 6 July 1856. The scribe William Ajax comments that the remarks made by President Benjamin Ashby "pleased all who could understand him." Ajax explains that "a summary of these observations were translated" into Welsh by John Treharn, the conference president. William Ajax would become the assistant editor of *Zion's Trumpet* in 1861 and would supervise the relocation of the press from Swansea to Liverpool where the last issue was printed in April 1862. See his page on the website at http://welshmormon.byu.edu/.

Fulfillment of Prophecies about Ancient Babylon 246
 Continued from page 221.

The Fall of the Great Babylon of the Latter Days. 247
 This is actually the concluding segment of "Fulfillment of Prophecies about Ancient Babylon" by William F. Williams. He makes the comparison between the Babylon of old and the Babylon of modern times and concludes that the "Great Babylon of the Latter Days will fall like a stone cast into the sea never to rise again,

just as ancient Babylon fell after a like stone was bound to a book, and which was cast into the river by the prophet Jeremiah."

(Editorial) 248

The first part of this editorial consists of Daniels's glowing report of the "General Council of the Presidencies of the Church of Jesus Christ of Latter-day Saints in the British Isles and the surrounding countries" held in Birmingham recently. He and his two counselors were in attendance along with six of the presidents of the Welsh conferences. He promises that further details will appear in *Zion's Trumpet*. In the second part Daniels emphasizes the urgency of getting the English version of *Marriage and Morals in Utah* in the home of every Latter-day Saint home in Wales and also of distributing it "generously among our neighbors the English." He then recommends the plan of John Kay by quoting Kay's letter to Daniels from Liverpool, dated 27 June 1856. Included in Kay's letter was a circular intended for "ministers, editors, officers, lawyers, merchants, craftsmen, etc." Daniels says in the final part of his editorial that he would have the circular reproduced in large quantities in English and in Welsh with the name and information of each conference president in Wales. In the 13 September 1856 issue of *Zion's Trumpet*, Daniels announces that the Welsh translation was then off the press and available for one penny each.

Letter from President D. Spencer—Journey of the Welsh Emigrants. 251

Excerpts from a letter written by Daniel Spencer on 22 June 1856 from a "Camp of the Latter-day Saints, near Iowa City. He gives many details about the Welsh who sailed with Dan Jones on the *S. Curling* just over two months before. Such information would be of great interest to those back in Wales who had plans to emigrate. See *Millennial Star* 18 (2 August 1856): 489–90.

Truth 253

Dewi Elfed Jones sends this bit of poetry to Daniel Daniels to be printed in *Zion's Trumpet* "for the instructional delight of the children of the muse among the Saints in Gwalia." The poem consists of two stanzas of 14 lines each. The structure is inverted parallelism with the first line of the first stanza and the last line of the second stanza being very similar, the second line of the first stanza and the second-to-last line of the second stanza being very similar, and so on in a chiastic format. The English translation for this poem and all poetry throughout *Zion's Trumpet* is merely informational and makes no attempt to imitate the rhythm, meter, or rhyme scheme.

Railway to Zion 255
    This poem of thirty-six lines is by Thomas Harris and is dated 5 April 1849.

Book Debts, June 30, 1856 256
    The outstanding book debts of twelve conferences are shown.

(No title) 256
    Daniels relays the news he received from Salt Lake City about what action is being taken to remedy the bad harvest of the previous year. The rain is increasing, however, and the forecast for refilling empty storehouses is encouraging.

Receipts for Books from July 17 to 24 256
    Payments from four book distributors are shown.

Contents 256
    A list of this issue's contents and their respective page numbers.

AUGUST 16

Constitution of the State of Deseret 257
    Continued from page 240.

Difference between the Baptists and the Latter-day Saints . 261
    The Welsh translation of this April 1841 essay by "A Baptist" that was printed in the *North Staffordshire Mercury*. See *Millennial Star* 18 (16 August 1856): 516–17.

Condition of the Conferences, &c. 263
> Thomas Rees sends a report of the Flintshire Conference from Brymbo, dated 1 August 1856. Because the ministers in the town of Mold had announced anti-Mormon lectures in English for the following week Rees requests that Daniels send "a brother who speaks English well, with instructions concerning the wisest way to act under the circumstances." In a letter dated 4 August 1856, Llanidloes, John Jones sends an account of his travels with Brother Treharn in Radnorshire. Because of the expense of traveling Jones asks that some of his money be sent to him.

(Editorial) 265
> The Welsh translation of the editorial on tithing in *Millennial Star* 18 (26 July 1856): 473–75.

Invitation to Become Saints 269
> A poem of nine 4-line stanzas with a 4-line chorus by Rachel Davies of Twynyrodyn, Merthyr. Poetry by women is very rare in *Zion's Trumpet*.

To Zion 271
> A poem of three 10-line stanzas by Aneurin L. Jones, the son of Dewi Elfed Jones.

(No title) 272
> Among the 4,395 Saints who had left Britain on eight different ships from 30 November 1855 to 6 July 1856 were 667 from Wales.

An Irishman and a Cardi 272
> A humorous 10-line poem by Thomas Harris, Georgetown, 1849. Georgetown is an area of Merthyr Tydfil and is the modern-day location of a stake center. This poem appears to be a space filler to complete the final page of this issue of *Zion's Trumpet*.

Receipts for Books from August 1 to 14. 272
> Payments from five book distributors are shown.

Contents. 272
   A list of this issue's contents and their respective page numbers.

AUGUST 30

Epistle by Orson Pratt 273
   The Welsh translation of this epistle by Orson Pratt, recently assigned to preside over the Church in Great Britain, Ireland, and all European countries. See *Millennial Star* 18 (23 August 1856): 529–32.

Circulating Tracts. 280
   The Welsh translation of an editorial from the *Millennial Star* in which Orson Pratt emphasizes the importance of tracts in propagating the gospel. He announces that the first two numbers of a new series of tracts—*The True Faith* and *True Repentance*—are now ready for circulation. See *Millennial Star* 18 (23 August 1856): 536 and *Millennial Star* 18 (30 August): 553.

(Editorial). 281
   The first part of this editorial is "Condition of the Conferences." Brothers Evans and Ashby praise the efforts of the Pembrokeshire Conference. Brothers E. D. Miles and David John are "traveling and preaching diligently." Brothers Israel Evans, J. Evans, and T. Jones have had large crowds in Cardiganshire. W. Jones and D. Davies report that things are going well in the Carmarthen and Llanelli conferences. Brothers John Kay and Thomas Williams from the Liverpool Office give high praise to the efforts of Brothers T. Harris and J. Davies in the West Glamorgan Conference. Evan S. Morgans, J. H. Davies, B. Davies, J. Morgans, and Noah M. Jones—all from South Wales—are now in North Wales preaching.
   In the second part Daniels reports that Israel Evans is now traveling throughout the North and that Benjamin Ashby is traveling throughout the South. In the third part Daniels reports that Joseph W. Tuckfield has gone to Aberystwyth to preach.

Letter from Sister Daniels 284
> This letter from Mary Daniels, the wife of Daniel Daniels, is dated 27 June 1856, Great Salt Lake City. She reports that mail transport was slow in coming from the Eastern States and that it had been nearly a year since receiving a letter from her husband. She learned of his call to remain longer than anticipated from someone who had read the news in the *Millennial Star*. "This news was not sweet to me at first," she writes. But she sees it as the will of the Lord and encourages her husband to do his best. She gives other news, especially of the Welsh, and sends her regards to a number of acquaintances still in Wales.

Happy Is the Mormon 286
> A poem of nine 8-line stanzas by John Davies, formerly of Merioneth.

(No title) 288
> Daniels reports that he has received news that the *Thornton* and the *Horizon* have reached America safely and will be crossing the plains in handcarts.

(No title) 288
> For lack of space the article "Difference between the Baptists and the Latter-day Saints" will not appear until the next issue which will also include a letter from Thomas Jeremy.

(No title) 288
> A new printing of the treatise "Divine Authority" is now available from the Liverpool Office.

(No title) 288
> Daniels reports receiving a letter from Ezra T. Benson, who is now in London and intends to visit Wales.

Receipts for Books from August 15 to 26 288
> Payments from two book distributors are shown.

Contents. 288
    A list of this issue's contents and their respective page numbers.

SEPTEMBER 13

Letter of Thomas Jeremy 289
    In this letter by Thomas Jeremy, dated 29 June 1856, Great Salt Lake City, he tells how things are going in general. Knowing that Mary Daniels had written a letter about the Welsh in Salt Lake City, Jeremy reports on such things as progress on the temple, the fifteen-mile canal being built to transport granite stones for the temple, and the positive outlook for this year's crops. He laments that because of the poor crops the previous year people have been too poor to send money for relatives in Wales to emigrate.

Letter of Gwilym Ddu 291
    Gwilym Ddu is the nom de plume of William Lewis, who had been in the first group of Welsh Mormon emigrants in 1849. In his letter, dated 26 June 1856, Great Salt Lake City, he expresses disappointment that Daniel Daniels would be staying longer in Wales longer than expected. He expresses concern that he had not been able to pay into the Perpetual Emigrating Fund to assist his daughter Mary to come from Wales to Utah, and he asks Daniels to investigate the possibility of sending her as a servant to an emigrating family in exchange for her help.

Letter of John Parry 292
    This letter dated 27 July 1856 was written by John Parry from Winter Quarters. He, his wife, and their one-year-old son had sailed on the *S. Curling* in April. He reports that everyone had survived just fine except for a few infants, his included. He was selected by Edward Bunker, the president of the third handcart company, to be one of the three captains of hundreds. They had landed in Boston and gone by train to Iowa City where they stayed for three weeks. They traveled by handcarts another three weeks to reach Winter Quarters and were making the final preparations to begin their trek to Salt Lake City. John Parry and his father had converted to Mormonism in September 1846 six weeks after being reproached by John's sister Sarah for not

allowing her to be baptized into the Church. He and his father both served as missionaries for two years in North Wales at which time his parents sailed to America with Dan Jones and the first group of Welsh Mormon converts. John, however, continued his mission for another seven years in Wales. From 1865 to 1868, he returned to Wales to serve another three-year mission. In 1877 he was appointed by Brigham Young to serve yet another mission—this time it was a building mission to be the master mason of the Logan Temple construction. In 1882, John died in Logan, two years before the temple was completed. See his page on the Welsh Mormon History website at http://welshmormon.byu.edu for more details of his life of service.

Feeling of a Missionary 294

This letter dated 25 August 1856 was written by Joseph Griffiths from the town of Builth Wells in Radnorshire. He tells of the strong opposition to his missionary efforts and gives great praise to John Jones for being "like a father" to him.

The Law of Tithing 295

A poem of four 8-line stanzas by T. Conway, Flint.

(Editorial). 296

In the first part of this editorial, entitled "News from the Valley," Daniels refers the readers to the letters by Thomas Jeremy and Williams Lewis at the first part of this issue to better understand that the reason friends and relatives in Utah had not been sending money to assist them in their emigration was because of lack of money caused by poor crops the previous year. He then gives some excerpts of a 30 June 1856 letter written by Brigham Young to Orson Pratt with greater detail concerning the crop failure of the previous year along with some other bits of news. The second part of the editorial is an appeal to all those wishing to emigrate to send their £1 deposit and information.

Flintshire Conference 297

This letter dated 1 September 1856, Rhosllanerchrugog, is signed by Thomas Rees, president of the Flintshire Conference, and Amos Clarke, his scribe. They tell the details of a successful conference despite "some of the Saints' enemies" who wished to cause a commotion.

The Priesthood. 298
A poem of twenty-one 8-line stanzas by Dewi Ioan Dyfed, formerly of Haverfordwest College. Dewi Ioan Dyfed is the nom de plume of David John, the young convert who until 29 January 1856 had been studying to become a Baptist minister.

Books for Sale. 303
A listing of Welsh Mormon publications available at the *Zion's Trumpet* office in Swansea: the Book of Mormon, the Doctrine and Covenants, the 1852 hymnal, various issues of *Zion's Trumpet*, the third volume of *Prophet of the Jubilee*, ten publications by Dan Jones, and nine publications by John Davis.

Marriage and Morals in Utah. 304
Daniels announces that the Welsh translation of Parley P. Pratt's *Marriage and Morals in Utah* is now available for purchase and dissemination. Included as part of the pamphlet is Daniels's plea to followers of other faiths to listen to the word of God as preached by the Mormon missionaries, "whatever that word may be," and to not believe the "hireling preachers" who "proclaim every lie about the Saints of the Most High God in order to keep [everyone] in darkness. Because the doctrine of plural marriage of the Church of Jesus Christ of Latter-day Saints was such a great impediment to missionary work in Wales, Daniels is following instructions from his leaders in Liverpool to give the work a boost.

Contents. 304
A list of this issue's contents and their respective page numbers.

SEPTEMBER 27

Letter of President D. Jones 305
Dan Jones writes this letter, dated 4 July 1856, to Daniel Daniels from Iowa City. Jones says that he was so exhausted from caring for over 700 people on the sea voyage that for three weeks

after reaching Boston no one knew for certain whether he would live or die. During the eight-day train trip from Boston to Iowa City one of the biggest challenges was to keep "wanton and evil men" from succeeding in enticing some of the sisters away from the group. Once in Iowa City the immigrants had to deal with numerous curiosity seekers who came from miles around to see the camp of Mormons. Jones expresses gratitude that thus far in the midst of the "sound of war" the Saints had been left in peace to go on their way.

Difference between the Baptists and
the Latter-day Saints 309
>   Continued from page 263.

Shutting Doors. 311
>   The Welsh translation of this brief article as it appears in the *Deseret News* for 25 June 1856, p. 1. A grandmother counsels her grandson to shut the doors of his ears, eyes, lips, and his heart in order to "keep out many cold blasts of sin."

(Editorial). 312
>   The Welsh translation of an article on tithing in *Millennial Star* 18 (20 September 1856): 601–3.

Letter to President Daniels 315
>   Dewi Elfed Jones writes this letter dated 21 September 1856 from Swansea to report his visits to various branches. He tells of the diligence of leaders and members in living the gospel and of the "insidious men" who are "raging under the effects of the 'cacoethe scribendi' (the 'scribbling mania') trying to vilify the glory of the organization of the redemption and the redeemed of God."

Tribulation of a Saint in Babylon 317
>   A poem of eleven 4-line stanzas with a 3-line chorus by Thomas Conway, Flint.

Longing for Zion 319
>A poem of four 10-line stanzas by Dewi Elfed. The poem is dated 22 December 1854, about six months before he was excommunicated from the Church.

(No title) 320
>The dates for eight conferences are shown.

Receipts for Books from August 27 to September 26 320
>Payments from four book distributors are shown.

Contents 320
>A list of this issue's contents and their respective page numbers.

OCTOBER 11

Consecration 321
>The Welsh translation of an article from *Millennial Star* 18 (27 September 1856): 609.

Verse to the Mormon 328
>A four-line poem by John Davies, formerly of Meirion.

(Editorial) 329
>The first part of this editorial, entitled "How to Warn the Whole British Nation in One Year," is the Welsh translation of the editorial by Orson Pratt that appears in *Millennial Star* 18 (11 October 1856): 648–51. President Pratt outlines the details of a plan to circulate pamphlets and information throughout all of Britain to inform all the inhabitants about the Church, its beliefs, and its meeting schedules.
>
>The second part is a directive for all who have plans to emigrate in 1857 to make their plans to sail no later than 25 May so as to arrive in the United States by May 1st.
>
>The third part is yet another plea from Daniels to all conference presidents to get their book debts cleared up by the end of the year.

In the fourth part Daniels gives his wholehearted support to Orson Pratt's scheme for flooding Wales with pamphlets and information.

Song of Longing. 334
A poem of five 8-line stanzas by D. A. Hughes, Llanelli. In bracketed comments following the poem is an invitation from Daniels to any "poetical writers" to send in "some of the tasty fruit of their fertile minds" to set on the table of the Trumpet.

(No title). 336
J. Jones writes from Brymbo of a mine accident that claimed the lives of thirty-four miners.

(No title). 336
Daniels calls for the names of those who have emigrated in different ways other than through his office during his tenure as president.

Addresses 336
The addresses for John Jones in Abergele and for David Davies in Llanelli are given.

Receipts for Books from September 27 to October 9. 336
Payments received from seven book distributors are shown.

Contents. 336
A list of this issue's contents and their respective page numbers.

OCTOBER 25

Consecration 337
Continued from page 328.

News from the Emigration 339
> The Welsh translation of this article as it appears in *Millennial Star* 18 (18 October 1856): 667–68. It was originally published in the *Council Bluffs Bugle*.

Home Correspondence 341
> The subtitle to "Home Correspondence" is "Conferences of the North." It consists of the 14 October 1856 letter written from Brymbo by John Jones. Jones was assigned to travel throughout North Wales and is able to give an account of his visits to various people and branches. He laments that there are only four members of the Church in the entire island of Anglesey, but he enthusiastically endorses the new plan of President Orson Pratt to flood the area with pamphlets.

Parable of the Disappointed Harvesters 342
> David Davies, Llanelli, presents this parable that involves a swaggerer, some harvesters, and a field. At the end he asks five questions and invites readers of *Zion's Trumpet* to submit their answers.

Letter of Israel Evans...........................344
> Israel Evans, first counselor to President Daniel Daniels, writes this letter dated 17 October 1856. He had visited all the conferences throughout Wales during the previous three months and gives a brief account of his visit.

(Editorial).................................345
> In the first part of this editorial, Daniels points out that many strong converts to Mormonism have been excommunicated for their transgressions. He warns the Welsh to beware of such deceivers among their own numbers. In the second part, entitled "The New Pamphlets," he declares his intent to publish Welsh translations of each of the pamphlets of President Orson Pratt. He then presents an excerpt from the first of the pamphlets entitled "The True Faith."

Patriotism, Freedom, and Truth 348
> A poem of eight 8-line stanzas by John Reynolds Jr., Heol y Felin.

Eisteddfod of the Saints 350
> "Eisteddfod" is a traditional Welsh festival of literature, music, and performance. The subtitle is "For the Bards and Men of Letters of the Saints, and Their Friends throughout all of Wales." The basic idea is that of competition in a variety of categories to determine the best competitor who then receives a prize. Thomas Harris, on behalf of the West Glamorgan Conference, extends this invitation for all Church members and their friends to compete in three categories: treatises, poetry, and renditions. This special "eisteddfod" is to be held on Christmas Day at the Hall of the Saints in Swansea.

Conferences 352
> The dates of four conferences are shown.

Contents. 352
> A list of this issue's contents and their respective page numbers.

NOVEMBER 8

Sermon, by President B. Young, Bowery, June 22, 1856 . . . 353
> The Welsh translation of this sermon as printed in *Deseret News* for 27 August 1856, 2–3.

(Editorial). 361
> The title of this editorial is "Epistle of President D. Daniels to the Saints in Wales." Daniels calls the attention of his readers to the importance of obeying the law of tithing and the urgency of distributing pamphlets on a large scale. Also he reminds everyone that the Welsh translation of President Orson Pratt's pamphlets will be published soon.

Home Correspondence. 364
> The first of the two reports is entitled "Conferences of the North." This is a letter from John Jones, who writes from Abergele, 26 October 1856. Jones tells of his visits to Machynlleth, Harlech, Porthmadog, and Rhuddlan. He gives high praise

to the missionaries and members for their efforts to sell pamphlets and spread the gospel. He reports several convert baptisms in Abergele, Flintshire, Caernarfon, and Merionethshire and calls for many more missionaries to be sent from South Wales to preach in the North. In his bracketed comment to Jones's request, Daniels says, "The call is earnest, and terrible will be the result of not going when one is able."

The second report is entitled "Pembrokeshire Conference." This is a letter from David John, who writes from Haverfordwest, 29 October 1856. Only ten months earlier David John had been studying to be a Baptist minister at the training school in Haverfordwest. He reports having several baptisms with many "yet quite close."

Attempt at Interpreting the Parable of the Harvesters 366
John Roberts, Merthyr, gives his interpretation of this parable that was presented by David Davies in the issue of *Zion's Trumpet* for 25 October, 342–43. He declares that the "swaggerer" is the devil, the "disappointed harvesters" are the sectarian preachers, the "field" is the earth, the "real owner of the field" is the Lord's, and his "authorized servants" are the Latter-day Saints.

Voice of the Weak 367
This poem of five 5-line stanzas is by N. Ddu. This appears to be Nathan Ddu or Dark Nathan, the nom de plume for Jonathan J. Thomas.

Eisteddfod of the Saints in Swansea 368
T. H. (most likely Thomas Harris) submits to the editor eight more topics for the upcoming "eidsteddfod" in Swansea.

Covers for the Treatises 368
Daniels announces that the Welsh conferences can obtain covers "printed and sown for the English treatises in Liverpool."

Contents. 368
A list of this issue's contents and their respective page numbers.

NOVEMBER 22

Sermon, by President B. Young, Bowery, June 22, 1856 . . . 369
    Continued from page 361.

Excerpt from the Treatise on True Repentance. 373
    Just over four pages from the Welsh Translation of the second in the series of pamphlets by Orson Pratt are quoted in this issue of *Zion's Trumpet*. The translator is Dewi Elfed Jones, now back in full fellowship in the Church.

(Editorial). 377
    In the first part of this editorial, Daniels reports on the visit of President Ezra T. Benson and the newly formed fund which Benson advocated as a means of raising funds to emigrate. In the second part he announces the appointment of Elder James J. Phillips to travel in the West Glamorgan Conference.

Editors of the "Hero" Repelling the Truth, and the Truth Repelling the Editors of the "Hero" 378
    Dewi Elfed Jones explains that he was prompted to write to the editor of *Zion's Trumpet* because of some letters that had appeared recently in the periodical "Hero." Jones refers to the authors of the letters as "half Saints at some time," suggesting that they were apostate Mormons. Jones chides the editors of the periodical saying that they had decided not to print his response to the erroneous information about the Mormons in their periodical for fear that "the honest and the sincere [would] have a fair chance of judging the fanatical partisanship of the *Hero* and its editors, and become enlightened about their made-up, distorted and impudent lies about the Latter-day Saints." "Sectarianism Ensnared" mentioned on page 379 is a reference to a lengthy and very sarcastic poem Jones had published over three years earlier in two issues of *Zion's Trumpet* (26 March 1853): 209–12 and (2 April 1853): 225–27. He mockingly refers to Thomas Price, a Baptist minister, as "his immersive reverence from Aberdare" and to Price's coeditor of the periodical, a Congregational minister, as "his sprinkling reverence from Aberaman." Price was the person who had taken issue with Jones's unprecedented decision

five years earlier to present the key and ownership of the Gwawr Baptist Chapel in Aberaman to William Phillips, the leader of the Mormons in Wales. In a legal battle the courts decided, despite Jones's fundraising campaign to build the chapel, that it would remain in the hands of the Baptists as one of their chapels.

Letter from the Plains to Israel Evans 380
    This letter is dated 31 August 1856, thirty miles east of Laramie. David Grant was a counselor to Edward Bunker in the third handcart company nearly all of which were Welsh. Grant writes only the positive aspects of the crossing to his friend and former missionary companion Israel Evans. Having traversed the plains in 1847 and again in 1848, this was Grant's third time to make the journey. Something that may well have added to his enjoyment of this crossing may have been eighteen-year-old Elizabeth Williams, who became his wife in a plural marriage just eleven weeks after reaching Salt Lake City.

Names of the Welsh Emigrants Who Went with the Handcarts across the Plains Last Season 383
    A total of 204 individuals are represented in this listing. There are 67 in the first group, 63 in the second, and 74 in the third. All of these had sailed on the *S. Curling* with Dan Jones and traversed the plains in the Bunker handcart company. Only 79 names are given, and others are listed as "wife," "child," or "children."

Contents 384
    A list of this issue's contents and their respective page numbers.

DECEMBER 6

Sermon by President B. Young, Bowery, June 22, 1856 385
    Continued from page 372.

News from the Valley 389
    The Welsh translation of this letter from Wilford Woodruff to Orson Pratt is dated 30 August 1856, Great Salt Lake Valley. See *Millennial Star* 18 (8 November 1856): 714.

Arrival of the Handcarts 391
>This letter by Thomas C. Martell is dated 27 September 1856, Great Salt Lake City, and is addressed to a Mr. Jones, a mutual acquaintance of Martell and his former missionary companion Henry Harries. Martell tells Jones that Harries is on his way back to Wales to serve another mission and will no doubt visit Jones, who lives in the town of Talog, Carmarthenshire, in a farmhouse named Rhydgarregddu. Martell expresses hope that Jones and his wife will "obey the calls of the Savior" and accept the message of Mormonism. Martell also tells of the grand reception the handcart pioneers received from Brigham Young and others leaders of the Church. He requests that Jones send the letter to Daniel Daniels at the *Zion's Trumpet* office in Swansea so that others will know of the arrival of the Welsh handcart pioneers in the Salt Lake Valley.

(Editorial) 393
>In the first part of this editorial, Daniels announces a number of changes in leadership positions. Israel Evans and Benjamin Ashby will be replaced by William Miller and James Taylor as counselors in the mission presidency. Also five conference presidents will be replaced.
>
>The second part has to do with the second treatise by Orson Pratt, which is now at the press. Daniels encourages all to do their part in the dissemination of the pamphlets.
>
>In the third part Daniels calls for a return of Welsh pamphlets to the *Zion's Trumpet* office, as about 100 of each are needed.
>
>In the fourth part Daniels instructs the book distributors for each conference to forward the packets of books to the branch distributors "with haste."

Early Polygamy among the Welsh 395
>This curious bit of information is taken from the *Modern Universal British Traveler*, page 671, which reports that in 1580 there was a 105-year-old man in a small village near Aberffraw on the Isle of Anglesey, who had three wives and two concubines and 43 children. No editorial comment is added to this brief article. One is left to speculate as to the reason for its inclusion in the Mormon periodical.

The Perpetual Emigrating Fund 396
This poem by J. P. Prosser, Cap Coch, has seven stanzas. The first three and the final two stanzas have ten lines, whereas the other two have just nine lines.

The Saints' Eisteddfod 398
Thomas Harris addresses this notice "To the Bards and Writers of the Saints, and their Friends throughout All of Wales" to advise them of nine more topics and prizes that have been added to the "eisteddfod" that is to take place on Christmas Day.

(No title)................................ 399
Daniels welcomes Elder Thomas Thomas back to Wales to serve a mission.

(No title)
The discourse of Ezra T. Benson in Swansea will appear in the first issue of the next volume.

(No title).............................. 400
Daniels reports reading in the *Mormon* about the visit of George A. Smith and Erastus Snow to about sixty or seventy of the Welsh Saints in Caseyville, Illinois.

(No title).............................. 400
Daniels also reports that in the account of the St. Louis Semi-annual Conference he saw the names of several elders from Wales. Among the names is that of William Henshaw, whom Daniels refers to as "the founder of the Church in Wales." In late 1842, Henshaw was sent by Lorenzo Snow on a mission to Merthyr Tydfil. His efforts during the next three years resulted in over four hundred convert baptisms. As early as 1840, however, there was a branch of the Church established in Overton, Flintshire, North Wales, on the border with England. But by 1845 when Dan Jones began his mission in North Wales the Overton Branch was no longer in existence. Thus Henshaw is deserving of the "founder" title. Despite his long missionary service in Wales, however, Henshaw eventually aligned himself with the RLDS

Church. See his page on the website at http://welshmormon.byu.edu for further details.

(No title)..400
Daniels comments on the "considerable effort" that has been made to establish settlements along the plains and the effect on future immigrants.

Receipts for Books from October 23 to December 3 400
Payments from eight book distributors are shown.

Contents..400
A list of this issue's contents and their respective page numbers.

DECEMBER 27

Sermon by President B. Young, Bowery, June 22, 1856 401
Continued from page 372.

(Editorial).......................................405
Daniels provides a few emigration notices for his readers to bear in mind.

Sermon 406
Continued from page 405.

Volume 10: 1857

Title page
> Although this is the final extant volume of *Zion's Trumpet*, publication of the periodical continued weekly until April 1862. But for the last four years of its publication, only seventeen isolated issues have surfaced. Benjamin P. Evans served as the editor for over three years until just before he emigrated in 1861, at which time William Ajax was put in charge of publishing *Zion's Trumpet*. George Q. Cannon, the president of The Church of Jesus Christ of Latter-day Saints in Europe, served as the official editor of *Zion's Trumpet*, but it was Ajax who shouldered the burden of getting a new issue of the Welsh periodical into print every Saturday. And thanks to Ajax's journal, we know that the press and the whole printing operation for *Zion's Trumpet* was moved to Liverpool in March of 1861. In a later journal entry, Ajax fixed the date of the final issue of the *Trumpet* as the one for 9 April 1862. Five weeks later Ajax and his wife were on their way to America. See his page on http://welshmormon.byu.edu/ for the link to his journal.
>
> The first nine lines of the title pages for *Zion's Trumpet*, volumes 1 through 9, read as follows:
>
> > Zion's Trumpet,
> > or
> > Star of the Saints;
> > Containing the
> > Principles of the 'Dispensation of the Fullness
> > of Times,'
> > in
> > Treatises, Letters, Accounts,
> > Poetry, &c."
>
> In volume 10, Daniels continues to use the same first three lines, but in place of the next six lines are these four:
>
> > Sounding the echo of the bidding of the Prophets and Apostles of the Church of Jesus Christ of Latter-day Saints—the Generals of the Latter-day Kingdom—the guiding light of the Saints.

The volume 10 (1857) title page was printed and distributed at the same time as the December 26 issue, along with the foreword and the contents.

The two scriptural quotations for volumes 1–6 are Jeremiah 51:9 and Isaiah 40:9. For volumes 7 and 8, Dan Jones changed these to Jeremiah 6:17 and Isaiah 18:3. For volume 9, Daniel Daniels used the Jeremiah and Isaiah scriptures, but for volume 10, he used Daniel 2:34 and Daniel 7:18.

The only other extant title page for *Zion's Trumpet* is the one for volume 13 (1860), which was printed as part of the issue for 29 December 1860. It contains no scriptural quotations—only the following ten lines:

Zion's Trumpet,
or
Star of the Saints,
Containing the
Principles of the Church of Jesus Christ of the
Latter-day Saints.
Volume XIII.
Swansea:
Printed and Published by B. P. Evans.
1860.

Foreword

Daniel Daniels refers to *Zion's Trumpet* as a "brightly shining Star" whose sounds over the years have been "true and consistent, with not a single one in vain." He says that all should rejoice that they have a "Prophet and Seer, whose voice resounds to the Saints in Wales through their Trumpet." He makes reference to the *Prophet of the Jubilee*, the forerunner of *Zion's Trumpet* that "began to declare the message of Heaven in Wales." He declares that apostates from the Church will be among the most wretched and that the faithful Welsh Saints will always have a place in his heart. He thanks all who have assisted him in the publication of *Zion's Trumpet* and announces that Elder Benjamin Evans is to be his successor as the editor.

The only other extant foreword for *Zion's Trumpet* after this one is the one for volume 13 (1860), which was printed as part of the issue for 29 December 1860. The author of this foreword is Benjamin P. Evans, who served as editor of the periodical during all of 1858, 1859, 1860, and the first dozen or so issues of 1861.

And since *Zion's Trumpet* was published weekly in its final years, Evans oversaw the publication of around 180 issues, more than any other editor. Although no complete volume of the periodical is extant for any of its final four years, a total of seventeen isolated issues have surfaced—three for 1858, five for 1859, six for 1860, and three for 1861. When Evans emigrated in April 1861, he was replaced as editor by George Q. Cannon, who presided over all the Church in Britain and Europe. Cannon, however, was editor of *Zion's Trumpet* in name only—his assistant William Ajax was put in charge of preparing the periodical for publication each week until its final issue, dated 5 April 1862. (See my *Welsh Mormon Writings from 1844 to 1862: A Historical Bibliography* [Provo, UT: Religious Studies Center, Brigham Young University, 1988], 72–79, for additional details of *Zion's Trumpet*.)

Because of its uniqueness, I am including here the English translation of Benjamin P. Evans's foreword for the third and final volume for which he was editor. Dated 29 December 1860 it was written just over three months before Evans, the final Welsh editor of *Zion's Trumpet*, left for America:

FOREWORD.

Since it is a custom in the world to write a foreword to every volume that is published, whether it is a volume of a monthly publication, a weekly publication, or a volume on some particular topic, we would be considered stranger than we actually are, were we to release this volume through the press without something of a foreword for it. We consider there to be a great deal of sense in the old saying, 'When in Rome, do as the Romans do,' and we have benefitted greatly from it. We know that one may adopt the manner of dress, eating, and behavior, while there, without partaking of the sins of the Romans, and if so, we can just as easily adopt the customs of Britain to the same extent, while in Britain, without partaking of the corruption of Britain, which will be better for us, if we do so, than were we to adopt the customs of Rome while in Britain.

But if we conform to the customs of the world in things like these, and recommend doing so to others, in wisdom, there is a great disparity between us and the entire world with regard to the 'great topic,' as it is known, and we are in no way recommending that anyone adopt the evil customs or principles, though they may be highly approved by the majority of men. We wish to be as far as this, at any rate, 'from the fashion.' We strike against all false principles and traditions, and we wish to get the world to do the same, which has fairly thrown us out of 'fashion,' as if we cared about that, since we are on the right path.

Perhaps some of our readers have felt inclined to complain about the printing of this volume, but not without cause, for it was very bad in some places. But let none, in their ignorance, place the blame on the printer, for he was not to blame, rather it was the letters, which because of that, are about to be thrown into the fire, to be returned to their original substance, in the same way that is done to some men, if they do not make a fine and blameless imprint on the volume of time. We are happy to think that there will be no room to complain about the printing of the 'Trumpet,' hereafter the fact, for the clothier is hard at it in making a new garment for him, one which will not be a source of embarrassment in any court in Wales or England. We hope that he will be welcomed to tell his story on every hearth, and that everyone will be ready to put a penny and halfpenny in his pocket each time he visits them.

We are sorry to have to try the patience of the sons of the muse more than we had wished. Although but little of the fruit of the muse appears in this volume, despite all that, some had to remain longer on the field of the pen before being released through the press, and that for lack of convenient space to put such. We have said many times that our chief master is Mr. Space, to whom we must humble ourselves each time he goes by. It is known also that we are publishing the translation of Apostle P. P. Pratt's 'Key to Theology' in this volume, which has placed us all the more in the clutches of Mr. Space than we would have been, had it not been for this. This was also the chief reason for the fruit of the sons of the muse to have to wait here so long before being allowed to proceed through the press. This will not be allowed in the future, therefore, let the poets strive to present us with a fruitful yield in our next volume, and there they shall have an immediate place in the barn. We earnestly desire the assistance of those who frequent the prose field, so that we may produce as much original material as possible, so that by doing so, we make our publication worthy of an extensive circulation, and an adornment for the Mission.

It is unnecessary for us to say anything about the work of this year, for one can see that by just turning to the index. It is our obligation to thank all the supporters of this volume of the 'Trumpet' for their effort on its behalf, and also we wish for them to refrain from putting their arms in the armory yet, for the battle is not over. We intend to begin again with renewed strength, after receiving our new battle garb, against Satan, and for the kingdom of God. Assist us, brave soldiers of Zion, to wage war bravely on the side of our Chief, and in this way secure for ourselves commendation when the battle is over, and when we have a crown of endless honor in his heavenly kingdom.

THE EDITOR.

Contents

An alphabetical listing of 102 major headings in the original Welsh. The English translation is also arranged alphabetically, making the order different from that of the original. There are 34 indented headings under "Editorial," 10 under "Letters," and 10 under "Songs, Verses, &c." Nine incorrect page references in the original are corrected in the translation of "Contents."

JANUARY 10

Summary of the Teaching of President Ezra T. Benson, in the Saints' Hall, Swansea, November 11, 1856 1

Ezra T. Benson had arrived in Britain several months earlier with Orson Pratt. Pratt was to replace Franklin D. Richards as the president of the Church in Great Britain and all European Countries, and Benson was to be his first counselor. Benson addressed the Welsh Saints in English at the gathering in Swansea, and William Lewis "recorded" the talk in some form of shorthand to be printed in *Zion's Trumpet*. Benson told of his conversion in Massachusetts and how his friends had left him. He encouraged everyone to be faithful in living the gospel and in preparing to emigrate.

(Editorial). 10

In the first part of this editorial, entitled "Pamphlets," Daniels gives instructions regarding the third pamphlet of the Orson Pratt series, *Water Baptism*, and other matters having to do with various publications.

The second part is entitled "Covers" and has to do with the covers for *True Repentance*, the second pamphlet of the Pratt series.

The third part, entitled "Emigration," is the Welsh translation of a lengthy article from the *Millennial Star* by the same title. See *Millennial Star* 18 (27 December 1856): 820.

In the fourth part, entitled "Notice," Daniels thanks those who sent information about those who had emigrated from Wales without notifying his office.

In the fifth part, entitled "Arrivals," Daniels gives the names of several recently arrived missionaries from Utah.

The sixth and final part is entitled "The New Year." Daniels writes of several worrisome happenings in various parts of the world and encourages the Welsh Saints to prepare themselves to emigrate as soon as possible. He then acknowledges his lack of skill to occupy his current office and gives his thanks to several brethren who have provided him with valuable assistance. He ends the editorial with an eight-line poem in which he wishes everyone a happy new year.

Song of Noah. 15

A poem of four 8-line stanzas by Pencrych about the urgency of proclaiming the gospel.

(No title). 16

A comment as to how many items could be purchased for emigration were one to forgo purchasing a daily threepence pint of liquor.

Address 16

The address for Abednego Williams in Merthyr Tydfil.

xciv CONTENTS

Receipts for Books from Dec. 4 to Jan. 5 16
    Payment for books from six book distributors are shown.

Ditto, for pamphlets 16
    Payment for pamphlets from seven book distributors are shown.

Contents. 16
    A list of this issue's contents and their respective page numbers.

JANUARY 24

Letter of Captain D. Jones 17
    Dan Jones wrote the bulk of this letter on 18 September 1856 from Fort Laramie. He was traveling across the plains with Franklin D. Richards and fifteen other returning missionaries on horseback and in fast carriages. Since leaving Florence two weeks earlier, they had already traveled five hundred miles. Jones reports that the Cheyenne Indians had killed Almon Babbitt and some others, but he emphasizes that all who were killed were enemies of the Saints. Jones wrote the remaining few lines of the letter on 27 September from the "Upper Crossing of the Platte."

"The Measure of the Stature of the Fullness of Christ" 19
    This letter written by Elder Evan Rees on 1 January 1857 from Nantyglo is actually a response to his father who had requested an explanation regarding the meaning of Ephesians 4:13. To answer his father's question, Rees quotes a number of scriptures and builds his argument in a very logical and step-by-step fashion.

Address of Henry Harries to the Saints in Wales 22
    Henry Harries converted to Mormonism in 1851 and went with a group of Saints to Salt Lake City in 1854. As he writes this 16 January 1857 greeting to his fellow Saints in Wales, he is at the *Zion's Trumpet* office in Swansea as a newly arrived missionary. He tells of his journey from Utah back to Wales and of the apostates who had been killed by the Indians. He assures those

who will be emigrating that they have nothing to fear as long as they remain faithful.

(Editorial) 25
In the first part of this editorial, Daniels reports the arrival of Elder Samuel Roskelley and Elder Henry Harries and states their assignments along with that of Dewi Elfed Jones. In the second part he makes a plea for book debts to be paid. In the third part he instructs the "presiding brethren" to submit their "numbers and financial stewardships" separate from their correspondence to spare his clerk the trouble of looking through long letters for the items of importance to him. In the fourth part Daniels explains, in answer to a question submitted by Sion Edwart, that Church members do indeed have a duty to pay tithing in addition to giving the occasional meal to a conference president or a traveling elder. And in the fifth part he warns the Saints not to receive any person who claims to be an office holder in the Church unless he has "an authorized appointment to travel throughout such a place."

Teaching of Apostle Benson 27
Continued from page 9.

Statistical Report 31
This report shows the twelve conferences in Wales, the names of their presidents, and various statistics as of 31 December 1856.

Book Debts, December 31, 1856. 32
A total of just over £418 is owed by the twelve conferences, the Liverpool Office and the Liverpool Welsh Branch.

Address 32
The address of E. D. Miles in Haverfordwest is shown.

(No title) 32
A call for the names of those who intend to emigrate.

Contents..32
   A list of this issue's contents and their respective page numbers.

FEBRUARY 7

"Paying Tithing"................................33
   On page 350 of the 25 October 1856 *Zion's Trumpet* is the announcement of a prize to be awarded for the best treatise on "Paying Tithing—its scripturalness—the blessings enjoyed from obeying it, and the failure that follows its opponents." The entry from John Jones was selected to appear in this issue of *Zion's Trumpet*.

(Editorial)......................................40
   In the first part of this editorial, Daniels exhorts Church members to be diligent in distributing pamphlets to their friends and neighbors. He explains that the combined individual efforts will be "mighty in their influence, and constitute the lever by which Babylon is to be turned upside down, and the kingdom of God established on its ruins."
   The second part is a short announcement of the brief visit of two missionaries to Wales before they emigrate.
   In the third part, Daniels announces that his counselors Israel Evans and Benjamin Ashby will soon be returning home.
   In the fourth part, he reports that Truman O. Angell and John Kaye visited Wales for a few days to learn the procedures of the iron and copper works. He comments on the excitement in Llanelli when word got out "that an angel was preaching in the Saints' Chapel!"
   In the fifth part, Daniels relays information from the 17 January issue of the *Mormon* about plans to establish settlements across the plains to render assistance to the handcart pioneers. He also mentions the rescue party sent by Brigham Young in behalf of the last handcart companies and promised to put more information in the next issue as he received it.
   In the sixth part, Daniels reports that repentance and baptism are being preached to all the Saints in Utah and that they are being asked to "show whether they wish to live their religion and serve God by truly building his kingdom." He declares that

the Saints in Wales need to show the same thing and urges conference presidents to prepare the members in their branches to "prepare to receive the word of the Lord." He then gives specific instructions as to how the conference presidents can conduct an investigation to ascertain the level of commitment among their members.

Teaching of Apostle Benson 45
Continued from page 30 in the previous issue.

Invitation of a Saint to His Relations 46
A poem of six 6-line stanzas by Thomas F. Thomas, formerly from Georgetown, a neighborhood in Merthyr Tydfil. He sends the poem from Pottsville, a town in Ohio, where many Mormon immigrants worked in the coal mines to make sufficient money to continue their journey to Utah.

Additional News from the Valley. 47
This issue of *Zion's Trumpet* was just about to be sent to the press when Daniels received a copy of the *Millennial Star* with more details about the Mormon Reformation then taking place in Utah. Thus he comments about the Reformation and how it will be initiated in Wales and promises to print the Welsh translation of the letters from Brigham Young and F. D. Richards in the next issue. He also gives additional information about the handcart companies that were rescued on the plains.

(No title). 48
The *Columbia* sailed from Liverpool on 16 November 1856 with 221 Saints and others on board.

Book Payments from January 5 to February 5 48
Book payments from six book distributors are shown.

Ditto for Pamphlets 48
Pamphlet payments from seven book distributors are shown.

(No title). 48
    The dates for four conferences are shown.

Contents. 48
    A list of this issue's contents and their respective page numbers.

FEBRUARY 21

Letter of President Brigham Young .49
    The Welsh translation of the 30 October 1856 letter of Brigham Young to Orson Pratt about the Reformation and how it is needed in England, Scotland, and Wales. Also included is the latest information about the last two handcart companies still on the plains. See *Millennial Star* 19 (14 February 1857): 97–99.

News from the Plains 54
    The Welsh translation of an article from the 31 January 1857 issue of the *Mormon* that contains the latest information about the rescue of the two last handcart companies during 1856.

(Editorial). 56
    In the first part of this editorial, Daniels comments on the "vehicle of lies" that is traveling "quickly on its greased, libelous wheels from one reverend and editor to the other" about the misfortune of the handcart companies. In the second part he informs the members of the Church in Wales that the Reformation is about to get underway.

Continuation of News from the Plains 57
    The final part of the article from the *Mormon*.

Reformation. 58
    The Welsh translation of the 4 February 1857 "Minutes of Meetings Held at 42, Islington, Liverpool, on Wednesday and Thursday Nights, 4th and 5th February, for the Purpose of Commencing the Work of Reformation in the Church in these Lands." See *Millennial Star* 19 (28 February 1857): 129–34.

The Measure of the Stature of the Fullness of Christ......64
> The first part of the 1 January 1857 letter written by Elder Evan Rees in answer to his father's question about the meaning of "the measure of the stature of the fullness of Christ" was printed in the 24 January 1857 issue of *Zion's Trumpet*. Daniels apologizes for failing to print the conclusion of the letter in this issue but promises to do so in the next.

(No title)..64
> Daniels apologizes for the delay in printing this issue of the periodical.

Latter-day Saint Psalmody............................64
> Daniels announces the publication of the first volume of this book "soon." There is no evidence that a book by this title was ever published by the Mormons in Wales.

Contents...64
> A list of this issue's contents and their respective page numbers.

MARCH 7

The Latter-day Work—Preparation 65
> The Welsh translation of this article from the *Millennial Star* 19 (7 March 1857): 152–53.

Farewell Address of Elder Israel Evans.................68
> Evans, an American elder with Welsh ancestry, bids a fond farewell to the Welsh Saints after serving as a counselor to Daniel Daniels in the presidency. He reflects back to the "huge void" left in the Church leadership with the departure of Dan Jones and all but two of the conference presidents a year earlier, and he heaps praise on the new leaders for filling that void very well. And he expresses his gratitude to the membership throughout Wales who gave him such kind treatment despite his inability to communicate with the vast majority of them in their native tongue.

(Editorial).................................72
 In the first part of this editorial, Daniels reminds conference presidents of the Reformation meeting to be held in the *Zion's Trumpet* office under the presidency of Ezra T. Benson, a counselor to Orson Pratt in the presidency of the Church in Britain.
 The second part consists of two letters from Richard Williams (corrected to Rice Williams in the 28 March 1857 issue, p. 112) to Daniel Daniels and excerpts of a letter from Rice Williams to his relatives. In the first letter to Daniels, dated 11 November 1856 from Salt Lake City, Williams expresses his joy at being in Utah. In the second letter to Daniels, dated 16 November 1856, Williams initially tells of the "great welcome" Dan Jones received on his return to Utah and then provides some information about the rescue of the handcart companies. And in the excerpts of Williams's letter to his relatives he first declares that Great Salt Lake City is a "much more excellent place" than he thought it would be. He then describes how the Reformation is working in Utah and closes with a prophecy given by Brigham Young to the effect that not many years hence the President of the Church would "have the right to place a President over the United States."

The Measure of the Stature of the Fullness of Christ......74
 Continued from *Zion's Trumpet*, 24 January 1857, 19–22.

My Dream.....................................76
 A poem of twenty 8-line stanzas by David John. The final three stanzas are printed three weeks later in the 21 March issue of *Zion's Trumpet*. In his dream an angel appears to him and answers his questions about religion. Because of the dream David John becomes an ardent supporter of Mormonism and is serving in Flintshire as a missionary at the time he sends the poem to be published in *Zion's Trumpet*. Only fourteen months earlier, he had been studying to be a Baptist minister at the training school in Haverfordwest. For more information and a link to the David John journals, see his page on the website at http://welshmormon.byu.edu.

News from Utah 80
  An update of the last two handcart companies to reach Salt Lake City.

Departure 80
  Information for those who will be leaving on the *George Washington* later in the month.

Address 80
  The address of James J. Phillips in Swansea.

Book Payments, from February 6th to March 5th 80
  Book payments from seven book distributors are shown.

Ditto for Pamphlets 80
  Pamphlet payments from six book distributors are shown.

Contents 80
  A list of this issue's contents and their respective page numbers.

MARCH 21

Report of the Reformation and Fasting Conference, which Was Held at the "Zion's Trumpet" Office, Swansea, Thursday, March 12, 1857 81
  Those in attendance at this high level meeting with President Ezra T. Benson, counselor to Orson Pratt in the presidency of the Church in Britain, were: Daniel Daniels and his two new counselors William Miller and James Taylor. His recently released counselors Israel Evans and Benjamin Ashby were there as well. Also John E. Jones, the representative for the conferences of North Wales; presidents of the conferences of East Glamorgan, West Glamorgan, Brecon, Llanelli, Carmarthen, Pembroke, and Cardigan; several traveling and local elders.
  This conference report occupies all sixteen pages of this issue of *Zion's Trumpet*. The purpose of the conference was to discuss how best the Reformation could be implemented in Wales.

William Lewis, the scribe who prepared the report for publication, was no doubt bilingual and probably used some form of shorthand to write down the talks and presentations. The main speaker was President Ezra T. Benson. Other speakers were Daniel Daniels, Israel Evans, Benjamin Ashby, William Miller, James Taylor, and John E. Jones. The scribe indicates that all the elders were able to express themselves during the conference.

(No title)..96
Using half the final page of this issue of *Zion's Trumpet,* Daniels announces his intention to publish the next issue within a week. He also gives strong encouragement to the presiding brethren to organize their Reformation meetings in a similar way to the one just held at Swansea and to make use of *Zion's Trumpet* and the *Millennial Star* in getting the Reformation underway in the areas over which they preside.

Address 96
The address of John Davies in Swansea.

MARCH 28

Liverpool Reformation Meetings 97
A continuation from page 63 of the 21 February 1857 issue of *Zion's Trumpet* of the minutes of the meetings held in Liverpool about the Reformation. Beginning five lines from the bottom of page 99, the English translation of the Welsh reads, "The Saints are backward in attending the sacrament meetings as they ought." This segment in the *Millennial Star,* however, reads as follows: "The Saints are backward in attending the meetings, unless there is an especial appointment made for someone extra to be there. They do not attend the sacrament meetings as they ought." Apparently the eyes of the translator of the English version into Welsh went from the first occurrence of "meetings" down to the second occurrence of "meetings" and the words in between the two occurrences were omitted from the translation.

Letter from the States..............................102
> This letter by John E. Rees is dated 4 February 1857, Pittston Ferry. Rees, originally from Cwmaman, tells Daniel Daniels of his rough journey from Liverpool to New York and of his joining with his brother and mother in Pittston Ferry, Pennsylvania. He reports that there is a branch of the Church in that mining town with about one hundred British members under the leadership of Benjamin Isaac. He predicts that because he and some of his children had been able to find work "immediately" that they were hoping to continue on to Zion by summer. He laments being unable to follow the progress of the work in Wales from his new location since he was without any issues of *Zion's Trumpet* to read.

The Way to Keep Peace in a Family...................103
> A list of ten suggestions to bear in mind in trying to resolve difficulties in one's family.

Death of President Jedediah M. Grant................104
> The Welsh translation of this notice as it appeared in the *Millennial Star* 19 (21 March 1857): 185–86.

(Editorial)..105
> Daniels pleads with all Church members to show their support for the Reformation by obeying the commandments and being more diligent in their callings. He requests that branch presidents read the editorials of *Zion's Trumpet* in their meetings and councils.

Instructive Chapter for the Censors of Utah.............107
> This is an editorial from the 24 January 1857 *Western Standard* then being published by George Q. Cannon in San Francisco, California. Cannon takes issue with the writer of a proposal to "partition Utah and apportion the different parts to California and the adjacent Territories." This idea was intended to keep Utah from gaining statehood and avoid "the deep disgrace" which would be inflicted upon the United States should Utah be recognized as a sister state. Cannon points out the hypocrisy in such a proposal coming from a resident of California, a state

where "corruption, whoredom and abomination of every kind are glaringly exhibited on all hands."

My Dream 110
> The final three stanzas of David John's poem for which the initial seventeen stanzas were published three weeks earlier in the 7 March 1856 *Zion's Trumpet*.

Departure of the Saints for Zion 111
> A poem of five 4-line stanzas by Aneurin L. Jones, Merthyr Tydfil. Jones was the son of David Bevan Jones, the Baptist minister from the Gwawr Chapel in Aberaman who converted to Mormonism in 1851, was excommunicated in 1855, and then accepted back in to the Church a year later. See the page for David Bevan Jones at http://welshmormon.byu.edu for further details.

(No title). 112
> A correction: Richard Williams on page 74 of this volume should read Rice Williams.

(No title). 112
> Daniels asks the book distributors to send him several specific issues from the 1856 volume of *Zion's Trumpet*. These were apparently needed to complete volumes for binding.

Book Payments. 112
> Payments from three book distributors are shown.

Affectionate 112
> Proof that absence does not cause love to wane.

(No title). 112
> Two enemies in particular to watch out for.

Contents. 112
> A list of this issue's contents and their respective page numbers.

APRIL 11

A Looking Glass, in which to examine ourselves, to see whether we be in the faith 113

> The Welsh translation of this article sent by Parley P. Pratt for publication in the *Mormon*. See *Millennial Star* 19 (4 April 1857): 221–24.

Credibility of the Book of Mormon, as Compared with that of the Bible 119

> The Welsh translation of this essay by C. W. Wandell that was first published in the *Western Standard* and then in *Millennial Star* 19 (4 April 1857): 208–11 and (11 April 1857): 237–39. This essay is much longer than the eight pages it occupies in this issue of *Zion's Trumpet*. Additional installments appear in later issues of *Millennial Star*, but no more appear in *Zion's Trumpet*.

(Editorial) 121

> The Welsh translation of Orson Pratt's editorial entitled "General Instructions to Pastors, Presidents, and Elders" that was published in *Millennial Star* 19 (11 April 1857): 232–33.

(Credibility of the Book of Mormon) 123

> Two and one-half pages of this essay precede the editorial. The final five and one-half pages follow the editorial.

Contents 128

> A list of this issue's contents and their respective page numbers.

APRIL 25

A Looking Glass, of Local Manufacture 129

> A letter written to Daniel Daniels by Dewi Elfed Jones, dated 8 April 1857, Merthyr Tydfil. Jones's letter is very similar in tone and content to Parley P. Pratt's "A Looking Glass, in which to examine ourselves, to see whether we be in the faith," the lead article in the April 11 issue of *Zion's Trumpet*. Whereas Pratt writes

about the Reformation as it applies to Church members in general, Jones directs his observations specifically at the members of the Church in Wales.

Fourteenth General Epistle 133
    The Welsh translation of this epistle by Brigham Young and Heber C. Kimball dated 10 December 1856, Salt Lake City. The translation from English into Welsh was done by Dewi Elfed Jones. At the end of the first installment of this epistle on page 141 of this issue is an indication that it will be continued on page 145, which is the first page of the following issue. Apparently the intent was to make the continuation of the Epistle the first item in the 2 May 1857 issue. The first item, however, turns out to be nearly two pages of encouraging accounts as to the progress of the Reformation in Wales, and the continuation of the epistle begins at the bottom of page 146.

Letter from Captain Jones. 142
    Dan Jones and his two good friends, Thomas Jeremy and Daniel Daniels, left Wales together on the *Buena Vista* in 1849 as part of the first group of Welsh Mormon emigrants. They returned to Wales together in 1852 as missionaries and served together in the presidency of the Church in Wales until April 1855, when Thomas Jeremy returned to his home in Utah. In April 1856, Jones returned to his home in Utah, leaving Daniels as the editor of *Zion's Trumpet* in his stead. Finally, in early 1858, Daniels was able to return to his home in Utah after an absence of nearly six years.

    Jones writes this 31 October 1856 letter from Daniels's home in Salt Lake City and tells him of several adventures he had during his journey from Wales to Utah, including the request he received to speak to a large gathering in the Tabernacle. Daniels comments in a bracketed note following the letter in this issue of *Zion's Trumpet* that Jones's letter was presented to the typesetter as soon as it was received. Daniels's wish for Jones to have "a long life and health" was not fulfilled, however, as Jones died just under four years later at age fifty-one.

(No title)..144
    Daniels gives instruction to conference presidents about selling pamphlets. They are not to sell the new series of pamphlets "to the world" (nonmembers of the Church) unless they agree to purchase the whole series. But they are permitted to sell the pamphlets of Dan Jones and John Davis however they wish.

(No title)
    Daniels comments that the letter of Dewi Elfed Jones at the beginning of this issue is a "complete answer to a variety of questions and complaints we have received" concerning the Reformation in Wales.

(No title)..144
    Daniels explains that the epistle of the First Presidency has made it necessary to publish a "supplement" to this issue of *Zion's Trumpet*. Only a week later, another issue was published that contains the remainder of the epistle "so that it may be read deliberately, accurately, and thoroughly in the meetings."

Contents..144
    A list of this issue's contents and their respective page numbers.

MAY 2

Home Church Accounts..145
    Daniels explains that his readers have been deprived in previous issues of the contents of letters from their "diligent and faithful brethren" who are "thundering the reformation wherever they walk." He then provides a few quotes from the letters of the following brethren: James Taylor, Benjamin Evans, Abednego Williams, W. Miller, S. Roskelley, J. Davies, and Bro. Jones.

Continuation of the Epistle..145
    The fourteenth general epistle continues from page 141 of the previous issue.

Repentance among the Saints. 156
> The Welsh translation of this article as it appears in *Millennial Star* 19 (2 May 1857): 281–84. Page 283 of this article in *Millennial Star* has the following bits of counsel:
>> Mind your own business.
>> Get the beam out of your own eye, and keep it out.
>> Purify your own hearts.
>> If you ache to slander some one, slander yourself.
>> Speak against your own corrupt doings.
>> Be ashamed and confounded because of your own evil deeds.
>> Do your neighbor good, or let him alone.
>> Let REFORMATION be written on your hearts.
>> Let life—eternal life—be your motto forever.
>
> The translator of these lines, probably Dewi Elfed Jones, elected to put these nine lines of counsel into a poem of four 3-line stanzas. The English translation of the poem is merely informational and not poetic.

Book Debts, March 31, 1857 160
> A list of the twelve conferences in Wales and the amount each one owes for books. The total is over £456.

Payments from March 6 until April 29 160
> The book payments from six book distributors are shown.

Ditto for Pamphlets 160
> The pamphlet payments from five book distributors are shown.

(No title). 160
> A call for volunteers for the "Mormon Army" of missionaries in Wales. The Captain Jones mentioned is not Dan Jones, who is now in Utah. Rather, it is John Jones, a missionary serving in North Wales.

Contents. 160
> A list of this issue's contents and their respective page numbers.

MAY 16

Letter from Elder Henry Harries 161
> This letter, dated 22 April 1857, Carmarthen, is from Henry Harries to Daniel Daniels. Since his arrival back in Wales as a missionary three months earlier, Harries had been questioned by worried Church members about the atrocities committed by the Indians on companies crossing the plains. He is using *Zion's Trumpet* as a general platform to provide his assessment to the Church membership in Wales. He provides details of several incidents to show that "the white men were more to blame than the Indians" in hopes of calming the fears that Church members had of making the journey to Utah. Harries then tells of meeting a great number of Welsh converts on his way back to Wales several months earlier and provides names and places of origin in Wales.

The "Daily Telegraph's" Slanders against "Mormonism" . . 164
> The Welsh translation of the refutation of charges against Mormonism by Joseph Ellis, the publisher of the *Daily Telegraph*, a London newspaper. This response appears in *Millennial Star* 19 (16 May 1857): 305–7.

Brecon Conference 168
> John Thomas writes to Daniel Daniels from Black Rock, Llanelly, Brecon, on 8 May 1857 about the condition of the Saints in that area. He reports that sixty Church members there are "in conformity with the Reformation." In *Zion's Trumpet* his name is misspelled as NOHJ THOMAS. This typographical error is corrected in the translation.

(Editorial) 169
> The first part of this editorial is a notice of the departure of the *Westmoreland*, bound for Philadelphia with 540 Saints on board.
>
> The second part is a notice that the East Glamorgan Conference has been divided into two. The new conference is to be called the Cardiff Conference.
>
> The third part has information about four conferences to be held during May and June.

In the fourth part, Daniel Daniels reflects back to the establishment of the Church in Wales. He is a convert of just under a decade and has witnessed many changes during this time. Although the numbers of convert baptisms have decreased substantially from the huge increase of several years ago, Daniels is pleased to report that during the previous six months 575 new converts have been added. And during this same time period, over £919 has been sent to the Liverpool Office from Wales. He encourages Church members to be faithful and to continue during this time of reformation.

In the fifth part Daniels relates news of the appointments recently made in the Federal offices of Utah as printed in the *Mormon* for 28 March 1857.

And he draws from the 25 April *Mormon* the latest information about the resignation letter of Judge Drummond and the commotion caused by his damaging accusations against the Mormons. Daniels also quotes extensively from a letter written by a "gentleman from Utah," not a Mormon, who defends the character of the Mormons and argues "in favor of the Saints in Utah being able to have officers of their own choosing."

Letter from Elder Israel Evans 172

Israel Evans, the former counselor to Daniel Daniels, writes this 16 April 1857 letter on board the *George Washington* as the ship neared the Boston harbor. He provides details of the crossing. He is obviously happy to see once again the land of his birth and writes, "I feel as if once again I am within my cozy home" and adds "I believe I speak the feelings of all on board."

(No title). 174

The 8 May 1857 letter of David John written from Rhosllanerchrugog follows immediately after the one from Israel Evans. John reports that he has "preached on the same topic for seven weeks, namely the 'Reformation.'" He writes that "if troubles arise in the midst of the people, these are most often caused by the ministers and the preachers."

Letter from Pastor Jones 175
> J. E. Jones writes this 11 May 1857 letter "alongside the road between Caernarvon and Cricieth, as happy as can be." He gives a report of the missionary efforts he is supervising in North Wales and pleads for more missionaries to be sent to strengthen the force. Daniels adds a bracketed reinforcement of Jones's request, declaring that those who answer the call "shall be blessed and strengthened."

(No title) 176
> An anecdote to the effect that people will put forth more effort to get money than to get eternal salvation.

Contents 176
> A list of this issue's contents and their respective page numbers.

MAY 30

The Public Shame of Judge Drummond 177
> The Welsh translation by Dewi Elfed Jones of this article as it appears in *Millennial Star* 19 (23 May 1857): 328–33.

Mr. Thomas Bullock, in Reply to Judge Drummond's
Charges 185
> The Welsh translation of this article as it appears in *Millennial Star* 19 (23 May 1857): 334–35. The bracketed comments of Orson Pratt, editor of the *Millennial Star*, in support of Thomas Bullock's truthful character, are also translated into Welsh.

TO PRESIDENTS OF CONFERENCES 188
> The Welsh translation of this brief paragraph by Orson Pratt requesting all conference presidents to send his (Pratt's) answer to Judge Drummond's Report "or any other articles of interest in any of our other periodicals" to editors of papers "respectfully requesting them to publish them."

News from Utah............................188
    The Welsh translation of these bits of news from Utah as they appear in the *Mormon* (9 May 1857): 2.

To Drummond and His Company 189
    A poem of four 4-line stanzas by Dewi Elfed denouncing Drummond and his ilk.

Letters from the Valley...........................190
    The first letter is from John S. Davis, dated 5 February 1857, Great Salt Lake City. Davis, the editor of *Zion's Trumpet* from 1849 through 1853, reports to Daniels that he is preaching the Reformation to all the Welsh in his neighborhood and that Dan Jones and Thomas Jeremy are his "fellow missionaries." These three are also encouraging the Welsh to learn English and "not to keep speaking Welsh, since that is an obstacle for persons learning another language."

    The second letter is from Hopkin Matthews, dated 20 October 1856, Ogden City. Matthews reports that he and his family had reached the Salt Lake Valley on 2 October after an "unusually successful journey across the plains and through the mountains." After giving the names of some of the Welsh who died, Matthews tells of the warm welcome they received after reaching the Valley. After Matthews's glowing report of the "abundant harvest of wheat, corn, potatoes, etc.," Daniel Daniels inserts the following bracketed comment: "What does the *Gwron* say now about the grasshoppers, I wonder." The *Gwron* (Hero) was a Welsh periodical whose editor had chided the Welsh Mormons for going to a place where the grasshoppers consumed their crops.

Payments for Publications and Pamphlets from
April 30 to May 29.............................192
    Payments from eight book distributors are shown.

(No title)....................................192
    Daniels announces his intention to publish the articles in this issue of *Zion's Trumpet* in the form of a pamphlet for the Saints to distribute them as widely as possible in response to Orson Pratt's

plea on page 188 of this issue. If such a pamphlet was published, none has yet surfaced.

Contents. 192

A list of this issue's contents and their respective page numbers.

JUNE 13

Letter from President B. Young. 193

The Welsh translation of a letter dated 1 March 1857, Great Salt Lake City, from Brigham Young to Orson Pratt, as printed in *Millennial Star* 19 (6 June 1857): 362.

Conference Accounts, &c.. 195

The first account is that of the West Glamorgan Conference held at the Saints Hall, Orange Street, Swansea. John Davies, the conference president, spoke of the "beneficent effects of the reformation" and of the necessity of "adding workers to the field." Daniel Daniels was present at the conference and spoke, also "earnestly expounding on the same topic." W. Powell from Llwyni spoke in English on the first principles. The report was submitted by John Davies and his scribe William Richards.

The second account is that of the East Glamorgan Conference, held at the Cymreigyddion Hall, the name given to the "long room" located above the "White Lion," a public house in Merthyr Tydfil, on 24 May 1857. Abednego S. William gave the opening address, and he was followed by William Miller, a counselor to Daniel Daniels in the presidency of the Church in Wales. William Miller and James Taylor, who spoke no Welsh, had replaced Israel Evans and Benjamin Ashby as counselors to Daniel Daniels two months earlier. Other speakers were David Rees, Samuel Roskelley, Dewi Elfed Jones, Benjamin Evans, and Evan Richards. The report was submitted by Abednego S. Williams and his scribe Aneurin L. Jones. The latter is the son of Dewi Elfed Jones.

(Editorial). 200

Since Daniels had received issues of the *Deseret News* up to 1 April 1857 and several letters from Utah, he presents a montage of news items having to do with events in Utah. The first item of his editorial is a long quote from a letter to Daniels from Franklin D. Richards. Apparently the Welsh Saints had given to Dan Jones a gift of some kind, usually money or clothes, to give to Richards and his counselors in appreciation for their service. Richards expresses his gratitude and his blessing for the gift. He also gives some detailed information as to how things were going for the Saints in Utah.

In the second item, Daniels presents more news items from the *Deseret News* focusing on the public works since Richards had given an account of the religious condition in Utah in his letter.

In the third item, Daniels quotes from a telegraph dated 18 May 1857 that had been sent from St. Louis to New York after the overland mail reached St. Louis from Salt Lake City.

The fourth item has a brief report of the widespread famine in part of the State of Michigan as reported in the *Mormon*.

The fifth item has to do with an earthquake in parts of California as reported in the *Deseret News*.

The sixth item is from the *Sacramento Age* and provides more details about the effect the earthquake had on the Mokelumne River, causing it to overflow its banks and spread destruction in the area.

The seventh item is about the attack of highway robbers on a sheriff in California as reported by the *Los Angeles Star*.

The eighth item is from the *Deseret News* about Captain Dan Jones and his latest activities associated with the *Timely Gull*, a sailboat belonging to Brigham Young.

In the ninth and final item, Daniels announces that the Welsh translation of the seventh and eighth pamphlets of the *True Faith* series by Orson Pratt accompany this issue of *Zion's Trumpet*. He then makes an appeal for book debts to be paid.

Accounts of Conferences, &c. 205

Three more conference reports are given. The first is one from Benjamin Evans about the conference held in Tredegar, Monmouthshire, on 4 June 1857. Speakers were Benjamin Evans, Samuel Roskelly, William Miller, and Henry Harries. Benjamin

Evans, the president of the Monmouthshire Conference, would later serve as the editor of *Zion's Trumpet*.

The second conference report, dated 1 June 1857, Denbigh, is from Pastor John E. Jones. Daniels playfully indicates that the letter is from Jones's "*Weekly Gazette*," a reference to Jones's frequent reports from his missionary travels. Jones reports an increase in animosity toward the Church and an increase in unemployment among many of the brethren. Jones describes the pleasure he has in working with James Taylor, a counselor to Daniel Daniels in the presidency.

The third report, also dated 1 June 1857, Denbigh, is from James Taylor. Although not a speaker of Welsh, Taylor declares that he is "managing splendidly among my adopted compatriots" and that he feels himself "as much a Welshman as anyone in the kingdom of God." He has kind words to say about the Saints in North Wales and the missionaries assigned to that area.

(No title) 208

Daniels laments that the verses of Dewi Elfed and a letter from the Valley were too late to be included in this issue but says they will be in the next issue.

Contents. 208

A list of this issue's contents and their respective page numbers.

JUNE 27

Letters from the Valley 209

The first letter, dated 30 March 1857, Great Salt Lake City, from Mary Daniels, is the first item in this issue which has a black border around each of its sixteen pages in memory of Parley P. Pratt, who had been brutally murdered six weeks earlier. Although Mary had expected her husband's return this year from his mission, she writes that she will be content and "pray daily for the will of God to be done" with respect to his mission. She also writes that their son Thomas and his wife "are well and prospering [and] have a daughter and two sons"—three grandchildren that Daniels had not yet seen. Mary also mentions a number of Welsh friends that send their regards to Daniels.

The second letter, dated 15 February 1857, Brigham City, Box Elder County, is from William Thomas to his mother and sisters who lived near Llanybydder. After describing his current condition in Brigham City, William encourages his mother and sisters to seek out the missionaries and "not to turn a deaf ear to the invitations of heaven." He writes that he has sufficient money to pay for their travel to Zion. [William Thomas's wife, Margaret Sophie Evans, is the younger sister of Sarah Evans Jeremy, wife of Thomas Jeremy. A few months after writing the letter, William returned to Wales on a mission. After his return, he and his wife joined with the Morrisites and went to Deer Lodge, Powell County, Montana.]

Ambush—Murder of the Apostle Parley P. Pratt 213
> The Welsh translation of these articles as they appeared in the *Millennial Star* 19 (4 July 1857): 417–20 and 426–27.

The Orphans' Lamentation, on Hearing of the Martyrdom of their Father 221
> The Welsh translation of this poem by Eleanor J. McLean as it appears in the *Millennial Star* 19 (4 July 1857): 427–28. Dewi Elfed uses poetic license in his translation and thus does not include the same phraseology as used in the English. My English "informational" translation of Dewi Elfed's Welsh rendition is different in many ways from the original. Here for comparison purposes is the original:
>
> > I heard a wail from out a distant mountain home;
> > It crept around a lofty mountain's rocky dome,
> > And ran along, o'er hill, and stream, and grassy plain,
> > Until it found the grave of one but lately slain.
> >
> > It was the voice of wives and children wild with grief,
> > Who sought to heaven, with prayers and tears, for kind relief;
> > For they'd learned, by a paper from a distant place,
> > The news that they no more could see a father's face.
> >
> > That in a land of *lust, profanity*, and *wine*,
> > Where once they dwelt beneath their native vine;
> > The father and husband had met a martyr's fate,
> > By the hands of *fiends*, surcharged with guilt and hate

That when his heart was pierced, he fell upon the ground,
Where there was none to raise his head, or bind his wound;
And though he lived for hours, he saw no faithful friend,
By whom he could his dying message safely send.

The wail increased until it reach'd the throne of God,
And ELOHIEM *Himself* did take His mighty rod,
And said, "I'll cut *them* down and blot *them* from the earth,
"Who've slain my Prophets on the soil that gave them birth.

"I'll send upon them *famine*, *pestilence*, and war,
"I'll call my legions from the northern realms afar,
"And they *shall hunt them* down in every land and place
"Stain'd with the noble blood of one of Joseph's race.

"The blood of Parley shall not long before me plead,
"For wrath on him and them who did the hellish deed;
"And e'er it cease to cry, that nation *shall atone*
"For every widow's tear, and every orphan's moan.

"And every drop of guiltless blood they ever shed,
"Shall quickly come upon their own devoted head;
"For once I have sworn, *by myself and by my throne*,
"*That in the 'Book of Life' their names shall ne'er be known!*"

Conference Accounts 222

David Davies, President of the Llanelli Conference, reports on the gathering held in Llanelli on 24 May. He gives the current number of members as 84.

Joseph Griffiths, President of the Cardiganshire Conference, reports on the gathering held recently in Cwrtnewydd. He gives the current number of members as 29.

(No title). 223

Daniels explains that the absence of editorial observations in this issue is due to the accounts of the murder of Parley P. Pratt. He encourages the Saints to be diligent in defending Pratt from false accusations.

Verses..224
> This poem by Dewi Elfed consists of six 4-line stanzas and is dated 31 May 1857. It is an elegy for his infant grandson who had died a month earlier.

Contents..224
> A list of this issue's contents and their respective page numbers.

JULY 4

War and the Mormons......................................225
> Daniels begins his six-page essay with the observation that the newsworthy massacre of European men by the Eastern Indians is not sufficient to draw the attention of the press away from the Mormons in Utah. He explains the nature of editors: "It is a compulsory fact that editors must have something interesting or disturbing always at hand, or they will not satisfy the corrupt appetite of their numerous readers." Daniels then proceeds to draw on a number of sources to portray the war of the press against the Mormons and gives considerable attention to the scandal surrounding Judge Drummond and his mistress in Salt Lake City.

Counsel to Elders..231
> The Welsh translation of this article as printed in the *Millennial Star* 19 (18 July 1857): 457–58.

(No title)...232
> Daniels alerts book distributors that they will soon be receiving information through the post.

(Editorial)..233
> "Exhortation" is the title Daniels gives to the first segment of this editorial. He encourages all Welsh Saints to make every effort to emigrate and join the body of the Church in Salt Lake City. He declares that "the only obstacle to the Salt Lake over there is the salt lake that borders us [here]."

In the second part of the editorial, Daniels encourages faithful members to preach, testify, and pay an honest tithe. He also explains that the profit from the sale of the pamphlet about the martyrdom of Parley P. Pratt will go to help his family.

In the third part of his editorial, Daniels gives an update on some of the Welsh who are living in Ogden and environs. Also he comments about Hector McLean, the assassin of Parley P. Pratt.

Teachings 237

"An Elder in Israel," the author of this article, declares that the building of the Kingdom of God "will come about through three grand principles." But he mentions only two of the three in his opening paragraph—the "increase of its subjects in number and virtue" and the "gathering of those from every nation, tribe, and language, to Zion." He proceeds to discuss at some length the first principle and then the second. And although the author neglects to name the third principle at the outset—"the preparation in Zion"—he does discuss it in the final part of his two-page essay.

Martyrdom of Parley P. Pratt 239

A poem of six 7-line stanzas by David John, writing from Flint, in which he laments the death of Parley P. Pratt. See the 7 March 1857 issue of *Zion's Trumpet* for "My Dream," a lengthy poem in which the former Baptist tells of his conversion to Mormonism.

(No title) 240

In the throes of preparing the semiannual report to send to his file leader in Liverpool, a frustrated Daniel Daniels reminds all conference presidents of the absolute need for keeping accurate information. "Remember, from now on," he instructs, "to keep track of the details, such as the names of things, persons, dates, etc., with regard to the expenses."

Contents 240

A list of this issue's contents and their respective page numbers.

AUGUST 1

Teachings, by President Heber C. Kimball, Bowery,
April 6, 1857 241

    The Welsh translation of this discourse by Heber C. Kimball as printed in the *Deseret News* for 22 April 1857, 4.

(Editorial).................................... 248

    In the first part of this editorial, Daniels reminds his readers that "the judgment of God has begun" and that "the prophecies of the martyred Seer, Joseph Smith, are being literally fulfilled." He recalls how the Gentiles mocked the Saints when the crickets destroyed the crops in Utah.

    Daniels then leads into the second part of his editorial by saying, "They rejoiced at the idea of the starvation of the Saints in Utah, but by today the tables have turned, as shown by the account of the 'Grasshoppers in Minnesota, U.S.A.'" He then quotes four paragraphs about this problem in Minnesota from the *Saint Anthony Express* as they appear in the *Mormon* for 11 July 1857, 3. Daniels then comments that if such plagues are bad for the righteous they will be even worse for the Gentiles.

    In the third part, Daniels reminds Church members that it is a "definite commandment" that they emigrate only through the Church program and that "all who go against the rules after this notice will forfeit their membership in the Church."

    The fourth part consists of an abridgment of an article in issue 32 of the *Millennial Star* that deals with the responsibilities of conference presidents. Daniels explains that the reason for not including a translation of the complete article is lack of space.

    The fifth part is entitled "Liberality," in which Daniels paraphrases Orson Pratt's instruction as printed in the *Millennial Star*. The Saints are encouraged to keep their homes open in order to have "the honor of lodging, feeding, and washing the feet of a servant of the Lord."

    The sixth part also has a title—"Conference Houses." Pratt explains that having fewer of these houses would result in more visits by conference presidents to Saints in their homes.

    The seventh part of the editorial is Daniels's encouragement to book distributors to collect the money for book debts and submit it without delay.

Teachings, by President Heber C. Kimball, Bowery,
April 6, 1857 252
   Continued from page 248.

The Temple Block 254
   The Welsh translation of this article as printed in the *Deseret News*
   for 20 May 1857, 5.

Book Debts, June 30, 1857 256
   A list of the outstanding book debts of the thirteen conferences.
   The West Glamorgan Conference's debt of over £130 is the largest. The total for all the conferences is over £544.

Book Payments from May 28 to July 31 256
   Payments from ten book distributors are shown.

(No title).....................................256
   Daniels makes an additional request for conference presidents to
   submit their reports as requested in the previous issue.

Addresses......................................256
   The addresses of David Davies in Llanelli and of Levi James in
   Swansea.

Contents.......................................256
   A list of this issue's contents and their respective page numbers.

AUGUST 15

A Nut or Two for the "Leader" to Chew On......257
   The *Leader* was a newspaper published in Pwllheli, North Wales,
   in which the editor had criticized the Mormons for not having
   established beliefs, for being "a mixture of paganism, Judaism,
   Christianity, Mohammedanism, idol worship, and atheism,"
   for having changing views of the Godhood, and for reaching to
   obtain the crown of Godhood. The author of this response—

presumably Daniel Daniels since the response is unsigned—answers each of the accusations with substantiating evidence. He quotes in its entirety a poem of fellow Mormon John Richards published in the 25 January 1851 *Udgorn Seion*, 35–36, in which the poet scoffs at the numerous misconceptions about God and ends with an appeal to him to hasten in bringing all his children to a knowledge of the "covenant" (Mormonism), in order for them to have a clearer understanding of his nature. (See my *Welsh Mormon Writings from 1844 to 1862: A Historical Bibliography* [Provo, UT: Religious Studies Center, Brigham Young University, 1988], 123–24, for additional details.) All the way through his response Daniels belittles the editor of the *Leader* for his absurd beliefs and assertions about Mormonism, and at one point he taunts, "How are your teeth as they crack the nuts, Mr. Editor?" Toward the end, Daniels says that he is sending a copy of "Who is the God of the Saints?" to the editor "so that we will not take up too much of our space in answering you." (For details of this twenty-four-page treatise by Dan Jones, see *Welsh Mormon Writings*, 171–73.) Because the editor of the *Leader* parrots only what others say about Mormonism and has nothing new to bring forth, Daniels ends his response with a suggestion: "We suggest, then, that you get a new name for the *Leader*, namely the *Follower*, and we expect to hear before long that it has no name in the world!"

A Few More Questions for Ministers to Answer 262

The Welsh translation of this article taken from the *Western Standard* as it appears in the *Millennial Star* 19 (15 August 1857): 526–27. Daniels prints this article in defense of plural marriage as a postscript to his previous article in reply to the editor of the *Leader*, and at the end he adds this caustic comment: "Come, Mr. 'Leader,' since you are so annoyed by the 'hallowed nest,' and compare the nest to which such a bird as yourself pertains with those of the 'hallowed nest.'"

(No title) 263

Daniels asks his readers to send him anything they come across about Mormonism that appears in any publication.

(Editorial) 264

    The first part of this editorial has to do with the troops that may be headed for Utah. The *New York Herald* reports that they may have been diverted to quell an insurrection in Kansas.

    The second part is entitled "Emigration Again." Daniels presents the names of some who have left on ships other than those organized by the Church, some of which were in violation of the rules. At President Pratt's request, Daniels asks his readers to send in the names of any others in this category.

    In the third part of this editorial, entitled "Instructions," Daniels carefully outlines the proper procedures and forms for submitting tithing money, book money, and the money for the Penny Fund. He ends this part with a stern notice: "Our patience will not endure much longer for those who delay in sending some of the things noted. Take warning."

    In the fourth part, Daniels relays the good news contained in some of the letters from the Salt Lake Valley that "the crops are remarkably abundant." He also says that "Brothers D. Jones and T. Jeremy send their fondest regards to the Welsh Saints."

    In the fifth part, Daniels announces the arrival of three missionaries from Utah to serve in Wales: Enoch Rees, William P. Thomas, and Richard G. Evans. The third line in this final part of the editorial is printed upside down in the original Welsh. This typesetting error is corrected in the English translation.

Poem 267

    Seventy-six lines of poetry by Dewi Elfed in which he expresses his disappointment at not having seen any new poetry by his "gifted brother," Nathan Ddu—the nom de plume of Jonathan J. Thomas—of Llywel.

Summer Song 268

    This is the poem—seven 8-line stanzas—with which Nathan Ddu responds to his friend's poem.

News from Utah 270

    The Welsh translation of this 29 May 1857, Great Salt Lake City, letter from Brigham Young to Orson Pratt as published in the *Millennial Star* 19 (15 August 1857): 524–25.

Sabbath School of Utah 272
> The account of an unusual event that took place on 1 May 1857 in Salt Lake City. The Sunday School teachers in the various wards and their students went on a procession to the slopes above the city to celebrate the arrival of spring. Afterwards they went to the Music Hall and were addressed by Elder Woodruff.

Contents 272
> A list of this issue's contents and their respective page numbers.

AUGUST 29

News from the Valley 273
> There are two items under this heading. The first is the Welsh translation of the 30 June 1857, Great Salt Lake City, letter of Brigham Young to Orson Pratt and Ezra T. Benson as printed in the *Millennial Star* 19 (29 August 1857): 556. The second is the Welsh translation of the 1 July 1857, Great Salt Lake City, letter of Wilford Woodruff to the editor of the *Millennial Star* as printed in the *Millennial Star* 19 (29 August 1857): 556–57.

Slavery Prospects in the United States 276
> The Welsh translation of this article as it appears in the *Millennial Star* 19 (29 August 1857): 557–58.

Emigration 278
> The Welsh translation of this article as it appears in the *Millennial Star* 19 (29 August 1857): 553–56.

(Editorial) 281
> The first part of this editorial is the Welsh translation of the article on tithing as it appears in the *Millennial Star* 19 (29 August 1857): 569–70. Daniels adds two paragraphs in total support of President Orson Pratt's instructions.
>
> In the second part, Daniels gives instructions to the conference presidents with regard to the sale of *Zion's Trumpet* and the Pratt pamphlets.

The third part is the Welsh translation of Pratt's instructions about the Penny Emigration Fund as printed in the *Millennial Star* 19 (29 August 1857): 570–71.

The fourth part is a notice that Elder William Jenkins is on his way to Wales to serve a mission.

In the fifth part of the editorial, Daniels expresses outrage at the "blatant and contradictory lies" about Mormonism printed in the *Herald Cymraeg* (Welsh Herald). The source was "one John Davies" who had been in Salt Lake City recently and was spreading vicious tales about the goings on there.

Daniels ends his editorial with an explanation to Brother John Bowen about a letter from his brother. John had requested that the letter be printed in *Zion's Trumpet*, but Daniels says he does not "feel that it is sufficiently free of subjectivity to appear before the public." (David D. Bowen, born 6 June 1822, Llanelli, is the author of the letter. His page on the website at http://welshmormon.byu.edu has a link to his lengthy journal.)

Contents 288
> A list of this issue's contents and their respective page numbers.

SEPTEMBER 12

Settlement of the Saints in Nebraska 289
> Daniels reminds his readers of the decision of Church leaders "to make new settlements along the broad plains and the desert that lie between the States and Utah." He then presents the Welsh translation of the 1 July 1857, Genoa City, Monroe County, Nebraska Territory, letter to the editor of the *Mormon* as it appears in the *Millennial Star* 19 (19 September 1857): 607. For the next two pages Daniels contrasts the virtues of the Saints with the "wickedness, deceit, oppression and misery" of their enemies.

Why Are the Apostates Flying from Utah? 293
> The Welsh translation of this article as it appears in the *Mormon* for 15 August 1857, 3.

(Editorial) 296
    At the beginning of this five-page editorial entitled "The Kingdom of God," Daniels observes that Sabbath after Sabbath the priests of the various religions throughout Wales constantly say the phrase "Thy kingdom come" in their repetitions of the Lord's prayer. He says that they also preach "that the country is sufficiently enlightened, with no need for additional revelation." After contrasting the beliefs and practices of Mormonism with those of the other religions, Daniels concludes with this counsel to his readers: "Do not pray any longer, 'Thy kingdom come,' for it has come, together with a revelation of the will of God."

Home Church Accounts 301
    The first account is that of the West Glamorgan Conference by John Davies in his letter dated 8 August 1857. Davies describes the constant efforts made by the Saints in his conference to adopt the principles of the Reformation and to warn their neighbors to repent and accept the gospel message. He reports that there are "unity, charity, and cooperation" in their midst.

    The second account is that of the Cardiganshire Conference by Joseph Griffiths in his letter dated 3 August 1857, Aberystwyth. Griffiths tells of his determined efforts to preach the gospel in the Aberystwyth area with Brother Joseph W. Tuckfield and in the face of considerable opposition. Daniel Daniels adds a note following the letter to the effect that Griffiths' diligence is "worthy of emulation."

    The third account is that of the Brecon Conference by John Thomas in his letter dated 8 September 1857, Llanelly, Brecon. Thomas expresses concern that a number of the Saints in his conference "are contrary and lazy, having lost the Spirit of the Gospel almost completely." He adds, however, that he and the faithful Saints will continue forward to the best of their ability.

Payments from August 1 to September 11 304
    Payments from eight book distributors are listed.

(No title) 304
    Daniels inserts three lines about the Indians going to war against the soldiers and adds that war is imminent in Kansas.

Contents..304
> A list of this issue's contents and their respective page numbers.

SEPTEMBER 26

Home Church Accounts.........................305
> This is a continuation of the Home Church Accounts from the previous issue and is a three-page letter from John E. Jones, dated 16 September 1857 and written from Llandudno. John E. Jones, called as the "Pastor over the Conferences of the North," reports to Daniel Daniels concerning the aggressive efforts being made by himself and several other missionaries to proclaim the gospel throughout North Wales. He had come across "hundreds and thousands of the works of D. Jones and J. Davies decaying by the boxful here and there throughout the Conferences," a reference to the numerous pamphlets published by Dan Jones and John Davis over the previous years that were meant to be distributed as a means of bringing converts into the Church.
>
> Pastor Jones and the other missionaries had been challenged by their leaders to "test the world" by conducting their missionary service without purse or scrip. Consequently, Jones gave to every two elders "a good bag full of books" to take to "the whole country, tracting every house, and preaching in the evening." He describes the result: "Sometimes they received food and hearty welcome; . . . other times they received nothing. Sometimes they would be in a bed, other times at the base of a hedge, in a haystack, in a barn, a sheepfold, or in the middle of a field."
>
> The missionaries serving with Pastor Jones are Thomas Jones (formerly from Aberystwyth), Edward Parry Jr. (from Llandudno), David Jones (Denbigh), Daniel Lewis, Edwin Price (Trefor), Robert Williams (Cefn Mawr), John Treharne, Hugh Evans, William Ajax, and David John. After their admirable service these missionaries were released so they could go to work to earn money to emigrate the following year.
>
> Despite his fierce loyalty to the Church in Wales, John Edward Jones later became a follower of Joseph Morris and ended up in Inyo County, California, where he died in 1897. See his page at http://welshmormon.byu.edu for more details.

Review, of the Treatise, Heresies and Deceptions of the
Latter-day Saints and the Book of Mormon, Exposed, by
the Reverend W. J. Morrish. 308
> The Welsh translation by David Roberts of the twenty-four-page pamphlet entitled *Heresies and Deceptions of the Latter-day Saints and the Book of Mormon, Exposed* by the Reverend W. J. Morrish was published in 1849 in Caernarvon. Now in 1857 several of the Church members in North Wales have informed Daniel Daniels that the pamphlet is causing "renewed commotion." At their request Daniels has agreed to "show as much of its inconsistency" in the limited space of this issue of *Zion's Trumpet* as he can. In typical polemical fashion, he refutes a number of the so-called heresies and deceptions that the Anglican vicar puts forth in his publication. In so doing, Daniels shows himself to be a first-rate polemicist on the same level as his predecessors Dan Jones and John Davis.

(Editorial). 313
> In the first part of this editorial, Daniels tells of his journey to the Brecon Conference and through parts of Monmouthshire and East Glamorgan in the company of his counselors and Elder A. Calkins from the Liverpool Office. He reports that "all true Saints" are living as they should, being blessed for so doing. But he laments that others are quite lax in keeping the commandments as they should. He gives particular attention to their dereliction in the payment of tithes and offerings and the negative effects this is having in the lives of these "half-hearted" members of the Church.
>
> In the second part, entitled "Religious Persecution," Daniels quotes a brief article from the *Cambrian* that tells of a group of Mormons who "upset their listeners so much with their corrupt and bizarre sermons" that they were assaulted by 200 or 300 people "with cabbages, potatoes, apples" and forced to retreat. Daniels refers to the newspaper as "the slanderous asp," and asks rhetorically where in the Bible is such behavior encouraged.
>
> The third part is a notice that locusts have been detected in Britain.
>
> In the fourth part, entitled "From the Plains," Daniels presents a brief report of the military expedition to Utah which "has

turned out to be a disgrace and a shame on the American government."

The fifth part is a brief comment about the good progress being made in setting up stations along the plains for the pioneer companies.

Reynolds Newspaper, Sectarianism, and Mormonism 315

Daniel Daniels quotes extensively from an article that appeared in the 13 September 1857 issue of the *Reynolds Newspaper*, a Sunday weekly published in London at the time by George W. M. Reynolds. The article, entitled "The Mormons and the Priests," declares that Nana Sahib and Brigham Young "have destroyed the peace, the appetite and senses of the religious *Times* forever." Thousands of British lives were being lost at that time because of a revolt in India led by Nana Sahib, and simultaneously thousands of British souls were being taken from the Isle of Britain by missionaries under the leadership of Brigham Young. A question appears in the *Times* as to what the priests in Britain were doing to allow their parishes to "be emptied of thousands of people under their noses." The column in the *Reynolds Weekly Newspaper* provides the answer: "They are doing what they usually do—they are defending the evils that exist, which tends to add to Brigham Young's numbers." The writer of the column then delivers a scathing rebuke to the priests who are "engaged in their old task of smiling at the wealthy, and frowning at the poor." Daniels then adds a brief postscript to the effect that although the author does not praise Mormonism, he says that it is "something substantial in exchange for the false sympathy, the forms devoid of passion, the religious husks, and the disheartening, powerless Christianity of those who, in the present day, are the commodities of the pulpit in the British Isles."

A "Living" for Sale 317

The tithe money received by the Church of England that is used to provide for the vicar of a parish is known as a "living," since it allows him to sustain life for him and his family. Daniels tells his readers of an "impudent statement" made by Punch in the *Times* about a "convenient opening for a lazy priest" that is for sale by an older priest who wishes to retire.

Chastity of a Priest of the Church of England 317
  Daniels explains ironically the "chastity" of the Reverend William B. Sutherland by telling of his custom of "seeking and ruining young women."

Success of the Kingdom of Christ 318
  A poem of sixteen 5-line stanzas by David John, who was serving as a missionary in Flint. The poem is dated 20 September 1857.

(No title). 320
  Instructions from Daniels to conference presidents about how to handle tithing and pamphlets.

Latest News 320
  Daniels happily reports that the crops are abundant in Utah and that the accusations against Brigham Young "have been refuted to the satisfaction of the President of the United States."

(No title). 320
  The dates for four district conferences to be held.

Contents. 320
  A list of this issue's contents and their respective page numbers.

OCTOBER 10

Teaching of President Brigham Young 321
  The Welsh translation of Brigham Young's address at the Bowery on 26 July 1857 as it appears in the *Deseret News* for 5 August 1857, 4.

News from Utah 326
  Daniels announces that he had received issues of the *Deseret News* up to August 12 and that the following day Elder S. W. Richards and four others had started off on their missions. He also tells his readers that the Saints had just experienced the most

plentiful harvest since their settlement in the Salt Lake Valley. He then devotes the remaining four pages of this article to providing details about the U.S. troops being sent to Utah by President Buchanan. He quotes extensively from addresses given by Brigham Young and Heber C. Kimball as they appear in the *Deseret News* for 12 August 1857.

(Editorial) 330

In the first part of this editorial, Daniels declares that "Zion is about to be delivered," echoing what he had just quoted in the previous article from Brigham Young and Heber C. Kimball.

In the second part, he announces that for the time being all emigration of the Saints to the States is stopped. But he predicts that the hiatus will be only temporary.

The third part is a brief announcement that the *Mormon* has ceased publication.

Daniels devotes the fourth part to giving instructions about subscriptions to *Zion's Trumpet* and the distribution of pamphlets.

Latest from Utah 332

The Welsh translation of the 4 October 1857, Liverpool, letter from S. W. Richards to Orson Pratt as it appears in the *Millennial Star* 19 (17 October 1857): 668–71.

(No title) 336

The troops of the Utah Expedition are afflicted with scurvy.

(No title) 336

Presidents Pratt and Benson will not be able to visit Wales as promised.

(No title) 336

Dates are given for four conferences to be held in South Wales.

(No title) 336

Dates are given for four conferences to be held in North Wales.

Payments, from September 12 to October 9 336
    Payments from six book distributors are shown.

Contents. 336
    A list of this issue's contents and their respective page numbers.

OCTOBER 24

Teaching of President Brigham Young 337
    Continued from page 326.

A Prophetic Warning to the Inhabitants of Great Britain . . 341
    The Welsh translation of this proclamation by Orson Pratt as it appears in the *Millennial Star* 19 (24 October 1857): 680–81.

Preaching to the World. 343
    In this 2 October 1857 letter written from Llangunllo, Dewi Elfed Jones tells Daniel Daniels of his missionary travels through numerous places without purse or scrip.

(Editorial). 344
    The first part of this editorial is the Welsh translation of the farewell address of Orson Pratt as it appears in the *Millennial Star* 19 (31 October 1857): 697.

    The second part is the Welsh translation of the greeting of Samuel W. Richards as he begins his duties as the editor of the *Millennial Star* as it appears in the *Millennial Star* 19 (31 October 1857): 697–99.

    The third part is the Welsh translation of the instructions about emigration as they appear in the *Millennial Star* 19 (31 October 1857): 699.

    In the fourth part instructions are given regarding the responsibility of Asa Calkin for money matters in Liverpool and the responsibility of S. W. Richards for other matters.

    The fifth part consists of an announcement that President Richards has called Elder Calkin as his first counselor and George G. Snyder as his second counselor.

The sixth part has information regarding the payment for the Pratt pamphlets.

In the seventh part Daniels points out that the "Bible worshipping sectarians" of the modern world fail to see that the prophecies regarding the destruction of Babylon are about to be fulfilled. He thus encourages Church members to be faithful and to "edify and comfort one another" and to continue to pray for the opportunity to flee from Babylon and take refuge in Zion.

Reasons Why Elder John E. Jones Is in Favor of Gathering to Zion 350

Elder John E. Jones writes a six-page explanation as to why he wants to leave Wales and join with the body of Saints in Salt Lake City. He presents nine major reasons with many details. Because of its length, the first part of Jones's treatise is printed in this issue of *Zion's Trumpet*, and the other part appears in the following issue.

Book Debts, September 31st, 1857 352

Outstanding debts for the thirteen conferences in Wales are listed. The total is just over £548. The error of giving September 31 days has not been corrected.

Contents. 352

A list of this issue's contents and their respective page numbers.

NOVEMBER 7

Reasons Why Elder John E. Jones Is in Favor of Gathering to Zion 353

Continued from page 352.

Teaching of Apostle Orson Hyde .356

The Welsh translation of Orson Hyde's discourse given at the Tabernacle, Great Salt Lake City, on 8 March 1857, as it appears in the *Deseret News* for 5 August 1857, 3.

(Editorial) 360
> In the first part of this editorial, Daniels reports the departure of Presidents Pratt and Benson along with some other missionaries returning to America. Daniels has kind words to say about President Pratt as well as about President Benson.
>
> The second part is entitled "The Troops and Utah." Daniels writes that the new president, S. W. Richards, is encouraging the Saints not to "worry their minds with this matter." Rather he suggests that they "redouble their diligence and trust in God."
>
> In the third part, entitled "Appointments," Daniels announces the appointment of Elders George G. Snyder and John L. Smith to travel under the direction of President Richards and "impart such instruction as may be deemed necessary."
>
> In the fourth part of his editorial, Daniels sums up the "Total News of the day" by presenting a list of the worst happenings imaginable, such as murders, whoredoms, violence, oppression, and pestilence. His final comment: "In short the world is going to hell at a gallop."

Farewell Address of Apostle Ezra T. Benson 361
> The Welsh translation of this address as it appears in the *Millennial Star* 19 (7 November 1857): 712.

Teaching of Apostle Orson Hyde 364
> Continued from page 360.

The Word of Wisdom 368
> Daniels emphasizes that it is just as important now to observe the Word of Wisdom as it ever has been.

Return of Books 368
> Daniels calls on book distributors to send certain issues of *Zion's Trumpet* to his office in order to complete volumes for 1856 and 1857 for binding. He has his typesetter put the issue numbers in oversized, bold print.

The Times 368
> Daniels tells his readers not to be overly concerned about all the newspaper reports of the "destructive and unfortunate happenings," but rather to "conduct themselves honestly before their God" to ensure His blessings for them.

Contents. 368
> A list of this issue's contents and their respective page numbers.

NOVEMBER 21

Signs of the Times 369
> This is a rather long conversation between Rhys, a member of the Church, and his friend Thomas, not a member of the Church. Thomas is very worried about the political and economic situation in Britain and asks Rhys to tell him how things are in America where he is making plans to go. Rhys explains that the Mormons are gathering in Utah, where they can practice their religion without persecution and where they can establish a Zion society. The conversation ends with Thomas promising to get baptized and start making plans to emigrate. The only indication as to the author of this conversation is "W. L." at the end.

(Editorial). 377
> The first part of this editorial is the Welsh translation of President Richards's article on finances in the *Millennial Star* 19 (21 November 1857): 745.
>
> The second part, entitled "News from Utah," is the Welsh translation of an article by the same name in the *Millennial Star* 19 (28 November 1857): 760.

Teaching of Apostle Orson Hyde 382
> Continued from page 367.

Teaching of President Heber C. Kimball 383
> The Welsh translation of a sermon given by Heber C. Kimball on 5 July 1857 as it appears in the *Deseret News* for 15 July 1857.

(No title). 384
> A brief notice about a riot in Nottingham where thousands of unemployed workers held a meeting in the marketplace and ended up stealing jewelry worth hundreds of pounds.

(No title). 384
> Daniels states that he has learned of disease and death in North Wales.

(No title). 384
> Daniels issues a call to Church members to be faithful in every way so they will be able to emigrate soon.

Payments from October 10 to November 20 384
> Payments from five book distributors are shown.

Contents. 384
> A list of this issue's contents and their respective page numbers.

DECEMBER 5

Spirit of the Times 385
> The Welsh translation of this article as it appears in the *Millennial Star* 19 (5 December 1857): 778.

A Prophet in Israel 386
> The Welsh translation of this article as it appears in the *Millennial Star* 19 (5 December 1857): 779.

American News – Utah Expedition. 388
> The Welsh translation of this article as it appears in the *Millennial Star* 19 (5 December 1857): 779–80.

Troubles of the Expedition........................389
    The Welsh translation of this article as it appears in the *Millennial Star* 19 (5 December 1857): 780.

Still More.......................................389
    The Welsh translation of this article as it appears in the *Millennial Star* 19 (5 December 1857): 780.

Patriotic Demonstration of Utah 390
    The Welsh translation of this article as it appears in the *Millennial Star* 19 (5 December 1857): 780–81.

Alarming Earthquake in Buffalo....................391
    The Welsh translation of this article as it appears in the *Millennial Star* 19 (5 December 1857): 781.

The Grasshoppers 392
    The Welsh translation of this article as it appears in the *Millennial Star* 19 (5 December 1857): 782.

(Editorial)......................................392
    In this very brief editorial, Daniels reminds the Saints that God is on their side and ready to bless them according to their faithfulness and obedience.

Contributions toward Emigrating and
Outfitting the Missionaries 393
    This is a list of pledges made by some Church members around Swansea and in the Pembrokeshire Conference.

(No title).......................................394
    Daniels asks the branch presidents of the West Glamorgan Conference to send the names of those who have made pledges directly to his office.

Teaching of H. C. Kimball 395
    Continued from page 384.

More Pledges, &c.. 400
    Ten more names of Saints from Cardiff are added to the list.

Contents. 400
    A list of this issue's contents and their respective page numbers.

DECEMBER 26

Proclamation of President Brigham Young 401
    The Welsh translation of this article as it appears in the *Millennial Star* 19 (26 December 1857): 822–23.

Pledges 403
    Three-and-a-half pages of names who have made pledges.

(Editorial) 406
    In this, his final editorial, Daniels writes: "After five years of heartfelt enjoyable labor with the Saints and our fellow nation, we have been granted the wish of our heart, namely the privilege of returning home to the servants and Saints of God, and our dear family in Zion." He requests the prayers of the Saints and encourages them to support their new leaders: Benjamin Evans, John Davies, and David John.

Contributions 407
    Daniels encourages all the Saints to look over the pledges and send a new pledge if they so desire. He comments: "Some believing gentiles have contributed and have pledged to contribute."

New Year's Gift 407
    Daniels declares this gift to be "The Trumpet weekly for the Welsh Saints, with the 'new old hands' to bring it forth!"

Appointments of Elders to Preside over the Welsh
Conferences, from January 1, 1858.................408

> The names of the new mission presidency are presented along with the names of the ten conference presidents. Thomas Jones is to be the Pastor over the Northern Conferences. The Monmouthshire and Brecon Conferences are to be joined under the name of the former. The Carmarthen and Merioneth Conferences are to be dissolved, and the alignment of the various branches with other conferences is shown. Daniels mentions that Joseph Griffiths is absent from the presiding circle because of illness. He also mentioned the following about John E. Jones: "The diligent and tireless labors of Pastor J. E. Jones are known to God and his children. More will yet be said about him." Daniels was no doubt greatly saddened when about four years later John E. Jones would leave Mormonism that he so passionately preached and become a follower of Joseph Morris.

Zion's Trumpet
Volume 9
1856

UDGORN SEION,

NEU

SEREN Y SAINT;

YN CYNNWYS

EGWYDDORION "GORUCHWYLIAETH CYFLAWN-
DER YR AMSEROEDD,"

MEWN

TRAETHODAU, LLYTHYRON, HANESION,
PRYDYDDIAETH, &c.

"A mi a osodais wylwyr arnoch chwi, gan ddywedyd, Gwrandewch ar sain yr udgorn."—JER. VI, 17.

"Holl drigolion y byd, a phreswylwyr y ddaear, gwelwch pan gyfodo efe faner ar y mynyddoedd, a chlywch pan udgano ag udgorn."—ESA. XVIII, 3.

CYFROL IX.

ABERTAWY:
ARGRAFFWYD, CYHOEDDWYD, AC AR WERTH GAN D. DANIELS,
1856.

ZION'S TRUMPET

OR

STAR OF THE SAINTS;

CONTAINING

THE PRINCIPLES OF THE "DISPENSATION OF THE FULNESS OF TIMES,"

IN

TREATISES, LETTERS, ACCOUNTS, POETRY, &c.

"Also I set watchmen over you, saying, Hearken to the sound of the trumpet."—Jer. vi, 17.

"All ye inhabitants of the world, and dwellers on the earth, see ye, when he lifteth up an ensign on the mountains; and when he bloweth a trumpet, hear ye."—Isa. xviii, 3.

VOLUME IX.

～～～

SWANSEA:

PRINTED, PUBLISHED, AND FOR SALE BY D. DANIELS.

1856.

FOREWORD.

Here is the ninth Volume of Zion's Trumpet in the hands of our readers. The experience of the uniqueness of its fascinating sound calls thousands to enlist under the banner of Jesus, and thousands to journey toward the strongholds of Israel on the tops of the Everlasting Mountains which, despite our own inability, have given us encouragement, through the help of our God, to blow for the ninth time, on the soldiers of the Kingdom of Jesus to teach more and more of its perfect organization. We are glad to understand that tithing, more fasting, saving, constant praying, and diligent working are occurrences, remarkable, among others, which are chronicled in our Ninth Volume. They become even more interesting in each additional volume in proportion to the success, the growth, the strength and greatness of the Kingdom of Jesus, and the overthrow of the kingdoms of the world.

Our present campaign is the preparatory work for the coming of our Great King in his glory, with his majestic host on high, to place vengeance on those who have refused the conditions of peace which we offer in HIS name.

The Trumpet of trumpets and the Star of stars is that of the Saints—it sounds the war cry of the King of kings and the Lord of lords against the great whore who has become drunk on the blood of his Saints. It sounds to those who have covenanted with God, through his messengers,

"Come out of her." To all others it says, "For the hour of His judgment is come."

Although our Trumpet is small, its voice is remarkable and important. If the great happenings of the Dispensation of dispensations and the Fullness of Times are interesting, then its sound will be of a similar nature, because the destruction of Babylon, and the rise and increase of Zion will be the constant topic of its cries. Its constant sounding of this kind until the thunderous sound of the Archangel shouts, "Babylon the great is fallen, is fallen"—and the light of our small Star, together with each one of its kind, to lead the wise men of this eastern country who recognize its light, to the Sun of Righteousness in the west, is the earnest prayer of your

EDITOR.

CONTENTS.

Address of F. D. Richards . . . 81, 150
" Dan Jones . . . 97, 110
Addresses 336
Arrival of Missionaries 15, 399
Arrival of the Handcarts 391

Bags for Emigrants 15
Books for sale 303

Circulating Tracts 280
Commemorative Certificate . . . 147, 156
Condition of the Conferences 263
Conference of Breconshire 171
" Monmouthshire . . . 171
" East Glamorgan . . 143, 214
" Carmarthen 189
" West Glamorgan . . . 165
" Flint 297
Consecration 321, 337
Constitution of the State of Deseret . . 234, 257
Covers for the Treatises 368

Debts 256, 333
Deseret Alphabet 171

Editorial	.	169, 265, 281, 393
" Time of the Emigration	. .	. 90
" Appointments	. .	. 393
" To Presidents and Distributors	.	90, 107
" To the Saints	.	185, 377
" Transporting Books	. .	. 26
" Changes	. 40, 105,	121, 137
" Circulation of the Trumpet	.	. 25
" General Conference	. .	. 57
" General Council	. .	. 248
" The Plan of President Pratt	.	. 333
" Tithing	.	232, 312
" Epistle of the Editor	. .	. 361
" Editor of Zion's Trumpet	.	. 107
" Feast	. .	. 155
" Departure	. .	. 14
" Conditions of the Conferences	.	. 281
" Notice	. .	. 170
" Departure of emigrants	.	. 90
" Good news	. .	. 201
" News from Utah	.	26, 296
" Marriage and Morals in Utah	.	216, 249
" Warning the World	. .	. 329
" State of Deseret	. .	. 233
" The Poor	. .	. 14
" New Pamphlets	.	346, 394
" Transgressing	. .	. 345
" The new year	. .	. 9
" The emigrating Saints	.	. 138
" The notice to emigrants	.	. 88
" The emigration	11, 73, 91,	153, 297, 333
" The 'Thornton'	.	. 171
Editors of the Hero	. .	. 378
Eisteddfod	.	350, 368, 398
Epistle of Orson Pratt	. .	. 274
Excerpt from 'True Repentance'	.	. 373
Farewell to Captain Jones	.	125, 127
Feeling of a Missionary	. .	. 2
Feeling of a young Saint	. .	. 79
Fulfillment of Prophecies	.	203, 218, 246
Gathering of the Saints	. .	. 62
General Epistle	. .	17, 28
Happy is the Mormon	. .	. 286
Hymn of Tribulation	.	157, 173

Instructions on the Emigration	58
Letter from the Plains	380
Letter of reconciliation	156
Ditto	231
Letters from —	
Brigham Young	241
Capt. Dan Jones	205, 305
Daniel Spencer	251
Dewi Elfed Jones	315
Gwilym Ddu	291
Israel Evans	344
John Jones	117
Response to it	118
John Parry	292
Mary Daniels	283
The Editor to his Printer.	135
Thomas Harris	159
Response to it	160
Thomas Jeremy	289
Longing for Zion	190, 319
Man Surprised	111
Marriage and Morals in Utah	177, 193, 304
Millennium	129, 161, 209
Minutes of the General Conference	33, 43, 74
News from the Emigration	339
News from the United States	45
Notices	108, 240
Opening of the Aberafan Chapel	184
Parable of the Harvesters	342
Its Interpretation	367
Peace	61
Polygamy	395
Prayer verses	119
Priesthood	298
Railway to Zion	255
Religious Freedom	231
Sermons of President Brigham Young	56, 65, 92, 353, 369, 385, 401
Shutting doors	311
Slave Trading	127
Song of Longing	334

Spaulding Story	122
Speech of President B. Young	113, 145
" D. Daniels	94
" Israel Evans	138
Statistical Report	47
The English Language	1
The Gathering of the Poor	49
The Hand of Providence	221
The Indian War	172
The Law of Tithing	295
The Maddocians	95
The Perpetual Emigrating Fund	396
To Zion	271
Tribulation of a Saint	317
Verse to the Mormon	328
Verse	136
Victory of the Saints over the World	141
Voice of the Weak	367
Western Standard	96
Word of Wisdom	7

ZION'S TRUMPET,

OR

Star of the Saints.

No. 1.] JANUARY 5, 1856. [Vol. IX.

THE ENGLISH LANGUAGE.

(From the "Star.")

It is natural for men to love the country they are born and educated in, to cling to the manners and customs of their fathers, and to think that the language in which they first learned to lisp their childish wants is the most perfect of any. It is well that this is so, for it tends to make men more contented with their lot, and we would not desire to have it otherwise merely for the sake of change.

Latter-day Saints are the Lord's peculiar people, raised up to accomplish his purposes in the earth, and the most perfect union is necessary to fulfill them. In order for a people to become perfect in union they must be one in everything which can influence their actions, whether of a religious, civil, social, or domestic nature. This can never be done effectually, without a general medium or language, by which one person can convey ideas or principles to another, in the same light in which they are received.

The Saints will some day be in possession of a pure language, of Celestial origin, such as Adam spake in the garden of Eden when the Lord talked with him in the cool of the day, and which will again be the medium of communication when men become sufficiently perfect to converse with the Gods.

[Price 1c.

If there is any one language on the earth, that assimilates nearer to this pure one than another, it has not yet been revealed to the world. Therefore there can be no utility in discussing the subject. It becomes the Saints scattered through the earth, to lay aside their national feelings, their prejudices in favor of their native languages and customs, merge all into the kingdom of God, and love that most which He favors, and which will tend to restore them to His presence. From among the multiplicity of languages, the Lord has seen fit to select the English as the medium through which to reveal the fullness of the Gospel in this Dispensation. The fact exists, the propriety of His doing so, man has no right to question. Into this language the Book of Mormon was translated by Urim and Thummim, and the revelations in the book of Doctrine and Covenants were first written as they were dictated by the Spirit of inspiration. It is the general language of the Saints in Zion, and the one through which the servants of the Lord continue to make known His will to the nations of the earth. No work can be translated from the language in which it was originally written into another, without losing much of its force and power. Therefore if the Saints would read the revelations of the Lord in these days, in their original beauty and excellence, they can only do so in the English language in which they are written.

To illustrate the subject more fully, let us consider the real position of the Scandinavian, Swiss, Italian, and Welsh missions. Those who have the presidential charge of them, have to bear the burden of being nearly the only channel through which the Saints can receive instructions from the authorities, and the only ones who can feel the weight of these instructions in all their original force. They in turn convey to the presiding Elders under them the knowledge they receive, and thus it has often to be reflected through several mediums, in order to be diffused among the people. No matter how diligent and faithful these mediums are, every secondary reflection must mar the beauty and brilliancy of the light which emanates from the fountain. If the people read the *Stierne, Darsteller,* or UDGORN SEION, the instructions they contain have all the necessary imperfections of a translation. If the Presidents of Conferences throughout those Missions understood English, a wide field of research in the works of the Church would be open before them. They could, by being able to read the "Journal of Discourses," the "Deseret News," the "Star," the "Luminary," and the "Mormon," drink deep of the rich instructions they contain, understand the general movements and policy of the Church better, and be, like an overflowing fountain of intelligence, ever ready to administer abundantly to those who have need. When they received instructions from their Presidents they could comprehend and carry them out with far greater efficiency and power.

This would greatly strengthen the hands of those who preside over such missions, and render their labors lighter and far more effectual. In this way the spirit of Zion could be more generally infused into the Saints. They would understand their duties and what was required of them better, simply because their instructors would be more capable of teaching them.

Not only the Presidents of Conferences where the English language is not spoken, but the President of each Branch, and the Traveling Elders should turn their attention to this subject, and let no opportunity pass of acquiring a knowledge of the English language, that they themselves may be profited, made strong in the faith, and thereby better able to feed with the riches of eternal life, those whom it is their duty to watch over and instruct. We particularly wish that young, enterprising brethren, whether engaged in the ministry or not, would consider this counsel as directly applicable to themselves, for in giving heed to it they will most effectually open the way, if they are otherwise faithful, to a rapid increase in wisdom, intelligence, and all those qualifications which will make them efficient in building up the kingdom of God, and doing good to their fellowmen.

The young will acquire a new language with far greater facility than persons of mature years, and parents who have a family of children should endeavor to have all, if possible, and one at least, acquire a knowledge of the English language. We presume that many of the Saints are so situated that this is not practicable, but there are thousands of opportunities neglected, because the importance of improving them is not appreciated. All the faithful anticipate, some day, journeying to the place of gathering. As soon as they leave the old world for the new, they are surrounded with innumerable perplexities, and subject to be imposed upon and suffer loss, for want of a little knowledge of the English language. Every possible care is used by those having charge of the emigrating Saints to avoid this, but it cannot always be done effectually, neither are they always in a position, particularly those who stop for a time in the United States, where their interests can be watched over.

It is evident to all, that the various nations of the earth must have the Gospel preached to them in their native language. One prominent reason for this is, that those who reject it may have the testimony of their own nation and kindred to meet in the day of final reckoning. Although the Lord may see fit to make the stammering tongue of a foreigner the feeble instrument of introducing the Gospel among a people, still it must be generally diffused among them by those who can preach it in the native simplicity and strength of their mother tongue. But after persons have obeyed the Gospel, and identified their interests with the kingdom of God, it becomes the duty of Elders laboring among them to teach them the necessity of early acquiring a knowledge of the English language, that they may receive that knowledge and instruction which can only be obtained through that source. Who can calculate what a Saint loses during the first year after his arrival in Utah, through not understanding the English language? The House of the Lord, and the Tabernacle of the congregation are there, where Apostles and Prophets minister in the holy ordinances, and expound more fully the principles, of exaltation and eternal life. The great object for which he has toiled and struggled for years is finally accomplished—he is at home with the Saints—but for a long time he can only in part reap the full benefit of his labors, because a barrier is in his way, which if he had surmounted previously, he would have saved one or two years of most valuable time to a Saint. To acquire a knowledge of any language requires patience and perseverance, but, as every Saint expects to be compelled by circumstances to acquire a knowledge of the English some day, delay in doing so is a continual loss which can never be repaired.

All the Saints of whatever nation, who can read English at all, should read the standard works of the Church in that language; and they should not fail of taking the "Star," the "Journal of Discourses," and such other Church periodicals as may seem desirable and suited to their circumstances.

Much more might be said on this subject, but we trust this is sufficient to enable the Saints who speak other languages to see the necessity of carrying out the suggestions we have made. If they will do so, an ample reward will naturally follow as they proceed, and they will be added upon with the knowledge which yields the peaceable fruits of righteousness, that intelligence which makes perfect, and that light which will guide men into the presence of the Father.

The attention of the Presidents of the Scandinavian, Swiss, Italian, and Welsh missions, is especially requested to this subject. They are also requested to procure translations of the above remarks, and insert them in the UDGORN SEION, *Skandinaviens Stjerene*, and *Darsteller*, and make their future appointments of Presidents of Conferences and Branches, and of Traveling Elders with a view of filling these offices as far as practicable with men who understand English, or feel interested in acquiring a knowledge of it.

LETTER FROM THE VALLEY.

G. S. L. City, August 27, 1855.

DEAR UNCLE D. DANIELS,—I saw a line in your letter saying that Hannah and Ann have again joined the Church, and that they are good Saints, &c., and that they wish me to forgive them and send for them, which I have decided to do, and I have sent word to Hannah regarding the matter; I have sufficient means to bring them, and I need them, for I always keep two servant girls in my house. I live next to the North West Corner of the Temple Block, the house next to the Temple, and I am building a new house now to the side of the house of Brother H. C. Kimball. This year I am making an *Astronomical Ephemeris* and an Almanac for the Church, and I live off my teaching. I heard that my youngest daughter died, and I was very sorry to hear that; I do not know where Mary is, but if you could arrange for her to come across I would prefer that to having a thousand dollars. Dear Eliza is a very fine lass, healthy and high-spirited. But where is Sister Ann Daniels now? I have not heard anything from her, except that she had gone to Glamorganshire, that she was usually desirous to come to Zion; if she is of the same mind now, allow her to emigrate at my cost, and I shall pay everything when you come to the Valley, and let this letter serve as "security" for the arrangement, and strive to send Mary with her if there is any way, and I shall repay it all honestly. I have nothing but the best love toward each one of them. Remember me to my brother Dafydd, and all his children; I hope that he is coming here this year; if not, I wish to hear from him, and tell him to send a letter soon containing information about his feelings, his intentions, &c., together with all the details about his children; I wish for them all to come here soon, for neither they nor we can enjoy a fullness of happiness until we come together,—here there is happiness for the Saints, and it is a big loss for them to remain in Babylon.

I wish for you to send a letter to me straightaway, and do not write anything to me in the letters of others; I prefer to pay the postage for my letter myself. Your family is healthy and comfortable, and everything is good, except that the climate has been unusually dry here this year, and the crops are not as abundant as you have seen them, but it is expected that there will be quite enough for food.

I wish to be very fondly remembered to Capt. Dan Jones; I heard that he has suffered heavy persecution in Wales since I left. O! dear Wales, who has taken out your eyes, that you cannot obey the truth? If they only knew the thousandth part of the respect, the praise, the honor, and the glory that Dan Jones has in the kingdom of God, yes, the situation in which he stands even now in the sight of Prophets and Apostles of the Almighty God, I suspect they would be considerably frightened, and they would fear until their hair would stand on end when they looked at him! I wish for the power of the Lord to be with him, and I believe that it will be, and that he will overcome.

I shall close now, wishing every blessing to be on you, and that you will be successful in getting my dear friends to the land of promise.

Yours sincerely,

THOMAS JOB.

WORD OF WISDOM.

Tune—*"Life and protection."*

There are still some foolish habits,
That yet continue in the world,
'Tis a very strange thing that God so long,
    Tolerates such a foolish thing.
        Drinking and getting drunk,
            And vomiting on the floor,
        And chewing tobacco,
        And smoking now.

'Tis a surprise now that man has not seen,
His own great foolishness;
He spends his money to purchase wine,
    Which makes him a fool.
        Drinking and getting drunk, &c.

Another spends every last penny,
To have tobacco in the corner of his cheek,
And if he can't get it he makes more noise,
    Than the Church bell.
        Drinking and getting drunk, &c.

Neither sensible or wise, rather man is a fool,
He pays for something that does him harm,—
He makes a god of his belly; and his tired back
    Has nothing to cover it well,
        Drinking and getting drunk, &c.

He raises some to wear a *veil*,
While he with his poor old clothes,
And his wretched family can get
    Only a base and miserable living,
        Drinking and getting drunk, &c.

There are some who wear fine silk,
And dine on delicious delicacies,
And he is feeding them,
    While his family are a pitiful sight.
        Drinking and getting drunk, &c.

Some must have snuff and tea,
And strong coffee every other with it,
With *rum* or *brandy* in it,
    To be quite in *style*.
        Drinking and getting drunk, &c.

Some great men have been seen,
Falling thus to the ground in misery,
And they are not on the parish,
    Because they were so foolish.
        Drinking and getting drunk, &c.

I heard one saying boldly,
That without tea she would die;
But remember the old grandmother,
   Who died at a hundred and two,
      Without tea or coffee,
         Nor tasting *rum* and milk,
      Nor snuff to harm her,
      Nor tobacco either.

She drank milk and whey,
And water with her barley bread,
She made soup just from vegetables,
   Better than anything these days.
      Without tea or coffee, &c.

She did not stay up late,
But got up early with the dawn,
And thus collected great wealth,
   By being wise like this.
      Without tea or coffee, &c.

There are *bome* and *organs* in the garden,
Mint, *savory*, and fair *goldmary*,
She cuts, dries these, following the bard's word,
   Makes a drink from these.
      Without tea or coffee, &c.

If a being with fine reasoning,
Never can convince a man like you,
Oh, take a lesson from a cow or dog,
   Or mule, or a wise horse,
      They refuse snuff,
         And the old, black tobacco,
      And the strong spirits,
      That are bad for us.

Give *joe* to the dear horse,
To a mule, a cow, a sow, or a dog.
None of these like it
   Nor pipe smoke either.
      They refuse snuff, &c.

Give *joe* to a goose, or a black cock,
Or a *pinch* of snuff to a cat or dog,
And *gin* or wine to a dear little lamb,
   You'll learn something from them.
      They refuse snuff, &c.

Give a *glass* of *rum* or strong brandy,
To the gentle sheep to see if it drinks,
To a wily fox, a lion, or a badger,
   You'll learn something from them,
      They refuse snuff, &c.

Offer tea, or red coffee,
To wild cats, or badgers,
Or put *joe* in the corner of their cheek,
    You'll learn something from them.
        They refuse snuff, &c.
All the fish of the sea, reptiles of earth,
And every creature wild and tame,
And the winged hosts of the heavens,
    All provide true teaching in this.
        They refuse snuff, &c.
Well, now then, Welsh folks, with haste,
Bid farewell to every craving,
Serve God every day of the month,
    And your place will be blessed.
        Refuse snuff, &c.
If this you do, God's favor you'll have,
His peace and all fitting knowledge,
And a blessed place to live forever.
    Enjoying the privileges of heaven.
        Refuse snuff,
            And the old, black tobacco,
            And the strong spirits,
            Which are bad for us.

Glan Teifi.   JOHN RICHARDS.

ZION'S TRUMPET,

OR

𝕾tar of t𝔥e 𝕾aints.

SATURDAY, JANUARY 5, 1856.

THE NEW YEAR.—Through the remarkable goodness of the Giver of every breath of life, here are we and our readers taking the first step over the threshold of a new year! And regardless of who can describe His feelings, we are incapable of expressing our feelings or our thoughts as we look back over the past year or what we perceive for the future. This we will say, that the beneficent effects we detect following the feeble voice of our TRUMPET encourage us to take it up again, and to strive to trumpet more loudly than ever—Come out of Babylon with haste, you children of Zion. Despite the shrieks of all the trumpets of great Babylonia that surround us that try to drown our voice with their raucous tones, we are not the least bit discouraged; the lovers of the truth in obedience to our voice escape to the only safe place, while the others like the ox to the slaughter follow their *fifes* and their *drums* to the clutches of a two-fold death.

This our new year, like a soldier who has slept the night after killing with all his might, awakens in the morning on the field of blood, underneath his full armor; rushing over the dead bodies of the previous day; in his lust for blood, he shouts—Give me, give me more food for my bloody sword to feast on! From the crown of his head to the soles of his feet, every member, joint and sinew of our world as a conquering soldier are writhing in deathly tortures, and every member believes that his own life depends on the death of the other. From head to toe, every member, joint and sinew of our world is like a conquered soldier writhing in the agonies of death, each member believing that its own life depends on the other dying. To him who understands the Signs of these dreadful Times there are obvious thick, black, red, and livid clouds in our skies, weaving a shroud for the nations of the world, such as will defy history to describe its like before; even so the ungodly do not see when adversity comes, but the wise foresee the storm from afar, and like doves, fly to their windows; and there sing praises to Him who provided for them, and led them to one small glade on the face of the troubled world, where its inhabitants live together in peace and wonderful vigor, which is *Utah*. Despite all this, doubtless the priests, editors, and teachers of false religion of Babel will show their jealousy, their wickedness and their hatred of true religion this year, and having seen clearly that their worst was beneficial to "Mormonism," we wish them good speed on their new year's adventure, and a fair wind to do the worst that they harbor in the dreadful pits of their deceitful hearts—onwards then, to the hilt, who will complain; God and the truth are on our side despite the ugly howl of all the world's wolves against us. He is our strength and our leader.

We shall add no more now, but we entreat the help of all lovers of the truth to fulfill our duties this year, whether by blowing through the TRUMPET, emigrating the poor, or any other thing which we are called upon to do for Zion; let us do it all through faith in our King, and we beg for the faithful prayers of our fellow-soldiers, for us all to be able to militate bravely and long enough to earn its "unfading crowns," and to have everlasting life to wear them.

The Emigration.—We wish for the Emigrants to the States to send to us their names, ages, occupations, dwelling places, and their deposit, as soon as it is possible; for we intend to be the first to go with them if a shipload can be obtained; and notice that the price for small children is ten shillings, and that 8 years, not fourteen, is the age that differentiates the price of the transport.

The suitability of the new plan of crossing the plains on foot is becoming more obvious the more it is examined, and with the blessing of the Lord and the precautions and wise plans of President Taylor on the other side, no one need fear failure and disappointment except from their own unfaithfulness in complying with them.

For more on this matter, we can do no better than to quote the following interesting observations from the *Star*, which together with an excellent letter of President Young in the previous issue, will make the hearts of the faithful, no matter how poor they may be, to leap for joy, and will tend to awaken the old sleepers to become worthy of the character of the faithful so they may have in their times, their part of the fatherly support and assistance of their generous fathers in Zion to bring them to safety. Here we see clearly the truthfulness of the promise of our elder Brother, namely, "Blessed are the meek, for they shall inherit the earth." May meekness be the chief characteristic of us all, so we may go to Zion to secure our titles to our eternal inheritances since only *meekness* will make us worthy of such. But the *Star* says:—

Perhaps it will be asked, 'Why has not this plan been adopted before?' Some of the reasons are obvious. The route to Utah is becoming more generally known, and there are many men who are familiar with its advantages and disadvantages, and more capable of judging what can be done, and more able to assist in carrying out new plans in a safe and judicious manner than they were before. The settlement of the country on the first part of the road by the whites for some distance, will save the emigration the trouble of hauling all their provisions from the Missouri river. The Saints in Utah are becoming every year more abundantly able to assist the emigration with teams and provisions on the latter part of the journey—of this, President Young gives the most cheering assurance; and last, but greatest of all, the faith of the Saints and the spirit of gathering has increased, and thousands now see the necessity of emigrating, and are willing to make any sacrifices for its accomplishment, who have heretofore felt quite indifferent, and as though, if they could not go pretty comfortably, they would rather not go at all."

One object of the P. E. Fund Company from the commencement of its operations has been to bring the expenses of the emigration down to the means of the greatest possible number. Another has been, to a considerable extent, to select mechanics and persons best calculated to build up and strengthen new settlements, and also those who could mostly help themselves, until the Saints were firmly established in their new home, and able to effectually carry out the ultimate design of the Company. Now the time has arrived when the funds of the Company can be applied to their legitimate object, and the faithful, long-suffering poor are the special objects of regard. Plans are being devised to effect the deliverance of the greatest possible number of these with the means at the disposal of the Company. This is the great object to be attained, and for which handcarts are to take the place of wagons and ox teams.

Every year the way opens up in proportion as the spirit of gathering increases, and the faith of the Saints enables them to overcome the increased difficulties and trials of the journey. The difficulties of gathering, and the amount of toil and hardship which the Saints will be willing to endure to get to Zion, have only *begun* to be developed. As there are no doubt many who years ago might have gone comfortably on their own means, but now would rejoice in the opportunity of getting there with handcarts, so there will be thousands in years to come who will be glad to flee there on foot, ragged and destitute, with a bundle under their arms, and nothing but a crust of bread to eat. Many who read this will live to see that time, and be overtaken in those scenes, unless they use all possible diligence.

Many men have traveled the long and weary journey of 2000 miles from the Missouri river to California on foot, and destitute, in order to obtain a little of the shining dust—to worship at the shrine of Mammon. Who, that appreciates the blessings of the Gospel, would not be willing to endure as much and more—if necessary, in order to dwell with righteous and reap the riches of eternal life? The Mohammedan will perform a long and weary pilgrimage of months and even years, and make every sacrifice that human nature can endure, to kiss the tomb of his prophet, and bring away a relic from the holy city of Mecca. The Roman Catholic will endure severe penance with the hope of saving his soul from purgatory. The Hindu devotee will suffer self-inflicted tortures of the most excruciating nature, to obtain the favor of his imaginary deity. And modern Christians, who trust to the frail bubble of a hope for salvation, will often endure much to prove their honesty of purpose. Then shall not the Saints, who have the revelations of heaven—the testimony of Jesus—the preludes of eternal joys—and can partake of the powers of the world to come—be ready to prove by their works that their faith is worthy more than the life of the body—the riches of the world—the phantoms of paganism—the creed of the false prophet, or the imaginary fantasies of modern sectarianism?

Although we are unable at this time to present our readers with the plan of our operations the ensuing season, we will endeavor to give a few facts which will enable them to answer some of the daily questions arising in their minds on that important subject.

All orders for persons to emigrate, by the P. E. Fund, to ensure our attention, must come from the President of the Company. The funds of the Company can only be applied to aid those who go directly through to Utah, under the direction of its agents, and cannot be applied to aid any going only to the United States.

The Company cannot, as it did last year, lend those who have ten, eleven, or twelve pounds, sufficient to go through with teams, as the funds of the Company must be appropriated to aid *those who have proven themselves worthy by long, continued faithfulness in the Church, whether they can raise any means of their own or not. These persons must be brought, so long as we can act within the means of the Company, no matter if they have a sixpence in the world.*

Last year, in order to accommodate the feelings of the Saints, and enable them to cross the sea with their friends and acquaintances, we sent Fund passengers with others on the same ship, but experience proved that the trouble and inconveniences arising therefrom more than counterbalanced the advantages. Therefore this season the P. E. Fund passengers will go in companies by themselves from here to the Frontier.

Persons ordered out through the President of the P. E. Fund Company, and who decline going, are reported back to him annually, with their reasons why. As on the arrival of such reasons the funds are liable to be otherwise appropriated, we do not feel authorized to forward the parties afterward unless the order for them has been renewed.

THE POOR.—The season of the year has now arrived when hunger and want press heavily upon the poor. Many of the Saints, we are aware, are in very destitute circumstances, and have to suffer in common with the multitudes that surround them. The Pastors and Presidents are specially required to see that arrangements are made in all the Conferences and Branches to prevent the diligent Saints from suffering in this inclement season from hunger and cold. "But whoso has this world's good, and seeth his brother have need, and shutteth up his bowels of compassion from him, how dwelleth the love of God in him?" Let the Saints who have impart to those who have not, and remember that he that giveth to the poor lendeth to the Lord, who in due time will repay him with increase.

DEPARTURE.—The Ship "John J. Boyd" sailed on the 10th of last month for New York, with 512 souls of the Saints on board, of whom 439 were from Denmark, Sweden, and Norway, 30 from Piedmont, and 43 from Great Britain.

The prices of passage on the "Emerald Isle" and the "John J. Boyd" were £4 5s for adults, £3 5s for children, and 10s for infants. The age of distinction between adults and children is 8 years, instead of 14 as heretofore. It is thought that the variations from the above prices will not be very considerable, though this is necessarily guided by the readiness with which ships may be obtained, and the abundance or scarcity of passengers. Persons had better send up their names, ages, &c., with their deposits of £1 each, immediately on their determining to go to the States, even though they may not wish to go by the first ship. This will better enable us to arrange for ships at the times most convenient for passengers. We shall send out another shipload about the latter part of January, if we have sufficient applicants for passage to make up a company.

NOTICE.—It is important for all who intend to cross the plains next season by the usual slow method of ox teams, and who wish us to secure cattle and wagons for them, so that they will be ready on their arrival on the Frontier, to forward the cash to us immediately on their deciding to want them, that we may be ready to secure them in time, through our agent there.

The price we estimate for this will be the sum required last year—£55 for a good wagon complete (except cloth for cover), two yoke of cattle, and perhaps one or two cows. The whole to be delivered at the place of outfit on the Missouri river.

ELDERS Asa Calkins, Joseph S. Scofield, and James Lavender arrived on the steamer "Pacific," on Sunday the 9th of last month. The brethren are in good health and excellent spirits, and we heartily welcome them to this portion of the earth, to labor a while in the gathering of Israel. Elder Calkins will engage in the business of the Office. The appointments of the remaining brethren will be given in the next *Star*.

BAGS FOR EMIGRANTS.—In answer to several inquiries about suitable bags for the journey instead of chests, we report that convenient bags with respect to size and manufacture, made to keep water out, for from 3s 6c to 4s 6c, can be obtained by contacting this Office.

MISCELLANEOUS, &c.

Payments toward the Debt of the West Glamorgan Conference from Dec. 13 to Jan. 2.—(The First Promises.)

	£	s.	c.		£	s.	c.
David Lewis, Swansea.............	1	0	0	J. Paliphant, ditto....................	0	3	0
Rebecca Knight, ditto.............	0	2	6				

The second Promises.

	£	s.	c.		£	s.	c.
John Perkins, Morristown........	0	5	0	Mary J. Cutliffe, Swansea........	0	2	6
John Evans, Treboeth..............	0	5	0	Thomas Fisher, ditto...............	0	3	0
Mary Evans, his wife...............	0	5	0	Enoch Lewis, Treboeth............	0	2	6
Thomas Davies, Ystrad...........	0	2	6	Jane Lewis, his wife.................	0	2	6
Elizabeth Davies, his wife.....	0	2	6				
Joseph Jones, Ystrad................	0	2	6	Total........	3	1	0
Ann Jones, his wife..................	0	2	6				

RECEIPTS FOR BOOKS FROM DEC. 18 TO JAN 1.—Thos. D. Evans, £3; Benj. Jones, £6; E. Middleton, £20 4s 2c; G. Roberts, £5 9s; Wm. Lewis, £10 14s; H. Roberts, £3 5s 7c; John Davies, £2 13s 1½c; Thomas Morgan, £4; Lewis Davies, £4 4s; George W. Davies, £54 14s 4c; Evan S. Morgans £1 11s 5c.

☞ As the movement of the grass on the prairies shows the direction of the breeze, the movements of the Conference Presidents will be indicated by their efforts to pay their book debts,—"By their fruits ye shall know them" applies here as well.

⁎ Send all letters, containing orders and payments, to *Capt. Jones,* "*Zion's Trumpet*" *Office, Swansea.*

CONTENTS.

	PG.
The English Language..	1
Letter from the Valley..	5
Word of Wisdom	7
Editorial,—The New Year,—The Emigration,—The Poor,—Departure,— Notice,—Arrival of Elders from Zion,—Bags for Emigrants................	9
Payments, &c.	16

SWANSEA:
PRINTED AND PUBLISHED BY D. JONES.

ZION'S TRUMPET,

OR

Star of the Saints.

No. 2.] JANUARY 19, 1856. [Vol. IX.

THIRTEENTH GENERAL EPISTLE OF THE PRESIDENCY OF THE CHURCH OF JESUS CHRIST OF LATTER-DAY SAINTS, TO THE SAINTS IN THE VALLEYS OF THE MOUNTAINS, AND THOSE SCATTERED ABROAD THROUGHOUT THE EARTH,—

GREETING:—

BELOVED BRETHREN,—Under the blessings of an overruling Providence, whose tender mercies are over all His works, we are again permitted to write unto you concerning matters and things pertaining to the kingdom of our God.

We have abundant reason for gratitude and thanksgiving unto our Father in Heaven, who hath shielded us from the power of the adversary, the stratagems and wicked devices of ungodly men. For a time the Saints have been left to pursue the even tenor of their way without molestation or hindrance from abroad, while peace and tranquility have reigned supreme in all the valleys of the mountains.

In May last, in company with a few of our brethren, we visited the southern settlements, counseling and instructing the people, among whom we are happy in believing that a general spirit of contentment and desire to do right extensively prevail, and although we found them with their crops almost entirely destroyed by the ravages of grasshoppers, rendering their hard exertions and the labors of their hands fruitless, still we heard

[PRICE 1c.

not a murmur, no complaining, but rather a firm and determined reliance upon the Lord of Hosts and their continued exertions for sustenance.

Although the crops were so generally cut off as late as from the 1st to the 10th and 15th of June, and though the small remainder afterwards suffered much from the drought, still the late crops of corn and vegetables and some late sown wheat have matured in sufficient quantity, it is believed to supply the wants of the community until another harvest; there will, however, probably, be a scarcity of wheat. All kinds of fruit trees have borne abundantly, although they also suffered through the ravages of grasshoppers and the effects of the drought.

Brethren, the Lord has touched us lightly; be advised by this gentle chastening, give heed unto the whisperings of the Spirit, and tempt not the Lord to bring upon us a heavier rod of discipline, that we may more fully escape those judgments of high heaven's King, which are now abroad upon the earth and being poured out upon the children of men.

When plenty shall again crown your efforts, let heaven's bountiful blessings be sufficiently appreciated to cause you to exercise the proper economy for their care and preservation.

The Indians in our settlements have been generally friendly; and though indications of hostilities will occasionally arise, still we have the satisfaction of believing that a good impression has been made upon them, and that the time is not far distant when we may more surely rely upon their peaceful disposition toward the whites.

The more we witness the workings of the peaceful policy which we have practiced, and endeavored to have our brethren practice toward them, the more we are convinced of its being the proper one, and best calculated to promote their interest and salvation, as well as ours. Besides being the cheapest, it is far easier, and exercises a better influence, to feed and clothe than to fight them.

Be merciful, therefore, and be patient to the poor, degraded, and ignorant children of the mountains and the plains. They are the seed of Abraham, unto whom pertain the promises; seek to enlighten and bring them back unto a knowledge of the Lord God of their fathers; remember that He is their God today, as well as anciently, and that He witnesses, with equal interest, the movements of the children of Israel, as when He gave them instructions from Sinai's consecrated mount, the Temple of Solomon, or Calvary's blood-stained soil.

The time of restitution approaches; be up and doing, therefore, while the day lasts, while there is an opportunity of rendering them assistance and doing them service, that you may hear the approaching words—"Inasmuch as ye have done it unto one of the least of these my brethren, ye have done it unto me."

While great exertions have been made, and are being made, toward converting the heathen in distant nations and upon the islands of the sea, if we have in our very midst a people just as worthy and intelligent, just as capable, and every way as much entitled to receive the Gospel, then let the words of life and salvation be extended unto them. Let the messengers of peace go and instruct them in the arts of civilized life, teach them to plant and sow, reap and mow, raise stock, build houses, make farms, and forsake their evil and pernicious practices, their wanderings and ill-paid predatory or hunting excursions.

Influence them to obtain a living without depending upon hunting, for that furnishes them a very precarious and scanty subsistence; give them your faith and prayers, as well as works; instill into their minds the spirit of peace and eternal truth, that the visions thereof may be opened to a knowledge of the Lord their God, and of Jesus Christ whom He hath sent.

At the same time, brethren, preserve yourselves from their treachery and savage fury, from their loathsome and degrading vices, and seek to elevate them in the scale of being to your own level, but never condescend to theirs, as is too often practiced by the whites. Show them that you are their superiors by your more noble and virtuous acts and bearing, and that you are not with them for selfish or unholy purposes. It is a pleasing sight to see so many of the children of the Lamanites in the families of the Saints, where they have the same opportunities and privileges as the white children, and we trust that the great good will result unto the rising generation through this source.

On the second day of September the Utahs and Shoshones met in this city and made a treaty of peace, which it is hoped will be permanent and prove of lasting benefit to all parties concerned—including the whites.

Near the Elk mountains, and on the left bank of Grand river, the Indians killed three men and some twenty head of cattle, and drove the settlers away; they came to Manti, and will probably not return this fall, notwithstanding they left nearly everything belonging to them in the possession of the Indians. With this exception there has been no actual outbreak during the season, although there have been a few hostile demonstrations and threatenings, whose cause is at present unknown. We trust that all matters will soon be satisfactorily explained and amicable relations restored, that the settlers may be able to return to their location the ensuing spring.

The endowment house in this city was dedicated on the 5th of May last, and received the name of the "House of the Lord." Since then endowments have been regularly given and are still continued, principally under the direction of President Heber C. Kimball.

The Church Historian house and office has been erected, and is now being finished.

A large amount of stone has been laid in the Temple foundation, which has been finished, ready for the basement story, but owing to want of stone, the work, since the first of August, has been and still is suspended. The teams engaged in hauling stone had to be turned away to range, in consequence of the feed's failing in the vicinity of the quarry and city.

We hope to obviate the occurrence of a similar suspension in the future, by availing ourselves of the Big Cottonwood canal, which, it is expected, will be ready for operations by the 1st of May next, and upon which we design bringing the granite stone for the further erection of the Temple.

A *Foundry* has been put in operation and has furnished very superior articles, mostly for machinery and mechanical purposes. Its operations have been much facilitated by the use of stone coal, large and valuable beds of which, of excellent quality, were discovered in the early part of the season, in Sanpete Valley, near Fort Ephraim, and a considerable quantity has been brought to this city; but it is located at too great a distance to become available at this point for general consumption.

Through the facilities afforded at the Public Machine Shop, cutlery of a good quality has been manufactured, also locks and many other articles for general use. Much more cloth than heretofore is being made in the various settlements, also leather, hats, cordage, brushes, soap, paper, combs, crockery, iron, and various other useful and self-sustaining articles are being organized from the native elements in flattering abundance.

Many good buildings have been erected during the season, among which we may mention the Court House, Warden House at the Penitentiary, and finishing the south wing of the State House at Fillmore, besides other extensive and permanent improvements both in city and country. Many mills and various other kinds of machinery have been put into successful operation.

The hum of industry has awakened the silence of these vast solitudes, and, while hill and dale resound with the woodman's song, with the tinkling bell of the headman's charge, and the rumbling caused by the husbandman's and artisan's toil, the clattering mills mingle their sounds with the roar of the mountain streams, while the Indian hies away to his secret spring by the mountain bush, or seeks his shelter among the *sage* of the barren plain. Thus, where but a few short years ago were heard naught but the howling world, the savage war whoop, or the raven's cry, we now hear many a nook and corner echoing with the sounds of civilized exertion, and behold them surrounded with all those appliances of wealth adapted to the white man's home.

In many lands, and among strangers, we have traveled many a weary mile, without purse, scrip, or murmur, to preach the Gospel of salvation to the people, and could scarcely find hospitable shelter for the night, but here we can travel throughout the length and breadth of the land, and seldom meet with any but Saints, those who have come out of the world to serve the Lord, keep his commandments, and do his bidding.

The aid of the P. E. Fund Company has this year been extended to some 1300 persons, nearly a fourth of this season's immigration. This operation, through the hard times in the English Conferences, and the great scarcity of money at home, has had a tendency to involve us somewhat in debt.

Many of the brethren here have sent for their friends, through the aid of the P. E. Fund Company, and they have arrived and are on their way hither; over 600 of this year's immigration are of this class. Now let the brethren who have sent, help us meet the liabilities which we have incurred on their account, and pay up their obligations to the fund.

Let those who feel an interest in the work of the gathering be liberal in their donations, and prompt in paying what they owe, that the Fund may be sustained, and our next year's operation be not crippled for the want of means.

The cry from our poor brethren in foreign countries for deliverance is great, the hand of the oppressor is heavy upon them, and they have no other prospect on earth through which they can hope for assistance. Many of them are long in the Church, and have been faithful in all things, acting in the discharge of every duty. Shall we turn a deaf ear to their appeals and leave them to linger in the midst of wicked Babylon, where, year by year, the perplexity and distress of nations, their wickedness, abominations, and corruptions, wars, pestilence, and persecutions are multiplied by waxing greater and greater, thus constantly tending more completely to hedge up the way and render their longer continuance in those lands more burdensome and oppressive than ever?

Let this question be answered by your acts, for to this resource are we driven, and unless we receive aid, either by donations or the payment of debts owing to the Company, we shall be obliged to measurably suspend operations the ensuing year. We have already extended relief to the utmost limit, and have almost entirely absorbed every available resource of the Church to aid in this matter; we trust, therefore, that you will make it a subject of careful consideration and prompt and proper action, for it is worthy of your most active benevolence. It has long engaged our attention and that of our Elders on foreign missions, has been the theme of our prayers and communications in time past, and commends itself to the attention of all Saints, as opening the only, at present known, effectual door of temporal salvation to the really destitute.

Thousands upon thousands of the immigrants who annually flock to the shores of America, though not of the wealthy classes, have means wherewith to come and subsist until they find channels of profitable occupation. But the P. E. Fund is designed to deliver the honest poor, the pauper, if you please, from the thralldom of ages, from localities where poverty is a crime and beggary an offense against the law, where every avenue to rise in the scale of being to any degree of respectable joyous existence is forever closed, and place them in a land where honest labor and industry meet a suitable reward, where the higher walks of life are open to the humblest and poorest, and where they can lay a foundation for indissolubly uniting themselves and their children in the progressive scale of human existence, "while eternity comes and eternity goes."

This is true charity, and should engage the efforts of every philanthropist, not only to feed the hungry and clothe the naked, but to place them in a situation where they can produce, by their own labor, their subsistence.

The world, at present, furnishes no place so well adapted as this for the exercise of such benevolence, no spot so suitable for the homes of the poor, no country more in need of their labor to bring into use its undeveloped and, we might almost say, unexplored resources, no government where institutions beckon the competition of the low as well as the high, of the poor as well as the rich nor where honesty, capability, and merit, instead of high birth, place, and worth, so often and so surely pave the way to honor and influence.

We have to regret the loss of many of the faithful, who have fallen victims to the power of the destroyer and pestilence, among whom we make mention of brothers W. W. Major and John Perry, of the English, Andrew L. Lamoreaux of the French, James F. Bell and lady of the Italian, and Jacob F. Secrist, of the Swiss.

While we mourn their loss, and deeply sympathize with bereaved families and friends, we rejoice that when they fell they were in the service of their Redeemer, and engaged in the promotion of his cause upon the earth. We trust, therefore, that they were taken for a wise purpose, and that they will meet the approval of the Judge of the whole earth, in the day of reckoning and recompense.

Elders Lyman and Rich are still in California, laboring in San Bernardino and other places in that State. Elder Orson Hyde is in Carson County, Utah Territory, where he has organized a Branch of the Church. Elder John Taylor is in New York, presiding and editing the "Mormon." Elder F. D. Richards is in Liverpool, presiding over the European Mission, and editing and publishing the "*The Star.*" Elder George A. Smith is still engaged as Historian and General Church Recorder, and, together with the remainder of the Quorum of the Twelve Apostles, and the Presidents of Seventies and others, is laboring in the various Settlements of Utah, directed from time to time as duty seems to require. Elder Orson Spencer is editing and publishing the "St. Louis Luminary," in St. Louis, Mo., and George Q. Cannon is engaged in the publication of the Book of Mormon in the Hawaiian language in San Francisco, California, where he also intends publishing a paper. Elder Dan Jones is publishing ZION'S TRUMPET in Swansea, South Wales; John Van Cott, the "*Scandinavian Star*" in Copenhagen; and Augustus Farnham, the "*Zion's Watchman*" in Australia.

The East India Missionaries have returned, or are on their way hither, having faithfully preached the Gospel, from two to five years, in that benighted country, with but little apparent success.

The work is still prospering in Australia, the Sandwich Islands, California, the British Isles, Denmark, Sweden, the North of Italy, Switzerland, France, the British Provinces, and in many parts of the United States. At Cape Town, South Africa, there is also quite a Branch of the Church.

A company of Saints left Sydney, Australia, for the purpose of gathering to San Bernardino and this place, but only a few have as yet arrived on our western coast, the vessel having put into Honolulu in distress and been condemned, thus retarding their anticipated speedy arrival to our peaceful abodes.

This is the first attempt at gathering the Saints from Australia, and we hope it will prove successful, for there are many more in that region who strongly desire to gather with the Saints in these Valleys, but cannot as yet obtain means of conveyance, trade, and commerce from our western coast with that country being very limited.

(Continued on page 28.)

ZION'S TRUMPET,

OR

Star of the Saints.

SATURDAY, JANUARY 19, 1856.

CIRCULATION OF THE "TRUMPET."—The majority of the Presidents of the Conferences decided in a council held lately that it is wiser to begin the present volume with about the same number as the previous volume, because of the following considerations:—

1st.—There will be hardly anything else published in Welsh.

2nd.—That the "*Route*" to the Salt Lake, and the "*Luminary*" have practically finished, with no hope that any others will replace them as far as is known.

3rd.—There will be many now expecting to emigrate who will change their minds, and will wish to have the TRUMPET.

4th.—The emigrants to the States can prepay for the remainder of the volume that will be published after their departure, and receive it after they arrive in the States.

5th.—Because hosts of the world are expected into the Church after the emigration who will be glad to receive it.

6th.—Because emigrants to Zion should make sure to obtain subscribers in their place before they leave, for *which no one should be unable to do* if he chooses to do his duty.

7th.—Because if its circulation is decreased it would be necessary to increase its price.

8th.—Because it was on the condition that two numbers would be received for its price to be decreased to a *penny*; and the Presidents judged that it would be better for their Saints to have *two* for twopence than to pay twopence for *one* number, and that it would be better for those who have a grain of the spirit of Zion to pay whatever it costs, than to be deprived of the priceless news and teaching that will come through it from there.

9th.—Because if use is not made of all these considerations, and if word is sent to the Office at the time of departure, their number will be decreased and the emigration will affect the circulation. Those who do not see the benefit of the objective, and who are not satisfied by these few reasons to begin with, let them inquire, and they shall have nine or ten other reasons!

———

TRANSPORTING BOOKS.—*How shall we transport our books with the handcarts?* is a frequently asked question. We answer, you can either leave the books with the Conference President, or someone else of your choosing: transport them to the camp, and leave them in the Office there until they can be sent for with the wagons next season, or some other way; those who have the means can hire their transport for about five pence per pound across the plains with those who go in wagons. There you have a choice of three ways, but for no reason should poverty or any other cause keep us from enjoying our books in Zion.

———

NEWS FROM UTAH.—We have gleaned the following from the "Deseret News" for October, newly arrived. The weather continued lovely until October: good health has been generally enjoyed throughout the settlements; the grasshoppers, &c., have destroyed the majority of the grain in some valleys, nearly all in other places, while others were greatly spared, so that on the whole it is said that there will be plenty of food if used frugally in Utah until the next harvest, although the chief dependency of many will be on the later crops of potatoes, Indian corn, turnips, melons, &c. The trees bore their fruit remarkably well; a substance not unlike the manna that rained on the Israelites is gathered from the leaves of the trees and the vegetables, from the rocks and the grass, from which is made a great abundance of sugar, and this makes up to some extent the deficiencies of the grain. Despite all this no murmuring or discouragement is heard from among the Saints, rather their dependence on the mercy of God, and their hopes for the future are clearly perceived in their tireless efforts to build the Temple, the public buildings and the forts.

We are sad to report that there are some rascals among the Indians who now and again disturb some of the distant settlements, stealing some of their animals, and they have killed three of the brethren in the new settlement made in the Elk mountains; the rest of the brethren fled for their lives, leaving their animals and their goods as spoil in the possession of the Indians. President Young has sent soldiers to defend the settlement that was threatened. All the camps of emigrants had reached the end of their journey successfully. The missionaries returned safely from eastern India and Australia, together with the chief authorities of Carson Valley, the Delegates who went to settle the northern confines of the Territory.

The new settlement of Las Vegas has been quite successful in everything they have tried to do; they had considerable rain which was a great blessing and help to their crops.

The California newspapers give high praise to the settlement of the Saints in San Bernardino, and they confess that the diligence, morality, and virtues of their Mormon neighbors there clearly gainsay the thousand malicious and false accusations spread about them. They have produced the best kind of cotton in Santa Clara, which will be of great benefit to the Territory.

By means of a comforting letter from his "better half," who sends her fond regards to her fellow nation, the Editor understands that the inhabitants of Sanpete are enjoying health generally; that the Indians have been peaceful, and that although hardly a bushel of wheat grew there the vegetables, &c., are supplying the needs of the inhabitants. He understands some other good news, namely that the wheat that was sowed last year is in good condition in the ground, and that it will do as seed for this year if it is watered in good time; this is valuable when seed is so scarce. Lately they have discovered an excellent material for making bells.

A Conference was held in Great Salt Lake City on the 6th, 7th, and 8th of October, where unity and an excellent spirit were enjoyed; we shall make space in our next issue for some of the interesting things that were discussed; until then study the instructive Epistle in this issue.

THIRTEENTH GENERAL EPISTLE, &c.

[Continued from page 25.]

The Saints are gathering home from every nation, kindred, tongue, and people; and while we are thus concentrating a heterogeneous mass of all kinds of people, from almost all nations, though animated by one general spirit, intention, and desire, it becomes one and all to be kind, courteous, and gentle toward each other, and seek to instruct the people, that they may be more strongly cemented in feeling, interest, peace, and union, as well as in faith, truth, and the bonds of the new and everlasting covenant.

It was to this end, and to effect more fully this object, that the last Conference appointed Elders to take missions to all the settlements throughout Utah that the people may become improved and cultivated in their taste and understanding, and in every grace and accomplishment; that they may be amalgamated in their views and feelings, be strengthened in their faith, and, by not omitting the small, and generally esteemed trifling, matters of practical life, that this generation of Saints may be found pure and holy, mild and equitable in their intercourse with each other, even polished shafts, after similitude of a palace.

Remember that it is the trifling things of this life which make up our existence, and that but a small number of great events transpire without them. They are, however small, the important little duties of life, upon the daily practice of which much depends to fit a people for the coming of the Lord Jesus, or to prepare them for an exaltation in the kingdom of our God.

Therefore, give heed unto the teachings of those we have sent among you, and let all strife, animosity, and contention cease in your midst; live your religion, and let peace, faith, charity, and good works abound.

To the Elders appointed upon these missions, we say, "Go forth in the spirit of humility and meekness, and teach the people in the things pertaining to their temporal as well as their eternal salvation; imbue the people with the spirit of holiness, cleanliness, order, and economy, with the Holy Ghost which leadeth into all truth."

To the Elders abroad, we say, "Be diligent in all your labors, be faithful in your testimony to the people, and when they receive the truth, teach them to live and practice their holy religion." It is easy to bear persecution, to contend for the faith, and even to die for it; the hardest of all is to live it, to be always actuated by its holy influences and practice it in all the walks of life. It is not a plaything or mere toy to believe, amuse ourselves with at our convenience, and then lay aside, but a tangible, everyday experience and solid fact, entering into every avenue of business, of pastime and repose, as well as into the spiritually religious exercises of the mind.

In fact we have no requirement or duty upon this earth only to serve God, keep his commandments, gather his Saints, and build up his kingdom thereon; for this we live, for this we expect to die. But the main difficulty with the Saints is to live their holy religion, and pursue that course which will ensure unto them its blessings and privileges, and that increase of faith, intelligence, and improvement which they may enjoy.

It is a small matter to devote and dedicate ourselves and all we have to the cause of truth, and the building up of the kingdom of God upon the earth, but it is of importance to rightly apply ourselves and our means where we may do the most good. It is important that we be obedient and passive in the hands of the servants of God, and when we have embraced the truth, and placed ourselves with all we have upon the altar to so remain, regardless alike of friend or foe, sunshine or shade, peace or war, plenty or famine and pestilence. It is our duty not only to profess and be believers, but to work out our salvation, continuing faithful in all things, even unto the end. When you enlist under the gospel banner, give the adversary a ticket of leave, and never again permit him an abiding place in your bosoms, never again place yourselves under his influence, neither anything which you possess; live to build up the kingdom of our God, and let your actions correspond with your professions.

We say to the Elders abroad, as well as at home, "Let these principles be instilled into your minds and the minds of all the Saints, and let them be amenable to the authorities which are placed over them, live humble before the Lord, deal justly and righteously, that the spirit of the Lord may richly abide in you."

When the Elders who are upon foreign missions wish to return home, and have no instructions to that effect, it is their privilege to meet together, make the question a subject of prayer and supplication before the Lord, and then act as shall be decided in council in accordance with the dictates of the Holy Ghost. It is your privilege to know the mind and will of the Lord concerning these matters, and by pursuing the proper course you will obtain it.

Let all things be done in order, and let all the Saints, who can, gather up for Zion, and come while the way is open before them; let the poor also come, whether they receive aid or not from the Fund; let them come on foot, with handcarts or wheelbarrows; let them gird up their loins and walk through, and nothing shall hinder or stay them.

In regard to the foreign immigration another year, let them pursue the northern route from Boston, New York, or Philadelphia, and land at Iowa City or the then terminus of the railroad; there let them be provided with handcarts, on which to draw their provision and clothing, then walk and draw them, thereby saving the immense expense every year for teams and outfit for crossing the plains.

We are sanguine that such a train will out travel any ox train that can be started. They should have a few good cows to furnish milk, and a few beef cattle to drive and butcher as they may need. In this way the expense, risk, loss, and perplexity of teams will be obviated, and the Saints will more effectually escape the scenes of distress, anguish, and death which have often laid so many of our brethren and sisters in the dust.

We purpose sending men of faith and experience, with some suitable instructions, to some proper outfitting point, to carry into effect the above suggestions; let the Saints, therefore, who intend to immigrate the ensuing years, understand that they are expected to walk and draw their luggage across the plains, and that they will be assisted by the Fund in no other way.

If any apostatize in consequence of this regulation, so much the better, for it is far better that such deny the faith before they start, than to do so for a more trifling cause after they get here; and if they have not faith enough to undertake this job, and accomplish it too, they have not faith sufficient to endure, with the Saints in Zion, the celestial law which leads to exaltation and eternal lives.

If this project is once fairly tested, and proves as successful as we have no doubt it will, the main expense of the immigration will be avoided, consequently thousands more than heretofore can receive assistance. Therefore, Saints and all returning Elders who undertake to come through with companies, consider this subject and prepare yourselves accordingly.

During the General Conference, just closed, the youngerly people were counseled to obtain their endowments and marry; hence we wish it understood that we are prepared to give the Saints their endowments in the House of the Lord, which has been built and dedicated expressly for that purpose; therefore, let parents, guardians, and bishops take this matter properly in hand, and counsel freely with the young people, and prepare them to receive their endowments and sealings. Young men, take unto yourselves wives of the daughters of Zion, and come up and receive your endowments and sealings, that you may raise up a holy seed unto the God of Abraham, even a holy and royal Priesthood who shall be born legal heirs thereunto, having a right to the keys thereof, and to administer in all the ordinances pertaining to the House of the Lord. Cease your folly and become men of God; act wisely and righteously before Him, and his choice blessings will attend you.

We exhort all the Saints to live righteously, to remember and keep their covenants with their God and with each other, to pay their tithing and make their consecrations in the spirit of liberality and in all good conscience, nothing doubting.

Keep the commandments of the Lord, observe the instructions and counsel you receive from those placed over you to preside, be faithful and industrious, economical and prudent; seek continually unto the Lord for wisdom, and train up your children in His nurture and admonition, that when we shall have finished our pilgrimage upon the earth, we may go hence in peace, having wrought righteousness and established justice thereon, and, through having fought the good fight and kept the faith, be prepared to come forth with a glorious resurrection to inherit eternal lives and exaltation, which may God grant, for his dear Son's sake. Amen.

BRIGHAM YOUNG,
HEBER C. KIMBALL,
JEDEDIAH M. GRANT.

Great S. L. City, October 29, 1855.

Payments toward the Debt of the West Glamorgan Conference from Jan. 2 to Jan. 15—(The second promises.)

	£	s.	c.		£	s.	c.
Daniel Lloyd, Abercenffig	0	10	0	David Llywelyn, Neath	0	5	0
William Evans, Llwyni	0	10	0	Hopkin Jones, Morristown	0	5	0
Isaac Evans, Cwmafon	0	2	6	Gwenllian Jones, his wife	0	5	0
David, son of J. Jones, Ystrad	0	5	0	Total	£2	2	0

RECEIPTS FOR BOOKS FROM JAN. 1 TO JAN. 15.—Edward Middleton, £14; Wm. Lewis, £3 10s; B. Jones, £9.

※ Send all letters, containing orders and payments, to *Capt. Jones, "Zion's Trumpet" Office, Swansea.*

CONTENTS.

	PG.
Thirteenth General Epistle, &c.	17
Editorial,—Circulation of the "Trumpet,"—Transporting Books,—News from Utah	25
Thirteenth General Epistle, &c.—(Continuation)	28
Payments, &c.	32

SWANSEA:
PRINTED AND PUBLISHED BY D. JONES.

ZION'S TRUMPET,

OR

Star of the Saints.

No. 3.]   FEBRUARY 2, 1856.   [Vol. IX.

MINUTES OF THE GENERAL CONFERENCE

Of the Church of Jesus Christ of Latter-day Saints, convened in Great Salt Lake City, commencing Saturday, October 6, 1855.

[And translated from the "Deseret News" by Thomas Harris.]

President B. Young presiding.

On the stand:—Presidents B. Young, H. C. Kimball, J. M. Grant.

Of the Twelve Apostles:—P. P. Pratt, O. Pratt, W. Woodruff, G. A. Smith, E. T. Benson, L. Snow, and E. Snow.

Seventies:—Joseph Young, H. Herriman, Z. Pulsipher, and A. P. Rockwood.

High Priests Quorum:—David Pettegrew.

Presiding Bishop:—Edward Hunter.

Presidency of the Stake:—David Fullmer, T. Rhoads, and P. H. Young.

Clerk of the Conference:—T. Bullock.

Reporter:—G. D. Watt.

Called to order by President B. Young.

Choir sang,—"The morning breaks, the shadows flee."

Prayer by President Young as follows:—"Thou God who dwells in eternity, even our God, the God and Father of our Lord Jesus Christ, and the Father of our spirits, it is thee whom we desire to worship and to whom we look, for we feel ourselves under obligations to thee, and owe to thee our being upon this thine earth.

We look to thee this morning in the name of thy Son Jesus Christ, whom thou hast given to be a ransom for our sins and for the sins of the whole world, and through whose name and atonement we expect life everlasting.

As thou has redeemed the earth and all things thereupon, we, thy creatures, who are endowed with intelligence, desire to worship thee in spirit and in truth, praying thee, our Father, in the name of Jesus Christ, for the light of thy Spirit to know how to worship thee, to know how to build up thy kingdom, to know how to approach thee acceptably, and in a manner that shall be acceptable to all holy beings. It is our God whom we worship, and we are assembled this morning in thy name to transact business pertaining to the building up of thy kingdom on the earth.

We feel thankful unto thee, our Father, that thou hast revealed thy will in this our day, that thou hast spoken from the heavens, and bestowed the holy Priesthood upon men, and again opened up the way of life and salvation, and that we are the happy partakers thereof.

Help us to appreciate the blessings that we enjoy. We have the privilege of assembling here to worship thee, with none to molest or make us afraid; thou has removed us far from our pursuers, from those that have sought to oppress us, and from those who have killed our Prophet and destroyed many of thy Saints. We thank thee that thou has removed us to these mountains. Help us to realize that our blessings are far above those of many of our fellows; while millions are sitting in darkness, in the regions and shadow of death, suffering for food, suffering through the oppression of kings and rulers, bowed down in their iron fetters, having not the liberty of speaking or acting, or scarcely of thinking, for themselves, help us to realize the blessings of having our birth and education in more genial climes and among more hospitable people, where the laws and government under which we were born have tolerated us in freedom of thought and speech; and on this happy soil, even America, where thou hast brought forth the fullness of the Gospel and the eternal Priesthood of thy Son, where thou has guaranteed to all the right to worship thee according to the dictates of their consciences.

We thank thee that we now enjoy that privilege. Help us to realize and appreciate these things.

While we look unto thee, our Father, and contemplate our circumstances, and contrast them with the circumstances of the inhabitants of other climes, we can say that we approach thee with shamefacedness when we look at thy Saints and those who profess to know thee, and at the same time behold that the little, frivolous, trifling affairs pertaining to this probation cause thy people to sin.

O Lord, we feel to beg and plead with thee to have mercy upon our weaknesses—be compassionate unto us.

And as we have assembled this morning for the purpose of transacting business in the capacity of a General Conference, we do pray thee, in the name of the Lord Jesus, that thy Spirit may influence each heart, that we may be enabled to worship thee in spirit and in truth, to forsake all our sins and vanities, and to leave off those things that mar our peace and grieve the Holy Spirit of the Lord Jesus, for we desire to be thy faithful children.

We pray thee that each heart may be suitably affected by the light of eternal truth, that we may understand thy will concerning us, that we may have a disposition to do thy will, to love the Lord our God with all our hearts, to love our neighbors, especially thy Saints, as ourselves to cleave unto righteousness and hate iniquity, and to do good even to our enemies. We pray that the influences of thy Spirit may attend us through our Conference, that the heavens may be propitious over our heads, and that the veil of darkness, even thick darkness, that covers the nations of the earth may be taken from us, that we may see and know things as they are, and understand the mind and will of the Lord concerning us, that we may understand thy ways and thy going forth among the inhabitants of the earth that we may read the destiny of man and the future destiny pertaining to us thy people, and to thy kingdom, and know and understand things past, present, and to come.

O Lord, we ask thee to let thy Spirit so rest upon us that each one who has assembled here to worship thee may have their spiritual strength renewed, that each one who shall speak before this people may be filled with the power of God, that the Holy Ghost may inspire each heart to speak, to hear, to sing, to pray, to write, and to do those things pertaining to the business transactions of thy kingdom acceptable unto thee, that thy kingdom may advance upon the earth, Zion be redeemed, and thine Israel be gathered, that we may be prepared for the coming of the Son of man, be the happy partakers of thy grace from day to day, and be counted worthy to be numbered with the sanctified, who shall enjoy the presence of the Lord Jesus with delight, and be caught up to meet him in the air.

Father in heaven, we ask for thy blessings upon those of thy Saints not now assembled here, who inhabit these mountains. Wilt thou comfort their hearts, inspire them, encircle them in the arms of thy love and mercy, and hedge them about by thy power; and be thou a munition of rocks round about us, towering between us and our enemies, that they may have no power over us.

Inasmuch as the wicked mingle with thy people here, we pray that thy Spirit may teach them the right way and convince them of the truth of the everlasting Gospel, though it is despised by men in high places, and set at naught by the nations; and though thy people and thy doctrine are held in derision, let those who are honest in heart have the light of thy Spirit, that they may be influenced to acknowledge that thou art God, and be inclined to seek after thy righteousness, that they may know and understand for themselves the influences that are of God and the influences not of God.

We pray thee, our Father in heaven, to bless all thy missionaries in the midst of these mountains, on this continent, on the islands of the sea, and upon other continents. May thy angels be with them, may they go before them and be round about them, that they may be preserved from the power of the enemy and be inspired from on high by the power of the Holy Ghost, that they may have power to do good and bring souls to the knowledge of the truth, and build up thy kingdom, and aid in preparing the way for the coming of the Son of man. We ask for thy blessing upon all those who believe in their testimony.

We realize, our Father, that the earth is thine and the fullness thereof, that the gold and the silver are thine, that the wheat and the fine flour are thine, that the cattle upon a thousand hills are thine, and that it is for thee to give, and for thy people to receive. We ask thee that thou wouldest so give that thy people may be gathered together from the islands of the sea and from distant lands.

Let thy Spirit rest upon thy Saints, that the rich may feel that liberality and that charity toward the poor which they should, and that the poor may feel a heartfelt gratitude to the rich who bestow means upon them, insomuch that they will render to each and every man that which is due, and not be covetous, neither be filled with idolatry; and may both poor and rich concentrate their efforts and means to the building up of thy kingdom, to the gathering of thine Israel in the latter days, to the redemption of Zion, the reestablishment of Jerusalem, and the bringing forth of salvation to the inhabitants of the whole earth.

We ask thee, our Father, to inspire us all to be of one heart and one mind, that our affections, faith, and efforts may all be united and engaged in building up thy kingdom, and in the establishment thereof on the face of the earth. Wilt thou bless and heal up the sick among thy people, and comfort their hearts. We would remember before thee those who are now upon the plains, journeying to this place, and ask thee to bring them safely to us; may the elements be favorable and propitious to them, and permit them to come to us without suffering, and let their hearts be inspired. Inasmuch as they suffer, toil, and labor to assemble with thy Saints, may they have thy Holy Spirit with them, and may thine angels be round about them. Bless and preserve their teams and all they have with them.

We pray thee, O Lord, to regard the interests of thy kingdom among the nations of the earth; hasten the gathering of Israel and the redemption of Zion; and may the remnants of the Lamanites feel the power of thy Spirit, that they may cease their wickedness and be divested of their bloodthirsty disposition, and receive hearts of flesh, that they may see and understand the ways of the Lord.

We dedicate ourselves unto thee, our wives, and our children, our houses and our lands, our flocks and our herds, with all that thou hast committed to our charge. We dedicate this Conference to thee, and pray for wisdom to transact the business that should be done, and that all things that are not right, and that are contrary to thy counsel and will, may be taken from our minds. May all hearts be concentrated in that which will please thee and advance thy kingdom, and cause and make the hearts of thy Saints to rejoice exceedingly that they live to be Saints in the latter days.

Hear us, O Lord, and answer these our supplications. Be with us through our meeting and through our future life, guide us to thy praise, and prepare us for thy kingdom and glory, and with the sanctified, bring us to thyself in thy kingdom. These, with all needful favors and blessings, we ask in the name of Jesus Christ. Amen."

Choir sang a hymn.

President B. Young addressed the congregation on the subject of faith, the Holy Spirit, the dealings of the Lord with this people, &c., and was followed by President Kimball, who spoke upon the principle of the Saints' living their religion, or the ordinances would be of no benefit to them.

The choir chanted—"Behold, a king shall reign in righteousness."—Isaiah.

Benediction by President Joseph Young.

At 2 o'clock in the afternoon, the meeting was called to order by President Kimball.

Singing by the choir, and prayer by President Grant. Singing.

Elder Nathaniel V. Jones, returned missionary, late from the Presidency of the Hindustan and Burman empire mission, related his travels in those lands, and stated that the Elders of the Church of Jesus Christ had traveled from the Himalaya mountains to near the southern limits of the Peninsula, and said that a Mr. Wilson, Episcopalian bishop of Calcutta, wrote to the clergy in all the military cantonments to forbid the "Mormon" Elders preaching there, and the clergy faithfully obeyed the bishop.

Elder John Young bore testimony to the truth of the Gospel, and spoke upon good works, agency, and revelation.

President Grant briefly discussed the text:—"Every man shall be rewarded according to his works."

Choir sang the anthem, "Hosannah in the highest."

Benediction by Elder E. T. Benson.

In the evening the Seventies met in their Council Hall, and the High Priests in the social Hall.

October 7, 1855, *at* 10 *in the morning.*—Called to order by President B. Young.

Singing by the choir. Prayer by President Kimball.

Choir sang,—"O my Father, thou that dwellest."

Elder Parley P. Pratt addressed the assembly on a part of the 21st chapter of Luke, and stated that what prophecies had been fulfilled, were literally fulfilled, and the remaining predictions will be in like manner fulfilled.

Choir sang, "Worthy is the Lamb that was slain."

Benediction by Elder George A. Smith.

At 2 in the afternoon, called to order by President Kimball.

Choir sang,—"Come, come ye Saints, no toil or labor fear."

Prayer by Elder Lorenzo Snow. Singing.

Elder Orson Pratt addressed the immense congregation on the divine authenticity of this latter-day work, the inspiration of Joseph Smith, and the divine authenticity of the Book of Mormon. During Elder Pratt's discourse, a blessing was asked on the bread by Bishop Edward Hunter, and on the water by Bishop L. D. Young.

Choir sang,—"Judge me, O Lord."

Benediction by President Grant.

October 8, 1855, *at* 9 *in the morning,* called to order by President B. Young.

Choir sang a hymn. Prayer by Elder Woodruff.

Choir chanted a Psalm.

Elder Elam Luddington, late from the Siamese mission, narrated the prominent incidents in his journeyings.

President B. Young remarked that he had been highly pleased with brother Luddington's narration, and that all the brethren who have returned have manifested the spirit of the Gospel, a fact comforting to the Saints, and more joyful to them than all the gold of India.

(*Continued on page* 43.)

ZION'S TRUMPET,
OR
Star of the Saints.

SATURDAY, FEBRUARY 2, 1856.

CHANGE OF CONFERENCE PRESIDENTS.—The time has come in which we expect the Presidents who were appointed to their task, to go to their various fields of labor, and we trust they will be there promptly, but inasmuch as their predecessors will not be emigrating for a few weeks, perhaps, we encourage them to make the most of that little time to come to a good understanding of the condition and state of their Conferences as thoroughly as possible; this is an opportunity for them to gain insights very easily which will cost them much searching if it is neglected, if not a loss to the cause or to the Saints of God; strive to assume the mantle one garment at a time as your predecessors divest themselves of it.

To our emigrating brethren, we say, strive to put your Conferences in order as much as you can; see to it that the Book of the Church in every Branch has been completed properly, so that the truly needed information about each member is registered, whether living or deceased; make sure that the Conference accounts are accurate lest there be misunderstanding between parties in the future with respect to that which was paid, or the remainder to be paid if there is any; that tidy and clear accounts in each branch show the contributions made by each person to each fund, and, especially examine the accounts of all the Distributors; and may the Saints have a basis, through clarity of accounts, to trust in their Presidents and their Distributors.

Brethren, the Lord has blessed your labor to be of great benefit to his people; thanks be to Him for the power; because of it, every effort you make to build this godly kingdom creates increasing love for you in the hearts of every possessor of the Spirit of God; you have done well, and for the sake of that good name which is a thousand times more precious than the world's gold, do not leave behind any influence on the world or the church except one which will be like the fragrance of spices to breathe. With your departure, may that Spirit which motivated you to serve the good of the Saints earlier increase more and more your desire to benefit them and bless them; God requires this, and may it be our pleasure as well as our benefit to do so, and thus he will open hearts to supply your needs and to carry you comfortably to Zion.

To the incoming Presidents, we say,—Brethren, strive to get the spirit and mind of your predecessors thoroughly, to obtain an understanding of the measures they put into operation according to the law of God. And instead of speaking a derogatory word about their arrangements, or pointing out to another a speck of their imperfection if you see one, improve on them if need be without anyone's knowing about it, and respect the Priesthood your brethren had as you do your own, for, with what judgment ye judge, ye shall be judged in time.

It is not greatness or wisdom in a man to begin in his field of labor by revolutionizing and disregarding that of his predecessor, rather it is a swelling of the "great I am," and a lack of wisdom, which bodes unfavorably for himself. Every President in his stewardship has the right to set measures in order to carry forth the work according to the wisdom that God gives to him under the circumstances, and while God approves that, let those who make changes take care to determine that God requires that. It is the special duty of the Saints, and a privilege for them to contribute according to their ability toward supplying the needs of their Presidents, and their generosity in the past leads us to believe that not much persuasion in this matter will be needed; but until the time of the emigration it will be their privilege to have two each to support, probably, for that is of benefit to them. In particular we entreat the Saints to pay attention to the emigration of the Presidents—we urge all, according to their ability to help them to go home like brave soldiers from the war, full of virtuous spirit, and fully armed, with perpetual wishes for them that the great Master who owns us all and our work will repay their generosity an hundredfold, and will soon take them, themselves, to make their home in Zion. These are the feelings that should be in all as they take leave of each other; and in order to facilitate the emigration of the Presidents, we ask their successors to seize the task quickly and energetically, to set wise measures before the Saints to this end, and put the noble influence of their spirits to work tirelessly until they complete the task, and that promptly.

We need not specify any measure or amount to this end; we believe there is enough wisdom among you to understand what is rightful, and that there is a desire among the Saints to do this; consequently, we rely on the incoming Presidents to be faithful in completing this, asking Him who requires this of them to repay them a thousand times better than any other can do, and confirm our belief, that, "verily, inasmuch as ye have done it unto one of the least of these my brethren, ye have done it unto me" will echo the whispering of Jesus' Spirit, gladdening their hearts according to their generosity.

We desire the cooperation of the double Presidency in favor of the emigration, that it will be their pleasure to support each other in the great work of easing the path of the Saints, helping as many as possible to leave the confines of Babel in haste; and to advise them and take precautions for them according to the instructions already given, and be ready to lead them properly from the country when the call comes to emigrate. Let all preparations possible be made while you can, lest the opportunity be lost because of the short notice to depart.

Lastly now, then, Dear Brethren, may you be filled with the Spirit of God; may the wisdom of heaven flow over your lips in perpetual feasts for the Saints; may your faithfulness and your diligence, your zeal and your kindness toward them force the Saints to emulate you, and may your good works honor the dear religion you represent. Let not the poisonous influence of partisan spirit find a place in your hearts, rather let your purity and godliness recoil from doing harm, and may your paternal care for Jesus' dear flock which he entrusted to your care for a moment, comfort the orphan and the widow, strengthen the feeble knees, foster every virtue, and tend to perfect the children in the image of their "Eldest Brother." May the seal and the blessing of our Father be upon all your accomplishments, your persons and your families, and also on your adherents, your co-workers and those who bless you, is and will be the prayer of your fellow servant.

MINUTES OF THE GENERAL CONFERENCE.

[Continued from page 40.]

THEN President B. Young took up the business of the Conference, when the authorities were unanimously sustained as follows:—

Brigham Young, President of the Church of Jesus Christ of Latter-day Saints, Prophet, Seer, and Revelator; Heber C. Kimball, first counselor, Prophet, Seer, and Revelator; Jedediah M. Grant, second counselor.

Orson Hyde, President of the Quorum of the Twelve Apostles, and Parley P. Pratt, Orson Pratt, Wilford Woodruff, John Taylor, George A. Smith, Amasa Lyman, Ezra T. Benson, Charles C. Rich, Lorenzo Snow, Erastus Snow, and Franklin D. Richards, members of said quorum.

John Smith (eldest son of Hyrum), Presiding Patriarch.

David Pettegrew, President of the High Priests Quorum, Reynolds Cahoon and George B. Wallace his counselors.

Joseph Young, Levi W. Hancock, Henry Herriman, Zera Pulsipher, Albert P. Rockwood, Benjamin L. Clapp, and H. S. Eldredge, Presiding Presidents over all the Seventies.

John Nebeker, President of the Elders Quorum, James H. Smith and Aaron Sceva his counselors.

Edward Hunter, Presiding Bishop of the whole Church.

Lewis Wight, President of the Priests Quorum, George Dockstader and William Whiting his counselors.

McGee Harris, President of the Teachers Quorum, Adam Spiers and David Bowman his counselors.

Alexander Herron, President of the Deacons Quorum, John S. Carpenter and Frederick A. Mitchell his counselors.

Brigham Young, Trustee in Trust for the Church of Jesus Christ of Latter-day Saints.

Daniel H. Wells, Superintendent of Public Works.

Truman O. Angell, Architect for the Church.

Brigham Young, President of the Perpetual Emigrating Fund to gather the poor; H. C. Kimball, W. Woodruff, O. Hyde, G. A. Smith, E. T. Benson, J. M. Grant, D. H. Wells, Edward Hunter, Daniel Spencer, Thomas Bullock, John Brown, William Crosby, A. Lyman, C. C. Rich, Lorenzo D. Young, P. P. Pratt, O. Pratt, F. D. Richards, and Daniel McIntosh, his assistants, and agents for said Fund.

David Fullmer, President of this Stake of Zion, Thomas Rhoads and P. H. Young his counselors.

Heman Hyde, Eleazer Miller, Phinehas Richards, Levi Jackman, Ira Eldredge, John Vance, Edwin D. Woolley, John Parry, Winslow Farr, William Snow, Daniel Carn, and Ira Ames, members of the High Council.

George A. Smith, the Historian and General Church Recorder.

Not one negative vote was given.

The President then spoke at some length upon the chastenings of the Lord, the principles that should govern those who have grain to sell, &c., and said, as we have now been together 3½ hours, we will adjourn for one hour.

At 2 in the afternoon, called to order by Elder E. Snow.

Singing by the choir.

Prayer by Elder Erastus Snow. Singing.

President J. M. Grant spoke a short time on the practical duties of Bishops and Teachers, the Big Cottonwood Canal, and expressed his anxiety for the time to arrive when he could preach the funeral sermon of all the drones.

Parley P. Pratt, Orson Pratt, Wilford Woodruff, Erastus Snow, Joseph Young, Zera Pulsipher, Henry Herriman, Joseph Hovey, Joseph L. Heywood, Jacob F. Hutchison, Horace S. Eldredge, George B. Wallace, Joseph W. Johnson, Thomas D. Brown, John Lyon, Jacob Gates, and William Snow (who answered to their names), and Richard Cook, Gilbert Clements, Levi Richards, Aaron F. Farr, William Gibson, Thomas Grover, Joseph Bates Noble,

George Woodward, Dominicus Carter, and Daniel D. Hunt, were unitedly and unanimously voted to go on missions to the Saints in Utah Territory.

Lorenzo Snow, Ezra T. Benson, and Phineas H. Young, were unanimously voted to go a mission to Europe next spring.

James Townsend was unanimously voted to go on a mission to Carson Valley.

President Kimball made a few remarks on the subject of the canal, marriage, &c.

President Young followed on the same subjects, and then called a vote of all who were in favor of completing the Big Cottonwood Canal, ready for the boats, between this and the first of May, and by the number of uplifted hands, all seemed willing to prosecute that work vigorously.

The President then continued on the subject of the P. E. Fund business, home trade, &c., and said, we will now adjourn this conference to the 6th of next April, at 10 o'clock in the morning, at this place.

President Kimball gave notice that in the morning he would commence giving endowments to persons from Iron, Fillmore, San Pete, and Weber Counties.

In the evening the Bishops, Priests, Teachers, Deacons, and their counselors met in the Tabernacle, and were instructed in matters pertaining to their duties by Presidents B. Young and Grant, and by Bishop E. Hunter.

T. Bullock, *Clerk of the Conference.*

NEWS FROM THE UNITED STATES.

The President says the perilous situation of the country domestically and abroad has forced him to exceed the bounds of Senate rule, and to transmit his Annual Address before the formation of the Senate, which, after some hundred attempts has failed to elect a Speaker.

The Address contains complex and threatening matters. The misunderstanding between them and this country causes the most definite and contrary contradictions, which tend to be contentious.

They assert that England does not have the right she claims in Central America, as it was agreed as a condition of the independence that neither party would interfere with the government or the possession of any part of them. England denies this, and extends her clutches across the Mosquito coast, Belize, part of Costa Rica even to the Bay Islands, which belong to the State of Honduras.

Despite giving serious consideration to the urging from England—that they adopt a generous and conciliatory spirit, although relative connections and the advantage of each are things that must be fostered, yet, says the President, unless an early decision is made on the matter, there is a danger that these connections will have to be broken, while the case appears as threatening as it is now.

Another case for contention, he says, was the English officials' challenging of the American law which makes them nonpartisan and noninterventionist in all disputes and wars of foreign nations, by coming to the States and enticing their citizens away to enlist them in England's army in her North American Territories. England admits, he says, to sending the aforementioned officials to gather men to her Territories, and make them into soldiers there, with a strict injunction that they not break any American military law, which was unavoidable, and called not only for a response beyond the persons sent who were opening on their government's responsibility, but also satisfactory compensation.

There is also a request for the dividing line to be drawn between the boundaries of the English Territories and those of the northern States, as they are once again treading on each other's corns, which was the cause of the previous war with Great Britain. Several serious (American) Senators judge that another war is inevitable.

Let the Saints clear the dust from their eyes while they can, and go as far to the west as they can see at all costs, before the pregnant cloud that darkens the western atmosphere spills its damaging bellyful on land and sea.

———

STATISTICAL REPORT.

OF THE CHURCH OF JESUS CHRIST OF LATTER-DAY SAINTS IN WALES,
FOR THE YEAR ENDING DECEMBER 31, 1855.

DAN JONES, President,]   [D. DANIELS, Counselor.
J. PARRY, Pastor over the Northern Conferences.

Conferences.	Presidents.	Scribes.
East Glamorgan,	Robert Evans,	George W. Davies.
West Glamorgan,	Thomas Harris,	William Lewis.
Monmouthshire,	Thomas D. Giles,	Edward Middleton.
Breconshire,	Thomas Morgan,	James Carter.
Llanelli,	Benjamin Jones,	Thomas Stephens.
Carmarthen,	Thomas Jenkins,	Isaac Jones.
South Pembroke,	John Price,	John Gibbs.
North Pembroke,	Thos. D. Evans,	Thos. D. Evans.
Cardiganshire,	John Richards,	David John.
Merionethshire,	John Davies,	John Davies.
Flintshire,	Lewis Davies,	Amos Clark.
Denbighshire,	John Parry,	William M. Jones.
Conwy Valley and Anglesey,	William Lewis,	Evan S. Morgans.

Conferences.	Br.	HP	Eld.	Pr.	Tea.	Dea.	Cut.	Died.	Emi.	Bap.	Tot.
East Glamorgan	27	0	263	63	82	53	300	19	117	232	1632
West Glamorgan	17	2	73	37	17	15	47	5	6	53	421
Monmouthshire	20	0	81	20	23	14	89	9	17	68	465
Breconshire	7	0	26	6	3	7	16	1	2	21	145
Llanelli	11	0	72	15	3	10	20	6	7	50	327
Carmarthen	7	0	22	7	2	4	29	3	8	21	126
South Pembroke	10	0	27	4	2	6	28	3	11	25	175
North Pembroke	4	0	11	2	0	1	5	3	10	3	32
Cardiganshire	5	0	16	3	2	0	25	1	3	3	80
Merionethshire	6	0	14	5	2	2	4	0	0	4	71
Flintshire	6	0	19	7	5	3	12	0	19	22	111
Denbighshire	4	0	14	3	4	3	7	3	7	8	106
Conwy Valley	3	0	10	4	3	1	3	1	7	6	48
Anglesey	2	0	11	6	0	1	5	0	5	3	46
Total	129	2	659	182	148	120	590	54	219	519	3785

MISCELLANEOUS, &c.

NOTICE TO THE EMIGRANTS TO THE STATES!!!—The ship

"Caravan," 1362 tons, has been hired to take the Saints from Liverpool to New York; it will begin its voyage on the 14 of February. The price of transport is £3 5s; under eight months, 10s. The emigrants must be in Liverpool Monday the 11th, and thus those who intend to take the Steamer from Swansea must be here Tuesday night the 5th, ready to leave on the 6th. Those who are in Monmouthshire and the works, must either leave from Newport at 20 minutes after 7 or 30 minutes after 10 Monday morning, or go to Abergavenny by 18 minutes after 8 or 30 minutes after 11 o'clock; the first is the best, if you can, in order to reach Liverpool before nightfall.

BOOK DEBTS FOR THE DIFFERENT CONFERENCES, FOR THE QUARTER ENDING, DECEMBER 31, 1855.

East Glamorgan, £41 15s 4c; West Glamorgan, £111 2s 8c; Monmouthshire, £22 17 5c; Breconshire, 16s 5c; Llanelli, £45 14s 6¼c; Carmarthen, £25 2s 3¾c; South Pembroke, £4 9s 7c; North Pembroke, £1 19s 1½c; Cardiganshire, £14 14s 10c; Merionethshire, £10 12s 10½c; Flintshire, £15 15s 2¼c; Denbighshire, £9 17s 8c; Conwy Valley, £4 12s 7¾c; Anglesey, £6 8s 9½c; Herefordshire, £4 2s 1c; Liverpool Welsh Branch, £3 2s 5½c; Office of the "Star," Liverpool, £6 4s 9c.—The total, £329 9s 7¼c.

RECEIPTS FOR BOOKS FROM JAN. 15 TO JAN. 30.—G. W. DAVIES, £3 11s; WM. LEWIS, £12 10s; THOS. D. EVANS, £1; BEN. JONES, £4 18s 9c; EVAN S. MORGANS, £2 3s 6c.

☞ For lack of space we had to leave out several things from this number until our next.

*** Send all letters, containing orders and payments, to *Capt. Jones, "Zion's Trumpet" Office, Swansea.*

CONTENTS.

	PG.
Minutes of the General Conference	33
Editorial,—Change of Conference Presidents	40
Minutes of the General Conference	43
News from the United States	45
Statistical Report	47
Miscellaneous,—Notice to the Emigrants to the States	47
Book Debts	48
Payments, &c.	48

SWANSEA:
PRINTED AND PUBLISHED BY D. JONES.

ZION'S TRUMPET,

OR

Star of the Saints.

No. 4.] FEBRUARY 16, 1856. [Vol. IX.

THE GATHERING OF THE POOR.
(From the "Star.")

We find our Savior when upon the earth constantly ministering to the poor, the sick, and afflicted. When teaching the multitude on the Mount he said, "Blessed be ye poor, for yours is the kingdom of heaven." His early disciples, those choice spirits who were the first to believe in his divine mission, were poor fishermen on the shores of Galilee. Among the poor of this world have ever been found the majority of the pure in heart—ready to receive and practice the truth. They are generally able to exercise more faith in the Lord than others, because they feel the need of it. Consequently they generally grow faster than the rich in the things of the kingdom. The Lord has ever manifested a peculiar regard for this class of creatures; hence say the Scriptures, "He that hath pity upon the poor lendeth to the Lord; and that which he hath given will he pay him again." It was not the rich man who went into Abraham's bosom, but Lazarus, who begged for the crumbs which fell from the rich man's table. The reason was that the rich man received his good things in this life and did not appreciate them, and Lazarus received evil things, but he worked righteousness in the midst of his afflictions.

It should be a source of great consolation to the poor Saints,

[Price 1*c*.

that while they are despised and persecuted by the world, the Lord has them in remembrance, and has chosen them out of the world as vessels of honor unto Himself, and is permitting them to pass through the fiery furnace of affliction, that they may come out like the gold seven times purified.

While the Lord has such regard for the poor, it follows that his servants, in every age of the world, should exercise similar regard toward them. Hence in the early periods of the Church the Lord instructed the Prophet Joseph to make provision for the poor. When the Saints were driven by mobs from Missouri, the Prophet Brigham was one of those who ceased not their exertions until the poor were gathered out from that land. When the Church was about to leave Nauvoo, at a General Conference held in the House of the Lord, President B. Young moved, "that they take all the Saints with them, to the extent of their ability, that is, their influence and property," which was seconded by Elder Kimball, and carried unanimously. The same spirit to assist the poor has continued to actuate these men, and many others, since that time, and it is the special business of the Bishops in Zion to look after them.

The great object has been continually to *gather the poor* and provide for them. For this President Young and the faithful in Zion labor and contribute liberally of their substance, for they realize that of such is the kingdom of heaven. It matters not how wealthy a man is when he obeys the Gospel, or how much of this world's goods he may take to the gathering place with him, in common with his brethren he must learn, by experience if necessary, to feel for the wants of the poor before he can receive a fullness of the blessings which the Lord has in store for the faithful. Then those who are poor have this assurance,—that they will the sooner be prepared for the reception of that abundance which the Lord is ready to bestow upon His people, as soon as they learn how to use it in wisdom.

In every plan devised for gathering the poor, the question has always been,—"In what way can the greatest good be accomplished? How can the greatest possible number be benefitted?" In doing this, ease and convenience cannot always be studied. If it would answer just as good a purpose, there is not an Elder in Israel who has endured the toils and hardships of journeying to and fro on the earth, who would not wish to see the Saints in these lands taken to Utah with every comfort and convenience that wealth could supply; but, strange though it may seem to some, it would not do the Saints themselves as much good as the anticipated difficult method of accomplishing the journey, neither would it subserve the purposes of the Lord as well. The road would be too easy, and too many would travel it for other motives than building up the kingdom of God.

While the Lord and his servants in every age of the world have manifested so much regard for the poor of his people, we take this occasion to remind the Elders in these lands, who are expecting to go home during the coming season of emigration, that their mission is not done when they are released from their present fields of labor, nor yet when they leave the shores of Britain. You have been here preaching the Gospel—the principles of the gathering, and using every exertion to call into action the energies of the Saints to accomplish their deliverance; and it will devolve on you to aid those who emigrate the coming season, to accomplish the task which lies before them. The poor have particular demands upon you. On your journey home you should constantly seek how you can aid them by your experience, direct and comfort them by your counsels, cheer them by your presence, strengthen their faith, and keep the spirit of union and peace in their midst, that the destroyer may have no power over them.

On your arrival in the United States, instead of feeling as though you had nothing to do but to get home yourselves, be in readiness to render any assistance or assume any responsibilities which those having charge of the emigration may see fit to place upon you. Make the interests of the gathering poor your interests, and be as anxious to see them safely home as yourselves.

Traveling across the plains with teams has always been trying to the patience and perseverance of the inexperienced, and traveling with handcarts cannot be expected to be any the less so. You cannot crown your mission with a labor more befitting your calling, or more consonant with the spirit of the Gospel you have been preaching, than to consider it your duty and privilege to assist the poor in gathering home. To toil along with handcarts through a journey of 1000 miles over the desert plain and rugged mountains, through streams and canyons, will be no easy task, even for those who are accustomed to the fatigues and hardships of mountain life, and the Saints who are willing to do it, with their aged and little ones, for the Gospel's sake, the Lord will make the objects of his special care and blessing. None of the emigrating Saints have ever crossed the plains who have had greater demands on the shepherds of the flock, than those who will travel in the handcart companies the coming season.

We do not make these remarks to the Elders because we anticipate any remissness on their part when called upon for the performance of any duty, but we deem it will stir up their pure minds, by way of remembrance to their privileges as well as duties, and we trust that they will feel the spirit of them all the way home to Utah. They are intended not only for those who have come from Zion, but for all who have been engaged in the work of the ministry in these lands, and who design to emigrate this season.

If those who are clothed with the garments of the Priesthood, and have the Holy Anointing upon them, flinch in the day of trial, who may be expected to stand? They are the ones who should ever be ready to shield the Saints from the onset of the powers of darkness. Are there enemies around the camps of Israel? Or, are the demons of pestilence stalking in their midst? The anointed of the Lord should be in the front of the battle, and by their faith and power with the Almighty, be able to rebuke the ravages of death. The Elders from Zion have received the keys and powers of salvation, and the Lord expects them to be used for the deliverance of his people who are in the midst of the nations, that they also may go up to the Lord's House and learn his ways more perfectly.

Let the Elders lay hold of the Lord in faith, and live up to their privileges by exercising the powers which He has bestowed upon them. When they go on board of a ship with the Saints, they should have power with the heavens to control the elements, and make everything on board contribute to their health, comfort, and peace.

It should be the same on the railroads, the rivers, and in the camps on the plains. The Saints look to you, and have a right to, as the angels of their deliverance. They expect you to be in the Lord's stead to them, like unto Moses when he led the children of Israel in the wilderness. By keeping your counsels, they should receive consolation in trouble, succor in the hour of danger, and be able to surmount every difficulty which opposes their progress. Therefore, discharge the responsibility like men of God, for it is upon you. Feed the Saints with the bread of eternal life, that their faith in the Lord may increase through you, and they realize more and more that He has clothed you with the powers of salvation.

We anticipate going home next summer, but the season will probably be considerably advanced, and business matters pertaining to the emigration will urge us on our journey. We still anticipate, however, much pleasure and satisfaction in associating with the companies of the Saints on the plains, and spending an occasional happy evening with them around the campfire under our Father's beautiful canopy, the starry heavens, which mobs have compelled the Saints to learn how to duly appreciate. We expect this privilege to afford us more joy and pleasure than any other events that will transpire on our journey.

It is our constant desire not to mislead the Saints concerning the difficulties of the journey to Utah. We wish them calmly to make up their minds that it is not an easy task, and to start with faith, trusting in Israel's God for success, and seek Him continually, by prayer and supplication, that measure of the spirit of faith and rejoicing which will enable them patiently to endure all things, and accomplish the desires of their hearts.

The Lord has promised that He will pour his Spirit upon the faithful of his people, in such measure as they may need, to cause them to endure with joy all the trials and difficulties which they may have to pass through. None have a stronger claim upon the Lord in this thing than the emigrating poor, if they will only fulfill the conditions of faithfulness. Thousands of the Saints will testify that the times of persecution, long and toilsome journeyings, and of other afflictions have been seasons of the greatest refreshings from the presence of the Lord, when the spirit of truth has most abundantly poured into their minds the intelligence of eternity, and that knowledge which leads to salvation.

While those Saints who neglect to call upon the Lord, and despise the counsels and reproofs of his servants, will journey to Zion with the spirit of contention in their hearts, grumbling and finding fault with everything and everybody about them, the souls of the humble and diligent will be continually feasted with comfort and consolation. When they rise up in the morning their hearts will be filled with joy and thanksgiving, and when they gather around their campfires at night, the sweet communion and fellowship of the Holy Spirit will rest upon them, and angels will watch over them, and administer to them in dreams and visions of the night. In after years the memory of the scenes they have passed through will be sweet, for they will realize that the Lord was with them, and that they have learned many useful lessons to guide them in after life.

By the Minutes of the General Conference in Great Salt Lake City, on the 6th of October last, published in this number of the *Star*, the Saints will learn the pleasing intelligence that Elders Ezra T. Benson and Lorenzo Snow have been appointed to succeed us in our labors in these lands. We feel to congratulate the Saints in the prospect of having two of the Twelve to labor among them. They are men of great faith, knowledge, and experience, and it affords us much satisfaction to learn that the responsible duties of our calling will soon roll from our shoulders onto those so much more capable of bearing the burden.

These our brethren will be fresh from the fountainhead. An increase of the spirit of Zion will burn in their bosoms, they will stir up anew the Gospel fire in these lands, and give a new impetus to the great work of the gathering. Let none of the Saints settle down to tarry here a little longer, thinking that all is peace and safety because two of the Twelve are coming in their midst, for they will come here with the spirit of the gathering burning like fire shut up in their bones. The great objects of their mission will be to gather Israel, and especially the poor. They will come with a full knowledge of the new plan of operations, devised and matured by the First Presidency in the councils of Zion, and go about the work with a faith and strength heretofore unknown in these lands.

The power of the Priesthood is rapidly increasing in the earth, and that increase is first felt in Zion, and like streams from an inexhaustible fountain, it is diffused through the earth by those who are sent abroad from that place. Some will, perhaps, query in their minds, "What is this power?" Why simply that which Christ referred to, when he bade his disciples tarry in Jerusalem until they should be endowed with power from on high. This is one reason why a continual change is taking place among the Elders, some returning home that the fire may be kindled anew in them, while others are sent to labor in their places. For this and other reasons, the Saints may expect that a great increase of faith and Priesthood will be brought to bear on the work of the Lord in these lands, under the administration of these our brethren. The Saints, instead of settling down at ease in Babylon, may expect to be stirred up to an increase of energy, faith, and good works. Where we in our weakness have failed to accomplish their deliverance, we trust that brothers Benson and Snow, by their greater experience and wisdom, will be enabled to devise more efficient plans for the gathering of the poor than we have been able to bring to bear on the subject. Inasmuch as those who are sent to the Saints have an increase of efficiency and power, they should endeavor to arouse their slumbering energies to increased exertions for themselves.

SERMON

By President B. Young, which was delivered at the October Conference in Great Salt Lake City, 1855.

As we have assembled in the capacity of a Conference to attend to business, we should earnestly seek to enjoy the spirit of our calling. We are called to be Saints, and if we have the spirit of Saints we shall have the spirit of our calling; otherwise, we certainly do not enjoy the privileges that the Lord designs we should. The Lord is ready and willing to give his Spirit to those who are honest before him, and who seek earnestly to enjoy it.

If Saints, assembled to worship God and transact business pertaining to his kingdom, should not have the aid of his Spirit, they would be likely to commit errors, and it would be strange indeed if they did not, and to do that which they ought not, even in business transactions; they would fall short of accomplishing their own wishes, and of course far short of fulfilling the designs of heaven. We see many led astray, because they have not retained the Spirit of Christ to guide them.

When any of this people, who believe the Gospel, forsake the duty which they owe to God and his cause, they are at once surrounded by an influence which causes them to imbibe a dislike to Saints and to the conduct of Saints; they receive a false spirit, and then the Saints cannot do right in their eyes, the ministers of God cannot preach right nor act right, and soon they wish to leave the society of the Saints, and that too, as they suppose, with a sanctified heart and life. They wish to withdraw from this, as they believe, wicked people, fancying all to be wicked but themselves, and wish to separate themselves until the people are as holy as they flatter themselves that they are, when they calculate to return again. Others will lose the spirit of their calling, and realize that they have lost it; they are wicked, and know it, and will have more confidence in others than in themselves. But the self-righteous will go away and wait until we as a people are sanctified and able to endure their presence, and think that then they will, perhaps, gather among us again.

People are liable in many ways to be led astray by the power of the adversary, for they do not fully understand that it is a hard matter for them to always distinguish the things of God from the things of the devil. There is but one way by which they can know the difference, and that is by the light of the spirit of revelation, even the spirit of our Lord Jesus Christ. Without this we are all liable to be led astray and forsake our brethren, forsake our covenants and the Church and kingdom of God on earth.

Should the whole people neglect their duty and come short in performing the things required at their hands, lose the light of the

Spirit of the Lord, the light of the spirit of revelation, they would not know the voice of the Good Shepherd from the voice of a stranger, they would not know the difference between a false teacher and a true one, for there are many spirits gone out into the world, and the false spirits are giving revelations as well as the Spirit of the Lord. This we are acquainted with; we know that there are many delusive spirits, and unless the Latter-day Saints live to their privileges, and enjoy the spirit of the holy Gospel, they cannot discern between those who serve God and those who serve him not. Consequently, it becomes us, as Saints, to cleave to the Lord with all our hearts, and seek unto him until we do enjoy the light of his Spirit, that we may discern between the righteous and the wicked, and understand the difference between false spirits and true. Then, when we see a presentation, we shall know whence it is, and understand whether it be of the Lord, or whether it is not of him; but if the people are not endowed with the Holy Ghost they cannot tell; therefore, it becomes us to have the Spirit of the Lord, not only in preaching and praying, but to enable us to reflect and judge, for the Saints are to judge in these matters. They are to judge not only men, they are to be judges not only in the capacity of a Conference to decide what shall be done, what course shall be pursued to further the kingdom of God, what business shall be transacted, and how it shall be transacted, and so on, but they will actually judge angels.

(To be continued.)

ZION'S TRUMPET,
OR
Star of the Saints.

SATURDAY, FEBRUARY 16, 1856.

GENERAL CONFERENCE.—We are happy to be able to announce that a General Conference will be held in the *White Lion* Inn, Merthyr Tydfil, to begin on Saturday, February 23rd, at half past ten o'clock in the morning. It is requested that all the Presidents especially, and as many of the Priesthood as possible, come from all the Welsh Conferences on that day. We have the promise of Presidents F. D. Richards, D. Spencer, C. H. Wheelock, &c., that they will honor the Conference with their presence, and we and they are confident that no one will neglect this opportunity to receive important and interesting teaching on their last visit to Wales before their departure from the country.

We wish for the Presidents to excuse us at this busy time for not giving them any more warning than this, and give this precedence as far as they can over any other engagements at that time.

INSTRUCTIONS ON THE EMIGRATION.

36, *Islington, Liverpool, February* 8, 1856.

IN CONSEQUENCE of Elder E. Snow's absence from St. Louis, and the death of Elder Orson Spencer, together with the disadvantages brought about by searching for, and determining a northern and more healthy route for the emigrants to go through the States to a point of outfit to start across the plains, we have been unable to lay before the Saints the following regulations:—

1st.—Iowa City, the capital of the State of Iowa, has been selected as the point of outfit for the starting across the plains. This is about the same distance as Mormon Grove from Great Salt Lake City. It is intended that both Perpetual Emigration Fund emigrants and those going through with their own ox teams shall fit out there.

2nd.—Emigrants will be forwarded from the port of debarkation to Iowa City on the northern route, and via Chicago and Rock Island.

3rd.—The P. E. Fund emigrants will use handcarts in crossing the plains, in which they will convey their provisions, tent, and necessary luggage, according to instructions contained in the "Thirteenth General Epistle" of the First Presidency in the *Star*, number 4, of the present volume [and the 2nd number of the TRUMPET of the present volume], also in a letter of President B. Young, and the Editorial in the *Star*, number 51, Vol. XVII [and the 26th number of the TRUMPET, Vol. VIII]. There will of course be means provided for the conveyance of the aged, infirm, and those unable from any cause to walk, but as the Presidency have informed us in the General Epistle, before referred to, that they "shall send men of faith and experience to the outfitting point, to carry into effect" the suggestions contained in the Epistle, we deem it uncalled for, on our part, to detail the minutia of that part of the journey, any more than to assure the Saints that their interests and greatest comfort will be consulted in the best possible manner by those men who will be charged with instructions directly from our beloved Prophet, brother Brigham.

4th.—It is determined to book through to Utah by the P. E. Fund Company and under the arrangements named and referred to in Section 3, all persons who desire it, for £9 each for all over one year old, and £4 10s under one year old, leaving it to the President of the P. E. F. Company to fix the final price after the expedition is closed and the cost of the same is known.

5th.—All P. E. Fund emigrants are required to bind themselves to repay the cost of their passage according to the "General Instructions" in the *Star*, number 2 of the present volume.

6th.—*Luggage*. Emigrants traveling in companies, under contract, on the American lines of railway last season, were permitted to carry free of extra charge 75 pounds each for one person over twelve years old, and 37½ pounds each for one person under 12 and over 3 years old, and none for those under that age.

Presuming the same quantities will be allowed this season, P. E. Fund emigrants will be able to include in their luggage such of their books as they may wish to take with them. Those who are ordered out by their friends in Utah, whose passage has not been prepaid, and those who may be selected here to go, cannot be allowed to take forward from the port of debarkation in the United States, more than the above named quantities of *luggage*. Those who prepay their passage, or those whose passage has been prepaid in Utah, if they have the means, to take their excess *luggage* across the States at about 10 shillings per 100 pounds to the point of outfit, where they can doubtless arrange for the conveyance across the plains by ox teams of that which they are unable to haul in their handcarts for about 6c or 7½c per pound if it costs the same as it did last year. Should it occur that any parties cannot arrange for all their luggage to be carried over the plains this season, they will be able to store it at Iowa City, or Kanesville, and order it to be forwarded to them another year. We recommend the emigrating Saints to dispense with and dispose of all their heavy wooden boxes, and to obtain oil-cloth bags to keep the water out. Where boxes are indispensable they should be made of tin, and be as small in size as possible.

7th.—As it is already so late in the season, and as we wish to hasten the emigration as much as practicable, it is particularly requested that all emigrants to Utah will now make their applications for passage at the earliest moment, providing their names, their deposits, &c., according to the "General Instructions." Those requiring us to provide their teams should forward their orders and the cash immediately, and the Fund emigrants who have prepaid should send their names and deposits, and their passage money as early as possible.

8th.—The through emigrants to Utah will not require to embark until the middle or latter part of March.

9th.—The present "Passenger Act" makes it penal for any person to be engaged, either directly or indirectly, in the sale or letting of passages out of the United Kingdom, unless duly authorized under the provisions of the Act. We, therefore, give notice that all applications from the Latter-day Saints for passage to America must be made direct to F. D. Richards, with deposits, &c., as detailed in "General Instructions," except by those in the London Pastorate, who may apply through his authorized Agent, Mr. W. C. Dunbar, 35 *Jewin Street, City, London*, and by those in the Welsh Principality, who may apply through Mr. Dan Jones, "*Udgorn Seion*" *Office, Swansea*, who also is his authorized Agent.

10th.—Pastors and President are requested to cause this Circular to be read and understood in all the Branches composing their Conferences at their earliest possible convenience.

F. D. Richards,
Daniel Spencer,
C. H. Wheelock,

*Presidency of the Church of Jesus Christ of
Latter-day Saints in the British Isles
and adjacent countries.*

PEACE!

PEACE! is the main topic of Emperors, Senators and Editors at present, while others shout, War! war! as this offer of reconciliation is no better than the previous one when the war was paused for an instant in the expectation that Russia would reconcile, while she, instead, made the most of the time to transfer war materials and soldiers through places they would not dare go afterward, nor from that time until now when it is again suggested to have a brief pause in the war until it can be seen what is next. If the Bear watched her advantage, prepared herself, and defied her enemies before, it is more than likely that she will do likewise again, while she has strength in her claws.

While our ears are stunned by the sound of war in the eastern world, we understand that the situation of Western America is no less so. As it is from an agitated *crater* spewing out the fiery *lava* of a *volcano* that one sees the contents of its enormous belly, one sees from the elements of harmful war brewing in Arkansas an indication of the inner contents of the great American Union.

On the 8th of last January some of the anti-slave-traders attacked the slave-traders in Kansas, and in the battle several of both factions were killed and wounded.

There was a battle recently in Oregon between 300 of the Indians and 400 American soldiers, and several were killed and wounded on both sides. In the Indian war on the Green River too the same thing is going on.

The American Senate had not formed recently, and when they do they have nothing better to do than to argue and demonstrate contentious, so-called political wit, as they have started to do, following their old habit.

Several Senators express their opinion with regard to England, that unless she moves back from her present position on the American Continent, war will be unavoidable. There was talk there that America intends uniting with Russia against the western European powers, but it was said that it was the whim of fanatics. Anyway, one of the main newspapers, namely the "New York Daily Times,"— "That in less than a year's time from when they intervene in matters on the Continent of America, they would see her banners flying where they would not want them; that the present is a dangerous time for them to threaten the United States, and that the aiming of the point of a spear can suck back a bolt of lightning!"

As the doleful sound of the wind's moaning and the appearance of black clouds in the sky before the awful storm that is coming causes the doves to flee to their windows, and the bees to their hive, the prophetic and threatening voices of the rulers of countries, and the signs of the "times of adversity" induce the Saints of Heaven to look and flee toward Zion at the opportunity.

GATHERING OF THE SAINTS.

BY GWILYM DDU FROM ZION.

The Day foreseen by holy Prophets
    And Patriarchs, has dawned above the confines of our world,
The keys of the last dispensation have been given
    To gather the children of Israel from every corner together;
The descendants of old Abraham, Isaac, and Jacob,
    Who for ages lived dispersed;—
"Thou shalt know thy seed among the gentiles,"
    Says an ancient prophecy by a prophet of God.

Now the missionaries of the God of heaven are preaching
    The eternal gospel to the people of the world,
All sent in divine authority,
    To every corner of the length and breadth of the earth;
And these are the "fishermen" and the "hunters" foretold
    Anciently by the old prophet through the Spirit of his God,
Gathering the Saints in the latter days,
    From among the gentiles where they have been living.

They are coming out of great Babylon before her fall,
    From countless places at the call of the God of heaven,—
As a cloud,—as mist and as doves,
    Swiftly to their windows they fly homeward;
The children of Ephraim to Zion, to the land of the west,
    And the ten tribes come home from the north each one,

> The children of Judah come to old Palestine
>> To erect their temple before the coming of the Son of Man.

> Old Satan will be bound, and our Jesus will reign
>> During a thousand years among his Saints,
> He will make them Priests to his Father, and Kings,
>> In the kingdom of heaven—(O privileged and true honor);
> The race of Abraham, Isaac, and Jacob, never again,
>> Will be scattered, say the words of the Lord God,
> But with their eternal King they shall reign,
>> Over the four corners of the earth, and from sea to sea.

MISCELLANEOUS, &c.

THE TEMPLE.—Twice as many stones have been used for the foundation of the Temple being built in Great Salt Lake City as were used to build the entire Temple that was in Nauvoo.

ONE of the state officials the American Government sent to Utah has obeyed "Mormonism," and already has two wives.

IT is said that the Czar is requesting the States to moderate between him and the allied powers. One wonders then which moderator "Jonathan" will get, who is powerful enough to moderate between the Southern and the Northern States? Unless he finds someone soon it is likely they will be torn to shreds, and who will complain of their fate?

THE Catholic Priests in Ireland are making a bonfire of Protestant Bibles and Testaments.

ACCORDING to the newspapers' prediction the atmosphere of the west is darkening, and the cloud that was like the palm of a man's hand some time ago is burdened with warlike elements, and it is quite likely that the British "Bull" will plunge its horns into its belly before long, at least the causes of contention have increased to five now, and when what holds them back is removed, that which was purchased will be done. Blessed are those who reach the western refuge before it pours.

A scoundrel by the name of James Brott was fined £50 recently in Dover, having been stood bail of £50 each against his appearance before the Quarter Sessions, for disrupting a Latter-day Saints service, and what man, who has a whit of respect for religion or a desire to worship God, will not thank the Magistrates for doing right for once, and hope that an example will be made of this wretch, as a warning to similar types who are so frequently employed by the Priests and Reverends of our country to disrupt the worship of their fellows who are more religious than themselves.

Payments toward the Debt of the West Glamorgan Conference from Jan. 16 to Feb. 13.—(The second promises.)

	£	s.	c.		£	s.	c.
Henry John, Morristown	0	2	6	Ben. Phillips, ditto	0	4	0
Ann John, his wife	0	2	6	Ben. Jones, ditto	0	2	6
George Cutliffe, Swansea	0	5	0	Esther Jones, his wife	0	2	6
David Davies, Traveling Elder	0	2	6	Thomas Jones, Cyfyng	0	2	0
Catherine Dear, Neath	0	2	6	Phillip Thomas, Alltwen	0	2	6
Wm Jenkins, ditto	0	2	6	Total	£1	10	6

Receipts For Books From Jan. 30 To Feb. 8.—Isaac Jones, £3 10s; John Davies, £1 7s.

☞ Conferences of the North will be held as follows:—Flintshire on the 2nd of March, Denbighshire on the 9th, Conwy Valley and Anglesey on the 16th, and Merionethshire on the 23rd.

☞ Because of lack of space we had to leave out some things from this issue until our next.

Addresses.—Daniel Daniels, "Zion's Trumpet" Office, Swansea.—Abednego Williams, Garden Street, Merthyr.

⁎ Send all letters, containing orders and payments, to *Capt. Jones, "Zion's Trumpet" Office, Swansea.*

CONTENTS.

	PG.
The Gathering of the Poor	49
Sermon of President Young	55
Editorial.—General Conference	57
Instructions on the Emigration	58
Peace	61
Gathering of the Saints	62
Miscellaneous	63
Payments, &c.	64

SWANSEA:
PRINTED AND PUBLISHED BY D. JONES.

ZION'S TRUMPET,

OR

Star of the Saints.

No. 5.] MARCH 1, 1856. [Vol. IX.

SERMON

By President B. Young, which was delivered at the October Conference in Great Salt Lake City, 1855.

[Continued from page 57.]

WE sit here as judges, and suppose that business which would prove injurious to this people should now be presented for them to decide upon, or suppose that the leaders of this people had forsaken the Lord and should introduce, through selfishness, that which would militate against the kingdom of God on the earth, that which would in the issue actually destroy this people, how are you going to detect the wrong and know it from the right? You cannot do it, unless you have the Spirit of the Lord. Do the people enjoy that Spirit? Yes, many of them do. Do they enjoy it in as great a degree as it is their privilege? A few of them do, still I think that the people in general might enjoy more of the Holy Spirit, more of the nature and essence of the Deity, than they do. I know that they have their trials, I know they have the world to grapple with, and are tempted, and I know what they have to war against.

But let us ask ourselves individually whether we fight this warfare to such a degree that we do overcome in every instance, in every contest do we come off victorious? Here we have to do with

[Price 1*c*.

our passions; here is fallen nature, that we can never get rid of until we lie down in the grave, it is sown in the flesh and will remain there, but it is our privilege to overcome that, and bring it under subjection in our reflections, in our meditations, and in all the labor that we perform, though we may be tried, tempted, and buffeted by Satan. It is our privilege to have power to rule, govern, and bring under subjection even our momentary passions; yes, it is our privilege so to live and overcome them that we never would have a temptation to think evil, or at least would never speak before we took time to think, but all would be in subjection to the law of Christ. Do we live up to this privilege?

People may ask, Are we not good Saints? Yes, I can say that this people are a good people, and they wish to be Saints, and many of them strive to be Saints, and many of them are Saints.

I realize the weaknesses of men; I am not ignorant of my own weaknesses, and this is where I teach everybody else their dispositions and the operations of the Spirit upon the inhabitants of the earth; to teach mankind is to teach myself.

This is a good people, they are a righteous people; yet there are some who are filled with folly, there are some who are inclined to do wickedly and seem to love wickedness; there are some who are filled with idolatry, and it seems as though it were impossible for them to overcome the spirit of the world, to keep them from loving it and from cleaving to it and to the things of the world. I will appeal to the people as judges, are you capable of judging in matters pertaining to the kingdom of God on earth, unless you have the Spirit of truth within you?

Some may say, "Brethren, you who lead the Church, we have all confidence in you, we are not in the least afraid but what everything will go right under your superintendence; all the business matters will be transacted right; and if brother Brigham is satisfied with it, I am." I do not wish any Latter-day Saint in this world, nor in heaven, to be satisfied with anything I do, unless the Spirit of the Lord Jesus Christ,—the spirit of revelation, makes them satisfied. I wish them to know for themselves and understand for themselves, for this would strengthen the faith that is within them.

Suppose that the people were heedless, that they manifested no concern with regard to the things of the kingdom of God, but threw the whole burden upon the leaders of the people, saying, if the brethren who take charge of matters are satisfied, we are, this is not pleasing in the sight of the Lord.

Every man and woman in this kingdom ought to be satisfied with what we do, but they never should be satisfied without asking the Father, in the name of Jesus Christ, whether what we do is right. When you are inspired by the Holy Ghost you can understandingly say that you are satisfied; and that is the only power that should cause you to exclaim that you are satisfied, for without that you do not know whether you should be satisfied or not. You may say that you are satisfied and believe that all is right, and your confidence may be almost unbounded in the authorities of the Church of Jesus Christ, but if you asked God, in the name of Jesus, and received knowledge for yourself, through the Holy Spirit, would it not strengthen your faith? It would. A little faith will perform little works; that is good logic. Jesus says, "If ye have faith as a grain of mustard seed, ye shall say unto this mountain, Remove hence to yonder place; and it shall remove; and nothing shall be impossible unto you."

A grain of mustard seed is very small; nevertheless if you had faith as a grain of mustard seed, and should say unto this mountain, Remove hence to yonder place, it would be done; or to that sycamore tree, Be thou planted in the sea; or to the sick, Be ye healed; or to the devils, Be ye cast out; it would be done.

Suppose that I had faith like a grain of mustard seed, and could do the things which Christ has said are possible to be done through that faith, and that another man on the continent of Asia had the same faith, we could not accomplish much because but two would have all the power of Satan to combat. Do you suppose that Jesus Christ healed every person that was sick, or that all the devils were cast out in the country where he sojourned? I do not. Working miracles, healing the sick, raising the dead, and the like, were almost as rare in his day as in this our day. Once in a while the people would have faith in his power, and what is called a miracle would be performed, but the sick, the blind, the deaf and dumb, the crazy, and those possessed with different kinds of devils were around him, and only now and then could his faith have power to take effect, on account of the want of faith in the individuals.

Many suppose that in the days of the Savior no person was sick, in the vicinity of his labors, but what was healed; this is a mistake, for it was only occasionally that a case of healing a sick person or casting out a devil occurred. But again, suppose that two-thirds of the inhabitants of Jerusalem and the regions round about had actually possessed like faith in the Savior that a few did, then it is very probable that all the sick would have been healed and the devils cast out, for there would have been a predominance of a good power over the evil influences.

Let two persons be on the continent of America, having faith like a grain of mustard seed, and let one of them be situated on the Atlantic and the other on the Pacific coast, and most of the sick would remain sick around them, the dying would die, and those possessed of devils would continue to be tormented, though once in a while a sick person might be healed, or a blind person be made to see. Now let each one of those individuals have another person of like faith added to him, and they will do as much again work; then let there be four persons in the east and four in the west, all possessing faith like a grain of mustard seed, and there will be four times as much done as when there was but one in each place; and thus go on increasing their number in this ratio until, by and by, all the Latter-day Saints have faith like a grain of mustard seed, and where would there be place for devils? Not in these mountains, for they would all be cast out. Do you not perceive that that would be a great help to us?

If I had power of myself to heal the sick, which I do not profess to have, or to cast out devils, which power I have not got, though if the Lord sees fit to cast them out through my command it is all right;

still if I had that power, and there was no other person to help me, the people would do as they do now, they would hunt me almost to death, saying, Won't you lay hands on this sick person? Won't you go to my house over yonder? and so on. I am sent for continually, though I only go occasionally, because it is the privilege of every father, who is an Elder in Israel, to have faith to heal his family, just as much so as it is my privilege to have faith to heal my family; and if he does not do it he is not living up to his privilege. It is just as reasonable for him to ask me to cut his wood and maintain his family, for if he had faith himself he would save me the trouble of leaving other duties to attend to his request.

Let this faith be distributed and it makes all things easy, but put one or two dozen men to hauling a wagon containing a hundred tons' weight and the labor is very heavy, whereas if the whole of the Latter-day Saints would put their shoulder to the load it would be moved easily. It is with the mental powers as it is with the physical, and that is why I wish you to consider the matter, and why I lay those things before you. Let the Latter-day Saints have faith and works, and let them forsake their covetousness and cleave unto righteousness.

I have given you a short discourse upon faith and practical religion, and now I say to the elders of Israel, to the bishops of the different wards, and to the presidents of the different branches, if there is any business you wish to bring before this conference, pertaining to fellowship and the conduct of individuals, you can have the privilege.

We were accustomed, some years ago, to attend to such business before our general conference, and it is our privilege to do so again, if we choose, or if there is any occasion.

In all high councils, in bishops' courts, and in all other departments for transacting our business, the Church and kingdom of God, with the Lord Almighty at the head, will cause every man to exhibit the feelings of his heart, for you recollect it is written that in the last days the Lord will reveal the secrets of the hearts of the children of men.

Does not the Gospel do that? It does; it causes men and women to reveal that which would have slept in their dispositions until they dropped into their graves. The plan by which the Lord leads this people makes them reveal their thoughts and intents, and brings out every trait of disposition lurking in their organizations. Is this right? It is. How are you going to correct a man's faults, by hiding them and never speaking of them, by covering up every fault you see in your brother, or by saying, O, do not say a word about his faults, we know that he lies, but it will not do to say a word about it, for it would be awful to reveal such a fact to the people? That is the policy of the world and of the devil, but is it the way that the Lord will do with the people in the latter days? It is not.

This is a matter that seems to be but little understood by some of the Latter-day Saints; it may be understood by a portion of them, but others do not understand it. Every fault that a person has will be made manifest, that it may be corrected by the gospel of salvation, by the laws of the Holy Priesthood.

Suppose that a man lies, and you dare not tell of it; Very well, says the man. I am secure, I can lie as much as I please. He is inclined to lie, and if we dare not chastise him about it he takes shelter under that pavilion,—he cloaks himself with the charity of his brethren, and continues to lie. By and by he will steal a little, and perhaps one or two of his brethren know about it, but they say, "We must cover up this fault with the cloak of charity." He continues to lie and to steal, and we continue to hide his faults; where will it lead that person to? Where will he end his career? Nowhere but in hell.

What shall we do with such men? Shall we reveal their faults? Yes, whenever we deem it right and proper. I know it is hard to receive chastisement, for no chastisement is joyous, but grievous at the time it is given; but if a person will receive chastisement and pray for the Holy Spirit to rest upon him, that he may have the Spirit of truth in his heart, and cleave to that which is pleasing to the Lord, the Lord will give him grace to bear the chastisement, and he will submit to and receive it, knowing that it is for his good. He will endure it patiently, and, by and by, he will get over it, and see that he has been chastised for his faults, and will banish the evil, and the chastisement will yield to him the peaceable fruits of righteousness, because he exercises himself profitably therein.

In this way chastisement is a benefit to any person. Grant that I have a fault, and wish it concealed, would I not be likely to hide it? And if the Lord would not reveal it I might cling to it, if I had not the spirit of revelation to discern my fault and its consequences. Without the influence of the Spirit of the Lord, I am just as liable to live and abide in false principles, false notions, and unrighteous actions as true ones. It is so with you.

If your faults are not made known to you, how can you refrain from them and overcome them? You cannot. But if your faults are made manifest, you have the privilege of forsaking them and cleaving unto that which is good. The design of the gospel is to reveal the secrets of the hearts of the children of men.

When men intimate to me, whether in public or in private, that their faults must not be spoken of, I do not know how worldly minded men feel in similar cases, but like Elijah, when he mocked the priests of Baal, I feel to laugh and make derision of such men.

Do you suppose that I will thus far bow down to any man in this Territory, or on the earth? Do you suppose that I will suffer myself to be so muzzled that I cannot reveal the faults of the people when wisdom dictates me to do it?

I fear not the wicked half so much as I would a *mosquito* in my bedroom at night, for he would keep me from sleeping, but for the unrighteous, those who will act the villain and conduct themselves worse than the devil, to insinuate that I have not the privilege of speaking of their faults makes me feel like laughing at their folly. I will speak of men's faults when and where I please, and what are you going to do about it? Do you know that that very principle caused the death of all the Prophets, from the days of Adam until now? Let a prophet arise upon the earth, and never reveal the evils of men, and do you suppose that the wicked would desire to kill him? No, for he would cease to be a prophet of the Lord, and they would invite him to their feasts, and hail him as a friend and brother. Why? Because it would be impossible for him to be anything but one of them. It is impossible for a prophet of Christ to live in an adulterous generation without speaking of the wickedness of the people, without revealing their faults and their failings, and there is nothing short of death that will stay him from it, for a prophet of God will do as he pleases.

I have been preached to, pleaded with, and written to, to be careful how I speak about men's faults, more so than ever Joseph Smith was in his lifetime; every week or two I receive a letter of instruction, warning me to be careful of this or that man's character. Did you ever have the Spirit of the Lord, so that you have felt full of joy, and like jumping up and shouting hallelujah? I feel in that way when such epistles come to me; I feel like saying, "I ask no odds of you, nor of all your clan this side of hell."

I have wise brethren around me who will sometimes say, "Don't speak so and so, be very careful, how do be cautious;" and I have been written to from the east; I have package after package of letters, yes, and wheelbarrows of them, saying, "O, Brother Brigham, I would beseech and pray and plead with you, if I only dare, to be careful how you speak. Would not this or that course be better than for you to get up in the stand, and tell the gentiles what they are? Would it not be better to keep this to yourself?"

Do you know how I feel when I get such communications? I will tell you, I feel just like rubbing their noses with them. If I am not to have the privilege of speaking of Saint and sinner when I please, tie up my mouth and let me go to the grave, for my work would be done.

It was for this that they killed Joseph and Hyrum, it is for this that they wish to kill me and my brethren; we know their iniquity, and we will tell of it when the Spirit dictates, or talk about this, that, or the other person and conduct at the proper time.

There are people in our midst who grunt at this course, and at the same time have evils that I think are hardly worth notice, for I do not think that such persons will be good for anything even should they happen to get into the kingdom of heaven, though I suppose they are good in their place if we can find out where it is, but as yet I am ignorant of it; I presume that the Lord knows where it is, but I do not. I wish to say to the elders of Israel, to all people, I shall tell you of your iniquity and talk about you just as I please, and when you feel like killing me for so doing, as some of the people did who called themselves brethren in the days of Joseph Smith, look out for yourselves, for false brethren were the cause of Joseph's death, and I am not a very righteous man. I have told the Latter-day Saints from the beginning that I do not profess my righteousness, but I profess to know the will of God concerning you, and I have boldness enough to tell it to you, fearless of your wrath, and I expect that it is on this account that the Lord has called me to occupy the place I do; I feel as independent as an angel.

(To be continued.)

ZION'S TRUMPET,
OR
Star of the Saints.

SATURDAY, MARCH 1, 1856.

THE EMIGRATION.—Allow us the pleasure of notifying the Saints who intend to emigrate this year, that President Richards has kindly permitted the Welsh Saints to emigrate on the same ship, whether they go with a wagon company, a handcart company, or to the States, and we shall have the privilege of going with them. Each one is requested to send his name and his deposit without delay. We hope that not one Saint will remain behind who has or who can obtain nine pounds, and that no one under six years old in the church who has five pounds is seen to be left behind.

We have the good news to report that the Perpetual Emigrating Society is offering to emigrate half the number who pay five pounds to the Perpetual E. Fund, if they have been faithful in the Church for six years or more, if they have no more than that; and the other half will be emigrated the next time. Let such come to an agreement among themselves as to who will go first, and if they cannot they will appeal to their Presidency, but in every case let *faithfulness* and *longevity* in the church tip the balance. Let those who do not have nine pounds hasten to snatch this opportunity! Seek out your partners quickly, dear Saints, before it becomes too late. Let all the others who have five pounds each, who have not been in the church for six years, make every effort possible to come to the States now. Since the end of March is the latest time that a ship should sail from Liverpool; and since the majority are ready now, and waiting for the others, you can see the great need for haste; there is not a day to lose when we consider the time that it will take to hire the ship, send notices, go to Liverpool, &c. Presidents, awake to your task immediately.

We expect to have the pleasure in our next issue of reporting who will be assisted to emigrate. It will not come a moment sooner for asking.

DISTRIBUTORS.—Good heavens! What is the reason that nearly all of you have agreed to no longer send any money for books this year? What is your answer?

MINUTES OF THE COUNCIL AND THE GENERAL CONFERENCE,

Of the Church of Jesus Christ of Latter-day Saints in Wales, held in the "White Lion" Inn, Merthyr, on the 23rd, 24th, 25th, and the 26th of February, 1856.

SATURDAY morning the 23rd.—Present—The Presidency of the Church in Wales—Dan Jones and Daniel Daniels, Israel Evans and Benjamin Ashby, American Elders.

Conference Presidents, except three from the North; several local Traveling Elders, &c., &c.

At 11:00 o'clock in the morning the President called the Council to order, reporting that we had been disappointed in our expectation of the presence of the Presidency of the British Isles, and several American Elders.

Elder Israel Evans prayed.

Elders William Lewis and G. W. Davies were selected as clerks for the Council and the Conference.

The Council was spent by President Jones in instructing the Presidents.

He spoke on the power of the government of the Priesthood over everything in the heavens and on and under the earth; the strait and narrow path is what Mormons have to walk. He reasoned about the indistinguishable connection of the business of the Church,—its commercial part and that which is called spiritual. The duty of those who are in different degrees of the Priesthood to govern themselves according to their superiors; they are like the cogs of a machine that turn and govern each other, from the Great Governing Wheel above. That the living Priesthood, and not the dead letter of the law, is our present Bible, and that it is by fulfilling its requirements through difficulties, and showing faith and effort in this that a President proves himself worthy of his office. On the necessity and the importance of being exact, attentive, and watchful, and diligent with regard to the distribution of the Books, and all the collections,—to see that there is temperance—that there is neither negligence nor overburdening. On the signs of the times, warning the world, the emigration of the Saints, and the coming of many into the Church.

In the hopeful expectation of the arrival of the aforementioned brethren, the next meeting was postponed until 6:00 o'clock. President Daniels prayed.

At 6:00 o'clock there were present also—from the Presidency of the British Isles—D. Spencer and Cyrus H. Wheelock the counselors.

American Elders—Joseph A. Young (son of the Prophet Brigham), Millen Atwood, J. B. Martin, and N. V. Porter.

Elder B. Ashby prayed.

President Jones addressed the congregation at the coming of the above Brethren, exhorting us to receive their teaching, since he gave his word it would be good, and he made way for President Spencer to speak, announcing that President F. D. Richards was on his way there, and that he would arrive before the end of the meeting.

President Spencer spoke on the fulfillment of duties which will qualify us to occupy the high circles in which God intends to have experienced and faithful men, and a little about the emigration, poverty and oppression of the Saints here, &c.

Elder J. A. Young commented on the importance of our callings in the various degrees of the Priesthood, and the great responsibility of each one.

President F. D. Richards came in when Elder Atwood was speaking about the privileges of the Gospel, and how great a price is paid to have them.

Elder J. B. Martin spoke about the living Priesthood and the fallibility of the dead letter of the law, and his experience under various persecutions of the Church.

President F. D. Richards greeted the Saints on his visit with them once again. He felt weary after traveling, and he encouraged them to prepare for the morrow.

President Jones encouraged the Saints to beware of intoxicating drinks in the places where they were lodging so they would not lose the Spirit and deprive themselves of the blessings of the Conference. Then President Spencer prayed.

Sunday morning the 24th.—President Jones made some preliminary remarks to bring the numerous congregation to order, requesting the Saints to make room for one another, and for those who were on the steps and on the road wishing to have a place to listen somehow. He requested those who did not understand English to be patient since it was in that language the brethren would speak.

President F. D. Richards wanted to know from a show of hands that the majority of the Saints understood English.

He spoke on the emigration, several present languages, and the future common language of the Saints. The advantages of learning the English language for the purpose of emigrating to Zion, &c., and the way to dig deep and lay a solid foundation for our salvation.

The meeting was closed with a prayer by Elder J. A. Young.

2:00 o'clock in the afternoon.—President Spencer prayed.

President Wheelock spoke about the English language, the emigration, and the sufferings that are before the Saints before they enjoy glory, and on the corrupt condition of Babylon.

President Richards in answer to the questions of the poor, said that more money that was collected for the P. E. Fund had been used to help out the poor, and that the Fund is not free from that debt yet, but that some will be helped from the money of the possessions, parts of which have been sold. Prayer.

Half past 6:00 in the evening. Elder M. Atwood prayed.

Elder N. V. Porter expressed gratitude for the privilege of visiting Wales. He encouraged the Saints to appreciate the teaching they had received, and testified that Joseph Smith was a Prophet and a martyr to God, and that Brigham Young was the lawful and worthy successor to him.

President Spencer rejoiced at seeing the growth and the improvement of what he had seen when he had visited Merthyr before, and he taught the way to be humble, bold and able, and he left his blessing on the Welsh Saints for their great kindness to him, encouraging them to beware of nationalistic feelings, and to strive to learn the English language.

President Jones wished for those learning English to take pleasure in doing so, and that no one would be burdened against his will. He translated some of the remarks of President Richards on "digging deep and laying a solid foundation," and he made his own observations on that. Since he is about to leave Wales, he wished for the Saints to sustain his successor as they had sustained him.

President F. D. Richards prayed.

Monday, at half past 10:00 in the morning, President Wheelock prayed.

President Jones called on the Conference Presidents present to report on their Conferences, and not to withhold anything that would be harmful to the cause.

President Richards wished for a report about Church members in the Conferences as well as non-members.

The Conferences were reported as all being in very good condition without exception. From which there was a considerable number emigrating, and signs of baptizing were widespread.

President Jones rejoiced as he looked back on the travels of Brother Daniels and himself, that there was never a contrary word or action, rather cooperation in love always.

Elder Israel Evans greatly commended the labor of President Jones, and he knew that he was emigrating under the blessing of God and the prayers of all the Saints for him.

Elder Benjamin Ashby told of his experience with Mormonism almost from his childhood. He felt to support the workers of righteousness everywhere, no matter how poor they might be, and to fight against the rebellious and treacherous spirit.

Elder J. A. Young expressed his great satisfaction as he listened to the Presidents reporting on their Conferences, and he spoke about personal salvation, and obedience to the Priesthood.

At 6:00 o'clock in the evening, a delightful *Concert* was held, in which all received great pleasure and beneficial teaching, through the recitations and songs, enchanting music from the choirs of Merthyr and Cwmbach, and a short but sweet lecture from President Richards on music, and his great praise for the high accomplishments of the Welsh in the arts.

Tuesday the 26th.—At 9:00 o'clock in the morning the Welsh Presidency held a Council with the outgoing and the incoming Conference Presidents, and a considerable amount of business was transacted successfully and unitedly.

At 11:00 o'clock, the Presidency of the British Isles, and the American Elders came in, and we continued with the Council.

President Jones taught earnestly and comprehensively on the importance of the calling and responsibility of the Presidents of the Conferences, and the details and the diligence required by the business of the Church. He counseled the President to make every effort to convince every Saint that had Nine Pounds to emigrate this year, and to get those who fall short of that, but who have sufficient to carry them to the States, to do so with haste. He announced also that half the number of those who give five pounds to the P. E. Fund will receive their passage to the Valley this year if they have been faithful Saints for over six years, and the other half will be given passage next year. [This is carefully explained on page 73 of this number.]

He was followed by President Richards, who expressed his complete satisfaction, and his certain knowledge of the approval, success, and smiles of God on the labor of President Jones in Wales during his two missions.

President Spencer added more details on this, reporting on the obvious improvement of the work and workers of God in Wales.

They said that President Jones would return to Zion happy

and successful, with the blessings of the God who sent him and prospered him on his head, and that the work he left behind would be a praiseworthy monument to his name, and that he would be called blessed by generations to come.

The Welsh First Presidency and Conference Presidents were blessed and set apart to their important areas of responsibility, and President F. D. Richards left his blessing with them, and this never-to-be-forgotten Council was brought to a close by prayer.

———

[We shall publish all the details we can of that which was done and said through the Conference in the following numbers of the Trumpet as soon as there is space.—Editor.]

———

FEELING OF A YOUNG SAINT.

I lost all my former friends,
    When I joined with the Saints;
Nevertheless, I have gained,
    And it is a wondrous honor to me.

If I have lost the smiles of my dear mother,
    And of my many relatives old and young;
I have received an even more valuable treasure
    That Jesus pure has promised.

In ignorance they wept,
    With a veil across their eyes;
But I was rejoicing,
    Having received strength from God by faith.

The things of the world concerned them,
    Namely the great and despicable mammon;
Of the treasures of heaven I sang,
    And the divine gift of grace.

They came to me, yes, twenty and three,
    And that on the same day,
Saying—"David, David, listen,
    People were clamoring after you!

"How could you join the Saints—
    The chief enemies of God?
To your father this news is hard to bear,
    It will be the death of him."

If this is a loss to him,
    Great gain it is to me;
And I shall testify before you,
    That you are the children of perdition.

I have already received the Spirit of God,
    A strong witness have I obtained,
And the same promise is given to you,
    From the King of all the Heavens!

Therefore, come dear friends,
    And give obedience now,
And then you shall have the Spirit of God,
    To uplift you and give you joy.

Unless you receive this there is no freedom,
    Just agony and pain;
I know now that truth stems from
    The man who was on the cross.

Therefore, I am all the more determined,
    To press forward,
And blessed be our God,
    For the favors of the Holy Ghost.

I shall leave Babylon before long,
    Across to Zion shall I go,
And there I shall worship my God
    With neither persecution, pain, nor fear.

Lately of Haverfordwest College.   DAVID JOHN.

CONTENTS.

	PG.
Sermon of President Young	65
Editorial,—The Emigration,—Distributors	73
Minutes of the Council and the General Conference	74
Feeling of a Young Saint	79

SWANSEA:
PRINTED AND PUBLISHED BY D. JONES.

ZION'S TRUMPET,

OR

Star of the Saints.

No. 6.]　　　MARCH 15, 1856.　　　[Vol. IX.

SUMMARY OF THE ADDRESS OF PRESIDENT FRANKLIN D. RICHARDS.

In a Council with the majority of the outgoing and incoming Presidents of the Welsh Conferences, which was held in the "White Lion" Inn, Merthyr Tydfil, Tuesday, February 26, 1856.

[Transcribed and translated by William Lewis, Swansea.]

I FEEL particular joy this morning, as I meet with my brethren in these circumstances in which we have come together. I feel myself among servants of God, that His Spirit is in our midst, and that He himself is aware of our deeds, and of the thoughts of our hearts. I feel thankful for the delightful time we have had together during our past conference.

I wish for the Spirit of revelation, the witness of Jesus to be with us this morning while we do a few things in his name, which we may make useful to the Lord, and beneficial to our fellow creatures.

We have not previously had such enjoyment here for quite a while. We have come here to you at the request of brother Jones to assist him to leave his departing blessing with you, and quite likely our own blessing as well; for we feel we are going to leave you in Babylon, among temptations and evil and harmful influences, which you have equally with your fellowmen to withstand; but

[PRICE 1c.

you have greater power than they to oppose them. You are the light of the world, and you are to be the eyes for the blind, and to see for them. You are to minister life to your fellow creatures who are in the dark, and who sin in their ignorance, and you are to inform them of that.

We strive towards your having invincible power, and being able to become unassailable castles, so that you may defend those over whom you have oversight; for we know that because of this the devil will aim his darts at you; that because you have more responsibility, you shall have greater opposition than those of our brethren who go down in the morning to the pits and other such places to labor and toil hard,—to work more like iron machines than human beings, sensitive and feeling, and who return home in the evening exhausted and desirous of rest, to the point of failing to exercise enough of their mental powers to learn the ways of the Lord. Therefore, you are to teach them, and you are to stand before them to defend them, and you are to be responsible for them. The devil knows that well, and it is at you that he aims; he is well aware of the increasing influence and power of Zion, and he will increase his corresponding opposition.

Brother Jones has been a tower of strength, defense and refuge for you; you have experienced that, and have always looked to him as such. You can feel the same way toward Brother Daniels his successor, and it is your duty to feel similarly toward all your brethren who are higher than you in the Lord. But, brethren, we wish for you to feel that you yourselves are the same to others,—that you have the care of Conferences, and that you must look out for the well being and success of your Saints, and nourish them with the bread of life. We want you to take the spirit and power of the influence that is felt here to them, and cause the gentiles to feel it to the ends of Wales,—from Cardiff to Holyhead.

Have the Conference Presidents chosen Counselors? [President Jones,—No, except for a few of them.] Neither are they essential in small Conferences, but only in large Conferences where the work of presiding is too much for the President to complete always on his own.

It is not necessary or beneficial to have them except where there are many tasks, and where one man cannot fulfill them. It has become a practice and a ritual here for every President to have counselors, when there is no need for them, except to go to some places to fulfill some of his purposes when he could not get time to go himself. For this task I have chosen Brothers Spencer and Wheelock. They go to places and do my will exactly as I would have done it myself. In this manner we wish for Brothers Ashby and Evans to take the Spirit of President Daniels their president with them, and let them consider it as if it were President Daniels and not they themselves,—to do that which they know he himself would do, and if they do this, they will win the favor of the people, and the favor of brother Daniels also, and the smiles of God will be upon them, but if they do otherwise, the consequences will be to the contrary.

Where a President has Counselors who do not know their place and he wants to do something, they will not move an inch until he convinces them that he is right, and they come to agree, and become willing to cooperate with him. It is like this in Branches and Conferences where there are Counselors who think they should be shoulder to shoulder with the President, interfering with things that in fact do not pertain to them in the least.

Now, Brethren, I want you to be desirous to know the mind and will of your President in Wales, and to go do it, no matter how you receive it, whether through Brother Israel Evans or B. Ashby, or even through a dream, just if you are certain that it is the will of your President. If I can understand through only a dream of the approval or disapproval of President Brigham of anything I do, or of his will to do anything, I am happy to come to understand so soon, so that I can make the most of the time to improve. It is not up to you to even doubt that which your superiors may say, or to doubt them in the least degree; rather it is your duty always to do that which you think will please your President.

In a vision I had some time ago I saw myself over in the Valley in a small room with Brother Brigham and his wife. He expressed his approval of some measures I had taken here, telling me to follow them. I continued to feel his approval until I was confirmed in it completely by a letter from Brother Brigham, which you all may have read, approving the approach I took, and supporting me to continue on and do as much as I could. Had it happened otherwise, I would go immediately and sustain higher authority in my heart, and I would seek twelve of his chief counselors if I could get them there, to determine what was wrong, for *there* would be the wrong, and not anywhere higher. This is how you also should feel, brethren, and you should do the same thing when you are praised or when you are chastised by your President, and live in such a way as to seek to do according to his mind and will, until by and by you yourselves are filled with revelations, and there will be hardly any need to ask you before you have anticipated it through the Spirit.

Beware of arguing and quarreling with your superiors, for by so doing the same spirit will fill the Branches of your Conferences, and you will have the difficult task of convincing each one of them before you can get them to obey you—they in their turn will argue and quarrel with you, and you will have to cast out of their midst the rebellious and contentious spirit before any good can come of them.

Do not be too hasty to chastise or to discipline the transgressor who has not been in the Church very long, or those who have not had many opportunities to know themselves; but for those who should know better you can give them the occasional clout or rap on the knuckles. When dealing with the former, remember in what condition you yourself were in when you came into the church,—you were as if you had been dyed in the wool in Babylon, in traditions, superstitions and foolish notions. While you consider that God, and God alone, has set you in your places, wash their eyes with 'milk and water,' and anoint them with 'eye ointment.' When you chastise them, make them feel that it is all for their benefit, that it is their best good that you seek, and they will love you for that. I understand that some have been cut off in Wales; when they came up and spoke in haste and without consideration in their anxious moment they were not spared, and they were not extended mercy in their unhappy hour, but they were cut away by those who were higher than they since they had the power to do that. The time is coming when there will be a careful examination of how we have used that power, and we are at present taking upon ourselves the responsibility for as much of it as we have. Therefore, let us be discreet and watchful, and let us always act according to wisdom as we behave toward those who are beneath us in their knowledge, their understanding, and their advantages.

As you behave with exactness in these things,—keeping yourselves in contact with those who are in authority over you, obeying their counsels, and seeking to understand what they suggest, and what they wish to set in action, and using properly the power you possess, you will do what we wish, toward getting all in order from one end to the other until the effect is felt throughout all creation. As brother Martin says, let the wires of the electrical informer be whole and faultless from one end to the other, and electricity will fly to the ends of the earth; thus goes the word of Brother Brigham.

You see then that the way for you to act toward bringing this about is by receiving from your superiors, and transferring it down. Now you know that a man cannot teach another the lesson he has received without first being able to understand it and learn it himself. You also know that it is a fact that the Lord has and continues to reveal the principles of the Gospel in the English language. Now, suppose that none of you in Wales could understand English except for brother Jones; you can imagine also that the Church in Wales would be small and weak, and its means sparse, and bro. Jones could not publish all he wanted through the *Trumpet*; the principles that you should receive would go like an overflowing stream that could not go through the same outlet to the wheel overflowing its channel and running in vain and uselessly; but if you were to open more outlets, the whole stream would flow down through them full force to the wheel, which would turn with greater speed and power and complete that much more work. Suppose next that you get every President over every Conference and Branch in Wales to learn and understand English as well as Bro. Jones, then they would read the *Star*, the *Journal of Discourses*, &c., as well as the TRUMPET; you would have that many more outlets from the same crystalline stream of the pure teaching from above, which would have the corresponding growing effect on the work of God in Wales.

May those who have and will come into the Church in Wales come to understand from you that as long as they do not learn English, there will be a curtain between them and the Saints in Zion, and the long-term benefits will be that they will not overburden you, rather they will do much for themselves by reading the books.

On one occasion lately, when I inquired as to the condition of Brother Jones, I learned that he was burdened to the ground with multiple tasks, worrisome cares with all their complications,—mounds of business of the emigration, publishing, presiding, and other church matters pressing on him until he fell sick, and I almost asked if you intended for him to put his bones down in Babylon.

When you go home to your various Conferences, take these teachings (about language) with you as a treasure for, and not an obligation on, the Saints, and do not say "they *must* learn English or be cut out of the church," or anything like that; rather appreciate and use it yourselves, and they will enjoy its appealing pleasures naturally, and they will follow your example, and within another year you will see that the power of God will have increased greatly in Wales.

Seek to have brethren working with you who are desirous of learning English. When you have mastered the language, you will be as much better off by understanding the two languages as is a man better off having two arms instead of one,—you can preach to the world in Welsh, and after they come into the Church you can help them to learn English.

Since the English language has been chosen as the means of communicating in Zion, and by having the Saints in every nation learn it, every kindred, tongue, people and nation in Zion will be able to understand, speak, and commune with one another. Would that not be wonderful, Brethren? [Yes, yes, was the answer.] Had the Lord chosen the Welsh language for that purpose, all the Saints would have to learn it, and I would learn it with the greatest pleasure.

We are going to place hands on the brethren (the Welsh Presidency) to bless them, to prepare them, and set them apart to their important stewardships,—to present to them a blessing that will be felt throughout the entire Church in Wales.

[He closed by encouraging the Presidents to be tender and kind with the weak Saints especially. To be eyes for them, and perceive for them further along than they can see. To show them how they can be frugal and save their shillings and pounds, and to make arrangements this way or that way for emigrating. To move as many of them as they can from their Conferences; in short, to consider their best good in all things, and be like parents to them, and to edify them in the most holy faith.]

President D. Spencer,—I consider your privilege to be great for getting the teachings you have received, that they will be a great blessing to you, that they tend to make you strong and powerful men, and enable you to minister life and salvation to those under your stewardship. I know that they are indispensable for your success, and that your labor would be vain without them.

[He supposed them to feel weak as he himself had felt when he first began his work in the ministry; nevertheless, they were the people God requested, and not the wise men of the world and the wealthy. Since it is most especially the poor whom God has chosen to be his people, he has sought men from among them who are well acquainted with their condition to minister to them, and among other things to encourage the Presidents, he said:—] You are aware of their afflictions, and have been in the coal pits, and different places of the kind, and share these experiences with them. If some of the ministers and the sectarian wise men had to go where you have been to save the people, they would be too disheartened; they would take fright and run away. Although you may feel weak, you are the men whom God requests, and He does not see any other group of men the way he sees you. When you go to the people, you can feel like giants,—you know their needs, and what is appropriate for them. You can lower yourselves to them, win their love, and raise them gradually to a standard of truth and righteousness. They will not fear you, rather they will reveal the feelings of their hearts to you.

Remember and feel the strength and power of the words of

Brother Franklin, and you will empathize with the needs of the people, and you will go out in the power of God to minister to them. I will tell you that each one of you is better than ten thousand sectarian priests and ministers put together, with all their wealth, their influence and their popularity. The Lord knows that, and that is why he has called you to the position you are in, and I want you to feel that and act accordingly, and may the Lord be with you is my wish, in the name of Jesus Christ, Amen.

[After the Welsh Presidency and Conference Presidents were blessed, &c., President Richards said that his heart went out to the faithful brethren of the North who were absent, because their distance was great and their means were sparse, perhaps.] But, (he said) the spirit, influence and blessings of this Council will go to them, and they will cause North Wales to feel it. The spirit will go to every Conference to all the Priesthood in Wales, who live righteously, and Wales will feel it again from one end to the other.

ZION'S TRUMPET,
OR
Star of the Saints.

SATURDAY, MARCH 15, 1856.

The Notice to Emigrants,—Which is found elsewhere in this number, merits the careful attention of the Saints—let the Presidents pore over it in detail, and take advantage of every opportunity to put it into action insofar as possible. Search out who has five pounds, and put that person in touch with another who has the same amount, and choose which of the two will get to emigrate this time and send his name together with the name of the other contributor to us, with careful accuracy, so that the other may emigrate next year.

Wherever there is a family who can contribute £5, £10, or more to the P. E. Fund, and does not know of another who can do the same, we know of several, who will allow us to select for them, for they can be sure through that of being able to send next time as many of the family as send £5 to us. By doing this, the amount which will take the rest of the family next time, all together probably, can be earned; at least they will save half the cost of emigrating by this means.

The reason why £10 is required to emigrate in this way while others are transported by the handcarts for £9 is because it is not known for certain how much money the journey will cost in this untested venture, and it is not possible to know until the participants reach the end of their journey, at which time it is expected that the emigrants will agree to pay the remaining cost of course. Another reason is because it will be necessary for the P. E. Fund Company to borrow the money to transport the other half of the emigrants probably the coming year, and more than likely they will need to pay interest on their loan; this shows the logic of making the aforementioned difference in their prices.

We are sorry too that more of the possessions donated to the P. E. Fund by the President and others have not been sold, so that more of the faithful Saints in the church for six or more years could be selected to emigrate this year; but our concern and that of others does not improve the matter one whit; and we did our best to sell more of them. We have sent to the Presidents the names of those selected for the great privilege of emigrating this year using the funds generated by the sale of the possessions, but if some fail to prepare to go according to the call, we beg for them to let us know by return *Post*, so that another may receive the opportunity promptly.

Let everyone strive to save as much as he can and we expect what remains after paying their debts and for going to Liverpool to be given to help pay for their transport; for it would be dishonest, as we said earlier when asking for the names of the deserving, to ask for the help of the P. E. Fund while pocketing their own money. May we be permitted once again to warn this class of emigrants against overburdening themselves with goods, rather, selling all they can do without on the journey lest they have to leave them before starting across the *Plains* or leave themselves with them.

Now, Presidential Brethren! is the time for you to show yourselves to be skillful and charitable by doing this speedily and precisely, for there is no time to be lost; otherwise, it will be too late for anyone to prepare to emigrate if they have the means.

We trust the green-eyed monster jealousy will not blast its poison at any of the Saints who cannot go themselves this time, along with their neighbors whom they consider little better than themselves, but rather that they rejoice that the departure of the others augurs well for the approach of their own deliverance if they remain faithful.

———

EMIGRATION TIME!—We intend everyone to be ready to leave their homes at the end of this month at the latest. And although the ship has not yet been chartered, we believe it will be possible to find one which leaves Liverpool in the first week of April. We have delayed the departure time until this last hour, in case anyone should be left behind who could go then.

It is understood from the previous TRUMPET that all the emigrants from Wales, whether by wagon, handcarts, or to the States, will be allowed to go together at the appointed time, if a large enough ship for all can be found.

———

DEPARTURE OF EMIGRANTS FROM WALES. On the 17 of February about 120 Saints sailed from Liverpool on board the ship "Caravan" for New York, all in good health and spirits; we had the pleasure of leading them on board the ship all with no mishaps in a spirit too desirous for the distant west to think of turning to look back as did Lot's wife longing for her home. They had fair winds for many days. A short and lovely voyage to them.

———

TO THE PRESIDENTS AND DISTRIBUTORS—We anxiously anticipate that it will be considered proper that our time in serving you through the TRUMPET is nearly over, that our business between you and the Offices ends with the next number, and that that consideration will prompt you, without our saying anything further to pay that which is owed by your Conferences to us personally, i.e., the money that we loaned to pay their debts for them, and that you will see to it that all the Distributors will send all they can for the books between now and then; so that through that we will be enabled to settle with others, and to finish our ministry in that, and to complete our book accounts somewhat similar to the order in which we wish to leave them to others. We rely on your good nature to do this favor to your old fellow-soldier, Brethren. There has already been considerable negligence this year in paying the book money and it has got rather too late to correct this for our benefit, apart from what can be done between now and the 28th of this month. So let's see who is first to buy that much time.

THE EMIGRATION.

36, *Islington, Liverpool, March* 5, 1856.

To the Latter-day Saints in England, Scotland, and Ireland, who have been members of the Church for ten years and above; and to those in Wales who have been members for six years and above.

BECAUSE so few of the possessions donated by President B. Young and others to the P. E. F. were sold, and because countless persons were sent for from this country by the Perpetual Emigration Fund Company, the means that are in our hands available for those of the aforementioned Saints who have attained worthy membership during the previously mentioned time are cut back. Consequently, the ones selected will be from among the most worthy and the most needy.

From among those addressed in this notice there will probably be many who wish to gather to Zion this year, but who cannot garner more than £5 each for themselves and for their children who are one year old and above, and £2 10s for their infants who are under one year old, which is insufficient for their passage further than the States unless they receive assistance other than what they have at present.

To assist such to achieve their objective we propose that they donate their means to the Perpetual Emigration Fund; and we offer on behalf of the P. E. Fund to provide passage for *half* their number to Utah this season, and we promise to provide passage for the *other half* next year, leaving it up to the Pastors and the Presidents, in consultation with the donors, to determine who among the latter will form the first half.

If those of the Saints to whom we refer in this notice prefer not to emigrate any further than the States, they have our approval and blessing to do so, the same as if they were to choose the plan suggested here. Our objective is to extend all the assistance we can to this group of Saints in their efforts to emigrate toward Utah. Nevertheless, perhaps some have relations or friends in the States whom they wish to join, and thus be of assistance to each other in the great work; therefore, let all decide in their own minds, and they shall take the way for which they exercise the greatest faith, and for which they enjoy the greatest measure of the Holy Spirit.

To Pastors and Presidents.—Send to us the names and other details of those Saints who are adopting the plan of sharing their money so a record can be made here separate from all the others.— Send to us the names and addresses of all the contributors, together with the money and the names, ages, occupations, and addresses of those who are chosen to go out this year without delay.

Read this Notice exactly in the meetings of the Saints, and make its objective known to all to whom it pertains.

F. D. Richards,
Daniel Spencer,
C. H. Wheelock.

The Presidency of the Church of Jesus Christ of Latter-day Saints in the British Isles and the surrounding countries.

SERMON

By President B. Young, which was delivered in the October Conference in Great Salt Lake City, 1855.

[Continued from page 57.]

Some of you have been brought before the High Council, charged with this fault and with that, and you say it is too much for you, that you cannot bear it. But you have got to bear it, and if you will not, make up your minds to go to hell at once and have done with it. If you wish to be Saints you must have your evils taken away and your iniquities exposed; this must be done if you remain in the kingdom of God. If you do wrong, and it is made manifest before the High Council, don't grunt about it, nor whine about your loving, precious character, but consider that you have none; that is the best way to get along with it. Myriads have scandalized me since I have been in this Church, and I have been asked, "Brother Brigham, are you going to bear this? Do you not know that such and such persons are scandalizing your character?" Said I, "I do not know that I have any character, I have never stopped to inquire whether I have one or not." It is for me to pursue a course that will build up the kingdom of God on the earth, and you may take my character to be what you please, I care not what you do with it, so you but keep your hands off from me.

As for the inhabitants of the earth, who know anything about Mormonism, having power to utter worse epithets against us than they do, they have to get more knowledge in order to do it; and as for those enemies who have been in our midst, feeling any worse than they do, they have first to know more; they are as full of bad feeling now as they can hold without bursting. What do I care for the wrath of man? No more than I do for the chickens that run in my dooryard. I am here to teach the ways of the Lord, and lead men to life everlasting, but if they have not a mind to go there, I wish them to keep out of my path.

I want the Elders of Israel to understand that if they are exposed in their stealing, lying, deceiving, wickedness, and covetousness, which is idolatry, they must not fly in a passion about it, for we calculate to expose you, from time to time, as we please, when we can get time to notice you.

During this Conference, I do not want to think where the Mormons have been, and how they have been treated, but I want to think of matters that will make my heart light, like the roe on the mountains,—to reflect that the Lord Almighty has given me my birth on the land where He raised up a prophet, and revealed the everlasting gospel through him, and that I had the privilege of hearing it—of knowing and understanding it—of embracing and enjoying it. I feel like shouting Hallelujah all the time when I think that I ever knew Joseph Smith, the Prophet whom the Lord raised up and ordained, and to whom He gave keys and power to build up the kingdom of God on earth and sustain it. These keys are committed to this people, and we have power to continue the work that Joseph commenced, until everything is prepared for the coming of the Son of Man. This is the business of the Latter-day Saints, and it is all the business we have on hand. When we come to worldly affairs, as they are called, they can be done in stormy weather, if we attend to the kingdom of God in fair weather.

SPEECH OF PRESIDENT DANIEL DANIELS TO THE CONFERENCE PRESIDENTS.

Swansea, March 10, 1856.

DEAR BRETHREN,—The frequent requirements of the business call for your most careful attention, for through fulfilling your duties you receive strength and power to become honorable in the important stewardships you have been appointed to.

I feel to remind you of some of the main things you have to fulfill. You no doubt remember the moving counsels you received in the last Merthyr Council, to diligently and tirelessly seek after all the Saints who can emigrate from your Conferences with a true effort this season. We wish for you to take the strength of life within you and seek to understand the condition of the Saints under your care, until you know how many have £9 each, to go with the handcarts.

May your teaching be like fire on the skin of those who are apathetic, motivating them to do their duties, until you get every officer and member to listen to the voice of, and to fulfill the counsels of the TRUMPET,—to sell their old statues, their stuff, and every unnecessary thing, and to make every lawful effort toward getting £5 each to donate to the P. E. Fund, either to be on their way this year or to get the privilege of making the journey next year, and to send the money here without delay. The chief objective of this address is to bring this about.

I trust that there are many in your Conferences who are able to do as noted above, but remember that there is no time to be lost in this matter.

We expect to receive that which was placed upon you at the Merthyr Council; some Conferences have already sent it.

Also, do not leave your book Distributors in peace, until you see the Branches free of debt, so that you and they will be ready when the call comes. The money for the books is not coming in as it should; there is some impediment somewhere,—search it out, and clear it away quickly, until you see the distributors beginning as if anew.

Brethren, it is required of us to be diligent not only with one responsibility, but with all of them. A work of very great consequences has been put upon us to fulfill. I am confident that you are in your fields of labor from morning till evening looking after the flock under your care, to ensure that the harvest will be carried forward in an organized fashion. See to it that the Saints fulfill all their family and church duties, and that they are feeding on the bread of life from above, so they will be working mightily while it is still daylight, so that we can finish the harvest and have the wheat into the barn in time. Think about the work of God night and day, and teach it to the people, reminding them frequently that the Temple is not finished, and that it is their duty and privilege to be able to contribute to it. Also, that God has given his law in such an orderly way to the Prophet Brigham with regard to the P. E. Fund, through which a multitude sings happily at the end of their journey; all that is needed is faithfulness, so that the last one will be brought home soon; and that is the true wish of your fellow servant,

D. Daniels.

THE MADDOCIANS.

Despite how much others may doubt the story that Madawg ab Owen Gwynedd discovered America before Columbus, we have gathered satisfactory proofs of the fact in our searches across the continent for the "Welsh Indians" during the past twenty years, and since we are determined to re-initiate at the end of this month a search with no turning back, if they are living on land, we beseech those who may have a more correct or more extensive story than that given by "Powell" or the "Triads" about the departure of Madawg from this country or by his descendants on the other side of the sea, to assist us in our venture; not their money, we do not ask that, rather for accounts which will help us to accomplish the objective which has cost us several hundred already.

If the editors of the "Times," the "Hero," the "Welshman," or any other man who holds dear his pedigree, see fit to put this request before the eyes of their readers, perhaps they will attract some to bring out their treasures from their old libraries to the light of the sun, and they will have the pleasure from that before long to read that the debate has been broken, the subject proven that the Madocians have come to the light also. Please choose whatever means you judge best to notify us; otherwise, direct responses to the Editor of "Zion's Trumpet" Swansea.

WESTERN STANDARD is the name of the weekly publication that George Q. Cannon intends to publish in San Francisco, California, for about £1 per year, and which can be obtained through the Office of the *Millennial Star*, 36, Islington, Liverpool. The skill and wisdom of the Editor is too well known for there to be any need to say anything about the interest of the publication, but only that it is under the auspices of the First Presidency in Zion, and that its advantages are such as to make it a *source* of news of this distant and golden country. All the best to this venture, and may its Editor be filled with wisdom from on high, and may his "WESTERN STANDARD" be spread across the world.

RECEIPTS FOR BOOKS FROM FEB. 9 TO MARCH 13.—Thomas D. Evans, 19s 5½c; John Richards, 3s 9c; John Gibbs, 12s 6c; Wm. Lewis, £6 5s; Thomas Stephens, £5 18s.

CONTENTS.

PG.

Address of President F. D. Richards 81
Editorial.—The Notice to Emigrants.—Time of the Emigration.—Departure of the Emigrants from Wales.—To Presidents and Distributors 88
The Emigration.. 91
Sermon of President Young.. 92
Speech of President Daniels to Conference Presidents.................................... 94
The Maddocians 95

SWANSEA:

PRINTED AND PUBLISHED BY D. JONES.

ZION'S TRUMPET,

OR

Star of the Saints.

No. 7.] MARCH 29, 1856. [Vol. IX.

SUMMARY OF THE TEACHING OF PRESIDENT DAN JONES, IN THE MERTHYR TYDFIL GENERAL COUNCIL, FEBRUARY 23, 1856.

The Council was called to order, and he said,—I feel great disappointment because our Presidency, [over the British Isles] and our other brethren [the American Elders] have not come punctually to our Council here according to our expectations, and I believe you feel the same way.

[After Elder Israel Evans had prayed, he said]—

Since our Presidency has not come, I think it best for us [the Presidency of the Church in Wales] to spend the time in instructing and teaching the various Presidents who are present.

Dear brethren,—your presence here today, and the cost and the trouble many of you have gone to to be here from afar, proves your love for this divine work, which I love so much that I can do no less than love those who love it to the extent they do. You have come here to receive a broader understanding of it, on which understanding its success depends in your Conferences.

I wish for the outgoing and the incoming Presidents of the Conferences instead of sitting mixed with the congregation to come to the front, so that when I speak I can see the whites of their eyes, I can gaze into their faces, and more than that, if I could, to look beneath their chins and read the thoughts and intents of their hearts.

7 [Price 1*c*.

We are servants of God, and sharers of the Holy Priesthood after the order of the Son of God,—of that Presidency which is to govern everyone and everything on and beneath the earth. It is on this power that we depend for every needful direction and understanding, and we rely on it for power to act. When we properly understand this, our own inability and deficiency of wisdom, we see the necessity of that and the obligations we have to be humble before the all-wealthy God who shares it. Past experience has shown us that the pleasure of our feelings and fantasies is not "Mormonism." Narrow is its way and strait is its gate. The more narrow the way we walk, the more strict are the commandments we receive, and the more difficult it is to keep them. The keeping of them depends on the direction and the understanding we receive, according to which we act; consequently, we see the importance of getting an understanding of the proper direction for ourselves, since the destiny of our souls depends on the following of it. The further we walk along this road the more it narrows, although our privileges and blessings increase,—or in other words, the greater our learning and our experience, the greater our understanding, and the greater our understanding, then, the greater our responsibility. It is not just our personal responsibility, but the responsibility of others that is on us also. We are representatives who have come here so that those whom we represent may receive instructions concerning the proper understanding of that on which their life or death depends. So that you may properly understand for them, and be mouths and ears to them, may you be an open heart, may the spirit of truth enlighten you in that, so that you may understand and receive every word that comes out of the mouth of God to you, and to the Saints under your care also.

It is true that the scriptures have been and continue to be good in guiding men toward receiving a fulfillment of the same promises which others received earlier. It is not on every word that has come out of the mouth of God but "every word that *comes*" that we live; it makes no difference how it comes, whether through writings, the ministering of angels, or through the living Priesthood. If we were to take the Bible as the only standard today, we would be obliged to search its pages in vain for direct instructions to correspond to our circumstances, but all we have to do is claim our privilege, and look to heaven for a sufficient measure of that Spirit which was available in the olden days to make the Bible.

The most particular part of our religion which we have to deal with today is the business,—the operational part, containing its affairs and all its negotiations. The religious sectarians differentiate between what they call religion and the temporal, the operational, or business. They consider that only the spiritual activities are those of a religious nature, and that only the spiritual part is religion, and that all else is material. I cannot perceive one whit of difference between the one thing and the other which we do for God—that it is not all spiritual. It is a fact that we do not carry out any outward action except through the inner motivation of the Spirit, and consequently, it cannot be any less than the spirituality which is in ourselves; and since the godly Spirit from above requires such duties of us, we believe there is sufficient spirituality in them for us to call them religion.

God says that his kingdom is a kingdom of order, and He was so good as to reveal it to his servant Joseph Smith. After receiving the organization, instead of trying to improve it by our own whim, our responsibility is to conform to it,—fit ourselves to the organization, and not the organization to us; conforming to it, and not going against it, will make us acceptable in the sight of its Great Giver. It is not the greatness of deeds of some kind according to our feelings, rather obedience to the call of God, no matter how little He asks, that constitutes religion before Him.

The business of this Church is to increase on the earth, especially in Zion. In Zion there are various stewardships, and every man fills his own stewardship by "Minding his own business" and not the business of anyone else. Before a man can "mind his own business," he is required to find out what his business is, and to know this depends on the one who is higher than he. Thus there is a wheel within a wheel for this perfecting machine to turn together in orderliness.

The European mission is a large wheel, and a large business pertains to it. Within it our little wheel turns in Wales, and within that wheel several others even smaller. The connection among all these wheels is such that when they turn faster or more slowly than they should, or when any confusion occurs, it affects all the others. We see the necessity then for all of us to understand one another, and govern ourselves by the wheel next to us, and for that one to govern itself by the next, and so on to the Great Governing Main Wheel which works the entire machine until there is harmony in all our turnings.

Brethren, those who preside over the Conferences, your duty is to get every little wheel throughout your Conferences, your own inner wheel first, to carry out the instructions that come out through the TRUMPET, down from President Richards, and all the other instructions, which constitute your Bible. Brethren, make them your textbook; you will be unable to fulfill your duties in any other way. It makes no difference what is required; when a sum of money is required from a Conference, the duty of that President is to seek to obtain it. "Yes, but you ask too much from us," says the President. Wait a minute then, for that is proof that either the one who gave the requirement is an unjust and oppressive man, or that the one who complains is not worthy of his office, that he tells a lie and that there is danger that he will teach others to be the same way. Complaining because of poverty, and looking for excuses to escape from the request is not the way for a President to win God's approval or that of his servants, rather his duty is to apply the same ability and effort he would have used for complaining to search out what advantages he may obtain in order to accomplish the task, and not search for excuses not to do it; while many have gone to the trouble to excuse and absolve themselves, they could have completed the task with the same or even less trouble. We are not to expect that everything will come easily. We are to make an effort and trouble yourself, and try to do it. After the sacrifice comes the blessing, and the God who requires it will open the way and prepare the offering. The servant is not better than his master. Even our Lord Jesus Christ got to suffer in the garden of Gethsemane; he suffered hunger, and he was tempted in the desert, but after that angels ministered to him. Through temptations He was perfected, and we ourselves will be perfected before we receive our glorification with him, after fulfilling our part of the same work. To do otherwise, namely, excusing ourselves, &c., is to listen to and to obey the devil, and the consequences will correspond.

Although I am sufficiently humble and grateful to listen to any good suggestion from a brother, yet, after the joint council is held, and the council has considered the matter, and has decided on the measures pertaining to it, the way and the means to complete them, from that moment on, the responsibility of each one is to set aside his own views and use all his wisdom and his influence to complete the task to the letter, according to the spirit and the decision of the Council where they were chosen; and no matter what the consequence may be, it will not depend on him. There will be an opportunity in this Council for each one to express his views or give any suggestion, but after we decide what course to take, if anyone goes out of the Council and utters an opposing word after that, we would consider him an opponent and a *traitor*, which would cause contention in the army of Jesus.

While some Presidents have had success in getting their Conferences to do well, others have complained excessively about their inability, but I believe that their problem is the unfaithfulness I noted earlier. What reason can he give for his idleness while his brethren are working? Do you think that some of the Russian soldiers could be permitted not to fight while the others are fighting? Could they pull back from the battle? No, I really don't think so; rather they would be punished as traitors. How much more so for the traitors in the kingdom of God then? Only the greatest ignorance would give to such a man the least excuse for failing to accomplish that which he had covenanted with God that he would fulfill.

It is not our own feelings that are to guide us, but the directions that come down from heaven together with the directions of the Holy Ghost. The Presidents must ponder seriously then, and put their senses to work in order to understand their duties, and see the necessity of that which is required; not to accomplish their duty because I ask them, or lest they be disobedient; I would not thank such in the least. The duty of a President is to see and understand the privilege of doing his duty, after understanding it thoroughly through the light of the Holy Ghost, an abundance of which he ought to possess, in order to foresee the beneficial consequences of doing so.

We were obliged frequently to request the same thing over and over again through the TRUMPET, and after that perhaps we would get all the details, and even some unnecessary details from some, but there would be one and just *one* thing lacking, and that would be the main thing I had requested perhaps, and the most important of all! "But who would have thought it!" they would say then. Brethren! we must *think*, it is reprehensible for us to fail to think about our duties. Our offices require our thoughts to be fruitful, and if they are not sufficiently so, we must cultivate them; that is the only way they will be fruitful.

I understand that some Branch Presidents are here also. It is the practice of many of you, in your great desire to fulfill a request of the President of your Conference, when you cannot get others sufficiently desirous of cooperating with you, to try to do it yourselves. It is to bless and not to curse your Saints that you preside over them, and that will depend on your effective leadership over them. The obedience of his faithful is the crowning achievement of leadership ability. A man who succeeds in winning others over to have the same vision as he and to cooperate with him is the worthy President, and the one who is most certain to win the battle. Would it not be foolishness for a General to lead his army into battle and say to his soldiers, Sit down here and I shall face the enemy myself. It would be no less foolish for a Branch President to try to do more than his own ability and let his Saints sit idly by.

Although it is the day of the "small things," and although it is the "small things" we as children accomplish, their importance to us is not any the smaller. They are the A B C to guide us to spell, and then to read. A thorough and faithful accomplishment of them, despite how small they may be, is the only way for us to receive greater things, and a higher responsibility, until from stewardship to stewardship we climb up as coequal with our elder Brother over the governments and kingdoms, and be "like him."

Some in particular among the "small things" are the various collections, especially for Conference Presidents, to oversee. They should not go to the Council just to talk about them; and when occasionally one is asked, What is the reason that so little has come from your Conference to the Fund, the Temple, or to something else? "Oh, I don't know! I have been mentioning them in the Council." Do not be satisfied with that, but go directly to determine what is the obstacle, and where you do not have hardworking men—those who practice their religion, but are instead a stumbling block in the road, turn them aside; examine them "to the hilt," and insist on removing the obstacle.

There ought to be a *daybook* and *ledger* in every Conference and Branch to contain all the details,—books of the Conference to contain contributions for the names of the branches, and books of the branch to contain the names and amounts of the contributors. If it were done in this manner, every Conference President could know where the deficiency is; it is his privilege to examine the books and it is his duty to search out and know how much each one in his conference is doing, and under what circumstances, so that he may distinguish between the faithful and the unfaithful in this or in any other duty, and that he may understand where to praise, counsel or chastise. From now on it will not be a sufficient excuse for anyone to say, "I said," &c. Similar precision is necessary when you look after the book distributor, and in places where this has been lacking, let it be reformed from now on, redouble the diligence to recoup the loss. Let the new Presidents look at that from the beginning of this first quarter, so it will not be over before they can know how things are, and the Saints have become numb from lack of care. Do not permit the distributor to give books out on credit, but on his own responsibility, lest he give an opportunity for some people through their dishonesty to refrain from paying, to lose the Spirit and to leave the Church because of it; but where that has been unavoidable, collect the deficiencies in the Branch where they occurred, and if that happens, do so in the quarter it occurs. While the President puts the Saints of his Conference to work, be careful not to throw the whole burden on their shoulders at once; this is not how they will do the most. You know that the best way to drive a steam vehicle is by feeding it a little coal at a time, as it takes it. Feed your Saints the same way at every opportunity you may have, keeping their hands constantly full, but not overburdened, neither too empty. A Conference without these things will be as useless as a harp with loose strings. Consider that your Conferences are like a harp in the hand of each one of you. If you do not tighten the strings sufficiently, you will not get them to sound musical; if you do not tighten each string according to its size and its situation, there will be no harmony, and if you do not tighten them to the point they break, they will delight with their music, and their sound will be a pleasure to hear in Conferences like this one. It is true that there is some unavoidable trouble and challenge in trying to keep them in tune,—every harpist has trouble and distress when it is hard for him to control the strings of his harp, but after he does so correctly there is hardly an end to his harp playing and his joy. Insist on keeping the strings of your small harps in such order that they will sound lovely and melodious,—your Conferences in order and full of work, so that you can go to your beds at night with your conscience clear, rejoicing in the approbation of God for your labor which will show in the success that will follow it.

Keep the debt for books down by not allowing it to increase,—let the string be in tune.

Judging from the present threatening signs I see in the east and in the west, the clouds laden with vengeance and judgment are, as it were, about to burst and pour out their contents, and perhaps that will happen earlier than we may think. Now, while it is fair weather is the time for you to work—to spread from your old dusty chests the books that are getting moldy and piling on top of each other,—those which contain spiritual nourishment for the soul, for want of which the people are starving. Take them to them so that which they do not expect will not come upon them, rather you will have warned them in every way you can devise, and you will have freed yourselves from them. It makes no difference to you what they do with the books, as they are to answer for that; your duty is to see that they receive them.

Perhaps some think that because they have worked quite well for a spell that they have an ample excuse for resting and not doing anything else until some special call may come some time later. Beware of this, Brethren. Whenever you see men believing thus, things are beginning to go quite badly. Remember the metaphor of the steam vehicle. May the Presidents be thorough and diligent in this,—to see that the business in all parts of his Conference may go forward in a constant and steady manner. They understand that walking to visit the homes of the Saints just to talk with them and enjoy themselves with them is not all they have to do to keep things in order. I cannot have even one day in which my mind is not full of the various important plans of the activities and concerns of my office. I see so many things that need doing in so many places that I almost find myself wishing to be personally in them all at the same time, as it is said about the god of the sectarians, that my head could be full of eyes and ears in front and behind, to see and hear all around me, and that I could have a thousand tongues, with all of them speaking at the same time, and a voice like a trumpet to declare the will of God to the people.

(To be continued on page 110.*)*

ZION'S TRUMPET,

OR

Star of the Saints.

SATURDAY, MARCH 29, 1856.

CHANGE OF THE WELSH PRESIDENCY.—We announce that the end of our stewardship among our dear Brothers and Sisters in Wales is at the door; that we have had almost the last opportunity to serve those who will remain here behind us, and that we finish our mission of three years and three months with unspeakable pleasure. We are happy to look back on everything that has been except for our own weaknesses, which are hidden, we believe, under the mantle of the love of our brethren, just as we do with those of every brother and sister within the church of our God in the confines of our own dear land, leaving with our heart warmed by the love we have for the least of them. As we look at the present in the face of the past, we are pleased that our conscience testifies that we have done what we could, and that our Blessed Master augments the pleasure even more by giving signs of his approbation and his blessing on our feeble efforts to build his kingdom and to benefit his dear children. Our hopes for the future increase our joy a thousand times more than all the rest. Before us is dear Zion with its hundred thousand advantages, virtues and pleasures—brothers of the same heart, and the most beloved family in all the world, and their outstretched arms welcoming us; around us there are about six hundred of our most beloved brothers and sisters, their breasts beating with a desire for a victory over all evil, in unity and peace who are beginning to run their course toward the adored home of their souls. Behind us we leave thousands of the same hopeful family busily preparing themselves to follow us, and with full hope, after a bitter separation for a small moment we shall all meet again in sweet gladness in the Temple of our Lord, to learn to live forever to praise him. Yes, our feelings, our situation, and all that is, by holding the past and the present to the mirror of the future, oblige our heart to thank the One who called us from darkness to the splendor of his gospel,—and hired us in his vineyard and blessed our labor because everything is as we have it today.

In the midst of all the work and the details associated with delivering up our stewardship, the business of the emigration, preparations for the journey, besides many things we shall not name, which consume our time, we believe we have sufficient excuses for our kind friends to excuse us for not trying to write down more of our feelings on our departure, which in any case it would be pointless to try to describe.

We are not to be blamed either for not going into detail concerning the duties which we would wish for the Saints to take pleasure in fulfilling; for you will have able men with pure hearts, servants of the same God, to teach you; listen to them together with that which has been written: their counsels to those who follow them will be like a fountain of living water to a thirsty soul. We shall not attempt to comfort those who remain except to assure them that the day will come when they will say,—"He did that which he was able to do to gather us to Zion," which is all we will say on that topic.

It is most likely known to everyone by now, that our dear Counselor and faithful brother Daniel Daniels is our Successor, and that Israel Evans and Benjamin Ashby are his Counselors; if not, be it known that these brethren are your Presidents from now on until further notice; and we thank, as do you, dear Saints, the God who gave you such men of a righteous heart to serve you. Obey their counsels, as you obey the words of God, for they are mouths for him to you, and obedience to them will secure everlasting life for those who do so. We confidently expect that great good will come about for the Welsh Saints through the service of those who have been appointed as Counselors in the First Presidency. We trust that the Saints will do their part to sustain them and obey their counsels, for they are men of God, and they will benefit you in proportion to the proper appreciation you give them for the excellent qualities they possess, for they have come from Zion to serve you. Only time can prove the personal benefit that will accrue to the Welsh by striving to understand the English language. Seize this opportunity to do so to the extent possible.

While you remember before the throne of grace any good your old servant has done for you, and you request any blessing for him, on which he depends a great deal, do not forget these my brethren in anything you seek. To have an interest in your faith, your trust, your prayers, and an opportunity to benefit you is still our chief objective, the certainty of which will abundantly repay all the cost of seeking it. That the holy Spirit of the good God who owns us all through the eternal covenant be in you, through you and around you, them and those of us who are leaving you until we are all brought together as one in Him eternally, is the most earnest, foremost and last prayer of your

Brother through Christ,

D. JONES.

ZION'S TRUMPET.—President Daniel Daniels is the Editor of the TRUMPET after this number; send all correspondence to him to this Office from now on, and let him know before the next issue the number if some need to decrease the number they receive because of the emigration; those who do not do so may expect to receive the present numbers.

TO THE PRESIDENTS.—Since the end of the first quarter of your ministry is drawing nigh, and lest you forget, we say to you again that the main treasurers of the P. E. Fund and the Temple are to add up their numbers on the last day of this month, and send here to the P. E. Fund the totals with their addresses and the names of the Branches.

NOTICE TO EMIGRANTS.

EXCERPT FROM THE LETTER OF PRESIDENT F. D. RICHARDS.

36, *Islington, Liverpool, March* 5, 1856.

Dear Brother Jones,—I have just returned from accompanying the "Enoch Train" and about 530 souls of Saints on board the ship. All the arrangements transpired in the most satisfactory and pleasant way: the ship and its company were *Number* 1, of the most excellent category.

The presiding care is on President Ferguson, assisted by Elders E. Ellsworth and D. D. McArthur, his counselors, and besides that he has the strong support of about eight or ten Presiding and Traveling Elders.

About twenty of the Saints were from Switzerland. The entire negotiation has been favorable thus far, and gives a hopeful promise for an excellent and comfortable voyage.

The Captain, who is quite a "*downcaster*," speaks to the point, and we hope they will receive God's blessing and that they will all succeed.

The main purpose of this letter, however, is to ask you about another ship. The prices for passage to the States are now £5 10s and £6 per person; ships are scarce and hard to obtain, and there is no present sign of a favorable change. I have succeeded until now in keeping the price of passage down at £4 5s, and I have been searching since three weeks ago to secure a ship for the majestic throng which is to go out under the Presidency of Captain Dan, and I have the first offer before me now for a new American ship which can carry out about 600 souls. Some merchants are trying to get it, and it can fetch any price it wishes to ask. If I don't get it, I don't know when in the world I can get another one, and if I do get it, I will be obliged to ask no less than £5 per person for all adults, and it is available to sail for Boston at any time it is convenient for us, say about the 19th of April.

The season is already getting late, and it is likely that 4 or 5, perhaps 6 shiploads will leave this spring on your ship.

In the face of all this the question is,—Is it better for me to secure this ship,—the "Saunders Curling," the owners of which said such good things about our people last year in the newspapers of New York,—as I have outlined or not? My mind is inclined toward the idea of getting it if the pockets of your candidates can bear it, since we know not how much worse off it would be for us were we to wait for another one. I transfer these observations to you so that I may have yours back.

You see the need for giving me a prompt response, so this important matter can be decided on without delay. . . . .

I am, your faithful co-worker in the gathering of Israel.

F. D. RICHARDS.

[It is more than likely that some of the emigrants will feel disappointment because of the postponement and the price increase suggested above, yet we believe that the Saints have sufficient wisdom to see that it is an unavoidable necessity; and under the circumstances we trust that the group of emigrants who are ready to start are patient and sympathize with the others who have failed to be as fortunate as they, despite their best efforts in that direction. Instead of being so selfish as to consider only our own opportunities, the fact that so many of the children of Zion are able to gather home this year like doves to their windows, in throngs too numerous to get enough ships in the chief port of the world to transport them, provides a source of joy and patience for those who properly value the privilege of getting to go.

We inform those who may fear that this delay will prevent them from crossing the Plains promptly, that that is a needless misgiving, for several additional weeks of time will be gained by going the way that will be used this year compared with the time taken to go along the old way through New Orleans, &c. And there is no danger that either President Richards or your own servant will start any of their brethren at a time inappropriate for the journey. President Richards does his best, and he can do no better than hiring the ship he mentions, and we have sent word to him to that effect, with a request that if possible he get the ship to get underway a week or two earlier than the time he names in his letter. His answer regarding that will be made available at the first opportunity, and all other pertinent notices of interest.

The foregoing circumstances make it necessary for us to call them to the attention of all the emigrants, and it would be wise for those whose means are scarce to sort themselves out accordingly. If anyone who fails to reach the above target of five pounds wishes to go to the States after every attempt has failed let us know of that without delay, and be content to remain either until he can get more money or until the price decreases, and, of the latter, the previous letter says there is now no likelihood, rather it looks as though it will get worse.

Furthermore, for encouragement to strive to take advantage of the opportunity offered, we are pleased to be able to give high praise to this splendid ship through our acquaintance with it, and to its Captain as a philanthropist who took pleasure in making the Saints happy who went with him previously. Its landing in Boston is not any disadvantage for the emigrants, but rather it shortens the voyage and the onward journey by rail. We expect more names after this; we do not yet have a full 600.—EDITOR.]

SUMMARY OF THE TEACHING OF PRESIDENT DAN JONES, IN THE MERTHYR COUNCIL.

[Continued from page 105.]

ANOTHER one of the most important duties of a President is to take the emigration of the Saints in hand, and promote it with all his might. The foreboding signs and the unstable condition of the western world,— harbingers of the bad times, are things for you to seriously consider, and show them to the Saints everywhere you go, encouraging them in every way you can to make every effort they can to emigrate; that there is not one kind of excuse for not going that anyone who has the means can offer. The gates are wide open, and the call is shouting loudly for all who can to come out; there is no requirement for them to stay here any longer to carry the work forward, but there is freedom for each one who can go and help many of the needy. Call the Presidents of the Branches, and all great and small; those who are considered pillars of strength and the backbone of the work in the places where they live, those who are generous, with their homes open to the Elders, those who contribute often to the Presidency, and the President,—all alike! Let the new President go like a new broom, and let him give a thorough sweeping to all those before him; let him not look at his own benefit, and the loss according to persons, &c., and God will take care of him, and at that time He will bless him with others in their place,—at that time and no sooner they will come in, and new places will be opened. We must rid ourselves of these old "stubborn ones" who now are more of an obstacle than assistance in bringing men to the Church,—the old Saints who have tired a long time ago in Babylon. It would be wonderful if we could disembody all the Branches of Wales through emigrating them; for as soon as we could do that we could go to the quarry to seek new stones,—at that time hundreds, yes, thousands would soon come to the Church, and they would be saved like pulling burning faggots from the fire. President Young has promised that they will come in at that time, and I for one believe him, and that is the most sure and definite verse I have to prove the point. We who have been in the Church a long time have grown old and grown so many horns on our heads, that the people are afraid to come near us. I intend to do my part toward bringing them into the Church, by giving my *Farewell Sermon* to them, which I shall do soon by showing my back to them instead of the face they hate so much, and I believe that that will be the strongest sermon of all to convince as many of them as will be convinced also.

Wm. Lewis, *Scribe.*

MAN SURPRISED!

What now is heard throughout the world?
Oh! there is some surprise for all of us!
There are some people called Saints,
Who are rushing over to the healthy land.

What, a healthy land,—who said that,
It caused amazement to many?
None other than the Saints who always say,
That God it is who calls them together.

What is the reason, tell us,
That the Saints will go so far as that?
The reason I shall tell you boldly,
It is our God who calls us.

It is your Father who calls, how is that,
O come now, let us know,
So that we too can come Home,
If yonder in Utah is the place.

Well, away with us all, happily,
By crossing the ocean now, in time,
So that we may have the blessed place,
According to the commandment of the King of Heaven.

Aberdare. PENCRYCH

MISCELLANEOUS, &c.

LET THE EMIGRANTS TAKE NOTICE!!!—By holding the press until now, we can report that on the 19th of April the ship will start from Liverpool. Wednesday the 9th, a week from next Wednesday, at 6:00 *o'clock in the morning* the Steamer will start from Swansea. Let the Presidents of Monmouth, Merthyr, and Brecon make arrangements for the best time to be in Liverpool by Monday the 14th of April. If we could know promptly the numbers who choose to go that way, we could seek information from the railroad Companies so as to facilitate the objective. This week the prices for passage across the sea have gone up for all ships except for the ships of the Saints to £6 10s, and there are still worse signs.

RECEIPTS FOR BOOKS FROM MARCH 14 TO 27.—Wm. Lewis, £3 18s; Thomas Rees, £2; Thomas Stephens, £3; E. S. Morgans, 8s..

☞ The East Glamorgan Conference will be held on the 20th of April. The others will be announced in the next number.

*** Send all letters, containing orders and payments, to *Daniel Daniels*, *"Zion's Trumpet" Office, Swansea.*

CONTENTS.

PG.
Summary of the teaching of President D. Jones in the Merthyr Council............97
Editorial,—Change of the Welsh Presidency—Zion's Trumpet—To the
    Presidents..105
Notice to the Emigrants...108
Summary of the teaching of President Jones (Continuation)................110
Man Surprised..111
Miscellaneous, &c. 112

SWANSEA:
PRINTED AND PUBLISHED BY D. JONES.

ZION'S TRUMPET,

OR

Star of the Saints.

No. 8.] APRIL 12, 1856. [Vol. IX.

SPEECH OF PRESIDENT BRIGHAM YOUNG TO THE TERRITORIAL SENATE OF UTAH,

Held in Fillmore City, Millard County,
December 11, 1855.

Gentlemen of the Council and House of Representatives,— In accordance with the adjournment of the last Legislative Assembly, we have met for the first time in the capitol, in rooms erected for legislative purposes of the seat of government. This part of the contemplated State House, being the south wing only, though it may answer for the present, has not those conveniences and that spaciousness and beauty which will be connected with the building, when finished in accordance with the original design. How far this may be accomplished through the aid of the general government I do not know, but presume that it will make still further appropriations for that object, as the present investment is upwards of 12,000 dollars in excess of the amount appropriated. Until further aid is extended by Congress, this excess should be assumed and paid by the Territory, since it is manifestly unjust that the contractors, and others who have expended their means and labor for this purpose should be obliged to wait the uncertain period of further appropriations, though the Territory would, probably, be reimbursed at some future time.

8 [Price 1*c*.

We are assembled for the purpose of considering the affairs of our young and thriving Territory, and of framing such laws, rules and regulations as may, in our united wisdom, be considered most salutary and beneficial to the interest of the public weal.

With a tribute of praise and thanksgiving unto that All-Wise Being who controls and governs the nations as he will, we invoke the spirit of wisdom to guide us in our deliberations. And while we render the full emotions of grateful hearts, for past mercies and blessings which have been extended unto us, we are thankful to Him who has preserved us from the bitter rancor and hatred of infuriated enemies, and given us a peaceful inheritance in these sequestered vales. Our hearts swell with gratitude for the privilege we enjoy of seeking and obtaining light and intelligence, that we may at all times, and in all places, be inspired by that spirit of wisdom and truth which emanates from Him who sits enthroned in sacred majesty, and dwells in the midst of his kingdoms. Though his chastening hand has been upon us, still it has been for our good, and we acknowledge it as the kind dealing of a tender parent who seeks the best interest of his children.

I have in my former communications to this body, suggested that laws should be plain, easy to be understood, and few in number. I am as yet unacquainted with any reason for changing my views upon this subject; on the contrary, as life gives me experience, and as experience furnishes knowledge and understanding, I find myself more fully confirmed therein. Neither should laws be too frequently changed, if we would enjoy a permanent and peaceful government. I am fully aware that matters of local and personal interest require alterations, and that, in a new country like this, where enterprise, development and progress so eminently characterize the people, legislation should keep even pace therewith, and not be bound down by contracted and selfish views, old and exploded policy, or traditional errors. Let a spirit of freedom and liberality pervade all our acts, and an enlightened and highly practical course of legislation will surely be the result of our deliberations.

We have a very good volume of laws, and I would recommend,

so far as they remain applicable to our wants, and are sufficient for probable emergencies, that we do not disturb them. No law, passed by the Legislative Assembly of this Territory, has been annulled by Congress, although it retains the power so to do, which is one of the most odious and contrary things to a republic government—a power so repugnant to and subversive of the principles of our free institutions that it should rarely, if ever, be exercised.

In order, however, to avoid this, as well as many other questions which might unfortunately arise only to perplex and entangle the relations so unreasonably, yet peacefully, existing in the present form of a dependent State, and to place ourselves, beyond cavil, upon the platform of equal rights, to have our own sovereignty and free government, based upon the principles sacred to every lover of American liberty as emanating from the people, I recommend that you take the initiatory steps towards our obtaining admission into the Union.

Preparatory thereto, it will be necessary to have the census of the Territory taken, and to hold a convention for the formation and adoption of a constitution. I am confident that this suggestion be taken into prompt consideration, that when you deem it wisdom to make an effort for our admission as a State, the incipient laws may be passed at an early day.

We trust that the present Congress will have wisdom to so far recognize the principle of self-government, and the genius of our free institutions, as to abolish in her territories that odious system of Colonial government which emanated from the British throne, and place them upon equality of constitutional rights enjoyed by the States in their internal regulations, election of officers and representation.

In accordance with a law passed by the Assembly in 1854–5, the Honorable Orson Hyde repaired to Carson county, accompanied by the Honorable Judge Stiles and marshal Heywood, and in connection with authorized persons from California approximately established the boundary line between this Territory and that State, in the region of Carson valley, and fully organized the county. The reports in relation thereto have been received, and will be laid before you at an early date. The compensation asked for service in determining a portion of our western boundary I trust will not be withheld, although it more properly belongs to the general government to defray such expenses, since it is more particularly its province to attend to the establishment of the boundary lines of the territories.

LETTER FROM THE VALLEY.

Fort Ephraim, December 9, 1855.

DEAR BROTHER JONES,—I take this opportunity to write to you, begging your forgiveness for not writing before this, but I have no excuse to offer for not doing so, just thinking that you are receiving the news every month from here through the Star, &c. Whether or not you forgive me, I know that the tender feelings of my heart are warm toward you, and wish for your success, not only in the things of this world, but in the things that pertain to your eternal exaltation in the kingdom of God.

It has been over three years since I last saw you, and I have no doubt but what you have seen much opposition to the Gospel of Christ in Wales this time. I was glad to hear from many that the wheels of the gospel of Jesus are turning quickly in Wales and are saving many continually. The glory of the principles of Mormonism, which are explained constantly by the servants of God here, have brought the affections of my heart to love them above all else. The earnest prayers of my heart are in behalf of the honest in heart in Wales, so they may obey the eternal gospel before the emissaries of peace are called home.

The signs of the times in these days are calling loudly on the Saints to be faithful, and the servants of God here testify that great things are at the door. We wish to see every Welshman who is honest in heart come here to learn to keep the heavenly law. The kingdom of Jesus is increasing in every part of the world, and it will spread across the face of the whole earth very soon. The time for the Saints to return to Jackson County is quickly drawing nigh, and is closer than many now think.

I was glad to see your brother Edward when he came to the City, but his health was quite low, and I feared that he would not live much longer. After he came back to the City from Fort Ephraim, I went to San Pete with him, and we are here now.

We have heard that you intend to come home to your family next year; I hope you have a successful journey. Jane and the children are well; I and my family are enjoying excellent health.

Since your brother is writing to you I shall not write any more at present. Tell everyone who asks about me that I am alive, healthy, and content in my heart, and remember me fondly to them all, especially to brother Daniels.

I shall not add any more at present, except to say that I and my family remember you kindly and lovingly.

   Yours in the new covenant,
      RICE WILLIAMS.
   Formerly from Swyddffynnon, near Tregaron.

LETTER OF JOHN JONES, MERTHYR, TO CAPTAIN DAN JONES.

Merthyr, March 22, 1856.

BROTHER JONES,—We feel truly thankful to you for answering our request, and letting us know what we must do in order to come back to the Church.

We know that we have been foolish in many things, and have said hard things about you, which caused you sorrow and uncomfortable feelings. We are sad and grieved now that that is the case, and we humbly wish your favor and your forgiveness for everything that we did to cause the least discomfort, and we wish to be embraced by you in your best feelings, and receive your faith and your trust in us, so that through that and other things we will be helped to stand and fight, and emerge triumphant the next time.

We wish to have the forgiveness of all of the Saints to whom we have caused the least unpleasant feelings and sorrow. Thus to our God against whom we have done the most we pray for forgiveness, and we ask for forgiveness from Him, from the Saints, and from you in the name of Jesus Christ, hoping there will never be a similar need to do this again.

We acknowledge that you did the right thing in cutting us out of the Church, and you could not have done better according to the prevailing circumstances; we recognize that you were justified in excommunicating us.

I have delayed until now to send this, because I have expected to see Mr. William Sims, and I have not seen him yet, but according to the last conversation between us I am giving his name.

We are your humble servants,

JOHN JONES,
WM. SIMS.

RESPONSE OF CAPTAIN DAN JONES TO THE FOREGOING LETTER.

Swansea, April 8, 1856.

DEAR BROTHER DANIELS,—In response to the request of John Jones in the foregoing letter for my forgiveness and my favorable feelings, I say that I am very pleased to find the merit in his repentance and his wish to enable me to forgive him on the grounds of justice, and I promise to keep my bosom wide open to welcome him very close to my heart in proportion to the sincerity and desire he shows to honor the laws which he has transgressed, to build the most precious kingdom, and to benefit my dear brothers and sisters he has grieved. No one can do that but he himself. My prayer is, and shall be while he truly deserves it, for our gracious Father against whom he has sinned a hundred thousand-fold more than against me, to forgive him, and strengthen him through a revisit of His Holy Spirit to always please Him, and to triumph over every enemy until he enjoys eternal life.

I believe that the Saints deserve and expect to be able to understand his feelings before they can agree with him and us, or embrace him as he wishes; consequently, if you were to publish his request in the TRUMPET, I believe that it would be beneficial in fostering trust and creating unity.

This only shall I add, that in all my dealings with him, as now, I have been keenly aware that I am a fallible man trying to walk the narrow way, something that requires all my energy and the assistance of the Spirit of God and my brethren to be able to enter in through the strait gate to the life, and I have never seen the day when I did not do to him as I wished for another to do to me had I behaved as he did.

It is reasonable to assume that the Saints will also ask for John Jones to reconcile with them according to the procedure of the church to receive him back in, as he should do and as he will wish to do, I believe. That is your business now, since it is not my church, rather God's church, and you are now the treasurer of this corner of it.

I would be glad if W. Sims himself had jointly petitioned with J. Jones, and although I do not doubt the sincerity of the letter, yet I am deprived of the pleasure of reconciling with him until he feels that seeking that is the first and foremost thing, and not something to delay until a convenient time. There is no intercession for the being that neglects his own duty. I seek only what God seeks, namely his best to undo the evil. Anything less is not repentance. Now I shall leave the matter in your hands; may your wise Master enable you to do according to His will, and I myself shall be satisfied.

Your Fellow Servant in Christ,

DAN JONES.

PRAYER VERSES OF THE TROUBLED SAINT IN BABYLON.

O GOD, O God, eternal Father,
When shall I go to fair Zion?
Within this Babylonian land
   I have wearied of living.

CHORUS.

O Father, deliver me from Babylon,
I have wearied, O I have wearied
   Of living any longer in this place.

O Father, I beg of Thee,
To sympathize with me,

And to consider my distress,
   In the land of great affliction.

It is troubles on troubles,
That weigh down my spirit night and day,
Daily I go about in sadness,
   In the land of great affliction.

I am violated and oppressed,
By those who are not Thy children,—
They cause my bones to dry,
   So great is my affliction.

Untruth is becoming more frequent,
And brotherly love is rarer,
Violence and oppression increase,
   In the land of great affliction.

Beloved justice and its pleasant home,
Are the objects of my heart's love,
For them daily I call out,
   In the land of great affliction.

O Father, I waited constantly,
To leave arrogant Babylon,—
My Father, do not ignore my request,
   In the land of great affliction.

Thy Saints are going home,
From the East, North, and from the South,
But I still am poorly placed,
   In the land of great affliction.

Six hundred now of the dear Welsh folk,
Are going over and leaving me,
In Babylon with my mournful cry,
   In the land of great affliction.

My lingering hope is growing weak,
And my soul saddens every day,
My constant grief increases,
   In the land of great affliction.

Thy pure angel has called me,
From Babylon to Thy Zion,
And I shall endeavor till I'm seen,
   Away from the land of great affliction.

CHORUS.

O Father, deliver me from Babylon,
I have wearied, O I have wearied
Of living any longer in this place.

Flint.   THOS. CONWAY.

ZION'S TRUMPET,

OR

Star of the Saints.

SATURDAY, APRIL 12, 1856.

CHANGE.—The change in the Welsh Presidency and in the Editorship of the TRUMPET is known to all who have read the announcement of the former Renowned Editor in the previous issue, and now we trust the Saints will sympathize in the most sincere way with our inability to function in such a responsible and important stewardship, and to fill it as did our more able Predecessor. We are far from being so conceited as to claim the same skill in a war as an old soldier who has been in the battle fighting with the family of the devil as if for life, and having done so from the first time the banner of Jesus waved over the hills of Gwalia until now, except for the time he was escorting a host of the Lord's Saints to their sure place of refuge, whom he had won from the possession of Satan to the Kingdom of our God in a few years, while editing the "Prophet." In the meantime the battle became so hot that you prayed to have the "old Captain back," and you were answered by the King of kings, who revealed to the General in Zion your situation and your desire to see him, and he was sent to you again, and we had the honor of coming with him and brother Thomas Jeremy from there to here.

You know how remarkable the sound of the TRUMPET was under the skillful editorship of its former Editor, and of the victories everyone won without exception who followed its direction—and all are evidences of the fitness of the trumpeter. He was always foremost in the army against the enemies of the truth, and the God of Israel strengthened his arm and gave him his Spirit to guide him in winning a spotless character, which was his shield of safety. He has gone and left us again; nevertheless, it is still necessary to blow through the

"Trumpet" while the war continues. Although it is said that Russia and Turkey have come to conditions of peace, let the Saints—soldiers of King Jesus, remember that no "peace" has been signed nor will it ever be between the Kingdom of God and the kingdom of the devil, until Satan is bound and every tongue comes to confess Christ as the King across the face of the whole earth. Victory is what every faithful desires and victory is what he shall obtain, and blessed is he who does his part under every circumstance as our former President did.

Not only did our President and Editor leave our midst, but many of the old faithful, mighty, and experienced soldiers have also gone, yes, some of the bravest. This is a change and a forever-to-be-remembered era.

Here we are poor weaklings and too grossly inexperienced, you Conference Presidents included, after having been set in our places to do the best we can, but we are not like those without hope; our protective fortifications and their foundations are more powerful and higher than mankind, all the host of Heaven is on our side, the soldiers are practiced with frequent experience, and readiness, obedience, and additional bravery of the army can make up for much of the deficiency.

Dear fellow soldiers, please complete the deficiency of your President and Editor who is at present unskilled, by keeping the divine armor shiny, and your swords sharp, and wage war to the sound of the Trumpet, through which we shall seek to blow only that which is most interesting and useful.

Now, then, let us all together concert our efforts until we retreat from the land of the enemy triumphant to the top of the tower of Zion, which is the heartfelt prayer of your

Humble servant,

Daniel Daniels.

THE "SPAULDING STORY" OR THE WORST BUGBEAR TO PREVENT A HOST FROM BECOMING SAINTS.

Esteemed Editor—I had the high honor of joining with the Latter-day Saints, and receiving for myself a satisfactory witness of the truthfulness of the Book of Mormon before I heard of the above Bugbear; thus it would be easier to shatter an adamantine rock with a rush arrow than for anyone to persuade me to believe that that Book was made from the "Spaulding Romance." But, not so for everyone; I have heard some intelligent people admit that the worst Bugbear of all was the above story to prevent them from believing in the divinity of the Book of Mormon. And it is a pity to think that thousands throughout the land at present, yes, in Wales, firmly believe that the Book of Mormon is a paraphrased "Spaulding Tale!" When I was first directed to this Bugbear, with a host of the sons of the devil shouting "Boo, boo," I already knew, by the best proofs that God has for his children, namely the vibrant, clarifying witnesses by the Holy Ghost, that the Book of Mormon had been written through or under the inspiration of Heaven. And yet I did not have satisfactory proofs for the world (although there are plenty available) of the divinity of the Book of Mormon, and that it was not a paraphrase of the "Spaulding Romance," any more than the blind man had to prove that Jesus Christ was the son of God; he could only say "where I was once blind, I can now see." His testimony did not satisfy them, any more than my testimony could satisfy my neighbors.

A hundred times I have felt my heart ache when preaching to my fellow nation, because I did not know how the story was devised that it was from the "Spaulding Romance" that the Book of Mormon was made. Now fellow officer, brother, or sister, if you are asked can you answer by whom and how the above fraudulent story was formed, a story that is preventing thousands from believing in "Mormonism"? Some will suppose, possibly, that it is not useful for them to know about the origin of the above story for themselves since they have a testimony of the truthfulness of the Book of Mormon, but they are mistaken, I think. If a brother were accused of being guilty of murdering a man in such and such a place the other day, and we know better, would it not be our duty to search for the witnesses and the proofs we have that our brother was not in that place on that day, in order to save his life? Yes it would, say all reason and humanity. Yes it would, says God himself. But how much more important is it here, when thousands of the honest in heart are in a condition of perdition for believing the above story, when we know that it is a lie. "It is certainly our duty if the story is as popular as you have noted," say many of the Saints now, probably. So popular, is it? What press in our country, and other countries, yes, and nearly the whole world, have not tossed this story out in some manner or other? What newspaper or publication has appeared without having its columns stained with this lying story, yes, and what pulpit or stool, if there were sectarian preachers on them, have not had the "Spaulding Story" recited with relish from them, and then swallowed voraciously by their listeners? What village or town is there whose walls and doors have not been bespeckled with an "announcement" that some "Reverend" or other is delivering a lecture on the "beginning of Mormonism!!"—"Admittance—Six Pence" or "Shilling each" mind you!!! And there they dress this white lady or the "Spaulding Story," by putting her on top of every post to frighten their listeners, poor things, not to believe in the divinity of the Book of Mormon. That's the way it is; and the Saints in general are too negligent to search out the details concerning the origin of the above story, to the point that many are unable to contest the assertions of the "Reverends," and to show better to their honest listeners.

It is true that the Saints can easily prove its divinity in another way, and by so doing prove the "Spaulding Story" false, and its inventors lying writers; but we have a duty to prove that in every way we can, until we dispel all unbelief about the matter.

With no reason to provide further details now, suffice it to refer the reader to the effective "Refutations" to the above story, which were published by our Dear former President Captain Dan Jones. These "Refutations" provide an account as to who fabricated the story,—where and by whom it was published, and the plans the children of the devil carried out to blacken our holy religion and the Book we know to be the word of God, until they lock themselves in, and are caught in their deceit. I would like for every lover of the truth to read the aforementioned "Refutations" carefully, and doubtless he will not find it without being thoroughly convinced that there was no more connection between the "Spaulding Romance" and the Book of Mormon than there was between it and the book of "common prayer," or the history of Henry the Eighth; let those who wish to save a sinner and hide a multitude of lies take a copy of the treatise to every Vicar, Curate, and Sexton who are ringing the clapper of this old bell daily, and if every sectarian "Editor," "Reverend," and "Jack" had a copy of it, it would have a better effect on their bowels to improve the colic which churns their insides than a tub of drugs and a whole lot of quacks. Do this, brethren, quickly, until the "Spaulding Romance" is exiled from our land, and anyone will be embarrassed to declare it any further.

Formerly from Georgetown. THOMAS HARRIS.

FAREWELL TO CAPTAIN JONES!

BY THOMAS HARRIS, FORMERLY FROM GEORGETOWN.

Now after bidding farewell to our President—kind father,
He who brought the word of life to the land of his birth,
My feelings are shattered—my heart is aching,
At parting, though but for a moment, with a hero for the truth.

My mind flies like a breeze across the ocean,
To Carthage, where the Captain was in the jail house,
In company of our dear Prophet and the Patriarch his brother,
Fearing not the edge of the sword, the world, or its haughty scorn.

Yes, he proved through his bravery on the land of America,
His zeal for Christ and his servants, and his love for the truth;
He sacrificed every honor and empty wealth of the world,
Giving himself and all he had to God and all his work.

He came here across the deep and brought his family with him,
To Wales—the land of his fathers, at the call of the King of Heaven;
He proclaimed the gospel—he labored night and day,
Until he had brought thousands into the family of faith.

All levels of Reverends appeared threatening frantically:
"We'll conquer the old *Captain*—we'll show his great deceit;"
But a thousand times they failed—no one can say less,
The "collegians" retreated before him with their mouths closed!

Then he went across the seas with a host of the Saints of our God,
From the midst of violence and oppression to dear Zion to live;
He led them paternally across the steep and rocky hills,
In the midst of every kind of tribulation—he was a strength to the Saints.

After arriving in Zion he was not fully content,
He ventured through the wilderness into the midst of the uncivilized host,
To search for the race of Madog lost in the tangled land,—
His intent was to transmit pure religion to them.

Before accomplishing his full purpose, Brigham gave kind counsel
To Captain Jones to return to Wales to us;
He did not see that as too much—he arose like a giant,
He did not say, '*I'll go if I can*,' but 'I AM READY NOW.'

Across the rocky mountains and the spacious seas he came,
Till arriving in Gwalia once again, without complaint, despite his journey;
His cup was overflowing—he shared it everywhere,
And the living waters he brought from yonder pure fountain.

He was here more than three years as Leader in the battle,
He sacrificed every feeling to benefit the Saints;
And they rejoiced upon receiving his true teaching,
Till an increase of love is now felt in their midst.

All the precious volumes he wrote will be
Witnesses of his diligence—never, never will they be forgotten;
And the thousands who were convinced by reading them,
Will be seen as a comfort to him happily on mount Zion.

Now *he has started* from Wales this week,
And the six hundred under his care are ascending the top of the billows;
That will again cause Satan to begin to weave
His hateful lies, and blow through his false prophets.

Where are the false prophets who testified that on their journey—
"That Captain Jones would sell all the Saints in Cuba" earlier?
If they have died their brethren are yet alive,
And it is strange if they do not unite in telling the same kind of lie.

Farewell our dear Pastor, our President, yes, our Father,
May you and your company be furthered to reach the land of Zion;
May every sail of the *Saunders Curling* be filled with an easterly wind,
To carry you quickly on your journey home.

Swansea, April 10, 1856.

STANZAS ON THE SAME TOPIC.

BY JOHN DAVIES, PREVIOUSLY FROM MERIONETH.

The joyful Captain who led us—leaves
    For a while of his own free will;
      He goes from his field in worthy fashion,
      He vanquished an ugly, rough throng.

A strong man and a support—was our Dan,
    He drew us from our tribulation;
      A moral man—one who grew greater,
      While he passed this way.

Through his vital godly teaching—we can admit,
    He increased our knowledge,
      And through him came nourishment to us,
      And unadulterated gems.

May daily success be our President's—
    And his thoughts on improvement;
      By living piously—cheerful Saint,
      Progressing to glory.

Swansea, April 4, 1856.

SLAVE TRADING OF AMERICA.

THE following decisions are contained in a recent proclamation of the Governor of the State of Mississippi:—"If the U. S. Senate (or the general government) prohibits slave trading in any way,—preventing it in any Territory; or from going where there was none before when there is an opportunity for it; interfering in any way against the sale of the slaves of one State in another State, or not receiving any Territory into the Union in its proper time such as a State because of its slave trading, the State of Mississippi will rise in its might for its rights, and insist on upholding them even if by force of arms."

While the one feeling (concerning slave trading) burns with bloody voracity in the States of the South, there is an equally zealous feeling in the north against it. All who have read the previous accounts on this topic understand that Kansas Territory is the battlefield between them. The South has sent and continues to send men to settle there, sending arms to them and military officers to lead them when the battle breaks out between them and those whom the North has sent for their purpose against slave trading, and to get Kansas as a "free Territory." "If we lose Kansas, we lose all to the east and west of it (says the South to their men), and we'll win it by the muzzle of the cannon and the tip of the bayonet if need be. Hanging is too good for the damned traitors of the North, &c." At the same time the North says to its own heroes, "Deliver Kansas from your savage aggressors by the power of your arms and the sharp proof of your bravery to the murderers, the thieves," &c., &c.

MISCELLANEOUS, &c.

THE EMIGRANTS.—The inhabitants of this town got an additional view, yes, an effective sermon, by seeing a host of the Saints of the Lord turning their backs on them and their faces toward Zion. Tuesday afternoon the streets of the town were speckled by them; it was a matter of surprise to the world to see their love and their unity—the one helping the other with their luggage, their children, &c., and no one rested until his brother had finished. Wednesday morning, the 9th, the host was seen on board the steamer, ready to start toward Liverpool, their hearts rejoicing, and saying in their conduct to those who wept after them—"Do not weep for us, rather there is greater cause for you to weep for yourselves and for your children." Our Revered Editor and President Daniels was with them like a father instructing them on board, and he went with them to Liverpool. In the afternoon Brother D. Jones departed on the steamer to meet them in Liverpool, to prepare comfortable accommodations for them, &c.; benefitting the Saints is food and drink to him. Success to them all, say thousands of others.—T. H.

CONFERENCES.—The East Glamorgan Conference will be held on the 20th of April, Breconshire on the 27th, Monmouthshire on the 4th of May, West Glamorgan on the 11th, Llanelli on the 18th, Carmarthen on the 25th, Pembroke on the 1st of June, and Cardiganshire on the 8th.

⁎ Send all letters, containing orders and payments, to *Daniel Daniels, "Zion's Trumpet" Office, Swansea.*

CONTENTS.

	PG.
Speech of President B. Young to the Territorial Senate of Utah	113
Letter from the Valley	116
Letter of John Jones	117
Response	118
Prayer Verses	119
Editorial—The Change	121
The worst Bugbear	122
Farewell to Captain Dan Jones	125
Verses on the same topic	127
Slave trading of America	127
Miscellaneous, &c.	128

SWANSEA:
PRINTED AND PUBLISHED BY D. DANIELS.

ZION'S TRUMPET,

OR

Star of the Saints.

No. 9.] APRIL 26, 1856. [Vol. IX.

THE MILLENNIUM.

BY THOMAS HARRIS, FORMERLY FROM GEORGETOWN.

We understand by this word any thousand-year period whether under the reign of evil or the reign of righteousness. But by "*The Millennium*" it is commonly understood to mean a particular thousand-year period mentioned in the scriptures, during which peace will reign—the great Sabbath of the creation, of which all the other sabbaths and *jubilees* are but types. It is written in the word of the Lord, that "a thousand years is as one day, and one day is as a thousand days with Him." Then we perceive clearly that seven thousand years is as seven days with the Lord, and the seventh, or the last thousand-year period is to be a sabbath or a jubilee through all creation; a place of rest and freedom from captivity and grief.

The first sabbath appointed for man was the seventh day, which was sanctified and set apart by the Creator, and it was to be understood by man as a day of rest for him, his family, and his servants, together with his animals, and also it is said that the Lord rested from all his labor.

Another sabbath was set apart for the children of Israel. (See Lev. xxv.) This was to be kept every seven years. It was a sabbath for the earth to rest from being cultivated, and even that which

[Price 1*c*.

had grown from it by itself was not allowed to be gathered in, but was to be free for all to partake of in the place where it had grown.

This seventh year was a rest not only for the earth, but it was a kind of jubilee, in which the creditor was to forgive his debtor—the servant was to be freed from his master, &c. The third sabbath or jubilee was the fiftieth year, counting seven years seven times (Lev. xxv, 10.)—"And ye shall hallow the fiftieth year, and proclaim liberty throughout all the land unto all the inhabitants thereof: it shall be a jubilee unto you; and ye shall return every man unto his possession, and ye shall return every man unto his family."

In any event, all these sabbaths were set apart by the Lord, and his people in ancient times got to enjoy them. Yet, says the apostle who wrote to the Hebrews, "For if Jesus had given them rest, then would he not afterward have spoken of another day." Here he refers to a future rest, of which all the sabbaths and the *jubilees* were but a foretaste. This rest is to be enjoyed by the Saints of God for a thousand years, during which time Satan will be shut in a bottomless pit, and he shall not deceive the nations any more until the time shall be fulfilled. The dead in Christ will be resurrected at the beginning of the these thousand years, and they shall reign with Christ as kings and priests until the thousand years have ended. That is the first resurrection. "Blessed and holy is he that hath part in the first resurrection: on such the second death hath no power, but they shall be priests of God and of Christ, and shall reign with him a thousand years." Whoever feels to read the twentieth chapter of the Revelation shall have many additional details in connection with the "Millennium," which are quite clear for the public to understand.

If the question arises in anyone's mind,—Where will these resurrected Saints reign during the Millennium? I shall say that the 10th verse of the 5th chapter of Revelation answers as follows:— "We shall reign on the *earth!*"

Now, the attentive reader sees that I have noted two important facts, namely the *time* and the *place*, (the time being a thousand years, and the place being on the earth). Now, reader, come along a little further, to search for other facts that are connected with this millennium of reigning on the earth with Christ.

The prophet Zechariah informs us that there will be "One Lord, and his name one, and He shall be king over all the earth." John also says that "all the kingdoms of this world are become the kingdoms of our Lord, and of his Christ." Daniel testifies that "The Kingdom and the greatness of the kingdom *under the whole heaven* shall be given to the people of the saints of the Most High." And in another place he says—"But the Saints of the Most High shall take the kingdom, and possess the kingdom for ever, even for ever and ever."

We can quote additional writings of the prophets to prove this, but if the reader is not satisfied with the testimonies of the three previous prophets, it is likely that he would not be satisfied were we to quote others.

From the previous quotations it appears that in the thousand years all the opposing governmental and religious formations that existed previously will be swallowed up into one perfect unity—one general government—with no laws but the laws established by God, and the Saints will administer in them; and the only priests belonging to this blessed period will be resurrected ones.

Perhaps the reader says:—Fear takes my soul! I stare in amazement!! I am dumbfounded!!! What! the European governments—the American republic—the oppressive Indian governments—the broad empire of China—the mixed kingdoms of Asia and Africa—the numerous tribes of the wilderness, and the numberless inhabitants of the islands. All—all to be annihilated—to destruction—or to become *one*—*one* political body—*one* peaceful empire—*one* Lord, and *one* King over the whole earth.

Yes, and something that will cause even greater astonishment to the world is to think that the various sects, denominations, beliefs, and faiths of men, scattered throughout the world, will all flee from before the brighter rays of divine truth, which will spread until they cover the face of the whole earth.

The thousands of superstitious, pagan rituals will all be swept away. The names of their countless false gods will fall into oblivion, never again to be mentioned.

On the earth there shall be *one* King, *one* Lord, and his name shall be *one*.

Can anyone acquainted with human nature, and with the present condition of the countries and religions of the world, believe that such vast changes will take place? A man is nearly brought to the point of shouting: *Impossible*. Nevertheless, there is no room for choice; rather, one must believe it all, or disbelieve the prophets.

Naturally, the reader is led to inquire by what means are such changes to take place—such wondrous and strange revolutions.

The first and foremost consideration that comes to mind by searching the prophets on this topic is that God will extend his hand a second time to restore the house of Israel and the house of Judah to their rightful nations, to God's favor, and to their own lands. They will be gathered from among every nation under heaven, with their silver and gold, and all their precious treasures, &c., in ships, steamboats, trains, on horses, mules, camels, and on swift beasts using every opportunity that can be invented. This gathering will take place with a strong hand, with an arm extended, and with the pouring out of wrath, and in short, the arm of Jehovah will be bared before the eyes of the nations, in signs, in wonders, in miracles, in revelations, in judgments, and in compassion.

The waters will be divided, and His people will be led through them on dry ground, as in the days of old. The mountains will feel his power, and they will melt like wax; and the kingdoms of the everlasting hills will shake at his appearance; for He will rend the heavens, and he will come down, and he will do awesome things—things that are not expected to occur. He will say to the north, "give up," and to the south, "keep not back; bring my sons from far, and my daughters from the ends of the earth." "He shall set up an ensign for the nations, and shall assemble the outcasts of Israel, and gather together the dispersed of Judah from the four corners of the earth." The power shown in the bringing of Israel from Egypt in days of yore will be nothing in comparison; it will hardly come to the memory or to the mind when compared with the majestic restoration which awaits that people. The fate of the nations hangs on this subject as if on an axis.

Their political and religious blessings, or their curses, yes, in fact, their existence depends on the path they take in connection with the work of God in gathering his people Israel. They can oppose, and be hurled to destruction like Pharaoh of old; or, they can assist, and be blessed as was Ruth. They can make a covenant and be partakers of the blessings with his chosen people; or they can cling to their superstitions, and their sectarian traditions, and by so doing discover that they war against God, until thrones are cast down, and judgment has given them to the Saints of the Most High God.

For scriptural proofs of these important topics, I direct the reader to read carefully the writings of the prophets, especially those of Isaiah, Jeremiah, Ezekiel, Daniel, and Zechariah. Some of the most interesting facts relating to these important topics are found in Isaiah xi, Ezekiel xx, Jer. xvi, Zech. xiv. The careful reader will perceive the truth of the previous observations, with no room for doubt, and much more in depth than can be said at present.

The *Second coming of the Messiah* has a close connection with the aforementioned restoration. His second coming will be *personal* and *visible*; as much so as was his first coming.

Enoch, the seventh from Adam, said that he would come with ten thousands of his saints.

Job testified that he would stand at the latter day upon the earth, saying, "in my flesh shall I see God."

Isaiah portrays him as coming in vengeance to smite the wicked; treading the people in his anger, and trampling them in his fury; that he will come as if in fiery war-chariots to destroy his enemies, and for the joy and redemption of his Saints, namely those who will shake at His word.

Daniel saw him coming on the clouds of heaven.

Zechariah foretold that his feet would stand upon the mount of Olives, for the deliverance of Israel, and to destroy their enemies; and that the mount would sink beneath his feet, and cleave, leaving a valley in its place; that all the saints would come with Him, and that Jerusalem and the Jews will be sanctified from that day forward; and that all the nations throughout the surrounding countries will go to Jerusalem once each year, to worship the King, the Lord of hosts, and to keep the feast of tabernacles.

Malachi testifies of his coming, asking who may abide the day of his coming, and who shall stand at his appearance, for he would be like a refiner's fire, and like fullers' soap, and he shall sit as a refiner and purifier of silver.

Peter foretold that Jesus should come in flaming fire, taking vengeance; also, that he would go to the Jews, after he was received by the Heavens until the times of restitution of all things.

Jesus also said that he would come with his holy angels, and that the powers of heaven would be shaken; and that great destruction would take place, like unto that which happened in the days of Noah, and in the days of Lot.

At the time he arose up from the grave the angels testified that he would come again in like manner as he ascended, personally, physically, and visible in the clouds of heaven.

The Revelations of John confirm the second coming of the Messiah, and even clarify when his enemies will see him, and that all kindreds of the earth shall wail because of him, and he ends his book by saying, "Amen. Even so, come, Lord Jesus." Now, it is a fact that all these witnesses without exception refer to his second coming, and not to his first coming; for many of them were spoken after his first coming, and all of them describe circumstances completely different to those which pertain to his first coming, and thus it is not possible that they refer to that.

Having given irrefutable proof that the thousand years will come in with the restoration of Israel—the rebuilding of Jerusalem—the second coming of the Messiah—the destruction of the ungodly, and the general establishment of a kingdom of peace across the face of the whole earth, I shall now describe a little about the nature of the "millennium," and the blessings that will be enjoyed under that blessed reign.

It is clear that those who are resurrected from the dead will be immortal beings; consequently, they will not take upon them the duties and enjoyment that are appropriate to a mortal state; rather they will dwell in the holy city, and they will be kings and priests, to administer the concerns of the government, and to assist the people. But those who will not have put on the garment of immortality, but who were kept alive until the second coming of the Messiah, they will possess the earth with all its riches and blessings, as did Noah and his family when they came out of the ark. They will sow their fields and eat of their fruit; they will plant vineyards and drink of their wine, they will build houses and cities and shall dwell in them. "The plowman shall overtake the reaper, and the treader of grapes him that soweth seed"; in short, they will "beat their swords into plowshares, and their spears into pruninghooks, and they shall not learn war any more." "The wolf also shall dwell with the lamb, and the leopard shall lie down with the kid; and the calf and the young lion and the fatling together, and a little child shall lead them. And the cow and the bear shall feed; their young ones shall lie down together: and the lion shall eat straw like the ox, and the sucking child shall play on the hole of the asp." The curse shall be taken from the face of the earth, and it shall become fruitful as paradise, when sickness and pains of every nature will be completely unknown throughout practically all the land; thus peace, joy, truth, love, knowledge, abundance, and glory will cover the face of the earth as do the waters cover the seas. God's tabernacle and his sanctuary will be with man, in the midst of the holy cities, and their cup will be brim-full with joy and rejoicing.

(To be continued.)

LETTER OF THE EDITOR TO HIS PRINTER.

Liverpool, April 20, 1856.

Dear Brother Harris.—At last I have obtained a spare moment to write a word to you. It has been a very busy time for us here night and day. We would give a detailed account of our journey from Swansea to here on board the "Troubadour," except that Brother Wm. Lewis has started back the same way as of yesterday, and I expect that he will arrive there tonight, when he will give the whole story to you. I hope that he arrives there well, and that he will find you all the same.

The ship "Saunders Curling" got under way yesterday (Saturday) from the Mersey river, at eleven o'clock in the morning. The steamer took her out to sea for 32 miles, and I accompanied her that far. All had good health and happy hearts, with the songs of Zion sweetly on their lips. It was a difficult task for me to take leave of all the old and faithful brothers and sisters, especially President Jones, after traveling sea and land with him, and working hand in hand with him for so long. Although their company was sweet, especially on a venture so desirable as "sailing toward Zion from the captivity of the land of enemies," I found strength to resist emotion when I thought about the others left behind longing for the same privilege. I arrived back here at nine o'clock at night.

The number of emigrants on board the "S. Curling" was 707. They are under the Presidency of Brother Jones.

Another ship, the "Thornton," is to get underway full of Saints on the second of May. I don't know when the next one will go after her.

You see that the great work of the emigration is going forward—the Saints are fleeing like doves to their windows. Their heads are full of songs and eternal joy, breezes of heaven fill the sails of their vessel, and the God of Jacob is at the helm.

I wish for you to put a brief account of the journey from Swansea to here in the TRUMPET, since there are things that pertain to it which are worthy of note.

I don't know how soon I shall be released from here to come there; I'll let you know.

I conclude, with my fond memories to you, and John Davies, and all the Saints.

     I am your humble servant,

              DANIEL DANIELS.

VERSE.

Through the gospel we have
 Bosoms full of joy,
And a pledge from our father
 Of his endless endurance;
Therefore let us all hold firm—
 There are unfailing promises,
That we shall possess a land
 Which is full of goodly blessings.

Alltwen.   D. W.

ZION'S TRUMPET,

OR

Star of the Saints.

SATURDAY, APRIL 26, 1856.

THE CHANGE we noted in our previous issue was one of the effects of the emigration. It has an effect in many places besides here. Our Presidents foresaw this, and they said that in the unforgettable Merthyr Council. We see now hundreds of our brothers and sisters starting for Zion. It was said that there was no reason for anyone to remain behind to offer support to the Elders and the cause, &c., and that God would see to that. We understood from them that the more frequent the emigration, the more would be baptized, which has restarted almost everywhere. We too tell the Presidents not to worry about themselves, or the cause of God, for He will send others in place of those who have left. About a hundred of them went entirely at the expense of the Fund. Since they were selected for their many years of faithfulness, this will offer encouragement for others to do likewise—to strive more diligently with the work, and to open their hearts and their pockets in proportion to their requests, so that they will be filled with the blessings of God.

The emigration will also have an effect on the circulation of the TRUMPET, which pleases us greatly, as it is the emigration of the Saints to Zion which is affecting it. Every President was given his freedom to send for as few of the TRUMPET as he wished. According to the few that we print at present, it is a task almost too difficult to produce them for a penny, except according to following reasons and conditions:—

1. Since issues will not remain on hand, and since the number is so small, it is reasonable for everyone to pay regularly for the books he receives.

2. We expect that no chief distributor will go for more than a month at most without sending payment. We wish for you, dear Brethren, the Presidents, to keep an eye on this, and on the payments of the Branches—to make sure that they are equivalent to the books received by the chief distributor.

3. Unless the payments that come in are equivalent to the number of Trumpets that leave the Office, it cannot be sold for a penny per issue. May the Saints feel their duty in this, and may the Presidents not be negligent in showing this to them, or in cooperating with us with all their hearts.

The Emigrating Saints.—Approximately 150 Saints went on the "Troubadour" to Liverpool. The majority of them were a bit sick for about 6 hours; but from Milford on we had a lovely and enjoyable time. There is no reason for the Saints to fear the steamer, as a bit of seasickness does a lot of good. The *Captain* and the *Mate* were extremely kind to the Saints, and gave a warm welcome to us; they deserve the gratitude of the Saints and the blessing of our God. They diminished the price of passage for some large families, which is encouragement for more to come this way. Hundreds of other Saints from the environs of Merthyr, Monmouth, and Brecon went successfully on the railroad to Liverpool. For more of the account of the emigrants have a look at our letter on page 135 of this issue.

SPEECH OF ELDER ISRAEL EVANS TO THE WELSH SAINTS.

Esteemed Editor,—With grateful feelings to God I take pen in hand to convey some of my thoughts by means of your Trumpet, at the outset of my ministry in the Welsh Principality.

I have wanted to visit Wales ever since I was a child, for this is the land of birth of my forebears, although they are not in the land of the living at present.

In the spring of 1853 I was sent on a mission to England, where I arrived January 13, 1854, together with Brother Jesse B. Martin. I was assigned to labor in the Warwickshire Conference, where I remained until the end of that year, at which time I was assigned to preside over the Derbyshire Conference, and at the end of 1855 I was sent from there to labor with you here. My heart jumped for joy when President Franklin said to me,—"Brother Israel—I want you and Brother Ashby to go to Wales to labor, and to learn the Welsh language, which will be an eternal blessing to you." After settling my accounts, and finishing my part of the business in the Conference, I started off with Brother Ashby on our journey to Wales. Many and varied were my thoughts I had before arriving in the land of Gwalia. With a light heart and a quick step I ascended the *Pier Head*, and I felt to ask,—Is this the land where my fathers lived, flourished and died? Did they leave anyone to keep their names in remembrance, and make them honorable among the people of God? The answers were—"Yes, this is the land of my fathers. You are the man who has come out boldly before men and devils to honor the Lord God of your fathers in the midst of scorn and wrath." When I have felt to say—"My fathers—where are they?" I feel as if their spirits are hovering around me, whispering in my ear—"They can welcome you in the land of your fathers, because you have the eternal Priesthood, through which you are an instrument in the hand of the Lord to make known to your brethren of the same blood the principles of life and salvation, and to gather them to Zion, where they can do our work for those of us who have gone through the trials of mortality without knowing of the true Gospel. We are looking anxiously at you who enjoy the privileges of the gospel on the earth, to do for us that which we did not have the opportunity of doing for ourselves, so that we may come forth in the resurrection of the just to inherit eternal lives and glory in the kingdom of God."

The knowledge I have of these things, when I ponder on them, inspires my soul with strength from the Lord, not my own, to be diligent and humble, obedient and determined in all that is required at my hand from the Lord or his servants.

I feel truly thankful for the privilege of being able to labor under your Presidency, for I know that you have the hearts of the Saints, and that their prayers for you ascend continually before the Lord of hosts, for you to receive strength and health, and for the blessings of the Lord to be with you in all your administrations, so that the mission may succeed according to the wishes of your heart.

I am pleased to say that the Saints have only the best feelings toward President Dan Jones, and that their prayers are for the Lord to pour out the blessings of heaven on him and on all who traveled to Zion under his care.

So far as I have become acquainted with the Welsh Saints, I have found them to be extremely warm-hearted Mormons, who are always willing to do everything that is required at their hands, and that speaks volumes of good things to me about them and those who have been laboring so successfully in their midst. That gives me joy and trust in the Lord continually, for I know that inasmuch as we are obedient and faithful in carrying out your counsels and teachings, thereby acknowledging the authority of the Lord, He will not leave us, but we shall succeed, and all will be well with us continually. And I say to the Saints,—Although several of those who were stalwarts in the Lord have emigrated toward Zion, yes, some who were strong fortresses to their people, have left us to stand against the opponents of truth without their presence, their prayers will be with us, and the fervent prayer of the righteous availeth much. The Lord is also with us to help us, for this is His work; and who can measure the arms of the Almighty? Therefore, dear Saints, let us feel willing to be faithful to the Lord wherever we may be, remembering the importance and greatness of the divine work we are engaged in, knowing always that it is necessary to work with all our might to be useful to the Lord to build his kingdom on the earth.

I feel truly grateful for the welcoming reception that I have received from the Saints in general. Please allow me to acknowledge that through the TRUMPET, and to say,—May God bless you for that. May our friendship comfort and encourage the one and the other, and to promote the work of the Lord. May whatever path we take be of such a nature as to perpetuate endless trust and brotherly love, in the one for the other, down to the last generation.

I conclude now, fearing that I may have trespassed on your pages; if so, I trust you will forgive me this once. The true wish of my soul, and my constant prayer to the Lord of hosts, is for your future success, that you may always be capable of fulfilling the daunting

challenge of your office.
  I am, as always,
    Your brother in the cause of truth,
            Israel Evans.

TRIUMPH OF THE SAINTS OVER THE WORLD.

BY JOHN DAVIES, FORMERLY OF MERIONETHSHIRE.

(Tune—*"The Delight of the Men of Harlech."*)

Strange! strange! how eager,
Are envious men,
To reject in disgraceful fashion
    Jesus, King of Heaven;
  The "wise men" join,
  With the mad men,—
All forever focused,
    On killing the righteous;
War, war is the forecast
Of the world's children, and Satan their chief,—
Everywhere they are mobilizing,
    Under his leadership.

Awake, awake, soldiers of Christ,
Let us take strength in his power,
Like heroes to overcome,
        Our cruel enemies;
    Now wave up high,
    Heaven's banner in the breeze.
And let us sound our beautiful Trumpet,
    To call everyone to battle;
Let us gather a great host,
And withstand with good heart,
Let us make the enemy fearful,
    Through the blue sword.

Soon, soon we'll be strengthened,
Sons of the forest will be civilized,
Tribes of Israel—they will be returned
        Back from the northern land
    They will walk in honor,
    Pomp and majesty,—
Terrible crags before their might,
    Will tumble into plains;

Hosts of heaven will come too,
They will ride from the land of bliss,
And we all shall fight in unity,
    Now in the party of the truth.

Shining, shining, will our arms be,
Waving high will be our banners,—
The sound of our trumpets will shake the
    Proud hearts of the world's children;
  Divine power will be seen,
  Like the fiery sun,
On us now,—O, Great Babel—
  Thy fate is frightful;
Thy inhabitants have wronged us,—
Thy kings and their glory,
We now thrust into oblivion,
    After tormenting us so long.

We shall march in all directions,
Our action will be felt, be felt
In our thorough victory,
    Over kingdoms of the world;
  We shall tear every government,
  Overturn their supremacy,—
Every tyrant now will descend,
  To disgrace and utter destruction;
We shall pay our enemies twice over,
Every heathen we shall destroy,—
Now we'll tread the dust of their bones,
    Always beneath our feet.

Now, now, we shall have peace and quiet,
Over us will spread the wings of peace,
And the light of our long happiness will break,
  In brilliant splendor;
  Jesus now reigns,
  He lays down just law,
And there will be peace to bring a smile,—
  Not one more face will fade;
The earth will give her produce,
To satisfy every need,—
And we shall walk like angels,
    Fully rejoicing.

As kings and priests,
The faithful will be placed,
They will be seen as leaders,
  Of great distinction;
  Then instead of sorrows,
  We'll always have pleasures,—

> Satan now will be on the ground,
>   And we on thrones;
> We can now carry out precisely,
> All our heavenly Father's will,
> And reign eternally,
>   Who will be greater than we.

Swansea, April 10, 1856.

THE EAST GLAMORGAN CONFERENCE,

WHICH WAS HELD in Merthyr, April 20, 1856. After Elder Abednego Williams, President of the Conference, had called the morning meeting to order, he gave some very appropriate instructions to the congregation. Then he called on the following Elders to report on the areas under their care:—John Llewellyn, Merthyr; Wm. Jones, Aberdare; David Pugh, Cardiff; and T. Rees, Pontytypridd. These brethren testified that the areas are increasing in virtues: that unity, love and obedience are thriving in almost every Branch, and that the world is searching more into the principles of the Saints than has been seen for years, especially in Cardiff and environs.

Then President Israel Evans gave a comforting account of the latest emigrants, from here to Liverpool, and said that he was concerned about the disappointment the congregation had received that our esteemed President Daniels had not yet returned from Liverpool. "But," said he, "we shall have the prayers of Brother Daniels over us, and thus the Lord will be with us." He expressed his joy that so many had emigrated, and if more had gone the work would go forward even more quickly.

It was proposed that we sustain all the authorities of the church as usual, without one dissenting vote. D. Pugh was approved to be Second Counselor to President A. Williams, and Brother John Price, Rhymney, is to assist Brother Stephens in writing an account of the Conference. It was decided that President A. Williams is to be the Treasurer of the funds of the P. E. Fund and the Temple Fund, and that Elders John Reynolds, Heolyfelin, and T. Evans, Merthyr, are to be *auditors* over the various accounts of the conference. The various statistics were read to the general satisfaction.

In the afternoon President Israel Evans was invited to speak, and in a very effective manner he commented on the duty we all have to preach to the world and do so in wisdom. He made some remarks with regard to financial matters, that all are to remember to begin their task in a timely fashion so they may do all things punctually, and for them to sacrifice every feeling that is contrary to the will of God, &c.

Then Elder Thomas Harris, President of the West Glamorgan Conference, was called to address the congregation. He commented that there is a great clamor in the world now because peace has been signed between Turkey and Russia; but he wanted the soldiers of Jesus to remember that Christ and Belial have not made peace, nor will they until the devil has been bound, and all the kingdoms of the world are under the government of King Jesus, &c.

In the evening President A. Williams remarked that the work of God had begun on the earth, and that he was certain that it would go forward. He showed the necessity the Saints have to come closer and feel more of a connection between each other so they can be of use to take this work around them, &c.

Then President Benjamin Ashby was called on to address the congregation, which he did in a very lively way. He showed that the kingdom of God is the same now as it was in the former days,—that through the Priesthood, man will receive eternal life. If an angel were to come to a man on the earth in these days, he would tell him the same as did the angel to Cornelius of old, to send for or go to one of the servants of God, &c.

The Conference was concluded, and all signs were that the blessing of God rested on what was done and said. JOHN PRICE, *Scribe*.

RECEIPTS FOR BOOKS FROM MARCH 31 TO APRIL 24.—Wm. Lewis, £3 6s 6c; Llywelyn Lewis, £1 5s; Thos. Rees, 5s; Thomas Jones, 11s 6c.

☞ We wish for those who have not paid their "Promises" in the West Glamorgan Conference to do so right away.—Brother James Tuckfield, Swansea, paid his 10s.

CONTENTS.

	PG.
Millennium	129
Letter of the Editor to his Printer	135
Verse	136
Editorial—The Change—The Emigrating Saints	137
Speech of Elder Israel Evans to the Welsh Saints	138
Triumph of the Saints over the World	141
The East Glamorgan Conference	143

SWANSEA:

PRINTED AND PUBLISHED BY D. DANIELS.

ZION'S TRUMPET,

OR

Star of the Saints.

No. 10.] MAY 10, 1856. [Vol. IX.

SPEECH OF PRESIDENT BRIGHAM YOUNG TO THE TERRITORIAL SENATE OF UTAH,

Held in Fillmore City, Millard County, December 11, 1855.

[Continued from page 113.]

The northern line of Utah has also been established, during the present season, by Professors Orson Pratt and Albert Carrington, and the Territorial Surveyor General, Jesse W. Fox, where it crosses the Malade, and by Prof. Pratt and Surveyor General Fox, where it crosses the Green river and the emigrant road east of the last named stream. There was no accompanying party from Oregon in either of the above cases, as the information was mainly desirable for determining the jurisdiction of this Territory at points where Oregon had no settlements within hundreds of miles.

[Then he gives an account of the revenue and the way it was used for public improvements, which was an encouragement to the public not to be delinquent in paying their taxes, since it was for the public the improvements were made.]

It has been proposed to open new channels of communication with us from the east through the tributaries of the Missouri, and from the south by way of the Colorado. Doubtless boats built expressly for the purpose will be able to approach our settlements many hundred miles nearer than at present. Should it be in your power by chartering

10 [Price 1*c*.

companies or rendering other encouragement to further any such enterprise, you will meet with my most hearty cooperation; I certainly deem it a subject worthy of your consideration. Schools for teaching children have flourished hitherto with but little aid or encouragement from the Senate. Should not the Legislature take this subject under advisement, adopting some well organized system which will provide at least a common education for every child, rich or poor, bond or free, in the Territory, and which will establish and keep in operation at least one school where the higher branches are taught?

I am aware that much has already been done and great good effected by private enterprise throughout the settlements generally. Though I am quite certain that no Territory so young as this can boast of so many or so good schoolhouses and schools, still there is a lack; much remains to be done. The Legislature has appropriated comparatively nothing for this object, and the appropriations of land by the general government are completely worthless for this.

None are so much interested in this matter as ourselves; it would therefore seem to be almost imperative upon our Legislature to extend its aid for the promotion of learning. And now, while we have peace and quietness in all our borders, is an opportune time to lay a foundation for the instruction of our children, which shall grow with our growth and strengthen with our strength, and extend its influence around the children of the poorest and humblest citizen, as well as the more opulent and wealthy.

Peace, quiet, gentle peace and a due degree of prosperity have thus far crowned our efforts.

The Indians, notwithstanding an occasional outbreak, are generally peaceful and friendly disposed.

On the 23rd day of September last, three of our people were killed by the Yampah Utahs near Elk mountain, at the settlement on the left bank of Grand River. A party of the Shoshones also exhibited signs of hostility at Forts Bridger and Supply, in Green River County.

Upon learning these facts, I issued a proclamation to the Nauvoo Legion, the *militia* of the Territory, to hold themselves in readiness and to send out such force as might be considered necessary to preserve peace, and to protect the settlements and the emigrants upon the roads.

A party, under the command of Major R. T. Burton, proceeded to the forts above named and remained in the vicinity until the immigrating companies had all passed and the Indians had left for their usual hunt among the buffalo. We call on the military more to preserve peace with the native tribes than to fight them, as it is well known that when a substantial force is in their immediate neighborhood, not infrequently their presence causes the Indians to check their depredations and seek for peace.

[He proceeds to show how much better it is to feed the Indians, to win them over through fairness, and to raise them into civilized circles, than to sink to their base condition—to wage war and spill blood, and that good consequences have proven the fact. He takes note also of the increase of the fortifications built through much of the assistance from the law that was passed in the previous session of the Territorial Legislature. He refers also to the praiseworthy effort of the people in the home manufacture of goods, and to their growth in doing that, and to the growth of the iron works. While the nations of the earth are warring and pulling down, he says that Zion is peaceful and industrious, and that it will flourish more than ever while Babel falls.]

COMMEMORATIVE CERTIFICATE,

Which was presented to Elder Dan Jones, President over the Welsh Mission of the Church of Jesus Christ of Latter-day Saints.

BY THE PRESIDENTS OF THE CONFERENCES.

DEAR BROTHER,—Since you are about to leave us on your return once again to the bosom of the Church, and to your dear family in Zion, the fullness of our own feelings, and of those over whom we preside, compel us to present to you this certificate, despite how inadequate it is, to demonstrate the genuine respect that we have for you,—our great appreciation for the bounteous and priceless blessings we have received through your ministry, and the infinite trust we have in you as a servant of the Most High God.

The goodness of God to us by calling you when in distant lands by a revelation through our revered Prophet Joseph Smith, and by sending you back to us with the light of the eternal Gospel to comfort our hearts, when we were wallowing in moral darkness, will light in us the flame of love and gratitude due to Him, while the hidden embers of his Holy Spirit burn in our bosoms.

While the memory persists of your having offered your life in Carthage Jail to save those most dear to us, and that in the midst of the heartbreaking scenes surrounding the broken bodies of the best men in Nauvoo, you did not deviate from the path of responsibility, but, unflinching like a magnet to its pole, at the cost of all worldly gain, you continued on your path across Continent and sea, and in 1844 you arrived with your valuable treasure among your compatriots,—in the land of your birth; your incomparable efforts to set up the banners of the Gospel of Peace on the hills of Gwalia; the steadfastness of the righteous purpose of your soul, and your triumph of winning nearly *four thousand* Britons to enlist under its banners during the brief span of five years, despite all the opposing energy of the Press, the Pulpit, and all the combined weapons of the adversary, are deeds that will make your remembrance forever dear, and augment your fame, and cause every lover of the truth to imitate your efforts to win eternal lives.

The clear and powerful arguments demonstrated in the nearly half million treatises, &c., which you sent through the Principality as emissaries of light, have won the trust and obedience to their injunctions of thousands from among every part, and have etched the name of their author on the tables of their hearts, there to remain so long as the inexhaustible fountain of light from which they originate continues to radiate its rays on their understanding.

You had the privilege in 1849 of returning with a tithe of the souls you harvested,—with the firstfruits of the Britons to the place of refuge of the oppressed,—to the threshing-floor in Zion, having been blessed with the faith and trust of every child of God you left in the field of your labor, and the fifteen hundred souls added to the Church in a few months after your departure were an indication of the healthy and strong condition in which you left it. Over the sea and across the uncharted Continent you led the adventurers of our race triumphantly over all the customary obstacles on a journey of 8,000 miles to the valleys of the everlasting mountains, there to be enlightened by the Chief Artisans of Zion, and your love and obedience to counsel were further manifest by going on a journey of a thousand miles at your own cost through the midst of savages, snow, and the dangers of severe weather. You had nearly three years to enjoy social fellowship, and dearer fellowship with those you love even more dearly, before the Lord, in answer to the prayers of a strong people, influenced his servants to send you once again to their bosoms. Neither home with its thousand delights, nor Zion with all its fascinations, nor wealth with all its offers constituted any obstacle in your way; again, you scaled the Rocky Mountains, you hastened across the Continent and the Atlantic Ocean, and into our midst, and the general thanks given to Him who sent you were but an abject demonstration of the indescribable joy we felt at your return in 1852.

Your tireless zeal to serve God in every way possible is truly praiseworthy; your rectitude in administering justice and mercy until it frightened the doers of evil, and the great success that has crowned your administrations during the three years you have been in our midst on your second mission are clear demonstrations of divine approval. To the one who has shown such philanthropy, faithfulness, and patriotism, he must have a feeling almost beyond delight as he leaves the Church as a whole in a healthy, pure, and successful condition in every way, with not a single division in it; that two thousand have been added to it; that a thousand have emigrated in the meantime, and that five hundred and fifty more await the pleasure of associating with you as you journey toward Zion.

Dear brother, we cannot describe the love we feel toward you for the valuable counsels we received through you,—through "ZION'S TRUMPET;" through its bold predecessor, "PROPHET OF THE JUBILEE;" a *viva voce* in Conferences, Councils, &c.,—all are explained more clearly by the strength of your love in enticing us and the Saints to imitate your virtues,—your honesty, soberness and saintliness; our *future lives* will testify more effectively of the consequences of your Missions of mercy to us, for which we pray to always be such that will increase your joy, until you receive in the resurrection of the just the prize due you for the priceless good you have done for your nation.

With heartfelt humility we wish for you to receive this Certificate of that which our language fails to describe, and which every self-denial on your part has made it impossible to reward financially; may it be preserved in your family Chronicles as evidence that Brother Jones has served well his nation, his God, and his Brethren; and may your posterity be persuaded to imitate their Father, and may every Welshman who loves his race be persuaded to say—"Well done, thou good and faithful servant," for as long as the world lives in his memory.

Farewell! that you may be escorted by Angels, served by elements, obeyed by everyone and everything on your return, and that you may be welcomed by God's honorable servants; and that the last of the seed of Gomer, with you and your respected family, may achieve victory over all enemies, and even over death, to inherit eternal lives will be our continual prayer.

[Here follow the names of the Presidents.]

A SUMMARY OF THE TEACHING OF PRESIDENT F. D. RICHARDS,

In a General Conference held in Merthyr Tydfil, on the 24th of February, 1856.

AFTER making a few introductory remarks to get the participants to make themselves as comfortable as they could, and after verifying that the majority of them could understand English, and after promising he would speak clearly and in a manner easy for them to understand, he said—

We have true cause to rejoice for this lovely morning that has dawned on our Conference,—the elements are as if smiling in peace on us, and if our feelings are united and peaceful in proportion, we shall have a lovely and beneficial time indeed. The way for our feelings to be thus is for them to be governed by the same spirit that rules over and orders the mighty elements by command of the Almighty, to whom we pray for it.

I have so many things to say to the Welsh Saints that I don't know with which one I shall start, or which one will be of the greatest benefit to you who are present, but I wish for the assistance of your prayers for the Lord to inspire me with his Holy Spirit to that end.

You look to me like you would like to go to the land of America and are longing to do so. Although I am not acquainted with you personally, or with your personal matters, yet I know your general needs, without associating with each of you separately, as the father knows the needs of his family without having to call all his children to him to ask them separately. However that may be, I am certain of one thing, and that is,—that all who possess the spirit of the Gospel feel that they are strangers here, and are desirous of gathering to the land of America,—to the place which God has prepared for you to have deliverance.

As regarding this gathering, there are things that are essential for you to understand in order to be able to prepare for the journey. All who intend to go on a journey have the practice of preparing for it, or to send messengers before them to announce their coming. John the Baptist was sent to prepare the way before our Savior. Now, there are preparations for the journey to Zion that are indispensable and of importance for you to know, about which I wish to speak, especially since Conference Presidents, Traveling Elders, &c., are here, and since I wish the principles and ideas I express to be circulated.

The first thing I wish to bring to your attention is.—The importance associated with little things. Although the Gospel of salvation is vast and extensive, yet it is composed of little things. This congregation is large in comparison to one man, but it is composed of *individual* persons; and on the same principle, this large body can be disassembled as it was assembled, if you but take out the small things or the persons one by one. It is the same with the great work of the Lord and the principles of the eternal Gospel. According to the material you saw with the small things,—gathering or scattering,—you will live or you will die. "Do not despise the day of small things." The Lord said through one of his ancient prophets, "My people are destroyed for lack of knowledge." There is no need for any of you to wonder how that can be, except for you to consider that the knowledge you possess is the cause of your presence here today, and that because of your knowledge you wish to go to the land of America, so that you will not be destroyed in Babylon. How would you have the desire to go had you not first learned about it? How would you have understood it had not Brother Jones or someone else come over to teach it to you? What would be the consequences had he not come to you and taught you? You would stay here to perish from lack of knowledge. What are the consequences of the knowledge that was taught? Let the fact of the congregation's presence here today answer the question,—you see its effects and workings which have captured your heart and mind—which have taken the leadership over all your operations,—your religious, family, business, and all of your affairs.

You have been blessed with an existence in this small part of creation, and have received the preaching of the gospel which is for a witness or knowledge in your midst, and to the extent you have obeyed some of its requirements you have enjoyed true knowledge. At the same time you are surrounded by friends and relatives, with whom you have become accustomed to the traditions and customs of your country,—you are bound to them through the family and societal ties, and through your language and country. Brother Giles opened the meeting by offering a prayer in Welsh. You and he understand English; nevertheless, if asked why it was done that way, you would say that you love the language of your fathers and your country more than any other language. This is a very consistent feeling with the nature of every speaker and countryman toward his own language: thus it is with me with regard to English. You see that things like this are personal, and encompass all even though they are at odds with one another. But when we obey the Gospel, we are completely governed by it, and not by the customs of one nation any more than by the customs of the other. The Apostle Paul says to every kindred and nation that came into the primitive Gospel that they were no longer to be Jews or Greeks, bond or free, &c., for they were all one in Christ Jesus. After you come into the Church of the latter days you wish to gather to Zion where there are no Jews or Gentiles, English or Welsh, but all will be "men of Zion,"—people of the Lord, who delights in blessing them. But before you go there, you should have prepared to enter into its blessings and its privileges immediately. The majority of those with whom you associate will speak English. Now, imagine yourselves meeting one of them, and with a heart full of brotherly love you take his hand to shake it, but you cannot greet him or understand whether it is with gentle or cross words he greets you, except as far as you can judge by his look, and he cannot understand any better from you. Would you not be glad to be able to say in English,—"Brother Brigham, I am happy to have this first opportunity to see you." Would you not be happy were he to bless you, wishing for that God who has kept you, and sustained you, and protected you until then, to bless and prosper you, and when he looked at you the Spirit of the Lord would run through your whole constitution? But imagine on the other hand that you could not speak English and that you would lose such a privilege because of that.

(To be continued.)

ZION'S TRUMPET,

OR

Star of the Saints.

SATURDAY, MAY 10, 1856.

THE present emigration and preparations for the coming emigration.—No doubt the Saints in Wales have been informed of that which is in the Notice of President F. D. Richards, for April 26, if the Presidents have properly carried out their responsibility in this. To be more certain we say again that the ship "Horizon" is to sail from Liverpool for Boston on the 23rd of this month. This will be the last company that will go through to Utah this year, and if there are some who wish to go, or who have not been advised after asking, let them send knowledge of that to us before the 15th. The remainder of the emigrants to the States will be sent out within about a week after that.

There is something else we are certain of, namely, the question that some will have afterwards,—How can we go the next time, and what preparations are we to make for that? We say to those to reread the answer to the same question in number 21 of the previous volume. Dear Brethren, the Presidents, read those directions again, and pray for the strength and the fullness of their spirit—you have not yet half completed them! We have heard and we know that baptisms have begun again in a lively fashion in several places, which is proof of the effect of the "last sermon" which was mentioned before. Now is the time to prepare for the next emigration. From County to County, from neighborhood to neighborhood, and from door to door, let the Saints be seen with the testimony of God in their mouths, soberness in their faces, and tracts in their hands warning their neighbors, until they expect the dread day to come. Let us work while it is daylight, as do the servants of God in Zion. They call earnestly for the Saints to flee somehow on the way toward Zion instead of staying in Babylon. The departure of nearly seven hundred of just the Welsh Saints this year in obedience to the call, with over one hundred of those poor and completely destitute, is proof that the storm is nigh. Oh! you say, Who were those who got the privilege, and how did they manage to go? We answer that some went from the south through Cardiganshire to Anglesey, and various counties of Wales, making the necessary preparations to which we have referred. Others have with all their might taken on the task of clearing the debts of their branches and their conferences. Others, although destitute widows, have fought the world for years, keeping a roof over the heads of the servants of God to keep them from inclemency of the weather and the merciless world, and providing something for them to eat to keep them from going hungry, and others have been so diligent in looking after the Priesthood that they could say, "Practically all that we could do, we have done."

The last word we heard from President Richards in Liverpool when accompanying the last shipload was, "This year's emigration is nothing in comparison to what it will be. It has annual increases ahead for as long as it lasts, and it will not stop until Israel is gathered out of these countries. Increase is what it has done from the beginning, and increase is what it will continue to do. To the extent that the rest of the Welsh Saints are faithful this year they will see many more than this of their poor who will get to go next time."

Summer is at the door, and we have been ready for a long time to receive the names of volunteers to fill the places of those who have gone happily to Zion, who have won eternal distinction in the army of Jesus. Who will go? Places are available to work or to travel as the need arises.

We see from the *list* of debts that £326 10s of book debt remains, despite the praiseworthy effort that was made from the end of the year forward. In light of this let us rejoice in the expectation that the old remaining Welsh giants, with the good news that is now stirring, double their diligence until this small amount amongst other things disappears quickly. The task will be made easier with the decrease of five hundred in the number of TRUMPET that are distributed, which will make it impossible for us to keep going for a penny per issue without full and regular payments, as we pointed out before. Let us transfer such a thing as "book debts" to oblivion from now on.

With the other things that are afoot, we see that there is plenty to do for yet a while, which will require diligence, generosity, and the unwavering determination of the Saints, and which will give us proof of the worthiness of the current Presidents.

The sooner the better that all begin on the proper and nearest way to Zion.

FEAST.—The First Presidency in Zion held a feast for the returning missionaries with their wives in the Social Hall, G. S. L. City, November 29, 1855. President J. M. Grant and five of the Apostles were present. The table was overladen with the best delicacies of Zion. They had a delightful and happy afternoon and evening of dancing, speaking, and singing, until the break of dawn. The women of Zion, who had to be content for several years before that without their dear husbands, while they were preaching the gospel of salvation and determining the fate of the nations of the earth,—never before had they seemed fairer, happier or livelier. Fatigue did not seem to affect anyone. Let the reader imagine the feelings of our experienced brethren, after being faithful in trials and tribulations on land and on sea, and then returning pure and spotless from the evils of Babel and being welcomed to Zion by Prophets and Apostles, and of hearing the splendid phrase,—"Well done, thou good and faithful servants, &c."

COMMEMORATIVE CERTIFICATE.—Upon receipt of advance payment of one shilling, we will send to the applicant a splendid copy in English of the "Commemorative Certificate," which was presented to our worthy and late President Dan Jones, made on blue silk in golden letters. We shall attend to the Presidents of Conferences first. Many will no doubt be disappointed since we have but 80 of them. Do not send for them without advance payment since they are not associated with the books of the Office. Send for them through the Conference Distributors.

LETTER OF RECONCILIATION TO PRESIDENT DANIEL DANIELS.

Swansea. May 3, 1856.

ESTEEMED PRESIDENT DANIELS,—As you know, there was a loving and reconciling conversation that took place between me and President Jones a little before his departure, where you, President Thomas Harris, and others were present; for such an opportunity I greatly rejoice.

I wish to remind you again through this letter, that I feel kindly from the bottom of my heart toward President Dan Jones. And allow me to say, there is neither peace nor ease for my spirit night or day outside the Church of Jesus Christ because I *know* that only within that Church am I able to work out my salvation.

With sincere repentance I acknowledge my many failings, and my awful offences of saying or doing the least thing in detriment of President Jones, and for that matter against you also, as authorities of the Church in Wales. Therefore, as you know, I requested clemency and forgiveness, which favor I have enjoyed.

Freely I can say that I was outside the Church in accordance with justice; and that President Dan Jones has behaved toward me in all his dealings with me in as just a manner as he could.

I have a free spirit and a pure heart towards all Saints in the West Glamorgan Conference, and all others, and I trust I shall find them, from now on, kind, loving, and forgiving, and that I shall have a larger share than ever of their frequent prayers on my behalf.

My heart is full of a desire to benefit all men in all places. I have confidence that God, the perceiver of my heart from the beginning, will bless me so that He will count me worthy of receiving all things, and all circumstances to work together for my good, which is what I love; and so that I shall learn perfectly to respect and appreciate all the advice of his servants, and to be thoroughly obedient to the eternal Priesthood in *all* that it asks of me.

With a sincere desire to be faithful in Christ's vineyard, and to build up His kingdom, and bring about much righteousness, so that I and my family, and my kindred, may be delivered quickly out of Babylon to the land of "Zion,"

  I remain,
    Genuinely yours,
      In the name of Jesus Christ,
        Dewi Elfed Jones.

P. S.—Before concluding allow me to sing a little of my troubles away, as follows:—

HYMN OF TRIBULATION.

 Building up the Church,
  Is the instinct of my heart;
 My spirit rests in it,—
  Longing caused my cheeks to flood;

Night and day my prayers,
    Go to my Father in Heaven;
He hears my groans,—
    I can enjoy His gifts.

Being deprived of blessings,—
    The huge privileges of today's children,
Weaken and soothe the heart,
    And overpower the free spirit:
Doors closed on life's paths!
    A severe dam against the light!
A cold cascade on fiery love!
    Grief where I once gave praise!

Like the wave battered by a hurricane,
    On the wild turmoil of the watery depths,
Was the dreadful calamity of my troubles,—
    My words fail to describe it.
Oh! my God. Thou alone,
    Knowest the nature of my heart;
In the hazy mist and fog,
    Thou hast been my strength.

Like a child crying yonder,
    For a second look at his father's house,
Groaning in my tribulation,
    With not an hour of solace,—
A thousand and more memories,
    Thronged in my mind,
With thoughts of *home* in my breast—
    Hard not to lose heart.

I never thought when starting,
    That this would be my part,—
In the deep I do not murmur—
    God still raises me to the shore:
This for me is a new test,
    To purify me on my journey,
To a more glorious splendor,—
    Again my eyes will be wiped of tears.

A strong hope anchored,
    In the capacity of God's bosom,
Was to hold me through all hardship,
    I experienced this—how strange it is;
This is what brought a song to my lips,
    For all the force of my great affliction,
Yes,—in the midst of oppression,
    I rejoiced many a time.

Through the confusion of my troubles,
    I bore witness to the best of my ability,
About the *truth of the principles*
    Of the pure gospel—of great worth;
Steadfast like the rock,
    I withstood the swell of the world's deceit,—
An order to save man from damnation,
    Was my great preoccupation.

This took root so deep in my heart,—
    It spread throughout my soul,—
It vanquished, despite all tribulations,
    The customs of the ways of the damned;
Violence and enticements failed,
    To take this from my living spirit;
The world and its temptations failed,
    To kill my love for my God.

                                        Dewi Elfed Jones.

TO PRESIDENT DANIELS.

Swansea, May 8, 1856.

Venerable President,—Since I know, to a greater extent than others, perhaps, concerning the case of Mr. Dewi Elfed Jones, and also because I came out against him when I saw him unworthy, I consider it my duty to him, and to the Saints in general, for me to make known my feelings in light of his return to the Church. After speaking to my satisfaction in private with Dewi Elfed Jones, and also after seeing him weighed carefully in the scales of the Presidency of the Church in Europe, and by the Presidency of the Church in Wales, I testify with a free spirit and forgiving heart, that I am completely satisfied at the humility and repentance of Dewi Elfed Jones; and I say to him that my soul is wide open to again receive him as a dear friend. May the Lord, who helped him to be so courageous and brave as to fight on behalf of the true principles when he first came to the church, now enable him once more to be faithful and useful on her behalf now and forever more.

    That is the true wish of,

            Thomas Harris,
      President of the West Glamorgan Conference.

RESPONSE OF PRESIDENT DANIELS.

With great pleasure and delight I can reveal publicly my warm acceptance of the letter of Dewi Elfed Jones. The good feelings, the full spirit, the humbling trial, together with the sincere repentance that are manifest in him provide not slight satisfaction to me. It always causes me joy of heart to witness worthiness for forgiveness and trust, and I can say on solid ground that I witness such worthiness fully in Dewi Elfed Jones.

That which President T. Harris said about him is true: Dewi agreed willingly with all things that were required of him; he has emerged from this like a man, and has proved to me and to all present that his chief purpose and his first delight is the building of God's kingdom. It is also right to declare my understanding that he continued to maintain and defend with vigor the principles of this religion the whole time he was on the outside; and a time is coming when he shall feel that this will be of greater benefit to him than his heart ever imagined. He has taught himself a lesson of experience of greater value than ever gold or silver could buy, and I wish for it to be a blessing to him forever. May the Lord give to him his Holy Spirit in great abundance, and strengthen him to overcome every evil, as he does his part to build the kingdom of God, and bring down the kingdom of darkness. I recommend him from my heart to the attention, goodwill and trust of the Saints, and pray for him while burying all that was, without further mention of it, so that we may be of one heart in supplicating in his behalf, that he shall have the strength to redouble his diligence until the gap caused during the time we have lost is fully made up.

Daniel Daniels,
President of the Church in Wales.

CONTENTS.

	PG.
Speech of President B. Young to the Territorial Senate of Utah	145
Commemorative Certificate	147
Summary of the teaching of President F. D. Richards	150
Editorial—The Emigration—Feast—Commemorative Certificate	153
Letter of Reconciliation &c.	156

SWANSEA:
PRINTED AND PUBLISHED BY D. DANIELS.

ZION'S TRUMPET,

OR

Star of the Saints.

No. 11.] MAY 24, 1856. [Vol. IX.

THE MILLENNIUM.

BY THOMAS HARRIS, FORMERLY OF GEORGETOWN.
[Continued from page 135.]

HAVING shown a little about the nature of the Millennium, we shall now go further to search for the signs of the times, in order to understand when that glorious period will come. And for that purpose we shall compare the present condition of the world with the future happenings according to the *prophecies* and their *fulfillment*. In this way Jesus said we could recognize when his coming would be nigh, even at the door.

Some of the early Saints in the apostolic age expected that this period would dawn in their own time; at least, Paul feared that some would deceive the Thessalonians, and lest that happen he wrote to them, saying, "Let no man deceive you by any means, for that day *shall not come*, except there come a *falling away* first." It was vain for them in that age to expect the Millennium or the Second coming of the Son of Man until the Gospel had *left* the earth. What, was the gospel to be taken from the earth after Christ had established it before He could come in his Second coming? Yes; and the need here is to quote some of the prophecies that prove that before going any further, so that the honest reader will have the opportunity to perceive that their fulfillment has *already*

[PRICE 1*c*.

taken place.

When the disciples of Christ asked what signs there would be of his coming, &c., he said, among other things, that they would be delivered up to be afflicted, and in the end they would be killed. Then since they were the vessels which contained the treasure, the power or the authority of preaching and administering the ordinances of the gospel, it was necessary, after they had been killed, for this power or authority to return to the heavenly Court from which it came.

Some of the prophecies which prove that the gospel would be taken from the earth before the second coming of the Son of Man are as follows:—"For I know this, that after my departing shall grievous wolves enter in among you, not sparing the flock; also of your own selves shall men arise, speaking perverse things, to draw away disciples after them"—Acts xx, 30. "Now the Spirit speaketh expressly, that in the latter times some shall depart from the faith, giving heed to seducing spirits, and doctrines of devils; speaking lies in hypocrisy," &c.—1 Tim. iv, 1, 2, 3. These are prophecies whose fulfillment is to take place long before the Second Coming of Christ or the Millennium. The unbiased reader will see that the fulfillment of them has already taken place. The primitive Saints had faith to listen to "every word that *proceedeth* out of the mouth of God"; but men have left that faith now, being satisfied with some words, or selected parts that *proceeded* out of the mouth of God earlier instead of that. The primitive Saints had faith to receive "these signs that follow them that believe, namely casting out devils, &c."; but men have *left* that faith now, shouting, "they are not needed." The primitive Church had faith to receive the laying on of hands to receive the Holy Ghost, after being baptized for the remission of sins, but men have *left* that faith now, and they say without any foundation, that such practices have ceased, and they, like their fathers, are "always resisting the Holy Ghost." The primitive Saints had faith to receive the gospel, not in word only, but in power and in much assurance in the Holy Ghost, but they have left that faith now, embracing "other gospels" which are in word only in its place. The primitive children of God had faith to receive the gifts of healing, working miracles, prophecy, discerning spirits, divers kinds of tongues, and the interpretation of tongues; men have *left* that faith also now, mocking and scorning those who profess to enjoy them. The primitive had faith to seek wisdom from God, but men have *left* that faith now, searching for wisdom in the colleges, &c. When the children of God were sick in the primitive days, they had faith to call the elders of the church to them, for such to anoint them with oil in the name of the Lord, believing that the prayer of faith would heal the sick, according to God's promise; but men have *left* that faith also, calling to them doctors instead. I believe that is sufficient to prove that the previous prophecy has been fulfilled, namely that men have left that faith which was once given to the Saints, and are giving "heed to seducing spirits, and doctrines of devils," because they do that by giving heed to any doctrine that is contrary to the word of God. Perhaps the reader is ready to ask—Is *that faith* necessary at the present time? I answer that it is necessary, for "without faith it is impossible to please God," says the apostle. And in another place he says—"Remember them which have the rule over you [the apostles], who have spoken unto you the word of God, whose *faith* follow," &c.

Another prophecy we shall quote here is,—"This know also, that in the last days perilous times shall come, for men shall be lovers of their own selves, covetous, boasters, proud, blasphemers, disobedient to parents, unthankful, unholy, without natural affection, trucebreakers, false accusers, incontinent, fierce, despisers of those that are good, traitors, heady, highminded, lovers of pleasures more than lovers of God; having a form of godliness, but denying the power thereof"—2 Tim. iii, 1–5. There is no inquiring reader who will doubt that this prophecy has been fulfilled to a great extent, so that there is no need to go into detail about each item contained in it. When many are stirred up to affiliate themselves with a religion, they search for the numerous congregation, and the beautiful chapels or synagogues, without looking for the correct principles or the consistency with the word of God, but being content with their religion if the walls of the synagogue have been beautifully adorned, and the due respect given to the gold ring, and that because they are *proud*. The hired leaders of the people are so covetous that they leave one denomination for the other if they understand that they can receive a higher wage, despite "breaking their truces" by so doing, thereby fulfilling the prophecy by being *covetous*. Let the reader understand that the apostle does not refer to those who are non-believers, but to those who "have a *form* of godliness," or some kind of religion of the work of men, "denying the *power* of godliness," namely the gifts of the Holy Ghost, or the power of God, "heaping to themselves teachers." The apostle also prophesied that they would be "ever learning, and never able to come to the knowledge of the truth." Thus it is in our days: I am acquainted with preachers and priests who have spent their entire lives learning, and yet they have not come to a knowledge of the truth, which is a literal fulfillment of Paul's prophecy.

After Jesus had set up his kingdom in the former days, the Saints had to "walk according to this rule," or to "observe all things whatsoever he had commanded them," but Jude said, when he was repeating the prophecy of Enoch about the Lord coming with ten thousands of his saints, that there should be "mockers in the last time, who should walk after their own ungodly lusts." All the different religious sects refuse to walk according to the plan and the apostolic teachings, thus fulfilling the prophecy of Jude by walking according to their own innate desires, *having not the Spirit*." All the religious denominations have "separated themselves," and they deny that they do not have the Spirit, or that it is lacking.

Having proved that the apostles would be killed, that grievous wolves would enter into the church, that the people would turn away their ears from the truth, and turn unto fables, and that the gospel would be taken from the world because the earth was not worthy of it, that all prophecies would be literally fulfilled, as they were spoken, we see that Paul has told the truth, namely that neither the Millennium nor the Second coming of the Son of Man would take place except there come a *falling away* first.

Next, to the signs of his coming; and I trust that the reader will read without bias, lest that day come when he is in his unbelief, and be punished for that as were the antediluvians of old, for "as it was in the days of Noah and in the days of Lot, so shall it be also in the days of the Son of Man."

(To be continued.)

WEST GLAMORGAN CONFERENCE.

THE above conference was held in the Saints' Hall, Swansea, on the 11th of this month. At half past ten the morning meeting was called to order, and it was begun with singing, and Elder D. Davies, Llanelli, prayed. Then the numerous congregation was addressed by President Thomas Harris something like the following:—Brothers and Sisters,—With joy I can report that I have pleasant feelings this morning, in light of how all things have agreed to be favorable to our Conference,—the summer-like weather,—a large gathering of Saints and Officers have assembled,—several Conference Presidents, together with the Spirit of a gracious God warming every heart, and cheering every face even at the beginning of our Conference, &c., &c.

Then he called on the following Presidents to report the condition of the various districts of the Conference.—

Elder John Jones, St. Brides,—Penybont District,—The Saints and Officers are in good condition. They possess godly zeal for the cause of God, which motivates them to the determination of willingly doing all that is asked at their hands by the servants of God. We preach out-of-doors almost everywhere in our area, and there are signs that our labors will be blessed with success.

Elder Rees Jones, Cwmafon,—Aberafon District,—I understand that there is unity and love among the Officers and the Saints in every Branch of the District; the experience we have had in the past is now effective power in our midst to stand against evil and enjoy our activity in goodness. With joy I can assure you today that there are satisfactory signs of growth in our midst in every sense.

Elder John Evans, Treboeth,—Swansea District,—The Saints in general feel good in this District,—many have emigrated, and several have been baptized in their place, and some of these have been called to the Priesthood, which is proof that the work is increasing. They are lively and going forward in the Morriston Branch under the leadership of Elder Hopkin Jones; there was a public baptism for one of the leaders of the Wesleyans last Sunday.

David Davies, President of the Welsh Branch in Swansea,—I can cotestify with Brother Evans about the condition of this District. Six were baptized in this Branch lately, and the officers are seen frequently and enthusiastically preaching in nearly every corner.

Elder Wm. Lewis, Alltwen,—Alltwen District,—There is a pleasant feeling in our midst as Saints, with a few exceptions, as can be expected among so many. Not as much attention as we would like has been given to preaching; therefore, we have taken books from house to house, and have had excellent success in that way.

President T. Harris,—I am highly satisfied with the current condition of the Conference. Not many of the "wise" have been called, still God has prospered the work remarkably in the hands of weak instruments; let none of us be discouraged because of our weakness, but let us take strength in our God, so that we may be stalwarts in Israel, for the work we have is great, yes, greater than anything that has ever been on the earth since the Creation until now, and it will succeed. If the world knew the thousandth part of its greatness, they would come, with the greatest willingness, with their valuable treasures to assist it, &c., &c.

The authorities of the Church were presented to the attention of the Conference, and all of them were received with the warmest approval, without one exception! President Harris remarked that the UNITY of the Saints is a wonder to the world, &c.

President Thomas Harris was approved to continue in the Presidency of the Conference, and it was voted that Elder John Davies, formerly of Meirion, be his Counselor.

President Israel Evans,—We should consider, when approving the Presidencies of the Church, that carrying out their counsels will make us worthy, and not just raising our hand; and if you disregard any Officer in the Church, by so doing, you disregard the one who sent him.

Elder Wm. Lewis was released from being the Distributor and Scribe of the Conference, and Elder John Davies was appointed in his place. Then the various statistics were read to the satisfaction of everyone.

After understanding from the reading of the Report that 20 were baptized during the quarter and after receiving strong exhortations from President Harris to be kind to strangers, the meeting was dismissed under the blessing of President Daniels.

At two o'clock, after singing, Elder Abednego Williams, Merthyr, prayed. Then President T. Harris announced that the greater part of the meeting would be spent preaching in English (since a great many gentlemen there had come to the meeting to listen), and he encouraged the Welsh to be patient.

President B. Ashby,—The world looks at the Saints as some who believe some strange or even anti-biblical things, but not because the Bible says the one thing and the Saints preach the other, but because they were sent by God. Yet this is what we can say about the various denominations,—It is not possible for their several doctrines and the Bible to be true, for they contradict one another. But we know that the Bible contains principles which must be followed before salvation can be obtained. Just having historical faith in Jesus Christ will not be sufficient, rather one must have firm belief in his words now before eternal life can be obtained.

He weighed the principles of the Saints, and those of some of the sectarian world, in the scales of the scriptures, and those of the sects were found wanting by more than four ounces per pound. Then he went forward by preaching the principles that begin a man in Christ, very effectively, and he concluded by bearing a strong testimony of the truth.

President Israel Evans,—The foregoing observations by my brother are true, if the Bible is true. If any sect had more or better principles than we, we would go to them to learn with the greatest pleasure.—It is judged that our principles are new or strange, but that is not the case, for what we believe is none other than that which was believed and practiced by the primitive Saints of God. We do not consider the Bible to be sufficient guidance, and in regard to belief we do not differ from our contemporaries in general, except that we believe that "revelation" from God is also needed, while they believe that the "*Common Prayer*," "Profession of Faith," and "Commentaries" are what is needed.—Who has seen time changing truth into lies? No one. How can our principles be erroneous now while they were true in days of old?

Then he referred to different scriptural promises, asking—Who has the substance pertaining to those promises now? . . . . .

President Daniels.—Important truths have been put before the congregation today, and our duty as Saints is to be diligent always in seeking to get our fellow men into the Church of God, by distributing tracts, preaching, or speaking in private; for the world will not be saved by looking at it, but it is necessary to make genuine efforts. All who do not preach in accordance with the Bible are not of God, and we know that no one in the world but the Saints are preaching in accordance with the Bible. Therefore, all who recognize that the Church of God is to save the world must be engaged in tireless efforts. I trust that all who are present have received sufficient exhortations in this Conference to stimulate them to be more diligent and relentless in their duties, for it is a short work the Lord will make on the earth. Therefore, may our works be found worthy of God's approval so that we may be delivered promptly from Babylon.

I can testify that Joseph Smith is a Prophet of God, and that it is a good people, under the protection of heaven, which lives in Utah.

It was then approved that the Presidents who preside over the Branches continue thus in the three coming months.

A mission was given to William Richards, Cwmbwrla, to go out to preach and make sure that the inhabitants of the Browyr area receive an offer of the Gospel of Christ in the fullness of its blessings. May the Lord prosper him to bring many to embrace the truth soon.

Also Jenkin Davies, Abercenffig, was called to go to Trefnewydd, near Penybont, to proclaim the good news, and bring the honest in heart to the Church of God. May the blessing of heaven be on his labor.

Elders Emrys Davies, Aberafon, and John Jones, St. Brides, were approved to be auditors over the various accounts of the Conference.

After starting the evening meeting in the usual manner, Wm. Jones, President of the Carmarthen Conference, was called on to speak; he remarked that the people of old practiced religion conscientiously and at the same time shed the blood of the Saints. He bore witness of the divinity of this work, explaining the principles of the gospel.

Abednego Williams, President of the Merthyr Conference, said,—You can understand Mormonism here better than in any other chapel in town. We believe the Bible completely, and despite that others say that we do not. Then he compared the plans of the world with the plan of the Son of God, and proved clearly that they are opposed to one another, &c., &c.

David Davies, President of the Llanelli Conference, showed the excellence of the Gospel of Christ over the gospels of the world. He said that the people complain that we preach the same thing, but, he asked,—In the name of reason, what shall we preach? if we were to say something other than what Paul said, "anathema maranatha" would pour its contents out upon us, &c., &c.

Then President Ashby presented some excellent teachings which showed that by doing good to his neighbor, man will gain happiness in his bosom, &c., &c.

President T. Harris thanked the congregation for their attentiveness in listening throughout the day, encouraging them in soberness to be obedient. The meeting was concluded with prayer by

JOHN DAVIES, *Scribe.*

ZION'S TRUMPET,

OR

Star of the Saints.

SATURDAY, MAY 24, 1856.

THE work of the latter days is great, and the workers are few; there are towns and villages, and many entire parishes in Wales without one of the servants of God to offer the gospel of peace to the people. God has called,—Who will go? and many have answered this year,—Here am I, send me! and because of that we have great reason to rejoice, for many of the deficiencies have been made up by our brethren,—but, there is still room. There are many who stand up to preach Mormonism, they say, but who have no connection with us, or with any other denomination either; it is sad to think that many in Wales are so far into tradition and prejudice that they believe that plan to be reasonable and orderly. They open their synagogues to enemies of the truth, and they permit such to ascend into their pulpits to blaspheme God and curse his people; and the eyes of the believers become cheerful as they listen to the lying stories of such, when they refuse to lend their ears to listen to the truth. All this is a loud call for soldiers of Jesus to come to the field in the strength of their God, and then they will make power—through their faith and their bravery, they will disperse the black mist until the honest in heart see the clarity of the gospel of our Lord—they will embrace it, and they will obey it, and they will obtain a testimony of its divinity, and then the foolishness of its blasphemers will become clear to all of them. Now, dear brethren, is the time to strive.

NOTICE OF THE BRITISH PRESIDENCY.—"In view of our approaching return to Utah, and the transfer of the business of our presidency, we call attention to the following Notice—

It is requested that the Presidents of Missions, and the Pastors and Presidents in the British Mission, will forward to us, prior to the 30th of June, all tithing collected, and the donations to the P. E. Fund, and Temple Offerings, for the quarter ending June 30, from the Saints under their respective jurisdictions.

Also that the Pastors and Presidents in the British Mission will see that General Book Agents forward to us all the funds possible to the credit of their respective Conferences prior to the same time.

All persons who have money on deposit at this Office are requested to communicate with us, stating the amount.

It is desirable that all individual obligations, whether for goods, cash, or postage, should be cancelled previous to the 30th of June, that we may not be under the unpleasant necessity of transferring such items to our successor for collection.

It is particularly requested, that all the remittances above contemplated, reach us before or not later than the 30th of June, as our accounts will be closed on that day.

F. D. RICHARDS."

We wish for the Welsh treasurers to send the above things to arrive here by the 27th at the latest.

THE ship "Thornton," Captain Collins, sailed on the 4th of this month toward New York, with 764 souls on board, of which there were 163 from the Scandinavian Mission.

NEW DESERET ALPHABET.—We understand through a letter from President Brigham Young dated December 24, 1855, that a number of books will be printed at the Liverpool Office in the New *Alphabet*, in which there is a letter to correspond to every sound, and no two letters of the same sound, and the new way of spelling will be taught throughout all the schools of the Territory; then one will be able to spell correctly according the sound of the letters, which will give a great advantage to the children, and also to speakers of other languages to read the English language easily. This is a strong encouragement to the Welsh to devote themselves to learning English.

CONFERENCES.—"The Brecon Conference was held on the 27th of April. The church part of the work of the day was done in unity and success, and I understood that they had carried it forward with their meetings and with their efforts in the past quarter.

In the evening the room was full of cheerful listeners. Those who spoke during the day were Elder J. Thomas, Conference President, Elders Evan Rees and Thomas Parry from Blaenau, together with your

Humble brother,

ISRAEL EVANS."

MONMOUTH.—We say the same concerning the Monmouthshire Conference in Tredegar the following Sunday, where we had the privilege of being present and seeing the same determination to consecrate themselves, their time, and their means to the work of the Lord to the extent required of them, for which He who owns the work will supply them with the ability and means to do so.

THE INDIAN WAR.

A LETTER from Joel Palmer, Superintendent of Indian Affairs in Oregon, says the following:—

"The present difficulty in Southern Oregon is wholly attributable to the acts of the whites," adding, "I cannot but feel it is our duty to adopt such measures as will tend to secure the lives of these Indians, and maintain the guarantees secured by treaty stipulations. The future will prove that this war has been forced upon these Indians against their will, and that too by a set of reckless vagabonds, for pecuniary and political objects, sanctioned by a numerous population who regard the Treasury of the United States as a legitimate object of plunder. The Indians in that district have been driven to desperation by acts of cruelty against their people. Treaties have been violated, and acts of barbarity committed by those claiming to be citizens, that would disgrace the most barbarous nations of the earth."

This is confirmed by a letter of Major General John E. Wool, who says that some people and soldiers have decided to drive the Indians out of the land, and two newspapers are advocating the same. That was begun without discriminating between enemies and friends, women or children, as long as they are red or Indians! They have stolen their animals, they have made all Indians a target for their arrows, to the point that the friendly Indians have become indignant, and have joined with the others in self-defense, and additional soldiers from the United States are being requested to withstand all these warring tribes. Through it all, one of the Indian chiefs, under a flag of truce, declared that he was for peace, stating that neither he nor his people wished to fight, but were forced to against their will, and if any of his young men had done wrong, he would make restitution: and he offered animals as food for the volunteer soldiers, who took advantage of his defenseless condition, and they killed him. They scalped him, cut off his ears and hands, and sent them to their friends in Oregon!

Time will tell what the Indians will do; they have begun to retaliate. The behavior is the same toward them in California, where there is another Indian war also. The account is found in the "New York Herald" for April 2 as follows:—

"On the morning of the 23rd of February, some of the Indians suddenly attacked the farms on the bank of the Rogue river, where ten or twelve of Captain Poland's soldiers were encamped, while the remainder were absent attending a ball four miles down river. It is said that the fight lasted nearly the whole of Saturday, and only a few of the white people escaped to give the account. All of the farmers were killed, and there was a terrible and general slaughter of women and children."

Let the Saints be thankful that such is not the case in the peaceful Territory of Utah, though it lies in the middle between the two places, ... Travelers are amazed at such influence the Mormons have over the Indians, so that only peace reigns between them. The Saints have clothed them and fed them, washed them and groomed them, teaching them skills, and in that way they have become peaceful and content.

"HYMN OF TRIBULATION."—*THE SECOND PART.*

ESTEEMED EDITOR,—As I had the time and opportunity the other day to sing away my "tribulation," please allow me again, this time, to sing Welcome Rejoicing, in the Church of Jesus Christ of Latter-day Saints, and here it is:—

"The pure breeze sings
Between the trees and the pleasant woods."

THE night recedes!—it had formed a mantle,
   Sadness and oppression for me,
See the fog is clearing!
   The storm flies away quickly;

Having reached the intended goal,
    Freedom came to my part;—
Thou my God, art guiding everything,
    For my welfare everywhere!

Our Lord's ways are above understanding!
    Above every order is, Heaven's Order!
"The one thing for another,"
    Is the order of His dispensation!
Without the bitter, what is the sweet?
    Without the night, what is day?
Without the enmity of a confining world,
    What is the peace of free privileges?

Let pain be given for pleasure,
    Let evil be given for goodness,
Leaving evil completely, restores
    Man to the bliss he enjoys;—
This explained the strength of Justice,
    In the First transgression.—
That Compassion from the heavens,
    Smiled lovingly upon us all!

Gold and silver must, to be purified,
    Be molten in the fire,
I must have Satan's temptations
    To be purified in turn!
After degradation, there is exaltation;
    After binding, there is liberation;
After crying and weeping
    There is rejoicing to enjoy!

A storm shows the strength and growth
    Of a root, once it is spread in the ground,—
Affliction shows the value of the pleasure,
    Which now is in my heart!
"Prove all things, hold fast," nevertheless,
    "That which is good,"—and disown the false;
God himself will carry me up,—
    He causes my heart to rejoice.

How sweet to encounter a fountain's source,
    After suffering prolonged thirst!
Happy respite, *from a foreign land*
    For the weary traveler!
Like a break in the cloud,
    Where I find sunshine's brightness—
Is the little rest for the mind,
    To feast joyously on endless fruit.

The wide doors of the light of life,
    Have opened in front of me!—
The delightful healthful breezes,
    Are winged, all spread out!
There the pale dawn is fading!
    Daylight spreads all about!
There the sun with its pure light,
    Gilds the distant hills!

Melodious songs are on the branches,
    Warbling among the leaves;—
Morning praise in anthems—
    Is not surpassed by my experience!
Living praises fill my heart!
    I give thanks with a free soul!
Peace flows into me like a river,—
    I have the light of "midday"!

May my virtues sprout into life,
    Above the growth of the fertile valley;—
Unmixed truth is what I embrace—
    It stays one color,—like a blue sky!
In its presence disappear completely,
    The world's greatness and glory!—
Riches, dignity and honors,
    Retreat like "the shades of evening"!

O! my God, I rejoice,
    In thy love—which endures;
Day and night I celebrate
    Truth which sets us free!
Every situation I encounter,
    Increases its worth for me,—
Its comfort in every weather,
    Gives me greater strength.

The old *dead religions of Babel!*
    Are all insufficient,
To give life securely,
    For one short hour!
False, all false—all their influence—
    Nothing at all, just full of vanity!
Sound without substance—devoid
    Of spiritual divine gifts!

Pure Religion is now culling,
    The world's traditions very nearly!—
The nations are driven mad
    Before the day of its winnowing!

The eternal power of the Great
 Priesthood of Heaven now shatters
The strong castles of unbelief!—
 All the glory of Great Babel!

That I am one of the subjects
 Of Jesus's kingdom, gladdens my heart,
And lights my whole soul.
 In fiery zeal throughout it!
Shattering the enemy's fortresses of deceit,
 Is the energy that fills my heart.
Having God's Governance to follow,
 And live forever in its peace.

While my feet are on slavery's soil,
 I shall not rest—I shall work,
Under God's power, and his protection—
 Then shall I have salvation;
Daily I shall ask for the strength of his Spirit,
 I shall testify for him at every step,
Here is the main comfort of my life—
 Love, for him, burns like a flame!

Swansea, May 22, 1856. DEWI ELFED JONES.

BOOK DEBTS FOR THE VARIOUS CONFERENCES FOR THE QUARTER ENDING, MARCH 31, 1856.

Monmouthshire, £30 4s 8c; East Glamorgan, £50 19s 10c; West Glamorgan, £101 1s 3½c; Llanelli, £46 11s 11¼c; Carmarthen, £22 18s 5c; Pembroke, £4 7s 4c; Cardiganshire, £15 14s; Merioneth, £11 1s 1½c; Flint, £15 3s 0½c; Denbigh, £11 5s 6¼c; Conwy Valley and Anglesey, £10 3s 11c; Liverpool Branch, £3 2s 5½c; Liverpool Office, 6s 9½c; Hereford, £1 13s 6c; Brecon, £1 17s 2c; Total,—£326 11s.

RECEIPTS FOR BOOKS FROM APRIL 25 TO MAY 23.—G. Roberts, £1 9s 6c; J. Treharn, £1 10s 6c; John Davies from Wm. Lewis, £4 5s 7½c; Hugh Roberts, £1; Wm. Jones, 15s; T. Stephens from Wm. Lewis, £18 7c; T. Rees, 10s 6c; John Gibbs, 1s 1c; Thomas Jones, 5s; T. Stephens, £4.

CONTENTS.

	PG.
The Millennium	161
West Glamorgan Conference	165
Editorial—Notice of the British Presidency, &c.	169
Indian War	172
Hymn of Tribulation	173

SWANSEA:
PRINTED AND PUBLISHED BY D. DANIELS.

ZION'S TRUMPET,

OR

Star of the Saints.

No. 12.] JUNE 7, 1856. [Vol. IX.

MARRIAGE AND MORALS IN UTAH.

An address written by Elder Parley P. Pratt, read in a Session of the Utah Legislature by Mr. Thomas Bullock, chief clerk of the House, in the Representatives' Hall, Fillmore, December 31, 1855. Members of the Legislature expressed their gratitude to the author by unanimous vote, and by a similar vote they requested that the Address be published in the "Deseret News."

(From the "Deseret News.")

Mr. President and gentlemen,—At the opening of the present session of our annual Legislature, I had the honor of being unanimously chosen Chaplain of the Council.

I was then and there laid under a solemn oath to faithfully perform the duties of this high and holy calling to the best of my abilities, and was also solemnly charged by the honorable President, Mr. Kimball, not merely to be fervent in prayer during the session, but also to contribute my mite in molding the moral and social institutions of our common country.

In accordance with these sacred responsibilities placed upon me, I have, with some pains, prepared this address, which I am extremely happy in having the privilege of laying before you; not merely, or principally for your sakes; but for the sake of the people of our Territory,—our nation, and the world.

As our young and rising Territory is preparing to enter upon

12 [Price 1*c*.

her sovereignty as a free and independent republic, and to assume her place amid the family of American States, it becomes her citizens, and especially those engaged in founding her institutions, to purify themselves and to come together with pure hearts and clean hands; and clothed with light as with a garment, lay a constitutional foundation, and make or adopt such laws as will tend to purify and exalt the people—establish righteousness and peace, and multiply and perpetuate a nation of freemen in the highest degree of moral, intellectual, and physical development.

No time-serving or mere temporary policy should enter into our composition, or influence us for one moment. We act, not merely or principally for ourselves or the living age; but for untold millions of posterity, and for ages yet unborn; who doubtless will be influenced by our institutions, and mold their morals, manners, precepts, and even their consciences more or less after the pattern we set them.

A wholesome moral atmosphere, and a conscience purified and enlightened by the Spirit of Truth are indispensably necessary to a permanent national growth, and to the strength and perpetuity of institutions.

The all-wise Creator, the God of Nature, has implanted in the human heart certain affections, which, under proper culture and direction, give rise to family ties; hence the necessity and importance of the moral and social relations and the institutions for their proper direction and government.

'Tis Nature's universal law, and the just and great commandment with blessing; that each and every species should multiply and fill the measure of its creation. Hence the growth of families, the germs of nations; and hence, as we before observed, the necessity of laws founded in wisdom, to guard, as it were, the fountain and issues of life.

In short,—moral and social affections and institutions are the very foundation of all government, whether of family, Church, or State. If these are perverted, or founded in error, the whole superstructure is radically wrong, and will contain within itself the seeds of its own decay and dissolution. These facts are not only self-evident, but are according to all experience: being exemplified in the decadence and dissolution of nations and empires of old; as well as in the general weakness and corruption characteristic of men and things in more modern times.

The Prophet Isaiah, in looking through the vista of long distant years, at length beholds the vision of modern "Christendom," or of the corruptions growing out of Roman sway. He exclaims: Isa. xxiv, 5, "The earth also is defiled under the inhabitants thereof; because they have transgressed the laws, changed the ordinance, broken the everlasting covenant."

We here inquire: What laws were transgressed? What ordinance was changed? and what everlasting covenant was broken,—the effect of which would defile the very earth under its inhabitants? This leads us back, in our researches, to the earliest institutions, laws, ordinances, covenants, and precedents or record touching marriage and the moral and social relations.

If we find laws, statutes, covenants and precedents emanating from God; sworn to by himself to be everlasting; as a blessing to all nations—if we find these have to do with exceeding multiplicity of the race, and with family and national organization and increase—if such institutions are older than Moses, and are found perpetuated and unimpaired by Moses, and the prophets Jesus and the Apostles, then it will appear evident that they were intended to be perpetual: and that no merely human legislation or authority, whether proceeding from emperor, king, or people, has a right to change, alter, or pervert them.

It will then remain to be shown by whom these institutions were changed or perverted: the direful effect of such change upon the nations, and the only course left for those who would survive the crash of nations and the wreck of worlds.

Our object, gentlemen, is to urge upon the statesmen and people of at least one state or government of our earth to avoid the rock and quicksands on which so many have made shipwreck—to restore the laws, the ordinance, and the everlasting covenant of our God: that her citizens may be purified and preserved by the same, and her institutions, being founded in truth, may be perpetuated forever.

I beseech, therefore, honorable gentlemen to hear me patiently. Abraham, the friend of God, lived in Asia upwards of four hundred years before the law of Moses was written on tablets of stone, or thundered from Mount Sinai.

To this man God gave laws, commandments, statutes, and judgments in an everlasting covenant. He said unto him, Genesis 12th, v. 2nd, "And I will make of thee a great nation, and I will bless thee, and make thy name great; and thou shalt be a blessing: and I will bless them that bless thee, and curse him that curseth thee, and in thee shall all the families of the earth be blessed."

And again, Genesis 17, verses 1–8. "And when Abram was ninety years old and nine, the Lord appeared to Abram, and said unto him, I am the Almighty God, walk before me and be thou perfect, and I will make my covenant between me and thee, and I will multiply thee exceedingly. And Abram fell on his face; and God talked with him saying, As for me, behold my covenant is with thee, and thou shalt be a father of many nations. Neither shall thy name any more be called Abram; but thy name shall be Abraham; for a father of many nations have I made thee. And I will make thee exceeding fruitful, and I will make nations of thee, and kings shall come out of thee. And I will establish my covenant between me and thee, and thy seed after thee in their generations, for an everlasting covenant, to be a God unto thee, and to thy seed after thee. And I will give unto thee, and to thy seed after thee, the land wherein thou art a stranger, all the land of Canaan, for an everlasting possession; and I will be their God."

In the foregoing promises it is evident that there is an everlasting covenant, touching the multiplicity of our species, government-making, or the raising up of families and nations, and their exceeding prosperity and increase: a covenant everlasting and unchangeable in which all nations should be blessed, if they were ever blessed at all.

In connection with this covenant we have reason to believe that God would reveal laws, statutes, and institutions which would be productive of the greatest possible increase of a wise, healthy, and virtuous posterity.

In the precedents recorded of Abraham and his posterity, two principles are conspicuous as being subservient to the carrying out of these ends, namely,—

First: a plurality of wives—

Secondly: An entire prohibition of all sexual intercourse, except upon the principle of marriage: a breach of which was considered a capital offense, punishable with death. God provided Abraham with Sarah, Hagar, Keturah, and several other wives not named. By this means he became the father of many nations, and his seed was multiplied exceedingly.

God also gave to Jacob, Abraham's grandson, four wives: namely, Leah, Rachel, Bilhah, and Zilpha; by which means he became the father of twelve tribes. The history of these things is so conspicuous in the Book of Genesis that we need not quote chapter and verse.

Now after Abraham had obtained all these wives, and had raised up children by them, the Lord bears testimony, Genesis 26:5, saying:— "Abraham obeyed my voice and kept my charge, my commandments, my statutes, and my laws." Here then, we have demonstration that a man living four hundred years before the law of Moses was given, had statutes, commandments, and laws given him of God; and that he kept them.

These laws evidently included polygamy or plurality of wives, from the fact that he had them, as a means of carrying out the promise of exceeding multiplicity. Here then, the matter is set forever at rest, that polygamy is included in the ordinance of marriage, and in the everlasting covenant and laws of God: and that, under proper regulations, it is an institution holy, just, virtuous, pure, and, in the estimation of God, abundantly calculated to bless, preserve, and multiply a nation.

Hence the laws of some of our States, which recognize polygamy as a crime, are at once both unscriptural and unconstitutional, as well as immoral. Common law in England, and in the United States, recognizes the Bible as the very foundation of all moral and criminal jurisprudence: and the Constitution of the United States, and of each State guarantees the liberty of at least an enlightened conscience, founded on the moral law of God as found in that Holy Book. Hence, should an individual, or a community, in all good faith regulate their marriages by the laws of God as given to Abraham, no State law can harm them while the civil courts are bound to abide that holy and sacred guarantee of the Constitution: namely, "Liberty of Conscience."

Having demonstrated the fact of an everlasting covenant made with Abraham and his seed, including plural marriage, and certain laws designed to multiply and bless many nations, and to be a blessing to all the families of the earth, we will not inquire after the penal laws touching morality, or the intercourse of the sexes.

The first intimation we will notice of this subject is found in Genesis 20, as follows,—"And Abraham journeyed from thence towards the south country and dwelt between Kadesh and Shur, and sojourned in Gerar. And Abraham said of Sarah his wife, she is my Sister: and Abimelech king of Gerar sent, and took Sarah. But God came to Abimelech in a dream by night and said to him, Behold thou art but a dead man for the woman which thou hast taken, for she is a man's wife. But Abimelech had not come near her: and he said, Lord, wilt thou slay also a righteous nation? Said he not unto me, She is my sister? and she, even she herself, said, He is my brother: in the integrity of my heart, and the innocency of my hands have I done this. And God said unto him in a dream, Yea I know that thou didst this in the integrity of thy heart; for I also withheld thee from sinning against me: therefore suffered I thee not to touch her. Now therefore, restore the man his wife; for he is prophet, and he shall pray for thee, and thou shalt live: but if thou restore her not, know thou that thou shalt surely die, thou and all that are thine." Here we have the law of God revealed by his own mouth, about four hundred years before the law of Moses was given; making death the penalty of adultery.

This penal law then, was part and parcel of the laws, statutes, and covenants under which Abraham and his neighbors lived, and it seems to have been an ancient and general law handed down by the fathers, to which Abimelech was no stranger; he did not plead his ignorance of the law, but the innocency of his intentions, and his ignorance of the true circumstances.

Again, Genesis, chapter 34, records a case of fornication, committed by Shechem the son of Hamon, the Hivite, prince of the country, with Dinah, the daughter of Jacob, the grandson of Abraham, and how he was punished. Two of the sons of Jacob, Simeon and Levi, took their swords and slew this fornicator and all the men about him, who had been accessory to the seduction of their sister, or who had consented thereto, and they took their goods for a spoil. They may in this case have superseded the bounds of the law, but still it goes to show with what abhorrence these sons of a chaste and plural marriage held the crime of fornication.

We will now inquire whether the law of Moses, or the gospel ever changed the covenant of Abraham, or disannulled the law of marriage, or the penalty of death affixed to adultery and fornication.

For this purpose we shall trace the subject down through the different ages and dispensations, bringing a few instances out of many, illustrative of the subject.

But first of all we will take the direct testimony of the Apostle Paul, found in Galatians, 3rd chapter, and 14th through 18th verses inclusive, which read thus—"That the blessing of Abraham might come on the gentiles through Jesus Christ; that we might receive the promise of the Spirit through faith.

"Brethren, I speak after the manner of men: though it be but a man's covenant, yet if it be confirmed, no man disannulleth it, or addeth thereto. Now to Abraham and his seed were the promises made, he saith not, And to seeds, as of many; but as of one, And to thy seed, which is Christ. And this I say, that the covenant that was confirmed before of God in Christ, the law (of Moses) which was four hundred and thirty years, cannot disannul, that it should make the promise of none effect. For if the inheritance be of the law, (of Moses), it is no more of promise: but God gave it to Abraham by promise."

(To be continued.)

OPENING OF THE "SAINTS' CHAPEL," ABERAFAN.

Mr. Editor.—I am happy to let you know that we, through the blessing of God and the instrumentality of President Thomas Harris, have secured a convenient place to hold our meetings in the town of Aberafan, in a chapel that belonged lately to the Wesleyans, the owner of which is John Richards, Esq., of the Court. After the enemies of the truth heard that the Saints had taken the Chapel, they went and tried to influence the gentleman not to give it to the Saints in any way. But all their efforts were in vain.

We opened the Chapel on the 18th of May, when we were able to see the kindness of our brothers and sisters from the surrounding Branches as they visited us on the occasion. Some of the Saints of Swansea hired a carriage to come here, because the schedule of the steamer would not get them here in time, and I venture to say that they were not disappointed, for they received excellent sermons from the brethren which took place in the public meeting of the day.

The morning meeting was begun with singing and prayer, and Elder John Davies, formerly from Machynlleth, preached; also Joseph Tuckfield, Swansea. In the afternoon the following persons preached: Elders Williams Lewis, Swansea; David Rees, former minister of the Baptists in Aberamman; and President B. Ashby from Salt Lake City. In the evening the following persons preached: Elders John Davies, Joseph Tuckfield, and Thomas Harris, Conference President, and the work of the day concluded. There were present many in attendance who listened politely and attentively. I say that the brethren preached in a splendid and edifying way, and my prayer is that He who owns the work may crown their labor with success. And as Bro. Tuckfield said in his sermon, that "This day is salvation come to this house," I am confident that the diligence and godliness of the Saints here are such that they will be worthy of their religion, and it will not be long before the "Saints' Chapel" will be overflowing with faithful Saints.

This is the wish and determination of your fellow servant,

Emrys Davies.

P. S.—We would like to notify the Saints in this Conference that our greatest delight will be to pay them a visit for a similar circumstance.—Emrys Davies.

ZION'S TRUMPET,

OR

Star of the Saints.

SATURDAY, JUNE 7, 1856.

TO THE SAINTS.—Brothers and Sisters,—The long dark night of tradition has traveled far—the truth has been revealed in its original simplicity and purity, like the morning star of the horizon, until the daylight dawns, and its rays of light spread, to distant degrees, across the dark frontiers of the universe, and soon the knowledge of God will have filled the earth as the waters cover the sea. The Lord has seen fit to send his Holy Angel to bring back the eternal gospel in the fullness of its blessings as in ancient times, to gather the scattered sheep of Israel into the same fold, and to restore to them "that faith which was once delivered unto the saints," and to send out his servants in these latter days with a message intended for all the nations of the earth, in order to prepare all who will listen for the Second coming of the Messiah, which is now at the door.

This magnificent work has been entrusted to us, dear Saints; we cannot complete it by our own strength—we must receive strength and life from God, and before receiving that, the heavens must see worthiness in us. Perhaps some may think and be content to receive membership in the church of God, and receive knowledge that this is the true religion, without doing anything further, except that which they see fit. We say to such,—that it is not by doing only that does man live, nor by doing only that will one get enough strength to do his part in the great work of the latter days, rather it is by listening to and obeying "every word that proceedeth out of the mouth of God." Dear Saints, are we mindful of that? Yes, say all. But, in some places, the fruits prove to the opposite. God has revealed in this age new and old things, and commands his servants to transmit them to the world. Do we, dear Saints, receive every principal taught to us through the appropriate transmission by the servants of God? If we find ourselves disputing and opposing such measures and principles, remember that we are doing that with the "words of God," and that we are on the way towards destroying the commandments of God by our own traditions and imaginations.

All the "words of God" which we possess have come through his servants, and the "words of God" through his servants now are as important to us as were those of his servants of old to the saints at that time, it is as necessary to 'hear every word' now as it was back then, for God desires that of us through them. Solomon says,—"Every word of God is pure; he is a shield unto them that put their trust in him." If we trust in the word of God through his servants, we will succeed. God is jealous of his word; in the days of old He commanded that all who even disregarded His word should be completely cut off. Because the children of Israel opposed the word of the Lord through Moses, the great God became angry and swore an oath, saying,—"Surely there shall not one of these men of this evil generation see that good land, which I sware to give unto your fathers." It would be good for us as Saints to ponder this, and remember that none of His words fall to the earth, and that membership of the church without obedience to every word is merely like incense without blood, or a censer without a sacrifice. He who receives these suggestions will be supported in the strength of God, and His word will be a shield to him, while he who disregards the word of God will have his knees knocking, and every joint of his body shaking, when the golden ligature of his knees breaks from the intensity of his agonies, for refusing to listen to the voice of God through his servants, and bend his ear to their teaching.

LETTER FROM THE VALLEY.

G. S. L. City, November 30, 1855.

MY DEAR RELATIVES,—I write to you this sixth time, trusting that I shall receive an answer that you are well, and enjoying your usual comforts, and even more. Now, I shall give you a little of my story to you. I suppose that you have heard so many stories about us that you have decided that you will not see me or hear from me ever again. Thanks to that God who has kept me, I am alive, and healthier than I have ever been. In my previous letters you received my story across the ocean and rivers to Mormon Grove, where I stayed for six weeks before starting across the Plains. On July 28th we got started under the presidency of Elder C. E. Harper, Thomas Jeremy, and others. They had charge of 43 wagons, and close to 500 people. We crossed the lands and waters very successfully, except for the occasional time when the wagon would be upside down because of the ineptness and carelessness of some among so many kinds of *drivers*. I had the honor of taking the wagon that was under my care without any misfortune to the end of the journey, for which I was given a rifle worth between three and four pounds.

On our journey we saw many Buffalos; we killed one. We saw many Indians; they were all very favorable to us; they had just had a battle with the soldiers of the United States, during which some on each side were killed.

Next, I shall give you a brief account of this place. On the 29th of October we came into view of this city and entered into it. My heart swelled with amazement upon seeing the excellence of a place built in so little time. The city is as big as the town of Swansea, and contains thousands of people. There is a big difference between this place and the towns of Wales and England, since there is but one "tavern" [*Commercial Hotel*] in the entire city! and no one [except travelers, &c.] pays much attention to it; each one is diligently at his work, with his mind on worshiping his God in soberness, and edifying himself. Neither does the law restrict anyone from drinking liquor, &c.,—each one is a free agent in this, and responsible to God for his work. A man who is sober, truthful, honest and hard working is the man who is respected here,—it is not money that elevates a man here, rather virtues. He who does not respect himself does not respect another, and can bid farewell to being respected by another. All who have been diligent here for two or three years live very comfortably in beautiful houses, [of their very own,] and have an abundance of every kind of food, and many animals. Sam, Grey House, has 2 horses, 4 oxen, 8 cows, some little calves and also a pig. Neli formerly from Esgerhir has 6 cows, 8 horses, 4 pigs, and 6 little calves, and she has married and lives in her own house, and has an abundance of food. Daniel lives in the north, and is the owner of cattle, horses, &c. It would take too long to name the riches of Zion,—in short, there is room here for all to live in happiness without being in debt to anyone, except to God himself, for anything. I have been in the Tabernacle twice. It is a beautiful place, and can hold from three to four thousand people, and each person can hear the preacher speaking. I have seen and heard the Prophet Brigham Young. He is a handsome man in appearance, having a great influence, and speaks as one having authority. All who listen to him will live. Even though he is the most prominent man here, yet the ungodly acknowledge his humility,—he humbles himself to be a servant to all, warning them of the evil and the good before they appear, and proofs of that are what have created so much trust in him.

I shall say a word about the farmers here. They enjoy the fruitfulness of as much of the beautiful land of this valley as they can cultivate. They raise wheat and India corn an hundred fold, and all kinds of fruit practically too numerous to name them. Looking at them is sufficient to fill a man's heart with wonder as he thinks of all the mercies that a little piece of land gives. The houses of the dwellers of Zion are filled with food. They pay tithing on all they own, but not for the personal benefit of anyone; rather for the general requirements of the Church, [such as building the temple, &c.]. The best land that is closest to the city has been taken. Land will be given out next year again from within 6 or 7 miles to the city: I put in my name for 30 acres in that place, since it is not too far for me to be able to come every Saturday to market, where we can sell our butter for 10c., and our cheese for 4c. per pound, our wheat for 8s. per bushel, bacon for 6 or 7c., and our beef from 4 to 6c. per pound. We can pay part of our tithing for this land by working on it to get water along it. That is not much, since there is a great difference in the prices of the lands here and there. You have to pay in addition to tithing [which is used for such a different purpose!] the poor tax, the road tax, the main tax, the *Income Tax*, &c., and the next day perhaps you will have to pay the rent,—things that are not to be found here. In light of the advantages of living here, I think I myself shall possess some wealth before long. At present I work on a farm, and I receive 4s. per day in wages, in addition to my food. One earns 8s. a day including food. A craftsman earns 12s. per day. If my brother-in-law Thomas were working here now, he would earn from 12 to 15s. per day. There is a place for my brother Dafydd to earn from £1 to £1 5s. for making a coat, and he will do better by farming. The wage for maids is from £15 to £20 per year and they do not have to work outside. * * *

I greatly wish to see all of my friends here; but no one more than you, of course. Do not worry about me, for I am healthy and content. I have not missed a meal ever since I left Esgerrhydd. I was received warmly by Mrs. M. Daniels: I have slept there and eaten there,—when I was without work she was very kind to me. Please show love to Brother Daniels, and give my fond regards to him. Brother Jeremy has been especially good to me, and also Sam Grey House and Ann.

Remember me to all of the Saints of my acquaintance. [He gives a list.] All the Welsh came across the plains safely, except for one, a child of Dafydd Williams.

D. F. THOMAS.

CARMARTHEN CONFERENCE.

THIS Conference was held in this town on the 25th of May. After beginning in the usual manner, the President called on the Branch Presidents to give the condition of the branches, together with the signs that are in their midst. All testified that the work is increasing, and that all are doing their best to carry on. They preach in the houses and outside the houses at every opportunity they receive.

All the authorities of the Church were sustained in the warmest love, recognizing that it is a privilege for them to be able to show their satisfaction and their pleasure by so doing.

The Representation shows that 44 have emigrated, and 3 have been baptized during the past quarter, and that the total is 90.

Elder Evan Morgans was set apart as first Counselor in the

Presidency of the Conference, Elder Dafydd Evans as Treasurer for the money of the P. E. Fund and the Temple, and Elders Hugh James and Isaac Jones as Auditors of the Distribution of books.

Useful and beneficial teachings were given by Presidents Daniels, Evans, and Ashby, and Elders D. Davies, Llanelli, T. Jones, Aberystwyth, D. Evans, Talog, and several others.

The kindness of the Saints of the town to our visitors was beyond my expectation; thanks to them from my heart. The Saints testified that this has been the best Conference yet.

WM. JONES, President.

LONGING FOR ZION.

(TUNE—"*Sweet Home.*")

I was a long time in Babel enjoying myself,
Where I learned from experience the world's twists and turns,
Where I loved friends and loved ones sweetly,
Now I am bidding farewell to it all.
    My home, O my home,
    Daily I long for Zion my home.

For all the glory and splendor of the world,
The poor are crushed to maintain it all;
The great oppressors ride over the weak,
To keep up unjust ostentation.
    My home, O my home, &c.

The earth groans under burdens like these,
Is it any wonder my tears form a lake?
I live in captivity and daily under a burden,
O who will be my deliverer from this?
    My home, O my home, &c.

It's easy to read my longing by seeing my mien,
I could not hide it now if I tried;
My whole constitution sadly bears witness,
That longing for Zion is increasing each day.
    My home, O my home, &c.

The heart that never felt anything but courage,
Is now transformed—Oh! the wheel has turned.
The feeling that once was indifferent has come,
In daily longing for Zion I'm trapped,
    My home, O my home, &c.

I'll desist, I'll desist from further yearning,
As I see no sign of a cure for my malady.
I cannot persist in such great longing,
For longing for Zion has overwhelmed me!
    My home, O my home, &c.

Hark! what whispering do I hear now?
O, Zion leaps forward—the day has dawned.
Listen! hear the command—Gather for home,
Again I am hoping to go over there.
    My home, O my home, &c.

There is a secret thread that the world has not felt,
Winding my heart to Zion all the time;
I trust, friends, that you will not blame me,
My longing for Zion is ever increasing.
    My home, O my home, &c.

The enemies persecute embracers of the truth,
Those who suffer injustice through the land,
The time draws near, what bliss if it were now,
For me to be delivered to Zion's fair dawn.
    My home, O my home, &c.

Justice and peace are in fair Zion,
And abundant blessings for the children of faith,
Glory and magnificent delight, a fine world,
And the Lord's wise men together in Council.
    My home, O my home, &c.

There's the ship that has sailed with a host in her bosom,
Far out of sight I am crying for her going;
May her sails be filled up—all hail to her journey,
While I remain with tears in my eyes.
    My home, O my home, &c.

Let us all now strive to finish our work,
So we may be worthy of joining the journey;

And arrive from the midst of old Babel and its plague,
To the Lord's Temple—O to have that honor.
  My home, O my home, &c. JOSEPH PROSER.

THE VOLUNTEERS.—Several of the brethren have gone out into the field, and we trust that more will yet go. We are glad that brother Noah Jones failed to feel at peace without returning to the field again: we shall give space for his verses—

What, what do I hear?
  A quiet voice that says,—
"You must go back again,
  Now hurry, and return."

The voice says—"There is a multitude
  Remaining in darkness,
Waiting to hear about the truth,
  Therefore, go and shout.

You who are young in every place,
  Rise up in strength,
With the Holy Ghost's valiant help—
  Go and show your courage." NOAH.

CONFERENCES OF THE NORTH.—The Flintshire Conference will be held June 15th; Denbigh, the 22nd; Conway Valley and Anglesey, the 29th; and Merionethshire, July the 6th.

CONFERENCES OF THE SOUTH.—East Glamorgan Conference will be held June 29th; Brecon, July the 6th; Monmouth, the 13th; West Glamorgan, (in the Saints' Chapel, Aberafan.) the 20th; Llanelli, the 27th; Carmarthen, August the 3rd; Pembroke, the 10th, and Cardiganshire, on the 17th.

RECEIPTS FOR BOOKS FROM MAY 24 TO JUNE 5.—E. Morgans, 7s 3c; J. Jones, 10s; W. Jones, 10s 6c; T. Rees, 3s.

☞ The Llanelli Conference account came to hand when it was too late to include in this issue. Sending everything promptly is best.

☞ The article of Elder Wm. F. Williams, Alltwen, came to hand, and it will appear in our next issue.

CONTENTS.

	PG.
Marriage and Morals in Utah	177
Opening of the "Saints' Chapel," Aberafan	184
Editorial,—To the Saints	185
Letter from the Valley	186
Carmarthen Conference	189
Longing for Zion	190

SWANSEA:
PRINTED AND PUBLISHED BY D. DANIELS.

ZION'S TRUMPET,

OR

Star of the Saints.

No. 13.]　　　　　　JUNE 21, 1856.　　　　　　[Vol. IX.

MARRIAGE AND MORALS IN UTAH.

Continued from page 183.

Again, in verse 29, (Gal. 3rd,) Paul says to the Gentiles—"If ye be Christ's, then are ye Abraham's seed, and heirs according to the promise." Here we have the most direct and positive testimony, in the New Testament, that the covenant and promise made to Abraham were intended for all time, and for the believing Gentiles, and all true Christian people; and that they were entirely distinct from the law of Moses, and were never disannulled, or changed, either by Moses or Christ. Hence we affirm that the law of plural marriage, and death as a penalty of adultery and fornication, has been in force through all time, and through every dispensation, from Abraham till the present, and that of right it should be of force among all truly Christian nations: that the carrying out of these holy laws in righteousness would greatly multiply and bless a nation; and that the breach, or change of them, would corrupt the world, and defile the very earth with abominations.

But, let us now come to historical illustrations. In chapter 25 of Numbers we have an account of Zimri, a prince in Israel who committed fornication with Cosbi, the daughter of Zur, a prince of Midian; and how Phinehas, the grandson of Aaron, the priest, took a javelin and thrust them both through the body, and slew them; and how the Lord staid the plague on account of this act;

13　　　　　　　　　　　　　　　　　　　　[Price 1c.

and rewarded Phinehas with an everlasting covenant of priesthood, for his zeal in this punishing the crime of fornication.

We should remember too that Moses, who was himself a polygamist, both in practice and as a legislator, was the Prophet and legislator, under whose administration this crime was thus severely punished.

In the first book of Samuel, and the first chapter, we find an account of Elkanah, and his two wives, Hannah and Peninnah; and of Samuel, the son of this pluralist, who was a promised child, devoted to the service of God and brought up in the holy temple. To this child came the word of the Lord against the house of Eli the priest, saying, (1 Samuel, chap. 3, verses 11–14.) "Behold I will do a thing in Israel, at which both the ears of everyone that heareth it shall tingle. In that day will I perform against Eli all the things which I have spoken concerning his house: where I begin I will also make an end. For I have told him that I will judge his house for ever, for the iniquity which he knoweth; because his sons make themselves vile, and he restraineth them not. Therefore I have sworn unto the house of Eli, that the iniquity of Eli's house shall not be purged with sacrifice nor offering for ever."

Here seems to be certain sins which the ordinances of remission could never cleanse. God swore that neither sacrifice nor offering should ever atone for them. What were these sins committed by the sons of Eli? The answer is found in the 2nd chapter of 1st Samuel. They, as Priests, robbed the sacrifices, and committed whoredoms with the women who came to the tabernacle; this they did repeatedly and would not repent. In the 4th chapter of said book we find the record of the fulfillment of the words of the young child, Samuel. Israel was worsted in a battle with the Philistines; the two Priests, the sons of Eli, Hophni and Phinehas, were slain; the sacred ark which they bore was taken by the enemy. Their father Eli, on hearing the news, fell backward, and his neck brake; and the wife of Phinehas died on hearing the same news. Here we have a most striking illustration of God's blessing on plural marriage, and of his curse and death, attendant on adultery and fornication.

Samuel, the son of Elkanah, the polygamist, was blessed as a holy prophet, to denounce death upon adulterers.

We next will notice a case of adultery committed by David, king of Israel, and how he was punished. 2 Samuel, chap. 12, ver. 7 to 14,—"And Nathan said to David, Thou art the man. Thus saith the Lord God of Israel; I anointed thee king over Israel, and I delivered thee out of the hand of Saul: and I gave thee thy master's house, and thy master's wives into thy bosom, and gave thee the house of Israel and of Judah; and if that had been too little, I would, moreover, have given unto thee such and such things. Wherefore hast thou despised the commandment of the Lord to do evil in his sight? Thou hast killed Uriah the Hittite with the sword, and hast taken his wife to be thy wife, and hast slain him with the sword of the children of Ammon. Now therefore the sword shall never depart from thine house; because thou hast despised me, and has taken the wife of Uriah the Hittite to be thy wife.

"Thus saith the Lord; behold I will raise up evil against thee out of thine own house, and I will take thy wives before thine eyes, and give them unto thy neighbor, and he shall lie with thy wives in the sight of this sun. For thou didst it secretly: but I will do this thing before all Israel and before the sun. And David said unto Nathan, I have sinned against the Lord. And Nathan said unto David, the Lord also hath put away thy sin: thou shalt not die. Howbeit, because by this deed thou hast given great occasion to the enemies of the Lord to blaspheme, the child also that is born unto thee shall surely die."

Here again we find death the penalty of adultery; but in this instance God in his mercy spared his life because it was a first offense, and because he sincerely repented. But He punished him very severely, in the death of his child, in taking his wives from him, and in denouncing rebellion and war in his own house.

In this instance as in all the former cases the same God who punishes adulterers with such severity declares in favor of polygamy, and expressly reveals the fact that he himself gave unto David's bosom the wives of his master, Saul.

These few instances must suffice to show that Moses and the

prophets did not alter the law of marriage, or the penal laws against adultery, etc., as existing in the everlasting covenant made with Abraham.

We next inquire whether Jesus Christ or his Apostles ever altered or abolished these laws. The 8th chapter of John, ver. 3–7, reads as follows—"And the scribes and Pharisees brought unto him a woman taken in adultery, and when they had set her in the midst, they say unto him, Master, this woman was taken in adultery, in the very act. Now Moses in the law commanded us that such should be stoned: but what sayest thou? This they said, tempting him, that they might have to accuse him. But Jesus stooped down and with his finger wrote on the ground as though he heard them not. So when they continued asking him, he lifted up himself, and said unto them, He that is without sin among you let him first cast a stone at her."

If Jesus had wished to abolish or alter this item of the law, this was a timely opportunity,—a point in hand: but so far from this, he ordered the woman to be immediately stoned: provided there was one virtuous man among all her accusers who was himself so pure as to be worthy to execute the law; but as none were found in that age of degeneracy, she went unpunished; but she was strictly admonished to sin no more.

Again, 1 Corinthians, chapter 5, ver. 5. The Apostle Paul in reference to a person in the Church who had committed fornication, exhorted the saints "to deliver such a one unto Satan for the destruction of the flesh, that the spirit may be saved in the day of the Lord Jesus."

This destruction of the flesh must have had reference to the death of the body; the man having justly forfeited his life, in accordance with the law of God. And "the spirit being saved in the day of the Lord Jesus," must have had an allusion to the great day of his second coming; thus showing that the fornicator, under the light of the Gospel, had forfeited his life in this world, and his salvation in the world to come, for at least eighteen hundred years.

Thus, under all dispensations, whether Patriarchal, Mosaic, or Christian, the penalty annexed to unlawful sexual intercourse appears to be the same, growing out of a fixed and unchanged law of God—a wise provision—a bright cherub with a flaming sword, as it were, to guard the chaste and sacred fountain or issues of life.

It is true that Jesus Christ and his Apostles, so far as their writings have come to us, have not dwelt on practical plurality in their own age, for the best of all reasons,—Judea was then a Roman province, under Roman laws, which were opposed to polygamy. On this account the Jews had greatly degenerated; they had corrupted their way and perverted the pure institutions of their more virtuous fathers. Hence John the Baptist and Jesus Christ reproved them sharply, calling them an evil and adulterous generation, who had made void the law of God by their traditions. But one thing is certain—Jesus Christ and his Apostles always approved of Abraham, Isaac, and Jacob, and the holy prophets of old, and bore testimony of their virtue and faithfulness, and represented them as honorable fathers of the faithful, and members or rulers in the kingdom of God.

Jesus said on one occasion to the Jews, "If ye were Abraham's seed ye would do the works of Abraham." On another occasion he said, "Many shall come from the east, and from the west, and from the north, and from the south, and shall sit down with Abraham, Isaac, and Jacob in the kingdom of God; but ye shall be thrust out."

Paul and the Apostles exhorted the saints to be like Abraham, the father of the faithful, whose children they were through the gospel; and if children, then heirs to the same covenants of promise.

Now we have already shown that the promises made to Abraham, to which the New Testament Saints were heirs, included exceeding multiplicity of children, and consequently of wives, as the means of carrying out the same.

But lest any might mistake this point of the covenant and promises, Jesus Christ himself has set it forever at rest. He says in Luke chap. 18, ver. 29 and 30, "Verily I say unto you there is no man that hath left house, or parents, or brethren, or wife, or children, for the kingdom of God's sake, who shall not receive many fold more in this present time, and in the world to come, life everlasting."

Men, brethren, and fathers—In this review we have proved—

First: An everlasting covenant made with Abraham, in which all nations should be blessed.

Secondly: That one main feature of this covenant pertained to the exceeding great multiplicity of our species, and to the organization, perpetuity, and growth of families, nations, and kingdoms.

Thirdly: That God, being the best judge of the means of multiplying, appointed a plurality of wives, for good and holy men, as a principal means of multiplying their seed, and forbade on pain of death, all sexual intercourse, except that sanctioned by the holy laws of marriage.

Fourthly: That the covenant and laws pertaining to marriage and virtue, or the moral and social relations of the sexes, as held by Abraham, Isaac, and Jacob were never altered or disannulled either by Moses or the prophets, Jesus Christ or the Apostles; consequently, that this covenant, and the laws, penalties, and promises there unto pertaining, are, or by right ought to be, still of force.

Fifthly: That all nations were to be blessed in these covenants and institutions; and that the gentiles were to become fellow heirs of the same by the gospel; through which they became the seed of Abraham.

And, sixthly: That to transgress these holy laws, change this ordinance, or break this everlasting covenant, would, according to Isaiah the Prophet, "defile the very earth, under the inhabitants thereof." We next inquire: What power has been guilty of such innovations? "Who has transgressed the laws, changed the ordinance, and broken the everlasting covenant?"

This we charge home upon Rome. She is the "fourth beast" of Daniel's vision: "She ruled the earth as with a rod of iron": "She made war with the Saints and overcame them": She changed the laws and institutions of both Jews and Christians: by her sorceries were all nations deceived: She, in short, is "Mystery, Babylon the Great, the mother of harlots and abominations of the earth." She licensed whoredoms; but forbade to marry; allowing to none of her citizens but one wife, and to many of them, namely, the clergy, none at all.

Every so-called Christian nation, including even Protestant England and the American States, has retained, at least this one trait of her superstitions and abominations. They have either permitted or licensed whoredoms; and strictly prohibited a plurality of wives. They have punished lightly, or not at all, that which was, under all dispensations, by the law of God considered a crime unto death; and have made a crime, and annexed a heavy penalty to that which, according to the Bible, was never recognized as a crime at all, either by God, Jesus Christ, the Holy Ghost, angels, Prophets, or Apostles. Yea, fellow citizens, the laws of some of our States, I am ashamed to tell it, would recognize as illegitimate the children of Abraham and Jacob; would take from them their wives; thus tearing asunder what God hath joined together; and would doom those holy patriarchs, themselves, to hard labor and solitary confinement within the walls of a prison for years; and then suffer their wives and children to be prostituted with impunity; and then, as if to crown the climax of inconsistency, such an order of things, taken together, would be called "virtue," and such institutions be dignified by the name of "Christianity." Such institutions have filled "Christendom" with whoredoms, her cities with abominations, and the world with disease and rottenness; till the words of Isaiah have been fulfilled: "The earth is defiled under the inhabitants thereof."

For instance, look at Paris, the capital of Christian France; one-third of the children born there are said to be illegitimate.

Look at the census of Europe, and even of our older States of this union: see the hundreds of thousands of females more than of males. All this surplus of immortal beings are doomed by the Romish law, prohibiting polygamy, to live single, and to never form those ties which would enable them lawfully and honorably to answer the end of their creation as wives and mothers. Nor is this all; under the present institutions men are trained to feel little or no obligation to marry; many of them choose to live single. This increases the number of females doomed to single life. Nor does the mischief end here; the present wars in Europe, alone, have deprived the world of perhaps half a million of men in the vigor of life—candidates for the sacred offices of husband and father: by which means the same number of females are, by the monogamic law, added to the prohibited list. All the surplus female population arising from these and other causes are, by the one-wife system, utterly prohibited marriage: and thus compelled to break the first and great command of God, namely, "Be fruitful and multiply."

Thus the laws of modern "Christendom," borrowed from Rome, have overwhelmed the nations with the grossest immoralities, with sin, and sorrow, and tears, and wretched loneliness and widowhood. The widows mourn, having no husbands; the virgins mourn, having no bridegrooms; children mourn, having no protectors; and families and nations mourn, having no confidence in themselves or each other. Virtue and confidence have fled; mercy weeps tears of blood; charity itself falters and is ready to yield to the cries of justice for vengeance on the earth.

What then, shall the righteous do? We reply, Restore the law of God—the new and everlasting covenant. Let every good citizen of both sexes marry at a proper age: bless them and say—"Be fruitful and multiply." Make death the penalty for fornication and adultery, thus throwing a shield around our families and sacred domestic institutions. Let the monogamic law, restricting a man to one wife, with all its attendant train of whoredoms, intrigues, deductions, wretched and lonely single life, hatred, envy, jealousy, infanticide, illegitimacy, disease and death, like the millstone cast into the depths of the sea—sink with Great Babylon to rise no more. Let every man and woman be virtuous, pure, holy, filling the measure of their creation. And let us go to, and fill these mountains; the States, North and South America; the earth; and an endless succession of worlds with a holy, virtuous and highly intellectual seed, whose hearts shall delight in the law of God.

Let our sons become the sons of God, through faith in Jesus Christ, and obedience to the Gospel; let His law be indelibly engraven on the tablets of their hearts; let them be indoctrinated in every principle of virtue and honor: that each may be a conservatory of chastity, and wield a savory influence in every circle of his acquaintance. Let them learn to respect themselves as sons of God, and the other sex as sisters—daughters of the Highest—holy vessels, eternal beings, destined as companions and coworkers in the great science of life. Let them be taught to aspire, by every principle of honor and integrity, to the Patriarchal throne, as heads of families and Saviors of men.

Let our daughters also obey the ordinances of God, and receive and cultivate the gift of the Holy Ghost, in every good and pure affection. Let them early understand the true relationship they are destined to sustain to the other sex. Let them be taught to respect them as brothers, worthy of their confidence and affection—worthy to become their savior and head, as Christ is the head of the Church. Let them be taught to respect and revere themselves, as holy vessels, destined to sustain and magnify the eternal and sacred relationship of wife and mother; to be the ornament and glory of man; and to share with him a never fading crown, and an eternally increasing dominion.

In short, let us educate our sons and daughters in all that is holy, and true, and virtuous, and pure, and lovely, and of good report; let us gradually and carefully develop in them the true affections and attributes of their nature; let us cultivate every intellectual and moral sense and faculty within them, and lead them gently onward in the great science of life and exaltation: that, when time shall be no more, we may rejoice with the untold millions of our posterity in the eternal mansions.

ZION'S TRUMPET,

OR

Star of the Saints.

SATURDAY, JUNE 21, 1856.

GOOD NEWS. Dear Brother and Sisters,—We have good news, this time again, which will bring you great comfort, by announcing that the Kingdom of the "Little Stone" is going forward,—the Kingdom which Daniel prophesied that God would set up in the last days, and which would never be possessed by any other people, but that the Saints of the Most High should receive it forever and ever.

Brother Israel Evans just returned from Pembrokeshire, where he preached the Gospel as a witness in practically every town and village. He lectured on the geography, the yield and the fruitfulness of the land, as well as the morals and customs of the people in Utah. He had numerous crowds listening to him, and he caused a considerable stir and inquiry among them.

We and he had the pleasure of being present in the Pembrokeshire Conference on the 1st of this month. The account of it, which was sent here, shows that 4 were baptized, and that 25 emigrated during the last quarter. Appointed as Traveling Elder was Brother Dafydd John, who has been in the Academy for years, until he was baptized by the Saints at a time when he was about to be ordained a minister for the Baptists. He received a confirming testimony of the divinity of the Church, and instead of a pile of old traditional sermons out of books, he has a Gospel which is strong and has the Holy Ghost. He is solid in the faith, as well as being meek, diligent and courageous in its defense.

We expect great success for the cause in Pembrokeshire, under the presidency of the faithful brother E. D. Miles, inasmuch as the love and devotion we observed there continue.

President Abednego Williams, Merthyr, says that there is an unusual enthusiasm there,—that they have, very recently, baptized over twenty as a beginning.

The account of the Llanelli Conference, D. Davies, President, shows that 107 have emigrated from there also with the most recent emigration. He says that the last Conference was the best yet.

West Glamorgan.—We quote the following good accounts from the letter of President Harris:—

"Dear Brother Daniels,—Sunday, the 15th of this month, I went to a District Council, where I found the brethren in good condition and determined to go forward with the work of God. They had advertised throughout the area that there would be preaching in the open air, but because the weather was unpleasant, we received permission to go to the hall of the "Dynevor Arms," Pontardawe, which was overflowing at a few minutes after two o'clock, with attentive and polite listeners, and at 6:00 o'clock, despite the large size of the hall, it was too small by half to hold the listeners. The Brethren who preached with me were Elders Thomas Evans, Cyfyng, Wm. Lewis, President of the Alltwen Branch; David and W. F. Williams, Alltwen; and judging from the look of the crowd, it can be said that much good was done that day for which the beneficial consequences will yet be seen. The brethren have determined to double their diligence in this place.

We had a lovely time last Sunday in Neath. At about 10:00 in the morning, hundreds gathered at the water's edge, when Brother John Jewry and I preached. Then I baptized in the crowd; and others promised to be baptized soon. At 5:00 o'clock in the evening, Bro. Jewry and I preached on the Quay to a large and polite crowd, who were surprised to understand that the doctrine of the Saints is completely different from what is published through the newspapers about it. The brethren and the Saints in the area have determined to increase the godly fire which has been lit in the town of Neath.

THOMAS HARRIS."

FULFILLMENT OF PROPHECIES ABOUT ANCIENT BABYLON.

THE PROOF which rises from the godly fulfillment of prophecy is that God is the same today, yesterday, and forever; and all his words will be fulfilled which were spoken and which will be spoken in every age through his servants the Prophets.

Babylon was the chief city of the old Babylonian empire, which was established by the first descendants of Noah, soon after the flood. It was expanded by Nimrod about two thousand years before the birth of Christ. It was added to greatly by Queen Semiramis, and it was strengthened and made more splendid by several queens that followed; but Nebuchadnezzar, and his daughter Nitocris, completed it as one of the wonders of the world, in incomparable splendor and glory.

Babylon was situated at the center of some broad and fruitful flatlands. It was divided into two parts, by the river Euphrates, which ran through its center, from the North to the south. These two parts were surrounded and enclosed by the same wall, which formed a perfect and complete square, sixty miles in circumference. It was remarkably strong—eighty-seven feet wide; and wide enough at the top for six carriages to run side by side along it, and three hundred feet high.

There were two harbors in it, one on each side of the river, and for each one a high wall, of the same thickness as the wall which surrounded the city. There were one hundred gates, of huge sizes, to go into the city, all made of brass.

The two parts of the city were connected by a stone bridge across the river.

To prevent devastation by the overflow of the river, two canals were made that conducted the excess water to the Tigris river. Large dikes were also made to keep the flood waters contained lest they break through and cause damage and destruction. The place from which the greatest part of the materials for this huge task was from the western side of the city, where an extraordinary lake was dug, which was thirty feet deep with a circumference of forty-five miles.

At each end of the bridge was a splendid palace; and from one to the other was an underground passage, which was dug under the body of the river. The size of the old palace, on the western side, was about thirty furlongs (close to four miles) in circumference, and it was surrounded by three different walls. Within the confines of this palace there were ingenious hanging gardens, and in them large walkways: one reached above the other until they were level with the wall of the city. They were intended to imitate a wooded land, to which end trees were planted in them in a sufficiently deep layer.

Near this palace stood the temple of Belus, the shape of which was four-cornered, and it was close to three miles in circumference. In the middle of it there was a huge tower—six hundred feet in height. This huge structure contained eight towers, each one of which was seventy-five feet high. There were steps around the outside of them going up to their highest point.

At the end of the temple there was a large golden idol forty feet high, and it was worth three-and-a-half million pounds. In it were a great many other idols, together with furnishings that were considered sacred. It is estimated that everything that pertained to this temple alone was worth forty million pounds.

These things showed something of the great power and wealth of the Babylonian empire, which, no doubt, was the strongest of the work of mortals. Babylon was called the golden city, the glory of kingdoms, and praise of all the earth. But, nevertheless, complete destruction was visited upon its pride, its wickedness, and its idolatry, according to the predictions of the holy Prophets.

Alltwen. WILLIAM F. WILLIAMS.

(To be continued.)

LETTER FROM PRESIDENT JONES.

On board the "S. Curling."
Boston, U. S. A., May 1856.

Dear brother Daniels,—May the fatherly goodness of our God enable me at last to fulfill my promise, namely, that we would write to you when we reached this port; and that you should learn something of our affairs while on this voyage.

Dear brother, believe me, that despite the multiple duties that rested on me, and the opportunity I had to do good, the memory of the pleasures we enjoyed together in former times inundated my mind nearly every day or night, and it would be a task too difficult for me, if I tried, to forget the Saints I left behind in Wales. I believe that they would be desirous, probably, especially the relatives of my fellow emigrants, of hearing about our experiences.

We were towed out of the river at Liverpool by a steamboat, April 19th. We had three days of calm weather and light wind, which was very favorable to allow the emigrants to get used to the sea gradually, secure the chests, &c., in their places. There are 707 of us, or I should say that as many as that started off, of which 560 are from Wales, 20 from Ireland, and the rest from England. We organized the ship into 11 groups, with a President over each one, whose duty was to see that men, but not women, arose at 5 o'clock in the morning to scrub the deck, so that all could arise to pray at 6 o'clock at the sound of the trumpet; I don't mean "Zion's

Trumpet," but the great brass trumpet that would practically wake the dead with its sound. A definite time was set for each group to cook in rotation, and in the evening, at the sound of the trumpet, all would come down to pray, that is, to worship our God. Every Tuesday and Thursday nights we would hold prayer meetings. Every Sunday morning the presidents would meet together in a Council to organize all matters pertaining to the circumstances. At three o'clock in the afternoon, sermons were given on the deck, and at 7½ in the evening, meetings of the Saints were held, and the Sacrament was distributed. In this manner we spent our time, or the devotional part of it, and we had great pleasure and benefit in this, and more blessings than would pay the cost of that. We frequently had fair wind in answer to our prayers, and I don't believe that so many people have ever before lived so happily united, gentle and devout for so long under such circumstances. There was hardly ever a cross or complaining word about anything during the time. It is a pleasure for me to be able to say this, and I love them all the more because of it.

With respect to our health I cannot offer so much praise; yet there is no room to place much blame: the greatest cause of sickness was eating too much of the good and strong food with no work to do to digest it. But the threatening consequences were anticipated from the beginning through the instrumentality of castor and olive oil mainly, together with the administering of the means which God set up for this purpose in his Church. The emigrating Conference Presidents from Wales, and other elders, were of great benefit through their faithful and constant administrations. Two children were born on the sea, one son to Thomas Dee, formerly from Llanelli, who was named Dan Curling Dee, at the request of his parents and the emigrants, and a daughter was born to a brother from England by the name of Reynolds, and the children and their mothers have improved exceedingly well. I had considerable trouble in getting parents to look after their children, especially the mothers to care for their infants, and bring them up to the fresh air: for negligence in this made the majority of the infants sick, and although I prepared a *mutton* and *beef* broth for the mothers, and arrowroot for the children almost every day, and despite every effort that was put forth, 5 of the infants died, at least three of which had no hope of getting better before leaving home. They were children of G. W. Davies, Jno. Lewis, Evan Davies,

John Basset, and Wm. Thomas. Because they confined the children too much in their beds, the "chicken pox" broke out among them, and it ran through the ship practically one after the other; but through the blessing of God on the administrations, and the treatment they received, no one died because of it; but we have cause to be grateful that is was not smallpox or worse. Eating too much meat and oat flour caused some to have diarrhea, but nearly all of them, by doing better, have recovered from that also.

The weather: After the first three days we had a strong tail wind which blew us close to 300 miles per day for 4 days. After that we had crosswinds for nearly a fortnight despite everything, and because there were 2000 tons of iron at the bottom of our ship it shook like a crow's nest on the top of a tree in a storm, and there is no one grumbling that they did not get their £5 worth of shaking. We had two days of summery weather, sunny, and warm, while the women were as busy washing their clothes and the men carrying water, and hanging them out to dry, as you've seen bees in Carmarthenshire gathering honey, and it's doubtful that so many sails on a ship have ever been up, or that there has ever been a sailor who knew the name of all of them. After the clothes had dried sufficiently, a fair wind came to push us gradually forward.

I had two faithful and able brethren as Counselors, John Oakley and Grant, brethren who had come with us from the Valley, as you know. Besides being President, I was unanimously elected to be *General Complainer* for everyone on the ship, and all promised not to try to steal my office from me; and as praise to their truthfulness and their honesty I must say that I was able to fulfill the office too well for anyone else to desire it anymore.

We were so fortunate as to get a good ship and a very kind and fatherly Captain. Thanks without exception were given to him by all and I hope that you yourself will have the privilege of getting one so philanthropic to carry you and your hundreds with you when you come after us.

It is considered practically a miracle that among 750 people during a month's time, no accident or injury happened to anyone, rather the tender and fatherly care of our God surrounded us against harm continually.

Now, dear brother Daniels, and all brothers and sisters—Behold the great sea that separates us; behold us where you would like to be, and on our way to the same place where we yet expect to meet you; therefore, let me testify once again from this distance that "Mormonism" is getting better all the time, the more we know of it; that the God whom we served while there with you, is here with us also, and that man's welfare, comfort, success, and happiness depend on obeying all his commandments. I am delighted to be able to believe that you, my dear brother, merit and have an abundant part in the faith and prayers of the Saints, and thus you are enabled to properly guide them in the ways of God, the walking of which will bring them safely and promptly to Zion.

My fond remembrance to you always and everywhere; to your Counselors, Evans and Ashby, to Thomas Harris, Wm. Lewis, and all in the house, and my old fellow laborers in the vineyard—the Presidents, and all the Saints.

Your Fellow Servant,
D. Jones.

MISCELLANEOUS, &c.

The Likeness of President Spencer is available in this Office. We know that all of the Welsh Saints desire and will have the privilege of recognizing the person from the likeness of him to adorn their libraries and their walls. We have purchased the number requested for the Welsh Saints to receive, in order to have the honor of assisting him to return home. The kinds, prices, and the profit are the same as the others.

☞ Let the presidents remember the collections, &c., by June 27. A bit of money for the P. E. F. arrived without naming the branches, &c.!

Payments from June 6 to 19.—G. Roberts, 10s; T. Stephens, £5; C. Harman, £1 6s; J. Gibbs, 10s; T. Jones, 8s.

CONTENTS.

	PG.
Marriage and Morals in Utah	193
Editorial,—Good News	201
Fulfillment of Prophecy	203
Letter from President Dan Jones	205
Miscellaneous, &c.	208

SWANSEA:
PRINTED AND PUBLISHED BY D. DANIELS.

ZION'S TRUMPET,

OR

Star of the Saints.

No. 14.]	JULY 5, 1856.	[Vol. IX.

THE MILLENNIUM.

BY THOMAS HARRIS, FORMERLY OF GEORGETOWN.

[Continued from page 165.]

It is true that no one knows the *day* or the *hour* that the Son of Man will come; nevertheless, our blessed Lord has been so merciful as to give indicative signs to the wise, those who are waiting for him, so that they would know the age and the generation in which he would come, and when the millennium would begin in which he would come, because "to you," he said, "it was given to know the signs of the times." His followers asked him what would be the signs that would foretell this lovely period, and he answered—"And *this gospel* of the kingdom shall be preached in all the world for a *witness* unto all nations; and then shall the end come." I have proved clearly and scripturally that the gospel of Christ, or "this gospel" which He preached, was taken from the earth after His time. Now the question rises in someone's mind that if it was taken from the earth, how did it come back afterwards? In response I say that John told of having a prophetic vision, which he received during his exile on the isle of Patmos, after receiving revelations previous to this vision, reporting that the earth would be destitute of "this gospel," following which he saw—"another angel fly in the midst of heaven, having [this] everlasting gospel to preach to every nation, and kindred, and tongue, and people

14	[Price 1*c*.

which dwell on the earth," which proves the statement that we examined previously, namely, that "every kindred, tongue, people, and nation" would be destitute of the eternal gospel; if otherwise, it would be a completely unnecessary work for a wise God to send an angel to the inhabitants of the earth to transmit to them that which they already possessed.

Now, I call the attention of the reader to the parable which Jesus spoke—"Now learn a parable of the fig tree, when his branch is yet tender, and putteth forth leaves, ye know that summer is nigh: so likewise ye, when ye shall see all these things, know that it is near, even at the doors." Presently, let us search to find out what these indicative signs are of the approach of the Millennium, and the Second Coming of the Son of Man, as the leaves on the fig tree are indicative signs of the approach of summer. Jesus said that "wars, and rumors of wars" would be heard of shortly before the end. What have we seen and are now seeing? Wars and rumors of wars from one corner of the world to the other practically. What else but the rumor of wars is heard from the extreme freezing borders of Kamshatka to the snowy mountains of Tierra del Fuego, yes, something that strikes fear and worry into the hearts of the inhabitants of China, India, Persia, Afghanistan, Greece and Turkey, &c. Also Jesus said that "nation shall rise against nation, and kingdom against kingdom, and there shall be famines, and pestilences, and earthquakes, in divers places," and that there would be "great tribulation." The facts that our reader knows about are sufficient to prove that nation has risen up against nation, and that the kingdoms of the world are in contention with one another: are not the horses of war being ridden into battle; does not the blood that colored the banks of the Danube prove that the words of Jesus are being fulfilled; are not the dead bodies that fill the trenches of Russia, the moan of the widows, and the cry of the orphans, who have lost their husbands and fathers on the field of battle lately, so many irrefutable facts to prove that peace has been taken from the earth, and that nation has risen up against nation, and kingdom against kingdom: in our days oxen are being slaughtered to feed the fighters—the common people are being starved so that avengers can be fed, and machines of destruction are being devised to send the inhabitants of the earth to their death in their thousands. War, wars, and rumors of still more fill the columns of the newspapers of the world; killing, burning, and murders of men, women and children, and new inventions to destroy human life with greater speed is the most frequent news I hear from practically every corner of the earth; the bloodhounds of war are howling, and the drinking horns of battle are at the mouths of kings and orators in the various senate houses of the kingdoms of the world; all this, with the sufferings of the starving poor, and the mourning for the deceased because of oppression prove that the great tribulation of the latter days has begun. The inhabitants of the world often shudder at the frightful earthquakes; frequently the earth is shaken and divided suddenly in various parts, by a series of turbulent shakings following one after the other with rapid thrusts, their sound spreading like the cracking of thunder in the atmosphere; frequently the earth is split into huge fissures, and castles are shattered into pieces, and cities broken into rubble, and men by the thousands are swept into another world without warning; plagues and deathly disease are bustling throughout the countries, suddenly moving numerous throngs of the earth's inhabitants to the world of spirits. The reader knows of a host of facts concerning these happenings with no reason for me to give further examples at present.

Who does not see that the facts noted are like a number of indicative signs of the coming of the Millennium, as the leaves indicate the coming of summer? But possibly someone says that the things I noted are those that were to take place in the days of Christ, but let such remember that which Jesus said,—"*Immediately* after the tribulation of those days shall the sun be darkened, and the moon shall not give her light, and the stars shall fall from heaven, and the powers of the heavens shall be shaken;" in another place, when reference is made to the same period, it is said, "And the sun will turn dark, and the moon will become as blood;" &c. All reasonable men believe that these things have not taken place, and thus they must acknowledge that those noted pertain to the last days, and not to the age in which they were spoken.

Another sign is, that "this gospel of the kingdom shall be preached." Many different false sects were preached in past centuries, but they were "other gospels"; Christ said "this gospel" because he perceived through the spirit of prophecy that over six hundred "other gospels" would exist during that time. He said very clearly that "*this* gospel," namely the gospel and "these signs" that would follow its believers, was the right one. He could say that the gospel which He preached contained apostles, prophets, miracles, gifts of healing, speaking with tongues, and faith to come boldly unto the throne of grace, nothing doubting, and seeking until obtaining, &c. Now, the reader observes that "*this* gospel," the gospel that contains the same officers and the one in which the same blessings would be enjoyed by its believers, would be preached in the latter days as a *witness* unto all nations, namely to every kindred, tongue, people, and nation that dwell on the face of the earth. Now, what do we hear? We hear being preached "*that* gospel" which contains apostles, prophets, &c., and the signs are following the believers; in these days, in every town and village in almost every country, the baptism of repentance for the remission of sins, and the laying on of hands to receive the gift of the Holy Ghost are being preached; in short, that gospel that Christ preached is being preached, which is not in word only, like the "other gospels," but it is being preached in power, and in the Holy Ghost, and in great certainty. This again is a sure and certain sign, like the leaves of the fig tree before the coming of summer, that the coming of the Son of Man and the Millennium are nigh, yes, at the door, which gladdens the hearts of the oppressed faithful, who longingly await the revelation of the sons of God.

Possibly some say that the things noted are not a sign of the coming of the aforementioned period—that wars, earthquakes, famine and pestilences have existed many times before. There is the taste of atheism with such a statement. It is true that all of them have taken place before and after the time of Christ; but they have come together in our age more particularly than in any previous age: such oppression as there is in our days has not been recorded in history since the beginning of the world: there is more envy among the kingdoms of the world, more atrocious massacres in wars, more destruction on land and sea, more machines being invented to destroy men, louder cries of widows and orphans, the poor of the countries are more numerous and more pitiful in their condition, and there is more pride and hatred among men now than there has ever been, and in the midst of this confusion pertaining to Babylon are the missionaries of peace, despite the scorn and derision, who lift up their voice, preaching "*this gospel* of the kingdom as a witness to all nations."

The true prophets of the last days are not to have fairer treatment than the true prophets of old, for Christ said that another sign of the approach of the millennium would be the appearance of *false* prophets. The reader notices again: until a few years ago the world was in peace, but wars came: until lately no one in the world acknowledged God, or had a knowledge of the truth, but God sent his angel with the eternal gospel, and since the Lord does nothing on the earth except he reveal his secret to his servants the prophets, he had to raise up servants or prophets on the earth, and He has done that in our age. Now, the reader can expect to hear tell of the *false* prophets appearing, for Jesus said that "*false* prophets shall arise;" remember that they themselves will not acknowledge that they are false. Oh no, they will appear as similar to the *true* prophets as the devil appears to an angel of light, until they "deceive many," says Christ, even "if it were possible, yes, even the very elect." From among which sect will they arise? It is quite likely that they will arise from our own midst as these men arose in the days of old, to speak perverse things, and to attract disciples after them. Let the Saints remember that it is necessary that these arise, for the words of Jesus to be fulfilled, and they may take that as another strong sign of the coming of the end.

The devil failed through bishops, priests, reverends, preachers, and all to prevent the success of the preaching of "*this* gospel of the kingdom," and the false prophets will fail also; but perhaps they will be so successful as to separate the chaff from the wheat, and carry the tares to the fire. It is necessary for the Saints and everyone to remember the words of our blessed Savior, who said,—"Beware of false prophets, which come to you in sheep's clothing, but inwardly they are ravening wolves." The reason they are so dangerous is because they are so similar to the true prophets,—coming to us "in sheep's clothing." But by their fruits shall ye know them,—"dreamers who defile the flesh, despise dominion, and speak evil of dignities, who are spots in your feasts of charity, when they feast with you, feeding themselves without fear: clouds they are without water, carried about of winds; trees whose fruit withereth, without fruit, twice dead, plucked up by the roots." Do they deny the doctrine of the Saints? No; but they acknowledge that Christ is the Son of God, and that Joseph Smith is his prophet, and that all the principles are true, but pay attention to their fruits,—they despise the present dominion of the Church, and they speak evil of those who are in authority in Zion, &c. This must be; therefore let the dear ones of God be on their guard.

THE EAST GLAMORGAN CONFERENCE,

WHICH was held in Cymreigyddion Hall, Merthyr, on the 29th of June, 1856. At half past ten in the morning, Elder David Pugh offered the opening prayer. Then President A. S. Williams addressed the numerous congregation, announcing that the morning meeting would be spent setting before them the authorities of the Church, and reading the statistics of the collections and the reports, &c.

Elder Israel—We are met here today to hold our Conference, and take care of matters of the Conference, and to covenant to uphold the authorities of the Church. Let no one raise his hand to covenant that he will obey the Presidents, if he does not intend to do so. Perhaps some by the name of Saints say they are willing to obey President Richards or President Daniels, but they are not willing to obey the Conference President; let such remember that that is nothing but inconsistency and hypocrisy. Branch Presidents ought to trust in the President of their Conference, and remember that it is not to them that the Conference President is accountable, but to those who have been set apart to care for them or to preside over them. If there is here any Branch President who feels unwilling to obey and carry out all the counsels that come through the Conference President, it is better for such to make himself known today, for it is impossible for success to be in the same place as he. The Branch President also deserves and must have the same trust and obedience from the Officers and Saints under his care, for without that they cannot be worthy of enjoying the blessings promised to the faithful here or in Zion.

All the authorities of the Church were sustained happily and unanimously.

Elders D. Pugh, T. J. Rees, W. R. Jones, and A. S. Williams testified that the Saints and officers in the Conference are in a remarkably good condition, and better than they have been for a long time. The Saints are determined to do their part to build up the kingdom of God, by giving themselves and their possessions to the service of heaven to perform the preparatory work for the second coming of the Son of God, which will turn out as a blessing for them, when the recusants and the mockers will lament, as did the antediluvians, when the work is finished and the door is closed.

The testimony of Elders John Llywelyn and Evan A. Richards were consistent with those of the brethren who pointed out the condition of the Conference.

After reading the statistics, the meeting was closed with a prayer by President Daniels.

At two o'clock, Elder Thomas Harris prayed, then Pastor J. B. Martin was called on to speak; he commented on the unity of the Priesthood, and the blessings that are enjoyed by the Saints by being obedient to it, and on the duty the Saints have to be generous in the Lord's work, and he expressed his joy in understanding that the Saints here, like those with whom he had labored in Bristol, &c., have had a strong awakening to the work of God.

Then President Daniels spoke with great power and persuasion. Important truths spilled over his lips, which gladdened the hearts of the Saints. And judging from the impact he had, it can be said that he is like the skilled craftsman, by the power of the Spirit of God, engraving every word on the hearts of his listeners.

The meeting was closed with prayer by David Davies, Llanelli Conference President.

At six in the evening, the prayer was offered by J. Thomas, Brecon Conference President. Then very fervent sermons were given by Thomas Harris, West Glamorgan Conference President; President Israel Evans from Salt Lake Valley; Benjamin Evans, Monmouth Conference President; and Pastor J. B. Martin from Bristol.

It can be said that we had an excellent Conference; the brethren received the power of the Holy Ghost to deliver the word with clarity, and we hope to see the beneficent effects from it all in the coming days.

We held the Tea Party the following afternoon, when several hundred of those who had tickets partook of the delicious tea and bran cake; and in the evening a Concert was held, which concluded the work of the two days. It is worth noting that the choirs of Merthyr, Cwmbach, and Aberaman did their part in a splendid way through all the meetings.

T. STEPHENS, Scribe.

ZION'S TRUMPET,

OR

Star of the Saints.

SATURDAY, JULY 5, 1856.

"MARRIAGE AND MORALS IN UTAH."—Dear Saints,—We live in an age in which God has revealed his secret to his servants the Prophets as in the days of old, after restoring the Eternal Covenant, and while feasting on the sweet meals of revealed truth which bring eternal life to us, we are surrounded by a host of zealous and false religionists who consider us to be "false prophets," and the most filthy and deceitful men on the face of the earth. They teach their children to recite the topic, as it is called, in the sabbath school to strike their fancy. The teacher asks, "Who are the false prophets?" The host of children shout loudly, in the old customary tune, "The - old - Lat - ter - day - Saints," &c. At the same time there are others who believe that the sectarian religions of our land are sound without any substance, and that the

Saints' religion of apostles, prophets, gifts, revelations, marriages and morals, and everything else is the religion that provides belief and power; but they fail to see through the principle of plural marriage: the poor things! What is the wonder? They have not had the opportunity to hear anything but the blasphemies of our enemies who themselves are full of adultery and fornication, and, like the man who has yellow fever, they see everyone else as having yellow fever also. Every Saint who has experienced the true eternal virtue knows how the holy principle of marriage and morals practiced by the Saints is maligned and mocked. Its connection with the beginning and increase, the health and strength of nations, yes, even *worlds*, is such as the foundation is to a building: through practicing it our world continued to increase and strengthen: through the perversion of it the world has begun and will continue to decline,—men will become still more corrupt and more scarce, until the earth will become empty, except for the few men who are left, namely those who have not transgressed the laws, &c. By living in accordance with it the giants of old in Israel were of the kind we read about in the account of judges and kings of Israel; and as we compare the length of life, or the physical strength and health of this age with that of the men of old, we ask ourselves, What is the cause of the difference? It is the perversion of this principle. What Saint then, who has a particle of love for God's cause, will allow such a pure and heavenly truth to be besmirched with the unhealthy filth of the corrupt men of our age, before coming to understand the virtuous substance in it? President Richards wishes for the new English pamphlet on this topic to have a place on *every hearth and family of Saints in Wales*. We have given the complete translation of it in our two latest issues. Tens of thousands of them are being ordered by the English Conference Presidents, who are striving in every way to circulate it, to show to the world, and as many as love virtue and chastity, that the marriage law and morals of the Saints are not just the pile of unwholesomeness as they are described. May it go to every family of Saints, and may its circulation be wide; and since the Welsh are encouraged, for their own good, to learn English, they will yet be happy someday to have secured a copy of this valuable treatise: let no Saint be without it, and do not leave any preacher or listener, or any intelligent person, without it or without an offer of it, so that all may be without excuse in the day of judgment, when they will be obliged to acknowledge that the Saints are a virtuous people, and that they should have known that. Let the Distributors send to the Liverpool Office for it, according to the direction of their Presidents. Be generous, brethren.

FULFILLMENT OF PROPHECIES ABOUT ANCIENT BABYLON.

Continued from page 205.

The following prophecies are to be had about the fall of Babylon,—Isaiah xiii, xiv, and xlv; Jeremiah l and li: we quote a few:—"And Babylon, the glory of kingdoms, the beauty of the Chaldees' excellency, shall be as when God overthrew Sodom and Gomorrah. It shall never be inhabited, neither shall it be dwelt in from generation to generation: neither shall the Arabian pitch tent there; neither shall the shepherds make their fold there; but the wild beasts of the desert shall lie there; and their houses shall be full of doleful creatures; and owls shall dwell there, and satyrs shall dance there: and the wild beasts of the islands shall cry in their desolate houses, and dragons in their pleasant palaces: and her time is near to come, and her days shall not be prolonged. For I will rise up against them, saith the Lord of hosts, and cut off from Babylon the name, and remnant, and son, and nephew, saith the Lord: I will also make it a possession for the bittern, and pools of water: and I will sweep it with the besom of destruction, saith the Lord of hosts. Thus saith the Lord to his anointed, to Cyrus, whose right hand I have holden, to subdue nations before him; and I will loose the loins of kings, to open before him the two leaved gates; and the gates shall not be shut; I will go before thee, and make the crooked places straight; I will break in pieces the gates of brass, and cut in sunder the bars of iron, and I will give thee the treasures of darkness, and hidden riches of secret places, that thou mayest know that I, the Lord, which call thee by thy name, am the God of Israel. Declare ye among the nations, and publish, and set up a standard; publish, and conceal not; say, Babylon is taken, Bel is confounded, Merodach is broken in pieces; her idols are confounded, her images are broken in pieces; because of the wrath of the Lord it shall not be inhabited, but it shall be wholly desolate: everyone that goeth by Babylon shall be astonished, and hiss at all her plagues: come against her from the utmost border, open her storehouses; cast her up as heaps, and destroy her utterly: let nothing of her be left. One post shall run to meet another, and one messenger to meet another, to shew the king of Babylon that his city is taken at one end. And Babylon shall become heaps, a dwelling place for dragons, an astonishment, and an hissing, without an inhabitant."

The observation of Herodotus and Xenophon, two famous historians, about the siege and subjugation of Babylon, agrees completely with the prophecies of Isaiah and Jeremiah. They say that Cyrus, together with a large army of the Medes and Persians, laid siege to Babylon; that the Babylonians trusted in the unshakeable strength of their walls, and because of their confidence they remained calm and unprepared against their enemies; that Cyrus planned to ensnare them by turning the flow of the Euphrates river to a large lake, and after the river had dried because of this stratagem the soldiers would go into the city along the river's bottom; also that the guards of the city had carelessly left some of the gates open, and that among all these things the army of Cyrus went in and took the city on the evening of a feast of idol worshiping being attended by the citizens, the nobility, the captains, the princes, &c., and that Cyrus and his soldiers quickly killed them while they were drunk; and that in this manner this famous city, never before conquered, was subjugated without the king's knowing, to whom messengers went to report the news, which he had barely heard before he himself was counted among the slain.

Babylon began to deteriorate soon afterwards: their extremely high walls were leveled to a fourth of their previous height; and it was reduced from an empire to a tributary city. Xerxes, the successor to Cyrus of Persia, took possession of all its treasures that were considered sacred; he spoiled its temples, destroyed its idols, which were made of precious metals.

Alexander set about the task of returning Babylon to its customary glory, and he intended to make it the capital city of a widespread empire. He put ten thousand men to work to restore the banks of the Euphrates, and the Belus temple; but Alexander's death put an end to the project. About one hundred and thirty years before the birth of Christ, the Parthian conquerors destroyed the fairest parts of Babylon. After the beginning of the Gospel dispensation, the inhabitants of Babylon were rare, and vast pieces of land within the walls were fertilized for cultivation. Babylon continued to deteriorate, her population continued to decrease, until the nineteenth century when her walls formed dens and shelters for wild animals to breed and to dwell, and thus Babylon was made a hunting park for the kings of Persia. From being the glory of kingdoms she became the greatest ruin, and after the passage of two thousand and four hundred years, before the eyes of every traveler she appears exactly as the sad scene described by the holy prophets,—the name and remnant were cut off from Babylon; neither shall the Arabian pitch tent there, neither shall the shepherds make their fold there; but the wild beasts shall lie there, and their houses shall be full of doleful creatures; where there are owls and dragons: she is a dry land and a wilderness—a burnt mountain—desolate—completely uninhabited—lakes of water—ruins—completely destroyed—a land where no man lives—everyone that goes by shall be astonished—the superstitious dread of evil spirits together with the fear of wild beasts, and the dragons in the midst of the ruins will keep the Arabians from pitching their tents and the shepherds from making their fold there. The royal palaces and habitations of the remarkable city, Babylon, are nothing but piles of bricks and scattered rubbish now! Instead of fine rooms, now there is nothing but dark caves, where the porcupines, the owls, the bats, and all kinds of ugly and evil creatures move. A stench comes up from there, and by the gates there are bones of sheep and goats scattered around. Nimrod's tower, or the temple of Belus, which was standing after the beginning of the Gospel dispensation, can be seen to some extent now. It was visited and depicted by some English travelers lately. The ruins show, to a great extent, the primitive splendor of the place; and even though the aforementioned Temple has been a ruin for many hundreds of years, its rubble now is about 245 feet high. On this ruin there are many pieces of molten brickwork that sound like glass when struck. From the top of this rubble one has a look at the rocky ruins of Babylon of old, which was at one time the glory of the kingdoms, and one cannot obtain a more perfect and complete view of the desolation than from here. From this we perceive that the greatest and most splendid work of mortals is brought to naught, and their highest monuments, their power, their skill, and their wealth are brought to the same level as the dust, and their rocky ruins are kept for the purpose of demonstrating and confirming the witness of the true God, as mentioned in his divine word. God's predictions through his servants the prophets seem so remarkable when we compare them with the events to which they direct our mind! The truth and divinity of the holy scriptures are shown so clearly! With such splendid propriety does the immortal Jehovah set out his foreknowledge in connection with that which came upon Babylon, for example, and in giving a challenge to the false Gods of all creation, and any of their supporters, to show anything similar! "Who hath declared this from ancient time? who hath told it from that time? have not I the Lord? and there is no God else beside me: a just God and a Savior: there is none beside me: declaring the end from the beginning; and from ancient times, the things that are not yet done: saying, My counsel shall stand, and I will do all my pleasure." Isaiah xlv and xlvi.

(To be continued.)

Alltwen. W. F. WILLIAMS.

THE HAND OF PROVIDENCE.

OF ALL the orders in the world,
    To bring about wise and beauteous virtue;
I never yet have seen in any place,
    One to equal the work of fair providence.
O! what a depth of riches there are,
    In the wisdom which comes from God!
Its work is found by night and day,
    In the design of every living creature:
From the enormous giant leviathan
    That plays in the watery depths,
To the great roaring lion
    That speeds through the vast wilderness;
From the living creatures seen on high
    Through the ten firmaments everywhere,
From the sharp-eyed eagle on strong wings

>   To the weary feeble reptiles.
> Among a myriad of tiny insects,
>   Is seen the evidence of its artful fingers,
> Skillfully arranging one by one
>   Their circles for each of these.
> Among the myriad colors of the flowers of the field,
>   Which are beautiful and delicately scented,
> And the trees that adorn the green earth
>   Is seen the hand of great providence;
> Gold, silver, minerals, precious pearls,
>   And the entirety of hidden treasures,
> That are found by searching the depths of the earth,
>   Show its skillfulness;
> The position of the stars, comets, sun and moon,
>   The order of the seasons, the dew and rain,
> Demonstrate the infinite store
>   Of ability in the gifted hand.
> Thus throughout the sublime creation
>   Are seen marks of its talent and power:
> Its subtle work in man's design
>   Is even more amazing to me;
> For though the world is overcome by evil,
>   And life is soured through this plague,
> It brings to us a remedy
>   From its lovely treasure to cure with joy:
> A baptism was given for full forgiveness
>   Of all the sins of the world's faults,
> And the Holy Ghost is our witness
>   To its continuing strength and virtue.
> Pure cleansing and consecration,
>   The holy ordinances of heaven,
> And the great joy of lasting peace
>   Are the powers of the strong gospel.
>
>   DARK NATHAN OF LLYWEL.

ANOTHER WITNESS FOR MORMONISM.

Pembrokeshire, June 7, 1856.

DEAR President Daniels.—There was a lot of talk through our neighborhoods here in Pembrokeshire, when I joined with the children and people of the Lord, regarding my "unparalleled fanaticism." Some said it was the effect of meditation in the academy that brought this about; others said that my purpose was "to take hold of the *deceit of Mormonism*, in order to expose it to the public;" but all united in one voice to say that I would not last more than a few days with the Saints. But by now several months have gone by, and the more in depth I research, and the more I ponder the doctrine of the Saints, all the more I see of its glory. This proves to me that glory pertains to it, and the faithful Saints will be brought from glory to glory by the Spirit of the Lord.

Now, I wish to announce to the public that I am staying safe in the most holy faith, and if the following lines are worthy of your attention, I would love to see them printed in "Zion's Trumpet."

> There is great love in my bosom,
>   Toward thee Pure Jesus;
> I have thy spirit warmly,
>   And it is burning like fire.
> Not a *strange* fire of the sectarians,
>   But a fire of the pure love of heaven,
> And through the help of the comforter,
>   Every day I cry to you.
>
> It tells me that "Joseph,"
>   Very diligently proclaims,
> To the spirits in prisons,
>   The freedom of full salvation.
> The Spirit says that thousands of those,
>   Will become free before long;
> They will receive their bodies to dwell in,
>   Yonder in Zion's holy land.
>
> It tells me to love the brethren,
>   And the sisters strong and weak,
> It says also that Jesus will come,
>   Down to his temple presently.
> It tells me to testify,
>   For Jesus, the true Son of God,
> That his priceless and pleasant Gospel,
>   Is now in the possession of mankind.
>
> God will impart its blessings,
>   As a witness to each one,

Who gives heartfelt obedience,
    To the commandments of the Son of Man.
They will no longer grope in darkness,
    As they travel over the earth,
But they will receive the Holy Ghost,
    With great strength and assurance.

By the Holy Ghost we shall not fear,
    The constant mockery and shame of the world,
And, "In the midst of fire and stones."
    All say, "We are happy."
Not to us, O gracious Lord,
    But to Thee be the praise,
For sending perfect order,
    To gladden under the Sun.

Who will declare longer that a deceiver,
    Was Joseph Smith, the servant of God?
He received the keys,
    Also the power,—it is true.
Whoever may deny that in anger,
    Let him also deny the rising of the sun,
It is the same evil spirit that leads him,
    To deny the merit of the Second Adam.

But, O! know this presumptuous man,
    God will call you to judgment for that,
You will be put in a dark prison,
    While we are free on Zion's hill.
But we thank our heavenly Father,
    That it is not yet too late,
And therefore give obedience,
    To the commandments of Great Jesus.

        DAVID JOHN, *Lately from Haverfordwest College.*

CONTENTS.

	PG.
The Millennium	209
The East Glamorgan Conference	214
Editorial—Marriage and Morals in Utah	216
Fulfillment of Prophecy	218
The Hand of Providence	221
Another Witness for Mormonism	222

SWANSEA:

PRINTED AND PUBLISHED BY D. DANIELS.

ZION'S TRUMPET,

OR

Star of the Saints.

No. 15.] JULY 19, 1856. [Vol. IX.

TITHING.

(From the Star.)

In the beginning, when the great plan for the salvation of man was decreed, one of the various doctrines or principles which were then ordained to be observed by him was that of paying tithes of his substance. And it was from this great law of heaven, that men originally obtained the idea of charging each other interest, commission, rent, &c.

"The field is the world," and for the use of this field, it has ever been the duty of mankind to pay to its owner ten percent of all they have been permitted to gather from it. In later times, when Israel failed to bring their tithes into the storehouse, the Lord charged them with having robbed him; *Malachi* iii. 8.

The Bible gives us but little information on any of the great leading principles of Gospel faith, as held by mankind, or revealed to them previous to the days of Noah; and it says as little about tithing as of any other of the doctrines which were revealed for the salvation of man, from the fall.

Paul states that the Gospel was before preached unto Abraham, and that among the most important doctrines observed by him was that of paying the tithe of his substance to the High Priest Melchizedek; "And he gave him tithes of all;" *Genesis* xiv, 20. This law continued to be strictly enforced by the Patriarchal fathers,

15 [Price 1*c*.

and was continued in Israel after they became a nation. Its mode of application to the people in those times is detailed in the law given to them by Moses, which was most religiously adhered to by all who lived in favor with God. Even after the departure of Israel into transgression, this ordinance continued as a great national characteristic, insomuch that the Pharisee in his prayer named it as one of his righteous acts—"I give tithes of all that I possess."

Some suppose that when Christ came the law of tithing was done away, from the fact that he gave no positive commandment, of which we have knowledge, that it should be continued. The reason that it was not taught to the Jewish disciples evidently was because the Jews at that time kept this law strictly. If Jesus Christ did not enforce it by a new commandment, he sanctioned it by his approval, for he said to the Pharisees, "Ye pay tithes of mint, anise, and cummin, but omit the weightier matters of the law; these ought ye to have done, and not to have left the other undone." Jesus taught the Jews those weightier matters of the law which they neglected; hence we hear but little of the law of tithing, which they were diligent in keeping. We find, by instances already referred to, that this law, like the one of sacrifice and burnt offerings, and the celestial law of marriage, was given long before the Ten Commandments, held sacred by all professed Bible believers, were delivered to Moses amid the thunderings and lightnings of Sinai.

Therefore, it is a law to all mankind, handed down from the beginning, and, if possible, made more especially binding upon the lineage of the Priesthood and the blood of Israel, than on the rest of the world, by special commandment and covenant. When the Holy Spirit of Promise lifted the veil from the visions of the mind of Jacob, and he beheld the glorious fulfillment of the promises which the Lord had given him—that his seed should become as numerous as the sands on the seashore or the stars in heaven, and that the good things of the earth should be multiplied upon him and his posterity, in the fullness of his heart he covenanted with the Lord saying, "of all that thou shalt give me I will surely give the tenth unto thee"; *Genesis* xxviii, 22. Hence this law of tithing is obligatory upon all the blood of Israel, by the special covenant of their father, Jacob, as well as by subsequent commandment given to them through Moses, which, as we have seen, was expressly sanctioned by Jesus Christ while on the earth.

The Roman Church and the Church of England teach and enforce the law of tithing, and, like many other principles which are good of themselves, but which men have perverted to evil purposes, they have been derived from commandments which the Lord gave to his Priesthood in earlier periods of the world, for high and holy purposes. When those who held this Priesthood, and practiced these laws in righteousness, became corrupt, they also perverted the laws and ordinances of heaven, and made use of them to carry out their own selfish purposes, without any regard to the object for which the Lord designed them. As the Kingdom of God becomes established, all these laws and ordinances, together with many important ones of which the world has not even a vestige remaining, will gradually be adopted by the Saints and carried out for the accomplishment of the purposes for which the Lord designed them in the beginning; and this is being done with the tithing among the Saints—it is appropriated to the purpose of establishing a nation of Kings and Priests to the Most High God, on the earth, by building temples, &c.

When the Priesthood was again restored to the earth through Joseph Smith, this commandment was made obligatory upon Israel in the last days. No person will ever inherit the blessings of Abraham, Isaac, and Jacob, until they learn to abide this law, and appreciate the blessings of so doing. If they never fulfill it they will be aliens from the commonwealth of Israel, and forfeit all right to an inheritance in the kingdom of God. Furthermore the Lord said, in a revelation to Joseph, "He that is tithed shall not be burned; for after today cometh the burning."

The dealings of the Lord with his people in every period of time when the Priesthood has been on the earth, and more particularly in this last dispensation, go to show that the fulfillment of the law of tithing is necessary in order to attain to that measure of salvation which every Saint indulges the hope of realizing. If any are saved without keeping it, it will only be "so as by fire." Though themselves should remain, their works will be like hay and stubble in the day of burning.

There have always been some in the Church who have felt too poor to pay the Lord his portion, and, while this has been the case with some who were really poor, it has been still more so with those who have had comparative abundance. Such Saints remind one of a greedy beggar who, instead of being grateful for favors bestowed, only clamors the louder for more. That is, their avariciousness increases in proportion as it is gratified. If such do not repent, when the day of reckoning comes, they will find a heavy balance of accounts against them, which they will have to pay to the uttermost farthing.

The importance of the law of tithing is wonderfully manifest in the dealings of the Lord with his people in this dispensation. When sick and comparatively destitute, in the city of Nauvoo, from their recent persecutions in Missouri, the Lord required his tithes of them; and it was with these accumulated mites of the poor that a Temple was built which cost a million dollars, in which the Lord bestowed the higher keys of the Priesthood upon the faithful, which has enabled his servants, in spite of mobs, infuriated by legions of devils from the regions of darkness, to bear off his kingdom on the earth, and administer salvation to scattered Israel.

During the life of the Prophet Joseph, and while the Saints were in Nauvoo, those who paid their tithing had privileges with regard to the ordinances of the Lord's house, which others had not; among which was the important one of baptism for their dead.

After the Saints had been driven from Nauvoo, and had, by the blessing of the Lord, begun to establish themselves in the valleys of the mountains, in a great measure away from Gentile influences, He revealed to them more fully the law of tithing; and they consecrated themselves, and their new home, anew unto the Lord, by keeping this law more perfectly. The Saints in Zion are required to pay their tithing, and if there are any who do not, they soon cease to have a name in Israel. The door of the House of the Lord is closed to such, and they find themselves cut off from the blessings of salvation—

from the only channel through which they can become Saviors upon Mount Zion, to themselves, their posterity, and to their dead.

A law requiring sacrifice was always necessary in ancient Israel to keep them in mind of their God; and it is equally necessary in modern Israel, to continually remind them from whom they receive their blessings. Were it not that the Saints were thus constantly called upon to sacrifice a portion of their worldly goods, which they have been taught to call their own, but the whole of which virtually belongs to the Lord, they would get fat and sick, and soon forget that the kingdom of God is to be established on the earth, or that it is necessary for them to do something in order to have an inheritance in it.

In proportion as the Saints in these lands have increased in knowledge and faith, the desire has increased in their hearts to be assimilated more and more in their works, as well as in their faith and feelings, to their brethren and sisters in Zion; and thus a great portion of them have been prepared for the reception of the law of tithing. We permitted several of the brethren in the ministry to introduce it into their fields of labor, several months since, and so large a proportion of the Saints in the Conferences where it has been introduced, have grasped it in their faith and worked to it, and have testified so abundantly of the many blessings which they have received through its observance, that we have been constrained, by the Holy Spirit, to recommend to all the Conferences to adopt this law practically; and we say to all who will be faithful in doing so, they shall be strengthened in the faith, have a renewal of the Holy Spirit upon them, and receive a rich increase of the blessings of the Lord. When they gather home to Zion they will discover that they have been doing a preparatory work here, which will have fitted them to keep in greater perfection the law of the Lord there—to adopt more freely than they otherwise would do, the measures which are there carried out, through which the faithful receive sanctification and blessing.

Tithing has hitherto been required in this country of those who have had more means than were necessary to emigrate them—while it has not been required of those who have had barely sufficient to do this. All tithing of this nature should still be forwarded to this Office, the same as heretofore, that the persons paying it may receive *credit* for the same in the General Tithing Office in Great Salt Lake City; but all tithings which are for less than £10 will be under the direction and control of the Conferences in which they are paid, subject to the counsels of those who may be over them in the Priesthood. Out of it the current expenses of the Branches and Conferences should be discharged, the various general funds sustained, and, after the apportionment of the Temple Offering to each Conference is paid, the balance can be appropriated to such objects as are required, for the spreading of the Gospel and the gathering of Israel. We trust that none will lose sight of the importance of the P. E. Fund, but let the payment of the Temple Offering, and the gathering of the poor be the two great leading considerations.

While laboring in this country, we have received letters from brethren who had more or less property, stating that they did not seem to enjoy the fruits of the Spirit, and to have that joy in the work of the Lord which many of their brethren appeared to receive. In most or all of these cases, it will be found that these men have not paid the Lord that portion of their possessions which is his due, and we would ask them what right they have to ask or to expect the Lord to bless them with the choice blessings of his Spirit, with revelation, knowledge, and wisdom, and the power to save themselves and families, in the day of affliction, if they are not willing to pay him the moiety of this world's goods which He claims at their hands. If such men do not speedily repent of having robbed God, and become honest with themselves, with the Saints, and with Him, they will soon lose the little light which they now have, and be given over to hardness of heart and blindness of mind, apostatize, and go down to death.

In conclusion, on this subject, we wish to remind the Saints that they should continually look forward, with the eye of faith, to the time when they shall have gathered home, where they will be expected to live up to the still higher law of consecration which is now being adopted by the Saints in Zion, and which all on that land will be required to keep who would attain to the glories and exaltations of the celestial kingdom.

LETTER OF RECONCILIATION TO PRESIDENT DANIEL DANIELS.

Rhymney, July 12, 1856.

Dear President Daniels,—In agreement with that which J. Jones wrote, I add that I am in complete conformity with the judgment of President Spencer in the Merthyr Council, and I do not see now how he could have done better under the circumstances; thus, I ask forgiveness of God and his Church for all my transgressions, and I request to have a place again, even if it is the lowest, in the Church of God, together with a part in your prayers that I might continue faithful in it.

I am, your humble servant,

Wm. Sims.

[It is our pleasure to perceive the beneficent effects of that Spirit which strives with man so long as there is some hope for improvement until justice shouts, "Leave him be." We are happy to understand that such is not the case for W. S., rather that he has listened to the still, small voice of the gentle Spirit of a longsuffering God, and through its light has come to agree with President Spencer regarding the behavior of President Jones in the matter under scrutiny. The decision that came to President Spencer was, "that Brother Jones had acted in a philanthropic, generous, just and honest manner, and had shown himself to be a benefactor of the destitute, at his own cost, (as we well know,) and had risked his own good name. We also know that the greatest friend of W. S. would be Bro. Jones, were he here to see the change. That the Lord may bless W. Sims, so that he may be as faithful as we once saw him to be before, and even more faithful, so that he may win glory in the kingdom of God is the prayer of the—*Editor.*]

Religious Freedom. It is necessary for political and religious freedom to open the way for the preaching of the Gospel, in every nation, and we rejoice at seeing new ways opening continually for the entrance into the midst of the nations of the old world. Because of the recent war, religious freedom has been granted in Turkey. This will also affect the gathering of the Jews, and the redemption of the land of promise.—*Star.*

ZION'S TRUMPET,

OR

Star of the Saints.

SATURDAY, JULY 19, 1856.

TITHING.—In this issue are the observations on this subject of our President F. D. Richards, who is an Apostle for Jesus Christ. They will be received happily, and their objective will be appreciated by each one who is intent on building the Kingdom of God, and receiving salvation therein; and he will not see anything he can do as being too much for its sake, while the short-sighted and the narrow-minded can perhaps look no further than their supposed present enjoyment nor feel inclined to do as much. One must sow before he can reap, and the one cannot reap what the other has sown. The farmer is sufficiently perceptive to see that he is not losing the seed that he sows, rather he is preparing to receive an hundredfold in the coming year. The faithful Saint expects not only an inheritance on the restored earth, under the reign of our Lord Jesus Christ, but also present blessings and assistance while he is dealing with the work. "This work must be finished," says a hymn that we sing: the more we do the sooner we will finish it; and "he who will not work, neither will he eat." Zion is to be completely built, the Kingdom of God is to be entirely established, Israel is to be totally gathered, Satan is to be thoroughly overcome, Jesus is to reign perfectly, and the fallen world is to be fully redeemed. "It is easier to say than to do," says an old proverb, and the previous saying is a great one; but how much greater is the fulfillment of it? This work has already cost the best blood of the nineteenth century, and the diligent efforts of twenty-six years, to have brought it thus far. Persecution and scorn, killing and burning, imprisonment and whipping, planting and building, sowing and reaping, traveling and preaching, moving and resettling have been some of the chief traits of our enemies and ourselves in the meantime. Several of the old heroes—the *pioneers*—those who as it were "broke the ice," have gone beyond the veil to rest from the pain and affliction of mortality, and we see new hands taking hold of the task. It is also a fact that until now Satan has not been bound, nor has his kingdom been shattered: is it likely then that we will have fair weather and idle time any different from our predecessors? There are not to be idlers in the kingdom of God; for it is not an intangible one like that of the sectarians: besides a king, it will contain subjects, laws and officers, towns and villages, houses and lands, cities and temples. Houses and temples will be built with tangible stones and huge, jagged rocks, and it will be necessary to dig them and to transport them. With the dust of iron and lead and the strength of arms is the common way to shatter kingdoms, and fortifications will be built with earth and stones. After Israel had done its best God comes to the field with his thunderings, his lightning, and his hail to make up the deficiency. In steamboats, ships, wagons, handcarts, &c., Israel will gather until God sends his angels to make up the deficiency. For all these things it is required to have workers, goods, money, &c. We read that it is with the Saints' tithing that these things are completed in Zion, and behold us here receiving the same unspeakable privilege. Who would not sow now while earthly time persists, so as to reap Christ's unfathomable riches in eternity?

STATE OF DESERET.—The movements of the "stone cut out of the mountain" are similar to that of a snowball making itself bigger and bigger: from being six members it became a neighborhood, then settlements and branches and a city; and after that, through the generosity of her enemies' voluntarily taking the trouble of turning her out of the city of Nauvoo, she became the Territory of Utah. This is Mormonism instead of being "finished and dead," and the Mormons, instead of "diminishing, scattering and starving," are "flourishing and multiplying and filling the earth." Among the emigrants from distant countries, the frequent, little emigrants from the other world, and those who were there already, there is a sufficient number to claim their own free and independent government, united with the rights of the great mother government which throws her protective mantel across all the States and joins them in one family. When they are received into the Union as a State, our readers will see by the translated articles in this issue that they will choose their own governor and make their own laws. At that time the privileges and punishments of the laws of God will be in force, as in ancient Israel. Then let the righteous rejoice,—those who long to see the will of God done on earth as it is in heaven, and let the transgressor fear and beware of the evil of his intent; for judgment will be laid to the line, and righteousness to the plummet, and neither root nor branch will be left for the ungodly in Zion, where He who is like a refiner's fire and fullers' soap will come to dwell. Perhaps it is after the judgment begins in God's house, and things are there made right, that Zion will be commanded to rise in her majestic splendor and her power, and with her iron horn and brass hoofs shatter the many nations. Is it not a privilege to have the opportunity to live according to some of the lesser laws now, so that we can adapt ourselves to receive the higher laws: and is it not obvious that if we cannot keep those we would be poor citizens in the State of Deseret?

CONSTITUTION OF THE STATE OF DESERET.

(From the "Deseret News.")

PREAMBLE.

Whereas all citizens of the United States have the right guaranteed by the Constitution to make those laws by which they are governed; and

Whereas, it appears from a census report, made pursuant to an act of the late legislature, that the Territory of Utah possesses a population sufficiently numerous to justify them in asserting their claims to this inestimable privilege;

Therefore, we the people, grateful to the Supreme Being for the enjoyment of life and mercy, and feeling our dependence on Him for a continuation of those blessings, do ordain and establish the following Constitution:—

ARTICLE I.

Boundary and Name.

SEC. 1. All that part of the territory of the United States now known as Utah Territory, and bounded as follows, viz:—On the west by the State of California, on the north by the Territory of Oregon, on the east by the summit of the Rocky Mountains, and on the south by the 37th parallel of north latitude, is hereby formed into a free and sovereign State, and named Deseret.

ARTICLE II.

Declaration of Rights.

Sec. 1. In republican governments all men should possess their natural rights, among which are those of enjoying and defending their life and liberty, acquiring, possessing, and protecting property, and of seeking and obtaining their safety and happiness.

Sec. 2. All political power is inherent in the people, and all free governments are founded in their authority, and instituted for their benefit; therefore they have an inalienable and indefeasible right to institute government, and to alter, reform, or totally change the same, when their safety, happiness, and the public good shall require it.

Sec. 3. All men shall have a natural and inalienable right to worship god according to the dictates of their own consciences; and the General Assembly shall make no law respecting an establishment of religion, or prohibiting the free exercise thereof, or to disturb any person in his religious worship or sentiments, and all persons demeaning themselves peaceably, as good members of this State, shall be equally under the protection of the laws; and no subordination or preference of any sect or denomination to another shall ever be established by law, nor shall any religious test be ever required for any office of trust under this Constitution.

Sec. 4. Any person of this State who may hereafter be engaged, directly or indirectly, in a duel, either as principal or accessory before the fact, shall be disqualified from holding any office under the Constitution and laws of this State.

Sec. 5. Every person may speak, write, and publish his sentiments on all subjects, being responsible for the abuse of that right; and no law shall be passed to abridge the liberty of speech or of the press.

Sec. 6. The people shall be secure in their persons, houses, papers, and possessions, from unreasonable searches and seizures.

Sec. 7. The right of trial by jury shall remain inviolate, and all prisoners shall be heard by self, or counsel, at their own election; and no person shall be held to answer a capital or otherwise infamous crime, unless on presentment or indictment of a grand jury, nor shall any person be subject for the same offense to be twice put in jeopardy of life or limb, nor be compelled in any criminal case to be a witness against himself.

Sec. 8. All penalties and punishments shall be in proportion to the offense; and all offenses before conviction shall be bailable, except capital offenses, where the proof is evident, or the presumption great. Excessive bail shall not be required.

Sec. 9. The writ of habeas corpus shall not be suspended, unless in case of rebellion or invasion, or the public safety shall require it.

Sec. 10. Treason against this State shall consist only in levying war against it, or adhering to its enemies, or giving them aid and comfort.

Sec. 11. The General Assembly shall pass no bill of attainder, or ex-post-facto law, or law impairing the obligation of contracts.

Sec. 12. The law shall not be suspended but by legislative authority.

Sec. 13. The right of petition by the people shall be preserved inviolate.

Sec. 14. The right of citizens to keep and bear arms for common defense shall not be questioned.

Sec. 15. Private property shall not be taken for public use, without just compensation.

Sec. 16. No standing army shall be kept up in this State in time of peace, and the military shall at all times and in all places be in strict subordination to civil power.

Sec. 17. The enumeration of certain rights shall not be construed to impair or deny others retained by the people.

ARTICLE III.

The powers of government of the State of Deseret shall be divided into three distinct departments, viz:—legislative, executive, and judicial.

ARTICLE IV.

Of the Legislative.

Sec. 1. The legislative authority shall be vested in a General Assembly consisting of a senate and house of representatives, the members of which shall be elected by the people.

Sec. 2. The sessions of the General Assembly shall be annual, until otherwise provided by legislative enactment: and the first session shall be as hereinafter provided.

Sec. 3. The members of the house of representatives shall be chosen biennially, by the qualified electors of their respective districts, whose terms of office shall continue two years from the day of their election.

Sec. 4. Senators shall be chosen in the same manner as the representatives, whose term of office shall continue four years from the day of their election.

Sec. 5. No person shall be a member of the General Assembly except he be a free, white, male citizen of the United States, and an inhabitant of this State one year preceding the time of his election, and has at his election an actual residence in the district he may be chosen to represent.

Sec. 6. The General Assembly shall have power to prescribe the number and make the apportionment of senators and representatives; provided the number of senators shall not be less than one-third nor more than one half of the representatives; and at its first session the General Assembly shall be divided by lot as equally as may be into two classes; the seats of the representatives of the first class shall be vacated at the expiration of one year, and of the senators of the first class, at the expiration of two years.

Sec. 7. Each house shall choose its own officers, and judge of the qualification, election, and return of its own members.

SEC. 8. A majority in each house shall constitute a quorum to do business; but a smaller number may adjourn from day to day, and compel the attendance of absent members, in such manner and under such penalty as each house may provide.

SEC. 9. Each house shall have all powers necessary for a branch of the General Assembly of a free and independent government.

SEC. 10. Each member of the General Assembly shall be privileged from civil arrest during any session, and in going to and returning from the same.

SEC. 11. Neither house shall, without the consent of the other, adjourn for more than three days, nor to any other place than that in which they may be sitting.

SEC. 12. The members of the General Assembly shall take an oath or affirmation to support the Constitution of the United States and of this State, which may be administered by each other, or by any person qualified to administer oaths.

SEC. 13. The veto power of the Governor shall be allowed by the General Assembly, except on bills which when reconsidered shall be again passed by a majority of two-thirds; and any bill vetoed by the Governor shall be returned within ten days (Sundays excepted) with his objections, otherwise it shall become a law, unless the General Assembly, by adjournment, prevent its return.

SEC. 14. Every law passed by the General Assembly shall take effect from and after its publication, unless otherwise provided at the time of its enactment.

SEC. 15. At the first election after this Constitution takes effect the voters of this State shall elect the same number of senators and representatives as are now elected to the Legislative Assembly of the Territory of Utah, and according to the present apportionment.

SEC. 16. The legislative power of the General Assembly of this State shall extend to all rightful subjects of legislation consistent with the Constitution of the United States and of this State.

ARTICLE V.

Of the Executive.

SEC. 1. The executive power shall be vested in a Governor, whose term of office shall be four years. A Lieutenant Governor shall be elected at the same time, and for the same term, who shall be the president of the senate.

Sec. 2. No person shall be eligible to the office of Governor or Lieutenant Governor, who has not been a citizen of the United States six years, and a resident of this Senate four years next preceding his election.

Sec. 3. The Governor shall be commander-in-chief of the militia, navy, and all the armies of this State.

Sec. 4. He shall transact all executive business with the officers of government, civil and military, and may require information in writing from the officers of the executive department upon any subject relating to the duties of their respective offices.

Sec. 5. He shall see that the laws are faithfully executed.

Sec. 6. When any office shall from any cause become vacant, and no mode is prescribed by the Constitution and laws for filling such vacancy, the Governor shall have power to fill such vacancy by appointment and commission, which shall expire when such vacancy shall be filled by due course of law.

Sec. 7. He shall also have power to convene the General Assembly by proclamation, when in his opinion the interests of the State require it.

Sec. 8. He shall communicate by message to the General Assembly at every session the condition of the State, and recommend such measures as he in his wisdom shall deem expedient.

Sec. 9. In case of disagreement in the General Assembly with regard to the time of adjournment, the Governor shall have power to dissolve the session by proclamation.

Sec. 10. No person shall, while holding any lucrative office under the United States or this State, execute the office of Governor, except as shall be prescribed by law.

Sec. 11. The Governor shall have power to grant reprieves and pardons, and commute punishments after conviction, except in cases of impeachment.

Sec. 12. There shall be a seal of this State which shall be kept by the Governor and used by him officially, and be called "Great Seal of the State of Deseret."

Trans. Dewi Elfed Jones.

ANNOUNCEMENTS, &c.

Presidents Orson Pratt and Ezra T. Benson have arrived in England. An urgent invitation to all Conference Presidents who understand English for them to meet in a Special General Council to be held in Birmingham, next Monday, the 21st. A Conference will be held there tomorrow, the 20th.

☞ Elder John Jones of Merthyr, (formerly Brecon), has been appointed to travel throughout the Conferences of the North, to preach to the world and instruct the Saints, as will be convenient for him. He is full of the spirit of work, and is likely to do great good; therefore let the Saints receive him and behave toward him accordingly. Elder Dewi Elfed Jones has also been appointed to travel through the Conferences of the South. We say the same thing about him as well.

Receipts for Books From June 20 to July 16.—T. Stephens, £4 3s 9c; E. S. Morgans, 11s 11c; W. Jones, 5s; J. Jones, 10s 7c; T. Rees, 9s; J. Treharn, 12s 6c; T. Jones, 5s; J. Davies, £3.

☞ For lack of space we had to omit the accounting of the book debts, and the Biannual Report because the Presidents did not send a copy here of that which they sent to Liverpool. Several bits of good news will appear in our next issue.

CONTENTS.

	PG.
Tithing	225
Letter of Reconciliation	231
Religious Freedom	231
Editorial—Tithing—State of Deseret	232
Constitution of the State of Deseret	234
Announcements, &c.	240

SWANSEA:
PRINTED AND PUBLISHED BY D. DANIELS.

ZION'S TRUMPET,

OR

Star of the Saints.

No. 16.] AUGUST 2, 1856. [VOL. IX.

LETTER OF PRESIDENT BRIGHAM YOUNG.

President's Office,
Great Salt Lake City,
April 11, 1856.

Elder Franklin D. Richards.

Dear Brother—We were much gratified, on the second of this month, by the arrival of your letter of last November 25 and 30, containing the welcome intelligence that my hill and other property had been taken, for the benefit of the P. E. Fund Company's operations the ensuring season. We always rejoice in the reflection that we are in any manner instrumental in rolling forth the work of the last days, building up Zion, and gathering Israel from their long dispersion. We feel honored and obliged that we have this privilege, and esteem it the greatest blessing that could be conferred upon us.

To be high heaven's messengers unto those who sit in darkness, carrying light and intelligence, salvation and exaltation to the benighted minds of mankind, is a commission of which the noblest among the noble might be proud, and it has always been considered by me, that all we could perform was but our reasonable service and a privilege. My poor brethren are welcome to all that I can do towards mitigating their condition, and I wish I had the ability to do a hundred, a thousand, yes, a hundred thousand times more than I have done hitherto, it would be a pleasure to me, and as free as the air we breathe. I wish that I could devote the remainder of my property in the same way, and then I would go to work and accumulate more; I would sell all that I have and devote the means to building up and rolling forth the kingdom of our God, if I had the chance to do so.

I hope, before this, that the remainder of the list sent has been taken, and that you will receive, or rather at this late date have received the money from brother Tenant for my place, as well as the other proffered assistance. The place will be ready for him to occupy when he arrives. I am going to add some little improvements to the place, by way of fencing, &c., during the summer.

Your prospects at the date you wrote were truly flattering, and you seemed to have the right idea in regard to the standing rules. Still we must be more careful than heretofore in regard to incurring debts, and keep more within our resources. The last year's operations were pretty hard upon us, but we shall get through with them, by the help of the Almighty. I find they have absorbed almost our entire resources, and still we owe. If those indebted to the Fund could and would pay up in available means, it would relieve matters at once; but this seems impossible; if we get any pay whatever form those assisted, it is in labor on the Public Works, or in some kind of unavailable means which usually finds its way into that channel. You are aware that these men have to be supported, with their families, while so laboring, and that alone consumes our available means—to provide tools and material to work with, clothing, &c., for themselves and their families. This labor balances the money advanced in Liverpool, and along the route, leaving us bare of ready means to operate with every year, except such as may be furnished in Europe, which *drafts* on us we have generally been able to meet, but these oftentimes are troublesome to pay, owing to the above causes. Hence, while we desire to do all there is to be done, we find it necessary to use a large discretion, not too closely to tie up our own hands, nor trammel and retard our entire operations by reason of an overanxiety to do too much, at once, in any one particular channel. I admit that the gathering is one of the most important items, and feel willing, and even anxious, to promote that interest in preference to many others; but while we emigrate, we must also build up and provide a Zion to live in, as well as gather people to it. A call was made during Conference, now just closed, for those brethren who feel disposed to aid the gathering, to advertise property that they felt willing to donate; the same as I did mine last fall, and some have come forward, lists of which will be forwarded to brother Pratt, and, after he leaves, be forwarded to the Liverpool Office. We trust that much may be accomplished by this new opening, in the deliverance of the Saints.

I am glad that you have resolved to avoid sending any more Saints *via* New Orleans; it sickens the heart to think of the distress and deaths which have attended the Saints upon that route. I trust that we may shortly be enabled to shun St. Louis, and the travel up the Missouri as well. We are in hopes that a line of railroad will soon connect the eastern cities with Kanesville, then the Saints can have a comparatively healthy country to travel in all the way, which, added to the improvements made in shipping by the new regulations, will very materially add to their health, comfort, and convenience. We very much desire to bring up a small quantity of supplies the present season, and, if possible, the woolen factory machinery, stored so long in St. Louis. We trust that you will be able to render whatever effective aid we may lack, in promoting these objects.

In your letter relative to the P. E. Fund business, of Nov. 25 and 30, you remark, that persons reported back would not be sent out without a new order from this Office. This is right, and will be attended to in due time, of course they cannot come this season. We have some few other names which will also be forwarded, in the season thereof. We contemplate making settlements along the route from Kanesville to this place, and at such other places as may be suitable, from this place to Carson Valley, with a view of establishing a daily express through the entire route. This, when once carried into effect, and grain is once raised at these stations, will very materially aid our emigration; as they can easily travel from station to station, and find both *food* and *friends*.

We would like some of the stations located this season, and have instructed brother Erastus to carry into effect, so far as may be practicable, this operation the ensuing season. If, on your way home you should find it in your power to aid him any in this matter, by counseling in regard to establishing stations, &c., without hindering your progress, it would be esteemed a favor. American brethren should be selected to preside, and no settlement should be allowed, only upon the basis of a good substantial fort, and cattle corral, well picketed in, that stock may be secure from Indians.

Our affairs remain about the same as usual; we are pursuing the even tenor of our way, doing the best we can, and trying to extricate ourselves from the forms and trammels of a Territorial Government, and emerging into a free and independent State.

The Convention closed their labors on the March 27, having formed and adopted a Constitution, and memorial to *Congress*, and elected Delegates to present them to the President and Congress, asking for our admission into the Union as a State. The proceedings of the Convention were laid before the people, in accordance with the law, for their approval or rejection, on the 7th of this month, and were unanimously sustained. The Hons. George A. Smith, and John Taylor were chosen Delegates. We are in hopes to have a favorable action upon our application, during the present Session of Congress, if, indeed, they have got or will get an organization, of which we have not yet learned. Brothers A. O. Smoot and Ira Eldridge will go down to bring up our supplies, the property left last season, and the woolen factory machinery if possible. To the accomplishment of these objects we also desire your effective aid, so far as you may be able to help.

I wish you to remember me to Joseph A., Edmund, James A., and all the *boys* as you shall meet them. Tell my son Joseph that I have not time to write to him at present, but often bear him in my mind and prayers before the Lord. I trust that he, as well as all the others, remain faithful and true to their covenants, and will return pure and spotless from the contagious and filthy abominations of the world.

We have been obliged to suspend operations upon the Public Works for want of food for the hands. Provisions are indeed quite scarce. The past year has been rather a disastrous one to us in many particulars, but if the Saints of the Most High will profit by the rich lessons it has kindly inculcated, it will prove an instructive one, and its results become a blessing instead of an evil. In addition to the loss of our stock, owing to the severity of the winter, the Indians have of late been quite troublesome, driving off considerable quantities of cattle and horses, and finally killing some seven or eight of our brethren, but all is quiet just now, and we hope will remain so. There are but few of the Indians engaged in this disturbance.

Praying the Lord to bless and preserve you,

I remain your brother in the
Gospel of Christ,

BRIGHAM YOUNG.

THE MERIONETHSHIRE CONFERENCE,

WAS held in Machynlleth, Sunday, July 6th, 1856. Present were Elders B. Ashby of the Welsh Presidency, J. Treharn, Conference President, T. Jones, President of the Cardiganshire Conference, &c.

It was learned that the Branches are in good condition,—feeling determined to go forward. No one was baptized during the last quarter: 24 emigrated, (besides children). The usual business was conducted in the morning meeting, (sustaining of the authorities, &c.,) unanimously.

We decided to have the afternoon meeting to ourselves, a Saints meeting where all could partake of the Sacrament, since it is very infrequent that their scattered condition permitted some of them to have such a privilege. An opportunity was given for the bearing of testimonies and practicing the spiritual gifts. Elder T. Jones instructed the Saints to live in unity and love, and from every word that proceeds out of the mouth of God. In this manner was the meeting concluded.

In the evening meeting the President encouraged the Saints to pray for the light of the Spirit of God, so that they could understand the principles delivered by the speakers.

President B. Ashby.—He felt that it was good to be with us. He showed that it was not difficult for the people to keep the commandments of the Lord, as they were not unreasonable or burdensome, after properly understanding how to fulfill them. That the Gospel had been given to men to do good as well as to save themselves. He called our attention to the efforts of our elders in spreading the work of the Lord, which are so worthy of our doing likewise. He spoke about tithing, pointing out that the poor are the instruments in His hand to fulfill his work in every age. His speech greatly pleased all who could understand him. A summary of these observations were translated by the President, who remarked further that it was an honor and a privilege to have part in the work of God to build his kingdom.

The congregation was dismissed under the blessing of Pres. Ashby, and all the Officers and Saints went home full of life and renewed determination to fulfill all which they had heard,—to pay their tithing, to warn their neighbors, and to make every lawful effort toward building the Kingdom of God on the earth, and to shatter that of the enemy.

John Treharn, *President*,
Wm. Ajax, *Scribe*.

FULFILLMENT OF PROPHECIES ABOUT ANCIENT BABYLON.

Continued from page 221.

We began with ancient Babylon in her glory and majesty—we pointed out her shameful sins and her insufferable abomination—the anger of the Lord toward her—his predictions, through his holy Prophets, of her destruction, and we brought forth various accounts which agreed with one another to prove their fulfillment, and then we looked back over the whole of it, and we noticed with solemn surprise and alarm the truthfulness, the omnipotence, and the immutability of the Great Jehovah.

In conclusion, we add only the following reasoning,—Inasmuch as this obvious fact remains about the fulfillment of the word of the Lord against ancient Babylon, if we find out that He had announced such a destruction closer to home,—yes, even to reach to us *ourselves*, if we do not escape, it is logical for us to rely with certainty on the fulfillment of that, and putting aside the frightful account of ancient

Babylon, after seriously considering that 'it was given to us for our instruction,' going as from the shadow to the substance,—to reflect on the ancient and the present prophecies about

THE FALL OF THE GREAT BABYLON OF THE LATTER DAYS.

The similarity between it and the ancient one is in

I. Her general government, her oppression, her violence, and her great power and wealth.

II. Her pride, her arrogance, her false religion or her idol worship, her atrocious sins, her malodorous abomination in the nostrils of the same just God, and in

III. Her similar atrocious fate.

In Rev. xvii she is compared (in verse 5) to a woman, under the name of "MYSTERY, BABYLON THE GREAT, THE MOTHER OF HARLOTS AND ABOMINATIONS OF THE EARTH." In verse 18 we learn that she is a *city*, and that her government reaches across the kings of the earth. The Church of Rome filled the role,—she oppressed and persecuted the Saints, and became drunk on their blood, and thus in about the year 570 A. D., the "woman," or the Church of God, and the "man child," or the authority to govern—the *Priesthood*, fled into the wilderness, where we leave them over a period of 1260 years, while we observe the Church of Rome filling the nations with her abomination and her false traditions that are now held by the various denominations of our country. All which were called "Christianity" in Roman-ese, Babylon-ese or a mixture, until the end of the 1260 years, namely until 1830 A. D., when the other angel that John saw, (Rev. xiv, 6,) came with the everlasting gospel to preach "to every nation, and kindred, and tongue, and people; saying, Fear God, and give glory to him; for the hour of his judgment is come," &c. The judgment is not to come only on the city of Babylon, nor the atrocious plagues noted in the book, but it is to come on all the nations that have taken part in her sins. The Lord has never destroyed any people without first warning them, and preparing a way for them to escape, and that is why He says, "Come out of her my people, that ye be not partakers of her sins, and that ye receive not of her plagues." The people of God were invited to come out of ancient Babylon, when they were persuaded by the rumor tellers not to go, as we read in Jer. li, 45, 46.—"My people, go ye out of the midst of her, and deliver ye every man his soul from the fierce anger of the Lord, and ye shall fear not the rumors that shall be heard in the land: a rumor shall both come one year, and after that in another year shall come a rumor." Various rumors are told in the present time to prevent the children and the people of the Lord from fleeing to Zion to hide from the persecution that is to come on Babylon; for we testify to all alike that after the preaching of the "everlasting gospel," or the "gospel for a witness" which the Saints have, the destruction will come which has already begun on Babylon, as Christ foretold (Matt. xxiv.) Remember that all this is the beginning of the afflictions, and this age or generation will not pass without all this being fulfilled—the plagues of the kind noted in the book of Revelation and other places will come, and Great Babylon of the Latter Days will fall like a stone cast into the sea never to rise again, just as ancient Babylon fell after a like stone was bound to a book and then was cast into the river by the prophet Jeremiah.

Alltwen. W. F. WILLIAMS.

ZION'S TRUMPET,

OR

Star of the Saints.

SATURDAY, AUGUST 2, 1856.

GENERAL COUNCIL.—A General Council of the Presidencies of the Church of Jesus Christ of Latter-day Saints in the British Isles and the surrounding countries, was held in Birmingham, on the 21st, 22nd, and 23rd of July, when the place was honored by the presence of three of the Apostles of Jesus Christ, namely Orson Pratt, Ezra T. Benson, and F. D. Richards, together with Elders Phineas H. Young, Truman O. Angel, &c., from the Valley in Salt Lake; also present were the Presidents of the following missions—namely, Wales, Ireland, France, Italy, Germany, Switzerland, &c., together with all the Pastors and Presidents of Conferences throughout England, and six of the Presidents of the Welsh Conferences. We have not written the details of the heavenly and effective teachings that were given there by the stalwarts of Israel, and it would be vain for me to do so now, since many of them will come out in the *Star* and in the Trumpet; but suffice it to say that the testimony of all present was that "never before was so much of the power of God in one Council in the British Isles felt." A godly fire was lit in the heart of every soldier who was present, and they were blessed with the power to carry it and kindle it in the heart of every Saint and honest man in all their fields of labor. From now on, the teaching of the servants of God will be more effective in being the scent of life to life or the scent of death to death than ever before.

We are happy to notify the Welsh Saints that brothers Pratt, Benson, &c., have promised to visit Wales before long.

Marriage and Morals in Utah.—The Church of God in every dispensation has been a light to the world, and thus we should be, since we are in possession of the light of the same divine Spirit. We see the world groping in darkness, and many of them imagine seeing crags on their path between them and the light that we possess that are impossible to climb. The solemn duty that we have is to move whatever obstacles that may be in their way, as much as we can, as we well know. How much easier is our task to move an imaginary thing through such a small feat as enlightening the person to see otherwise—and how much greater our punishment if we do not. An obstacle of this kind in the eyes of the world is the doctrine of plural marriage that we believe, and which is practiced in Utah. For the purpose of enlightening those who love light more than darkness— following the examples of godly men whose behavior the Bible approves rather than the whims of superstitious fanatics who have neither logic nor scripture as a foundation of their false traditions, the Fount of Light has inspired his servant P. P. Pratt to write the treatise on "Marriage and Morals in Utah," which is further to be translated into Welsh and made into a pamphlet, to be spread as far as the circulation of contrary tales, and further if possible. Also, the wish of Presidents Richards and Pratt more than once for us was for the English tract,—"Marriage and Morals in Utah," to have a place with every family of Saints in Wales, and to distribute it generously among our neighbors the English: we hope that the Presidents have given this serious consideration. We commend for their attention the plan of bro. John Kay, who wrote the following letter to us:—

20, *Rupert St., Everton,*
Liverpool, 27 *of June,* 1856.

ELDER D. DANIELS.

Dear Brother,—At the request of President Richards I send this *Circular* to you, which I am sending to ministers, editors, officers, lawyers, merchants, craftsmen, &c., of Liverpool, and throughout my Conference, and I am enclosing with it, as you see, a pamphlet entitled "Marriage and Morals in Utah." It is President Richards's belief that this method of bringing this important topic to the attention of people of common sense will tend to induce them to look in greater detail into the principles of our holy religion.

I had 500 of the circulars *lithographed* for £1. I intend to assign apportionments for the officers to distribute to the people.

Leaving the matter to your consideration, I remain

Your brother in the Lord.
JOHN KAY.

WE WISH for the Welsh Presidents to act in the same way. If they raise a sum of money, according to the number they request for the circular, and send it to us, we will get a circular inscribed for every Conference President in Wales, with the name and information of each one on his circular, which will be done in Welsh and English according to the request of the Presidents.

The content of the circular is a kind of informational letter, in printed writing, to be sent with the pamphlet, in an *envelope,* for the recipients to become acquainted with the principle. Some English Presidents have already taken hold of the plan.

The pamphlet will come out in Welsh soon. It will be about 16 pages, and, if large numbers of it are ordered, it will be a penny per copy to the public. An unusually generous profit will be given to the distributors; the profit will go to the author, P. P. Pratt.

LETTER FROM PRESIDENT D. SPENCER.—
JOURNEY OF THE WELSH EMIGRANTS.

Camp of the Latter-day Saints,
Near Iowa City, June 22, 1856.

President F. D. Richards.

Dear Brother—In reply to your favors of May 8 and 27, I am happy to inform you that everything moves along well with us, even better than I could have anticipated. . . . . .

I am expecting the passengers of the *Thornton* in a day or two. I received, on the 20th, a message of their arrival, but without date, and the telegraphic element becomes very lazy when it points its course westward. From New York a messenger will arrive here some days ahead of his own message sent to announce his coming.

It will give you much joy to learn that the *handcart* experiment is now being fairly, and so far, most successfully tested. Captain Edmund Ellsworth left here on the 9th, with 274 souls, accompanied by Elders Oakley and Butler as assistants. Captain D. D. McArthur left on the 11th, with 221 souls, accompanied by Elders Crandall and Leonard as assistants. These, numbering in all 497 souls, embraced 104 of the *S. Curling's* company, and their fitout was 100 handcarts, 5 wagons, 24 oxen, 4 mules, 25 tents, and provisions to Florence. Brother Ferguson visited their camps 35 miles out, and accompanied them during a portion of a morning's march. He reports that, though their first two days' travel were good marches for strong men, considering the sandy roads, he never visited a camp of traveling Saints so cheerful and happy. All were full of faith in God, and the fulfillment of His promises through his servants, and what few doubts existed in the minds of half-weakly believers had all vanished when they saw the reality before them. The weak and feeble had already begun to gather strength; the sick were fast recovering, and the power of God was made abundantly manifest in the pouring out of his Spirit upon the people. Much credit is due, not only to the brethren in charge of the companies, but to the native Presidents of Conferences, who emulated each other in setting an example of putting in practice the theories they had taught their flocks in their fields of labor in their own country. The remainder of the *S. Curling's* company of P. E. F. passengers will leave tomorrow. Their number is about 320 souls. They are organized with Elder Edward Bunker as their Captain, assisted by Elders David Grant, John Parry, and Geo. W. Davis. To fit out these companies, brothers Grand and Kimball succeeded in purchasing, in the vicinity of Weston, a few cattle and mules, which, including traveling expenses, average nearly 85 dollars per yoke for oxen, and 120 per head for mules. Since then cattle have lowered some in value, and brothers Van Cott and Grant have purchased about sufficient to fit out the independent handcart and ordinary dependent companies, at an average of from 38 to 65 dollars per yoke; cows will cost from 15 to 18 each. These will be furnished at the Bluffs with the thorough fitout. They have also contracted for young stock to supply the demands already made at the rate of 7 dollars for yearling and 12 dollars for two-year-old heifers; dry cows 15 each. Brother George has also purchased and brought in 16 head of mules at 110 dollars, which, with seven or eight which brother Van Cott has got, will make sufficient for a mule team to each 500 of the Fund companies, and for those who will cross the Plains with you. . . . . .

I am looking for Brother Van Cott daily, with the general drove of cattle, from which I expect to supply the ordinary passengers who are here, as well as those coming, with whose names you have furnished me. The first company of wagons left Florence about the 6th of this month, of which, by my appointment, Elder P. C. Merrill took charge. Elder Peterson's company were expected to accompany them. Elder Joseph France left in company with Captains Ellsworth and McArthur, with the appointment to take charge, on his arrival, of such of the Saints congregated there from St. Louis and other parts, as would form the second company of wagons.

Business having called me down to St. Louis a few days, I was much rejoiced, on the 14th, to meet brother Erastus, together with brothers G. A. Smith, E. T. Benson, Orson Pratt, and the other brethren bound eastward. Brother Erastus accompanied me here. He leaves tomorrow for St. Louis: he is in tolerable health. I expect he will meet the *Horizon's* company at Boston, and, having a copy of that portion of your letter pertaining to the business of that company, will give it the necessary attention. I will continue to draw upon you, as heretofore, until I shall have completed the money part of the season's operations. I shall expect to meet you at Florence, and will endeavor to have the mules harnessed and whip in hand on your arrival, and a crust of bread in pocket. . . .

The health of the camp is unusually good this season. My own is also excellent. Truly the Lord has been with us, and has favored the opening of the new route. Since we have taken the making of the handcarts into our own hands, it is getting along beyond our best calculations. Brother Webb has been most faithful and successful in the charge of this department. The Church goods, sent by the *Thornton*, were already ordered to this place, and will have the proper attention.

Brothers Ferguson, McAllister, Grant, Webb, and the brethren generally, join me in much love to yourself, brothers Cyrus, Little, Dunbar, Linforth, Calkin, Williams, Turnbull, and all the Saints.

May success be multiplied to you in all your exertions is the wish of

Your faithful Brother in Christ,
DANIEL SPENCER.

TRUTH.

HONORABLE EDITOR:—Here is a taste for you of a cross-harmony *cywydd*, which I composed accidentally, side by side in confusion, for the *instructional delight* of the children of the muse among the Saints in Gwalia, and others who may wish to see and read "ZION'S TRUMPET," which is easily obtained for a low price and handy. If you can place it in some corner of a page, here it is at your service.

The just word of truth,
Through the Atonement it turns for peace;
It has smitten our misery,
Yes, to protect our earth!
The *false* runs through the gloom,
And to the black holes of goblin;
To good men come gifts,
From the Lord's wish to benefit them;
From black pain—from penance they go
To sing to glory!
Jesus will come to choose,
He'll call after the thronged best;—
Dear one,—Lamb of heaven
To keep company with Him.

Parallel like this:—

With Him to keep company
Lamb of heaven—a dear one
The thronged best—he calls after
And Jesus will come to choose
To glory to sing
From penance they go—from black pain;
To benefit them—from the Lord's will,
Good gifts come to men:—
Black goblin goes to holes,
Through the gloom runs the *false*.
For our earth's protection, yes,
He smote our misery!
He turns for peace, through the Atonement,
The truth—just Word.

Swansea, June 5, 1856. DEWI ELFED JONES.

[We consider the above to be worthy of imitation by several of the "children of the muse," who write to the "Trumpet," as far as its adherence to the rules goes: they have taken care to keep room for improvement.—ED.]

RAILWAY TO ZION.

The road to Zion was made by Jesus,
The vast rail is in divine truth;
From here to there it reaches,
Its end is in a blessed land.
Faith, repentance is the *station*,
And water baptism is ever the door;
No one here needs to be paid
Only walk the path indicated by Jesus;
The Holy Ghost is the *ticket* there,
And all can have it if they ask,
And through the officers' laying on of hands,
It can be had as before and clearly;
And God's law is the engineer
Who operates this to Mount Zion.
Through dark caverns and dangers
Quickly it goes to mount Zion.
The love of God is the fire,—truth is the steam,
Which propels the machine at speed;
And all who go to Zion in it,
Must come to Christ in obedience to him.
If you want to sit in the front row
The pure law of heaven must be kept,
If this is too fine for you to go away,
You can keep the earthly law.
And if you refuse the whole lot,
The underground is still to come,
Where thieves and liars will be,
Together with all who are felons.
To the true station you must come
To have life, although there is no compulsion.
O! men come from the black darkness,
The carriage awaits to receive you.
In through the door you have to go,
And be sure to get your ticket;
Then you'll go without taking too long
Very safely to the end of your journey.

Georgetown, April 5, 1849.   Thomas Harris.

BOOK DEBTS, JUNE 30, 1856.

Brecon Conference £2 2s 10c; Monmouth, £36 0s 2c; East Glamorgan, £57 0s 5c; West Glamorgan, £102 12s 3c; Llanelli, £48 0s 4c; Carmarthen, £22 11s 2c; Pembroke, £4 15s 10c; Cardigan, £15 0s 3c; Merioneth, £8 10s 9c; Flint, £15 3s; Denbigh, £10 15s 11c; Conway Valley and Anglesey, £9 17s 2c. The farthings are not listed.

MISCELLANEOUS, &c.

WHEN this issue was going to press, we received news from the Valley, for May 28, reporting that President Young intends to send 14 wagons up to Oregon to fetch dry fish to help food supply which is so scarce because of the disaster of the year before. Bro. Rich, in San Bernardino, prepared to send corn to the Territory if the pinch of the food shortage became too intense. They were greatly comforted by the remarkable, heavy showers of rain, and the unusually warm weather that ripened the abundant crops and offered an encouraging forecast of refilling their empty storehouses. They intend to begin harvesting before the middle of summer. The potatoes and green vegetables appeared to be very favorable, and there was an abundance of pasture the like of which had not been seen for two years.

RECEIPTS FOR BOOKS FROM JULY 17 TO 24.—T. Jones, 10s; T. Stephens, £4 14s 3c; E. S. Morgans, £1; C. Harman, £2.

CONTENTS.

	PG.
Letter of President Young	241
Merionethshire Conference	245
Fulfillment of Prophecies	246
The Fall of Babylon	247
Editorial—General Birmingham Council—Marriage and Morals in Utah	248
Letter from President D. Spencer	251
Truth	253
Railway to Zion	255
Book Debts	256
Miscellaneous, &c.	256

SWANSEA:
PRINTED AND PUBLISHED BY D. DANIELS.

ZION'S TRUMPET,

OR

Star of the Saints.

No. 17.] AUGUST 16, 1856. [Vol. IX.

CONSTITUTION OF THE STATE OF DESERET.

[*Continued from page* 240.]

Sec. 13. All grants and commissions shall be in the name and by the authority of the people of the State of Deseret, sealed with the Great Seal of State, signed by the Governor, and countersigned by the Secretary of State.

Sec. 14. A Secretary of State, Treasurer, Auditor of Public Accounts, and Attorney General, shall continue in office for the term of four years, and shall perform such duties as may be assigned them by law.

Sec. 15. In case of impeachment of the Governor, his removal from office, death, resignation, or absence from the State, the powers and duties of the office shall devolve upon the Lieutenant Governor, until such disability shall cease or the vacancy be filled.

ARTICLE VI.

Of the Judicial.

Sec 1. The judicial power shall be vested in a supreme court, district courts, and such inferior courts as the General Assembly may from time to time establish.

Sec. 2. The supreme court shall consist of a chief justice and two associates, two of whom shall be a quorum to hold courts.

Sec. 3. The supreme judges shall be elected by the General

Assembly for the term of six years after the first election under this Constitution. At said first election one shall be elected for two years, one for four years, and one for six years.

Sec. 4. The judges of the supreme court shall be conservators of the peace throughout the State, and shall exercise such other jurisdiction and appellate powers as shall be prescribed by law.

Sec. 5. Until otherwise provided by the General Assembly, the State is hereby divided into eleven judicial districts, as follows:—

Great Salt Lake and Summit counties shall compose the first judicial district.

Utah and Cedar Counties	" second "
Juab and San Pete	" third "
Millard and Beaver	" fourth "
Iron and Washington	" fifth "
Carson	" sixth "
Humboldt, St. Mary	" _____ "
Greasewood and Malad	" Seventh "
Cache and Box Elder	" eighth "
Weber and Davis	" ninth "
Green River County	" tenth "
Tooele, Shambip, and Deseret Counties	" eleventh "

Sec. 6. The judges of the district courts shall be elected by the electors of their respective districts, whose term of office shall be two years, and shall have such jurisdiction as may be prescribed by the General Assembly.

Sec. 7. The style of all *process* shall be "State of Deseret," and all criminal prosecution shall be in the name and by the authority of the people of the State.

ARTICLE VII.

Of Elections.

Sec. 1. All male persons over twenty-one years of age having a residence of six months in this State, being citizens of the United

States, shall be entitled to vote.

Sec. 2. Electors shall in all cases, except treason, felony or breach of the peace, be privileged from arrest on the days of election, during their attendance at such election, going to and returning therefrom.

Sec. 3. No elector shall be obliged to perform military duty on the day of election, except in time of war or public danger.

Sec. 4. No person in the military, naval, or marine service of the United States, by being station in any garrison, barrack, military or naval place or station within this State, shall be entitled to vote, unless otherwise provided for by law.

Sec. 5. No idiot or insane person, or person guilty of any infamous crime shall be entitled to the privilege of an elector.

Sec. 6. The first general election under this Constitution shall be held at such times as the acting Governor of this Territory, by proclamation, shall appoint for the election of a governor, lieutenant governor, representatives in the Congress of the United States, members of the General Assembly, and all other officers of this State, as provided for in this Constitution. Said election shall be conducted and returns made in accordance with the existing laws of the Territory of Utah, at the time when said election shall be called.

Sec. 7. The first meeting of the General Assembly shall be as directed by proclamation by the Governor elect, and subsequent sessions shall be held as provided by law.

ARTICLE VIII.

Of the Militia.

Sec. 1. The militia of this State shall be composed of all able-bodied male citizens between the ages of eighteen and forty-five years, except such as are or may hereafter be exempt by the laws of the United States, and shall be armed, equipped and trained, as the General Assembly may provide by law.

Sec. 2. All commissioned officers of the militia shall be elected as the General Assembly shall prescribe, and shall be commissioned by the Governor of the State.

ARTICLE IX.

Amendments of the Constitution.

If at any time the General Assembly deem it necessary, and for the best interest of the State, that this Constitution be revised, altered, or amended, they shall cause such proposed revisions, alteration, or amendments, to be published in the same manner as provided for notices of elections, and submitted to the votes of the Commonwealth at their next general election; and if a majority of said electors shall vote in favor of such proposed revisions, alterations, or amendments, the same shall thereafter become parts of this Constitution, otherwise this Constitution shall remain unaltered.

ARTICLE X.

Miscellaneous Provisions.

SEC. 1. In order that no inconvenience may arise in passing from a Territorial to a State government, it is hereby declared that the present organization, laws, and everything pertaining to the Territorial government of Utah shall remain in full force and virtue in law, until superseded by the action of the State government under the provisions of this Constitution.

SEC. 2. The compensation of the Governor, Lieutenant Governor, Judges, members of the General Assembly, and all other officers shall be as may be prescribed by law.

SEC. 3. All officers of this State may continue in office until superseded by their successors.

SEC. 4. The officers created by virtue of this Constitution shall take an oath or affirmation to support the Constitution of the United States and of this State, and to faithfully perform the duties of their office.

SEC. 5. The General Assembly shall encourage education.

Resolution.—Resolved, that the Constitution and other documents of this Convention, together with the names of the Delegates to Congress, be laid before the people of this Territory by the Members of this Convention, on the 7th of April next; and if approved by the people, then the doings of this Convention shall be considered valid; if disapproved, then they shall be null and void.

Trans. Dewi Elfed Jones.

DIFFERENCE BETWEEN THE BAPTISTS AND THE LATTER-DAY SAINTS.

(From the history of Joseph Smith.)

One of the Baptists wrote to the *North Staffordshire Mercury* as follows:—

"Sir—In a late publication, you reported the case of some persons who were taken before T. B. Rose, Esq., for disturbing a congregation of Latter-day Saints, or believers in the "Book of Mormon." A teacher of that sect, on being asked by the magistrate wherein they differed from the Baptists, replied, "In the laying on of hands;" but declined making an honest confession of those peculiarities which separate them as widely from the Baptist, as from every other denomination of the Christian Church. This was certainly prudent; but as the Baptists feel themselves dishonored by such an alliance, they would be unjust to themselves were they to leave unanswered such a libel upon their denomination. The following very prominent marks of difference will enable your readers to judge for themselves.

"I. The Saints admit all persons indiscriminately to baptism, encouraging them to pass through that rite, with the promise that great spiritual improvement will follow. They baptize for remission of sins, without waiting for credible evidence of repentance for sin. But the Baptists admit none to that ordinance who do not exhibit this qualification in the most satisfactory manner; and if they found a candidate looking to the water of baptism as having virtue to cleanse him from sin, he would be put back until better instructed.

2. After baptism the Saints kneel down, and their Priest, laying on his hands, professes to give them the Holy Ghost. If effects similar to those produced by the laying on of the Apostles' hands were seen to follow, skepticism must yield to the force of such evidence; but in their case no such effects are produced; the baptized sinner is a sinner still, though flattered and deluded with the epithet "Latter-day Saints." The Baptists regard such mummery with as much disgust as all Christians do.

3. Having, as they suppose, the extraordinary gifts of the Spirit, the Saints consistently pretend to have the power of working wonders, and profess to heal the sick with holy oil; also to the power of prophecy. As most moral evils bring with them their own remedy, these lofty pretensions will ruin them in due time, by opening the eyes of the most deluded, as in the case of the countless sects of impostors who have appeared upon the stage before them. It need not be added, that the Baptists stand far removed from such conceits, and have no part in them.

4. Not satisfied with the Bible as a complete revelation from God, the "Latter-day Saints" have adopted a romance, written in America, as a fresh revelation, and have added a trashy volume of 600 pages to that Book, which we are forbidden to add to, or take from, under the most awful penalties! But even this is not enough for their impious presumption. They have published a monthly magazine, in which "new revelation" are served up fresh, as they arrive, for the use of all who can swallow them. The disgust with which the Baptists regard such a melancholy exhibition of human folly and wickedness, separates them to an impassable distance from such people.

5. In order to carry on this order of things, the Latter-day Saints have appointed two Priesthoods. "The lesser, or Aaronic Priesthood, is to hold the keys of the ministering of angels, and to administer in outward ordinances. The power and authority of the higher, or Melchizedek Priesthood, is to hold the keys of all the spiritual blessings of the Church,—to have the privilege of receiving the mysteries of the Kingdom of Heaven,—to have the heavens opened

to them,—to commune with the general assembly and Church of the Firstborn,—and to enjoy the communion and presence of God the Father, and of Jesus, the Mediator of the new covenant," (see page 13). So that, in this wonderful Priesthood, they have provided for an ample supply of new things, in endless variety, and without end, from the hands of wretched men, who blasphemously aspire to a dignity which belongs along to Him who is the only "Priest forever after the order of Melchizedek."

The fear of trespassing upon your valuable columns, Mr. Editor, prevents my enlarging upon these and very many other points of difference; but enough has been done to show your readers, that no two sects can differ more widely from each other, than the Baptists and Latter-day Saints; and that to confound them in any way together is not only unjust to the former, but involves them in the disgrace of being partakers in a bold imposition, or a pitiable delusion, which they regard with equal abhorrence and disgust.

A BAPTIST."

[In our next issue, the difference that exists between the Baptists and the Former-day Saints.—ED.]

CONDITION OF THE CONFERENCES, &c.

Brymbo, August 1, 1856.

DEAR brother Daniels,

I take this opportunity to make known to you the condition of the Flintshire Conference.

There is a great effort in every Branch to preach, while the devil and his servants agitate and oppose us. I was in Treffynnon last Sunday, where we preached to a host of listeners. Some became unruly because of the testimony that Joseph Smith was a Prophet of God, and the constable came to subdue them. From there I went on my journey toward Mold. There I found the weakest Saints quite frightened from the attack of the reverends who had come with the express purpose to the field in their pomp and greatness the previous Sunday to mercilessly attack poor Mormonism, to condemn it, to kill it, and to announce its burial the following Monday and Wednesday nights. I intend to announce its resurrection after that. Since the speaker is English, and there is no permission to ask a question or say a word during the oration until the end, I wish for you to send a brother who speaks English well, with instructions concerning the wisest way to act under the circumstances, and if it would be good to take the *Town Hall* and announce a debate.

Yours faithfully,
Thomas Rees.

Llanidloes, August 4, 1856.

Dear brother Daniels,

Here is another letter in your hand from John Jones. I feel better and better each day, and my heart is in the work more than ever. One thing that is different now that I have not felt before, is more intensity of the Spirit of God in preaching, for which cause I am constantly hoarse, since I am preaching out of doors. . .

I was received by the Saints as happily as ever, and we had meetings full of the Spirit of God. Brother Treharn and I were in Radnorshire looking at the condition of the brethren who were preaching to the world there. . .

Brother Treharn and I found two excellent Saints, man and wife, within two miles of this place; they have lived here for a year not knowing that there are Saints nearby. The wife was in a Saints meeting we held in this place last night: we intend to establish a Branch here before long. We preach here tonight, then we intend to go around to Ffestiniog. . .

There is an especially good feeling toward the payment of tithing,—all the Saints I have seen are happy in their hearts. Their President, brother Treharn, is a man who is practically all heart, and a good one at that. The two of us have spent quite a lot of time and money in traveling so much, therefore I wish for you to send some of my money to me.

My regards to all of you from the depths of my heart.

Your brother in Christ,
JOHN JONES.

ZION'S TRUMPET,
OR
Star of the Saints.

SATURDAY, AUGUST 16, 1856.

WHEN the spiritual organizations of men come from the bosom of the Father to take tabernacles upon this earth, their bodies are the first portions of this planet which are given them to improve upon and bring into subjection to the laws of their Creator. It was natural, just, and necessary, for the benefit of his children, that the Lord should establish an eternal law of tribute, by the payment of which his subjects might give a material acknowledgment of their allegiance to Him, or by the refusal of which they might deny that allegiance. This is a primitive principle on which the law of tithing is founded, and when men come to a knowledge of it, they have an opportunity of proving their loyalty to the God of heaven, or of showing that they refuse allegiance to Him. The Lord does not require the tenth of the substance of his people, for his personal benefit, for their spirits and bodies and the earth on which they dwell all belong to Him; but it is required of them for their own good that they may be constantly reminded of their Creator, Lawgiver, Protector, Provider, and Savior. He has also condescended to have this portion used, under his wise supervision, for the direct benefit of those who pay it, in building temples and sustaining the administration of ordinances, necessary for their salvation; hence, those who refuse the Lord his portion not only sin against Him, but against themselves, and treat the manifestations of his goodness with contempt.

This law, from the beginning, has pertained to the eternal Priesthood; and therefore it is an eternal law, binding upon all the generations of men, and none will attain to the blessings of salvation until they abide it.

In a former number of the *Star*, we showed that Abraham kept the law of tithing, that Jacob covenanted with the Lord that he would pay Him the tenth of all that He should give him, and that this law was embodied in the Mosaic economy, and sacredly kept by ancient Israel. Inasmuch as the blessings which the Lord promised to Jacob were prospective, and were to be fulfilled upon his generations, as well as on himself, the covenant which he made with the Lord, to pay Him tithes of all, was, on his part, an everlasting covenant—binding upon his generations after him, and for the fulfillment of which they are responsible through the covenant of their father. The Patriarch, Jacob, will stand forever at the head of his generations, and, as we are informed in the revelation on celestial marriage, he, with his fathers Abraham and Isaac, has already entered into his glory, and is seated on his throne; we may rest assured that he will see that this covenant is strictly fulfilled, by all who have an inheritance in his kingdom. This is a point which should be deeply impressed upon the minds of all who bear the name of Latter-day Saint, for if they have not found it so already, they will find it a point on which their salvation is staked—one of the tests by which they will have to prove their claim of belonging to the house of Israel. Inasmuch as the Saints are taught this law, and are required by the Priesthood to keep it, and do not, to that extent they forfeit their claims to the blessings of the Gospel, and prove themselves recreant to the faith they profess.

As we have before stated, the law of tithing is only a preparatory work, to fit the Saints to live under the higher one of consecration. But the law of consecration will not do away with that of tithing. Obedience to both must be rendered by all who would attain to the blessings of eternal lives. While, under the law of consecration, everything which a Saint possesses will ever be ready, at the call of the Priesthood, to be used for building up the kingdom of God; they will, at the same time, be required to pay a tenth of all that the Lord shall make them stewards over. We are not aware that anything is said in the Scriptures on the subject of consecration, until Christ came and opened up the Gospel Dispensation. It is recorded that a rich young man came to Jesus, saying, "Master, what shall I do that I may inherit eternal life?" There are some peculiarities embodied in this simple question which are generally overlooked. The young man did not ask what he should do to obtain a portion of salvation—a glory of the moon or of the stars; he appeared to be ambitious to attain to the highest glory, to exaltations and dominions—to the blessings of eternal lives. He evidently had not counted the cost of the prize he was seeking, for, after Jesus had enumerated the commandments, he said, "All these things have I kept from my youth up; what lack I yet?" Jesus said to him, "If thou wilt be perfect, go and sell that thou hast and give to the poor, and thou shalt have treasure in heaven, and come and follow me." This was equivalent to telling him that it was necessary to sacrifice all that he yet held dear—his worldly possessions, his honorable position in society, and his good name, and devote the remainder of his life to spreading the Gospel and building up the kingdom; but the young man, like many others, went away sorrowful. In his estimation eternal life was not worth the sacrifice.

This rich young man, if he has not yet done so, has a sacrifice to make, equivalent to the one which Jesus demanded, before he can inherit eternal life. Every son and daughter of Adam, who obtains the highest blessings of salvation, will find it necessary to make the greatest possible sacrifices.

As further evidence that the spirit of consecration pertains to the Gospel, we read in Acts iv, 34, 35, "Neither was there any among them that lacked: for as many as were possessors of lands of houses sold them, and brought the prices of the things that were sold, and laid them down at the apostles' feet." We do not learn that this was required of the early Saints, but we are left to infer that it was the spontaneous fruits of the Holy Spirit which rested upon them. The Spirit of sacrificing is the legitimate spirit of the Gospel; as proof of this, every faithful Saint has only to remember that when the

Holy Ghost was poured out upon him, in rich effusion, he felt like giving liberally of his substance to further the work of the Lord, and there are hundreds in these lands, as well as in Zion, who have often regretted that they had not more to give. This is the measure of the spirit of the Gospel which every Saint should strive to live in.

The time has come when the Saints in this country are required to cultivate, more diligently than heretofore, the spirit of obedience and sacrifice. For this purpose the Lord has made it manifest that the law of tithing should be introduced, that it may serve to separate the chaff from the wheat, and that the Saints may have an opportunity of proving, to a greater extent than they have yet done, whether they are worthy of being gathered home to Zion.

We will mention a few things concerning those Saints who are not willing to abide the law of tithing. They need not expect that the Lord, through his servants or by his providences, will grant them special favors in opening up their way for gathering home, for it is not probable that such will be worth much when they get there. If there are any who have not sufficient faith to pay their tithing here, they will not be likely to pay it there, or endure the many other requirements that will be made on them, which if they do not fulfill, they will be cut short in blessings, find that they are in the wrong place, and, no doubt, will soon seek an atmosphere more in accordance with their worldly views. They need not expect to grow in faith and in the revelations of the Holy Spirit, and thereby increase in wisdom and the knowledge of the principles of eternal life, but they may expect that the spirit of the Gospel will leave them, the little light that is in them depart, the shades of darkness veil their understandings, and that they will lust after the things of this world, apostatize and be cut off from the household of faith, and have no hopes of salvation until they have paid the penalty of transgression, begin to do their first works over again, and come up by keeping those commandments which they now reject.

The Saints will do well to continually bear in mind, that when they have learned well to practice the law of tithing, there is still another glorious lesson before them—to learn the law of *consecration*.—*Star*.

The pamphlet about *Marriage and Morals in Utah* will come out as soon as we have orders for a sufficient number of it. Some Conference Presidents have sent for about a fourth of the number they should have requested, "*supposing* that it will be only for the Saints." We would like to have stronger language to portray the desire of our Presidents that it be spread everywhere the contradictory tales have reached. Preaching the Gospel to every creature is our duty, and, at present, among other things, preaching this important topic of the Gospel to the thousands of precious souls in the various Counties of Wales who are blinded by the servants of the devil, until they believe that the Saints are satisfying degraded passions, and not respecting and keeping within the rules and limits of the laws of the God of Nature, which are not violated by even the dumb animal, while man, although in the form and image and possessing to a great degree the same attributes and instincts of his Great Creator, perverts them for his selfish and corrupt purposes! Instead of the other species filling the measure of their creation in righteousness and cherishing them, behold them wandering along the "garden of Christianity," as it is called, being deprived of their crown and their comfort—their chastity, and no one to complain to! Those who should do that look at the supposed mote in the eye of Utah while our eyes see daily this frightful beam in their eyes. Presiding brethren, who have the care of entire counties, have you understood your duty and your responsibility in this matter? Time will tell.

INVITATION TO BECOME SAINTS.

> There are worries in my heart
> As I find you dear friends,
> In your pride as you rush along
> To be first into prisons.
> > O how privileged you'll be,
> > To share with the Saints,
> > And to escape from slavery
> > Where no pain nor disease flies,

Why do you refuse true reasons,
Giving credence to traditions,
And ignoring the precious words
Of our Lord, and his ordinances?
    O how privileged you'll be, &c.

Christ has stated definitely
That forgiveness comes through baptism;
And through the laying on of hands, believe it,
The Spirit and its comfort are to be found.
    O how privileged you'll be, &c.

Come obedient to the conditions,
And abstaining from sins,
That you may be adopted
Under the protection of eternal God.
    O how privileged you'll be, &c.

Then you will be free children
You can claim all the blessings;
Your doubt will fade completely
Before the powers of true testimony.
    O how privileged you'll be, &c.

The Spirit of God in his blessings
Will give you great comforts,—
Faith, wisdom, and knowledge,
The gift of healing and prophecy.
    O how privileged you'll be, &c.

You'll have tongues and their translation,
Explanations through revelation,
And the power of God working miraculously
Through the strength of the spiritual gift.
    O how privileged you'll be, &c.

Do not feed on empty husks
While there is plenty of every delicacy;
Refuse sectarianism,
And feed on Mormonism.
    O how privileged you'll be, &c.

Come all, and do not slumber;
Flee to the refuge of the true fold,

Before you're caught by the storm,
As the Sodom folk once were,
　　O how privileged you'll be,
　　To share with the Saints,
　　And to escape from slavery
　　Where no pain nor disease flies.

Twynyrodyn, Merthyr.　　　　　　　　　　　RACHEL DAVIES.

TO ZION.

Tune,—Sir Dark Harry.

O sheltering Zion,
Best of the world's lands,
This is a pleasant abode;
Here the Saints will be
In their beautiful dwellings,
In pleasure, with joyful mien—
God and his peace will overspread the ground
And the Saints will enjoy His blessings every hour,
O! soon the heavenly dawn will break—
Blessed hours will gladden the heart.

Sweet waters,
Beneficent Heaven,
Let us rejoice in one song:
Large and wide fields,
All alive with produce,
Splendid growth—with fine grain.
Beautiful mountains surround them
And over them blows the free healthful breeze,
Spreading the scents of the soft flowers.
Over the meadows—a fair sight.

Seemly cities
Under our God's protection,
Their appearance is commendable,—
Well maintained temples,
Adorned with pearls,
And gilded will be there.

>   This for the Saints is a land of deliverance,
>   From God's harsh vengeance—from plague and disease,
>   Which is poured down on Babel—what an honor!
>   Who can say as much—the day will dawn?

1853.   ANEURIN L. JONES.

MISCELLANEOUS, &c.

THE Counting of the emigration of the Saints from these countries to America, during the past season, from the 30 of last November to July 6, shows that 8 ships have sailed, and 4395 have emigrated. There were 667 from among them from the different counties of Wales.

AN IRISHMAN AND A CARDI.

>   THIS Irishman stood with a Cardi
>   Close to the bank of the river Teifi;
>   When Pat asked quite steadily,
>   "Is this side the other side?"
>   "O no, you fool," said the Cardi,
>   "Have you lost your mind, you Irishman?"
>   "Well, is that one side over there?"
>   "Yes, of course," replied the Welshman;
>   "Well, now (said Pat) I swear that
>   This can only be the other side."

Georgetown, 1849.   T. HARRIS.

RECEIPTS FOR BOOKS FROM AUGUST 1 TO 14.—T. Jones, 10s; W. Jones, £1 10s; J. Gibbs, £2; J. Davies, £2; J. Thomas, £3.

CONTENTS.

	PG.
Constitution of the State of Deseret	257
Difference between the Baptists and the Saints	261
Condition of the Conferences, &c.	263
Editorial—Tithing—The New Pamphlet	265
Invitational Song	269
Song—To Zion	271
Miscellaneous, &c.	272

SWANSEA:
PRINTED AND PUBLISHED BY DANIEL DANIELS.

ZION'S TRUMPET,

OR

Star of the Saints.

No. 18.] AUGUST 30, 1856. [Vol. IX.

EPISTLE BY ORSON PRATT,

To the Saints throughout Great Britain, Ireland, and all European countries, greeting—

Dear Brethren—With feelings of gratitude to God and love to you, I again resume my pen, to inform you of my appointment to the Presidency in these lands. At a General Conference of the Saints, convened in Great Salt Lake City, Utah Territory, on the 6th of April 1856, I was, by a unanimous vote, appointed to the Presidency in these countries; and soon after received a "Letter of Instruction" from President Brigham Young, of which the following is an extract—

"President's Office,
Great Salt Lake City,
Utah Territory,
April 10, 1856.

Beloved Brother Orson Pratt—You are hereby instructed and authorized to forthwith repair to Liverpool, England, and take charge of "The Latter-day Saints' European Publishing and Emigration Office" in said City, and the Presidency of the Latter-day Work in the British Isles, and in those regions of the country whose missions have heretofore been more immediately under the supervision of said Presidency.

To assist you in said duties, you are counseled to call to

18 [Price 1*c*.

your aid, Elder Ezra T. Benson, one of the Twelve Apostles, and recommended to select him as one of your counselors, and his labors will be under your counsel and control. You are also at liberty to command the services of Elder James A. Little, who is now in the Liverpool Office, and to call around you such other assistants as the business and your judgment may require.

Brother Asa Calkin will be your chief *Clerk*, until the period when he should be released or relieved by someone sent from this place; in the meantime, it would be well that the other clerks be promising, faithful young men, and placed under the tuition of brother Calkin, that, peradventure, we may be able to avoid the necessity of sending clerks from here. . . . .

I pray God, the Eternal Father, to bless you in all duties with His Holy Spirit, to open your way to the accomplishment of every laudable undertaking, and to lead your mind in the way of all truth.

BRIGHAM YOUNG.
President of the Church of Jesus
Christ of Latter-day Saints."

In compliance with these instructions, I left Great Salt Lake City, on the 22nd of April, in company with Elder Benson and many other missionaries, designed for this country. Five of us arrived in Liverpool on the 13th of July. And having notified the principal presiding authorities in the Pastorates, Conferences, and foreign Missions, we assembled in Special Council in Birmingham on the 21st, 22nd, and 23rd of July. From the reports there given, I became more fully informed of the condition and general welfare of the Saints throughout England, and upon the continent.

In the years 1848, '49, and '50, I was blessed with the privilege of occupying the same official position in this country, and has seemed good to the Lord to again confer upon me.

I receive the great responsibility with which I am entrusted with a heart overflowing with gratitude to God and the Saints; but, at the same time, with fear and trembling in consequence of my own inabilities and weakness, which are, perhaps, known to myself more than to many others. One thing I have most effectually learned, that man, however great his natural abilities and acquirements, is, without the Holy Spirit, a poor, weak, frail being, and as nothing in the sight of God. But clothed with the wisdom of heaven, and armed with the power of God, he is like the mighty torrent from the mountain gorge which sweeps all before its resistless current. Without the Holy Spirit, he is like the autumn leaf which withers in the cold, and falls from the tree that gave it birth; but with the Holy Spirit, he is like the mighty oak that braves the storms of winter, and stands firm in the midst of the raging elements. He speaks, and his voice is heard, and the power thereof is felt by the Saints throughout the earth; while the wicked fear and tremble; for something whispers to their hearts that "God is there."

The morning that I bade farewell to our beloved President, B. Young, while inquiring at his mouth for some word of counsel and instruction, relative to my duties in this land; he replied, "Seek earnestly for the Holy Spirit, and it will show you what to do." What answer could have been more true and appropriate than this? What can be of more importance to the servant of God, than to enjoy communion with a Spirit pure and Holy, that will never deceive, but will show him plainly what he should do? Is communion with this Spirit a fiction? No. It is a heavenly joyful reality. The very thought of being instructed from such an unerring source, fills the soul with inexpressible happiness. It is my constant prayer, and my most fervent desire, that the counsels of the Presidency and the whisperings of the Holy Spirit, may be my sure Guide in all my ministrations among you, and that all my instructions to you, my counsels, my writings, and my conduct both in public and private, may be dictated and inspired by the Holy Ghost. If such be the case, I can benefit you in the name of the Lord; if otherwise, I shall be only as sounding brass, and all my efforts will be in vain. Saints, will you help me by your faith and prayers, to obtain a great measure of the Spirit, not only for my sake, but for your sakes, that God may make me a blessing to you, through the ministration of the Holy Apostleship, in imparting the words of life—the gifts of the Spirit, that you may be strengthened and comforted with the knowledge of spiritual things, with a knowledge of your duties, with a knowledge of the law of God, and be more fully prepared to endure the glory and presence of God, in that future world to which we are all fast hastening?

In accordance with the instructions of President Young, I have appointed Elder Ezra T. Benson, one of the Twelve Apostles, my first Counselor. Elder Benson will travel much among you, and you will be greatly blessed through his ministry, as one of the faithful Apostles of the last days. He is, when filled with the Spirit, in the language of Scripture, "a son of thunder," and gives forth his testimony in the wisdom and power of God. May God Almighty bless him among the Saints in Great Britain, and make his voice to be heard like the sound of a mighty trumpet, awaking the Saints to life and energy; and among the wicked may it be like the voice of terrible thunder, arousing them from the death-slumber of ages.

I have also appointed Elder James A. Little my second Counselor. His duties will be more confined to the Office, to assist in the editorial department of the *Star*. Elder Little, though young, is a man of the most sterling integrity, and his heart is full of wisdom and truth; for God is with him; his soul shall be enlarged as the ocean, and his light shall break forth as the noon day; his writings shall be inspired by the Spirit of Truth, and be highly esteemed and sought after by the Saints. Brother Little, be encouraged, for thou art beloved of the Lord, and in Him shall be thy strength, henceforth and forever.

The Saints in this country have been blessed above measure, by the wise counsels of that great and good man, Elder Franklin D. Richards, my predecessor, who has, for a long time, presided with great wisdom and dignity in your midst. The holy Apostleship has been highly honored by him. His heart has been a fountain of truth, and his bowels have yearned with sympathy and compassion for the poor Saints. By his wise counsels and suggestions, thousands have been delivered from oppression and starvation, and sent to a land of peace and plenty. His counsels have been like those of a father to his children; his teachings have been like the refreshing showers of spring, quickening, animating, and giving renewed life to the trees of the Lord's vineyard. Through him the Holy Spirit has been shed forth like the dews of heaven upon the land of Joseph, imparting a morning freshness to the landscape. May the God who appeared to Abraham and blessed his seed forever, also bless brother Franklin and his generations; may his sons be among the chief men of Israel—wise Counselors in Zion, and Rulers in the kingdom of our God.

I shall endeavor, so far as circumstances and the Spirit of the Lord dictates, to carry out the wisely-devised plans of brother Franklin for the prosperity and welfare of the Saints, hoping that my feeble labors may also be blessed, and that God may also work by my instrumentality for your good.

I should take great satisfaction and pleasure in visiting all the Conferences and foreign Missions under my charge, were it compatible with the multiplied duties constantly devolving upon me, and which seem to require my attention at the Office in Liverpool.

The authorities and Saints should use every laudable exertion to spread the printed word, as this is one of the mighty engines of the last days to enlighten the world, and to build up the kingdom of God. The tract entitled *Marriage and Morals in Utah* is worthy of being circulated by hundreds of thousands; also many other tracts, with which you are familiar, would be of more extensive usefulness, were they more widely diffused among the people. The influence of the press in England and America is very powerful, either for good or evil. And, so far as we can bring it to bear, it is powerful in the kingdom of God, to stay, and in some measure control, the mighty torrent of opposition which is arrayed against the Saints, and which occasionally breaks forth, and threatens to overwhelm us in its angry floods. Let the Saints, therefore, seize upon the masterly facilities offered by the art of printing, and spread light and truth in every dwelling throughout the land. In so doing, they will soon see the fruits of their labors, manifested by increased inquiries, by increased congregations, and by increased numbers of the honest who will be added to the Church.

Let every member of the Church pray earnestly that he may

bring, at least, one soul unto repentance every three months, and at the end of the year, we will find our numbers quadrupled, our strength and force greatly augmented, and our funds for doing good vastly replenished.

In consequence of the many thousands that have been helped from this land, during the last two years, the funds of the Office have been greatly diminished, many heavy debts have been contracted, and we are surrounded with many perplexing embarrassments; yet, it is to be hoped, that the Saints will be prompt to help in every time of need; and that funds may roll into the Office by thousands, that the good work of gathering the poor may continue with increasing prosperity.

The Saints in Utah, feeling for the welfare of the poor in this country, have, many of them, with a liberal zeal, and with hearts full of benevolence, contributed farms, city lots, private dwellings, and public storehouses, to the amount of many thousand pounds sterling, to the Perpetual Emigrating Fund Company; and the avails of all these properties, if they can be sold to the wealthy among the Saints in these countries, will be used at this Office to emigrate the poor of our people. We exhort the wealthy Saints to purchase themselves inheritances in Utah, and thus they will throw into the P. E. Fund available means to help their poor, downtrodden brethren from this country to Zion. If our brethren in Zion can afford to give their property for the benefit of the poor, you certainly ought to be willing to purchase for the same benevolent object. I have a transcript of all those donated properties at the Office, and shall be most happy to dispose of the same to you, if possible, in time to send out several thousand Saints next spring, in season to get across the Plains early. The City lots, farms, and houses for sale, vary in value from one or two hundred pounds to two or three thousand: Come on, my brethren, and suit yourselves; now is a most favorable time for you to secure a home in Zion and to do good. The cries of the poor are to you for deliverance. Will you become their deliverers, and secure to yourselves mansions and everlasting habitations among the righteous? Or do you prefer the fate of the rich man, far away from Abraham's bosom—in torment? The choice is your own, and you alone must abide the consequence. If you refuse this blessing, God will open some other way for the deliverance of His Saints; for He will hear their cries and provide for them; and your blessing, that you might have received, shall be upon the heads of those more worthy. This is not applicable to those who would be glad to do, but whose property is in circumstances unfavorable to a present purchase, but it is intended for the covetous—the greedy lovers of filthy lucre—who think more of their riches than they do of their souls. It is such that may well fear and tremble! for their hour is coming! and the days of their misery are fast hastening!

Wickedness is greatly on the increase, and great Babylon is now festering in her own filth and corruption. It becomes all the Saints to take strict heed to their ways, lest they are overcome, and pollute themselves and partake of the sins of these wicked nations, and perish with them. Blessed is that man who, when surrounded with temptation and wickedness on every hand, still keeps himself pure and virtuous before God. Such shall flourish like the choice grape vine, which sendeth forth its green branches in all directions, and beareth great clusters of rich, delicious fruit. His seed shall be greatly multiplied, and his generations shall be blessed forever. But cursed is that man who, after he has received his endowments, defileth himself with women, and regardeth not the sacred and everlasting covenant of life; for such shall wither away, like a branch pruned from the tree of a vineyard, which beareth no fruit, but is well nigh unto burning. "Woe unto all them who commit whoredoms, saith the Lord God Almighty, for they shall be thrust down to hell." Oh, my brethren and my sisters, let not virtue and purity of heart depart from you; for they are your strength and safeguard in Babylon, your glory and honor in Zion, your endless increase of eternal lives in the world to come.

To the Traveling Elders and Missionaries, I say, idle not away your time; labor with your mights, for the end of the harvest soon cometh; let your voices be heard in the morning, and at midday, and in the shades of evening, crying repentance unto all people;

let the halls and chapels, and private dwellings, resound with your warning voice; let the streets, the lanes, and highways reverberate the glad tidings; let the high places, the hills, and the mountains re-echo the joyful sound; let the mansions of the great and noble, and the gorgeous palaces of queens and kings, hear your testimony, till, by the power of God, the nations shall be broken in pieces, thrones be cast down, and old Babylon itself be made to shake, and tremble, and totter, and fall to rise no more. Call on the Lord day and night, for the wisdom and might of His Spirit; for the power of the Holy Ghost which giveth utterance; for the spirit of prophecy to forewarn the nations; for spiritual gifts to impart to the Saints; for revelations of the knowledge of God; for angels to protect and guard you, and to minister to and for you; for the Lord to rend the heavens and come down, and save His people and redeem the earth. Oh, how great the work to be done! Oh, how diligent ought we to be in doing it!

May blessings, and righteousness, and strength, and salvation, and the gifts and powers of heaven, be increased and multiplied upon you, until you are exalted to sit on thrones of power, and reign forever and ever, is the fervent prayer of your humble servant,

ORSON PRATT,
President of the Saints in Great Britain
and all European Countries.

CIRCULATING TRACTS.

(From the Editorial of the "Star.")

DURING our former Presidency in these countries, we were led to notice, in a particular manner, the powerful and beneficial influence, resulting from an extensive circulation of tracts and pamphlets upon the principles of our religion. Then, in the short period of about two years, the Church of the Saints in these lands considerably more than doubled their numbers. Meetings were generally crowded, and hundreds were anxiously inquiring to know the truth. Let the

Branches of the Church pursue the same course again, and we cannot but believe that it will be attended with the same happy results; besides, it will have a tendency to make all the members of the Church, both brethren and sisters, diligent and useful in spreading the truth.

The first and second Numbers of a new series of tracts, on the first principles of the Gospel, are now ready for circulation. The title of the first number is, "THE TRUE FAITH"; and the title of the second is "TRUE REPENTANCE." We are in hopes to issue one number every two weeks, until the series is completed. Saints, if you wish to see your numbers quickly doubled or quadrupled in these countries, spread, with an untiring zeal, the printed word, and seek most diligently to save yourselves and your neighbors. When you labor with your might, God will labor with you. When you become idle or slack, God will slacken his hand in crowning your efforts with success. Each number will contain 16 pages. Price, 2c., or 14s. per hundred.

ZION'S TRUMPET,

OR

Star of the Saints.

SATURDAY, AUGUST 30, 1856.

CONDITION OF THE CONFERENCES.—We have received lately, letters from several of our hardworking and faithful brethren in the ministry in this part of Christ's vineyard.

Brothers Evans and Ashby say that the Pembrokeshire Conference is unanimously serving the Lord,—paying their tithing, and building the kingdom in every way. Brothers E. D. Miles and David John are traveling and preaching diligently, despite their bloodthirsty enemies who are seeking their lives; they are having numerous throngs to listen attentively to them.

Brothers Israel and J. Evans, and T. Jones, have been preaching by the sea in Cardiganshire, and they have had large crowds listening attentively to them, and who have purchased all the tracts they had, asking for more. There is a promising prospect for the people in those parts; but there is a great need for laborers in their midst. We consider that it was a great honor in receiving a visit from their "king." The condition of the Carmarthen and Llanelli Conferences, according to the account of their presidents, W. Jones and D. Davies, is similar to that of Pembrokeshire—tithing is coming regularly. Brothers John Kay, of the Valley, and Thomas Williams, from the Liverpool Office, visited parts of the South Conferences. They were greatly pleased in the diligent labor of brothers T. Harris and J. Davies, in the West Glamorgan Conference. They were pleased with their visit to Merthyr, Cardiff, and Monmouthshire. Great was their praise for the singing in Merthyr: they said that they would be glad for the Presidents to seek to imitate that in their various Branches.

Through a letter from brother E. S. Morgans, of Anglesey, we understand that he, and brothers J. H. Davies, B. Davies, J. Morgans, and Noah M. Jones, who left everything in the south to go there to build the kingdom of God,—some to work and the others to travel, are testifying continually, along with the other faithful elders who are there; but they complain at the stubborn Methodists, for disregarding the God's counsel against them, by not receiving their baptism from them. We put some of the account of the Meirion and Flint Conferences in our last issue.

All shows that the Kingdom of God in Wales is increasing, through the blessing of God on the efforts of his servants. Brethren in the ministry—you who have consecrated yourselves, your time, your labor, your disposition and everything, to God's cause, take heart; for His angels are at your side, when you are carrying out your duty, and He himself is aware of all that you do and suffer for His Cause. Let the fruitfulness of the trees you are tending in his vineyard bear witness of your diligence. You have had the honor of treating them and nourishing them; but remember that you are also responsible! Look to yourselves if you allow the godly sap that comes to you weekly and every two weeks to go in vain.

If you are negligent, the fruit of your labor will be lackluster and out of season. It is not any old time, when everyone else has almost finished, that a President is to speak of starting to fulfill that which God's Priesthood asks.

We call your special attention to the Epistle of our President Orson Pratt. Remember that its reading is not for amusement; but to put into practice without delay, as with every other instruction that comes. Then the trees under your care will bring early fruit, which is always the most choice.

We are always glad to hear of your adventures, dear brethren, and take pleasure in chronicling your names, and your praiseworthy deeds, so that you will be objects worthy of emulation by the coming generations.

ELDER Israel Evans is now traveling throughout the North, and Elder B. Ashby throughout the South. We would like for all the Welsh Saints, whenever the one or the other of these brethren comes into your midst, to do your best for them while you have them; for they bring life and salvation with them.

ELDER Joseph W. Tuckfield, from Swansea, has gone to Aberystwyth to work, in order to assist in preaching the Gospel in those parts. Success to him.

LETTER FROM SISTER DANIELS.

Great Salt Lake City,
June 27, 1856.

MY dear Husband—I received your kind letter, dated November 21, 1855, on the 12th of last May. I was very happy to learn from it that you are happy and enjoying good health. Thanks to the Lord for having restored your health from the fever you had. I hope you will take care of yourself until you are released from your calling and that you will be able to return to your loving family, according to our prayers, and praise the name of the Lord for his many blessings.

It had been nearly a year since we received a letter from you, because the mail transport is so uncertain. We were here for six months without getting one from the Eastern States, nor are there any signs that it will be any different until a daily one from the 'Mormons' themselves begins to run, which is likely to take place soon: there are great efforts being made to that end.

They are presently completing the task of making a canal from South Cotton Wood to furnish water to the lands of this city, and it extended to part of the city about a week ago. There will be another canal before long to bring the granite to the temple.

I was very confident that we would see you this year, but I learned from Bro. John Davies, the printer, that he had come across an account in the *Star* to the effect that Bro. Jones had been released and that you had been called to preside in his place. This news was not sweet to me at first, but, as you said in your letter, "that the will of the Lord be done, and his counsel be respected," is my wish, although it may not always be in accordance with the feelings of human nature."

I shall expect frequent letters from you from now on.

We learned through the newspaper—*The Mormon*, that many will be immigrating this year with handcarts. We saw the names of many of them, and many of the Welsh among them. May the Lord keep them on their journey.

There are good signs for food for men and for the animals. The harvest has begun, and it will someday be a "cash" harvest.

About half of our *lot* has wheat growing on it, and it is excellent; the same for the peas, potatoes, &c. We have been eating peas in abundance for days. My son, Thomas, planted them for me in March while Dafydd was in Box Elder.

We wintered our cattle in Box Elder. Dafydd had a great deal of trouble to keep them from dying. Hundreds of animals died last winter. The snow was on the ground for about five months. A year-old bull of Thomas's died, and one of Dafydd's work oxen in Willow Creek while coming down from Box Elder, and one cow also. Five of our calves died also; and we lost one cow; we don't know whether it is alive or not. We still have seven head of cattle, one two-year-old bull, three six-month-old bulls, two bulls, and three calves still alive.

We have a team of work horses, one two-year-old mare, and two excellent one-year-old mares.

We have not experienced a shortage of bread, cheese, meat, or butter, although a general shortage is predicted, for the grasshoppers have destroyed practically all of this year's crops.

The Prophet Brigham and his Counselors have made predictions, and exhorted "the people to store the products of their fields carefully, lest the scourge of disobedience smite them with a famine," so that everyone could remember the words that he and others said. It is good that they have done this, for after the famine came Brigham Young and others were seen contributing generously, saying to the needy, "*Come on boys*," and telling them that their white flour would increase further. One brother contributed all he had in his barrel except for the residue on the bottom. A while later when his wife went to shake it,* to her surprise, she found the barrel half full. She asked her husband if he had put flour in the barrel. He said that he had not. He himself went to see and found that it was as his wife had said. This reminded me of the story that you sent of the dream you had there about the shortage here when you saw the angels ministering to the Saints, &c.

My son, Thomas, and his family are living in Box Elder. As I said before, one yearling bull of his died. He still has a fine team of oxen, five head of cattle, together with heifers and calves. He has two children: Mary Jane and Thomas.   .   .   .

All the Welsh in this place are well, and send fond regards— the two brothers Jeremy and their wives; Daniel Thomas from Esgerhydd, and David Williams from Ystrad.

Remember me to my sisters, their husbands and children, and to your brothers and your sisters also, and to your mother if she is still alive. I hope they will come soon to the way of life. I say once again that I have come to the only way that leads to eternal life.

I wish for you to remember me to Sarah Williams, Cerbyne, and Anne Lewis, Cwmcoch, and their families, and to the family at Llawbarth, the family of the *Plough*, and my former neighbors, and all the Saints regardless of who they are.

Henry Harris, formerly from Talog, sends his kindest regards to you and to the family at Rhyd-y-garreg-ddu, and wishes you to make every effort to bring them into the Church, so that they can come across the same time as you to safety.

With wishes for your temporal and spiritual success I remain

Your loving wife,

MARY DANIELS.

*In the foregoing example we see that God is the same to the Saints in these days as He was when he blessed the meal in the barrel and the oil in the cruse.—Editor.

HAPPY IS THE MORMON.

(Tune—"Pop Goes the Weasel.")

Although everyone under the sun,
    Feels completely dissatisfied;
And is bedeviled by headshaking,
    Happy is the Mormon.
He never tries in his life,
    To please the unwise ones;
He walks by the mind of God,
    Happy is the Mormon.

Let the world's chief mockers join,
    They bellow like goblins;
"The Saints have naught but utter deceit,"
    Happy is the Mormon.
Let the proud lift up his head,
    Swelling most cruelly;
Let another make a great rebuke,
    Happy is the Mormon.

If preachers "of great talent,"
    Shout in services;
"That the Saints are full of fraud,"
    Happy is the Mormon.
Let them travel each town and land,
    And tell their stories,
Coldly shouting with ugly cry,
    Happy is the Mormon.

When trials and tribulations come,
    Again from enemies,
Ones without religion, only a figment,
    Happy is the Mormon.
He suffers pain and scorn,
    Needlessly at times;
To bring comfort to his brother,
    Happy is the Mormon.

When traveling many places,
    To benefit men;
Although adversity's his lot,
    Happy is the Mormon.
When at times he is seen,
    I tell you, in tight corners,
With nowhere to rest under the sun,
    Happy is the Mormon.

Let savage and civilized nations,
    Battle in their thousands;
And they fight in their anger,
    Happy is the Mormon.
Come pestilence and black hunger,
    Let them destroy horribly;
Let the great throng go to the grave,
    Happy is the Mormon.

As he knows that so it shall be,
    Signs and signals,
And that God will justly give them,
    Happy is the Mormon,
From the disaster will escape,
    All who are faithful—
When beyond plague and pestilence,
    Happy is the Mormon.

When the hills leap like rams,
    The waves of the deep roar;
When the world shakes from its bases,
    Happy is the Mormon.

> When the "summer" goes completely,
>   The world ignites in sparks;
> When elements melt like wax,
>   Happy is the Mormon.

Formerly of Merioneth.   JOHN DAVIES.

MISCELLANEOUS, &c.

A LETTER from the camp says that the companies of the ships *Thornton* and *Horizon* have arrived there safely. The handcart companies were to start across the Plains, July 14.

☞ WE were obliged to omit the article on the *Difference between the Baptists and the Latter-day Saints* this time for lack of space. The *Letter from Brother Jeremy* will be in the next.

"DIVINE AUTHORITY."—A new printing of this treatise is ready, and available in the Liverpool Office.

☞ WE have just received a Letter from Apostle Ezra T. Benson, from London, giving an account that the halls of the Saints there are filled with listeners eager to hear the truth. After spending about six weeks on the Continent, he intends to come to Wales.

RECEIPTS FOR BOOKS FROM AUGUST 15 TO 26.—Thomas Stephens, £5; John Thomas, 8s.

CONTENTS.

	PG.
Epistle by Orson Pratt	273
Circulating Tracts	280
Editorial—Condition of the Conferences	281
Letter from Sister Daniels	283
Song—Happy is the Mormon	286
Miscellaneous, &c.	288

SWANSEA:
PRINTED AND PUBLISHED BY DANIEL DANIELS.

ZION'S TRUMPET,

OR

𝔖tar of the 𝔖aints.

No. 19.] SEPTEMBER 13, 1856. [Vol. IX.

LETTER OF THOMAS JEREMY.

Great Salt Lake City,
June 29, 1856.

Dear Brother Daniels,—I have just returned from your house, and there I had the great pleasure of reading your lengthy letter to your wife; I am glad to understand that you are enjoying good health, which is one of the precious gifts of your God. Since your wife is sending you a letter herself with the letter carrier that leaves here next Tuesday morning, I shall not give you news about them to you, but I shall just say that they are comfortable, and the Lord is prospering them, and David is a big, strong and brave man much like his father.

I had the pleasure this morning of hearing two of the Apostles of the Latter Days addressing the Saints in the *Bowery*, namely P. P. Pratt and Amasa Lyman. After Apostle Pratt had given a brief account of his mission through the southern settlements of this Territory, he then remarked on the great strength and power that follows the Saints of God, who are anointed in his holy Temple, although they may not have felt much at the time, but were anointed for the time a call would come for the power of that anointing as in the case of David of old, killing Goliath, &c.

The topic of Brother Lyman was most especially to exhort the Saints to beautify the dwelling place of Zion more and more

[Price 1*c*.

continually, so that there will be no cause for us to be ashamed when Zion comes down from above. He exhorted all of us to follow our revered President Brigham Young in building, planting, &c., so that Zion may be glorious, for no doubt the great will come from among the nations of the earth.

The work of the Lord is prospering here, though not as quickly as we would like, for the grasshoppers destroyed the greater part of the grain crop last year; yet great preparations are being made to complete the Temple. There is a great canal under construction to bring water from the Big Cottonwood to this city, in order to transport the *granite stones* in boats; the canal will be about 15 miles long.

The work will increase here more than double after we get our harvest in. The crops this year are unusually good; it is believed that there will be twice as great a yield in the crops this year throughout the Territory than in any previous year from the time the Saints first arrived here.

The advantages of the Saints here have not been as good as they wished in order to send for their relatives and the deserving Saints from there, but things will get better soon. Let the Saints there remember that Zion has not been built yet; until then strength of arm and shoulder will be necessary to carry the work forward, for the time is short and the labor is great, and it is as much as we can ever do to get ready before the Lord Jesus comes to visit this earth. O, how lovely, brother Daniels, it is to be able to labor in the vineyard of our God; may the Lord bless you with the strength and power of the Priesthood which you received here; may the angels of the Lord protect you day and night from our enemies and wicked men, for there has never been a good man on our earth who has not had enemies. You are remembered by here in the house of the Lord, and several of the faithful brethren ask me, "When is Brother Daniels returning?"

When I returned here I had a great reception from President Young and his Counselors, and others; the first thing they said was—"*God bless you brother Jeremy.*" Things like that were a great comfort to me if not to anyone else.

I wish for you to remember me to the dear Saints there a thousand times over, but to no one more than to President Daniels. I wish for you to give my best to my sisters, and to their husbands and their children, and to all who may ask about me. My family is of the same heart as I in wishing to be remembered to you. Give my best to your Counselors, and Brother Thomas Harris and his family.

If you deem this writing worthy to appear in the TRUMPET, it is at your service.

I shall rest for the present time.

I am, as always,

Your brother in Christ,

THOMAS JEREMY.

LETTER OF GWILYM DDU.

Great Salt Lake City, June 26, 1856.

DEAR BROTHER DANIELS,—I was promising to myself much rejoicing and mental pleasure this coming autumn, inasmuch as we were expecting your return home from your mission; but when we learned the story from the "Star" we were disappointed in our expectation; but inasmuch as your mission will continue, and it is unlikely that we shall have your association this season, yet we rejoice together as Welsh brothers and sisters, that it has fallen your lot to be the President over our fellow nation in the land of our birth. May the gracious Lord keep you and impart to you the Spirit of your holy calling is my sincere and constant prayer, yes, I dare say, the prayers of all your acquaintances from among the Welsh, together with other nations in Zion.

I shall not take it upon myself in this letter to write about much of the news to you, since Sister Daniels will write that. There are better signs for sustenance of men and animals this year than there was last year, since we are not troubled by grasshoppers so frequently, although they have destroyed some few in some places of the Territory this year, but nothing in comparison to last year.

I am a bit concerned about my daughter, Mary, at present, since she has revealed in a letter to me her wish to come away; and I answered her that I would pay her expense as I did with Henry; but the way appears to be closed at present, since the Public Works have been idle since the last part of last year, which was brought about by the scarcity of food because of the grasshoppers and the drought. If the work had continued I would have paid into the Fund before now, and then I could send for her by next season. Also the rules of the Fund are more strict now than they were; one must pay in full now before sending for someone. I do not know how things will turn out next fall; it is said that the Public Works will begin after the harvest, but it will be late at that time to send for her by the next season. I wish for you, dear brother, if you see any chance to send her as a servant to someone, that is, if that is not a trouble and a hindrance to you, for I consider that the weight of your calling is already great without anyone burdening you with some errands like this. I have paid Capt. Davies and Brother Sykes; I built a house for each of them last year, and I am still willing to do my best in behalf of Mary.

The Neff family mentions you frequently and they send their regards. Ann and I were glad to see your letter and to learn that you have seen her mother. May the Lord bless your effort to bring some of them if not all, to gain salvation. Dear brother, I long to see you and have your association.

Your loving brother,
WM. LEWIS.

LETTER OF JOHN PARRY.

Winter Quarters, July 27, 1856.

DEAR BROTHER DANIELS,—According to your wish, I herewith send a little of our story to you by letter, hoping that you will forgive its brevity and its mistakes, for I am in a great hurry.

I am pleased to let you know that I and my wife are well, and that the camp in general is enjoying extremely good health. It is not useful for me to give an account of our voyage across the ocean to you, since that has already been done by others. But I will say that we had an unusually stormy voyage, yet no one died except a few infants. We came across in about five weeks, to Boston, which is an unusually beautiful town. We came from there to Iowa city on the Railroad. All were healthy, except for a few infants, among which was my own little child. We were eights days traveling on the Railroad, and we stopped in Iowa city for three weeks; then about three hundred of us started towards here. Edward Bunker is our President, and three of us have been set as Captains of hundreds. We arrived here with our handcarts in about three weeks quite successfully, about 300 miles, with no deaths except for one infant, although we had some old people, from eighty to one hundred years old, who were carried in the wagons with the provisions.

Several grumbled because there was not an abundance of food given out, and some stayed behind because of it; but I lived on what was given out, and worked as much as any man in the camp, and you understand that I am alive, and looking better and healthier than I ever did before, although I consider the rations quite small; at the same time there was wisdom in that, for practically all of us had more *luggage* or dishes than were allowed. And through that plan the unnecessary things were sold for butter and bacon, &c., so that we are now ready to start across the plains, although we must yet scale back on several things.

I do not think that anyone remained behind except for those who were unable to pay anything toward their own transportation. Plenty of food is allowed for us from here to the Valley, besides that which is anticipated for our arrival.

We have been here since a week from yesterday, and we intend to start for the Valley next Tuesday if we can get everything ready for the journey.

America is a beautiful and attractive land, with an abundance of everything except for inhabitants. I have not seen anyone who is repenting for having left the old country, rather they praise God for their deliverance from it. We have heard that the prospect is for a particularly good harvest in the Valley this year. Everything is well with us. The handcart companies are going forward *first rate*. It is easier for us to walk twenty miles per day now than it was for us to walk ten at the beginning, and all are increasing in strength and health, according to the prophecy of the Prophet Brigham.

I don't have time to write more now; I cannot find time to write to those I promised. I wish for you to remember me to all the Saints in Wales, especially my brothers and sisters in the North. I would really love to see them receive redemption from the cruel captivity of Babylon to the glorious freedom of the children of Zion.

Thomas Morgans is with me now, and he sends his fond regards to you. And I send my warmest regards to you and to your Counselors, and to the Conference Presidency of Denbighshire and to the Saints under their care. I wish for your success in all things.

I am your brother in Christ,
JOHN PARRY.

FEELING OF A MISSIONARY.

Builth Wells, August 25, 1856.

MR. EDITOR,—I am pleased to have the present opportunity to give you a brief account of my travels through the country. I am fully determined to complete the counsel I received from you with regards to laboring among the world, although I am frequently under many difficulties. I preached out-of-doors last night to several attentive listeners. I have not baptized anyone as yet, but there are several in this town, and in other towns, who believe the principles, but they do not have enough courage at present to obey, because there is no Branch established here; I have faith that some will come out before long. The enemies of the truth are causing great confusion in some places of Radnorshire, heckling me when I preach, and they encourage their children to shout and scream, until the honest in heart feel, and come to understand that all this is a device of the devil, to prevent men from listening to a servant of God preaching the eternal gospel in the fullness of his blessings. I am heartened by the Spirit of God, until I feel brave in the heat of battle, having full assurance that God is with me.

Brother John Jones, formerly the President of Brecon Branch, was with me preaching like a giant in Llanfair and Rhayader, &c. Brother John was like a father to me as long as he was here, and my wish is for the blessing of the Lord to follow after him.

I feel well with the work of the Lord, and thankful to have part in this great and important work. I take great delight frequently in going aside in secret to pray to the Lord. This in haste from

Your humble brother in Christ.
JOSEPH GRIFFITHS.

THE LAW OF TITHING.

(M. N.—8.7.)

HAIL and welcome the law of Tithing,
    Come forward to have your share,
You have been much despised
    And attacked in many places;
Now you have visited Wales,
    In your great nobility,
And in the name of him who created
    All of heaven and earth below.

You were warmly welcomed,
    By the venerable Abraham,
And he taught his family,
    To exalt you in perfection;
Jacob also glorified you,
    Respecting you everywhere,
And from all his property daily,
    You received a tenth part.

No one can honor you
    Without the faith of old Abraham,
These are they who truly embrace you,
    And love you like a mother;
All who lack the faith as noted,
    Perceive you mistakenly,
Considering you as oppression,
    Plundering them of all their standing.

> But those who possess a part
>   Of the dear precious faith,
> Believe that it's their welfare you seek,
>   And you elevate them each day;
> They believe too all the laws,
>   Which are to come from Zion dear,—
> They'll not transgress, and will not fail,
>   In all the subjects of heaven above.

Flint. T. CONWAY.

ZION'S TRUMPET,

OR

Star of the Saints.

SATURDAY, SEPTEMBER 13, 1856.

NEWS FROM THE VALLEY.—We call the attention of our readers to the letters that are at the beginning of this issue. There are many brothers and sisters in Wales who were promised by their relatives in Zion, that they would send for them before now, but have not done so, for which reason many are disheartened and are losing hope that they will ever be sent for. But through the letters of brothers Thomas Jeremy and Wm. Lewis, the Saints understand that this delay has been caused by the hard times there have been in Utah Territory lately because of the grasshoppers, &c. We understand also through the "Deseret News" and through several letters besides the aforementioned, that there are better signs for a more abundant harvest than have ever before been seen.

We quote the following from a letter written by B. Young to Orson Pratt, dated June 30:—

"The Indians are quiet, and many of them are busily engaged in agricultural pursuits; those hostile in the spring, with the exception of Tintic, have come in, and he is expected shortly.

"The harvest will commence shortly, a little barley will be cut this week, and some wheat next, but not much before the 15th or 20th of July. Provisions, of course, continue quite scarce.

"Water is quite scarce for irrigation, which will cause the loss of some grain. We have brought the Big Cottonwood down, so that it can be brought to the *five-acre lots* and the east part of the City, and are still working more or less on that Canal, which will, eventually, prove of great benefit to this City, not only in furnishing water for irrigation, but for the transmission of *granite rock* for building purposes. We hope to get it into operation this fall.

"The health of the community is generally very good, and the crops generally look well. We shall forward teams and provisions to meet the emigration companies so soon as we can get sufficient harvest, from which we can obtain supplies of flour."

―――――

EMIGRATION.—All Saints who wish to emigrate this autumn, are instructed to send to us, immediately, their £1 deposits, names, ages, where born, occupations, and addresses. We shall probably send out a ship some time in October; and desire to know at least one month before it sails, how many passengers wish to be accommodated. The ages of all infants under twelve months are required.

―――――

FLINTSHIRE CONFERENCE.

Rhosllanerchrugog, September 1, 1856.

MR. EDITOR,—The above conference was held in Mold, Sunday the 24th of August, when we had the association of several brethren and officers with whom we had not been previously acquainted. The Council was held in the morning; it was begun with singing and a prayer by Elder Samuel Parry, Rhos. Then President Thomas Rees spoke on the purpose for our having come together, and about the privilege of meeting together to deal with the work and service of the Lord in these days.

Then the scribe was called on to read the report, the total of which is as follows—Elders 19, Priests 3, Teachers 5, Deacons 2, Baptized 2, cut off 3, scattered 9, total 103. After that we were encouraged by brother Israel Evans; he taught enthusiastically and warmly about the work of God on the earth. Then all the authorities of the Church were unanimously sustained, and then we received profitable and beneficial teachings from Israel Evans and from President Thomas Rees. The morning meeting was concluded with singing and a prayer by Griffith Roberts.

Sermons were given to a very large congregation by brothers Griffith Roberts, John Jones, and Israel Evans. In the evening brothers Noah Jones, Griffith Roberts, John Jones, and Israel Evans preached. Some of the Saints' enemies had come together there, wishing to cause a commotion, but despite that, some received the truth. Only two were baptized that night, with signs for more. The brethren received the power of God's Spirit to preach the gospel throughout the day, and the honest in heart took pleasure in hearing them. The work of the day was concluded with a prayer by John Jones.

T. REES, President,
A. CLARKE, Scribe.

[We received another letter from Elder J. Jones, which contains the same account as the previous one. We are very glad to learn of the success and the good signs that are following the labor of our brethren in the North.—ED.]

THE PRIESTHOOD.

There is some great disturbance,
    In the camp;
Those with great gifts now,
    Fear our stand;
The power of the Priesthood is,—
    It will conquer,
False religions of all kinds,
    Hallelujah.

This one yields authority,
    Over the Saints;
While our mien is joyful,
    For our privileges:

It governs undeniably,
    All the worlds,
This one exalted our dear Father,
    Up to heaven.

Without it God could not have
    Created the planets,
Nor given them according to their nature,
    Holy laws;
On our little orb,
    Are found,
Countless thousands,
    Very clearly.

Of objects large and small,
    To our astonishment,
Through its power they now exist,
    From the Deity;
Laws of nature under the heavens,
    Are governed.
By the strong Priesthood,
    For our comfort.

Noble power of a high order,
    It presides,
It is a branch of the foremost one,
    Who will deny it?
There are blessings galore in it,
    Praise for religion,
This will be the basis of the Lord's throne,
    For ever more.

Jesus our dear friend was called,
    As a Priest,
Through a sacred oath by his Father,
    And consecration;
An infinitely higher post was given,
    To the Rose of Sharon,
Than to the Priests of high degree,
    Through the order of Aaron.

Up to the Father's great throne,
    It can ascend,

And the lowest realm as a blessing,
    It governs;
There is no beginning to it, hark,
    It is eternal,
It is not some nebulous shadow,
    It has substance.

Through almost the whole universe,
    Cannot be found
Its parents, nor any proud ancestry,
    Which exist;
If I look ahead through faith,
    In ages to come,
I shall find no end to its day
    Through the centuries.

Since Christ our heavenly Lord,
    Possessed,
This office while on earth,
    He bestowed;
The same order on myriad hosts,
    Of human kind—
I shall see them at journey's end,
    Over in Zion.

To the desert the woman went,
    To hide away,
Because the old dragon every day,
    Was bothering her;
Truly there she stayed,
    For centuries,
And darkness across the land,
    Spread out.

Back to heaven—divine senate,
    Was taken,
The true strong Priesthood,
    To the throne;
This the serpent and its wrath,
    Could never spoil.
Through our world to it is sung,
    The sound of Hosanna.

A bright light was seen yonder,
    Appearing,
There are myriad blessings nearby,
    Awaiting us;
Well, prithee, what was it—
    Shedding light,
For a very loud shout,
    Was heard there.

It was an angel in heaven,
    Coming down,
And he had the Gospel,
    In authority;
And to the Prophet Joseph Smith,
    He revealed it,
His name will be revered for ever,
    For what he received.

Elijah has come,
    To the continent,
All that previously existed,
    Will be restored;
And the boy child also came,
    In great power,
I'll give praise along the way,
    To Christ Jesus.

Joseph, the great Seer,
    Received it,
And on hosts on the earth,
    He bestowed it;
For the strong angels of heaven,
    Substantially,
Ordained him,
    An Apostle.

A stone from distant Gomorrah,
    Which was in the earth,
Was broken untouched by hand,
    Recently;
It rolled from wave to wave,
    Conquering,
Till it came to this island;
    To give us joy.

All mankind's wisdom,
    Will be abolished,
Through the strength of God's Priesthood,
    It will be vanquished;
Now it's seen in a clear light,
    That truly,
The great ones were dreaming,
    Who gave explanations.

The boy child is now in power,
    Within Wales.
The lovers of big salaries,
    Are trembling;
False teachers of all sorts,
    And the bishops,
And religious counter to God,
    Fear Zion.

Because I am one of the Saints,
    I give praise,
Ineffable is the privilege,
    Which I own;
Namely to have an office in God's Church,
    A spiritual office,
It is not a feeble human one,—
    It is most powerful.

Let us Saints join with one voice,
    To give praise,
To our holy Father in heaven,
    And glory;
For the synagogues of the earth,
    Will be shattered,
And the cries of all the "Reverends,"
    Will be silenced.

Thanks be, I see a Temple yonder,
    In the Valley,
Where the King will come later on,
    Quite suddenly;
While I shall go with happy song,
    When I'm called,
Within its sacred walls,
    Such is my aim.

Lately of Haverfordwest College.   DEWI IOAN DYFED

BOOKS FOR SALE

BY D. DANIELS, IN THE OFFICE OF "ZION'S TRUMPET," SWANSEA,
And the Prices to the Branches and the Conferences.

Book of Mormon, bound 4s;—4s 3c.

Doctrine and Covenants, bound 3s,—3s 3c.

Book of Hymns, most handsome binding 2s 3c,—3s 5c.

    Ditto, second best 2s, 2c.

    Ditto, strong calfskin 1s 9c;—1s 11c.

Zion's Trumpet, Vol. I—IV., bound 3s each. Vol. V., 1s 10¾c. Vol. VI., 2s. Vol. VII., 2s 10¼c, unbound. Also Volume VIII., the same price. Profit of 1 issue of every 20 to the Branches.

Prophet of the Jubilee, Vol. III., unbound 2s.

Pamphlets written by Capt. Jones.

The Scriptural Treasury, bound 3s;—3s 2c. Unbound 2s 4c;—2s 5c.

Who is the God of the Saints, per hundred 17s 6c;—19s 10c.

The Old Religion Anew, £1 18s;—£2 6s.

Proclamation, per hundred 10s;—11s 6c.

Refutations to the Spaulding Story about the Book of Mormon, per hundred 14s 2c;—15s 10c.

Unpopularity of Mormonism, per hundred 6s;—7s 6c.

Guide to Zion, per hundred 11s;—12s.

What is Mormonism, per hundred 3s;—3s 9c.

What is Saving Grace, per hundred 3s 6c;—3s 11c.

Invitations, per hundred 1s 10c.

Pamphlets written by John Davis.

Book of the Church, 11s each.

That which is in Part, &c., per hundred 6s;—7s.

First General Epistle, per hundred 6s 6c;—7s 6c.

Treatise on Miracles, per hundred 6s;—7s.

Treatises on Miracles. No. 1–6, per hundred 6s;—7s.

Preaching to the spirits in Prison, per hundred 5s 6c;—6s 6c.

Go and Teach, per hundred 1s 8c;—1s 10c.

Conversations, per hundred 2s 9c;—3s.

Prove all things, per hundred 2s 9c;—3s.

"MARRIAGE AND MORALS IN UTAH,"

HAS just come off the Press. Its price for the Conferences is 7s per hundred; for the Branches 8s per hundred; and to the public 1c each. Let no faithful Saint be unwilling for anyone of his neighborhood to be ignorant of the contents of this pamphlet. Let everyone strive his best to disseminate this pamphlet according to the counsel of God. We have put the following on its wrapper:—

"Friends,—Do not let the influence of false religion stir up your passions to disregard our message to you; for it is an irrefutable truth that God has spoken from heaven that which you must do to be saved. If you were to do every other thing which every sect commands, and neglect the commandments which God has revealed, you would not be saved. Eternal life never was, nor is it promised except ONLY through obeying EVERY WORD THAT *COMES* FROM THE MOUTH OF GOD, whatever that word may be. The religion of whosoever changes one jot of the commandments of Jesus Christ cannot be divine even if they were professed or praised by the world, or if all the human wisdom of the world were to claim the contrary; consequently, for the sake of your eternal salvation do not be beguiled into believing them. Also, if every preacher, author and editor join together in affirming this, do not believe them, for they are our enemies—hireling preachers, who treat the Word of God deceitfully, and lest their business fail, they proclaim every lie about the Saints of the Most High God in order to keep you in darkness, and to prevent you from going to listen to and understand the doctrine of the Saints, and to hear the word of God preached as it is in Jesus. Let your feet be free from the traditional fetters of the fathers, and go to listen to the Latter-day Saints, those who preach in your neighborhoods—and open your doors to the servants of the King of Glory to come in to preach the gospel of peace, which will bring a witness to you through the Spirit of God of your approval before him."

CONTENTS.

	PG.
Letter of Thomas Jeremy	289
Letter of Gwilym Ddu	291
Letter of John Parry	292
Feeling of a Missionary	294
Law of Tithing	295
Editorial—News from the Valley—emigration	296
Flintshire Conference	297
The Priesthood	298

SWANSEA:

PRINTED AND PUBLISHED BY DANIEL DANIELS.

ZION'S TRUMPET,

OR

Star of the Saints.

No. 20.] SEPTEMBER 27, 1856. [Vol. IX.

LETTER OF PRESIDENT D. JONES.

Camp of Israel,
Near Iowa City,
July 4th, 1856.

My dear Brother Daniels,—As you see I am still alive, although you fear by now, perhaps, because of my long silence, that I am on the *Plains*, or in the other world. The truth is, the care of the 700 people who were entrusted to my care had so heavily overburdened me, that, by the time I reached here, I had hardly enough strength in me to live any more, and it was not for nearly three weeks that I nor anyone else knew in which world I would be the next day. By now, through the goodness of my God, there is hope that my life will continue who knows how long. Thanks be to him for that.

I wrote to you at length from Boston. Thank you for your comforting letters from there, and I received one here too, which proves that neither the ocean nor the continent has diminished the love which has bound us together for so long, and inseparably I hope.

We came from Boston to here in eight days by railway, and for £2 6s. each, half price for those who were under 14, and bringing a hundred pounds at no charge.

The common people of this country treated us humanely, although some wanton and evil men tried to entice some of the sisters away in every place where they had a chance, and in several

20 [Price 1c.

towns, such as Buffalo, Toledo, Chicago, and Rock Island, especially the last, we were obliged to mount an armed watch on the carriages, on Saturday night, and fight with crowds of hounds such as those that were once in Sodom throughout the Sunday with arms, clubs, pitchforks, and swords in order to keep them from rushing on the sisters, and indeed all the brethren fought well until victory, and although we had very little *help* from the Sheriff and his army, he was kind enough to give us the freedom to defend ourselves, and no sooner was that obtained than the little Mormon army rushed into the middle of the throng, outing a swathe before them as wide as the road, and *guess* who was leading them. The next day it was proved before the Mayor that these bloodhounds had sworn allegiance to each other in order to help each other to steal the fairest of our women to serve their own devilish purpose, and it was thanks to the power of arms and the bravery of my fellow soldiers that they did not succeed. In the first town I mentioned I had to assemble a few select men and clear the *station* before us, with the permission of the *Station Master*, of the savages who were rushing into the midst of and *insulting* the sisters when they were changing carriages and their goods, and they threatened to cut the throat of the first who came into their midst to that end. Oh, how thankful I was to be able to settle the company on this sacred ground, in the midst of Saints and brethren where they would be safe. I felt as though my work was almost over, and the innocent little flock spared from the teeth of wolves, and brought safely to the fold each and every one. Apart from that worry, we came this far comfortably, cheaply and successfully, peacefully and without complaint and with unity and love increasing among us. In a word, I cannot praise too highly the dear brethren, and there were not too many exceptions among the other sex, and those few almost cost the best lives in the camp. Only damnation, trouble and pain follow the devil of love on the road to Zion, and this is the main *hobby* of the evil one in order to ruin the young and torment their leaders who give them better counsel. But enough about that, although we have to guard the camp here with a strong force in order to keep the foxes out at night, and you would laugh to see the occasional one in the snare. Thanks be to our God that the faces of all the Presidents who are here (and they are here from the four corners of the earth, now on their way home) are set like flint to defend and safeguard the chief adornment of the other sex at all costs.

Three companies set out with the handcarts some weeks ago, one of them from Wales, about 300 in number, about three weeks ago. They left in the midst of loud shouts of Hosannah and rejoicing. I escorted them the first day and their only concern was that I would not be allowed to go with them: because of this many cried; but I was advised to stay here to help President Spencer, &c., to start the companies before us. Over two thousand people have come here from England, after me: over a thousand have started out for the far west; three companies of men on foot, comprising about 1500 people, intend to leave next week.

I was appointed to supervise the wagon and carriage camp, including nearly a hundred teams, or at least to start it until President Richards catches up with us, and I intend to start this week. In their midst are between 150 and 200 Welsh people all at *first rate*. Yet the strong western winds here have winnowed some chaff on this threshing floor, or the occasional wheat seed to the doorstep to hide until the next sowing season. No one has been excommunicated as yet, and only one of the 707 has died, namely Sister James of Tredegar, and a few infants as I noted before.

Our dear President Spencer is proving himself to be a better man all the time the greater the burden that rests on him, so that everyone here considers him invaluable.

Services are held here every Sunday, and throngs came from the country and the towns to them, including many Welsh people among others who live near here. The meetings are often in the evenings, and there is a prayer night and morning in every tent at the sound of the bugle for that purpose. There is remarkable unity and brotherly love here through everything, whatever language, race or nation, hardly any difference is seen. Nearly all the remainder of the American Elders who came here across the *plains* the same time as you and I, are now on their way home under full sail as conquering giants; and if you were here too, the *ranks* would be nearly full.

People come hundreds of miles here for the express purpose they say of seeing for themselves if the wonders they have heard about us and our camp are true: carriagefulls of them are seen here almost every day and hour, and they all marvel at the scene before them, and indeed our big white city on the top and the slopes of a beautiful hill and open country looks very fine, especially when the sun shines on it; it glitters rather like that city which John once saw from the top of that mountain. The large round tents are in straight rows, with their number above the door; the square tents are as straight in other rows, and the wagons with their white, red, black, yellow, and multicolored covers are a round wall meeting each other, and their tents another wall outside that. Everything inside and out, and even the roads are kept as clean and pure as though you were in a nobleman's park. Not infrequently heaven rains down tears of joy profusely on our heads, until there is scarcely a dry thread on anyone, in the midst of which echo back through the air the shouts of the songs of Zion mainly from the sisters when the water streams from their gowns of silk and satin. Although there are in this *pickle* scores who were brought up too delicately almost to tread the ground at home, let alone lie on the ground in our Father's great bedroom with no cover but His blue airy coverlet. They get neither cold nor chill, and it is all merely delight to them; they rise from their beds sometimes with the dew of heaven like incense smoke rising in columns from their clothes, a monument to their sacrifice for the gospel of Jesus, while praise to God issues from their lips and no complaint.

President Snow visited us recently from St. Louis, having just returned from the Valley.

No doubt O. Pratt, Benson, and Phineas Young have arrived there with you by now; when you see them, give them my very fond regards.

All news from the Valley is very comforting, and while peace reigns there, over here nothing is heard but the sound of war with forces from the Eastern States swarming toward Kansas to meet the forces of the slave traders of the South on a battle ground which is already scarlet from men's blood, yes, *men* who were nursed on the same breasts, and were nourished from the same valleys have swords locked together on their own hearths, and their father cannot understand who is at fault, who is to be helped, but rushes his armies to kill both sides as they please! While the poor things are quarreling about the soil which will fill all their heads before long, the Saints are thus left in peace to go safely home through the middle of them this year again! Great is the wisdom of our God and the precaution of his shepherds.

You will hear from me again from Council Bluffs. Until then, dear brother, Farewell; the Lord bless you with every competence to fulfill our important position to His satisfaction, to your own and to all the Saints', and bless those who bless you and all our fellow workers.

This with fond remembrance to all, the brethren in the Office, and all the Officers and the Saints, is the fervent desire of
Your dear brother in Christ,
D. JONES.

DIFFERENCE BETWEEN THE BAPTISTS AND THE LATTER-DAY SAINTS.

(From the History of Joseph Smith.)

WE will now attempt to show the difference between the Baptists and Former-day Saints.

1. The Former-day Saints baptized for remission of sins, Acts ii. 38. The Baptists baptize only those who are supposed to have their sins forgiven before they are baptized.

2. The Former-day Saints admitted all persons indiscriminately to baptism, as soon as they professed faith and repentance, encouraging them to pass through that rite, with the promise that great spiritual improvement would follow, Acts ii. 38–41. But if the Baptists found the penitent believer looking for remission of sins through that rite, they would be put back to "get religion" where they could find it.

3. After baptism, the Former-day Saints prayed for, and laid hands on the disciples in the name of Jesus, and professed to give them the Holy Ghost, Acts viii. 17, also Acts xix. 6. The Baptists say, "They regard such mummery with as much disgust as all Christians do."

4. Having, as they supposed, the extraordinary gifts of the Spirit, the Former-day Saints consistently pretended to have the

power of working wonders, and professed to heal the sick with holy oil; James v. 14, 15. Also to the power of prophecy; 1 Corinthians, from chapter 12 to 14. It need not be added that the Baptists stand far removed from "such conceits," and have no part in them; nor in anything pertaining to the gifts and power of God: or, to use the Apostle's own words, "they have a form of godliness, denying the power."

5. Not satisfied with the Bible as a complete revelation from God, the Former-day Saints have added a volume of several hundred pages (the New Testament), to that book, which (according to the Baptist logic) Moses forbade them to add to, or take from; Deut. iv. 2. But even this was not enough; but new revelations were served up almost daily, fresh as they arrived, for all those who could swallow them. "The disgust with which the Baptists regard such things, considering them but a melancholy exhibition of human folly and wickedness," separates them to an impassable distance from the Former-day Saints; and how, with all these differences, the Baptists should ever have been thought, by themselves, or anybody else, to be the Church of Christ, is difficult to imagine!

6. In order to carry on their strange work, or order of things, the Former-day Saints had two Priesthoods. The Aaronic Priesthood administered in outward ordinances, as in the case of John the Baptist. The power and authority of the higher, or Melchizedek Priesthood, was to hold the keys of all the spiritual blessings of the Church, as Jesus said, "I give unto thee the keys of the kingdom of heaven—whatsoever thou shalt bind on earth shall be bound in heaven," &c. They were to have the privilege of knowing the mysteries of the kingdom of heaven. "To you it is given to know the mysteries of the kingdom"—to have the heavens opened unto them—to commune with the general assembly and Church of the Firstborn; and to enjoy the communion and presence of God the Father, and of Jesus the Mediator of the new covenant; Heb. xii. 22, 23, 24. So that in this wonderful Priesthood, they have provided for an ample supply of new things, in endless variety, and without end, from those who are and were counted the offscouring of all things;

and who, as the Baptists would insinuate, "did aspire to a dignity," which they say, "belongs alone to Him who is the only Priest forever after the order of Melchizedek."

The fear of trespassing upon the time and patience of our readers, prevents our enlarging upon these and many other points of difference; but enough has been said to show, that no two sects can possibly differ more widely from each other than do the Baptists and Former-day Saints; and to amalgamate the two systems in any way is not only an act of injustice—but would involve the Baptists, who by the by are an honorable body, in the disgrace of that sect which was "everywhere spoken against."

SHUTTING DOORS.

(From the Deseret News.)

'Don't look so cross, Edward, when I call you back to shut the door; grandmother feels the cold wintry wind; and, besides, you have got to spend all your life shutting doors, and might as well begin now.'

'Do forgive me, grandmother! I ought to be ashamed to be cross with you. But what do you mean? I am going to college, and then I am going to be a lawyer.'

'Well admitting all that; I imagine Squire Edward C—— will have a good many doors to shut, if ever he makes much of a man.'

'What kind of doors? Do tell me, grandmother.'

'Sit down a minute, and I will give you a list.

'In the first place, the door of your ears must be closed against bad language and evil counsel of the boys and young men you will meet with at school and college, or you will be undone. Let them once get possession of that door, and I would not give much for Edward C——'s prospects.

'The door of your eyes, too, must be shut against bad books, idle novels, and low, wicked newspapers, or your studies will be neglected, and you will grow up a useless, ignorant man; you will have to close them sometimes against the fine things exposed for sale in the shop windows, or you will never learn to save your money, or have any left to give away.

'The door of your lips will need especial care, for they guard an unruly member, which makes great use of the bad company let in at the doors of the eyes and ears. That door is very apt to blow open; and if not constantly watched, will let out angry, trifling or vulgar words. It will backbite, sometimes worse than the winter's wind if it is left open too long. I would advise you to keep it shut much of the time till you have laid up a store of knowledge, or at least till you have something valuable to say.

'The inner door of your heart must be well shut against temptation, for conscience, the doorkeeper grows very indifferent if you disregard his call; and sometimes drops asleep at his post, and when you may think you are doing very well, you are fast going down to ruin.

'If you carefully guard the outside doors of the eyes, ears and lips, you will keep out many cold blasts of sin, which get in before you think.

'This shutting doors, you see, Edward, will be a serious business; one on which your well-doing in this life and the next depends.'

ZION'S TRUMPET,

OR

Star of the Saints.

SATURDAY, SEPTEMBER 27, 1856.

TITHING.—Should any Latter-day Saint be excused from paying tithing? As this question has arisen in the minds of some, for their satisfaction we design answering it in a plain and brief manner.

The law of tithing is an eternal one, obligatory not only upon the Saints, but upon every son and daughter of Adam, so far as they have a knowledge of it, without any regard to their position or circumstances, whether they be high or low, rich or poor, Saint or sinner, Jew or Gentile. One tenth of everything which men obtain belongs to the Lord, and should be placed in the hands of his servants, to be used in the way He may direct, for the building up of his kingdom.

The tithing is a tribute which men owe to the Lord for the use of the earth which He has created for their benefit; and they should consider the payment of it as a continual acknowledgement that all they have belongs to him, and is only loaned to them for their use. Taking this view of the case, whether they obtain much or little from the elements which surround them, they equally owe a tenth of it to the Lord; and that too, whether it amounts to only one farthing, or to tens of thousands of pounds.

The question has been asked us, whether those Saints should pay tithing whose income is so small, that if they do it they will either have to go without bread, or run into debt in order to live? We think the above has answered this question plainly, but will further add, that the Lord, in revelations on the subject, has excused no class of his people from the payment of this tribute, and if He has not, we certainly have no right to. It is a matter that lies directly between every man and his God. It is the duty of the servants of the Lord to instruct the Saints in the law of tithing, the same as in other commandments which they are required to teach them, then the responsibility of keeping it rests with them, and they will be rewarded according to their works.

The question now arises, what will be done with the poor whose income is so small, that if they pay their tithing they must suffer for bread? We answer, let those who have more abundantly, administer to their wants. The Bible tells us, "He that giveth to the poor shall not lack: but he that hideth his eyes shall have many a curse;" and in a revelation to Joseph Smith, the Lord says, "Wo unto you rich men, that will not give your substance to the poor, for your riches will canker your souls; and this shall be your lamentation in the day of visitation, and of judgment, and of indignation—The harvest is past, the summer is ended, and my soul is not saved!"

It is incumbent upon those who minister in the offices of the Priesthood to instruct those who have it in their power to assist the needy and destitute in their duty in this respect, and to give them an opportunity of showing their love to the Lord and his kingdom by administering to his poor.

In places where the Saints are all in an impoverished condition, or where the means contributed by the more affluent proves insufficient for the wants of the needy, they should be assisted out of the proceeds of the tithing.

Great care, and a judicious discrimination will be found necessary in the use of funds for this object, in order to prevent the indolent and unworthy from reaping the benefit of what is only designed for the Lord's poor—the diligent and faithful Saint. None should receive assistance except those who pay their tithing, and are found approved by their works before the Lord and their brethren; and great care should be exercised that no impositions are practiced by persons who may join the Church for the sake of obtaining bread.

It is the duty of all men who have it in their power to assist the worthy poor; and it is especially the duty of the Saints to assist those of the household of faith, who are weighed down with poverty and affliction.

We say to the poor, if you would enjoy in rich effusion the gifts and blessings of the Holy Spirit—if you would prove to the Lord that even in affliction you are determined to serve him, and to prove him, and see if He will not pour out his blessings upon you as He has promised, and if you would yourselves belong to the poor whom Jesus meant when he said, "Blessed are the poor, for theirs is the kingdom of heaven"—*pay your tithing.*

We say to the rich—If you would not have your wealth canker your souls—if you would not have it prove a curse instead of a blessing, and lead you down to death—if, when earthly treasures fail, you would have some laid up in heaven—pay your tithing, and administer to the wants of the needy. And we say to all—If you ever expect to enjoy the blessings of the faithful in Zion—to enter into the House of the Lord—to receive the keys and powers of eternal life—to be the means of welding together the broken links of your generations—to become Kings and Priests of the Most High God—to be saviors upon Mount Zion, and finally to receive an inheritance on the earth after it is sanctified, purified, and become the dwelling place of the Father—pay your tithing, and prepare your hearts to turn everything that you have over to the Lord whenever He calls for his own, which He now permits you to be stewards over. Unless you do these things, your course in this kingdom will soon be run; your light will be shrouded in darkness; and the star of revelation, which would have led you on with increasing strength to the brightness of eternal glory, will be lost altogether to your vision.—STAR.

LETTER TO PRESIDENT DANIELS.

Swansea, September 21, 1856.

REVERED PRESIDENT DANIELS:—In accordance with my duty, here for you is a little of my story and my adventures visiting the Branches, together with other places where I taught and preached the word of life.

First of all, I can testify to you that I have never in my life felt more completely at one with the great work of God than at present. I feel that I am continually receiving more strength and power, and more understanding and light of God's Spirit. My constant prayers are for my heavenly Father to open the eyes of my understanding, and to make it active in His law, and to bless me with wisdom and discernment to properly share his words, and to recognize the appropriate time, the means, and the opportunity to deliver them and declare them for the edification of the Saints, and to swiftly cleanse myself from the blood of all with whom I have had dealings in the course of my labor. The importance of this is always on my mind. I feel grateful to God, through Jesus Christ, for the sublime privilege of being able to labor in his vineyard.

Your counsels, and those of Evans and Ashby have been, and

continue to be valuable and priceless to me, as I have carried them out under the guidance of the Spirit of God which has been a blessing to me personally, to the Saints, and to all those who are persuaded to recognize the truth.

The Saints whom I have visited in the various Branches throughout the different Conferences, with the exception of a very few, are feeling extremely good and resolute.

"The law of tithing" is being received and practiced by the Saints generally. Many of these began paying their tithing at the first *hint* that was given them and have willingly and promptly paid not only the *tenth*, but also the *fifth* in order to build the kingdom of God, and to win for themselves the honor and the blessings refused by those who are too indifferent and mean-spirited to obey this commandment.

The obedient willing ones feel their breasts swelling with love, happiness and joy, testifying that all they have is, as it were, already on the altar, yes, even their life is ready to be sacrificed whenever the Lord may ask it of them, while those who are not experienced in the work of God, are inclined to complain, "without seeing any further," and go deeper and deeper into darkness. . . .

It is a million times better to accept the word willingly than to be obliged to believe it and receive it because of the pressure of ill health, distress, restricted emotion, difficult circumstances, poverty and misfortune, &c. God loves and blesses a cheerful giver. . . .

There is plenty of work wherever I go. The Presidents of Conferences and Branches, the Elders, &c., are also very diligent. They preach in the open two and three times every Sunday, and many other times—hundreds come to listen, yes, thousands at times—an excellent hearing everywhere.

It seems that throngs wish to be baptized. There is a new excitement among the people, as if they were in constant pain—emotionally uneasy—unable to sleep until the wee hours of the morning—quietly inquiring of Jesus' servants about the means of restoring man to the presence of God.

Although I received hardly any opposition when I preached out-of-doors, yet I did meet with some who were filled with anger, hatred, envy and animosity toward the truth. These are insidious men; they want to backbite in secret, except for the occasional one who is sufficiently foolish and reckless to run before the puff of his own arrogance, vehement and raging under the effects of the *cacoethe scribendi* so they cannot help but show their weakminded scribing in the newspapers, &c., trying to vilify the glory of the organization of the redemption and the redeemed of God. These childish men in their attack on the Saints always vanish like "water bubbles" and the foam of the wave, absorbed in their own foolishness—completely devoid of the ability to accomplish their wicked purposes in order to do business with those who listen to them.

Ha, ha, sectarianism is in a great frenzy—the gift of preaching has become hollow and boring—the days of the beast have swallowed them alive—and the time of their overthrow now brings near the fall and collapse of Great Babylon, the mother of whores and the abomination of the earth.   .   .

Presently hardly anything but a bark is heard against the polygamy of the Mormons. How short-sighted must the sectarians of the age be, how ignorant of the patriarchal order and its purpose, and its associated blessings!   .   .   .

No doubt the treatise of Apostle P. P. Pratt will silence every tongue, and it will enlighten and convince those who are without prejudice. Success to him and to Mormonism to fill the world.   .   .

Yours in the New Covenant,
Dewi Elfed Jones.

TRIBULATION OF A SAINT IN BABYLON.

O God, O God eternal Father,
When may I go to dear Zion:
Within the Babylonian world
  I have tired of living.

Chorus—

O Father, redeem me from Babylon;
I have tired, O I have tired
From living in it.

O Father, I beseech thee
To sympathize with me,
And to consider my tribulation
    In the land of great affliction.

Tribulations upon tribulations
Weary my spirit night and day;
Daily I walk despondently
    In the land of great affliction.

I am overcome and oppressed
By those who are not thy children;
They dry my bones,
    So great is my affliction.

Iniquity is spreading,
And brotherly love is diminishing;
Tyranny and oppression are increasing
    In the land of great affliction.

Dear justice and its beloved home
Is the object of my spirit's love;
For them is my daily cry
    In the land of great affliction.

O Father, I have waited for so long
To be able to go from arrogant Babylon:
My Father, do not disregard my petition
    In the land of great affliction.

Thy Saints are going home
From the East, North, and from the South;
But I am still lowly in my place
    In the land of great affliction.

Ships that emigrate hosts
Are still going and leaving me
In Babylon in the despondence of my cry—
    In the land of great affliction.

My lingering hope is weakening
My soul each day, and making it sad;
And I am losing heart
    In the land of great affliction.

Thy dear Angel has called me
From Babylon to thy Zion,
Nevertheless I cannot come
    Out of the land of great affliction.

    Chorus—
O Father, redeem me from Babylon;
I have tired, O I have tired
From living in it.

Flint.   Thomas Conway.

LONGING FOR ZION.

    Tune—*O Pure Bird.*

How sweet it was many a time,
    To sing myriad cadences,
At close of day with a sound heart,
    To loved ones and friends;
Sweet music and antiquity,
The customs of my native land,
Favorite bards, wise writers,
Were once my constant topics,
    "A better land" is now my secure topic,
This is what I've set my heart on.

The ceaseless tumult of the sons of violence,
    The MEEK mourn,
Under the oppressive feet of the children of lust,
    Unfortunately beaten:
Traditions,—frightful persecutions,
Overfill the land of my fathers,
Cruel war,—heavy judgments,—
Plague and pestilence destroying men;—
    O! if only I could see the dawn of the day,
I could be free in ZION.

I live here in a captive state,—
    The world is worse and worse each day;
The governments of this world,
    Are like the rule of the restless wave;

There will not be peace or happiness,
To be had any more, nor safety,
Ever for men—except in Zion,
Where God saves the faithful,
    That's where the world's best are,
And the love and desire of my heart.

God is calling his children together,
    To the freedom of the LAND OF PEACE,
The pure of heart there will have,
    Glory and happiness,
After being underfoot bleeding,
The poor are seen there singing,
The blessed, heavenly creatures
Will be in all the cities of Zion—
    Dear Land,—dear land of the world's best,
That's where lies my heart's desire.

Swansea, Dec. 22, 1854.   DEWI ELFED.

MISCELLANEOUS, &c.

CONFERENCES.—The East Glamorgan Conference will be held Sept. 28; Brecon, Oct. 5; Monmouth, 12th; West Glamorgan (in Swansea) 19th; Llanelli, 26th; Carmarthen, Nov. 2; Pembroke, 9th; Cardigan, 16th.

RECEIPTS FOR BOOKS FROM AUGUST 27 TO SEPTEMBER 26.—T. Rees, 15s; G. Roberts, 16s 8c; E. S. Morgans, £1 17s 10s; John Treharn, 16s.

CONTENTS.

	PG.
Letter of President D. Jones	305
Difference between the Baptists and the Saints	309
Shutting Doors	311
Editorial—Tithing	312
Letter of Dewi Elfed	315
Song—Tribulation of a Saint	317
Song—Longing for Zion	319
Miscellaneous, &c.	320

SWANSEA:
PRINTED AND PUBLISHED BY DANIEL DANIELS.

ZION'S TRUMPET,

OR

Star of the Saints.

No. 21.] OCTOBER 11, 1856. [Vol. IX.

CONSECRATION.

(From the *Star.*)

The earth is the Lord's and the fullness thereof; the world, and they that dwell therein.—Psalm xxiv, 1.

Sacred history opens with the declaration of the inspired penman:—"In the beginning God created the heaven and the earth." We are also informed that He made it to bring forth fruit and herbs of every kind. The beasts of the field and the inhabitants of the sea are the works of His hand; and last of all came forth man, in the similitude of his Maker—"In the image of God created him; male and female created He them."

In receiving their life and being from the Creator, mankind became his debtors to that amount. But the sum of man's indebtedness to Him is not to be told by the figures of a primitive creation. Though the love, munificence, and majesty of God are even there written in characters whose big meaning the most gigantic human mind cannot grasp, and though the weight of man's obligations to Him in receiving the invaluable gifts of life, with all his fine and wonderful faculties of spiritual and bodily organization, and the dominion and lordship of the whole earth, is enough to bow the proudest of earth into dust, yet the primitive creation is only the first *item* of the great sum. At every step which we take from this point that sum assumes a form more compound;

21 [Price 1*c*.

higher proportions are added to it, and every act of God, in blessing and sustaining those whom He has created, strengthens his claim upon them, and makes them, if possible, more fully His.

Not only is man dependant upon the Almighty for his birth, but the faintest breath of his nostrils, every pulse of his heart, and the sustenance of his body, whether derived from fruit, herb, grain, or flesh, all come from the same bountiful hand from whom he received being. By Him was the economy of nature originated, and by Him it is continued. The whole machinery of the world is moved by His Spirit, and by it the earth brings forth—producing all the necessaries and luxuries for the support of life and the delight of the senses. We live and move by the will and according to the wise arrangement of Him who feeds the raven and takes account of the sparrow. But men in their ingratitude forget their God, and in their pride overlook their complete dependence. They point to their cities, railroad, telegraphs, ships, storehouses, &c., with self complacency; they look on their rich fields of corn as the full ears wave in the summer breeze, appearing like nuggets of gold, and with thoughtless vanity boast, "These are the embodied ideals of our brains and the works of our hands, and this ripe harvest is the fruit of our labor. In their imaginary greatness and independence their Creator is hid from their eyes, and they fancy how much the universe is indebted to them, and how tangible is their right to possess the earth, and use the riches that are hid in its bowels.

Man is continually unlocking the floodgates of corruption, and vitiating the pure stream which flows from the fountain of goodness. From false religious and political systems, and from scientific inventions, turned to evil purposes, comes a world of sorrow and woe. God said, "let there be light," and the earth was filled with the reflection of His own glory; but man has drawn a veil of darkness over it, and when a ray of original brightness crosses his benighted path, to make life endurable, that ray comes from Him who opened the primeval morn. He who gave to us our being also gives strength and fatness to the land; and causes vegetation to blossom and the sun to ripen it.

He illuminates our path as we prosecute our daily labors, and inspires us to unlock the treasure mines of the earth. He it was that hid those treasures there and compounded the elements which form the basis of chemistry; He also wrote in space those characters which furnish food for the study of the astronomer, constructed the anatomy of man, and organized the physical body of the world. It is His beautiful construction of nature—His chemistry, architecture and mechanics, that are continually giving us hints enticing us with their secrets, and charming the heart and intellect with a revelation of their wondrous mysteries. Let God and his Spirit be withdrawn from creation, and with a tremendous crash it would rush again into chaos and break into pieces all organized being. How true therefore is the saying of the Psalmist—"The earth is the Lord's and the fullness thereof; the world and they that dwell therein."

We do not for a moment suppose that any professor of religion will in plain language oppose our views on this matter, or deny the justness of the inspired words of David. We believe that all Christendom will *formally* subscribe to the claims of God upon that which he has created and still sustains. Indeed, if severely pressed home upon them, we doubt if many of any class of men would have the hardihood to altogether deny those claims and the solidness of our position.

But that acknowledgment would amount only to words. It has ever meant but little when made by the ungodly, nor does anybody pay much attention to it when spoken by the Christian world of the present day. The fact is, the nations serve God with their tongues, and honor Him with their lips, but their hearts are far from Him. Their words are those of believers, but their lives are those of Atheists. Men live as though there was no God; they have altogether forgotten Him; and oftentimes, both in theory and practice, he who is called Atheist better deserves the name of Theist than those who profess to serve Him.

"The earth is the Lord's and the fullness thereof; the world, and they that dwell therein." But where is the Christian nation whose society and institutions give an honest and tangible embodiment to this truth? Out of the Church of Jesus Christ Latter-day Saints, where are there a people whose whole lives are devoted to the glory of God, whose time, talents, energy, wealth, persons, and families, are all consecrated to the glory of His name, and for the ushering in of the great millennium—the universal reign of Christ upon the earth? Indeed, where is the nation whose past history, present existence, systems, and religions, stand as a monument—a living testimony that its acceptance of the doctrine which David taught is any other than half-hearted, spurious, and hypocritical? There is not one of them who dare say that it is practically consecrated to the glory of God, or who has even begun to travel in that direction.

We do not doubt that there are some few individuals among every sect who are wholehearted in their profession of this truth; and who to the best of their knowledge and strength, do really live to the honor of their Creator and for the good of mankind. But these are few, few indeed. It is true there are plenty of forms of godliness and articles of faith; plenty of chapel going, church building, praying, preaching, and chanting. But what does all this amount to? Who can conscientiously say that such nothingness is a fair acknowledgment and discharge of man's obligations to his Maker: that is so far as we can pay a debt of boundless love and blessing which is ever accumulating? Who will say that this is a fulfillment of the duty which the human family owes to their Heavenly Father, Preserver, and Savior.

Instead of the churches of sectarian Christendom being consecrated with all their possessions, wealth, and influence, to the glory of God, and for the salvation and good of mankind, the people have to consecrate millions of their money yearly to support them; and there are few who would undertake to prove that these have given an equivalent of good to mankind or service to God for the immense worldly endowments which they have received. Suppose every movement of these churches and the official acts of their ministers tended directly to good, yet, even by the common standard of business transactions, their craft has been insolvent a thousand times. The most sordid, mercenary men of the world would scarcely have the conscience to receive such immense wages for so few and worthless labors, as the servants of these churches have given to their duped employers—the people. Indeed, judging them as we would a banking firm, a great commercial house, an insurance society, or a company of railway speculators, these bastard Christian organizations would by common consent be denounced as huge impostors; and bishops, clergy, and dissenting ministers would have to take their places as felons along with those gigantic banking swindlers of recent and general notoriety. Going no farther back than the dawn of Protestantism in England, its so called religious societies have many times consumed the whole produce and riches of this princely land—this nation of merchants and almost boundless wealth. And for what purpose have all the millions gone which these vampires have sucked from the heart of this country? Has it not been to enrich an apostate Priesthood, to weave the web of their craft, and to adorn mystic Babylon with the robes of grandeur, and the bewitching garments of an harlot; not used to beautify the sanctuary for the presence of the Lord, but to seduce the nation and to make it drunk with the wine of the fornication of the great whore?

It is an incontrovertible fact that civilization, development, education, and every movement tending to the elevation of mankind, and therefore indirectly to the glory of God, instead of having come from any of the established churches of apostate Christendom, or from any of their sectional branches, have originated among the lay members of society. It is true that something of this is due to the protest of religious reformers, such as Luther, Wesley, and others, against the prevailing corruptions of established churches; but the good which has resulted from this source is of a negative and not of a positive nature—from the exposure of corruptions and the breaking of the chains of priestcraft, and not from the introduction of any genuine system of civilization or religion. Indeed, since the apostasy from ancient Christianity, as it came in purity by the teachings of its great master, and by the power of the Holy Ghost, human development has ever come in contact with all the established and dissenting churches which men have built up in the interim of that long night of spiritual darkness, and it has in turn been sternly opposed by them and their ministers. If any good has come from this source, it has been through men acting from their humanity, their love of truth and science, and in the character of reformers. But whenever those churches have stood in the quality of organizations and interpreters of a perfect theology, they have assumed a mission which did not belong to them, for at the best they are but the representatives of states of transition. So true is this that those very sections who have protested against the parent, because of its corruption and enmity to God and man, have in their turn been protested against by their offspring for the very same reason. Thus it appears, as before observed, that the good which has come from that source has been of a negative nature—the breaking of strong chains and the introduction of systems more compatible with the spiritual development of man than those protested against. Many sterling wholehearted men have engaged in these works of transitory reformation, and so even have tyrants and bad men. The one class have tended to weaken priestcraft by their virtues, and the other by their tyrannies and evil passions have assisted in breaking down old barriers, and thus a way has been opened for further improvement and greater liberty. In no other sense than this can it be admitted that sectarian Christianity has tended either to the good of mankind or to the glory of God, neither have professors of religion been as organized bodies consecrated to these ends. Individuals have unquestionably served God to the best of their knowledge and privileges, and with full purpose of heart have devoted their lives to benefit their fellows, but the professions and claims of any of the sects to have thus done are hypocritical, and indeed are a mockery both to God and man.

No genuine and direct movement for the elevation of mankind has ever come from apostate churches. The good from that source has been of a negative character, and has come in an indirect manner. The Reformations, which have from time to time taken place in the religious world, have been like those movements which society make for the correction of criminals rather than for the education of its uncommitted members. Those whom the world call reformers have been merely pioneers of that civilization which tends directly to the glory of God and the salvation of man.

It is evident that society has received but very little benefit from the intrinsic value and operations of any of those systems and churches which have been—though most unworthily—called Christian. Is it to them that the nations owe their science, commerce, knowledge, enlightenment, and greatness? No, every one of common information knows that in them the philosopher, the reformer, and the man of enterprise and discovery, have met deadly foes—similar to those which Christ and his apostles met in the Pharisees of old. This is perfectly consistent, for false religions and priestcraft will ever be opposed to truth and development, no matter whether they come embodied in the Gospel of salvation, in wholesome education, commerce, manufacture, enterprise, or science. It is neither the sects nor their ministers who take the lead in bestowing upon mankind the positive blessings. It is not they who bridge the mighty ocean with ships, extend the arena of the known world, and link nations together in something like a common family, thus indirectly working out and preparing the way for the removal of the confusion and scattering of Babel.

It is not they who girdle the earth with railroads, run veins of electric wires through seas and continents, build manufactories, and invent machinery, which perhaps God will use in removing the curse—"Man shall live by the sweat of his brow." It is not to them that the nations owe their glory, their education, improvements, or any liberal institutions which they possess. All this is due to secular government and private enterprise.

It is true that many professors of religion engage in these movements, but then it is in their lay character. They do it as merchants, votaries of science, artisans, and politicians; and, as before observed, when laboring in these directions they find their own religious systems and priests oftentimes their enemies. Moreover, society owes more of its science, enterprise, wealth, and greatness, to what is called the world, than to any of the members and priests of sectarian churches; and it is also a stubborn fact that science, reform, enterprise of every kind, and all philanthropic movements, find most of their disciples and true friends among deists, atheists, secularists, and the many different shades of heterodox thinkers. This is generally realized more or less; but the most pious and silly endeavor to persuade themselves that religion is too spiritual to mix with and bring forth earthly good; and it would seem they imagine that evangelical alliances, Bible and tract societies, class, prayer, and preaching meetings, and certain feelings, views, and forms of expression to be the ultimatum of Christian life, and the sum and substance of the Gospel. These considerations remind us that the Prophet Joseph in a vision beheld that the glory of the moon was in the economy of salvation allotted for the honorable of the earth, while the lesser portion in the scale of exaltation is prepared for sectarian religionists.

The very existence of secular government and private enterprise is a proof that, although society pay their priests well, and profess much religion, the people do not in reality feel that their creeds and ministers tell much either to the glory of God or the elevation of mankind, for while they pay and support these, they take the practical good of humanity into their own hands. These sectarian churches do not even come up to the world's standard of appreciation of the great truth—"The earth is the Lord's and the fullness thereof; the world, and they that dwell therein"; for while the labors of the latter indirectly tend to the glory of God and the good of man, the former as churches and priests do not, neither would many like to see what the earth and its inhabitants would be had these held undivided sway.

(To be continued.)

VERSE TO THE MORMON.

The Mormon constantly seeks,—from God's support,
In the day of wrath he succeeds;
He sees the end of every enemy,
Above black anguish he escapes safely.

Formerly of Meirion. JOHN DAVIES.

ZION'S TRUMPET,

OR

Star of the Saints.

SATURDAY, OCTOBER 11, 1856.

HOW TO WARN THE WHOLE BRITISH NATION IN ONE YEAR.

(From the Editorial of the "Star.")

To the Pastors and Presidents of Conferences, and Branches of the Church of the Saints throughout Great Britain.

Dear Brethren—feeling an anxious desire to see the great work of our God roll forth in these countries with greater power and rapidity, we, after mature reflection, submit to you, for your consideration and adoption, a *plan* which we are fully convinced will be one of the most potent and powerful auxiliaries that can be adopted by the Saints, in connection with the ministry, to faithfully and speedily preach the Gospel to the whole of this nation.

The plan we propose is as follows—

First: Let, at least, FIVE MILLIONS of the inhabitants of Great Britain be notified by handbills, in the course of a year, of the places where, and the times when the Latter-day Saints' meetings are held. By this extensive method of notification your two thousand chapels or places of public worship will, most undoubtedly, be continually filled to overflowing.

Second: Let, at least, FIVE MILLIONS of the people be supplied, during each year, with a printed catalogue of some of the most important Latter-day Saints' publications, including their prices, and a notification that they can be procured at each of your public meetings, and at other places such as you may choose to name.

Third: Let each of, at least, FIVE MILLIONS of the inhabitants, during every twelve months, have the loan of one or more of the pamphlets, printed for circulation; let each retain the loan for the period of one week or more, or purchase the same if he chooses. Brethren, after you have read these three propositions, you may be ready to hastily exclaim, "The plan is indeed a good one to spread the Gospel, but very difficult, if not impossible, to carry into execution." You may inquire, "How can it be possible for the Saints to print Five Millions each, of handbills, catalogues, and pamphlets?" We answer, that it is entirely unnecessary to print so large an amount. Suppose the Saints in Great Britain number twenty-five thousand; let each of these be supplied with two pamphlets for weekly circulation, or according to that average. With two pamphlets to each Saint, fifty thousand habitations would be weekly supplied. We may very safely estimate that as an average, two persons in each habitation would read, or hear read, the contents of such publication; and on the cover of which they could also read the notifications of the places and times of meetings, and a catalogue of some of our printed works. Thus one hundred thousand could be weekly informed; and in fifty weeks, fifty hundred thousand or Five Millions be favored with our printed doctrines, together with the catalogue and handbills upon the covers. And all this immense circulation of true principles, and important notifications could be brought about in one year, simply by each Saint having TWO pamphlets, and circulating them weekly.

Now if each Saint had, not only *two* pamphlets, but two of each number of the series which is chosen for circulation, the inhabitants warned would be doubled for every additional number in the series; for instance, if there be five in the series, twenty-five millions, equal to the whole population of Great Britain, might be benefitted in one year.

Now we shall send to each Conference, among the British Saints, double the number of each of the pamphlets, selected for circulation, that there are members in said Conference. For instance, if there be one thousand members in a Conference, we shall send them two thousand of each pamphlet.

We will now prescribe the plan for each Conference to pay for these pamphlets. You are all well acquainted with the plan that brother F. D. Richards introduced among you to avoid multiplied contributions and to do them away, and to have the greatly varied contingencies and expenses of the Conferences, borne out of the one general fund, raised by the weekly tithings of the poor. This is the Lord's plan; and by it, you have found it much easier to pay your Chapel rents, help the poor, sustain your traveling ministry, pay your Temple donations, and scores of other things too numerous to mention. Among the many items of expense, drawn from this general fund, we will now include the *item* for pamphlets, which is one of the most important among all the others, when traced out in its vastly extended results.

To accomplish ends of such overwhelming importance, and hasten the warning message of the Gospel among the British nation, we hereby counsel all the Presidents of the respective Branches of the Church, each week to reserve from the weekly tithing fund, at the rate of ONE FARTHING for every member that belongs to said Branches, as a *Pamphlet Fund*; let this fund be monthly or quarterly forwarded by the President of each Branch or the President of the Conference, to the General Book Agent of the Conference, who should immediately forward the same to our Office. Each Conference will be responsible for this fund, sent through the General Book Agent, the same as for other publications.

On these pamphlets, sent for circulation, neither the general nor sub-agents can receive any profits, as they do on the other publications. But the respective Presidents of Branches are to receive them at the Liverpool prices, as the properties of the Branches. The expenses of the General Agent, or Presidents of Branches for carriage, wrapping paper, &c., should be met out of the General Tithing Fund of the Conferences or of the Branches, the same as other contingent expenses.

Each President of a Conference should see that all the pamphlets, intended to be circulated in each Branch, are securely and nicely covered with colored covers; on the front page of which should be printed the *Title*, and also the *two lines* of print running up and down the back of each pamphlet in the New Series. On the back page should be printed the Times and Places of holding the Meetings in the Branch, near the places where they are to be circulated; also a request for the Reader to keep the same clean, and a statement that it will be called for unless purchased. On the inside of the covers should be printed a catalogue of some of the most important of our publications, together with the prices, and the places where they may be procured. These covers should be about the quality of the covers on the "Pearl of Great Price." The expenses attendant on this should also come out of the General Fund.

The Presiding authorities should see that all these pamphlets are kept in constant motion every week, *and that every man, woman, and child* in the Church who is able to walk to his neighbor's door, should do what he can to circulate the truth. Some can do much more than others; therefore let the pamphlets be judiciously distributed among the Saints, according to what they have time and circumstances to perform; and let each know his own district for circulation, so as not to interfere with that of his brother or sister; and let no one be fainthearted or fearful; for it is only the valiant who will enter the celestial kingdom.

We shall probably reprint several of the old series of pamphlets, with some alterations, which will be chaptered and paged, to agree with the New. And the whole will form, when completed, a series with an index, adapted for binding. The whole number in the series may be from twelve to twenty.

We propose furnishing these pamphlets, in quantities as above stated, as soon as they can be printed, and wait for our pay at the rate of a Farthing a week from each, as before stated, unless the Conferences can, without inconvenience, pay sooner.

The results of this universal exertion on the part of the Saints, will, without doubt, cause hundreds of thousands to investigate the Latter-day Work, that would otherwise remain in ignorance.

Scores of thousands may thus be brought into the Church, and be gathered to Zion, and who will assist with their means to gather the poor and roll forth the Latter-day Kingdom. The Funds that would thus be replenished, would most probably be ten, twenty, or fifty fold more than the mere item of One Farthing a week expended. Then, again, if each Saint should sell only one pamphlet in two months, this alone would meet the expenditure of One Farthing a week. We say, then, to all the Presiding authorities, officers, and members, go ahead in this good work, and the Lord your God will see your exertions, and abundantly bless you; and through your diligence, He will cut His work short in righteousness, as predicted by the prophets.

Our God has placed the power in us, to do much good, or little, or hide our talent in the earth and do nothing. When we work for Him, He will work with us. Urge on, then, the weekly tithings; the surplus funds will be the means of gathering thousands annually.

We say to the Welsh, translate the new series of tracts, and publish of each a number, equal to double the number of Welsh Saints who cannot understand English. We say to the Scandinavians—Do likewise. Let all the Saints put their shoulders to the Big Wheel, and we will, in the *strength of Israel's God*, turn the nations of Christendom upside down, and shake out the righteous from their midst.

ORSON PRATT, *President.*

EMIGRATION.—All Saints who intend going to Utah in 1857, must make their calculations to sail from this port, at least, by the 25th of March, so as to land in the States by the 1st of May.

BOOK DEBTS.—Since this Office has great debts owing to the Church, and since they must be paid at the end of the year, we would wish for the greatest effort that can be made, Presiding Brethren, to get your Conferences free with us by then, so that we will be enabled to do the same with the Church of God.

We are delighted to understand that some have seen the need for this, and have begun the task. We trust that this *hint* is sufficient for every President who is always ready to carry out whatever God asks, so that he may prove his fitness for this important and honorable post that he occupies.

We have gone as easy as possible with the burdened Conferences from the time right after the emigration until now, so they could have fair play to free and strengthen themselves, and to enforce the tithing, up until this recent time when the last quarter of the year has begun.

THE PLAN OF PRESIDENT PRATT speaks and shows so well for itself, that it is unnecessary to add our observations, any more except to report further that President Pratt, in a recent letter to us, counseled the

Welsh Saints not to leave any kind of their Welsh pamphlets lying idle; rather they are to be kept moving around weekly with his own new series which are soon to be translated into Welsh.

It will be seen that our Presidency takes a confident view of the conviction and conversion of thousands through the general effort that is made.

It is considered that the dispatch of two pamphlets for every member, and a payment from them of a farthing each per week, is a reasonable thing for the most burdened Conference to receive and achieve, and anyone is free to do whatever they wish.

We have no fear but what the Welsh Saints will be foremost in the battle and participants in the spoils. As armed regiments with all varieties and kinds of their pamphlets, and confident in their God, they will be seen attacking the kingdom of Satan and freeing its prisoners from the chains of darkness.

Presiding Brethren, see that you have a pamphleteering regiment in **EVERY BRANCH**, and see to it that there is no pamphlet left idle. Insist on as many types as you can get.

There are still several kinds of splendid pamphlets of the renowned brother Davis in the Office: who would like them? Also a collection of the works authored by brother D. Jones, bound, 6s 4c each. Including "Treasury" and "History of the Church." We have but a few—fewer than one for every President.

SONG OF LONGING.

Tune—*"Black Bird."*

O! hear my elegy!
    Burdened in Babel's land,
I've wanted to be in fair Zion
    For a long time.
And O! how captive I am
    In a poor and sad state.
From wanting to come to you
    To the Temple of Jesus Christ!

When will the long hours come
    To an end to set me free.
O! if only I were on my journey
    Coming over, what success!
O brothers, hear my lament!
    And see how captive
I am, and come quickly to bring me
    To great Mount Zion!

If I could have this gift
    O brothers, it would be an honor!
I would be content
    In Zion with the Saints!
I continue to be
    Faithful, but I am tired,
And almost too bound to carry the yoke
    So badly am I treated!

Longing to come to the better land
    Makes my cheeks wet!
The time is far advanced,
    And the earthen tent gets worse!
Everything is wearying,
    And the circumstances lower;
And the breath also becomes shorter,
    Till it fails many months!

O if only I were moved
    Completely from where I am!
Truly I would thank
    All of you while I live!
Oh! oh! when will the long
    Time come to an end
To take me yonder to Mount Zion?
    O! let it come soon! Amen.

Llanelli.   *(Formerly of Penydaren.)*   D. A. HUGHES.

[We shall be pleased to receive, any time, from our poetical writers, some of the tasty fruit of their fertile minds to set on the TRUMPET's table; but, nevertheless, we would like a variety—something with Longing for Zion, &c.—ED.]

MISCELLANEOUS, &c.

A Letter from bro. J. Jones, from Brymbo, dated Oct. 1, tells of the happening of a frightful accident, the previous day, in the Pendwll pit, by the breaking of water from an old working. It filled the whole works, and 34 yards up the pit, in one hour. The majority of the workers, poor things, escaped through an old air chamber from which they were pulled up on a rope. There were 13 inside without any hope in this world for them. They were pumping water all night, and yet no let-up in it was seen. There were hundreds of people there day and night. There is no need to say how heartbreaking the sight was!

☞ Send to us, without delay and without fail, the names and details of those who have emigrated in different ways, except through this Office, *after* the end of bro. Jones's stewardship, and at all times henceforth, together with reporting about those who did not emigrate after sending their names here, so that our books will be accurate.

Addresses.—Mr. John Jones, 4, Water Street, Abergele, Denbighshire.

Mr. David Davies, Mr. C. Harman, CilHeol, near Town Hall, Llanelli, Carmarthenshire.

Receipts for Books from September 27 to October 9.— T. Stephens, £5 15s 6c; J. Thomas, 12s; T. Rees, £1 10s; T. Jones, 14s; J. Davis, £2 15s; G. Roberts, 11s; T. S., again, £2 13s 11c; W. Ajax, 15s.

CONTENTS.

	PG.
Consecration	321
Verse to the Mormon	328
Editorial—To the Presidents—Emigration—Book Debts—Plan of President Pratt	329
Song of Longing	334
Miscellaneous, &c.	336

SWANSEA:
PRINTED AND PUBLISHED BY DANIEL DANIELS.

ZION'S TRUMPET,

OR

Star of the Saints.

No. 22.]　　　OCTOBER 25, 1856.　　　[Vol. IX.

CONSECRATION.

(Continued from page 328.)

THERE is in man a spirit—the inspiration of the Almighty. He has planted in the soul a thirst for excellence—an irresistible impulse to progress. He moves upon the mind to interrogate nature for her secrets and to adorn and beautify the earth. In their development the people call authoritatively to their rulers for reform and wrest their liberties from the hands of tyrants, and God in his infinite wisdom and goodness gives all things a direction for His own glory, and for the exaltation of the children of men. Nevertheless how few there are who of their own free will are consecrated to the honor of their Maker, Preserver, and Redeemer. How few do their works in the name of the Lord, and practically acknowledge the vast debt which they owe to Him.

The merchant stands simply in the character of a merchant, the artisan acts in the name of himself or of his craft, the man of science reveals his knowledge as a scientific man, and not as a servant of God; the legislator administers by the voice of the people, or by the right of hereditary descent; kings wield scepters placed in their hands by invasion and conquest, and sit on thrones established in blood and tears; nobles inherit wealth and lands from warrior fathers, who gained them by sword and rapine. None act in the name of the Lord, none are living wholly

[PRICE 1*c*.

consecrated to His glory, among all the kingdoms of the earth, except in that one which He Himself has established in these last days, and even its subjects are only just beginning to travel in that direction. Where is the nation whose lands, cities, railroads, ships, wealth, and science are all laid on the altar of consecration? The great hold lands and possessions by the sanction and gift of human authority, and kings and nobles possess inheritances of blood, but where are they who hold title deeds from the King of the Universe?

Men live as though they were their own creators, or had purchased from the Almighty "the earth and the fullness thereof." Mankind do not consecrate themselves to their Maker and preserver; neither does anyone profess that such is the case. The fact is, society is practically atheistic, rulers and subjects, priests and people. Men live to themselves and not to the glory of God.

Brethren—Latter-day Saints, we must consecrate ourselves—our lives, energies, wealth, talents, wives, families, and all that we are or have unto Him who has thrice purchased us—by creation, by preservation, and by the blood of his Only Begotten. Let no one deceive you, neither deceive yourselves in this matter; consecration is the order of a celestial kingdom. He who is not prepared to abide this law, whose soul is not thus enlarged by the Spirit of the Almighty, has need to seek earnestly for wisdom and power from the Holy Ghost to enable him to be equal to the race set before him, and worthy of the inheritance and exaltation prepared for the sons and daughters of God. Unless he does this, without fear and trembling at the thought of laying himself with his all upon the altar, as an offering unto the Father of Saints, he had better step aside and become a candidate for a lower glory, lest, at beholding the height for which the righteous aim, he become dizzy and fall to a depth far beneath the point from whence he started. The exaltation to the dignity of Kings and Priests of the Most High is too high a pinnacle for such to reach.

"The earth is the Lord's and the fullness thereof; the world, and they that dwell therein," and He will have His Saints to practically acknowledge it. *By consecrating themselves wholly and undividedly to Him is the only way by which they can become heirs of God and joint heirs with Christ.*

NEWS FROM THE EMIGRATION.

(From the *Council Bluffs Bugle.*)

It may not be uninteresting to some of your readers to learn something of the movements of the emigration to Salt Lake Valley this season. (Last August.) A few days since, in company with Colonel Babbitt, Secretary of Utah, and several citizens of this place, we visited Florence, N. T., and there found encamped about 500 of the "faithful," all in good health and spirits, intending to start in a day or two on their long journey. (They left on Monday, the 18th.) From Captain Willey, and assistant Captains McGaw and Savage, we learned that the train had been but three weeks in coming from Iowa City, and that all were healthy, cheerful, and contented.

Having seen several handcart trains pass through this city, and cross the ferries at Elk Horn and Loup fork, we could not help but remark the enthusiasm which animated all classes and ages. This train seemed to be better provided with camp equipage, and outfit of provisions, &c., than those which preceded it.

We saw the butcher dealing out a splendid beef to the crowd, and were informed that the allowance was one half pound each, one pound of flour per day, and the usual quantities of molasses, sugar, &c., &c. Many, however, have private supplies, which enable them to live very comfortably.

It may seem to some that these people endure great hardships in traveling hundreds of miles on foot, drawing carts behind them. This is a mistake, for many informed me that after the first three days travel, it requires little effort for two or three men or women to drag the light handcart with its moderate load of cooking utensils and baggage.

It is, also, a fact, that they can travel farther in a day, and with less fatigue, than the ox teams.

These trains are composed of Swedes, Danes, Germans, Welsh, Scotch, and English, and the best evidence of their sincerity is in the fact that they are willing to endure the fatigues and privations of a journey so lengthy.

First, they have toiled wearily o'er the hundreds of miles which separated their native hills from the European seaport from which they were to embark—then see them on crowded ships, braving the dangers of the broad Atlantic—afterwards, they travel patiently one thousand inland miles to Iowa City, thence to start on foot for a journey over hill, plain, desert, and mountain, fourteen hundred miles, to reach the "Happy Valley."

This is enthusiasm—this is heroism indeed. Though we cannot coincide with them in their belief, it is impossible to restrain our admiration of their self-sacrificing devotion to the principles of their faith.

But we have forgotten Florence, not destined, like its beautiful Tuscan prototype, to be universally worshipped as the most lovely of European capitals, rejoicing in her magnificent palaces, her glowing paintings and speaking statuary,—but to be known in this our practical work-a-day world, as one of the most important towns in the Territory of Nebraska.

Three months ago there were but five buildings, there are now about forty, and as fast as labor and material can be obtained, they will continue to build. Before winter, probably 150 houses will have been erected.

The steam sawmills are doing their best to supply lumber, but the water mill on Mill Creek moves lazily for lack of "copious showers." Another stream mill will be put up this fall. There are two brick yards near at hand, a lime kiln, and a quarry of superior building stone. To James C. Mitchell, Esq., who has labored for nearly two years to make Florence a town, in fact as well as name, is most of the credit of its improvement and growth to be attributed. We cordially wish it success and prosperity.

P. S.—Since the above was written, we notice the following arrivals in this city, en route for Salt Lake:

On Monday, the 18th of this month, 56 handcarts and 5 ox teams;

on the 20th, 30 ox teams; and on the 21st, 60 handcarts and several teams.

About 400 have already left Florence; the above trains contained about 800 persons, and a large number are still expected, *via* St. Louis.

HOME CORRESPONDENCE.

CONFERENCES OF THE NORTH.

Brymbo, October 14, 1856.

DEAR BROTHER DANIELS.—I received your letter last Saturday. Since I wrote to you previously, from Llanrwst, I have been in the company of brother Ajax through Bethesda, Bangor, and to Amlwch, in Anglesey, and preached there to a large crowd.

Anglesey, as you know, contains tens of thousands of inhabitants. There are only four of the Saints in the midst of all this number, as far as we know. We baptized one while on our journey there.

Brother, my heart bleeds in thinking that so many in Anglesey lie in darkness, because there is nothing we can do for them, except to leave them like that; for it is impossible for us to be there and in other places where there are Saints.

I have prayed to the Lord to open some way; that he will send his Spirit to soften the hearts of as many as twelve from the South to come to Anglesey, and Caernarvon.

After we preached in Amlwch to several Religious sects I heard some testify that they had never imagined that the principles of the Saints were so scriptural. May the Lord send hosts of workers to the great harvest of the North, *amen* and AMEN.

I was in Abergele, Saturday night, when my heart was greatly gladdened as I read the letter from you and bro. Israel Evans.

Sunday, I went to Mold, and I came this far yesterday. I preached here last night. You see that I am not idle; rather I walk every day and many of the nights as well, and assist the Presidents, the best I can, in all things.

I saw the STAR which contained the plan to distribute pamphlets on Sunday the week before last, and I read it and taught it in the Council of the "Ajax Conference." *All right*, brother; my heart rejoices in the plan. We stand ready for the task.

I find the Presidents and the Saints of the same spirit as myself. The Saints, with us, are book sellers already, and before the end of this month all the pamphlets you sent will be sold, and you shall have payment for them.

Some wish to have more of the new pamphlet, but since there are so many of the old pamphlets on hand, with some new ones yet to come, we believe that it is better for us to do our best with them.

There is faithfulness here; with all their heart the Saints of the North are carrying forth the work of the Lord in selling pamphlets as well as in every other way. We are determined to do our best to fulfill all the counsels that come out through the TRUMPET to the letter, believing that this is the only way for us to hope for success in the work of the Lord.

In the General Councils that are held monthly, we intend to gather in all the money for books from the various Branches, so they will not lie idle.

I would be glad to see Brother Israel Evans up here again. When the Saints ask "when is President Daniels coming up here?" my answer is, "Oh, sometime between now and the end of the Millennium."

Yours in the work,
JOHN JONES.

PARABLE OF THE DISAPPOINTED HARVESTERS.

LATELY a company of men happened to go on a journey to some part of the Principality to ask for work in the harvest.

Each one of them had his sickle in his hand bound with a grass rope to protect the edge.

They had a hard journey for many days until they came to a land where there were many *farmers*.

This armed army walked around the broad, ripe fields desirous of attacking the yellow heads that stood directly before them, but when they bent with the breeze they seemed to be greeting their strange visitors who were aiming so threateningly at them. At last they noticed a gentleman, as they supposed, standing in a gap in the hedge. They mistook him for the owner of the field; but he was an arrogant swaggerer—an *intermeddler*, who lived on his deceit. The harvesters asked him very humbly for work. The "gentleman" cast an English look at them, and, he said, "Where you come from?" They answered him. "What you ask *per acre* for harvesting?" They stated their price. "*All right*; I have much of harvest work—all those fields there—I live in big *palace* over there. I make *agreement* with you to harvest all the corn. You give five pounds for me to keep until you finish my work. I meet bad men, who go away before finish." Each one looked in his pocket, and among them all, they came up with the five pounds, and they gave it to him. "Now then, (he said) go to field, and begin to harvest at the bottom end, and remember do good job. Come up that palace after to have food, drink, and sleep. You have five pounds back after finishing the *job*, and also pay. Good morning for you now," and away he went with the five pounds in his pocket.

No sooner had he left than the harvesters rushed to the field, and it was not many hours before they had "left their mark," and they were perspiring profusely, praising the *job* and the "gentleman" every other with no small rejoicing.

In the afternoon the real owner of the field came in his greatness and sway from his dwelling place, and, to his great surprise, he saw men harvesting his corn. He knew that he had not sent them. Therefore, he sent his servants to them to send them away; but they asserted that the owner of the field had authorized them, and that they would not cease, but they threatened the poor servants with their sickles, and not before fighting a heated battle, and the coming of the owner himself to the field with his powers, were they obliged to flee without food or pay but a frightful expectation of being caught and punished for their rebellion.

Questions
1. Who is the swaggerer?
2. Who are the disappointed harvesters?
3. What is the field?
4. Who is the real owner of the field?
5. Who are his authorized servants?

Llanelli. DAVID DAVIES.

LETTER OF ISRAEL EVANS.

Swansea, October 17, 1856.

PRESIDENT DANIELS,

Dear Brother,—After visiting all the Conferences in the Welsh Mission during the last three months, I now present you with a brief account of my visit.

On my visit to the North, among the faithful and true-hearted Saints, I enjoyed myself greatly. I found the Saints increasing in faith and good works. The principle of tithing, which was planned under the direction and wise counsel of President Ashby on his visit there, is increasing. All who had begun acting according to this heavenly law were firm in their testimony that it had proved a blessing to them.

Brother John Jones, my co-traveler, and I, nurtured the principle of tithing, showing to the Saints the necessity of their obedience to this law, and the beneficial results that would be sure to follow, and I am thankful to God for blessing us with his Spirit in teaching them, and his people with an inclination to fulfill it.

Brother Jones and those who are with him in the North are good men—such ones who do their best to fulfill all your counsels to them.

We baptized several while on our journey through the Conferences, and there were promising signs for more when we left. I understand that some have been baptized after that.

After returning, I had the honor of being present in some of the Conferences of the South where I found that the same good spirit and feeling abound—the tithing is increasing—there is a general desire for spreading the pamphlets. I trust that great good will be done through the combined faith and effort of the Officers and the Saints, and that many honest souls will be brought from darkness to the light of the truth.

I am glad to say that the work of the Lord in this Mission is increasing in an encouraging manner. The Saints, with a few exceptions, will be, as long as the wheat and tares grow together, determined to live according to the laws of heaven, as they are made known to them. My earnest prayer is that they will continue thus, for that is the only way to life.

ISRAEL EVANS.

ZION'S TRUMPET,

OR

Star of the Saints.

SATURDAY, OCTOBER 25, 1856.

TRANSGRESSION.—Among the multitude of truths which were brought to light through the revelation of the Gospel of Jesus Christ, one has proved very plainly in these latter days that the man who has practiced evil cannot stay long in the Church of God.

Men can achieve light and understanding—they can have the heavens open before them, and enjoy visions of eternity, &c., and nevertheless, although they are partakers of the highest blessings of heaven, by turning to, and following evil, they fall back to murky darkness, they lose all light, and they even forget the Church of God. They use every influence in their power to oppose and obstruct this work whenever they turn to shameless sin, hypocrisy and arrogance.

Perhaps someone will wonder that the characters noted can fall to such an extent.

Lucifer, the "Son of the Morning," was the first *dissenter*. Although he was once an angel of light, yet, through his wickedness and his rebelliousness he became Satan—he was lifted up above all things that were called God—*he* wanted to be God, or an object of worship.

There are others, according to their different degrees and positions in the Church of God in these latter days. We shall name the following of note.—Sidney Rigdon, James J. Strang, Gladden Bishop, Martin Harris, Brewster, Charles B. Thompson, Cutler (*the negro preacher,*) Oliver Olney, Lyman Wight, &c., &c.

Each one of the above was cut off from the Church for his shameful and rebellious transgressions. After they were excommunicated each one of them claimed that he was the Prophet, and he tried to attract disciples after him.

No doubt others will yet rise, and they will pull some who are of the same bent after them; but the true children of God will be kept safe, and that will only make them grow in their testimony, and make them cleave firmly to the work of God, until every enemy is overcome.

We understand that accursed creatures, in different guises, are trying to deceive the Welsh Saints, and beg. Beware of such.

THE NEW PAMPHLETS.—We intend to publish one of these every fortnight, or earlier if we can, until they all come out. We trust that the first call has been sufficient for all the Presidents to prepare volunteers in every Branch to go out in the name of our God to get more soldiers for the army of Jesus. Our Presidents are full of godly fire having just come from a Temple of God, and they prophesy in the name of the God of Israel that hundreds of thousands of pamphlets which will be distributed throughout these islands will cause no small stir—that the houses of worship of the Saints will be filled with eager listeners, and that hosts will be brought to the light of the Gospel. We trust, as we said before, that no pamphlet of any kind pertaining to our principles will be left idle. The following is an excerpt from the pamphlet that is now on the press.

"THE TRUE FAITH.

1. It is the intention of the author in this chapter to define and simplify the great principle, called Faith. This is not an abstract principle, separate and distinct from mind, but it is a certain condition or state of the mind itself. When the mind believes or has confidence in any subject, or statement, or proposition, whether correct or incorrect, it is then in possession of faith. To have faith is simply to believe. Faith and belief, therefore, are synonymous terms, expressive of the same idea.

2. Faith or belief is the result of evidence presented to the mind. Without evidence, the mind cannot have faith in anything. We believe that a stone will fall, when unsupported, on the evidence of past observation in relation to the falling of heavy bodies. We believe that day and night will continue on the evidence of past experience

in regard to the uniformity of nature's laws. We believe that space is boundless, and duration endless, on the evidence, presented by the mind itself, which at once perceives the absurdity of either space or duration being limited. We believe in all self-evident truth, on the evidence that all opposite propositions to these truths are absurd. We believe in all the great truths of science, either on the evidences of our own investigations, or on the researches of others. We believe in historical facts on the evidence of the historian. Faith in every fact, statement, truth, or proposition which we have confidence in, is, in all cases whatsoever, derived from evidence. Therefore, without evidence, faith can have no existence.

3. Faith is of two kinds, namely, *false* and *true*. A false faith is the result of giving credence to false evidence. A true faith, the result derived from true evidence.

4. The faith of Cain in offering the fruits of the ground was false, derived from some incorrect evidence, in relation to offerings or in relation to the conduct necessary to obtain a blessing. The faith of Abel in offering the firstlings of his flock, was founded upon the evidence he had from the word of God that such an offering would please Him. The faith of the Egyptians in the doctrines of the magicians was the result of false evidence, strengthened, and, as they supposed, confirmed by the numerous miracles wrought by their evil hands. The faith of Israel in the doctrines of Moses was founded upon true evidence, and hence, was pleasing in the sight of God. Faith in idols and in the mythologies of the heathen, is the result of a false traditionary evidence. Faith in the true God is founded upon true evidence. Faith in false doctrines, and in the creeds and articles of religion, invented by human wisdom, is the production of traditionary evidence, not to be depended on. Faith in every word of God, whether ancient or modern, is always produced by evidence that is true, and calculated to give the greatest assurance to the mind.

5. As evidence precedes faith, the latter should be weak or strong in proportion to the weakness or strength of the evidence. Where the evidence is accompanied by circumstances of a doubtful nature; or where it relates to things which are, in some degree, improbable in themselves; or where there is an opposing

evidence of nearly the same influence or weight; or where there is only circumstantial evidence—faith should be weak. On the other hand, where the evidences are direct; where they relate to events or things, not improbable; where they are accompanied by favorable circumstances of a confirmatory nature; where no evidences, of any influence or weight, are in opposition—faith should be strong. The weakness or strength of faith will, therefore, in all cases, be in proportion to the weakness or strength of the impressions, produced upon the mind by evidence. It is often the case, that the judgment becomes so weak and beclouded, that the evidence, however great, and clear, and lucid, and demonstrative, produces no sensible impression upon the mind. Hence, faith does not always exist in impaired or vitiated minds with a strength proportioned to the degree or force of evidence."

PATRIOTISM, FREEDOM, AND TRUTH.
(Tune—*"Break of Day."*)

The call goes out to nearly all
    Of Gwalia's stirling sons,
To set aside their useless work,
    And honor the Lord God.
By listening to his wise advice,
    And his sage's pure words,
The dullest eye will brighten,
    As will the blindest mind.

The man who truly loves his God
    Who respects his good laws,
Attempts to bring blessings to all
    Within the country's bounds.
He feeds the starving poor,
    He clothes the naked,
He takes the feeble to his breast,
    And teaches the foolish wisely.

He anoints the wounded one,
    And tends His wounds;
He forgives the repentant man,
    And welcomes him home.
The damaged heart he makes well,
    And the sad face happy.

And instead of grief he places
    Joy in the bosom.

And if you entreat his favor
    He'd see a feeble weakling,
He'd not trample him down in the dust,
    But would raise him up.
He does not hurt his brother's good name,
    He shies away from this;
He administers between man and man
    Justice everywhere.

A lovely, blessed time's ahead
    When God's family will be seen
Without ire or malice in their midst,
    But all living in peace.
Oppression will nowhere be felt,
    And there will be no ugly villains;
But freedom will reign from sea to sea
    O dawn the happy day!

Jubilee will be proclaimed to the captive,
    Light to the land of gloom,
To the sick will be offered pure health,
    And death will lose its strength.
And where terrible war once was
    All will live in peace;
And the dead will come (oh wondrous work)
    Up from the doors of the grave.

The false traditions of the world
    Will be conquered by the truth;
All tricks and treachery will be made clear
    In pure divine light.
Untruth will all its supporters
    Will be exiled from our midst;
And unity there'll be twixt brother and brother,
    And confidence—not its illusion.

Those who dwell on earth, heaven's angels,
    And the beautiful Seraphic choir
Will all together sing sweet pure hymns
    Of praise to their worthy Lord.
The sun, the moon, and the many stars,
    The earth and the vast seas;
And the big wide creation,
    Will praise him in their tongue.

Mill Street.   JOHN REYNOLDS, JR.

EISTEDDFOD OF THE SAINTS.

FOR THE BARDS AND MEN OF LETTERS OF THE SAINTS, AND THEIR FRIENDS THROUGHOUT ALL OF WALES.

BE it known that an Eisteddfod will be held in the Hall of the Saints, Swansea, on next Christmas day, under the patronage of the venerable President D. Daniels, when the successful contestants will be given prizes for the following topics:—

TREATISES.

For the best Treatise on the Inconsistencies of the Religious Denominations. Prize, from Mr. D. Davies, Llanelli,—Volume of "Old Sermons of the Inconsistencies."

For the best Treatise on the Condition of the troubled Kingdoms of the world. Prize, from Mr. T. Harris, Swansea,—*An English-Welsh Dictionary, by William Evans; second edition, Improved by the late Rev. Mr. Richards, of Coychurch, Glamorganshire*, bound.

For the best Treatise on "Paying Tithing—its scripturalness—the blessings enjoyed from obeying it, and the failure that follows its opponents." Prize from Mr. D. Daniels, Hymn Book of the Saints, best binding.

POETRY.

For the best poem on "Praise to John Richards, Esq., Court, Aberafan, for his kindness to the Saints in Aberafan." Prize, from Mr. Thomas Harris, Swansea, "The Dawn," complete, but unbound.

For the best poem on "Tribulation of the Saint tests the world." Prize, from Mr. Dewi Elfed, "The Pearl of Great Price."

For the best poem on "Manner of debate among an Atheist, a Sectarian, and a Saint, (to be no fewer than 25 verses.) Prize, from Mr. John Davies, formerly of Meirion, "Scales of the Bards."

For the best poem on "Manner of debate between a Sexton and a Saint." Prize, from Mr. T. Harris, Swansea, "Life in America."

For the best poem giving an account of Hepburn (*The Anti-Mormon Lecturer*) and the Reverends trying in vain to obstruct Mormonism. Prize, from Mr. D. Davies, Llanelli, "History of the Martyrs."

For the best poem giving the "Tribulation of the Saint going from house to house distributing Pamphlets." Prize, from Mr. T. Harris, Swansea, "Doctrine and Covenants." (The composition is to be no fewer than 50 verses.)

For the poem that gives the best portrayal of "Hatred of the religious denominations toward each other." Prize, from Mr. T. Harris, "The Betrayal of Immersion."

For the best poem giving an "Account of a Saint visiting his Methodist father." Prize, from Mr. T. Harris, Volume of commentary on Romans.

For the best poem on the "End and abomination of tobacco and snuff." Prize, from Mr. T. Harris, a volume of "Commentary on 1 Corinthians."

For the best poem "To the Drunkard." Prize, from Mr. Wm. Lewis, Swansea, "The Scriptural Treasury."

For the best poem on "The Secret of the Reverends' pains on seeing their hope of profit about to fail." Prize, from Mr. Dewi Elfed, "Dr. Pritchard's Memoirs."

For the best poem on "Mormonism confusing the sects." Prize, from Mr. Dewi Elfed, "Pearl of Great Price."

For the best poem on "Empty husks of false brethren especially the feast of Editors of Welsh Newspapers and Monthlies," to the tune of "*Mind your own business*," or some other tune. Prize, from Mr. Dewi Elfed, "Pearl of Great Price."

RENDITIONS.

For the best performance of "Joseph the Seer." Prize, from Mr. T. Harris, "A Poet's Porfolio, and Minor Poems, by James Montgomery."

For the best performance of "Sectarianism in the Snare." Prize, from Mr. T. Harris, "Report of the Debate Fair of Rhymney."

We wish for the competitors to be present, so they may read their own compositions. If they cannot be present, they must send someone else to do so in their place.

Some songs will be sung skillfully between the recitations of the various compositions, &c., Mr. A. L. Jones, President of the Aberdare Choir, has definitely promised that he and his choir will be present. We would be pleased if other choirs came also to take part in the day's proceedings.

Children of the muse will be free to sing on whatever topics using whatever meters they wish, strict or free, besides the ones named above.

If anyone wishes to orate, sing, or recite on some topic, in Welsh or English, we notify them to let us know ahead of time.

It is expected that the compositions and names of all the competitors be sent a week beforehand to the hand of "Thomas Harris, 2, Clifford Place, Whites' Garden, Swansea."

The compositions will be the property of the Eisteddfod; and some of the winners will appear in the Trumpet from time to time.

Prizes for the winning competitors will be presented on the day of the Eisteddfod.

If others yet wish to give topics and prizes, send them promptly by the publication of the next issue: it will be too late after that.

The doors will be open at half past ten in the morning, at two in the afternoon, and at six in the evening. Tickets, sixpence each. The profit will go to the expense of the Conference, and the account will be given in the following Conference.

Yours respectfully,
Thomas Harris,
President of the Conference.

MISCELLANEOUS, &c.

Conferences.—The Merionethshire Conference will be held November 23rd; Conway Valley and Anglesey, 30th; Denbighshire, December 7th; Flintshire, 14th.

Receipts for Books from October 10 to 22.—T. Stephens, £2 10s; M. Vaughn, £3; Wm. Jones, £1 5s.

CONTENTS.

	PG.
Consecration	337
News from the Emigration	339
Conferences of the North	341
Parable	342
Letter of Israel Evans	344
Editorial—Transgressing—New Pamphlets	345
Song—Patriotism, &c.	348
Eisteddfod of the Saints	350

SWANSEA:
PRINTED AND PUBLISHED BY DANIEL DANIELS.

ZION'S TRUMPET,

OR

Star of the Saints.

No. 23.] NOVEMBER 8, 1856. [Vol. IX.

SERMON,

BY PRESIDENT B. YOUNG, BOWERY, JUNE 22, 1856.

I am happy for the privilege of rising again before you to converse upon those things that pertain to our peace, that most deeply interest us in our reflections and in our lives; it is a matter of constant joy and comfort to me.

It gives me great pleasure to look upon the congregations of the Saints, while I reflect that some of us have been faithful in this Church for many years, have preached to the Saints and to sinners, have called upon people to repent while the finger of scorn has been pointed at us and all manner of evil has been spoken against us falsely. And many times the elders, while laboring faithfully in preaching to the people, would not find where to lay their heads, no doors open to receive them and no one to feed them, yet they have traveled and searched until they have found a great many that ought to be honest in heart, a great many who have embraced the gospel.

It has been a hard labor upon many of the Elders of this Church to accomplish what has been done, to preach this gospel to so many people in so many different nations and kingdoms.

If the miles our missionaries have traveled were counted they would amount to a great sum, and if you could know how many days they have been without eating, while calling upon the people

[Price 1c.

to repent, you would find them to be a great number.

If the troubles of this people from the commencement of this work, from the early history of the Prophet and the persecutions of the Saints, could be presented before this congregation, you would be astonished; you would marvel at them. You would not believe that a people could endure so much as this people have endured, you would think it an impossibility for men and women to endure and pass through what a great many in this Church have. Truly it is a miracle that we are here.

Taking these things into consideration, and viewing our present circumstances and the privileges we enjoy, there is not a heart, that fully realizes what we have passed through and the blessings we now enjoy, without praising God continually and feeling to exclaim— 'O, praise the name of our God.'

True, many think and feel that we have hard times here, that it is a hard country to live in. We have long, cold winters, and we have a great many difficulties to encounter—the Indian wars, the cricket wars, the grasshoppers, and the droughts.

What we have suffered during the two years past comes before us, and now the prospect is gloomy pertaining to sustenance for man.

How many are there who feel and say like this? "Were it not for Mormonism, I should know at once what to do; I know the course I would pursue." What would you do, brother? "I would pick up my duds and leave; I would sell what I have here, if I could, and if I could not, I would leave it." These are the feelings of some.

I will tell you what my feelings are, they are, praise God for hard times, for I feel that it is one of the greatest privileges to be in a country that is not desirable, where the wicked will pass by.

Now, do we all realize this? No, we do not, though I have no doubt but that some do. I will tell you what will make you realize it; to suffer the loss of all things here by the enemy's coming along and driving you out of your houses, from your farms and fields, and taking your horses, cattle, farming implements, and what little substance you have, and banishing you from this place and sending you off five or six hundred miles, bereft of all you possessed, without suitable clothing and provisions for the journey.

Then you go to work and toil and labor with all your might, for a few years, to get another home, and then let another set come and drive you out of that place, taking your cattle, your farms and all you have, telling you that they want your possessions, and by the time they had thus driven you four or five times, as they have many of us, and made you leave everything you have, and threatened you with death, and watched for you by day and by night to get a chance to kill you, and they suffered to go at large with impunity, and would kill you in open daylight if they dared; after having passed through fifteen or sixteen years of this persecution, you would thank God for hard times, for a country where mobs do not wish to live.

Many of the people in these valleys have no experience with these things, and I would be very glad to have such persons escape those trials, if they could receive the same glory and exaltation that they would if they had passed through them.

I look upon the people, and, as I frequently say, I have compassion upon them, for all have not experience. It was told you this morning that you could not be made perfect Saints in one day; that is impossible. You might as well undertake to teach a child every branch of English literature during its first week's attendance at school; this cannot be done.

We are not capacitated to receive in one day, nor in one year, the knowledge and experience calculated to make us perfect Saints, but we learn from time to time, from day to day; consequently we are to have compassion one upon another, to look upon each other as we would wish others to look upon us, and to remember that we are frail, mortal beings, and that we can be changed for the better only by the gospel of salvation.

As it was observed this morning, we ought to be ourselves and not anybody else. We do not wish to be anybody else, neither do we wish to be anybody but Saints. We wish the gospel to take effect upon each one of us; and we can change in our feelings, in our dispositions, and natures, to the extent that was observed by President Kimball in the comparison which he made.

A man or a woman, desiring to know the will of God, and having an opportunity to know it, will apply their hearts to this wisdom until it becomes easy and familiar to them, and they will love to do good instead of evil. They will love to promote every good principle, and will soon abhor everything that tends to evil; they will gain light and knowledge to discern between evil and good.

The person that applies his heart to wisdom, and seeks diligently for understanding, will grow to be mighty in Israel.

Call to mind when you first embraced the gospel, how much did you then know compared with what you now know? Could you detect error then as now? Could you then understand the operations of the different spirits as you can now understand them? I know what your reply would be to these interrogations.

In the first rise of the church, when the gifts of the gospel were bestowed on an individual, or upon individuals, the people could not understand but that the giver of the gift gave also the exercise of it; how much labor the elders that understood this matter have had to make it plain to the understandings of the people.

Take, for instance, the gift of tongues; years ago in this church you could find men of age, and seemingly of experience, who would preach and raise up branches, and when quite young boys or girls would get up and speak in tongues and others interpret, and perhaps that interpretation instructing the Elders who brought them into the church, they would turn round and say, "I know my duty, this is the word of the Lord to me and I must do as these boys or girls have spoken in tongues."

You ask one of the Elders if they understand things so now, and they will say, "No, the gifts are from the Lord, and we are agents to use them as we please."

If a man is called to be a prophet, and the gift of prophecy is poured upon him, though he afterwards actually defies the power of God and turns away from the holy commandments, that man will continue in his gift and will prophesy lies.

He will make false prophecies, yet he will do it by the spirit of prophecy; he will feel that he is a prophet and can prophesy, but he does it by another spirit and power than that which was given him of the Lord. He uses the gift as much as you and I use ours.

The gift of seeing with the natural eyes is just as much a gift as the gift of tongues. The Lord gave that gift, and we can do as we please with regard to seeing; we can use the sight of the eye to the glory of God, or to our own destruction. The gift of taste is the gift of God; we can use that to feed and pamper the lusts of the flesh, or we can use it to the glory of God.

The gift of communicating one with another is the gift of God, just as much so as the gift of prophecy, of discerning spirits, of tongues, of healing, or any other gift, though sight, taste, and speech are so generally bestowed that they are not considered in the same miraculous light as are those gifts mentioned in the gospel.

We can use these gifts, and every other gift God has given us, to the praise and glory of God, to serve him, or we can use them to dishonor him and his cause; we can use the gift of speech to blaspheme his name. That is true, and I have as good a right as brother Kimball, to say that what I am talking about is true.

These principles are correct in regard to the gifts which we receive for the express purpose of using them in order that we may endure and be exalted, and that the organization we have received shall not come to an end but endure to all eternity.

By a close application of the gifts bestowed upon us, we can secure to ourselves the resurrection of these bodies that we now possess, that our spirits inhabit, and when they are resurrected they will be made pure and holy; then they will endure to all eternity.

But we cannot receive all at once; we have to receive a little here and a little there. If we receive a little, let us improve upon that little; and if we receive much, let us improve upon it.

If we get a line today, improve upon it; if we get another tomorrow, improve upon it; and every line, and precept, and gift that we receive, we are to labor upon, so as to become perfect before the Lord.

This is the way that we are to change ourselves, and change one another, pertaining to the principles of righteousness.

As brother Joseph observed this morning, 'Joseph must be Joseph; Brigham must be Brigham; Heber must be Heber; Amasa must be Amasa; Orson must be Orson, and Parley must be Parley'; we must be ourselves.

What should we be, and what are we? I will take the liberty of saying a few words upon this. We were created upright, pure, and holy, in the image of our Father and our Mother, in the image of our God.

Wherein do we differ? In the talents that are given us, and in our callings. We are made of the same materials; our spirits were begotten by the same parents; in the begetting of the flesh we are of the same first parents, and all the kindreds of the earth are made of one flesh; but we are different in regard to our callings.

In the first place we may vary with regard to our organizations pertaining to the flesh; brother Kimball explained this morning why and how we vary.

Let a man be devoted to his God and to his religion, and his wives with him, and he is very apt to have children that will grow up in the nurture and admonition of the Lord. If the whole of the father and mother in all their acts is devoted to the building up of the kingdom of God on the earth, if they have no desire but to do right, if righteousness reigns predominant, then the spirit that is within them controls, to a certain extent, the flesh in their posterity.

Yet every son and daughter has got to go through the ordeal that you and I have to pass through; they must be tried, tempted and buffeted, in order to act upon their agency before God and prove themselves worthy of an exaltation.

Though our children are begotten in righteousness, brought forth in holiness, they must be tried and tempted, for they are agents before our Father and God, the same as you and I.

They must bring this agency into action; the passions and appetites must be governed and controlled; the eye, the speech, the tastes, the desires, all must be controlled.

If the people would thus control themselves in their lives, it would make a great alteration in the generations yet to come.

But we cannot clear ourselves from the power of Satan; we must know what it is to be tried and tempted, for no man or woman can be exalted upon any other principle, as was beautifully exhibited in the life of the Savior.

According to the philosophy of our religion we understand that if he had not descended below all things, he could not have ascended above all things.

As he was appointed to ascend above all things, his Father and his God so brought it about, by the handiwork of his Providence, that he was actually accounted, in his birth and in his life, below all things.

Did he descend below all things? His parents had not a house nor even a tent for him to be born in, but were obliged to go to a stable, doubtless because they were denied the privilege of a house.

The Son of Man could not be born in a house, and the poor mother in her distress crawled into a manger, among the litter that had been left by the cattle.

Others may have been born in as low a state as this, but it is hard to find anybody, among the civilized portions of mankind, that gets any lower.

But in the opinion of the people they were not considered worthy of anything better, and by some means it happened so, though they did not know why, neither did the people.

The history of Joseph and Mary is given to us by their best friends, and precisely as we will give the history of the Prophet Joseph. We know him to have been a good man, we know that he performed his mission, we know that he was an honorable man and dealt justly, we know his true character.

But let his enemies give his character, and they will make him out as one of the basest men that ever lived. Let the enemies of Joseph and Mary give their characters to us, and you would be strongly tempted to believe as the Jews believe.

Let the enemies of Jesus give his character to us, and, in the absence of the testimony of his friends, I do not know but that the present Christian world would all be Jews, so far as their belief that Jesus Christ was an impostor and one of the most degraded men that ever lived.

Jesus descended very low in his parentage and birth; but the question may be asked, did he condescend to be reduced in his understanding?

By the same reasoning I would believe that he did. I would believe that he was one of the weakest children that was ever born, one of the most helpless at his birth; so helpless that it might have been supposed that he would never grow to manhood.

What is his history? Read for yourselves the account given by his friends. It is said that Josephus has given a pretty just account of Joseph and Mary, of the apostles, &c., but he has only given just about as good an account of Jesus and his parents as some person in London lately has about the "Mormons" and Joseph Smith their Prophet, though he gives a pretty fair account.

Take a man in Paris or in London and let him write a history of Joseph Smith and the Latter-day Saints thirty years after Joseph figured on the earth, for the history of Christ by Josephus was written several years after he was crucified, and he would come as nigh to the truth, perhaps, as Josephus did in the history he has given of Jesus and his apostles. Josephus was a pretty fair man, but he knew but little about them.

What account would Jesus have given of himself, could he have transmitted his own statements? Such as every good man would, for he would have told the truth; but now we have to take his history from his friends and from his foes. What history do we get from the Jews? I will venture to say that no man living on the face of the earth, capable of using language to portray the character of any individual that lives on the earth, could paint a worse character than they have given to Jesus Christ. Compare that with all that has been said against Joseph Smith, and you will find that the wisdom of this generation will have to succumb to that of the Jews, for they portrayed the meanest character in the history they have given of Jesus; but let that pass.

You can discern that we have to control ourselves, that by the gospel we can actually do so and reform. Each man and woman, by the spirit of truth, can conform to that principle to improve until we will know and understand the things of God, so as to save ourselves by the commandments and will of God.

The gospel is simple, it is plain. The mystery of godliness, or of the gospel, is actually couched in our own ignorance; that is the cause of the mystery that we suppose to be in the revelations given to us; it is in our own misunderstanding—in our ignorance. There is no mystery throughout the whole plan of salvation.

(To be continued.)

ZION'S TRUMPET,

OR

Star of the Saints.

SATURDAY, NOVEMBER 8, 1856.

EPISTLE OF PRESIDENT D. DANIELS TO THE SAINTS IN WALES.

Kind Saints,—With great pleasure and delight I write my feelings to you at this time once again, with gratitude for the pleasure I have had in laboring together with you during the past portion of this year, acknowledging God for giving his Holy Spirit so abundantly to us in the work of his vineyard.

I am glad to see so many, in light of the revelations and the new laws, for us, which come from Zion, through the holy Priesthood, respecting and honoring the law of Tithing, and by so doing respecting its divine Author, not only in word, but in deed and truth. At the same time I am sorry that I cannot say the same thing about every Branch of every Conference.

The last quarter of this year is nearly half gone, while in it there is great work yet to be done. Its end will reveal the fruit of the labor of each Branch in Wales, at which time I am confident that not a single one of them will be ashamed at the opening of these books on the floor. It would be good to remember also every day and night that there is a record book in heaven also, in which the deeds of each one while in the body are chronicled, in much greater detail and perfection than here on the earth; also perhaps it will show even the thoughts and intents of our hearts.

Dear Saints, who have not as yet obeyed the law of tithing, I implore you once again not to delay any further, so that your names will be written in heaven and on earth, yes, before the end of this year, among those who have proved themselves ready supporters for the cause of Jesus Christ by their works, for nothing else will do—according to our works will we be judged. Is it not possible for each one who has been called to this high calling of being Saints, and having their names on the book of the Church of God, to see eye to eye together, and walk hand in hand by the same rule, and obey the heavenly laws as they come out to us from time to time? All but the blind can see that this is how it ought to be, and we trust that this is how it will be from now on with everything that comes out of the mouths of the inspired and holy Apostles and prophets of God in this dispensation.

Brothers and sisters, inasmuch as the purposes of God have not been fulfilled with regard to warning the dark and ignorant world of his plan to save it once again, God only knows if it will not be the last time for us, I call on you to yet make a great effort in this campaign to spread pamphlets across the entire face of the country, and bear vigorous witness of the Spirit more powerfully than ever, until we overcome the servants of Belial who are increasing their effort to thwart the work of the Lord, and, in spite of them, so that hosts of the honest may be brought out, before they pull the cords too tight to get every grain of wheat out from among the tares before the day of burning. Two of the Apostles of Jesus, and other missionaries, have just come from God's Zion full of godly fire to lead the army of Mormons to the battle against false teachers and false religion, testifying that as the Saints receive this spirit and this faith for the powerful truth of their religion, and cooperate with all their might, in the name of the God of Israel we will turn the nations of "Christianity," as it is called, upside down.

Let not anyone go out except of his own free will, and in full faith and confidence in the God of Israel. The old time of the early days is returning, in one sense—we hear the sound of convincing and baptizing several from every corner, we hear meetings filled with listeners, and enemies coming to oppose, grumbling when they see success starting afresh as it were to crown our labor, and the dawn that is now breaking promises a fair noon full of the warmth of the sun of righteousness to smile on the cause of God in Wales once again.

You are all aware that we intend to translate the series of new pamphlets of our renowned President Pratt, and of the excellent plan to distribute them and to pay for them. People cannot refuse the pamphlets of the Saints now with the excuse that they fear the Saints are profiting from their pennies, but so that our hands can be clear from their blood, they can offer them on loan. We are happy to understand that in some places there is no cottage, house, or palace where intelligent beings dwell, that has not been offered a witness of Jesus some way or another. O! how great is the privilege of the faithful Saints in those places. O! if we and they could understand that by doing that they are laying the foundation for the Priesthood and an endless kingdom!—that those who scorn them and refuse them now, will lick the dust under the feet of the royal Saints of Jesus, who gives them the kingdom and the greatness of the kingdom under all the heavens. Our present enemies will be glad for the privilege of being lowly servants at that time!

The first treatise, "The True Faith," is just about ready. We wish for our brethren to prepare themselves, their wives, and their children to distribute it with the other pamphlets, when they come out, so that the Welsh Nation will not be further behind than other languages in fulfilling the wish of the apostles of Jesus Christ.

It has been said before that it is good to gather every pamphlet in the "old Stock," and put them in among the assembled pamphlets, and keep them in constant circulation with the new ones that come out.

The longest time possible is allowed to pay for them. Even though the Welsh Office perhaps does not go according to the rule of the English Office, since it is weaker, yet, we do not set a greater weekly sum on the conferences to pay for the pamphlets than will be necessary to carry on the work of printing, and we wish for the Presidents to understand specifically that we cannot make do with a halfpenny less than the amount set for their conferences, since we are asking for the least sum possible.

That health, strength, and a blessing be added on the head of each faithful person who wishes to win a crown and part in the kingdom of Jesus when the whole world ends, which will come sooner than we think, is the heartfelt wish of,

Your humble fellow servant,

DANIEL DANIELS.

HOME CORRESPONDENCE.

CONFERENCES OF THE NORTH.

Abergele, October 26, 1856.

DEAR BROTHER DANIELS.—I came here last night and received your letter in my hand immediately. I started from Machynlleth on Tuesday, and when I came to Harlech I saw brother Treharne; he had traveled a great deal around the country selling pamphlets, and had not sold very much, but despite it all the brother is full of the Spirit of the Gospel, and his whole heart is with the work of the Lord, and striving through the heartland of the Methodists, to carry the principles of eternal life to his fellow men.

All the Saints and their officers are very united, and selling books as much as they can, and there is not one dwelling in which men live that has not received the books of this Church.

I sent the two brothers who were in Porthmadog to Dylife to labor, and the two others are going to Flintshire; it was better for them to go there than to come to the South, although that was their chatter. It would be wonderful if you could get a few more to come up to Ffestiniog and Porthmadog in the place of these; and also a dozen or two to Anglesey and Caernarvon, and about the same number to Denbigh and Flint,—the harvest is great.

Today I was in the Rhuddlan Council, and I had a Council to my heart's content,—the officers were full of the Spirit of the Lord as I taught about the nature of fasting and prayer by Jesus and the servants of God in every age of the world.

The brothers and sisters have done their work with the books and pamphlets, so that there is not one house in Newmarket parish that has not received a book, or the offer of one, and the situation is similar in general, except perhaps not so thorough in every place as in this one. Nearly all the pamphlets have been sold, and tithing is increasing everywhere, and there is evidence that God is blessing all who do His will.

Several are believing in every Conference, and I anticipate many baptisms soon. We are baptizing regularly—3 have been baptized here, 7 or 8 in Flintshire, 3 or 4 in Caernarfon, and 3 or 5 in Merionethshire since the last Conference.

My best regards to you and all the family, and all of the Saints.

Your brother in Christ,

JOHN JONES.

[We have invited as many of the brethren of the South who can go, to send their names here, and go out to assist these brethren who have so much of the weight of the work on their shoulders, so they may inherit the exaltation and glory that awaits such faithful ones. The call is earnest, and terrible will be the result of not going when one is able.—EDITOR.]

PEMBROKESHIRE CONFERENCE.

Haverfordwest, October 29, 1856.

President Daniels,—With regard to the success, nature, and condition of this Conference, you have that through the letters of brother Miles.

We have baptized several lately, and we believe that many are yet quite close. We received a letter last night from Fishguard, that there is yet another one who wishes to receive his baptism,—many seeds have been planted there from time to time, and it is clear that many of the honest have received it, so it is sure to work on their hearts convincingly, despite all the "Reverends" who become very agitated whenever they see us.

I had believed in the religion of the Saints for years, but, despite that, I never imagined it to be so powerful as I have already proved it to be, and thanks to God for it. Strange how all the "teachers" who "have been heaped together to teach" shake before Mormonism, much like the flower that shakes in a storm. The glory of all their silly pronouncements wilts before the gentle and loving words of Mormonism, much like a blade of grass in the fierce heat of the noonday sun. But how much greater their pitch black deceit appears when the Mormon Sun comes to the *Meridian*. I am grateful, then, for a substantial religion, which contains unspeakable strength, and incomparable glory.

Miles and I join together in sending our love to you, and also to brothers Harris and Lewis in the Office. We would really love to see President Daniels in our Conference.

I am, your obedient servant in Christ,

DAVID JOHN.

ATTEMPT AT INTERPRETING THE PARABLE OF THE HARVESTERS.

FIRST,—I think that the swaggerer mentioned is the devil, because of his title, and also his work in agreeing with the harvesters, which he did not have a right to send anyone to harvest that which belonged to another. It was not good for the harvesters to mistake him by his outward appearance for the owner of the field, for they were disappointed in doing so.

Second,—"The disappointed harvesters." The Parable does not mention that anyone had sent them to the field, rather they had gone without being sent, the same way that you went, Mr. Davies, before coming to the Saints. They are your former sectarian-preaching brethren.

Third,—"The field." Jesus said that this world is the field.

Fourth,—"Who is the real owner of the field?" The earth and its fullness is the Lord's, and the world that dwells therein.

Fifth,—"Who are His authorized servants?" I shall say immediately that they are the Latter-day Saints. I trust that Mr. D. Davies will be satisfied with this

From his well wisher,

Merthyr. JOHN ROBERTS.

VOICE OF THE WEAK.

THOU who hearest the voice of the weak,
    Incline thine ear and listen to my cry,
And come quickly now to my aid,
    To guide my steps toward home,
From the lands of Babel—home of strong oppression.

I am weary—my God well knows,
    For I have tired of this affliction,
My trailing withered heartstrings,
    I drag bruised and feeble from my bosom;
O see me sicken, I am pulling against the current.

What, after all my sufferings,
    Must I die far from my country?
Did thine arm sustain me so long,
    Against oppression, ire, and betrayal,
For me yet to die far from goodly Zion?

For so long Thou wert to me, Lord,
    Ever better than father or brother,
I call upon thee now always,
    For Thou art merciful to the weak and poor,
From the midst of old Babylon's trouble and scorn.

> And I shall look toward Zion,
>   Where the Lord's sacred Temple is seen,—
> How great is the Almighty's mercy,
>   Who's to say that I won't go across the sea,
> And go to her and sing amid her choir.   N. Ddu.

EISTEDDFOD OF THE SAINTS IN SWANSEA.

Mr. Editor,—I wish for you to publish the following topics in addition to those that were published in the last issue,—

For the best treatise (in English) on the History of the outstanding Apostates from the Church of God in every age of the world. Prize from Mr. Israel Evans, "Snow's Poem."

For the best treatise on Obedience and Disobedience. Prize from Mr. D. Davies, Llanelli,—English volume of the Jewish History, bound.

For the best song on Cleanliness. Prize from Mr. D. Davies, Llanelli,—Volume of the Chronicle, bound.

For the best song to a Virtuous Woman. Prize from Mr. William Thomas, Llanelli,—Jones on Baptism, bound beautifully.

For the best song on the Consistency that exists between the Stick of Judah and the Stick of Ephraim, or the Bible and the Book of Mormon. Prize from Mr. E. D. Miles, Haverfordwest,—The Scriptural Treasury.

For the best song to the Presidency of Wales. Prize from Mr. D. John, Haverfordwest,—Commentary on the Hebrews, by McLean.

For the best song on the clear difference between the gathering of the Saints to Zion and that of the Jews to Jerusalem. Prize from Mr. David John, Haverfordwest,—The Scriptural Treasury.

For the best song on the Fall of Babylon. Prize from Mr. Charles Harmon, Llanelli,—History of the Highlanders.   T. H.

Covers for the Treatises.—We now understand that the Welsh Conferences can get covers, &c., printed and sown for the English treatises in Liverpool. Therefore, they send the particulars of their Branches, the number they order, &c., there to get them. We will need the particulars for the Welsh covers here in the same way.

CONTENTS.

	PG.
Sermon	353
Editorial—Epistle of President Daniels	361
Home Correspondence—North—Pembroke	364
Attempt at interpreting the Parable of the Harvesters	366
Voice of the Weak	367

SWANSEA:

PRINTED AND PUBLISHED BY DANIEL DANIELS.

ZION'S TRUMPET,

OR

Star of the Saints.

No. 24.] NOVEMBER 22, 1856. [Vol. IX.

SERMON,

BY PRESIDENT B. YOUNG, BOWERY, JUNE 22, 1856.

(Continued from page 361.)

Brother Joseph Young, in the forenoon, touched upon one principle that I wish to talk about, i.e., our future state—futurity.

From time to time our fathers and our mothers leave us, their bodies are consigned to the silent tomb; our prophets are taken from us; our companions are taken away; our brothers and sisters leave this world.

The organization that pertains to this life decays, it becomes lifeless, we lay it down. Disease fastens upon our children, and they are gone.

I said a few words upon the principle of affection last Sabbath; now I wish to say a few words with regard to our lives hereafter; I will extend these remarks further than our existence here in the flesh.

We understand, for it has long been told us, that we had an existence before we came into the world. Our spirits came here pure to take these tabernacles; they came to occupy them as habitations, with the understanding that all that had passed previously to our coming here should be taken away from us, that we should not know anything about it.

[Price 1c.

We come here to live a few days, and then we are gone again. How long the starry heavens have been in existence, we cannot say; how long they will continue to be, we cannot say. How long there will be air, water, earth; how long the elements will endure, in their present combinations, it is not for us to say.

Our religion teaches us that there never was a time when they were not, and there never will be a time when they will cease to be; they are here, and will be here forever.

I will give you a figure that brother Hyde had in a dream. He had been thinking a great deal about time and eternity; he wished to know the difference, but how to understand it he did not know. He asked the Lord to show him, and after he had prayed about it the Lord gave him a dream, at least I presume he did, or permitted it so to be; at any rate he had a dream; his mind was opened so that he could understand time and eternity. He said that he thought he saw a stream issuing forth from a misty cloud which spread upon his right and upon his left, and that the stream ran past him and entered the cloud again. He was told that the stream was time, that it had no place where it commenced to run, neither was there any end to its running; and that the time which he was thinking about and talking about, what he could see between the two clouds, was a portion of, or one with, that which he could not perceive.

So it is with you and me; here is time, where is eternity? It is here, just as much as anywhere in all the expanse of space; a measured space of time is only a part of eternity.

We have a short period of duration allotted to us, and we call it time. We exist here, we have life within us; let that life be taken away, and the lungs will cease to heave, and the body will become lifeless. Is that life extinct? No, it continues to exist as much as it did when the lungs would heave, when the mortal body was invigorated with air, food, and the elements in which it lived; it has only left the body. The life, the animating principles are still in existence, as much so as they were yesterday when the body was in good health. Here the inquiry will naturally arise, when our spirits leave our bodies where do they go to? I will tell you. Will I locate them? Yes, if you wish me to. They do not pass out of the organization of this earth on which we live. You read in the Bible that when the spirit leaves the body it goes to God who gave it. Now tell me where God is not, if you please; you cannot. How far would you have to go in order to go to God, if your spirits were unclothed? Would you have to go out of this bowery to find God, if you were in the spirit? If God is not here, we had better reserve this place to gather the wicked into, for they will desire to be where God is not. The Lord Almighty is here by his Spirit, by his influence, by his presence. I am not in the north end of this bowery, my body is in the south end of it, but my influence and my voice extend to all parts of it; in like manner is the Lord here.

It reads that the spirit goes to God who gave it. Let me render this Scripture a little plainer; when the spirits leave the body they are in the presence of our Father and God; they are prepared then to see, hear, and understand spiritual things. But where is the spirit world? It is incorporated within this celestial system. Can you see it with your natural eyes? No. Can you see spirits in this room? No. Suppose the Lord should touch your eyes that you might see, could you then see the spirits? Yes, as plainly as you now see bodies, as did the servant of Elijah. If the Lord would permit it, and it was his will that it should be done, you could see the spirits that have departed from this world, as plainly as you now see bodies with your natural eyes; as plain as brothers Kimball and Hyde saw those wicked disembodied spirits in Preston, England. They saw devils there, as we see one another; they could hear them speak, and knew what they said. Could they hear them with the natural ear? No. Did they see those wicked spirits with their natural eyes? No. They could not see them the next morning, when they were not in the spirit; neither could they see them the day before, nor at any other time; their spiritual eyes were touched by the power of the Almighty.

They said they looked through their natural eyes, and I suppose they did. Bro. Kimball saw them, but I know not whether his natural eyes were open at the time or not; bro. Kimball said that he lay upon the floor part of the time, and I presume his eyes were shut, but he saw them, as also did bro. Hyde, and they heard them speak.

We may inquire where the spirits dwell, that the devil has power over them? They dwell anywhere, in Preston, as well as in other places in England. Do they dwell anywhere else? Yes, on this continent; it is full of them. If you could see, and would walk over many parts of North America, you would see millions on millions of the spirits of those who have been slain upon this continent. Would you see the spirits of those who were as good in the flesh as they knew how to be? Yes. Would you see the spirits of the wicked? Yes. Could you see the spirits of devils? Yes, and that is all there is of them. They have been deprived of bodies, and that constitutes their curse; that is to say, speaking after the manner of men, you shall be wanderers on the earth, you have to live out of doors all the time you live.

That is the situation of the spirits that were sent to the earth, when the revolt took place in heaven, when Lucifer, the Son of the Morning, was cast out. Where did he go? He came here, and one-third part of the spirits in heaven came with him. Do you suppose that one-third part of all the beings that existed in eternity came with him? No, but one-third part of the spirits that were begotten and organized and brought forth to become tenants of fleshly bodies to dwell upon this earth. They forsook Jesus Christ, the rightful heir, and joined with Lucifer, the Son of the Morning, and came to this earth; they got here first. As soon as Mother Eve made her appearance in the garden of Eden, the devil was on hand.

(To be continued.)

EXCERPT FROM THE TREATISE ON TRUE REPENTANCE.

1. Repentance is one of the gifts of God to fallen man. And in treating upon this subject, it will be assumed, on the strength of the word of God, that man is a fallen, sinful, lost being; degraded, ruined, and cast out from the presence of God; subject to His justice, wrath, and the penalty of His holy laws, which consign him to an eternal death and misery; and that a plan of salvation was devised and offered to him, to redeem him from his sins, and restore him to the favor of God. One of the conditions of this plan is a true and genuine Repentance.

2. The great and infinite sacrifice, made by the Son of God, for the sins of the world, has purchased for man the gift of Repentance, which, if properly received and exercised, will give him a claim upon the mercy of God against whom he has sinned. But without Repentance, mercy can have no claim on the sinner.

3. Repentance does not atone for past sins; neither could it have been a condition of pardon, if Christ who was innocent, had not suffered for the guilty.

4. Without the Atonement, Repentance would have been useless; mercy could not have been exercised, without interfering with the great attribute Justice.

5. It was not the design of Jesus, in atoning for the sins of the world, to save man in his sins; neither to pardon him in a state of impenitence. But the design of the atonement was to offer mercy on the condition of Repentance. Therefore, without Repentance, man must suffer the penalty of his sins, the same as if no atonement had been made.

6. That the sinner may have a clear understanding of the nature of Repentance, we shall divide the subject into four branches, namely,

First, The evils and sins to be repented of.
Secondly, The nature of the sorrow connected with true Repentance.
Thirdly, The confession necessary for the penitent.
And lastly, The promise and determination to sin no more.

7. We shall examine, First, *The evils and sins to be repented of.* An

innocent being who has committed no sin, cannot repent; neither can anyone repent who is not convinced of sin. Sin against God is a transgression of his law. A person unacquainted with the law of God may ignorantly transgress it, and have no idea that he has done wrong. Such a person, while unconvinced of sin, will feel no need of Repentance.

8. Without a knowledge of the revealed law of God, a person cannot always discern between good and sinful actions. It is true, that the light which is in every man that comes into the world, will enable him, without the aid of the revealed law, to distinguish, in some small degree, between good and evil. But there are many evils that could not be known short of the revealed law. The light of conscience will make manifest some of the more glaring evils; but this light becomes greatly obscured by neglect and by constant violation of its teachings, so much so, that persons may become almost or wholly insensible to the dictates of conscience; many actions which were once considered evils, will, by constant habit, be considered virtuous; while many practices once considered good, will, by tradition and habit, be transformed into evils. A heathen entirely unacquainted with the revealed law, would, if he were always to follow the still small voice of conscience, receive more and more light, and be able to discover many important truths, and to distinguish between virtue and vice more clearly than those who are constantly violating the monitor within them. But with all the light that he could glean, independent of revelation, he would be far from understanding the sinfulness of many actions, and would be entirely ignorant of the nature of others, in regard to whether they were sinful or not; and he would also be wholly uninformed in regard to a future judgment, and the penalties to be inflicted upon sinners; and without a knowledge of these things, he could not repent acceptably as the Gospel requires.

9. Where there is no knowledge of the revealed law of God, sinful actions will not be punished to the same extent as where the laws and their penalties are known; for the apostle says, "Sin is

not imputed when there is no law." (Rom. v. 13.) That is, sin is not imputed to the same extent, and they are not punished with the same severity, as those who are acquainted with the law. Hence, the Savior declares that he who knoweth the master's will and doeth it not, shall be beaten with many stripes; while he that knoweth not, and yet doeth things worthy of punishment, shall be beaten with a few stripes. The apostle also says, "For as many as have sinned without law shall also perish without law; and as many as have sinned in the law shall be judged by the law." (Rom. ii, 12.) The heathen, therefore, will perish without law, and be beaten with a few stripes, because they obeyed not the light that was in them; but the penalty of the revealed law will not fully be executed upon them, and it will be more tolerable for them in the day of judgment, than for those who have sinned, having the law, and who are to be judged by the law, and have the sentence of the law executed upon them. Such, without Repentance, will suffer eternal torment and everlasting banishment from the presence of God. And they will have weeping, and wailing, and gnashing of teeth.

10. Having learned that man is convicted of sin by the law, let us next endeavor to ascertain what sins the present generation are guilty of, in order to learn whether they have any need to repent; we will, for the present, pass over the sins of the heathens, and enumerate some of the evils existing among Christian nations where they have copies of the revealed law, existing by millions, and where almost every family can read the sacred pages of the same.

11. The Divine law says, "*Thou shalt not kill*". Now it is not the individual who murders who is a lone criminal, but all those who sanction the same. When the Saints were murdered in Missouri and Illinois by the marshaled hosts of the wicked, who were urged on by the highest authorities of those States, it is a notable fact that thousands of professed Christians, and many Christian ministers of different denominations, were directly engaged in those most wicked and horrid murders. When the great Prophet of the Lord was taken unlawfully from his peaceful avocations, and

torn from his family, and carried with a number of others, into the mob camp, and was sentenced to be shot the next morning, who was it that sanctioned and urged on these diabolical deeds? We reply, that among the vast hosts of those who made no profession of religion, there were no less than SEVENTEEN preachers of different orders who were in this council, and most strenuously urged the cold-blooded murder of the Prophet and his friends, in the presence of their own families upon the public square. Have these preachers, and the thousands of professors of religion who took such an active part in the foul murders of the Saints, been disfellowshipped by their brethren throughout the world? No, they are still, the most of them, retained in the respective churches to which they belonged. But were those who immediately participated in these bloody persecutions, the only ones guilty? Were there not hundreds of thousands in Christendom, who in their hearts sanctioned these things, and who still continue to sanction them? Will the persons who committed these murders and shed the blood of the only prophets which God has sent to the earth for more than a thousand years, be the only ones condemned as murderers in the day of judgment? No. Every person who has in the least sanctioned these things will suffer with the murderers, unless they repent. The Savior said that the blood of all the prophets which had been shed upon the earth, from the days of righteous Abel, until the blood of Zacharias, which was shed between the temple and the altar, should be required of that generation. Why? Because they sanctioned the murder of contemporary prophets. The approbation given to the murder of the prophet Zacharias, and other prophets sent directly to them, was just as wicked as though they had actually killed all the former ones. So likewise, God will require of every individual on the earth, who in the least sanctions the murder of Joseph the prophet, or of any of the Saints, the blood of those holy men at their hands; and not only their blood, but the blood of those righteous persons that has been shed upon the earth in any age, will be required at the hands of those among this generation who give countenance in their hearts to these wicked deeds. This, therefore, is one among the many sins which hundreds of thousands are guilty of, and of which they must most heartily repent, or else the blood of the prophets and the Saints will ascend up to heaven against them, and in the great day of judgment, they will receive their portion, not only among hypocrites and unbelievers, but among murderers, whose deeds they have sanctioned.

ZION'S TRUMPET,

OR

Star of the Saints.

SATURDAY, NOVEMBER 22, 1856.

To the Saints,—Beloved Brothers and Sisters,—With great pleasure and delight we are able to inform you of the very great and valuable blessings the Officers and Saints received, in several Conferences, through the visit of President Ezra T. Benson, who is one of the "sons of thunder," full of the divine fire, with his bosom as if burning with love for the brethren in every place. His eyes were like fountains of waters as he looked on so many thousands here who are longing for their better home on Zion's mount, who stay here as if confined for lack of means. But after waiting long, hour after hour, the dawn broke with the visit of Apostle Benson; he taught and showed the way that all can deliver themselves from the captivity of Babylon, by each one throwing into the newly formed fund by the name of the "Penny Fund," no less than one penny weekly, but up to sixpence. He said that that is the way for us to proceed from now on, beginning now.

Also, the Apostle gave a very important command that every family should keep a book, and record in it that which each member of the family gives to the aforementioned fund each week.

Furthermore, that the brother that is appointed to gather funds in the Branch, keep a book in the same way, and record carefully, fearing the Lord, so that nothing will get lost.

Also let everyone record the money given as a fast offering,—it will all go for the same purpose.

Appointment.—Elder James J. Phillips has been appointed to travel according to the direction of President Thomas Harris, in the West Glamorgan Conference.

D. Daniels.

EDITORS OF THE "HERO" REPELLING THE TRUTH, AND THE TRUTH REPELLING THE EDITORS OF THE "HERO."

Dear President Daniels:—What impelled me to write these lines to you as Editor of "Zion's Trumpet" is as follows:—

I recently wrote and sent a letter to the "Hero," addressed to the Editors, and reviewing the various querulous letters that had appeared in it, from some sly and unreliable types—who had been half Saints at some time. These were rendered shameful in their printed appearance, having been under the distorted gaze of the one-sided, perverse editors,—illusory and deceitful under the mantle of malice,—plotting to deceive men deliberately into believing falsehoods; and intended to cast a poor light on the Saints, and that done purposely to enrage the enemies, and to incite the cruelty of their father's children, to persecute and destroy the children of the light.

One could think from their style that they felt compelled about something important or unimportant. But by the time I started to raise the edge of their mantles, and reveal their deceit, there we were jumping, and kicking, and getting cross, and banging heads together; and never was there such pain, my good fellows!

The content of the truths in my letter took hold of their consciences—it worked through their marrow and their bones,—their sinews and their flesh. And since they were familiar and acquainted with deceit and transgression, at this point his immersive reverence from Aberdare, and his sprinkling reverence from Aberaman,—the editors of the "Hero," while cognizant of the intractable facts of my letter, they decided to cast it away, hide it and reject it, lest the honest and the sincere have a fair chance of judging the fanatical partisanship of the "Hero" and its editors, and become enlightened about their made-up, distorted and impudent lies, about the Latter-day Saints.

What is their excuse for this? Let every living person take note. Behold! here it is—"Dewi Elfed Jones's letter, a true image of its author." Ha, that is an unwitting truth. "A different image from theirs"—yes, completely. I am so pleased with this much truth from the lips of those who usually speak harsh words of vanity about the Saints! *Well done.* What else? My "image in my letter" has caused them to "let the cat out of the bag," like "a barber's cat full of wind and froth." I portrayed previously the "Exhibition in the belly of the preacher," or "Sectarianism Enared." I never imagined then that there were cats in there! Good heavens!

But when they saw my "image" once again, and the drawing of my hand, in black and white, it worked and pushed this out of them, according to their own depiction, yes, the force and the substance of their principles came out, in a feline way, windily, and full of froth. Oh! Oh! ministers, are they not, having failed to find anything to disprove my letter, unable to withstand the weight of the truths contained in it without fighting in opposition against a "barber's cat full of wind and froth."

Who would have thought that celebrated (?) reverends like T. Price, Aberdare, &c., were so weak and feeble—unable to stand over truth, without feeling their jaw dislocating, and spouting such substantial sense as a "barber's cat." Unless they cease this, they will no doubt be held in their day of tribulation, in company with the "owl, the bitterns, and the cats answering each other" within the walls of the ruined houses of Great Babylon, when the refuge of lies will be swept away, and the shelters of those who loiter there will be destroyed.

They can bet their beards, that they were in a half-swoon, while in T. Price's parlor, staring in alarm at my "image in *my* letter," with fanciful eyes, cheeks swollen with the gnawing of their guilt for refusing the truth—about to split from anger and rage, against the Saints. And finally, after foaming for a long time, having to spray out, and issue frothy threats in the form of "the barber's cat," against those who through the force of truth undermine the hope of profit of false teachers—devoid of any form of godliness—deceivers of men, about the most important thing. Remarkably similar too, to their manner in the *Preaching Match*, in battle refinery, or a singing festival, affected by the "fervor" under the influence of the *Black Prince*, "like a barber's cat full of wind and froth," spitting preacherly babbling across the people, and foaming the froth of false doctrine over their congregations.

O Price, Price! is this the end, the extent of the strength and soul of your religion! Spreading deceit before your congregations—ensnaring the innocent with lies about the Saints—refusing the truth with ireful wrath—making commerce out of the history of God's word in the past—distorting the straight path of truth, and turning your ear away from listening to it, and making your own and others' invented stories into a market-place, and all in the end, according to the testimony of your own polluted lips, no better than "a barber's cat full of wind and *wabbling*."

Be aware that your pride will be brought low, in your own destiny, as you deserve, as a lover and embracer of deceit and impudent refuser of the Truth—Repent quickly, and turn to a safe place with a determination not to sin any more.

I shall have an opportunity to send you the content of the letter you refused in printed form, for the sake of those who wish to find the Truth, and have deceit and falsehood entirely driven from the face not only of the land of Gwalia, but also of the whole earth; and know that none of you interests me, poor things, for

    Your weapons are shaving foam,
    Never anything—all false.
        Yours, as ever,
            DEWI ELFED JONES.

LETTER FROM THE PLAINS TO ISRAEL EVANS.

30 Miles East of Laramie, August 31, 1856.

Dear Brother—I thought I would use the few spare minutes I have to write to inform you of the success of this small company of

Saints. You no doubt have heard concerning our successful voyage across the ocean, and our landing with all healthy, with the exception of a few infants who died at sea and going across the States, and of our arrival at Iowa City about the 1st of June.

We left Iowa City about the last day of June, 300 of us in number. We traveled 7 or 8 miles the first day, and we thought that to be a very difficult task. After we had been traveling for about a week, we went 10 miles per day, which we thought was a lot; but before we reached Winter Quarters we were able to cover from 15 to 20 miles per day more easily than we covered 7 or 8 at first. It was hard work at first, because of our long idleness previously.

As we came from Iowa City to Winter Quarters we had a considerable number of defections. Whenever we camped near a settlement, the settlers would come to us and try to get the Saints to stay, giving them all kinds of good offers if they would stay, telling them that everyone was starving in the Valley, &c. Well, they attracted some away, but we were glad to get rid of them. My heart rejoiced when I saw some of them stay behind, and if any who were Saints remained behind, they would come along again when they had had their fill of the Gentiles. These happenings remind me of the account of the devil offering the whole world to our Savior when he actually didn't have a foot of it for himself.

We reached Winter Quarters July 19, in exceptionally good spirits and good health. While we were fitting out there, old sister Brookes died, and, also, brother David Davies, [formerly from Newton, Glamorgan,] and they were buried in the Saints' cemetery.

We left Winter Quarters July 30th, all in good health and spirits, 225 in number. Some of the Saints remained behind there, with permission.

From Iowa City to Winter Quarters we had three wagons, and from there on, four, loaded with provisions; besides that, each tentful (20) of persons had to carry four hundred pounds of flour on their carts.

You can see that we had traveled only a month's time, and we had accomplished nearly half the journey. We determined to reach the City by Saturday, the 4th of October, God willing, so as to be there by Conference.

I shall give you my thoughts as to what I know about the handcart system: I have traveled this country with horses and oxen, but I have never traveled so quickly as I have thus far this time by handcart. I know that this is the best and fastest way for the Saints to cross the Plains and the Mountains, and if there could be a settlement every 150 or 200 miles, from which they could get their supplies, and do away with the wagons, they could carry their provisions with them so far as that; they could travel faster and easier, and they wouldn't require so many guards: besides that, the oxen cannot travel as fast as men and women after they get used to traveling.

We each have a pound of flour per day, with a lot of tea and coffee during the week. I don't remember how much.

We killed three large buffalo, and we have already eaten all of them. Last Saturday we slaughtered an excellent fat cow, and we have 5 more oxen to slaughter. We intend to slaughter one each week. With those, and with the buffalo we will get on the Sweetwater, we will live splendidly. Besides other food the Company has 14 milk cows, and they have their milk. You see that we live quite well; but you know that this is a land so beautiful and healthful that we can eat our whole rations, and then look around for more. Well, we have heard that more for us is on our way, and as soon as it comes, we shall have a pound-and-a-half or two pounds for each of us every day.

We met some brothers yesterday; they said that Brigham had sent out two wagons loaded with flour the same day they started out, namely the 11th of this month, and that he intends to send out 5 wagons every week loaded with flour to meet the emigrants, until he understands that they have all been satisfied. We expect to meet the first one in about a week.

The milk cows, as you know, supply us with the best and most trouble-free food we could get—we don't have to carry it.

Elder Bunker purchased two milk cows, and I purchased one, to use for ourselves—and we have found them to be a great blessing for us; we gave 25 dollars each for them. The brothers we met yesterday told us that we could sell them in the Valley easily for 40 dollars each; so there is profit both ways; but the greatest profit is using them on the Plains.

It is getting late, so I shall put aside writing for the time being, and I shall finish the letter in, or close to Laramie.

September 2—We are within a few miles of Laramie; we intend to go past there today. The camp is full of health and good spirits.

The D. D. McAllister Company is about 75 miles ahead of this one, and that of E. Ellsworth is about 100. They were all healthy a few days ago.

Elder Bunker sends his regards to you and to brothers Daniels and Ashby. He has proved himself to be a father to this people: he has been guided by the Holy Spirit the entire time: I am proud to have such a man as my President crossing the Plains. We have been in unity in everything, ever since we left Iowa City.

Brother Israel, I have gone through it *first rate* ever since we parted company in Liverpool. I have traveled so much and had such good success with these people that it will be hard for us to leave one another.

Remember me to brothers Daniels and Ashby, and all the *boys*. Tell them that D. Grant has gotten fat and strong by pulling the handcart.

I shall conclude, praying to God that he will bless you with every needful blessing, and gather you and those who are with you to your mountain home in peace and safety.

Your fellow laborer in the Kindgom of God,

DAVID GRANT.

NAMES OF THE WELSH EMIGRANTS
Who went with the Handcarts across the Plains last Season.

CHIEF CAPTAIN,
Edward Bunker.

CAPTAINS OF HUNDREDS

The 1st hundred, David Grant: 2nd, G. W. Davies: 3rd, John Parry.

The first Hundred,—David Grant   Thomas Rees, his wife, and 8 children   Daniel Lewis   Rees Llewellyn and his wife   Daniel Thomas, his wife, and his mother   Enoch Lewis, his wife, and 2 children   W. J. Lewis, (Anglesey) his wife, and his sister   Elias Lewis and his wife   Mary Llewellyn and 4 children   Henry Jenkins, (died August 23.)   Martha Jenkins and her daughter   Wm. James (age 71)   Elvira

Thomas and her son   Owen Jones   Elizabeth Hughes   Elizabeth Davies   Thomas D. Evans, *Commissary for the Hundred*.   Priscilla Evans   John Cousins and his wife   John Thayne and his wife   James Morgans   William Morgans   Hannah Walters and 3 children   John R. Roberts and his wife and 3 children   Robert A. Roberts   Elizabeth Lane   John Davies   David Davies, (died July 24,) his wife, and 2 children, who went forward   John Butler and his wife   Isaac Rees and his wife   William Morgan and his wife   David Evans   Thomas Giles and his son Joseph.

The second Hundred.—G. W. Davies, and his wife   John D. Roberts, (*Commissary*,) his wife, and 2 children   John James, formerly from Sirhowy, (*Sergeant of Guards*)   Sarah James   Morgan Evans and his wife and his child   Moses Evans and his sister and 3 children   Margaret Rees   Thomas Evans, his wife, and 5 children   Thomas Phillips, his wife, and 5 children   William Jenkins, his wife, and 3 children   David Lewis, his wife, and 2 children   Abram Evans, his wife, and 6 children   Nathaniel Evans, his wife and his child   David Evans, his wife, and his mother   John Parry (formerly from Aberdare)   James Bridge   John Edmunds   Thomas Axton, his wife and his child   Letitia Williams   Thomas Morgan (Commissary) and his wife.

The Third Hundred—John Parry, former Pastor over the Conferences of the North, the Captain, and his wife   John Parry, Mariam, his wife, and 4 children   John Williams, his wife, and 4 children   Edward Parry and his wife   William Jones, his wife, and his child   David Roberts, (Commissary,) his wife, and 5 children   Thomas Jones, Pantmawr, his wife, and 6 children   Hannah Job, and her child   Richard Williams   Sarah Walters   Susannah Roberts   M. N. Morris and his wife   Thomas and John Jenkins   Joseph Chappel, his wife, and his child   John Williams, his wife, and his mother   Samuel Brookes and 3 of his children, (Emma Brookes died August 23.)   William Edwards   Hopkin Matthews, his wife, and 5 children   Thomas Jarman, his wife, and 3 children   Anna Butler, widow, and 2 children   Owen Owens   Margaret Jones   Thomas Evans, Sr.   Thomas Evans, Jr.—Rees Llewellyn, *Clerk*.

CONTENTS.

	PG.
Sermon	369
Excerpt from the treatise on True Repentance	373
Editorial—To the Saints—Appointment	377
Editors of the Hero, &c.	378
Letter from the Plains	380
Names of the Welsh Emigrants	383

SWANSEA:

PRINTED AND PUBLISHED BY DANIEL DANIELS.

ZION'S TRUMPET,

OR

𝔖tar of the 𝔖aints.

No. 25.] DECEMBER 6, 1856. [Vol. IX.

SERMON,

BY PRESIDENT B. YOUNG, BOWERY, JUNE 22, 1856.

(Continued from page 372.)

You cannot give any person their exaltation, unless they know what evil is, what sin, sorrow, and misery are, for no person could comprehend, appreciate, and enjoy an exaltation upon any other principle. The devil, with one-third part of the spirits of our Father's Kingdom, got here before us, and we tarried there with our friends, until the time came for us to come to the earth and take tabernacles; but those spirits that revolted were forbidden ever to have tabernacles of their own. You can now comprehend how it is that they are always trying to get possession of the bodies of human beings; we read of a man's being possessed of a legion, and Mary Magdalene had seven.

You may now see people with legions of evil spirits in and around them; there are men who walk our streets that have more than a hundred devils in them and round about them, prompting them to do all manner of evil, and some too that profess to be Latter-day Saints, and if you were to take the devils out of them and from about them, you would leave them dead corpses; for I believe there would be nothing left of them.

[Price 1c.

I want you to understand these things; and if you should say or think that I know nothing about them, be pleased to find out and inform me. You can see the acts of these evil spirits in every place, the whole country is full of them, the whole earth is alive with them, and they are continually trying to get into the tabernacles of the human family, and are always on hand to prompt us to depart from the strict line of our duty.

You know that we sometimes need a prompter; if any one of you were called by the government of the United States to go to Germany, Italy, or any foreign nation, as an ambassador, if you did not understand the language, somebody would have to interpret for you. Well, these evil spirits are ready to prompt you. Do they prompt us? Yes, and I could put my hands on a dozen of them while I have been on this stand; they are here on the stand. Could we do without the devils? No, we could not get along without them. They are here, and they suggest this, that and the other.

When you lay down this tabernacle, where are you going? Into the world of the spirits. Are you going into Abraham's bosom? No, not anywhere nigh there, but into the spirit world. Where is the spirit world? It is right here. Do othe good and evil spirits go together? Yes, they do. Do they both inhabit one kingdom? Yes, they do. Do they go to the sun? No. Do they go beyond the boundaries of this organized earth? No, they do not. They are brought forth upon this earth for the express purpose of inhabiting it to all eternity. Where else are you going? Nowhere else, only as you may be permitted.

When the spirits of mankind leave their bodies, no matter whether the individual was a prophet or the meanest person that you could find, where do they go? To the spirit world. Where is it? I am telling you. The spirit of Joseph, I do not know that it is just now in this bowery, but I will assure you that it is close to the Latter-day Saints, is active in preaching to the spirits in prison and preparing the way to redeem the nations of the earth, those who lived in darkness previous to the introduction of the gospel by himself in these days.

He has just as much labor on hand as I have; he has just as much to do. Father Smith, and Carlos, and bro. Partridge, yes, and every other good Saint, are just as busy in the spirit world as you and I are here. They can see us, but we cannot see them unless our eyes were opened. What are they doing there? They are preaching, preaching all the time, and preparing the way for us to hasten our work in building temples here and elsewhere, and to go back to Jackson county and build the great temple of the Lord. They are hurrying to get ready by the time that we are ready, and we are all hurrying to get ready by the time our elder brother is ready.

The wicked spirits that leave here and go into the spirit world, are they wicked there? Yes.

The spirits of people that have lived upon the earth according to the best light they had, who were as honest and sincere as men and women could be, if they lived on the earth without the privilege of the gospel and the priesthood and the keys thereof, are still under the power and control of evil spirits, to a certain extent. No matter where they lived on the face of the earth, all men and women that have died without the keys and power of the Priesthood, though they might have been honest and sincere and have done everything they could, are under the influence of the devil, more or less. Are they as much so as others? No, no. Take those that were wicked designedly, who knowingly lived without the Gospel when it was within their reach, they are given up to the devil, they become tools to the devil and spirits of devils.

Go to the time when the gospel came to the earth in the days of Joseph, take the wicked that have opposed this people and persecuted them to the death, and they are sent to hell. Where are they? They are in the spirit world, and are just as busy as they possibly can be to do everything they can against the Prophet and the Apostles, against Jesus and his kingdom. They are just as wicked and malicious in their actions against the cause of truth as they were while on the earth in their fleshly tabernacles.

Joseph also goes there, but has the devil power over him?

No, because he held the keys and power of the eternal Priesthood here, and got the victory while here in the flesh.

Before I proceed further, I will give you an illustration. Send a man that is used to magnetizing people, and see if he can magnetize an Elder in Israel, one that is full of the faith, or a faithful sister in the Church of God. Could LeRoy Sunderland, one of their greatest characters, magnetize one of the Latter-day Saints? No. He might as well try to magnetize the sun in the firmament. Why? Because the priesthood is upon you, and he would try to magnetize you by another and lesser power.

The principle of animal magnetism is true, but wicked men use it to an evil purpose. I have never told you much about my belief in this magnetic principle. Speaking is a true gift, but I can speak to the glory of God, or to the injury of his cause and to my condemnation, as I please; and still the gift is of God. The gift of magnetism is a gift of God, but wicked men use it to promote the cause of the devil, and that is precisely the difference. You may travel through the world and make inquiries where the Elders have traveled, and you cannot find an instance where the devil has gained power over a good and faithful Elder through this power. He cannot do it, because the faithful Elder of this church holds keys and power above that which is used by those who go round lecturing on magnetism, and operating upon all who will become passive to their will. They have not the same power that the faithful Elders of Israel have, for those elders have the eternal priesthood upon them, which is above and presides over every other power.

When the faithful Elders, holding this Priesthood, go into the spirit world they carry with them the same power and Priesthood that they had while in the mortal tabernacle. They have got the victory over the power of the enemy here; consequently, when they leave this world they have perfect control over those evil spirits, and they cannot be buffeted by Satan. But as long as they live in the flesh, no being on this earth, of the posterity of Adam, can be free from the power of the devil.

When this portion of the school is out, the one in which we descend below all things, and commence upon this earth to learn the first lessons for an eternal exaltation, if you have been a faithful scholar, and have overcome, if you have brought the flesh into subjection by the power of the Priesthood; if you have honored the body, when it crumbles to the earth and your spirit is freed from this home of clay, has the devil any power over it? Not one particle.

This is an advantage which the faithful will gain; but while they live on earth they are subject to the buffetings of Satan. Joseph and those who have died in the faith of the gospel are free from this; if a mob should come upon Joseph now, he has power to disperse them with the motion of his hand, and to drive them where he pleases. But is Joseph glorified? No, he is preaching to the spirits in prison. He will get his resurrection the first of anyone in this kingdom, for he was the first that God made choice of to bring forth the work of the last days.

This office is not taken from him, he has only gone to labor in another department of the operations of the Almighty. He is still an Apostle, still a Prophet, and is doing the work of an Apostle and Prophet; he has gone one step beyond us and gained a victory that you and I have not gained; still he has not yet gone into the celestial kingdom, or if he has, it has been by a direct command of the Almighty, and that too to return again so soon as the purpose has been accomplished.

(*To be continued.*)

NEWS FROM THE VALLEY.

Historian's Office, Great Salt Lake City

August 30, 1856.

President Orson Pratt,—Dear Sir,—The eastern mail arrived on the 28th of this month, and brought many letters from our friends at Washington, and other parts of the globe, with the Star, the Mormon, and many other papers, which gave us the general news of the day, and showed us that the political state of the atmosphere at Washington, and throughout the nations, was anything but calm and serene. We heard but little from our handcart emigration, or any of the back companies. Philemon C. Merrill and company arrived on the 16th of this month; as far as we could learn all was well. I had an interview with Dr. J. Clinton, who was well and in good spirits.

The weather has continued dry since we last wrote. Our wheat harvest is gathered, and proves to be a much better crop than we could have expected, considering the drought; the heads were well filled, even where the wheat was so short that it had to be pulled, which has been the case with many acres this season. Our corn crop looks quite well. The potato crop is nearly a failure, they mostly run to vines; beets and garden vegetables look well. This season is not our *peach*-bearing year, yet some orchards will bear a middling crop—some very fine apples in the orchards.

President Young's apple trees are, some of them, loaded, and he has a good crop of *peaches*; his grape vines are loaded, and I think he will have two or three thousand pounds of grapes this season.

It is a general time of health in this Territory, excepting a company that came in from the Mississippi, who brought the smallpox with them, but it has not spread much yet, and we hope it will not.

A company arrived from Carson Valley on the 28th of this month; they report that Murray, who was tried for murder last winter, was killed by the Indians, also a man by the name of Reddin.

Your family is all well. Brothers Bates and Luke Johnson are about to start on a mission of about one month, with Seth M. Blair to Ruby Valley on an exploring expedition to open a new route to Carson Valley. They expect to meet brother Enoch Reese with a company from Carson to cooperate with them.

Our Agricultural and Manufacturing Society are making quite an exertion to promote home manufactures in this Territory, as the time has come when we see that we are under the necessity of making, in a great measure, what we use. The various Wards of the City and Territory are forming auxiliary branches of the same; intending to manufacture all they can for home consumption.

During this month Elder Parley P. Pratt, and a few others, have been appointed on missions to the States. Thomas Bullock, Bernard Snow, and some others are sent to Europe.

The Agricultural and Manufacturing Society held their annual fair on the 1st of October, at which there will be an exhibition of stock, agricultural products, farming and gardening implements, manufactures, ladies' work, machinery, and fruit. A plowing match will take place on the Governor's land near the City, about Conference time. There will be premiums awarded for the best of each named class; also for the best essays on agriculture, horticulture, pomology, and home manufactures. We expect the fair will be as extensive as the occasion.

Brother Willes, the Territorial inspector of schools, has returned from a tour to the north, and reports the favorable results consequent upon the cooperation of the authorities in the various settlements; also the establishment of Sabbath schools, and the organization of Literary societies.

Among other improvements in the City, a new baptismal font is now being built, near the endowment house in the temple block.

Yours truly, &c.,

W. WOODRUFF.

ARRIVAL OF THE HANDCARTS.

Letter from the Valley to Mr. Jones, Rhydygarreg-ddu, from Elder T. C. Martill.

Great Salt Lake City, September 27, 1856.

Mr. Jones,—Dear Sir,—My dear friend Henry Harries (formerly of Talog) started from this City, Friday, the 10th of this month, on a mission to Wales. I accompanied him for about twenty miles. As I returned back I felt like a bird with one wing, for the unity that existed between us was similar to that of Caleb and Joshua. Several missionaries are traveling together with him, some who were sent on missions to different parts of England. If all goes well on their journey, they will likely reach Liverpool by about Christmas.

I am sure you will be happy at the visit of your brother to the land of his birth, and that he also will be extremely happy of having the honor of coming on such a glorious mission to his loved ones. I comfort myself, hoping (although his departure is unpleasant for me) that it will be beneficial to many of my fellow nation.

I pray to God that you and your worthy wife will have faith to believe and obey the calls of the Savior, through which they will preach to you the word of the covenant. My prayer is not only on your behalf, but on behalf of all who wish to do the will of God.

A company of Saints from England arrived here yesterday with the HANDCARTS. Great was the joy that was everywhere; they were extremely happy to see the Valley, and we were just as happy to see them having arrived safe with the handcarts, over such a long journey.

When the news came that they were not far from the Valley, President Brigham Young, and others of the leaders of the Church, together with many hundreds of Saints, went to meet them about fifteen miles outside the City. Many soldiers also went out to lead them in, and musicians, who played in a brass band, preceding them into the City. Before reaching their campsite, thousands were ready to receive them. They were welcomed with loads of foodstuffs of various kinds, and lovely fruits, such as Peaches, Melons, &c. Another company is expected to arrive in about four days, the majority of them from Wales. We heard that some from Carmarthenshire are among them, namely John Edwards, Ffynnon-ddrain, and Edward his son, and Thomas Jones from Llanelli, &c.

It is unnecessary for me to give you an account of this land, because my dear brother Henry Harries has done that in his letters, and that which he has not yet told you, he will let you know better than can be done through the means of paper and ink.

I expect a letter from Henry Harries before long, but I will not be able to answer it before he arrives in Liverpool, for I will not know where to address it.

Give my kind greetings to Mrs. Jones and the family, to your father-in-law, and the people of Pantycendy and Posty. When you have the chance give my greetings to my parents, to my faithful brother Daniels, who leads the Saints in Wales; his wife and the children, and the Welsh in general greet him. Give my greetings to Isaac Jones and his family; it would be very lovely for me to be able to greet all the Saints of Carmarthen.

I do not have the time to write more at present: I must visit the Welsh who have arrived recently. I will be happy to receive a letter from you.

Yours respectfully,
T. C. Martill.

P. S.—I intended to write to President Daniels, but I do not have time; therefore, be so kind as to send the foregoing letter to the Office of the Trumpet, Swansea; perhaps some will be glad to hear that the Handcarts have arrived here safely.—T. C. M.

ZION'S TRUMPET,

OR

Star of the Saints.

SATURDAY, DECEMBER 6, 1856.

APPOINTMENTS OF THE PRESIDENTS OF THE CHURCH IN WALES FOR THE YEAR 1857.

Elders Israel Evans, Benjamin Ashby, Thomas Harris, William Jones, Thomas Jones, Griffith Roberts, and Thomas Rees were released from their various presidencies.

Elders William Miller and James Taylor are appointed to succeed Elders Israel Evans and Benjamin Ashby as Counselors to the President of the Mission.

Elder John Davies, formerly from Meirion, is appointed to

succeed Elder Thomas Harris, formerly from Georgetown, in the presidency of the West Glamorgan Conference.

Elder Thomas Rees, Flintshire, is appointed to succeed Elder Wm. Jones in the presidency of the Carmarthen Conference.

Elder Joseph Griffiths is appointed to succeed Elder Thomas Jones in the presidency of the Cardiganshire Conference.

Elder Hugh Evans, Newmarket, is appointed to succeed Elder Griffith Roberts in the presidency of the Denbighshire Conference.

Elder David John, Pembrokeshire, is appointed to succeed Elder Thomas Rees in the presidency of the Flintshire Conference.

The foregoing Appointments will take effect on the first of next January. Let the appointed brethren go to their new fields of labor promptly. Let the brethren who are released strive to transfer all the numbers and everything in the most correct, clear, and understandable way they can, and let their successors be precise in seeing that everything is done well. The other Presidents will continue as they are.

All the Presidents of the Conferences in Wales have been faithful and diligent during the year that is about to end; and through their efforts, and those of the worthy Saints who listened to their voices, the Church has increased and strengthened in principles, knowledge, great and praiseworthy deeds, and also in numbers.

May the God of Israel prosper the faithful brethren who are released to emigrate, and through their humility and their readiness to listen to the voice of God they will yet be seen as brave soldiers in his kingdom in Zion.

Remember the Annual Reports, the Emigrating Fund, and the Temple promptly.

D. Daniels.

New Pamphlets.—The second treatise, namely "True Repentance" is now at the Press. The first, namely "True Faith," before now is in the hands of our readers. It was priced very cheaply, at the wish of President Pratt, so that no one will do any more than pay for its preparation and printing, for the Welsh Saints to make the same effort toward it for their part. Since only one or fewer will be printed for each Welsh member, we think it will be easier for the Conferences to pay for them. Its price to the distributors is twopence per number, and no profit, but the Conferences are to compensate them for postage and expense. We expect full payment back, by, or before the following number comes out, so that we do not fail to complete the work. From the weak Conferences we will try to make do with the payment of a penny and a halfpenny per number, and to wait for the rest. If we work together God's blessing will be on us, and the honest in heart will flock to the Church by our light, after we take it to them. We understand that praiseworthy efforts are being made to distribute the pamphlets, especially in the North—the sisters, until now, are carrying the day over the brethren, especially with the treatise "Marriage and Morals in Utah." We think that the Pamphlet Fund is at work in its strength by now. Send the pamphlet money in separately.

———

PAMPHLETS NEEDED.—We wish to know without delay from our distributors, what kinds and how many of the Welsh pamphlets they can return to the Office, because we need about 100 of each kind, except for a few of the pamphlets of John Davis.

———

TO DISTRIBUTORS.—We wish for the Conference Distributors to send the packets of books to the Branch distributors with haste, so that our counsels through the TRUMPET can be carried out promptly. Presiding Brethren of the Conferences, devise the best way for this, and more blessings will follow.

———

EARLY POLYGAMY AMONG THE WELSH.

(From the *"Modern Universal British Traveler,"* page 671.)

NEAR Aberffraw there is a small village, known for being the birthplace of Dafydd ab Howell ab Iorwerth, who lived there in the year 1580, although he died soon after that, and he was at that time 105 years old. He had three wives and two concubines. The total number of children he begat lawfully was thirty-six; by his concubines, seven. His oldest son, Griffith ab Gwilym, who was 84 years old, had a large number of children and grandchildren; his youngest son was two years old, living in the same parish, and there was 82 years difference between him and his brother. There were about 88 persons who descended from the old man, and who were alive at the same time and in the same place; and it is said that about 300 persons total descended from him, and were born in his time. He was small in stature, good appearance, and was rarely troubled with sickness, moderate in what he ate, lived by toiling, and frequently used his skill in fishing and hunting. His hearing, his sight, and indeed all his senses, were intact until about an hour before his death.

THE PERPETUAL EMIGRATING FUND.

Tune—*"Pure Bird."*

The great eternal wheel has come
    To set the captive free,
And its warm bosom—
    And a host from shame to bliss;
The Fund will emigrate
Its loved ones to escape.
It takes men over to Zion,
To the happy land—where there is plenty
Of all varieties, which makes man
    Into one to delight in.

The Perpetual Emigrating Fund
    Was formed through the dictate of the Council,
And was revealed by our Father,
    For the benefit of every land and border;
What good would teaching us do,—
Powerful rhetoric and preaching,
Without the great care of the Lord now,
Through the Fund for the poor;
This opens up the way
    For the Saints to mount Zion.

The whole aim of its organization,
    Is clear enough to us,
It is to deliver humankind,
    To their fitting home to shelter,
While the frightful wrath of the Lord,
Is disturbing with disaster,
Across the earth in his anger,
Against the disobedient and vain world,
While the family of God each one
    Is full of joy in plenty.

When wars with grievous shouts come
    To the public to the ends of the earth,
The Saints will all be seen contented,
    With not one in loss or care;
Every day the obedient know,
That the Lord is a savior,—
That there is a Fund that saves,
And that they can go in her bosom,
    With not one left in custody.

This Fund will be before long,
    A great surprise to the world,
Thousands will be saved in one day
    When the pressure comes;
Thousands upon thousands there will be,
Of every tribe and tongue and people,
Gathered from wretchedness,
Through the auspices of this very one,
    Under the protection of Jesus our king.

Thousands have gone over there,
    With the Fund's helping hand,
To their summery, warm inheritance,
    From the evil world of Babylonia;
There is no way to express
How many this could gather,
If there were unity and faithfulness
To cooperate in wisdom,—
Our work would be a miracle to the world,
    If we put together our courage.

> Every farthing given into its care,
>   Is directly put to use,
> It won't be long until someone feels the value
>   Of the sacrifice from its support;
> Let us immediately put arm and shoulder,
>   To work with the Lord,
> By striving with all our might,
>   Together until it is filled,—
> There is room for all to give a helping hand,
>   To launch it in generosity.

Cap Coch.　　　　　　　　　　　　　　J. P. PROSSER.

THE SAINTS' EISTEDDFOD.

TO THE BARDS AND WRITERS OF THE SAINTS, AND THEIR FRIENDS THROUGHOUT ALL OF WALES.

To the list of topics and prizes that were added in the previous TRUMPET, I yet wish to give the following. Although there is but a short amount of time before the day of the Eisteddfod (Christmas), still the bards have the same fair play.

For the best translation of the song "*Dear Zion,*" published in the *Star*, number 22, of this year. Prize from Mr. Israel Evans, "Voice of Warning."

For the best song to the Penny Fund, no fewer than 10 stanzas. Prize from Mr. Israel Evans, "Spencer's Letters."

For the best song to the Tithing, in English, no fewer than 10 stanzas. Prize from Mr. John Jones, formerly of Brecon, "Voice of Warning."

For the best song on Polygamy, no fewer than 10 stanzas, in the meter of "*Pop goes the Weasel.*" Prize from Miss Eleanor Ellis, Machynlleth, "Harp of Zion," and five shillings from Mrs. Margaret Davies, Cwmafon.

For the best song on the Necessity of woman to choose a righteous man as a husband and defender. Prize from Miss Catherine Ellis, Machynlleth—Hymn Book.

For the best song of praise to the Presidency of the Church in the Welsh Principality. Prize from Miss Cathrine Arthur, Machynlleth,—

English Hymn Book,—and a Volume of Zion's Trumpet, bound, from Mr. Emrys Davies, Cwmafon.

For the best song on the Effort made from time to time to preach the Gospel in the Merioneth Conference. Prize from Mr. John Treharne, Merioneth,—Body (the death) of Theology.

For the best song on the Feelings of the Saints who emigrated to Zion with the Handcarts. Prize from Mrs. Martha Jones, Cwmafan,—Five shillings.

For the best song to the Presidency of the West Glamorgan Conference. Prize from Mr. Hopkin Jones, Aberafan, a Book of Mormon, bound.

It is requested that the contestants send their compositions in according to the instructions given previously.

I wish for those who desire to take part in the public performances of the day to send their names in beforehand, together with the names of the topics they wish to discourse, sing, recite, or debate about. I am happy to report that several have sent in the information already, and all signs are that those who attend will have a delightful day. Some out-of-town brethren will be present, among which our able brother John Jones, formerly from Brecon.

Meetings to begin at 10 in the morning, 2 in the afternoon, and 6 in the evening. Tickets for 6c each.

Yours truly,

THOMAS HARRIS.

MISCELLANEOUS, &c.

ELDER Thomas Thomas, formerly from Llanelli, Carmarthenshire, has arrived on a mission to Wales from the Great Salt Lake Valley, in good health and spirits. He has letters of approval from the First Presidency, and the Presidency of the British Isles, and has been appointed to labor in Wales. Welcome to him. The field is vast, and there is a great need for diligent laborers. May God strengthen him to be a blessing to the Saints wherever he may go. Accept him as a servant of God.

THE discourse of President Benson, in Swansea, is too long to put in this volume of ours. It will come out in the first issue of the next volume.

A LETTER from Apostles George A. Smith and Erastus Snow in the "Mormon," dated, October 21, 1856, says that they visited the Welsh Saints in Caseyville, Illinois. Elders W. M. Lewis and Walter Roach met them in the Railway Station. In the evening, about 60 or 70 of the brethren sat down to a feast for supper. Then there were Welsh songs and salutations by the Welsh, and in English by the Apostles. The meeting ended at 11:00 o'clock at night. After that, the Apostles went to see the coal works.

IN the account of the St. Louis Semiannual Conference, we read the names of several of the Elders who were in Wales earlier. William Henshaw (the founder of the Church in Wales), belongs to the High Council, and Robert Humphries is a Bishop. Henry Lewis was sent on a mission to Iowa to labor among his Welsh compatriots; bro. Roach was called to succeed him in the presidency of the Welsh Branch of Caseyville.

CONSIDERABLE effort has been made to establish settlements along the Plains. When the goal is achieved, the tribulations of Babylon will no doubt cause those who could have gone comfortably to Zion to rejoice at the opportunity to go barefoot, with their food on their backs.

RECEIPTS FOR BOOKS FROM OCTOBER 23 TO DECEMBER 3.—Thos. Stephens, Merthyr, £7 11s 6c; W. Jones, Carmarthen, £1 5s; G. Roberts, 8s; C. Harman, £4 8s 3c; Thos. Rees, £1; Wm. Ajax, £3 3s; John Jones, 16s; John Davies, £1 10s; John Treharne, £1 7s 4c.

CONTENTS.

	PG.
Sermon	385
News from the Valley	389
Arrival of the Handcarts	391
Editorial,—Appointments—New Pamphlets, &c.	393
Early polygamy among the Welsh	395
The P. E. Fund	396
The Saints' Eisteddfod	398

SWANSEA:
PRINTED AND PUBLISHED BY DANIEL DANIELS.

ZION'S TRUMPET,

OR

Star of the Saints.

No. 26.] DECEMBER 27, 1856. [Vol. IX.

SERMON,

BY PRESIDENT B. YOUNG, BOWERY, JUNE 22, 1856.

(Continued from page 389.)

No man can enter the celestial kingdom and be crowned with a celestial glory, until he gets his resurrected body; but Joseph and the faithful who have died have gained a victory over the power of the devil, which you and I have not yet gained. So long as we live in these tabernacles, so long we will be subject to the temptations and power of the devil; but when we lay them down, if we have been faithful, we have gained the victory so far; but even then we are not so far advanced at once as to be beyond the neighborhood of evil spirits.

The third part of the hosts of heaven, that were cast out, have not been taken away, at least not that I have found out, and the other two-thirds have got to come and take bodies, all of them who have not, and have the opportunity of preparing for a glorious resurrection and exaltation, before we get through with this world; and those who are faithful in the flesh to the requirements of the Gospel will gain this victory over the spirits that are not allowed to take bodies, which class comprises one-third of the hosts of heaven.

Those who have died without the Gospel are continually afflicted by those evil spirits, who say to them,—"Do not go to hear that man Joseph Smith preach, or David Patten, or any of their associates, for they are deceivers."

Spirits are just as familiar with spirits as bodies are with bodies, though spirits are composed of matter so refined as not to be tangible to this coarser organization. They walk, converse, and have their meetings; and the spirits of good men like Joseph and the Elders, who have left this Church on earth for a season to operate in another sphere, are rallying all their powers, and going from place to place preaching the Gospel, and Joseph is directing them, saying, Go ahead my brethren, and if they hedge up your way, walk up and command them to disperse. You have the Priesthood and can disperse them, but if any of them wish to hear the Gospel, preach to them.

Can they baptize them? No. What can they do? They can preach the Gospel, and when we have the privilege of building up Zion, the time will come for saviors to come up on Mount Zion. My brother Joseph spoke of this principle this forenoon. Some of those who are not in mortality will come along and say, "Here are a thousand names I wish you to attend to in this Temple, and when you have got though with them, I will give you another thousand," and the Elders of Israel and their wives will go forth to officiate for their forefathers, the men for the men, and the women for the women.

A man is ordained and receives his washings, anointings and endowments for the male portion of his and his wife's progenitors, and his wife for the female portion.

Then in the spirit world they will say,—Do you not see somebody at work for you? The Lord remembers you, and He has revealed to his servants on the earth what to do for you.

Is the spirit world here? It is not beyond the sun, but is on this earth that was organized for the people that have lived, and that do, and will live upon it. No other people can have it, and we can have no other kingdom until we are prepared to inhabit this eternally. In the spirit world those who have got the victory go on to prepare the way for those who live in the flesh, fulfilling the work of saviors on Mount Zion.

To accomplish this work there will have to be not only one temple but thousands of them, and thousands and tens of thousands of men and women will go into those temples and officiate for people who have lived as far back as the Lord shall reveal. If we are faithful enough to go back and build that great temple which Joseph has written about, and should the Lord acknowledge the labor of his servants, then watch, for you will see somebody whom you have seen before, and many of you will see him whom you have not seen before, but you will know him as soon as you see him.

This privilege we cannot enjoy now, because the power of Satan is such that we cannot perform the labor that is necessary to enable us to obtain it.

When we commence again on the walls of the temple to be built on this Block, the news will fly from Maine to California. Who will tell them? Those little devils that are around here, that are around this earth in the spirit world; there will be millions of them ready to communicate the news to devils in Missouri, Illinois, California, Mexico, and in all the world. And the question will be,—"What is the news? There is some devilish thing going on among the Mormons, and I know it. Those Mormons ought to be killed." They do not know what stirs them up to this feeling, it is those spirits that are continually near to them.

We all have got spirits to attend us; when the eyes of the servant of Elijah were opened he saw that those for them were more than those that were against them. There are two-thirds for us, and one-third against us; and there is not a son or daughter of Adam but what will be saved in some kingdom and receive a glory and an exaltation to a degree, except those who have had the privilege of the Gospel and rejected it and sinned against the Holy Ghost, they will become servants to devils.

How long will they exist? I do not know, neither do I care. Every one of this people, with the Saints that have lived before us, from the days of Adam until now, and those that may come after us, all say, 'build up the kingdom of God.' What for? To save the inhabitants of the earth, to get them all back into some kind of a kingdom where they can be administered to, and not have this organized matter return again to its native element, for we wish this work to be preserved.

You know that when you make a farm you dislike to see it overrun with weeds, and it would hurt your feelings to see your homes, barns and other property destroyed. True, you can make more, but how do you suppose the Lord feels, who is much more compassionate than we are, when he sees the devil gaining an advantage over his creatures to lead them away to destroy them? Do you not suppose that the bowels of his compassion yearn over this people, and that he is angry with the wicked? Do you not suppose that he often feels like saying, 'O, my children, why do you not hearken to what I tell you, and take hold of the principles of life, and cease pursuing a course that is calculated to destroy you? I have labored to bring forth this organization, and I do not wish to lose my labor, but I desire to have you hearken to the counsel I give to you and prepare yourselves to endure forever and come into my presence, and if you cannot do that and abide a celestial law, at least abide the law of a kingdom where I can send angels to you, and I will send you comfort and administer unto you, and will raise you up and make you glad and happy, and will fill you with joy and with peace.'

It is our business to live our religion, and it is all that we have to do. "But," says one, "I thought we had to raise grain." I have told you, many a time, that I would not give you anything for your faith, unless you add works. How are you going to work to build up the kingdom?

I now wish to leave the subject we have been considering, for I think I have talked enough about it for the present, and tell you how to prepare yourselves to build up the kingdom of God and save the honest in heart.

Here we are in the valleys of these mountains, and I say that there is not a people on the earth that would live here but the Latter-day Saints, and it seems almost more than they can do to stay here. Now if they would be as swift to hearken to counsel as they are to get rich, and as they are in pleasing their own dispositions, we should not see the hard times that we now see.

When we first came here we had not been two weeks on this square, before the Big Cottonwood canal, which we are now building, was just as visible to me as it ever will be when it is completed, and you will yet see boats on it. It has to be there, what for? To sustain this people. Do you think we want the water that is now wasted in those natural channels? Say, sisters, do you think we want any more water for irrigation? Yes, you do, for your peas are drying up, and you are not likely to have many cucumbers for pickling.

Has this people been as swift to hearken to counsel as to get rich? No, and many of you would rather pray the Lord to send rain, than to appropriate, by your labor, the waters that are continually flowing from these canyons. I tell you now, as I have before said, I do not have much faith to pray for rain; and if I had faith and power to bring rain upon the crops in these valleys, I would not do it. Why? Because it would throw many of you into lazy, slothful, idle habits, and every Gentile that came through here would covet your farms, and would say, "this is the finest country we ever saw, how rich you are, how your cattle thrive upon the hills, your grain grows almost without labor in cultivating the earth."

(*Continued on page* 406.)

ZION'S TRUMPET,

OR

Star of the Saints.

SATURDAY, DECEMBER 27, 1856.

EMIGRATION—For lack of space we are obliged to leave several emigration notices until our next issue. We shall give a few. From the handcart emigrants £3 per person is requested now—the rest is to be paid in the States. In addition to the £3 a prepayment of £1 toward the sea crossing is needed, the rest of which is to be paid in

Liverpool. It is anticipated that the cost of the sea crossing will not be any more than the usual. Names and payments will be received until the 1st of February—it will be too late after that. Those who have paid £5 for the purpose cannot be emigrated this time. Further details will be given.

SERMON.

(Continued from page 405.)

They would soon begin to desire your inheritances, those houses and this city, and it would be but a few years before we would have to leave or contend with them. As it is now, there is no people that would live here, except the Latter-day Saints. And they are decidedly the best people upon the earth, even though I sometimes chastise them, and what I say is true, for a few deserve chastising.

I do not believe that the city of Enoch made greater advancement, in the same period of time, than this people have done in the twenty-six years of their career, which is saying a great deal for them. Who else would live here? Nobody. Put Gentiles here and tell them that they had to be confined here, and they would consider themselves in a worse prison than a penitentiary.

Do some of the brethren murmur a little, and say if it were not for Mormonism, they would do thus and so? What of that? Is there any other people would do as well as you do? No, not another.

When I find fault with the people for not hearkening to counsel, it is because I want them to live so as speedily to obtain the reward of righteousness, and not have to wait so long for it.

This is a good people, though there are some in our midst who do not do right. Plant the Gentiles here, and you would soon see cutting throats and hear the sharp crack of the *rifle* at the water sects. There would be far more fighting for water than there is among the 'Mormons,' though some of them steal it now.

Many of the brethren feel as I do; if I had my crops growing and somebody should come along and steal my water, I should say, "You will raise grain, will you not? Well, go ahead, for we shall get it, if you raise it."

Here sits a man I can now look upon who says I am a greater despot than the Emperor of Russia. Maybe I am, for should I see the poor suffering, I could knock open flour barrels better than Alexander II, and give the contents to the poor with a better heart than he could.

Who in the wide world could live here more peaceably than we do? Nobody; and I thank God for hard times. Do you suppose that the Gentiles want this country? No, they say, it is a Godforsaken country, and I say hallelujah, for it is the very country I prefer, and country where nobody else will live but those who are willing to keep the commandments of God.

I wish to be tyrannical enough, if that is the proper term, to make you good men and good women. Go to with your might this year, and see if we cannot prepare for another. This is a great Saint-raising country; we have seen wheat grow here almost spontaneously, and there could not be a better Saint-raising country.

If a person is honest before God and has more than he needs for his own use, and does not covet it, he will make a distribution to those who have not, and there need not any person go without necessary food. I know that there are many here who have given out much flour, and they have by no means suffered on account of their liberality. There is a man sitting on the stand who says that his wife has scraped the bottom of the flour barrel, and on the next morning has gone to scrape again, to give out more to the poor, and found it half full. She asked him if he had put it there; he answered, no. Well, said she, I scraped it out last night.

The Lord wishes to try you; shall we say that we will hoard up the blessings of God, that we may be able to say that we have a large amount to ourselves? No, but divide them out, and do so with an honest heart, in all humility; and let those who receive blessings receive them with an honest heart, in all humility and thankfulness. Some who have, will withhold, and some of the poor are covetous and will grab a little here and there and lay it up, or waste it. If you continue in covetousness, your substance will shrink and waste away.

Let the poor, those who have to depend upon their brethren for bread, after they have done all they can to obtain it themselves, be thankful, and take no more than they require to use in a frugal manner. By taking such a course, no person would suffer. With some there is a fearfulness, a want of faith and confidence in God, and a stingy close-fistedness; this is the cause of many's being so pinched. As I have often done, I again invite those who are distrustful and fearful that God is going to forsake this people to leave, if they do not wish to be Saints and repose confidence in the God of the Saints. I wish such characters would leave; I shall be glad if they will leave. I would not have them stay; I would rather give them flour and help them to leave, because they are a curse to the Saints. And if the devil puts it into their hearts to leave, I know there will be a certain portion of those evil spirits go with them, and still we shall always have plenty more coming.

All I ask of you is to apply your hearts to the gospel of Jesus Christ and be Saints; I will not ask anything else on this earth of you only to live so as to know the mind and will of God when you receive it, and then abide in it. If you will do that, you will be prepared to do a great many things, and you will find that there is much good to be done.

We have not time to spend foolishly, for we have just as much on our hands as we can probably do, to keep pace with that portion of our brethren who have gone into the other room.

And when we have passed into the sphere where Joseph is, there is still another department, and then another, and another, and so on, to an eternal progression in exaltation and eternal lives. That is the exaltation I am looking for. May God bless you. Amen.

CONTENTS.

	PG.
Sermon	401
Editorial—Emigration	405

SWANSEA:
PRINTED AND PUBLISHED BY DANIEL DANIELS.

Index

A

Aaronic Priesthood, 262–63
Abel, 347
Aberafan, opening of chapel in, 184
Abimelech, 182–83
Abraham, 180–82, 193, 197–98, 225
adultery, 182–83, 193, 195–96, 200
agency, 359
Agricultural and Manufacturing Society, 391
agriculture
    in Salt Lake City, 188, 390–91
    of southern settlements, 17–18
alcohol, 76
Alexander the Great, 219–20
alphabet, 171
Anglesey, 341
animal magnetism, 388
Annual Address of President of United States, 45–46
apostasy, 161–62
apostate churches, 325–27
apostates, 345
Ashby, Benjamin
    called to Wales, 139
    missionary efforts of, 283
    speaks in conferences, 78, 144, 167, 169, 245–46
    in Welsh First Presidency, 83, 106–7

Atonement, 373
Australia, gathering of Saints from, 24–25

B

Babylon
    fall of, of latter days, 247–48
    fulfillment of prophecies about ancient, 203–5, 218–21, 246–47
    "Prayer Verses of the Troubled Saint in Babylon," 119–20
    "Tribulation of a Saint in Babylon," 317–19
baptism(s), 261–62, 309, 366
Baptists, 261–63, 309–11
Belus, temple of, 204
Benson, Ezra T., 54–55, 240, 274, 276, 288, 377
Bible, 167–68, 225–26, 262, 309–10
Big Cottonwood Canal, 20, 45, 297, 405
Blair, Seth M., 390
blessings, of Saints, 34–35
bodies, 401
Book of Mormon, the, 122–25, 262, 309–10
books
    debts for, 333
    for sale, 303
    transporting, 26

branches, Dewi Elfed Jones's visits to, 315–17
branch presidents, 102, 214–15
Brecon Conference, 171
British nation, preaching to whole, 329–34. *See also* England
British Presidency, notice of, 170–71
Brott, James, 64
Bunker, Edward, 252, 382, 383

C

Cain, 347
Calkin, Asa, 15, 274
calling of Saints, 55–57
Cannon, George Q., 24
Caravan, 47–48, 90
Carmarthen Conference, 189–90, 282
Caseyville, Illinois, 400
celestial glory, 401
chapel, opened in Aberafan, 184
chastisement, 70–73, 84–85, 92–93
chicken pox, 207
children, death of, on *Saunders Curling*, 206–7
churches, apostate, 325–27
Church leaders
    Franklin D. Richards on, 83–85
    satisfaction with, 66–67
Church of Jesus Christ of Latter-day Saints, The. *See also* gospel
    David John as witness of, 222–24
    differences between Baptist Church and, 261–63, 309–11
    growth of, 233
    operations of, 99–104
Church of Rome, 247
Clinton, J., 390
communication, as gift, 357
Conference Presidents
    appointments for 1857, 393–94
    award commemorative certificate to Dan Jones, 147–50
    change of, 40–43
    counselors to, 82–83

Conference Presidents (*continued*)
    Daniel Daniels's speech to, 94–95
    Dan Jones on, 78, 100–101, 103, 110–11
    obedience to, 214
conferences
    condition of, 281–83
    dates for, 320, 352
    Ezra T. Benson visits, 377
    Israel Evans visits, 344
Conferences of the North, 341–42, 344, 364–65
consecration, 266–67, 321–28, 337–39
constitution, of State of Deseret, 234–40, 257–61
Conway, Thomas
    "Prayer Verses of the Troubled Saint in Babylon," 119–20
    "The Law of Tithing, 295–96
    "Tribulation of a Saint in Babylon," 317–19
Cosbi, 193
covetousness, 164
cows, 252, 284, 382–83
Creation, 321–23
Cyrus, 218, 219

D

Dafydd ab Howell ab Iorwerth, 395–96
Daniels, Ann, 5–6
Daniels, Daniel
    Dewi Elfed Jones's letter of reconciliation to, 156–57
    on Dewi Elfed Jones's return to Church, 160
    and emigration, 128
    epistle of, to Saints in Wales, 361–64
    speaks at East Glamorgan Conference, 215
    speaks at West Glamorgan Conference, 168
    speech of, to Conference Presidents, 94–95
    in Welsh First Presidency, 106–7

Daniels, Daniel (*continued*)
    William Sims's letter of reconciliation to, 231
    as *Zion's Trumpet* editor, 107, 121–22
Daniels, Mary, 189, 283–85
David, 195
Davies, B., 282
Davies, David
    "Parable of the Disappointed Harvesters," 342–43
    speaks at West Glamorgan Conference, 166, 169
Davies, Emrys, 169, 184
Davies, Jenkin, 168
Davies, J. H., 282
Davies, John
    called as Conference President, 393–94
    "Happy Is the Mormon," 286–88
    "Stanzas on the Same Topic," 127
    "Triumph of the Saints over the World," 141–43
    "Verse to the Mormon," 328
    and West Glamorgan Conference, 167
Davies, Rachel, 269–71
Davis, George W., 252
Ddu, Gwilym, 62–63, 291–92
Ddu, Mary, 291–92
Ddu, N., 367–68
dead, redemption of, 402
death, 23–24, 369–72, 386–89
Dee, Dan Curling, 206
Dee, Thomas, 206
Deseret. *See* Utah
Deseret alphabet, 171
Dinah, 183
disappointed harvesters, parable of, 342–43, 366–67
discernment, through Holy Ghost, 65
"Divine Authority," 288
doors, closing, 311–12
dream, of Orson Hyde, 370
Dyfed, Dewi Ioan, 298–302

E

ears, door of, 311
earthquakes, 211
East Glamorgan Conference, 112, 143–44, 214–16
Eisteddfod, 350–52, 368, 398–99
Eldridge, Ira, 244
elections, in Utah, 258–59
Eli, 194
Elkanah, 194
Ellsworth, Edmund, 251, 252
Emerald Isle, 15
emigration. *See also* Perpetual Emigrating Fund Company
    and Australian Saints, 24–25
    bags and luggage for, 15–16, 59–60
    Brigham Young on, 241–44
    on *Caravan*, 47–48
    and changes to *Zion's Trumpet*, 137–38
    of conference presidents, 40–42
    Daniel Spencer's letter detailing, 251–53
    of Dan Jones, 78–79
    Dan Jones on, 110–11, 205–8, 305–9
    David Grant's letter detailing, 380–83
    departures, 14–15, 90, 128, 136–37, 138, 171
    D. F. Thomas's letter regarding, 186–87
    First Presidency on, 30–31
    Franklin D. Richards on, 151
    funds for, 88–90, 94–95, 278–79
    and gathering of poor, 49–55
    information regarding, 11–14, 15, 90, 112, 405–6
    instructions regarding, 58–60, 73–74, 297
    John Parry's letter detailing, 292–94
    and learning English, 3–4, 76, 152–53
    names of Welsh emigrants, 383–84
    news regarding, 108, 288, 339–41

emigration (*continued*)
    postponement and price increase for, 108–10
    preparations for, 153–55, 333
    "Railway to Zion," 255
    records concerning, 336
    reduction in, 91–92
    and relations with Indians, 146–47
    "Song of Longing," 334–35
    statistics on, 272
    and transporting books, 26
Endowment House, 20
endowments, 31
England. *See also* Great Britain, preaching to all of
    contentions between United States and, 45–46
    war with, 61, 63
English language, 1–5, 76, 85–86, 152–53
Enoch Train, 108
eternal life, 267
eternity, 370
Evans, Dafydd, 190
Evans, Hugh, 394
Evans, Israel
    as counselor to President Daniels, 83
    letter from, 344
    missionary efforts of, 202, 281–82, 283
    speaks at East Glamorgan Conference, 143, 144, 214–15
    speaks at Flintshire Conference, 298
    speaks at general conference in Wales, 77
    speaks at West Glamorgan Conference, 166–68
    speech of, to Welsh Saints, 138–41
    in First Presidency of Wales, 106–7
Evans, John, 166, 281–82
Evans, T., 143
evidence, faith and, 346–48
evil spirits, 371–72, 385–86, 387, 401–2
exaltation, 267, 385
eyes
    door of, 311–12
    gift of seeing with, 357

F

faith, 67–69, 162–63, 346–48
false faith, 347
false prophecies and prophets, 213–14, 216, 356–57
famine, 256, 285
"Farewell to Captain Jones!" (Harris), 125–26
Farnham, Augustus, 24
fast offerings, 378
faults, revealing, 70–73
feast, for returning missionaries, 155–56
"Feeling of a Young Saint" (John), 79–80
fig tree, parable of, 210
First Presidency. *See also* First Presidency of Wales, change of
    gives notice regarding emigration, 91–92
    thirteenth General Epistle of, 17–25, 28–32, 58–59
First Presidency of Wales, change of, 105–7
Flintshire Conference, 263–64, 297–98
Florence, Nebraska, 339–40
food shortage, 256, 285
fornication, 183, 193–94, 200
foundry, 20–21
France, Joseph, 252
freedom of religion, 231
futurity, 369–72

G

gathering. *See also* emigration
    of Israel, 132–33
    during Millennium, 132–33
"Gathering of the Saints" (Ddu), 62–63
general conference
    Brigham Young's sermon at, 55–57, 65–73, 92–94
    minutes of, 33–40, 43–45
general conference of Saints in Wales
    announcement regarding, 57–58
    Franklin D. Richards's address at, 81–88
    minutes of, 74–79
General Council, 248–49
General Epistle of Presidency, Thirteenth, 17–25, 28–32, 58–59

gifts of the Spirit, 309–10, 356–57
God
    building up kingdom of, 29, 404
    consecration to, 321–25, 337–39
    location of, 371
    repentance and law of, 374–75
    word of, 98–99, 185–86
gospel. *See also* Church of Jesus Christ of Latter-day Saints, The
    mystery of, 361
    restoration of, 185
government, of Utah, 237–40, 257–58
Grant, David, 252, 380–83
Grant, Jedediah M.
    in general conference minutes, 44
    and Thirteenth General Epistle of Presidency, 17–25, 28–32, 58–59
grasshoppers, 26, 285
Great Britain, preaching to all of, 329–34. *See also* England
Griffiths, Joseph, 294–95, 394

H

handcarts, 251, 307, 339–40, 382–83, 392
"Hand of Providence, The" (Dark Nathan), 221–22
Hannah, 194
"Happy Is the Mormon" (Davies), 286–88
Harris, Henry / Harries, Henry, 285–86, 391–92
Harris, Thomas
    Daniel Daniels's letter to, 135–36
    on Dewi Elfed Jones' return to Church, 159
    "Farewell to Captain Jones!," 125–26
    "An Irishman and a Cardi," 272
    "The Millennium," 129–35, 161–65, 209–14
    "Railway to Zion," 255
    reports on West Glamorgan Conference, 202–3
    "The 'Spaulding Story' or the Worst Bugbear to Prevent a Host from Becoming Saints," 122–25
    speaks at conferences, 144, 165, 166, 167, 169

harvesters, parable of disappointed, 342–43, 366–67
healings, 67–69, 262
heart
    applying, to wisdom, 356
    door of, 312
Henshaw, William, 400
Hero, 378–80
Herodotus, 219
High Council, 92–93
Holy Ghost, 56–57, 65
Hophni, 194
Horizon, 153–54, 288
"How to Warn the Whole British Nation in One Year" (Pratt), 329–34
Hughes, D. A., 334–35
Humphries, Robert, 400
Hyde, Orson, 24, 370–72
"Hymn of Tribulation" (Jones), 157–59, 173–76

I

inactive members, chastisement of, 84–85
Indians
    relations with, 18–20, 27, 146–47, 187, 245, 296
    war with, 61, 172–73
"Invitation to Become Saints" (Davies), 269–71
Iowa City, Iowa, 58
"Irishman and a Cardi, An" (Harris), 272
Israel, gathering of, 132–33

J

Jacob, 226–27, 266
James, Hugh, 190
Jeremy, Thomas, 289–91
Jesus Christ
    Atonement of, 373
    Brigham Young on, 359–61
    and gathering of poor, 49–50
    and laws concerning marriage and adultery, 196, 197
    miracles performed by, 67–69
    to reign during Millennium, 131–32
    Second Coming of, 133–34, 209
    tithing and, 226

Jewry, John, 203
Job, Dafydd, 6
Job, Thomas, 5–6
John, Dafydd, 202
John, David
    "Another Witness of Mormonism," 222–24
    called as Conference President, 394
    "Feeling of a Young Saint," 79–80
    missionary efforts of, 281
    reports on Pembrokeshire Conference, 366
John J. Boyd, 14–15
Johnson, Luke, 390
Jones, Aneurin L., 271–72
Jones, Dan
    announces change in Welsh First Presidency, 105–7
    Church service of, 24
    commemorative certificate awarded to, 147–50, 156
    and emigration, 78–79, 128
    "Farewell to Captain Jones!," 125–26
    Franklin D. Richards on, 82
    Israel Evans on, 140
    letter from, 205–8, 305–9
    persecution suffered by, 6
    reconciliation with Dewi Elfed Jones, 156–57
    speaks at general conference in Wales, 75–78
    "Stanzas on the Same Topic," 127
    summary of teaching in Merthyr Tydfil General Council, 97–105, 110–11
Jones, Dewi Elfed
    on *Hero* editors, 378–80
    "Hymn of Tribulation," 173–76
    letter from, 315–17
    "Longing for Zion," 319–20
    repentance and return of, 156–60
    "Truth," 253–54
Jones, Edward, 117
Jones, Isaac, 190

Jones, John
    called to Conferences of the North, 240, 344
    letters from, 117–19, 264–65
    missionary efforts of, 295
    reports on Northern Conferences, 341–42, 364–65
    and West Glamorgan Conference, 165, 169
Jones, Nathaniel V., 38–39
Jones, Noah, 192, 282
Jones, Rees, 165
Jones, T., 245, 281–82
Jones, William, 169
Jones, W. R., 215
Josephus, 360
jubilee, 130
Judah, gathering of, 132
judgment, 57

K

Kansas, 127–28
Kay, John, 250, 282
killing, law against, 375–77
Kimball, Heber C.
    in general conference minutes, 45
    sees evil spirits, 371–72
    and Thirteenth General Epistle of Presidency, 17–25, 28–32
kingdom of God, building up, 29, 404

L

language, 1–5, 76, 85–86, 152
Las Vegas, 27
Lavender, James, 15
law of God, repentance and, 374–75
law of Moses, 180–81, 183, 193, 226
"Law of Tithing, The" (Conway), 295–96
laws, Brigham Young on, 114–15
learning, without coming to knowledge of truth, 164
Lewis, Henry, 400
Lewis, William, 136, 166, 167
Lewis, W. M., 400

life after death, 369–72, 386–89
lips, door of, 312
liquor, 76
Little, James A., 274, 276
little things, 151–52
Llanelli Conference, 202, 282
Llywelyn, John, 215
"Longing for Zion" (Jones), 319–20
"Longing for Zion" (Proser), 190–92
Luddington, Elam, 40
Lyman, Amasa, 289–90

M

Madawg ab Owen Gwynedd, 95–96
Maddocians, 95–96
magnetism, 388
"Man Surprised!," 111–12
marriage, First Presidency on, 31
Marriage and Morals in Utah, 177–83, 193–201, 216–18, 249–50, 269, 277, 304
Martill, T. C., 391–93
Martin, J. B., 76, 215
McArthur, D. D., 251, 252
meekness, 12
Melchizedek Priesthood, 262–63
Merionethshire Conference, 245–46
Merrill, Philemon. C., 252, 390
Merthyr Tydfil general conference
    Dan Jones's teaching in, 97–105, 110–11
    Franklin D. Richards's teaching in, 150–53
Miles, E. D., 202, 281
militia, of Utah, 259–60
Millennium, 129–35, 161–65, 209–14
Miller, William, 393
miracles, 67–68, 262
missionaries and missionary work
    among Indians, 19–20
    call for, 169–70
    and call for unity, 28–29
    calling of, 44–45, 168
    feast for returning, 155–56
    First Presidency's report on, 24–25
    hardships of, 353–54
missionaries and missionary work (*continued*)
    Israel Evans called to, 138–39
    Joseph Griffith's report on, 294–95
    language and, 4
    Orson Pratt on, 279–80
    in Pembrokeshire, 202
    prayer for, 36–37
    before Second Coming, 209–12
    spirits and, 402
    through distribution of pamphlets, 329–34, 362–64
    volunteers for, 192
Mississippi, 127
Mitchell, James C., 341
Monmouthshire Conference, 171–72
morals. *See Marriage and Morals in Utah*
Morgans, Evan, 189–90, 282
Morgans, J., 282
mortality, 358
Mosaic law, 180, 181, 183, 193, 226
Moses, 194
mules, 252
murder, 375–77

N

New Orleans, 243
New Year, 9–11
Northern Conferences, 341–42, 344, 364–65

O

obedience, 185–86, 214
order, 99
oxen, 252, 284, 382

P

Pamphlet Fund, 331, 332
pamphlets
    circulating, 280–81
    Marriage and Morals in Utah, 216–18, 249–50, 269, 277, 304
    and missionary work, 329–34, 362–64
    in Northern Conferences, 365

printing and distribution of, 346
pamphlets (*continued*)
 True Faith, 281, 346–48, 363–64, 394–95
 True Repentance, 281, 291, 394
parables(s)
 of disappointed harvesters, 342–43
 of rich man, 267
Parry, John, 252, 292–94
"Passenger Act," 60
passions, bridling, 65–66
"Patriotism, Freedom, and Truth" (Reynolds), 348–49
peace, 61–62
Pembrokeshire Conference, 202, 281, 366
Pendwll pit, accident at, 336
Peninnah, 194
Penny Fund, 377
"Perpetual Emigrating Fund, The" (Prosser), 398
Perpetual Emigrating Fund Company
 Brigham Young on, 241–43
 Franklin D. Richards on, 76–77
 funds for, 13–14, 88–90, 94–95, 107, 208, 278
 instructions regarding, 58–59
 purpose of, 12
 repayments and contributions to, 22–23
 "The Perpetual Emigrating Fund," 398
persecution
 of Saints, 354, 375–76
 in Wales, 6, 316–17
Phillips, James J., 378
Phinehas, 193–94
plural marriage, 181, 193–200, 216–18, 395–96
poor
 caring for, 14, 18–19, 37, 408
 and emigration funds, 278–79
 gathering of, 49–55
 tithing and, 228, 313–14

Porter, N. V., 77
Pratt, Orson, 39, 240, 273–80, 329–34
Pratt, Parley P.
 in general conference minutes, 39
 Marriage and Morals in Utah, 177–83, 193–201, 249–50, 269, 304
 reports on mission, 289
"Prayer Verses of the Troubled Saint in Babylon" (Conway), 119–20
premortal existence, 372, 385
Price, John, 143
Price, T., 379–80
pride, 163–64
priesthood
 in Baptist versus LDS churches, 262–63, 310–11
 Dan Jones on, 75, 98
 increasing power of, 55
 "The Priesthood," 298–302
 tithing and, 266
"Priesthood, The" (Dyfed), 298–302
primitive Saints, 162–63
private enterprise, 328
progression, spiritual, 357–58
prophets, 213, 376. *See also* false prophecies and prophets
Proser, Joseph, 190–92
Prosser, J. P., 398
Public Machine Shop, 21
Pugh, D., 143, 215

R

"Railway to Zion" (Harris), 255
redemption of the dead, 402
Rees, Thomas, 215, 263–64, 297–98, 394
Reese, Enoch, 390
Reformation, 326–27
religious freedom, 231
repentance
 of Dewi Elfed Jones, 156–60
 of John Jones, 117–18
 treatise on true, 373–77
 of William Sims, 231
Restoration, 185

resurrection, 130, 134–35
revelation
  Brigham Young on, 56–57
  continuing, 185–86
Reynolds, John, 143, 348–49
Richards, Evan A., 215
Richards, Franklin D.
  Brigham Young's letter to, 241–45
  Church service of, 24
  on emigration, 58–60, 91–92
  Orson Pratt on, 276–77
  teachings in Merthyr Tydfil general conference, 150–53
  and general conference in Wales, 76–77, 81–88
Richards, John, 7–9
Richards, William, 168
rich man, parable of, 267
rights, in State of Deseret, 235–36
Roach, Walter, 400
Roberts, John, 366–67
Rome, 199–200
Russia, 61, 63

S

sabbath, 129–30
sacrifice, 13, 267–68
Salt Lake City. *See also* Utah
  developments in, 20, 290
  letters from, 5–6, 186–89, 289–92, 391–93
  news from, 296–97, 389–91
Salt Lake Temple, 20, 63
Samuel, 194–95
San Bernardino, California, 27
Sanpete, Utah, 27
Sarah, 182
Satan
  to be bound during Millennium, 130
  being led astray by, 56
  as first dissenter, 345
  power of, 389
  resisting, 65–66
  and war in heaven, 372, 385

satisfaction, 66–67
Saunders Curling, 108–10, 136–37, 205–7, 251–52
science, 327–28
Scofield, Joseph S., 15
scriptures, 98–99
sealings, 31
Second Coming, 133–34, 209–12
secularism, 327–28
seeing, gift of, 357
sexual intercourse, 181–83, 193–99
Shechem, 183
Shoshones, 146
Sims, William, 118–19, 231
sin, repentance and, 373–77
slavery, 127–28
small things, 102
Smith, George A., 24, 244, 400
Smith, Joseph, 375–76, 386–89
Smoot, Abraham O., 244
Snow, Erastus, 252–53, 400
Snow, Lorenzo, 54–55
"Song of Longing" (Hughes), 334–35
southern settlements, 17–18
"Spaulding Story," 122–25
Spencer, Daniel
  Franklin D. Richards addresses, 87–88
  gives notice regarding emigration, 58–60, 91–92
  letter from, 251–53
  likeness of, 208
  speaks at general conference in Wales, 75–76, 77
Spencer, Orson, 24
spirits
  evil, 371–72, 385–87, 401–2
  following death, 371–72, 386–87
spiritual gifts, 309–10, 356–57
spiritual progression, 357–58
spirit world, 371–72, 386–87, 402–3
"Stanzas on the Same Topic" (Davies), 127
statistical report(s), 47

T

Taylor, James, 393
Taylor, John, 24, 244
Temple Offering, 230
temple(s). *See also* Salt Lake Temple
    and redemption of dead, 402
    tithing and, 228–29
temporal affairs, as spiritual affairs, 99
temptations, fighting, 65–66
territorial senate of Utah, Brigham Young's speech to, 113–16, 145–47
Thomas, D. F., 186–89
Thomas, Thomas, 399
Thornton, 137, 171, 251, 288
time, 370
tithing, 225–30, 232–33, 265–68
    practice of, 188, 344, 361–62
    reception of law of, 316
    teachings on, 312–15
    "The Law of Tithing," 295–96
tongues, gift of, 356
"To Zion" (Jones), 271–72
tracts. *See* pamphlets
transgression, 345–46
translation, imperfection of, 2–3
trials
    Brigham Young on, 353–55, 358–59, 407
    of southern settlements, 17–18
"Tribulation of a Saint in Babylon" (Conway), 317–19
"Triumph of the Saints over the World" (Davies), 141–43
Troubadour, 136, 138
True Faith, The, 281, 346–48, 363–64, 394–95
True Repentance, 281, 394
"Truth" (Jones), 253–54
truth, learning without coming to knowledge of, 164
Tuckfield, Joseph W., 283

U

United States
    news from, 45–46, 205–8
    slavery in, 127–28
    Utah's admission into, 115, 244
    war with, 61
unity
    First Presidency calls for, 28–29
    language and, 1–2
    prayer for, 37
Utah. *See also* Salt Lake City
    Brigham Young's speech to territorial senate of, 113–16, 145–47
    conditions in, 21–22, 187–89, 233–34
    constitution of, 234–40, 257–61
    contribution of property in, to PEF, 278
    developments in, 20–21, 290
    food shortage in, 256
    "Longing for Zion" (Jones), 319–20
    "Longing for Zion" (Proser), 190–92
    Marriage and Morals in Utah, 177–83, 193–201, 216–18, 249–50, 269
    news from, 26–28, 284–85
    public works in, 244–45
    "Railway to Zion," 255
    Rice Williams's letter from, 116–17
    settlement of, 404–5, 406–7
    "Song of Longing," 334–35
    statehood of, 115, 244
    stewardships in, 99
    "To Zion," 271–72
    trials in, 354–55

V

Van Cott, John, 24, 252
"Verse" (D. W.), 136
"Verse to the Mormon" (Davies), 328
vision, of Franklin D. Richards, 83–84
"Voice of the Weak" (Ddu), 367–68

W

war in heaven, 372, 385
war(s), 61–62, 210–11
Western Standard, 96
West Glamorgan Conference
 news from, 202–3
 payments toward debt of, 16, 32, 64
 summary of, 165–69
Wheelock, C. H., 58–60, 91–92
wickedness, 71–73
Williams, Abednego, 143, 144, 169, 214, 215
Williams, Rice, 116–17
Williams, Thomas, 282
Williams, William F., 203–5, 218–21, 246–48
wisdom, applying heart to, 356
Woodruff, Wilford, 389–91
word of God, 98–99, 185–86
"Word of Wisdom" (Richards), 7–9

X

Xenophon, 219
Xerxes, 219

Y

Young, Brigham
 bowery sermon of, 353–61, 369–72, 385–89, 400–408
 calls Orson Pratt to European Publishing and Emigration Office, 273–74
 D. F. Thomas on, 188
 Franklin D. Richards's vision of, 83–84
 and gathering of poor, 50
 in general conference minutes, 40, 44, 45
 general conference prayer of, 33–38
 general conference sermon of, 55–57, 65–73, 92–94
Young, Brigham (*continued*)
 letter from, 241–45
 speech to territorial senate of Utah, 113–16, 145–47
 and Thirteenth General Epistle of Presidency, 17–25, 28–32
Young, J. A., 76, 78
Young, Joseph, 244

Z

Zacharias, 376
Zimri, 193
Zion's Trumpet
 change in editorship of, 107, 121–22
 circulation of, 25–26, 137
 emigration and changes to, 137–38

Zion's Trumpet
Volume 10
1857

UDGORN SEION,

NEU

SEREN Y SAINT;

Yn udganu dadseiniad o eurchiadau Prophwydi ac Apostolion Eglwys Iesu Grist o Saint y Dyddiau Diweddaf—Cadfridogion Teyrnas y Dyddiau Diweddaf—goleuni arweiniol y Saint.

CYFROL X.

Edrych yr oeddit hyd oni thorwyd allan gareg, nid trwy waith dwylaw, a hi a darawodd y ddelw ar ei THRAED o haiarn a phridd, ac a'u maluriodd hwynt.—Daniel ii, 34.

Eithr Saint y Goruchaf a dderbyniant y freniniaeth, ac a feddianant y freniniaeth hyd byth, a hyd byth bythoedd.—Dan. vii, 18.

ABERTAWY;

ARGRAFFWYD A CHYHOEDDWYD GAN DANIEL DANIELS.

ZION'S TRUMPET

OR

STAR OF THE SAINTS;

Sounding the echo of the bidding of the Prophets and Apostles of the Church of Jesus Christ of Latter-day Saints—the Generals of the Latter-day Kingdom—the guiding light of the Saints.

VOLUME X.

Thou sawest till that a stone was cut out without hands, which smote the image upon his FEET that were of iron and clay, and brake them to pieces.—Daniel ii, 34.

But the Saints of the Most High shall take the kingdom, and possess the kingdom forever, even forever and ever.—Dan. vii, 18.

SWANSEA;

PRINTED AND PUBLISHED BY DANIEL DANIELS.

1857.

FOREWORD.

Upon presenting the tenth volume of our small, brightly shining Star into the hands of our readers, we address them on the growth of the light of 'Mormonism' through it, from the first day it appeared until today.

Certainly everyone who has become accustomed to the sounds of *Zion's Trumpet* will acknowledge that they have been true and consistent, with not a single one in vain. Its reliable warning shouts are so clearly in conflict with the multitude of dissonant and inconsistent voices of the Babylonians, who one day say one thing, and the next the total opposite.

The thoughts, opinions, arguments, and contrary assertions of the preachers, editors, and politicians are as unstable as the sand of the sea, and their ways just as fickle. They do not see the future, and they do not agree about the present, while the people perish for want of vision. Let the Saints rejoice, then, that they have a Prophet and Seer, whose voice resounds to the Saints in Wales through their Trumpet.

We call the attention of the Saints back to the time when the 'Prophet of the Jubilee' began to declare the message of Heaven in Wales, and to follow the story along through all the volumes of the Trumpet, and we ask, Has their prediction of the growth of the kingdom of God and His judgments fallen to the ground? Is there any sign that the funeral sermons of Mormonism that were preached the entire time by the revered ministers and priests of the sects will be proved right?

Quick and remarkable has been the increase of Mormonism, or the Latter-day Kingdom of God, and the fall of oppression. The faithful Saints can hardly be ready to accept the sudden changes! But what about the idlers in and the apostates from this church? Of all the wretched ones, these will be the most wretched; for the testimony they have will gnaw like a worm in their hearts, while the judgments of God will be to their shame upon them, and the door of deliverance will be shut!

During the five years of our mission in Wales we have perceived examples of the faithfulness and devotion of the Welsh Saints with the work of our God that will never be deleted from our memory, which have filled our breast with love for them, a love we shall yet try to prove, though we will be far away, in any endeavor that love and desire can invent.

We received the editorship of the Trumpet (January, 1, 1856) from experienced and approved hands: we deliver it now to such hands—to those of our worthy successor, Elder Benjamin Evans. As to us, we thank our assistants, our correspondents, and our kind and willing subscribers, trusting that they will be sympathetic with us in our weakness and lack of skill.

That the privilege of the Saints may be to finish their labor in Babylon, and follow us soon to Zion, is the most earnest and final prayer of the

EDITOR.

CONTENTS.

A Looking Glass.	113
A Prophet in Israel	386
Address of Ezra T. Benson	361
" Henry Harries	22
" Israel Evans	68
American News	47, 54, 188, 273, 288, 327, 388
Announcements, &c.	144
Apostates, why they fly from Utah	293
Chastity in the Church of England	317
Death of Jedediah M. Grant	104
Debts	32, 160, 256, 352
Emigration	278
EDITORIAL:—	
Appointments	408
Arrivals	13, 42
Business	25
Contributions	393
Debts	25
Departures	80, 169, 360
Distributing pamphlets	40, 331
Earthquakes	203
Emigration	10, 32, 347
Error	348
Famine	203
Farewell Address	344
Farewell	42
Financial	377
From the Plains	56
Instructions	121
Introductory	345
Journey	313
Judgments of God.	246

Missionary	286
Mormon, the	331
News from Utah	42, 27, 80, 200, 266, 320, 332, 379
Notice	348
Pamphlet Covers	10
Pamphlets	9
Reformation	43
Signs of the Times	348
Sound of the Trumpet	330
The Perpetual Emigrating Fund	284
The World and the Press	286
Tithing	25, 281
To the Presidents of Conferences	251
Total News	361
Troops to Utah	264, 361
Visitors	42
Fourteenth General Epistle	132
Home Church Accounts	145, 168, 174, 175, 195, 206, 223, 301, 305
Instructive Chapter for the Censors of Utah	107
Kingdom of God	296
Light-mindedness	159
Living for Sale	317

LETTERS from—

Brigham Young	49, 193, 273
Captain Dan Jones.	17, 142
David John	174
Dewi Elfed Jones	129
From the United States	102
From the Valley	72, 190, 209
Henry Harris	161
Israel Evans	172
John E. Jones	175
W. Woodruff	274
Miscellaneous, &c.	16, 48, 64, 112, 336, 368, 384
Parley P. Pratt, his murder	213
Paying Tithing	33
Peace, How to Keep it	103
Pledges of Contributions	393, 400
Preaching to the World	343
Prophetic Warning to the Inhabitants of Great Britain	341

vii

Questions for Ministers . . .	262
Reasons for Emigrating	350
Reformation	72, 81
Repentance among the Saints . . .	156
Review of an Anti-Mormon Treatise . .	308
Reynolds Newspaper, Sectarianism, and Mormonism .	315
Sabbath School of Utah . . .	272
Settlement of the Saints in Nebraska . .	289
Signs of the Times	369
Slander of the Daily Telegraph . . .	164
Slavery Prospects in the United States of America .	276
Spirit of the Times	385
Statistical Report	31

SONGS, VERSES, &c.—

Death of David John Griffiths . .	224
Departure of the Saints . . .	111
Invitation of a Saint to his Relations . .	46
Martyrdom of Parley P. Pratt. . .	239
My Dream	76
Orphans' Lamentation, the . .	221
Success of the Kingdom of Christ . .	318
Summer, the	268
To Drummond and his Company . .	189
To Nathan Ddu of Llywel . . .	267
Teaching of Apostle Ezra T. Benson . .	1, 45
" Heber C. Kimball . . .	241, 383
" Brigham Young . . .	321, 337
" Orson Hyde . . .	356, 364
Temple Block	254
The Latter-day Work	65
The Measure of the Stature of the Fullness of Christ .	19, 74
War and the Mormons	225

ZION'S TRUMPET,

OR

Star of the Saints.

No. 1.]　　　　　JANUARY 10, 1857.　　　　　[Vol. X.

SUMMARY OF THE TEACHING OF PRESIDENT EZRA T. BENSON, IN THE SAINTS' HALL, SWANSEA, NOVEMBER 11, 1856.

[Which was recorded by William Lewis.]

WITH your kind attention, brothers and sisters, I shall make a few observations, and I know not but what I shall take a topic to begin with, which will be words of wisdom to the Saints, and to all others who wish to listen.

I think it will open a broad field before me. Saints, look here, and give me your attention while I speak. If you had sought for as long as I have sought to preach, you would also wish to have attention. I do not expect, of course, that I shall be able to command that much of the attention of others that may be present. Well, in the revelations of Jesus Christ, order is the first law of heaven, and without order, it is impossible to edify this congregation.

We have come here for the purpose of worshiping God: I have come to speak to you in the name of the Lord, and not in my own name, or by my own power, or to speak to you my own words of wisdom, but those about which I have experienced their truth and their necessity, and those which the Lord wishes to reveal to his people—it is about those that I wish to speak tonight.

[PRICE 1½c.

I feel thankful for being greatly blessed and privileged to be able to stand before you this afternoon. I have traveled about eight thousand miles [meaning on his present mission] to preach to this people, and I have had a prayerful heart and have been praying all along the way. Before leaving, I consecrated all that I have to the Lord. I felt that I was but a steward over it. It was not I who produced or created it; rather it was a blessing which God placed in my hands. I did not do this according to the sectarian manner—I presented it to the hands of the servants of God, for He himself was not personally there.

Our mission is to tell this generation that we are dealing with the work of the Lord in the latter days. This is the message which the angel, whom John saw, was to bring in the latter days. When John was in the visions of the Almighty on the Isle of Patmos, he saw that an angel was to fly in the midst of heaven, having the everlasting gospel, to preach unto them that dwell on the earth. He was to cry with a loud voice for the people to fear God—to worship Him, not to worship gold or silver, goods or chattels, or anything of the kind, but to worship Him who made the heaven, the earth, the seas, and the springs of water, and all that exists. We know that it is God who brought forth all things that are.

There is nothing that we eat, drink, enjoy, or possess, that was not made and given to us by the Lord. Should we not, therefore, obey and worship Him? Should we not receive his Prophet when he sends him? Is this being done? No. Why? Because, as the prophet says, darkness shall cover the earth, and gross darkness shall cover the minds of the people. Therefore, a curse hath devoured the earth, and they that dwell therein are desolate; therefore the inhabitants of the earth are burned, and few men left. Isaiah was a great Prophet. Jesus referred to him often, and Ezekiel, and all the other old prophets, who supported his sayings. When the Jews spoke with him, he understood their thoughts and directed them to the scriptures and the prophets, encouraging them to search them, for they testify of Him, and if they believed them, they would believe in him also. He was certain of that, yet the people at that time behaved as they do now, refusing and mistreating the servants of God, those who have come to benefit them and to save them.

I have come on a mission to preach the gospel to the children of men, and to benefit them. I began with a prayerful heart, and I have continued thus during my entire journey, until tonight. I have always tried to preach the mind and the will of the Lord to his Saints, through his Spirit. What is his Spirit? Who has it, and who is without it? Jesus says, Suffer the little children to come unto me, and forbid them not, for of such is the Kingdom of Heaven. Do they destroy or harm them? Does a man do so, when guided by the Holy Ghost? He does not; he will be humble, harmless, and childlike: he will turn away from every evil, and he will feel willing to set down his life and his all to seek the Kingdom of God and his righteousness, after which all these things will be added unto him.

Well, is not the Gospel of Jesus Christ plain and simple? Has not the Lord spoken to the people in these latter days? Cannot every man and woman who know how to gather food to sustain life and can find their way in the streets, understand when God speaks? Yet, they do not perceive the gospel. How can this be? Paul says, if his gospel is hid, it is hid to them that are lost; in whom the god of this world hath blinded the minds of them which believe not, lest the light of the glorious gospel of Christ should shine unto them. And why has the god of this world blinded them? Because it is the things of the god of this world they seek first before they seek the Kingdom of God and his righteousness.

Well, someone says, do you not want the things of this world? Yes, but we seek first the gospel—the Kingdom of God and his righteousness, and then we expect to have all things added unto us. Although we do not receive so much of the luxuries and enjoyment by so doing, yet, we shall do without them until we first receive the Kingdom of God and His righteousness.

You profess that you have received the gospel—that you have been generously blessed, and that you are subjects of the Kingdom of God. I ask, do you live in such a way as not to violate the rights of any of your brothers and sisters, or those of anyone else? If you live thus, I can testify to you that it will not be long before all these things shall be added unto you to once again supply all your needs.

You see that I have not come to preach any strange gospel to you, or to give any teaching other than that which these my brethren give to you. For what reason would I change my religion? Can you obtain enough gold in old England, or in the whole world, to give to me for my religion? No, you could not. For all of that I would not change the least bit of what I have received in my experience from the time I embraced the gospel. If I lost the gospel, I lose my salvation. And what if I were to lose my salvation? I will lose all my gold and my silver as well. But if I live my religion, I know that all things will be added unto me. I trust implicitly in the words of Jesus and the Apostles, and I shall take my chance with what they have. My lot is cast with these people, and my fate is bound with theirs. I am in the hands of my brethren; they can send me anywhere, or do whatever they wish with me.

I enjoy more fulfillment in this gospel than in any other. I enjoy more fulfillment speaking with you this afternoon, than if I were feasting this evening on all the luxuries this town could offer, or receiving all the honor it could bestow upon me. If that were to come to pass, it would end up like a bubble on the wave; but after presenting to the people the word of God in the power of his Spirit, I shall sleep comfortably with a conscience as pure as the driven snow, having lovely dreams and visions from the Almighty, and being happy and safe. Then, if I am called beyond the veil, I shall have work to do in the spirit world. What if all of this generation were to do the same? How blessed they would be.

I have not come here to mock or to pull down, to confuse or to darken the minds of the people, rather I bring the light and the blessings of the Gospel. If my words are consistent with the word of God, and with your reasoning, and if the Spirit jointly testifies of the truth to you that they are true—you will receive them, and let the rest of the world go its own way. If we do not claim our Savior now, He will not claim us before his Father. What are relatives,—wives or children, fathers or mothers, in comparison with the gospel of Jesus Christ? When I first embraced it, my friends left me, and I left them as well, and they did not see me for another ten years, at which time they were glad to see me, although they had at first called me a foolhardy man for going to the west with the people, about which they said would perish. I was living in Massachusetts before I went to the West; it was a very long journey at that time. I was willing to go to the ends of the earth if required, and I prayed for others to be so disposed, but not in public. I have always been prayerful from my youth; I call upon my God humbly every day—that is the way to receive revelations and peace—that is what Daniel did, until he was able to interpret dreams. His wisdom was beyond that of the king, and the wise men of Babylon. He received dreams, visions, revelations, and wisdom from the God of Heaven through his diligence and his humility—through fasting, prayer, and living his religion. Do you not think he kept the Word of Wisdom? I think he did, and, if he had them, I think he threw away his pipe and his tobacco, did away with his box of snuff, and broke his bottle of whiskey.

Do you suppose that the people in these countries are going to live for the coming ten years as they do now? I do not think they will. The spirit that is in me prompts me to warn the Latter-day Saints—to shout with loud voice and encourage them to live their religion; to serve their God completely, and with an undivided heart, and declare to those who do not keep these words of wisdom that they will certainly apostatize. What is wisdom? To understand and act appropriately. If we do not do so we will of necessity go backwards and apostatize, and it is likely that we will turn and oppose this work as some do now. [There was an apostate speaking against "Mormonism" in the town at the time.] But, will such succeed in overrunning this kingdom? We know they cannot. We know that God has called and ordained a Prophet, and has given him the keys and power of his kingdom on the earth, and that the Prophet has ordained others, and those still others, &c., until we ourselves have received the power and the authority. We know that whatever the servants of God seal on earth is sealed in heaven, and that whatever is bound or absolved on earth is bound or absolved in heaven. The God of the hosts of heaven is with this work—it is He who owns it, and not we. It is useless, then, for a man to raise his feeble arm against the Almighty. I tell you that he is digging in a ditch where the potatoes are few, and he will soon be digging where there are none. He will dwindle away, and he will sink into the earth, and he will lose his influence, even with his own friends. Let them slander, let them print, let them speak, and let them do whatever they wish until they go to hell; they will be no better, for God is with this people, and He will continue to be also, so long as they do right, and nothing that is brought against them will succeed. I know that, and I would not be a Mormon unless I knew that Mormonism is true.

I must join together with you tonight, and say a word to our friends. I have spoken, particularly to the Saints, things that will humble you if you do them.

I am not asking anything from you that the early Apostles did not ask. I ask you to repent of your sins, to be baptized for the forgiveness of them, and to come into the kingdom of God with pure hearts to serve Him. I testify that the keys, blessings, and the power of the kingdom has been given to the children of men—to this people, so that whatever they bind or absolve on the earth, will be done in a like manner in heaven. I honor and fulfill all the ordinances of the gospel of Jesus Christ. I ask all men and women to believe their own Bibles, those which they have had in their homes for so many years, and if they believe them, they will become Mormons, and if they do not become Mormons, they must deny their Bibles. I declare, if you believe your Bibles—believe in the Son of God, repent of your sins, and receive your baptism, receive the gift of the Holy ghost, which will open your understanding, so that you may see and perceive and know for your selves that Mormonism is true, if you come truly and sincerely; otherwise, the administration of the ordinances will be no more beneficial to you than the ashes of a blade of grass.

You say that we, the Latter-day Saints, are overly zealous. Yes, we are very zealous. An old proverb says, "Be sure that you are right, and then go forward with all your might." But the big challenge that people have, once they have joined, is to continue in that manner.

Brothers and sisters, how can I continue properly? I shall give the key word to you. You are aware that two opposing powers are contending for you, and incline you toward some thoughts and acts. If the feeling that is inspired within you is full of love toward any being, it is surely a divine attribute—every inclination toward benefiting a being or doing any good deed is a divine attribute. When we feel thus, and understand that which is good, why do we not go straightaway and do it? The good Spirit persuades you as quickly or even more quickly than you could act. If we knew that, not one bit of the opposing spirit would reside in us—we would sin no more or be moved to sin, while completely under the influence of the Spirit of God, any more than the angels or God himself would do, and we would be as perfect as they in our sphere. Jesus says to his disciples, "Be ye, therefore, perfect, even as your Father which is in heaven is perfect." He did not ask as much from them as from the angels, but according to their understanding, their experience, and their ability—to be perfect in their sphere. Thus I say to the Saints,—Be perfect. How, you say, can I be perfect? By living your religion; for that is perfect. Has there ever been, is there now, or will there ever be in me any doubt about the religion or the gospel I have embraced? Not a bit. I progress and improve in it from day to day and from week to week, as quickly as I wish and try to do so. The principle of progressing is Mormonism. Do you, Saints, intend to continue for the ten coming years in the same manner as you have spent the last ten? No, I do not think you do. If you do not progress, you will no doubt retrogress, and suffer the consequences. Remember then the words of wisdom.

The Word of Wisdom—what is it? It is to live according to the light and knowledge that you have, and by so doing, an unburdened conscience is to be had toward God and men, and not without doing so. Why do we not believe that we can do so, and fulfill it? What do we lack? Trust in God. Jesus says that if two or three come together in his name requesting that which they need he would not withhold it from them. We must have this faith, and follow it and perfect it with our deeds. Can this be done? Yes, it is just a matter of taking care of the first thing that is before us every day, and to cease worrying about whatever may come the following day. I do not ask God what I have to do next week, but I try to work out my present salvation—that which I have to do today. Before coming here tonight, I did not pray concerning tomorrow, but I said, "O, Lord, give me wisdom and strength tonight to reveal thy mind and will to this people." If I do well today, I shall be more able to do even better tomorrow, and thus I shall improve and progress. What use is it for us to try to improve the past—we cannot call yesterday back. Let us better ourselves; there is no need for us to follow the same old path all the time. You know that people are more learned now than they were earlier. In the old days, when they sent the lad to the mill with a bushel of wheat, they would put a rock in the other end of the bag to counter-weigh the wheat: since then they have learned a better way—to divide the wheat in the two ends of the bag. This is reform and improvement. If we do our duty, we shall improve ourselves and progress also; if we do not, we shall go backwards.

I said that we lack faith and trust in God. He says that His business is to provide for his Saints. I frequently ask the following questions and receive the following answers—"Brother, or sister, when do you plan to go to the Valley?" "I do not know." "Do you expect to wait as you are for another five or ten years?" "Well, there are no better signs before me."

Despite that, the Lord says that it is His business to provide for his Saints. It would be a very strange thing for him not to think about them as he did about Moses and the children of Israel. Moses preached to them, and called them out; and, although they were slaves and poor, they believed and put their faith in God to soften the hearts of their neighbors to assist them to go out, and through their faith they crossed the Red Sea. Do we not worship the same Almighty and immutable God? Do we not obey the same powerful Gospel? Do we not have the same strong faith, and would it not produce the same consequences now as it did formerly? Certainly it would. How shall you get it? By living your religion.

I ask you again, do you keep the words of wisdom? Are you being wise? Jesus says, Be ye wise as serpents, and harmless as doves. Are you harmless toward, and loving of, the children of men? Permit me to ask you heads of families, are you living your religion? You claim to be part of the best group of people there is. Show me any people in any place that are united with the principles of truth and holiness, and you shall show Mormons. If you lower yourselves to the poor practices of the nations you shall go down to their level, yes even lower. We need to live our religion and show our righteousness—our good and majestic works before men. The sectarians have prayed and wailed greatly for many centuries, but we ought to have something better; we need to live humbly, prayerfully, watchfully, and diligently.

(To be continued.)

ZION'S TRUMPET,

OR

Star of the Saints.

SATURDAY, JANUARY 10, 1857.

PAMPHLETS.—The third pamphlet—"Water Baptism" is just about ready. If the Conferences who have not yet sent here a single halfpenny of pamphlet money, and the others who have sent only part of it, would act according to the conditions offered, we would be enabled to move the work forward. In asking the Saints to make an effort to warn our fellow countrymen, neither the author nor the publisher were lacking in their joint efforts and sacrifices, if they were sacrifices, by making the pamphlets as cheap as possible, so that the blessing of God may follow their labor, because they said *come* and not *go*.

It is understood that the money for "Marriage and Morals" is not mixed in with that for the pamphlets.

We would like for the Chief distributors who have sent the number of the pamphlets they have on hand, to send also the number of those which are on hand in their Branches, and those who have not sent any number, to send the number of all of them put together. Let brother E. D. M. send the names of the *several different sorts* which he has on hand.

By having the information right away we can know which pamphlets are out of print, and which we can publish.

We do not think it wise for the brethren of Cardiganshire to keep the "Defense" on hand, but to spread it in those areas of the County that need it. Perhaps it would disabuse many honest minds; while, looking at it from the other side, it can count against those whose responsibility it is to distribute it.

Covers.—The price of the English covers for "True Repentance" from now on is two shilling per hundred. We expect full payment for them as soon as possible after receiving them, with the money for the pamphlets. We trust that the persons named on them are of a worthy character of the religion they profess: this is important.

Emigration.—(*From the "Star."*)—This Office will not send any P. E. Fund emigrants to Utah, during the year 1857. All the funds that the Company can command will be exhausted in discharging the heavy liabilities, incurred in sending out over two thousand souls, in the year 1856. The Saints will bear in mind that two thousand persons cannot be sent to Utah without incurring an expense of about eighteen thousand pounds sterling. It will probably require nearly two years from the present time, before the P. E. Fund Company will have discharged the debts contracted by last season's operations.

There were several persons last season who deposited with the P. E. Fund five pounds each, on the condition that they should be emigrated in 1857. We are sorry to be under the necessity of saying to all such, that the state of the finances will not permit their emigration the coming season. In case any of these persons desires to withdraw their deposits, they are at liberty, at any time, to do so; but if they can let them remain in the Office a year or two more, it will confer a great favor; and they shall be remembered among the first to be hereafter sent by the Fund.

The President of the P. E. Fund Company has sent us the names of some of the Saints whom he requests should be emigrated by the Fund during the coming year. We sent letters, notifying these persons of the President's request, hoping, at the time we gave them the information, to have been able to send them; but we are now compelled to say to all those who have received such letters, that the Company will not have means to forward them in 1857.

In relation to this subject, we give the following extract from a letter to us by President Brigham Young, dated G. S. L. City, August 30th, 1856.

"In regard to Emigration per P. E. F. Company the ensuing year, we wish to say to you, not to borrow money to aid in the Emigration, and draw upon us, as has been the practice heretofore, with the view of our realizing funds from the debts of persons brought over; or in any manner from debts owing the Fund; for it is impossible for us to realize any money from this source; and the operations of the Company have absorbed everything in the shape of available means, for the last two years, which we can control in every department.

"We cannot longer stand this constant drain, without reimbursements from those who are owing the Fund. We are, therefore, necessarily obliged to operate exclusively within the resources of the P. E. F. Company, instead of borrowing, and then paying out of tithing money, as we have had to do under the existing practice. The stock and wagons are our only resources from the Fund, at this end of the route, except a donation once in a while. Last winter the stock died, and you are aware that wagons are unavailable in this market.

"We truly feel to assist the poor Saints to come home to Zion, and think that we have proven this by our work; but it is not wisdom to absorb every other interest, pertaining to the building up of the kingdom of God, in gathering the poor, which is only one branch of it." . . . .

"You are aware that the Woollen Manufactory has been lying in storehouses in St. Louis, for years, and we have had to pay storage, amounting to thousands of dollars. It is our wish to bring this machinery across the Plains, as it is now needed in this Territory for manufacturing purposes.

"We also desire to do all that we can on the Temple, another year, as we have done nothing on it this year, and we must have some supplies, to assist this work. We are determined to nurse our general Church business a while."

To all Saints, purposing to go through to Utah on their own means, we say that teams can be ordered through us, and will be supplied at the point of outfit for the Plains by our agent. We think £55 will cover the cost of one wagon—with bows, yokes, and chains, four oxen, and one cow—perhaps two. All who wish us to order for them, must inform us immediately, and send the needful that we may transmit the same by our agent. The 1st of February will be as late as we can receive orders for this season.

To all persons who wish to go through to Utah on their own means, by the handcart train, we say, that we shall only receive from them cash sufficient to pay their passage to the States. At the port of disembarkation, Elder John Taylor will receive their passage money, and make all necessary arrangements for their provisions and conveyance by railway to Iowa City. It will, however, be indispensably necessary, if you intend crossing the Plains, to have handcarts, teams, provision wagons, cows, beef cattle, provisions, tents, &c., in readiness at Iowa City, so as not to be detained a day, for anything. To accomplish this, you can order all these things through us, and they can be supplied at the point of outfit for the Plains, by our agent. We do not know exactly the cost of all these articles; but we think £3 per head for all over one year old, will supply the outfit from where you leave the railroad, at Iowa City. Should it, however, prove to be too little, you can make up the deficiency to the agent upon your arrival at the place of outfit. Should it be too much, the balance can be refunded to you at the same point.

All, therefore, who intend going in this manner, should send to our Office £1 per head, as the usual deposit to secure a passage over the ocean; and £3 per head additional, to be forwarded by our agent to secure your outfit, on or near the frontiers. No deposits will be received, for emigrants intending to go through to Utah this season, later than the 1st of February.

The probable cost for adults, from the ports of disembarkation to Iowa City, including the necessary provision, may not vary much from £2 10s; it may be a few shillings cheaper than this. The expense across the Atlantic we hope will not be more than last season.

It is intended to have this season's emigration leave the frontiers in May and arrive in Utah in July. This will give the Saints several months after their arrival to make preparations for winter. . . . .

The Pastors, and Presidents of Conferences and Branches, will see that the Saints are fully instructed in regard to their emigration, so that everything may be accomplished in its time and season; this will avoid confusion, "which bringeth pestilence."

All persons intending to emigrate to Utah this season, who have deposits in our Office, and who have not already informed us of their wishes, are requested to notify us of their intention, on or before the 1st day of February next; otherwise, they may be disappointed in their expectations.

NOTICE.—Thank you very much to those who sent information to us about those who emigrated unknown to us after the end of the stewardship of brother Jones. If there is anyone from among those emigrants by the name of Ruth Rees or some others who have emigrated from the Monmouthshire Conference or some other Conference, we thank their President if he would send the details to us. And by the way, we say that we expect the names of all the Welsh emigrants who have paid deposits to come through this Office from now on.

ARRIVALS.—Brothers William Miller and James Taylor arrived here some time ago, and have earnestly begun their important stewardships. They have our greatest trust as fathers in Israel,— precious gifts of our Lord to his Saints, and we wish for the Saints to thank God for the privilege of having them in place of the faithful brethren who are leaving us. At present they are on a journey through Brecon and Monmouth.

Brothers Henry Harries and Samuel Roskelly have not arrived, but we expect them any day.

THE NEW YEAR.—1857 shows signs of being an unforgettable year among the remarkable years of this greatest and last Dispensation. Who can say what will happen during it? Who, but the watchmen on the towers of Zion, who have seen the destructive host of hell coming to harvest man like the grass of the field, and who have forewarned the people? Who but the great Prophet and Seer of our age, twenty years ago, at a very unlikely time, who foresaw and foretold of the breaking of the great American Union—the rise of slaves in rebellion against their masters, and the outpouring of arduous war on all the nations of the earth? No one. Now what do the newspapers of our day publish that is more important than the conflict of the North and the South of America? The threatened breaking of the Union—the reddening of the green surface of the land of Kansas with the blood of the two factions of the same nation—the men of the South, and the men of the North of America? What else? The contention of the strongest kingdoms of the world with each other—Persia and England deciding to meet one another, and clash on the jagged, rocky mountains of Herat, to cover the atrocious massacres on the banks of the Danube, Sinope, Alma, Inkermann, Balaclava, and Sebastopol with ten-times uglier bloody scenes, as a mantle covers the face of the sun; while the malicious bear of Russia behind the bush watches for its advantage to take revenge on the British lion in its weariness and weakness. The Prussian giant wishes to establish the fate of Switzerland with one blow, while France is ready to jump to the battlefield on the side of the latter, despite her respect for the former.

Frightful stories of highway robberies, house break-ins, frequent rapes, hideous murders, and executions of one another are sumptuous feasts for the corrupt taste and filthy stomachs of the children of the whore; but the cauldron's contents are not as tasty without a greedy netful of the worst slanders that could be woven in the hellish den, the work of the hired 'reverends' and 'editors,' about the innocent followers of the Lamb.

O, Babylon! Babylon! The cry of the widow and the orphan, the poor and the oppressed, and the shout of thousands of souls of godly martyrs beneath the altar are about to be answered!

Saints of the Lord, say Amen, and may "come out of her" be your loudest call to honest souls again this year.

Your humble and inexperienced trumpeter acknowledges his lack of skill to occupy such an honorable and high office, especially when he remembers his worthy predecessor. He thanks brothers Thomas Harris, Dewi Elfed, William Lewis, the bards, and his generous and amiable subscribers, for their energetic assistance, which, together with the promising signs for improvement and progress in every part of the good work in Wales encourages him to make the attempt for yet another year, and to trumpet from the heart—

> For a happy new Year for the Saints,
>   May their privilege be to live better;
> May each one's heart's desire
>   Be to go to the far west.
> Let all work constantly now
>   The work is great indeed,—
> No one who keeps an idle hand
>   Will go over to the land of Zion.

SONG OF NOAH.

The people are stirring,
    Small and large,
Some host is opposing,
    Through the Northland now;
They assert there is no need
    For baptism on the journey,—
Without this they seek bliss
    For long eternity.

But listen, errors
    Are steering everyone through the place,
They do not want to believe
    In the words of the King of heaven,
Or to give heed to his counsel,
    By coming to baptism of water,
Where forgiveness is found,
    The poet is quite sure.

The Church of our God
    Is governed in these days,
In accordance with the command
    Of the man who was on the mount;

In her are apostles,
> And undeniably prophets.
And God gives knowledge
> To the honest in our land.

For this reason, faithful brethren,
> Who are now in the land of Babel,
Let all of us lift up our heads
> With boldness to speak the truth,
And testify strongly
> To all wherein we dwell,
That God is calling his people
> Across the sea to live.

Pencrych.

MISCELLANEOUS, &c.

A Pint of liquor costs 3c per day; for one year, the total would purchase two shirts, two pair of stockings, two pair of shoes, a fustian jacket, a waistcoat, a pair of trousers, a cap, a flannel undershirt, a piece of rough cloth, a cloak, a neckerchief, two pair of cotton *sheets*, and two large blankets.

Address—Mr. Abednego Williams, 1, Graham Street, Merthyr Tydfil.

Receipts for Books From Dec. 4 to Jan. 5— Edward D. Miles, 7s 3c; T. Rees, £1; T. Stephens, £8 11s 6½c; J. Jones, 10s; Thomas Jones, 15s 8c; John Davies, £3 12s 6½c.

Ditto, for pamphlets,—M. Vaughn, £2 10s; T. Stephens, £8; E. D. Miles, £1 12s 9c; T. Jones, 8s 4c; G. Roberts, 12s 6c; W. Ajax, 7s; J. Davies, 7s 6½c.

CONTENTS.

	PG.
Address of President Benson	1
Editorial—Pamphlets—Covers—Emigration—Notice—Arrivals—New Year	9
Song of Noah	15
Miscellaneous, &c.	16

SWANSEA:
PRINTED AND PUBLISHED BY DANIEL DANIELS.

ZION'S TRUMPET,

OR

Star of the Saints.

No. 2.] JANUARY 24, 1857. [Vol. X.

LETTER OF CAPTAIN D. JONES.

(With Brother Henry Harries.)

Fort Laramie, September 18, 1856.

Dear Brother Daniels.—While the animals are grazing and I am preparing for breakfast, I shall write you some of my news again, and since I have possessed neither pen nor ink for weeks, do your best to understand the scrawls of this lead. The last time I wrote to you was from the region of Elk Horn, at that place where we had that memorable *Stampede* when going to the valley last time. Since that time I have much to tell, if time permitted. Even so, you, and many other dear brethren, especially the work of my God which is under your care, have not long been out of my mind. Let Him whose work it is bless it, and prosper it daily, is my constant prayer, for I love its welfare eternally.

It is not yet a fortnight since we set out from Florence, on this journey, and we are already over five hundred miles toward its end, and everyone is fit and well. Because of all the demands and fuss of setting thousands of other Saints on their way on this journey, I have hardly had time to remember that it was toward my home in Zion that I was going, where my dearest ones live, yes my beloved await me, who have yearned to see me many times for four years and three days; no, it was like a dream for me to be on the way to dear company and godly brethren, there to enjoy the glory of

2 [Price 1½c.

salvation in Zion. Do you know, brother Daniels, what awakened me most, and forced me to believe I was really, returning there now? What would you say if you saw the buffalo by the thousand prancing around you, if the wolves showed you their snarling teeth from all sides, and the antelope their white coats—if you saw the tops of the distant mountains beyond the magnificent plains? Then, I think you would believe too, although amazed, that it is not a dream. Well, I have the provable signs of every look forward that Zion is still onward—ever onward.

We travel quite differently from the other companies. We go at a gallop always through everything that meets us—often fifty miles or more in a day and ten or a dozen of those before daybreak, and as many or more at night. The Indians are so hostile along the route we followed, that we scarcely dared stop at night, for fear they would fall upon us and kill us. We rested, for the most part, in daylight, when we could see from afar those who approached. By doing that, we escaped many a danger.

Several small companies have been killed by the Cheyenne, (Indians) this year on the road we traveled. When we called in Fort Kearney, an individual came there who had traveled 50 miles on foot while out hunting, and informed us that a whole company had been killed, among whom was that Thomas Margetts who created such ungodliness among the Saints in London, and was excommunicated for that. His wife and baby were also killed, and another returned apostate from the Valley called Cowdy, and his wife and child.

A few days before that, the Indians attacked A. Babbitt's camp, and killed every soul except one young boy who was a faithful Saint, who gave me a detailed account of the whole thing. He says that one woman from St. Louis, and her baby, were killed while in their bed in the wagon. The Indians shot everyone else belonging to the company, and they plundered the most valuable provisions, and forty oxen. I saw the wagons, the traces of the bullets, and the blood. All those who were killed were enemies of the Saints, except the woman and her baby, and she had been excommunicated in Saint Louis. They took her body away, but they left her underclothes there bloodstained and torn. A short while before that, they rushed on the *mail*, which fled before them to the doors of Fork Kearney, throwing out clothes,

&c., along the way, to delay them. The army rushed out of Fort Kearney to meet them; they killed ten of them and the rest fled more fiercely than before. Another company of Californians were killed, all but one; and lastly, they have got Col. Babbitt, secretary of Utah territory, himself in custody, after all his boasting. We saw the eagles eating his flesh and that of the two who were with him. Despite the fury of these wild men, it is a fact worth proclaiming to the ends of the earth, that not so much as one of all the thousands of Saints who are on this road, and almost on every side of the place of slaughter, has been harmed. They have not stolen one of their animals, and I have not seen any of the Saints afraid of them in the least; rather in the midst of a throng of three thousand of their warriors, brothers and sister, and children too, cheerfully shaking hands, and they (the Indians) laughing, shouting *Mormon good good, no shoot Indian*.

Upper Crossing of the Platte, September 27th.

I failed to get this ready for the *mail* in Laramie, and I shall now have the opportunity to send it to you with the company of missionaries who are on their way to England, &c.

I met here, (at the upper crossing of the Platte) my brother (Edward Jones) and his team [of horses], and I waited, so that we could take the threshing machine home with us.

Encouraging news from the Valley comes to meet me every day. All of my family are well, and yours too.

The company is about to start—short *stories*, aren't they? May the God of our fathers bless you, and everyone I know, is ever my prayer.

Your Brother,

D. JONES.

"THE MEASURE OF THE STATURE OF THE FULLNESS OF CHRIST."

(Answer of Elder Evan Rees to a question of his Father.)

Nantyglo, January 1st, 1857.

MY DEAR FATHER.—At your request I shall attempt to give the explanation you requested concerning verse 13 of chapter 4 of Ephesians—"Till we all come in the unity of the faith, and of the knowledge of the Son of God, unto a perfect man, unto the measure of the stature of the fullness of Christ." The question, if I understood it properly, is "what is meant by the measure of the stature of the fullness of Christ," &c.

I confess that in the saying is an incomprehensible mystery, except to such ones who comprehend *what man is in his originality* or in his innate beginning. Certainly the Apostle understood this secret thoroughly, before he would presume to reveal his assertion and his and the Ephesians' reaching from their imperfect state to arrive at the perfect and blessed condition of Christ.

This leads us to think that the human race has a legal right to the inheritance of Christ, and, by reading the previous verses, to understand that the Head of all intelligent beings has a desire to set them in possession of it, which is revealed in his sending of his authorized servants especially for the task. He has put an ambitious mind in man, who, naturally, asks himself, Who am I? Where did I come from? If there is a better condition before me, what is my lower condition now? Why this attention of myself, I wonder?

When some inheritance or earthly position comes about for a poor man, it generally happens because he is an heir or a legal relation to the giver or the possessor of such, and frequently trouble is taken to trace the origin of this man to have proof of his legal right.

In our tracing of the origin of man we have an account in the holy scriptures, that the human race are the offspring—sons and daughters of the Most High God. We know that this is not in the carnal sense. In what sense are we the offspring of God, then? It is a fact generally accepted that man has a body and a spirit, and the two are not one, although the latter dwells in the former, any more than a person and the house he inhabits are not one. Then we are led to trace further where our *spirits* came from, since God is not our father in the carnal sense. "That which is born of the flesh is flesh," says our divine standard, while it also says that God is a spirit (John iv., 24) and the FATHER of our *spirits*. Hebrews, xii, 9—"Furthermore we have had fathers of our flesh which corrected us, and we gave them reverence; shall we not much rather be in subjection unto the Father of spirits, and live?" Further, Psalm lxxxii, 6—"I have said, Ye are *Gods*, and all of you are *children of the most High*. What comparison is there between lowly and mortal man and the almighty God, who governs the elements as he wishes? What is the difference between them? It is like unto the difference that exists between a man who is mature in age, ability, and understanding, and a weak and innocent baby. A benefactor sends a child to school, where he is disciplined, from lesson to lesson, if he is obedient, until he progresses, as he ages, so that when he reaches the age of a man, he will be qualified to be as high as his father, who will rejoice to set him as his equal. On the other hand, if the child is disobedient, refusing education, he will not be enabled to stand in place of his father, who, out of mercy for him, will set him in some place appropriate for him. Some disobedient sons are sent to the army or the navy, &c., and they are cut away with a meager portion.

It is acknowledged that Jesus Christ existed before in heaven, and he condescended to come down to a lowly manger, to receive a body of flesh, to fulfill the great purpose of the redemption. We read that Nebuchadnezzar saw the Spirit of Christ in the fiery furnace with the three boys. Jesus says himself, "Before Abraham was, I am;" and in Hebrews, iv, 3, we read that he was *"before the world was;"* John xvii, 4.—"I have glorified thee on the earth: I have finished the work which thou gavest me to do. And now, O Father, glorify thou me with thine own self with the glory which I had with thee *before the world was.*" (Read the entire chapter.)

If the Spirit of Christ, our older brother, was before the world was, and dwelt in the house of his Father, why were not we, his youngest brethren, there also?

Christ is called, because of his distinction and his glory, a *star*. The scriptures frequently compare beings to stars, because of their goodness and their light. Those who turn many souls to God are promised that they will shine like the stars of heaven in glory, forever and ever. It was promised in Numbers xxiv, 17, that a star, (namely a person or being) would come out of Jacob, &c. A church of persons was compared to stars. When the devil had not yet fallen, he was called Lucifer, the son of the morning. We learn that he drew after him the third part of the stars of heaven, or the fallen angels. In Rev. xxii, 16, Christ is called a Bright and Morning Star. Could it be that there are additional morning stars? We learn that Jesus was the firstborn among *many brethren.*—Rom. viii, 29.

It was not only our Older Brother who prayed when in his bitter trial, but we learn that others did as well. When Job was under severe discipline in this earthly school, his kind Father visited him, and asked, to comfort him, "Where wast thou when I laid the foundations of the earth? declare, if thou has understanding, who hath laid the measures thereof, if thou knowest? or who hath stretched the line upon it? when the *morning stars* sang together, and *all the sons of God* shouted for joy." Where was Job at that time, I wonder? Singing together with the others of the sons of God, or the *morning stars* for the privilege of coming to become flesh on the face of the earth, which he had helped to create; thus he became like unto his Father.

The first chapter of Genesis shows that multiple Gods were there, saying *let us*, and not *let me*. Such a comfort to a child of God when in the bitterness of his trial in this school! It was his choice and his request to come to it, although he does not remember; for, like his oldest brother, "in his condescension his understanding was taken from him," until he became a weak and innocent babe.

We trust that the foregoing is sufficient to convince the honest believer of the bible of the pre-existence of our spirits, and of the *origin of man*, together with that which is added that God said to the old prophet Jeremiah (i, 5.)—"Before I formed thee in the belly, I knew thee; and before thou camest forth out of the womb I sanctified thee, and I ordained thee a prophet unto the nations."

If it pertained to the subject, I would add that the spirits in the pre-mortal world had rules to live by, before Lucifer, the son of the morning, and a third of them, could rebel, and fall, and that some of the good spirits, in light of that, were more valiant than others, and were highly elevated, and were appointed to chief offices here. Jesus, the eldest of them, was chosen to be first, and a Savior to all his brethren. The Psalmist says, (xlv, 7.) "Thou lovest righteousness, and hatest wickedness; therefore God, thy God, hath anointed thee with the oil of gladness above thy fellows."

(To be continued.)

ADDRESS OF HENRY HARRIES TO THE SAINTS IN WALES.

"Zion's Trumpet" Office, January 16, 1857.

Dear Saints in Wales.—Having received my appointment by the First Presidency, in Zion, to visit the land of my birth, and authority to administer in the Church ordinances that pertain to my office, I started from Great Salt Lake City on the 10th of last September, in the company of about 27 other missionaries who were sent to different parts of the earth, to preach the gospel, &c. I say that they are all principled men with their whole will in the work of the Lord. O! how lovely it was to travel together with such men who walk in such unity and cooperation, that it brought down from heaven merciful blessings on us! We crossed the plains quickly and successfully, and I can say that the hand of the Lord was abundantly manifested toward us, and toward all the companies of the Saints that we met on their way to the Valley while others who were enemies of the Saints and apostates from them were killed, and their animals and all their possessions were stolen by the Indians. The Indians gave terrible treatment to the bodies of some apostates who had started from the Valley a little before us with full intent to do whatever harm they could in a deceitful way. They did their utmost to try to discourage the immigrating Saints on the plains, and persuade them to turn back with them, that men were starving in the Valley, &c. Despite it all, they did not succeed in turning back a single one. The Saints felt splendid, especially when we came with the truth, and proved to the contrary, that those apostate and intentionally evil liars were bad men galloping to destruction. Before many days our words were confirmed as a testimony to the Saints, and a warning to all such men—those men were dismembered by the Indians. The hand of the Lord was clearly delivering all his Saints, while four companies of the others were killed, of the kind we have noted, together with wicked and vile gentiles who pulled down the judgment of a just God on them.

The faithful Saints need not fear anything, for *all things* work together for good to them that love God. I saw clearly the hand of the Lord toward me in the States opening the way before me to have a way for me to get my transport across the sea. I traveled hundreds of miles there, and I met friends in almost every place I went. The Welsh were in several of those places, faithful Saints, and sent their regards, &c., to their relatives and their acquaintances here. They are too many to mention here; but I shall notify all when

I have the privilege of seeing you face to face. Almost all of them were doing well, and feeling splendid, especially in the following places,—Florence, Nebraska Territory, Gravois, Missouri, Caseville, Illinois, Pottsville, and Minersville, Pennsylvania, and Williamsburg, New York.

From New York, we sailed on board the ship *Guy Manwaring*. We had a quick voyage of only 21 days. It was brutally rough at times, but on the whole it was not as bad as the sea voyage as the Apostle Paul had to Melita. Not one life was lost or the ship either; but the *cargo*, the sails, the *life boats*, and many of the sailors were damaged—they were hit by the waves, and the bones of some were broken. No harm came to me, nor was I frightened. The reason for that was because we were blessed before starting,—we were assured, on the condition of our faithfulness and our appropriate behavior, that we could return to Zion in peace. We knew that we had not crossed our boundaries, and consequently the blessing was certain for us, and to the faithful forever. I trust that you will live faithfully, so that you may have the blessings that are in store for the faithful and for no one else.

It is a great blessing, in my view, to get to walk on the land of Zion, although the old Babylon was beautiful and rich to the natural eye; but to me it is loathsome to hear the blasphemy, the swearing, and the tumult, to see the violence, the oppression, the stealing, the murdering, avarice, prostitution, drunkenness, &c., that are carried on here. I hope that the time is short that I will remain here, and not just myself, but all of the Saints. Yonder is the place—yonder is my home, and that of all others who love righteousness, sobriety, peace, and tranquility.

I ask for a share in the prayers of the Saints, so that I may be able to carry out these principles, and teach them to others, so that I may have clean hands from all others, and that you and I will be able to enjoy together and rejoice in Zion.

May the Lord bless you, and keep you, and may he bring you out of Babylon, is my wish, in the name of Jesus Christ. Amen.

HENRY HARRIES.

ZION'S TRUMPET,

OR

Star of the Saints.

SATURDAY, JANUARY 24, 1857.

ARRIVALS OF MISSIONARIES.—Elder Samuel Roskelley arrived when our previous number was at the press.

Elder Henry Harries, "Talog," arrived Tuesday night, the 13th, in excellent health and spirit. Certainly the Saints will take a great interest in his Greeting to them; and his words from brothers and sisters, and families and friends, when there is a bit of a *chit chat* beside the fire, will be welcome.

ELDER Samuel Roskelley is appointed to travel through the Brecon and Monmouth Conferences, and the area of Cardiff and the East Glamorgan Conference; Elder Henry Harries is appointed to travel through the Carmarthen, Cardiganshire, and Pembrokeshire Conferences; and Dewi Elfed Jones is appointed to travel through the upper area of the East Glamorgan Conference, and through the West Glamorgan and Llanelli Conferences.

The above brethren are to go according to the direction of the Presidency of the Conferences where they are sent.

BOOK DEBTS are still increasing. We trust that the beginning of the new year is the beginning of the efforts to delete them from sight.

BUSINESS.—Numerous tasks oblige us to request our presiding brethren to write their numbers and financial stewardships separate from their correspondence, &c. It is not just once in the day that the *Clerk* must read a long letter from one end to the other to get hold of the one financial *item* among others that may be in it, and search as if for a needle in a haystack.

Send the following things separately, and on different paper—requests for books—payments—names of emigrants, church happenings, &c., in the most comprehensive and succinct manner possible.

PAYING TITHING.—"To the Editor of 'Zion's Trumpet,'"—Dear Brother.—I wish for you to answer the following question for me, so that it may give more satisfaction to the few who ask it, namely "is it a duty for the Saints to give the occasional meal, &c., to a Conference President, or a Traveling Elder, in addition to paying tithing?"

I am,
SION EDWART———"

We concede that it is as much as the occasional Saint can do to pay his tithing, and maintain his family, while others can easily do much more than that. Our understanding of duty is all that a man can do. If two men are in possession, the one of a remaining penny, and the other of a remaining pound, and if the Lord were to ask for all that each one of them could impart, it seems to us that it would be as obligatory for the one to give his pound as completely as it would for the other to give his penny. If we do only what the law requires of us, how much greater will be our righteousness be than that of the Scribes and the Pharisees? Jesus did not consider that it was any more to ask that rich man to sell what he had, and divide it among the poor, than it was for the two mites of the poor widow to be received. The law of tithing applies to every man and woman in the world, and the time will come when the disobedient nations will be obligated to pay it as a tribute to Zion. Should not the Saints do better than the children of the world? When they do all that is required, and do no more, it will be said in the end that they are "unprofitable servants."

We trust that every Saint has sufficient light of the eternal gospel to perceive his duty, and for his benefit to strive to fulfill it. Our feeling toward the work of God is, if we were to possess the whole world, our soul would have no better feast than to give the whole thing to establish the government of the Lord in it. What great feat is giving a meal while we know that the flour has not failed in the tub, and that the blessing of the God of Israel is on our contributions to Him. Yes, to Him, we say, not to the President or the travel Elder, and the time will come when the giver and the receiver will be paid a hundredfold for their trouble in this world, not to mention eternal life in the world to come.

Let us live above the law, for it was included because of transgression, and remember the Apostle's advice by the way, which is "Be always abounding in the work of the Lord, forasmuch as ye know that your labor is not in vain in the Lord."

WARNING.—Let not the Saints receive, into any Branch of the Welsh Mission, any person who pretends to be an officer; and let them not assist such a one, no matter what he was, unless he has an authorized appointment to travel throughout such a place.

TEACHING OF APOSTLE BENSON.

(Continued from page 9.)

DO you call your families together in the morning to pray; or, do you sleep too late to be able to do so? Do you keep order in your homes?—to have all of your family to bend the knee before the Lord? *Do you live your religion?* Have you thrown away your tobacco pipe? I, or we have spoken of that. Have you done away with your snuffbox, your whiskey bottle, together with every thing or deed that tends to sadden or trouble the Spirit of the Lord or your brethren? What kind of look would I have preaching from this pulpit and *chewing* tobacco in the corner of my mouth? How does it suit the Elders of Israel to go about preaching with pipes in their mouths? Will those who smoke and chew tobacco, or who drink intoxicating liquors and hot drinks, go to Zion? or, if they go there, will they do any good there? I ask this to the young, healthy, strong, and fit people.

Put away these things, and you will be blessed. If I were to ask of the old grey-haired brother here if he is accustomed to such things, he would say that he is not. Compare that with what some young people say [in a plaintive tone]—My desire is so weak—the craving is so unbearable—I *cannot* do without it.

Others have kept the Word of Wisdom for a time, and then have broken it again. They remind me of the story of an old, well-known drunkard who lived in Massachusetts. He went to *sign* the temperance pledge. (Our sectarian friends are so detailed as to classify temperance and other good things of the kind, on their own, *separate* from that which they call religion. Thus, one thing is temperance, and *something else* is their religion, according to that reasoning. My religion contains everything that is good. If I present any truth that does not pertain to my religion, it must be an *irreligious* deed, and if so, an *ungodly* deed. But, to return to our story—) The drunkard was not received into the temperance union except on the condition that he go past a tavern without going in. The drunkard was energized, past the tavern he went without hesitation for a little ways, when he stopped suddenly, and tapping praise on his belly, he said, *Well done*, resolution, come back to the tavern to have a *treat*.

Whatever you sow, that shall you reap. If wheat is sowed, wheat is reaped—if potatoes are planted, potatoes will be obtained. If you sow to the flesh, you will have corruption: if you sow to the Spirit, you will obtain eternal life. That is the word of the Lord.

The Gospel is perceptible, clear and simple. What does it require of Latter-day Saints? To keep the Word of Wisdom that I am preaching tonight. Am I asking the elderly sisters to give up their tea, and other such things? No, except they feel to do so. But I speak to those who are younger. Perhaps they ask, What shall we do with the money that we thus save? it is not a sufficient amount to put in the Liverpool Office toward our emigration, and it is burning in our pockets—we *must* spend it!

They must purchase beautiful bonnets and ribbons, or some other frivolous things of the kind: they *must* spend the money if they are obliged to spend an evening formulating how. I say to the poor Saints how the Lord intends to deliver them—*on the penny principle*. I shall come so low as a penny. Save your remaining pennies, sixpences, shillings, &c.; throw them into the penny treasury, and you shall be delivered.

Some have received and kept the principle of tithing, and they have not found themselves poorer by so doing, but richer in faith and in the blessings of the eternal Gospel. They know how much they possess by sowing so generously. Through that the Temple of the Lord will be built where they will receive their endowments—they will have the power of the eternal Priesthood, which will cause them to savor life to life—as saviors to their ancestors as far back as they can find one, and also to save their posterity. If you do not do that, there will be some others who will. The principle of tithing was revealed on the Fishing River, about twenty years ago.

What else is required of you? For you to preach the Gospel, distribute pamphlets, and testify with all your might. Do you think that it is only a few Elders who should preach the Gospel? You, sisters, can preach it secretly, by spreading pamphlets, bearing your testimony, and inviting and bringing people here, to this hall, to hear the preaching of the Gospel. You need that which the Sectarians call a *reformation* in Swansea, and this is the time for it, which you are opposed.

Many have preached the Funeral Sermon of Mormonism, and have dug her grave; but when they went to bury her *she was not there*! Nor will she be buried; but she will grow and spread from sea to sea, and after that the Elders will go to every part of the earth. Indeed, Mormonism exists in many places besides Swansea. I have traveled several thousands of miles across European countries—Sweden, Norway, Germany, and Denmark, and what I heard was "Mormonism here, and Mormonism there—the Mormon Elders in practically every town." They are also along the face of the American Continent, with a sufficient number in Utah alone to form a State; and if we were all there, we would form three or four states. We have gone in through the narrow end of the horn; we have swollen and increased, and there is no use trying to blow us back; we must come out through the wide end.

Many times I have asked, "Brother, or sister, when do you intend to go to Zion?" "O, when they take me." "Well, who are they? Are you not as much THEY as anyone else?" The matter became clear immediately. What if "they" were to do something about that, then? Which one would seem better—for young, healthy, and capable people to go to work and earn a way to transport themselves, or for them to be snatched away in mass, and put down in the Valley, and given a sack of flour to begin their lives, and by the time they eat the flour they are ready to apostatize, perhaps? It would make some sense to take such as the old brother who is at my right.

I ask this sensible congregation, Where are the means to emigrate this people, if not in your own midst? Nowhere. Yet, there are some in their midst who have the means, but they lack the heart to contribute it.

The Saints in Zion, empathizing for their captive brothers and sisters in Babylon, have donated, for their emigration, that which they have, namely thousands of dollars worth of possessions, to the P. E. Fund, intending for them to be purchased by the wealthy saints, to deliver the poor, without any loss to themselves. But, have they purchased them? I have traveled thousands of miles lately, and I have found only one buyer to purchase about 300 dollars worth. We see, then, that the wealthy are not going to do much of the work of the Lord.

I see your condition, that you are poor. Jesus said that the poor will have the gospel preached to them. Can you see, then, how great is your privilege? If you had been born and raised in wealth and luxury, who knows but what you would refuse the gospel also? The work of the Lord is to be done by the poor. What will you do in the face of that, then? Treasure up your wasted and remaining pennies that you can spare, toward your emigration. The voice of the spirit is "gather out of Babylon, O ye Saints." Get a book, a good man, who will keep a correct account of your names, and your payments to the Penny Fund—one who will not keep anything for himself, if you can find him, and when enough is saved, away with you, or wait another year to preach the gospel, if you feel to do so.

When I left the Valley, on my current mission, I presented all my possessions to the church, to the hands of my brethren. How could I have done anything more logical? What is more inconsistent than for a man to entrust himself, body and spirit, to the church, but then to keep his possessions separate for fear of losing them, saying, "let the church take my all, but don't let it touch my possessions!" What if the Saints were to bring their all into it? I dare say to you that they would not wait long before all the things they need would be added unto them.

(To be continued in our next.)

STATISTICAL REPORT

OF THE CHURCH OF JESUS CHRIST OF LATTER-DAY SAINTS IN WALES, FOR THE YEAR ENDING DECEMBER 31, 1856.

President.—Daniel Daniels. Counselors.—Israel Evans and Benjamin Ashby.
Pastor over the Conferences of the North.—John E. Jones.

Conferences	Bran.	S.	HP	Eld.	Pr.	Tea.	Dea.	Cut.	Died.	Emi.	Bap.	Tot.	Pres.
Brecon	7	0	0	24	3	3	3	7	1	10	9	132	J. Thomas.
Monmouth	13	0	0	63	21	22	10	23	3	65	34	377	B. Evans.
East Glamorgan	27	1	0	221	55	55	39	170	22	207	168	276	A. Williams.
West Glamorgan	18	1	1	66	13	16	11	15	4	35	38	370	Thos. Harris.
Llanelli	6	0	0	38	8	4	8	5	2	81	12	195	Dd. Davies.
Carmarthen	6	0	0	13	6	1	4	6	0	31	6	80	Wm. Jones.
Pembrokeshire	10	0	0	30	4	4	5	27	3	25	26	168	E. D. Miles.
Cardiganshire	5	0	0	10	3	2	0	2	0	1	5	75	Thos. Jones.
Merionethshire	4	0	0	10	4	2	1	1	0	24	10	57	J. Treharne.
Flintshire	6	0	0	24	2	3	4	9	0	12	13	106	Thomas Rees.
Denbighshire	4	0	0	13	2	3	1	2	0	26	6	89	Gr. Roberts.
Conway Valley and Anglesey	5	0	0	13	6	4	1	2	0	11	11	84	Wm. Ajax.
Total	111	2	1	525	127	119	87	270	35	528	338	3010	

The above abbreviations stand for the following words:—Branches, Seventies, High Priests, Elders, Priests, Teachers, Deacons, Excommunicated, Died, Emigrated, Baptized, Total.

BOOK DEBTS, DECEMBER 31, 1856.

	£.	s.	c.
Brecon	5	15	2
Monmouth	50	17	10
East Glamorgan	84	10	5
West Glamorgan	118	4	11
Llanelli	54	2	11
Carmarthen	24	14	3
Pembrokeshire	.6	8	1
Cardiganshire	16	0	10
Merionethshire	10	14	7
Flintshire	15	14	5
Denbighshire	15	10	8
Conway Valley and Anglesey	10	14	2
Liverpool Office	1	10	0
Liverpool Welsh Branch	3	2	5
	£418	0	8

The Halfpennies are not included.

ADDRESS—E. D. Miles, Dew St., Haverfordwest.

☞ Let all who intend to emigrate send in their names, &c., here in time for us to be able to send them to Liverpool by the 1st of February, or they will be too late.

CONTENTS.

                                                                                         PG.

Letter of Captain Jones ... 17
Address of H. Harries ... 22
Editorial—Arrivals—Book debts—Business—Paying Tithing—Warning ... 25
Teaching of President Benson ... 27
Statistical Report ... 31

SWANSEA:
PRINTED AND PUBLISHED BY DANIEL DANIELS.

ZION'S TRUMPET,

OR

Star of the Saints.

No. 3.]　　　　　FEBRUARY 7, 1857.　　　　　[Vol. X.

"PAYING TITHING."

ITS SCRIPTURALNESS—THE BLESSINGS THAT ARE ENJOYED BY OBEYING IT, AND THE FAILURE THAT FOLLOWS ITS OPPONENTS.

(One of the Entries of the latest Eisteddfod of the Saints in Swansea.)

Here is my attempt at the great and difficult task of making what is called a pamphlet. I see my topic divided into three headings, so that it may be clear to all, and I shall do my best to comment on each one of them without any introduction, except this; I wish to have the spirit of the topic, and clarity of thought, in as few words as possible, and the sympathy of all to forgive me of language errors in every sense if they have a mind to do so: I search for the spirit of the topic, and not for the language or the prize. I was thinking of writing about it, even before I saw it in the "Trumpet," as a topic of the Eisteddfod competition.

I. *Paying Tithing, its Scripturalness, or as I understand it as well, the Scripturalness of Paying Tithing*. By this I do not consider every verse that mentions tithing as being necessary, but scripture, and I think that a few are as good as many, because the scripture was given under the inspiration of God, and though there are contradictions in the *Bible*, the scriptures are one; therefore, one will do as well as a hundred, and the way that we determine that a scripture will be the verse we quote is by the standard of *Revelation*; there is nothing else to be had in this world, given by whatever means. But

[Price 1½c.

lest some think that there are not several verses to be had, the places where they can be seen are in Gen. xiv, 20; Lev. xxvii, 30—32; Neh. x, 37; Num. xviii, 21—24; Deut. xii, 6—11, 14, 23—28, 26, 12; Neh. xiii, 5—12; 2 Chron. xxxi, 5—12; Neh. xii, 44; Isa. vi, 13; Amos iv, 4; Mal. iii, 8—10; Deut. xiv, 22; 1 Sam. viii, 15. From the foregoing verses, we see that tithing is a possession of the Lord, and that he gives it as a possession of the Priesthood. "This is the inheritance of the sons of Aaron, saith the Lord, throughout all their generations," and for as long as the priesthood of Aaron is on the earth, and for as long as there is service in it for the salvation of men, namely preaching, baptism, and the outward things of the church of God on the earth, and the forgiveness of sins, the healing of the sick, and the ministering of angels, revelations are indispensably necessary for the salvation of mankind, and these blessings are in connection with the lawfulness of the service of the office of Aaron. Now, if one must have salvation before being saved, one must have the ordinances to obey, and these must be administered lawfully, and be known before by the authorized servants of God, who labor for God, and in the name of God, which work is for the glory of God and the salvation of mankind. All acknowledge that it is not more just to receive the blessings connected with righteous service, than it is to pay for the service, which is tithing, and as long as the generation of Aaron is on the earth and as long as man has a duty to obey the Lord, and the service of the Aaronic priesthood is necessary, that is how long tithing is to exist. Also, as long as there is power in the word of God, and falsehood that needs to be eliminated, and an offering is necessary to be given, and priests to minister, that is how long tithing needs to exist; yes, as long as the Lord causes men to repent, and sin has not been forgiven, and as long as the priesthood of Aaron remains with the last of his posterity, that is how long tithing needs to exist.

1. Tithing should be paid, because God gives more than the worth of the labor. It is man who tills the earth, through plowing, leveling, sowing, planting, and watering it, but it is God who gives the increase, and the abundant crop is greater than the worth of the labor, still it is God who gives it, expecting for them to do justice with Him, by paying back to him one part in ten, but they do not

acknowledge God, and they hate his laws. Therefore, the sermon of Peter is preached, "Repent and be baptized for the remission of sins," together with tithing.

2. Tithing should be paid, because all men are in a position that they can pay it. The way we prove this is because all without exception waste more than twice what God asks in tithing on unnecessary things. I consider every unnecessary thing a waste, in connection with food, drink, clothing, or anything which is commonly used by us but which we don't need, and God does not justify anyone for failing to fulfill his duties, even if he cannot, if waste is the reason for that, since it can be done, if we properly use things, our duty is to do so, and it is justice to pay our tithes to the Lord.

3. Tithing should be paid, since the Lord asks only that which is just. The silver, the gold, and the animals for a thousand years are the Lord's; the earth and her righteousness is the Lord's. Man, then, is but a steward over the things God gives to him, and since it is He who owns all things, "All souls are mine," says the Lord. Man is not the owner of anything, and in fact, he does not even own himself. Thou shalt truly tithe all the increase of thy seed, that the field bringeth forth year by year, the tithe of thy corn, of thy wine, and of thine oil, and the firstlings of thy herds and of thy flocks. And to bring the firstfruits of our ground, and the firstfruits of all fruit of all trees, to the house of the Lord. Since the Lord is the owner of all the great farms, let us be honest servants, to give to him the things that he requires, for he cannot ask anything but what is his, and that which he now asks is tithing.

4. We ought to pay tithing, since it is a commandment for us to do so. The vision and the purpose he has in this is our own welfare; that is all the great objective. Also, if we find that God asks us to do something, that is sufficient to prove that that man has the ability to do so, and the hearts of all should jump for joy at having the privilege of being considered worthy to do something with his work. We should not be compelled to do any duty out of fear of punishment, rather out of love; and he who loves God, and keeps his commandments, is accepted of him, and it is impossible to gain acceptance, and disregard tithing, by not paying it.

5. Tithing ought to be paid, because the circumstances of the

church of God on the earth are such that require that; also, it is not just from the Saints the Lord requires tithing, but from every living man on his earth that lives on it; yet he more definitely asks those who have covenanted with Him through baptism, and have assumed the responsibility, according to the covenant, and the service of the priesthood. The Lord requires tithing from the poor as well as from the wealthy, and also the poor should tithe first, so that their effort in the midst of their poverty becomes a means of encouraging the wealthy to follow them, and so that their tireless and conscientious efforts, in the midst of scorn, persecution, and poverty ascend to their merciful Father, and sound like silver bells in his ears, until his bowels move in compassion so that he can delight in pouring out his Holy Spirit, in a spirit of the same nature, so that the wealthy might feel for them, and out of respect for the commandment of their God, so they could not be kept from opening their hearts, and fulfilling the needs of the poor, and supplying them with all things; but unless the poor feel for themselves, God will not feel for them, and pour out his spirit on such who can do that as well, namely to gather them as heirs of Zion to their own land, which is indispensable; and that is done through tithing. "Bring your tithing into the storehouse," says the Lord. "This shall be an eternal law through all your generations."

6. The principle of tithing is necessary to prove the honesty and conscientiousness of all men. Tithing will strike against the soul of the world (avarice); this is what the merchant, the businessman, the craftsman, and every worker strive for; out of money one achieves honor and glory, good food, splendid clothes; the comforts of the world depend to a great extent on money. That is the chatter and campaign for all, of every level and character. Although it is so great in the sight of men, to the point that they imperil their domestic situation, and their lives which are more precious than all the world, the Lord does not narrow his way or his order to please anyone, but let us say to all, "gold and silver are the Lord's," and despite how dear they are you must tithe them. Also let us consider that necessary qualifications are required for tithing, and unless a man has these in his possession, the profit that God intends for man to receive through tithing will not be enjoyed. If a man does not receive a benefit, which is the true purpose of God in connection with all the duties, it is

better for a man to refrain, even though his gold and his silver, as gold and silver, are as good as the best, and also they answer just as good a purpose. But in order for us to be blessed, we must act by faith, trust, and love for the principle, and remember honesty first and foremost. It is easy for us when by ourselves, to do things we do not do when many can see, and in the light, but let us remember that the sun of God always shines, and on us everywhere, and there is no secret that will not be made obvious, and also the unseen deeds of a man will be brought to light, for him to receive his prize and his glory, just as the unseen bad and dishonest deeds will bring public loss, disgrace, punishment, and shame in the light. Conscientiousness then is peace, and on this axis every man will be approved, in every duty, and it is impossible for anyone to be conscientious when he does not accomplish those things that are taught him. Tithing is taught to all the Saints as a heavenly law, and the peace of God is in connection with the duty, and great peace, in connection with great blessings.

II. *The Blessings that are enjoyed by obeying it.* One of the greatest blessings that man can obtain in the present situation is work, and whenever a man is out of work, it can be said of him, *he is a poor man indeed*, for he has no foundation for wealth. All the blessings of this life are founded on work, whether on his own or that of someone else. It is also reasonable and scriptural that all the blessings of a better life are based on the same nature of the thing, namely work, although the work can be totally different. Work is what fits a man to do work; work with one's hands is what hardens and adapts the hands, instead of the hands wearing out from rough and hard work, and the hands harden and become still more fit. So it is with a man when he walks, the feet harden; and carrying, the arm and shoulder are what make greatest what is strongest and more fit; so it is with the man in thinking, remembering, and writing, it is appropriate to say, *practice makes master*, with all things, and the greater the work, the faster the increase, (in moderation). We can say that the strength, usefulness, fame, wealth, and glory of all men in this world and the world to come, depends on work. The greatest loss then that a man can suffer is to be without work. Paying tithing is work, obedience to the Giver of the work after obtaining it is to do it, and in connection with doing it are the blessings.

1. The nature of the blessings that are enjoyed, corresponds to the nature of the things that are tithed, and it is a double blessing; the ninth part of the ten, of which the tenth part was a sacred prayer for them, blessed to answer the purpose greater than the ten, with success following to obtain eleven or more in the place of ten. "Prove me now herewith, saith the Lord of hosts, if I will not open you the windows of heaven, and pour you out a blessing, that there shall not be room enough to receive it." That which is tithed by its nature will be blessed. Everything that comes from the earth is tithed; therefore, the Lord says, "and he shall not destroy the fruits of your ground; neither shall your vine cast her fruit before the time in the field. And all nations shall call you blessed, for ye shall be a delightsome land, saith the Lord of hosts." Mal. iii, 10—14. We see from the above that the blessing of having a delightsome land, which constitutes blessedness, is connected with paying tithing. If we want beauty and blessedness on the earth, let us start on the way of making it, by paying tithing.

2. The manner in which blessings are enjoyed. God who governs all things, and whose spirit is in all places, and through His spirit every blessing that is enjoyed is given; at times he governs circumstances until they are acknowledged as miraculous, even by those who are not Saints. It is the Spirit of God that keeps families healthy and peaceful, bringing growth, strength, cleanness, and health in the children from the food they eat, influencing the mother to think of the most nutritional food, and cooking it in the best way. It is not the nature of the food in and of itself that satisfies or strengthens anyone, but the spirit that is in it. For example, the five loaves and the two fishes fed five thousand, in addition to women and children. A bit of bread and a bit of fish is not a sufficient meal for a man, unless that bit has as much of the spirit as would be in a usual meal; in that case it would do sufficient to strengthen just as well. It is the spirit that keeps alive, that strengthens, and spirit that feeds spirit, and we know that many live well, healthy and comfortable, and perhaps a family of six, from the same amount of money as a family of no more than four. What is it that causes this? I attribute it to the spirit that is around and within the family, and in connection with everything that has to do with it, food and clothing, and that they have the right

and legality of all the blessings they need, if they keep the law of the spirit. Honest tithe payers have a right to all the blessings of the earth.

3. Certainty of the enjoyment of blessings. All the promises of God are all yea and amen, in connection with every duty. The saint who believes that the principle of tithing is a heavenly law, and who believes that this law is now in effect, and who knows that God is united with his promises, has been, and is now blessed; that is sufficient certainty which makes the connection with tithing. The forgiveness of sins, the gift of the Holy Ghost, visions of the ministering of angels, in this age, and everything, in connection with the law of God, and the promises of God before he fulfills them, were and are enjoyed; this is how men enjoy blessings through tithing, and there is no basis to doubt that, for the truthfulness of the Lord has been proved in other things. "Heaven and earth shall pass away, but my words shall stand forever; I shall pour you out a blessing, that there shall not be room enough to receive it."

III. *The failure that would follow its opponents.* Everything that has a blessing connected with it when it is done, also has a curse when it is not done, corresponding in its size to the blessing, success in reverse is failure. It is possible for men not to do something without opposing it, but it is impossible for anyone not to do something without disregarding it. By not obeying, a man deprives himself of blessings, but the man who opposes deserves curses, as deserving as are the obedient of blessings. Tithing and the necessary blessings connected to it is a duty, and nine of every ten parts are the legal right of every man, and those who oppose this truth are punished. "Ye are cursed with a curse, for ye have robbed me, even this whole nation." (Mal. iii, 9.) Now let us comment on plundering as theft.

1. Stealing takes away the right of every man to have the blessings of government, and makes him unacceptable as a citizen, and unworthy as a member of society, and imprisons him as a criminal. The just merit of such is punishment. "Ye are cursed with a curse." This saying is appropriate, for every curse is a failure, whether it has to do with temporal or spiritual matters. The failure that follows the opponents of paying tithing deprives them of the blessings that are connected with paying tithing, namely food, clothing, wealth,

honor, and glory. Also, the rebel loses the Spirit of God, then he loses happiness, enthusiasm, affection, harmony, and health; and unhappiness of every kind comes in, to his mind, to his family, and to his society, and he becomes desirous of denying the entire faith, and opposing it. With all of this he becomes uncomfortable with himself, his family, and the entire society, falling into transgressions more and more with each passing day, until at last he is rejected by his family, and all of his acquaintances. Little by little he is opposed by all lovers of righteousness, so that he opposes the counsel of God, and all his own detest him because of his surrounding failure, and the poverty he has drawn to himself, and the grievous consequence of that seen on his family, and after a while he loses the entire faith given to the Saints, and the Spirit of God, and he is out of the church, under condemnation, and the day of his punishment is about to dawn. This is the perfection of failure, and all this awaits the opponents of God's commandments, of which the payment of tithing is one.

JOHN JONES.

ZION'S TRUMPET,

OR

Star of the Saints.

SATURDAY, FEBRUARY 21, 1857.

PAMPHLETS, &c.—*"Be faithful in good works"*—(From the "*Star.*")—According to the plan which we have laid before the Saints, a large number of Pamphlets are now in the Conferences, and we presume that they are generally being put into circulation among the people. The plan is an extensive one, and is calculated to do a proportionate amount of good, wherever continued and efficient efforts are made to carry it out. This rests upon the Elders and Saints in the various Conferences. Some of the people will, doubtless, refuse to receive and read these Pamphlets, and may treat many of those who carry the truth to them with contempt and abuse. But as they cannot come under condemnation until they have an opportunity of obeying or rejecting the truth, the Lord requires those who have received it and know something of its value, to give them that opportunity inasmuch as circumstances will permit. The Saints, in order to obtain salvation themselves, must do their duty, and clear their skirts of the blood of this generation. Therefore we exhort them to be diligent in this and all other duties that are required of them, in order to preach the Gospel, gather Israel, and build up the kingdom of God. Seek diligently for the light of the Holy Spirit to lead and guide you in all the duties of life. Set yourselves and your households in order; make Zion within yourselves and in your habitations. Then go forth and preach the Gospel, distributing Pamphlets, and also to your daily labors, with the Spirit of peace and goodwill burning in your bosoms; you will then have power to draw the honest in heart to the same great fountain of light from which you derive joy and comfort.

It is by faith and good works that we are to obtain our own salvation. In the kingdom of God our inheritances will be given to us according to the exertions we make to establish that kingdom on the earth. It is the united and constant efforts of the Saints, guided by the powers of heaven, that is to overthrow the power of Satan, and redeem the earth from his dominion. The Elders of this Church should preach the Gospel, and the Saints should visit from house to house, leaving the printed word, and when opportunity offers, bearing their testimony that God has again revealed his will from the heavens, and sent Apostles and Prophets to declare the way of life and salvation to the children of men. These individual efforts, when considered singly, appear small, and not productive of very great results, but when the multitude of them are all concentrated for the attainment of one object, they are mighty in their influence, and constitute the lever by which Babylon is to be turned upside down, and the kingdom of God established on its ruins. It becomes the Saints, therefore, to be diligent in all these apparently small things, out of which the great whole of this latter-day work is made up, and thereby obtain the fulfillment of the promise, that he who is faithful over a few things, shall be made ruler over many. This life, with its trials and sorrows, will soon pass away. As we become conscious that its last sands are leaving the hourglass of time, how pleasing it will be to review its changing scenes, and be able to say within ourselves that we are satisfied with life, having striven to do good and work righteousness according to the light that has been given to us. When the final account comes to be settled, if we find that our sins have gone before us to judgment, and that there is a *balance* in our favor in the accounts of this probation, we shall indeed be a thousand times repaid for all our labors here.

ARRIVALS.—Elders Henry Lunt and A. M. Musser are on a brief visit to Wales before they emigrate.

THE SAINTS are aware that our faithful brothers Evans and Ashby intend to return home this season. We wish the help of the Saints to this end *beyond* that which was assigned them, if possible, and their fervent prayers for them that the God of Israel will be with them to guide them through all trouble they may encounter.

BROTHERS Truman O. Angel and John Kaye visited with us recently for a few days. They went to see the iron and copper works to take note of their procedures, &c. There was considerable excitement in Llanelli because of the word that got out that an angel was preaching in the Saints' Chapel!

NEWS FROM UTAH.—In the "*Mormon*" for January 17, we learned that as many of the Twelve as are in the United States have decided to unite in their efforts to establish settlements across the Plains. Each settlement is to contain, at least, 50 able men, who can build forts, and defend themselves against enemies. They are to have every kind of farm tool to take with them, so they may raise wheat and all the necessary food for the emigrants. A handcart company cannot go through to Utah without receiving assistance along the way. Elders F. D. Richards and D. Spencer arrived before the Conference, and they reported the true condition of the companies which they passed on the plains. The first business transacted in the Conference was to invite volunteers to take teams with food to meet the immigrants, and to start off that very day. About 250 teams went out, with 26,688 pounds of flour, in addition to other food and blankets and warm clothing. The emigration was unreasonably late, and we fear there will be accounts of some of the last emigrants suffering. Perhaps we will have more information by the time we print our next issue.

A REFORMATION in the members of the Church of God is

something that should be a daily happening. To our sadness, all too often, proof is provided of the truth of the parable that compares the Kingdom of God to a net that is cast to the sea, that catches every kind of fish, which are separated after the net is brought to shore. The unpleasant sound of the quarrels and the hardening of hearts of the brothers and sisters in the Church of God towards one another, puts every Saint's teeth on edge who is a clean habitation for the Holy Spirit to dwell in, worse than the sound of the sharpening of a hundred thousand saws. The foul smell of the corrupt deeds of those who wear the name of religion like a mantle to be set aside when they wish is repugnant to the taste of those who love righteousness, and hate iniquity, and the lukewarmness of those who are neither one thing nor the other is like *vomit* to those who feel as God himself does.

AFTER the heavy threshing that has been taking place on the threshing floor, namely Zion, for some time, much chaff has been blown in every direction, and the shucked wheat has come forth in its purity. Repentance and baptism for the remission of sins is being preached to all the Saints of Utah, and they are being asked to gird up their loins and show whether they wish to live their religion and serve God by *truly* building his kingdom. This life is a testing situation, and a time for working; and the Saints are not to expect idleness and leisure if they are to achieve the highest feat in Christ Jesus, of which we have yet to gain scarcely any idea. Who ever heard of a lazy man being a godly man? or a lazy Saint being of any worth in this Church?

Besides encouraging you to consider the translation of the teaching of our President, we say, Prepare yourselves, for the word of the Lord is about to come from Zion, and it will not return to Him in vain. Let the diligent rejoice, let the doer of evil fear, and let the sluggish reform; for judgment is about to be set by a measuring type, and justice weighed in this country, as it *has begun in Zion*. The square and the compasses will be set against every stone in the building in Wales, and its rough edges will be cut away, and if it does not bear being trimmed, it will be thrown on the heap. Goodness gracious! is there any reason that a great work is cut out for many persons, and only some fulfill it, and the others, not only do they themselves not work, but they want to prevent others from doing so as well. They are like the year-old frog riding the two-year-olds.

We say to the Presidents of Conferences, Prepare your Branches to receive the word of the Lord. Let your query in every Branch be,

I. Is the President himself a good man and diligent *enough*, and an example to all the other officers? If he is not, let him be taken out of the way, and another put in his place.

II. Are all the officers in unity, and keeping their sickles shiny? Is there work being cut out in front of them—preaching, distributing pamphlets, visiting the Saints, &c.? Are they living frugally, fasting, purifying and sanctifying themselves in their conduct and increasing the godly particles of the Holy Ghost from within and around them, and in the invincible power of the Priesthood? If not, it is much better to have their offices taken from them and given to those who will use them.

III. Are the Saints alive? Are they free from slander and contention? Not infrequently such problems are neglected and considered small, until they grow and flood entire branches with a torrent of strife. To prevent this, the teachers, or the senior officers acting as teachers, should search out such things, and administer impartial justice. Ask them also if they are doing all they can by kindness and by seeking to persuade and induce before they administer the last letter of the law.

IV. Are all without exception who have any *income* paying their tithing to the Lord? If they are not, let there be no slackening of preaching, persuading, inducing, enlightening, or convincing, until it is done. Deal gently where there is inexperience and weakness; but where there are "old heads" who know the will of their Lord, and do not do it, beat them with many blows from sticks, until they are beaten to their obligations, or out of the church.

V. Let every Conference President of the South send a report, at least monthly, of the condition and the progress of his Conference, with the number who are paying tithing, together with the amount. Also the amount of debt of the Conference, if there is any, and to whom the Conference is indebted. Pastor J. Jones is to give an account of the Conferences of the North as often as he is able. Also requested is the status of tract distribution, preaching, baptizing, and also the weeding, and every account of interest.

In closing, we wish for every Conference President to prove his worthiness to *be able to continue* in his important office by doing these things. Let not the Offices forget about the publications and pamphlets, so that are encouraged to move the work forward. May our house be clean,—every piece of furniture in its place, and everyone clean and happy "minding their own business," so that we are fit to receive the word of the Lord; for, remember, *He is coming*.

TEACHING OF APOSTLE BENSON.

(Continued from page 30.)

Unless God, the owner of the earth and its fullness, can impart whatever He wants to his children, when will He see fit to receive it? By acting according to this principle I expect to possess everything I want,—wives, children, gold, silver, houses, lands, and every other good thing. They belong to the Lord, and they will not be given eternally to anyone except to those who hold the priesthood. Thus, you see that we do not have the cart before the horse, but each thing comes along naturally in his own time, although we may have to suffer and lay down our lives first.

I feel good tonight; there are many good people who will come into the church after this. Others may roar and spew out their "exposure of Mormonism" all they wish. That is what we want to do. We are on hand to expose it as much as we can to those who wish. I am not exposing some of its principles; and were the people who go to hear our enemies to come here to me, I could say that we tell them the truth; but if they prefer to hear anything bad about us, and if they love lies, they can go and gorge themselves on them, and go to hell.

Go to work, brothers and sisters; the elements that surround you are full of copper, silver, gold, and all needful things, and secure enough to pay your transport, so that you may deliver yourselves from the captivity of Babylon.

If the penny principle could begin here from this time forth, one year after next March, thousands of Saints could leave these countries because of it. Can you not, according to your understanding and your wish to free yourselves, gather sufficient faith to fulfill it? If you did not know where to turn for your next meal, and if starvation stared you in the face, unless the Lord were to help you, would you not exercise faith, and would you not pray for manna and quail? I should think you would, but it would be because you were forced to do so.

Seek, therefore, for words of wisdom from the Lord; act according to them, and gather home.

May you have the fullness of the Kingdom of God, and salvation in it, is my prayer, in the name of Jesus Christ. Amen.

INVITATION OF A SAINT TO HIS RELATIONS.

I imagine hearing the groans of the weak,
Sighing, and shouting, "oh! where is the place
For us to receive deliverance from the midst of oppression,
That smothers us now and crushes our breast.
    Where, where can we live,
On the face of the earth, under the protection of our God?"

I am ready to answer your lament,
And I shall now give the counsel for your sake;
I shall say truly now, without any plea,
Where you and I can have the total protection of heaven.
    Come, come, all together,
Come, hasten to Zion from old Babylon.

Through baptism by immersion your soul will live,
And the laying on of hands—you will receive the spirit of our God,
You shall be led happily from the midst of the world,
You shall be brought to Zion cheerfully together;
    Happy, happy will be your countenance,
In Zion cheerfully, in the enjoyment of the feast.

I have traveled far, far from my country,
With my longing for Zion, where relief is to be had;
Listen, you relations, and the Saints in joy,
Come, hasten to Zion from old Babylon.
    Come, come, all together,
You will come to Zion from old Babylon.

The cups of wrath are hanging down,
Above the wretches who now refuse,
To give obedience to the gospel of peace,
That now calls them to come to the feast.
    Come, come, all together,
Come, hasten to Zion from old Babylon.

Do not fear to travel across the lands and sea,
If you are faithful, you shall have the care of our Lord;
His care shall be over you, while you are on the earth,
The gospel will save you every minute—every hour.
    Come, come, all together,
O! come to Zion from old Babylon.

THOMAS F. THOMAS,

Pottsville, U. S. A., *Nov.* 30, 1856. *Formerly from Georgetown, Merthyr.*

ADDITIONAL NEWS FROM THE VALLEY.

As we were about to send this issue to the press, we received the Star that contained letters from Presidents Brigham Young and F. D. Richards.

They are full of consuming fire of the Lord. The chief topic of all the territory is about the REFORMATION that is to be. The servants of God preached with such power that they were obliged to refrain from saying more, because the people were groaning from "fear of the Lord." The exhortation of our Presidents in this country is to clean the church first, preaching a general *reformation* to the Saints in the power of the Lord, and give the truth, plain and strict to them, for our Prophet says that the Saints in this country, also, are too cold and sluggish with their important responsibilities.

A translation of both, together with the observations of President Pratt will be given in their entirety in our next issue. In the meantime, Presiding brethren in Wales, prepare yourselves and the Saints, through prayer and fasting, to receive the word of the Lord, which is like a two-edged sword. It will shortly be seen that none but the *diligent workers* will have the privilege of accomplishing work, and proclaiming the warning message of the Lord. Drink abundantly of the spirit of Zion, so that its effect will be felt through every abode in Wales.

The number of the two latest handcart companies of emigrants was about 900 souls. A snowstorm caught one of the companies in the *Sweet Water*. There were several feet of snow on the ground, and assistance just *barely* came in time for the two companies, says the mail, which came past for them. They were taken up into the wagons, wrapped in warm clothing, and fed abundantly, by the dear brethren who went voluntarily, and at their own cost, to complete such a loving task. President Young expected each one of them to come soon, "without their having to suffer much." He was quite unwilling for them to get such a late start across the plains.

MISCELLANEOUS, &c.

THE SHIP "COLUMBIA" sailed from Liverpool, November 16, 1856, with 221 Saints and others on board. One son was born on the voyage. They reached New York, January the 1st, after a voyage of 45 days.

BOOK PAYMENTS FROM JANUARY 5 TO FEBRUARY 5.—Wm. Ajax, Anglesey, 15s; Denbigh, 13s. and £1 8s. 4c. (Oct. 22, 1856); C. Harman, £2 14s. 1c.; J. J. Phillips, £1; A. L. Jones, £3; J. Gibbs, 3s. 4c.

DITTO FOR PAMPHLETS.—T. Stephens, £10 4s; John Treharn, 16s. 8c.; William Jones, £1 18s.; C. Harman, 15s.; D. John, £1 10s.; W. Ajax, Denbigh, 16s. 8c.; Anglesey, £1 5s.

MERIONETH Conference will be held, February 22; Conway Valley, &c., March 1st; Denbigh, the 8th; and Flint on the 15th.

CONTENTS.

	PG.
Treatise on Paying Tithing	33
Editorial—Pamphlets—Arrivals—News from Utah—Reformation, &c.	40
Address of President Benson	45
Invitation of a Saint to his Relations	46
Additional news from the Valley	47
Miscellaneous	48

SWANSEA:
PRINTED AND PUBLISHED BY DANIEL DANIELS.

ZION'S TRUMPET,

OR

Star of the Saints.

No. 4.] FEBRUARY 21, 1857. [Vol. X.

LETTER OF PRESIDENT BRIGHAM YOUNG.

EXHORTATION TO THE SAINTS IN EUROPE TO HUMBLE THEMSELVES—GET THE SPIRIT OF GOD—LAY ASIDE VAIN PHILOSOPHY—PREACH THE FIRST PRINCIPLES OF THE GOSPEL, AND WARN THE INHABITANTS OF JUDGMENTS TO COME.

President's Office, Great Salt Lake City,
October 30, 1856.

Elder Orson Pratt.

Dear Brother,—Your letters of July 6th and 31st, and August 5th, containing lists of persons not coming, who were sent for, and reasons why, were received on the 6th of this month.

Our immigration is late; the last two companies, consisting of over 900 souls, have not yet arrived. There is snow on the Mountains, and on the Plains.

We have sent out large supplies of teams, flour, other provisions, and clothing, so that we think they will all come in safely, without much suffering. Brother Smoot has not yet arrived, but is between here and Bridger, with plenty of *teams*.

The immigration is too late; this is an evil that must be remedied in future. We now give you positive instructions, that, so

4 [Price 1½c.

far as you control the immigration to come across the Plains, you are not to permit any company to leave the Missouri river later than the first of August, and it is far more preferable that they leave early in June or May. If they could start that soon, they would arrive here in time to aid in the harvest, and have an opportunity to lay up some provisions for winter; get wood, &c.; whereas now a great portion have to be sustained by charity almost a year, before they can do much for themselves.

Every year, large numbers of men and teams, and great quantities of provisions are sent back to meet the immigration; this is an outlay which is now considered, as it has always been, gratuitous; but it is a heavy task upon the people, and is becoming a serious public detriment. It prevents thousands of acres of wheat from being sown in the fall, which would, if more generally practiced, save an immense amount of labor in watering, beside producing a much larger amount of wheat, earlier harvest, and of superior quality. It prevents people from getting up their wood for winter; hence arises a vast deal more labor, to say nothing of suffering and expense, all of which, or at least a large share, would be avoided by having the privilege of performing this work in the proper season, when teams can find grass to eat, and have good roads to travel. Thus, you perceive the great disadvantages resulting from such late immigration; not only to the emigrants, but to all Israel; all of which might be avoided by an early start. Hereafter, therefore, let this be your motto—"Take time by the foretop, and if you do not do quite so much, do it better." But if you will do as we tell you, you will do more, as well as better.

Listen! There is a great reformation needed in England, Scotland, and Wales; the Saints are dead, and do not drink at the living fountain; the fire of the Almighty is not in them; and we make the same observation in regard to the Elders who are sent to preach.

Brother Orson, and brother Ezra, humble yourselves before the Lord of Hosts, and get the Spirit of the Almighty to fill you up;

receive the Holy Spirit, and let it live in your bosoms, and pour it out upon the people; arouse the people, the old and the young; the Elders and the Priests; the Seventies and High Priests; the Teachers, and Deacons, and all the Saints, to a sense of their obligations; cause themselves to sanctify themselves before the Lord of Hosts; make them practice cleanliness in their persons and houses, that the power of the Highest may rest down upon them. Let brother Benson and yourself, as much as possible, go through all the Conferences and Branches, and stir them up; and call and ordain Elders, and send them forth into the neighborhood, parish, and town, into every ward of the cities, and let the Elders meet often and pray, and talk about the things of the kingdom, and get the Holy Ghost. Trim off the dead branches, so that the tree may thrive, grow, and expand; so that it may furnish the living waters, where the Saints can come, and drink of the fountain.

Make the Elders, the Priests, Teachers, and Deacons work; cause them to awake from their stupor, and redeem the time they have lost while asleep; throw the arrows of the Almighty at them till you get them right; till you get them fired with the Holy Ghost; till you get them aroused and active, and see if the Lord does not pour you out a blessing greater than there is room to receive.

Be humble, and seek unto the Lord as children; put away your vain philosophy, and strip yourself for the Kingdom. Preach Christ, and him crucified—preach life and salvation unto the Elders; the Saints first, and then unto the people. Begin at home in the Office—purify and regenerate them; get the fullness of the Spirit, and the power of the Highest to rest down upon you, and then go forth to the people, and let a reformation be stirred up among the Saints; fire up each other, and then all the Saints; let all participate, and when they have sufficiently cleansed the inside of the platter, let them cleanse the outside, and renew their covenants in the waters of baptism and abide in the truth, and be alive in the Church, and Kingdom of God.

Let the Elders go forth into every nook and corner of the land, faithfully warning all men to repent and turn unto the Lord, preaching the first principles of the Gospel, being filled with the Holy Ghost, let them be active in their duties. Call up the past only to spur onward to the future; let *bygones* be *bygones*, and awake to newness of life.

Brother Benson, kick the scales from the eyes of the old Saints! and from the young Saints, and from the honest in heart, who come to hear the words of eternal life and salvation from the lips of the servants of the Lord. Counsel much together, abide in great faith, and be filled with the Holy Spirit, the testimony of Jesus, and of Joseph; and call upon the people to repent.

Dear Brethren, receive our exhortation in the spirit of meekness, that you may be strong. Be faithful and true, and put away selfishness, covetousness, and every besetting sin, that you may be pure in the sight of God our heavenly Father.

Work! labor for Zion! her welfare and her interests, and for the salvation of the people. Convert the Saints over again. We feel assured that they need it, or at least a good share of them do, and it will do none of them any harm. If any of them have got a little of the Holy Ghost, a little more will not hurt them.

We tell you they are dull; they are so here, as well; but we are awaking; let them awake in Europe also; let the sinner be afraid, and the hypocrite fear, and tremble, and let the first of the Almighty consume the wicked and ungodly, that their place may be no more known upon the earth.

We wish to have T. O. Angel return early in the spring; so that the work of the temple may be pushed forward another season.   .   .   .

Let brother J. A. Little be set as General Emigration Agent in the States the ensuing year. Say to him, that if he cannot get the companies off before the first of August, from Florence, to let them wait over another year, for *we are determined* to stop this *late* starting across the Plains. Ascertain the number, &c., of emigrants, as soon as possible, so that brother Erastus Snow may have all things in readiness for them to start directly across the Plains. Also let brother Taylor assist with his excellent abilities. . . .

We have just received an *express* from Captain Willie's company of handcarts; they are supposed to be now about Green river, as the express left them on Sunday morning, the 26th [of October] near the South Pass. We have no late tidings from brothers Martin, Hodgetts, Hunt, and William Walker. The Willie company had a pretty severe time in a storm which lasted two days, and then cleared up cold; the relief sent was timely, but none too soon. We sent, however, just as soon as we learned that they were coming, which was not until brothers Franklin, Spencer, and others arrived on the evening of 4th of this month.

We have also forwarded, since that time, a great many teams, designing to pick them up, and bring them all in.

The weather still continues to moderate, and this express informs us, that there is no snow in the road; it also gets better as they come this way. Brother George D. Grant, with eleven wagons and the best mule teams, went on to meet brother Martin, [Captain of one of the last companies we think.—ED.] not knowing where that would be. Let this be a lesson to us in the future, not to start companies across the Plains so late. It is a great mistake. The first three companies came through in good time, and were extremely successful, and they were quite late enough. [We think that the Welsh were the third company.—ED.] We had no idea there were any more companies upon the Plains, until our brethren [F. D. Richards, &c.] arrived, presuming that they would consider their late arrival in America, and not start them across the Plains until another year, but so it is, and now too late to remedy. . . .

If you, brother Benson, and the other brethren, go forth with the spirit of reformation through England and the British Conferences, as we have suggested, you will find a large increase of members, and means donated to the benefit of the work: you will find your hands untied, and be out of debt, and able to help us all that we shall require, and also be able to operate efficiently and successfully, in regard to emigration. Instruct the poor Saints to gather up and cross the seas, if they can get no further, and then they can make their way along; a great many would not be in the States over a year before they could fit out a team of their own and come on without help; others, perhaps, in two years might do the same. Instruct them in these things, and open every effectual door that you can to gather the Saints, aside from the aid furnished by the P. E. Fund, and then let that come in to the aid of such persons as cannot help themselves.

Praying the Lord to bless you and preserve you and your Council forever, I remain, truly, your brother in the Gospel of Christ.

BRIGHAM YOUNG.

NEWS FROM THE PLAINS.

(From the "Mormon.")

On the assurance of a telegraphic dispatch, we announced last week the arrival of the Salt Lake mail at Independence, but by correspondence we learn that it was only the conductor, Mr. Ferguson, that had arrived there December 29th, the mails having been left at Marysville.

How long the mails were detained or what have become of them we know nothing, but this much we do know, that we have not received either letters or papers from Utah since the above announcement. We regret exceedingly that anything should have prevented the speedy delivery of this mail, as many, with ourselves, are deeply interested in receiving definite intelligence of the *true position* of the late emigrants on the plains, and the circumstances attending the latter part of their journey.

We have read of the sufferings of travelers and surveyors on the plains and in the western territories from the early fall of snow, piercing cold of an unusually severe winter, and are apprehensive that the latter portion of our emigration has not escaped. The accounts of the Mormon suffering on the plains, are written with such rejoicing and unmistakable enmity to Mormonism that we entertain the hope that the calamity is much less than our enemies wish it. As the Saints are ever deeply interested in the well-being of their brethren we shall, in the absence of Salt Lake advices, quote from an outsider:

"Correspondence of the 'St. Louis Republican.'

Independence, January 4, 1857.

The arrival of the Salt Lake mail here, on the 29th of December, I neglected to mention when I last wrote you. From the conductor, Mr. Ferguson, I have obtained a statement of the trip, which, considering the character of weather and amount of snow on the plains, was one requiring no little fortitude on the part of those in charge of the mail, to bring it safely through. Accompanied by Mr. Briggs, and a few others, the conductor left Salt Lake City on the 1st of November. A few miles from the city, at the canyon of Wasack Range, they found snow to the depth of two or three, and even eight feet, through which they were compelled to travel for some distance, and, after much detention, reach Fort Laramie on November 19. They desired an escort, but none being provided, they pushed on; at Cottonwood Spring they met the outward-bound mail, [on their way to the Valley] under the charge of Jones. A little after that they encountered a snowstorm of much violence, impeding their progress, so much so that they were ten days in making 85 miles; they arrived at Fort Kearney December 11.

On their way in, near Bear River, they met the third handcart of 'Mormons' going west.

The fourth and fifth trains were met at the three crossings of Sweet Water, in a very different condition from those in advance. They were suffering beyond measure for the want of provisions and on account of the cold. They were very badly clothed, and in consequence of the hardships, many of them were dying; in one camp they buried fifteen in one day. The mode of burial, since they could not dig the frozen ground, is to lay the bodies in heaps, and pile over them willows and heaps of stones. President Brigham Young, learning something of their condition, dispatched some men and provisions to their relief; but these were met by the mail party returning to the city again, having been turned back by the violence of the storms they encountered. What the poor creatures will do, or what will become of them, it is hard to tell. Under delusion, they have left their homes in foreign lands, and to satisfy a whim of the Governor, undertook a journey of thousands of miles, not half provisioned or fitted for a trip that even in good weather is difficult enough, let alone at this inclement season of the year."

(To be continued at the end of the Editorial.)

ZION'S TRUMPET,

OR

Star of the Saints.

SATURDAY, FEBRUARY 21, 1857.

News from the Plains.—The vehicle of lies certainly travels quickly on its greased, libelous wheels from one reverend and editor to the other, and here is yet another sweet tidbit. Think not that our enemies are not rejoicing as usual, while, once again, they sing the elegy for the "wretched decease of Mormonism," as they say. So many of these remarkable "Mormons" have died, and lived, and died again, and yet live, until by now the Saints have lived too long next to the forest to be frightened by owls. This latest tale is again swollen and enlarged much like the one about "Jane's son John who vomited from his belly *three* whole crows." By asking the one who told the story, it turns out that he had heard from another that it was *two* crows, and the other had heard from another that it was *one*, and by going to the first, "certainly" he says, "I said something as black as a crow." We shall not add to the observations quoted from "The Mormon," any more than to bring them to the attention of the Saints, and encourage them to prepare for the next shriek that will come from the mouths of the unclean birds who feast on nothing but the stinking carcass of the lie.

THE REFORMATION.—We are glad to inform the Saints that we are expecting President Benson to begin the general reformation of the Church in Wales in this Office. We are confident, without multiplying words, that the Presidents and the Saints are preparing by much prayer, fasting, and pondering on their levity and indolence, and their frivolous words, and their improper deeds in the sight of the Lord, so that we might have more of the Holy Spirit, because there is something that exists that requires us to possess it before we can stand, either here or in Zion.

(Continuation of News from the Plains.)

"No local news of interest. Thermometer six degrees below Zero on Saturday morning." J. M.

The spirit of the above is manifest to everyone; of that, therefore, we take no notice; but while we think it very probable that numbers of the Saints have died on the plains, as by recent dispatches, we are certain that others have died, through being caught by an early winter. We think it quite as probable that the losses will turn out to be much less than such a gloomy account would warrant us to apprehend.

The mail conductor says he met the third company at Bear River, the fourth and fifth companies at the three crossings of the Sweet Water—the two latter in a very bad condition. Previous to meeting them, he says that he met the teams with provisions, clothing, &c., from G. S. L. City, returning, because of the violence of the storms they encountered, leaving it to be inferred by: "What the poor creatures will do, or what will become of them;" that the two last companies had been abandoned to their own impoverished resources. This may be true, but we don't believe it. In addition to the confidence we have in the perseverance, the bravery, the humanity of the Utonians, we have information that confirms our doubts in the mail conductor's or correspondent's conclusions.

The *Western Standard*, of San Francisco, California, publishes a letter from President Wilford Woodruff, of G. S. Lake City, dated

November 5th, *five days after this mail conductor left*, in which he states that two men had arrived in the city from the third company, and that before they left, the assistance from Great Salt Lake City had arrived.* Though we cannot dispute the assertion that the mail conductor met a company returning, we are confident that out of nearly two hundred and fifty teams sent out from the city with provisions, blankets, clothing, &c., some of them would fulfill their mission. There is, in our mind, on this no manner of doubt. The conductor says that the fourth and fifth companies were met at the crossings of the Sweet Water, and they were traveling west, which, being placed with the fact that the assistance had reached the third company, which was only some days in advance, there is not the slightest doubt that the emigrants would get assistance. Another thing should be borne in mind, that the last company, Hunt's company, had fifty wagons. These, no doubt, had both extra provisions and clothing.

We are prepared to hear of deaths by the way; but of starvation from lack of food we don't believe it. Our opinion, which we have more than once expressed before in this paper, was and still is that the emigrants started too late; but we sincerely hope that when all is known, things will be much better than some anticipate.

*See the latest Letter of President Young in this Issue.

REFORMATION.

MINUTES OF MEETINGS HELD AT 42, ISLINGTON, LIVERPOOL, ON WEDNESDAY AND THURSDAY NIGHTS, 4TH AND 5TH FEBRUARY FOR THE PURPOSE OF COMMENCING THE WORK OF REFORMATION IN THE CHURCH IN THESE LANDS.

Wednesday, February 4th, 7 *p.m.*

The following brethren having convened—
Presidents Orson Pratt, and Ezra T. Benson; Elders James A. Little, John A. Ray, Phineas H. Young, William G. Young, Truman O. Angel, John Kay, Miles Romney, C. R. Dana, James Marsden, Matthias Cowley, Asa Calkin, George Turnbull, Thomas Williams,

and E. W. Tullidge; Priests, William H. Perkes, and John Graham—

President Pratt arose, and explained the object of the meeting. He said—

"On Monday, the 26th of last month, I received a communication from President Young, stating the position of affairs in Zion, in which we are given to understand that the Saints in Utah are stirred up to reformation, and the renewal of their covenants. From this communication, we find that the work of reformation is progressing rapidly there. The President has also written to us to commence the same work here in this country, and throughout the mission, and to begin here in this Office. I have accordingly sent for brother Benson, and we have concluded to bring the brethren of the Office together, that we might pray together, repent of our slothfulness, renew our covenants, and be baptized. I am happy to see so many others here to unite with us on this occasion."

He then opened the meeting with the following prayer—

" Our Father, who art in heaven, we thy servants have assembled together from the various fields of our labor in thy ministry, for the purpose of humbling ourselves, and commencing anew to worship thee, and renewing our covenants, calling upon thy name with all our hearts, that we may receive the abundance of thy Spirit to cause our hearts to rejoice.

"O God, the Eternal Father, we pray thee to look in mercy upon us who have named thy name, and are most of us absent from our families, and the Presidency of thy Church, on foreign missions. We feel thankful that thou hast permitted us to receive a communication from thy servant, President Young, calling upon us to repent of our sins, and reform, and renew our faithfulness and diligence. We feel thankful for the work of reformation going on there, and that we have received thy word, showing us our situation before thee. He has pointed out the condition of the missionaries and thy Saints. He has represented us as being dull, and dead as pertaining to the things of thy kingdom.

"O God, the Eternal Father, inasmuch as thy servant has thus represented our situation, and has called upon us to repent and turn away from our sins, even so we desire to comply, and for this purpose we have assembled together, that we may confess our sins—that we may renew our covenants, and be determined to keep thy commandments—in order that our sins may be forgiven, and that we may receive the renewal of the Holy Spirit in our hearts. Give us power that we may search ourselves—that we may know ourselves—that we may find out every sin that is lurking within us—that our faith may become great—that we may be filled with the Spirit, and that we may know by its teachings every duty devolving upon us. We pray that when we become converted, thou wilt enable us to strengthen our brethren—to preach to them repentance—to point out their errors, and the necessity of being obedient to thy word, that they may enjoy more of thy Spirit; and to cut off those who will not work righteousness, and obey thy word—that thy Spirit may be more abundantly poured out—that the word of God may spread—that the arrows of the Almighty may reach the hearts of thy people, and of the honest in heart—that thy hand may be made manifest—that thy works may be shown forth in thy Church—that the honest in heart may see the good works of thy people, and glorify their Father in heaven, and that thousands may come forth with broken hearts and contrite spirits and obey the truth.

"May thy Spirit be poured out upon us this evening. Remove from our minds all darkness and dullness. Let the energy of the Holy Spirit be with us to instruct us. May our hearts be purified and strengthened, and may we feel that thou art with us, to bless us and to do us good.

"Bless thy servants who are appointed to preside over thy Church in these countries. We feel that we need thy Spirit to enable us to instruct thy people and give them counsel—and that we have no counsel or wisdom of our own. We ask that we may be filled with the spirit of revelation, and that thou wilt give us such instructions as will benefit the Saints.

"Hear us in these our humble breathings—be propitious to us, and bless us. We ask these things of thee, in the name of Jesus Christ. Amen."

President O. PRATT said—

"You have all read President Young's letter. I feel that it is of the utmost importance to carry out its instructions, according to the letter and spirit. So far as I understand, it is necessary for us to put away the evils we may have been practicing—to cease from everything that is wrong—to renew our covenants, and be baptized. I feel that I would like to hear the mind and feelings of all present on the subject."

President Ezra T. Benson said—

"I feel the necessity and importance of the reformation. It caused my heart to rejoice very much, when I read the letter. I jumped up and shouted, 'Glory! hallelujah!' Although I have tried to preach reformation wherever I have traveled, I have felt that the Saints were sleepy, dull, and slothful in attending to their duties, and unless there were some excitement more than usual, not more than half the Saints would attend the prayer and sacrament meetings. It has seemed out of the power of the presiding officers to get the people together. I feel that this move is necessary, and I am glad that it has come. I am determined to get a renewal of the power of God. I believe I shall if I do my duty, and cooperate with those who are over me. I have the best of feelings toward all my brethren and sisters, and I want to do them good. In order to be able to do good to them I must do good to myself first. In order to infuse the Spirit into them I must have it myself. I am willing to comply with any suggestions the President may make. If I have not traveled and preached enough, I am willing to try it again and do more. If I have not climbed high enough on the tree, I am willing to climb a notch higher. I feel as good as I know how; still there is a chance for me to feel better. If I have had a little of the Spirit, I can still have a little more. When an Elder has enough of the Spirit of God, the people, and the world know that he is preaching by the power of God, and that is the man that will be talked about. When a man is preaching by the power of God, mobs may rage, but they cannot touch him. The Devil will howl. Then let him howl on.

"If we are going to have a reformation, let us have one indeed. Let us get heated up, that it may not be like hammering cold iron; and let the reformation be both spiritually and temporally. I want it to take place in temporal things as well as spiritual! and not to put the cart before the horse.

"I would to God we had every Pastor and President here. We

would lock them up in a room, and keep them there three days and three nights, and would hammer and pound them until we got them into some shape. It is the Pastors and Presidents who are asleep as well as the people. They think themselves the biggest men in the world, if they can walk about in a first-rate suit of clothes. Do they dig about the people, and know how the money is disbursed? Do all the Presidents consult their Pastors about their business? Some do, and some do not. They buy watches, and chains, and so forth, and do as they please. I would they were here, and then they should stay here till they got the Spirit of God into them. I want to see this reformation become thorough, spiritually and temporally. Let us take a position to render an account of our stewardships.

"Brother Brigham knows the people are not living in the lively exercise of their duties, and we also know it. They are dead, and must resurrect them. There is a great deal to be done. A great many understand the Gospel, Priesthood, authority, &c., in theory; but talk about it practically, and you find that they are as far from it as sectarianism is from heaven. They are stereotyped, and carry out a fixed form in their meetings just like the sectarians. When I read the 6th chapter of Moroni, I find their meetings were controlled by the power of the Holy Ghost. How is it among the Saints here? Let brother Pratt or myself go into a meeting, and you would see some President get up and extol us to the highest heaven, and preach the preliminaries of a discourse for us, and take up all our time. Oh! look out! President Benson! One of the Twelve Apostles! &c. I feel to cut myself loose. I will bear it no longer. I will have the Priesthood respected.

"This letter has put fire on to fire: and, with the help of God, I am on hand to kick the scales from the eyes of the people.

"I feel that God is here. We will have a glorious time. God help us to reform, to be spiritually minded, and to perform every duty required of us, in the name of Jesus. Amen."

Elder JAMES A. LITTLE said—

"I am happy to be meet with my brethren. Brother Benson has expressed my views. It has long appeared to me that the Elders and Saints are stereotyped. They are bound to a certain system, and whether it is right or wrong it makes no difference. Many have thought and acted as though these forms were all there was of 'Mormonism.' I have endeavored, with my imperfections, to do the best I could; and I have tried to get more of the Spirit. I want it, and I believe I shall get some more. The President's letter fired up my spirit and filled me with joy. The Lord bless you all. Amen."

Elder JOHN A. RAY said—

"I feel thankful for the privilege of meeting with this Council. Since I was called upon this mission, I have sought the Spirit of the Lord to guide, direct, and strengthen me. I know that I have not been as faithful as I should have been. I have not enjoyed as much of the Spirit as I would like. I realize that I can do no good unless aided by it, and I am dependent on the arm of the Lord to strengthen me. It is thus with all the Elders—they will never do any good unless the Lord employs them. I was thankful when I read the President's letter. It is a privilege for us to renew our covenants. I wish to enter into covenant with the Lord—endeavor to lay aside every sinful thing, and I pray that the kingdom of God may roll on with mighty power. I feel that the Saints are dull, and that there is a great reformation needed before the work can go forth. I am willing to make an effort to reform, and get more of the Spirit to aid me in the discharge of my duties."

Elders Phineas H. Young, John Kay, C. R. Dana, Miles Romney, James Marsden, William G. Young, Truman O. Angel, Matthias Cowley, Asa Calkin, Thomas Williams, E. W. Tullidge, and George Turnbull, and Priests William Perkes, and John Graham, several expressed their thankfulness for the privilege of renewing their covenants, and their determination to exercise renewed diligence in their performance of their duties, and contend for more of the Spirit of God than they have had theretofore.

(To be continued.)

MISCELLANEOUS, &c.

The Measure of the Stature of the Fullness of Christ.—We are sorry that the abundance of the news from the Valley and the Plains have obliged us to leave out of this Number the continuation of the above topic; but we hope that the measure of patience of the Author is sufficiently abundant to pardon us this time, while we promise to put it in at the next opportunity.

We hope that our readers will excuse our tardiness in bringing out the 'Trumpet,' when we inform them that the cause of that is, that we are waiting until the last minute, while expecting important News.

Latter-Day Saint Psalmody.—Let the Saints be aware that it is intended to publish the first Volume of this book soon. Its price to Subscribers will be 5s.; to others 7s. 6c. We hope that the coming out of this Book will be supported, by a large distribution of it. Send orders and payments for it to the Liverpool Office.

CONTENTS.

	PG.
Letter of President Brigham Young	49
News from the Plains	54
Editorial—News from the Plains—the Reformation	56
The Reformation	58
Miscellaneous	64

SWANSEA:
PRINTED AND PUBLISHED BY DANIEL DANIELS.

ZION'S TRUMPET,

OR

Star of the Saints.

No. 5.] MARCH 7, 1857. [Vol. X.

THE LATTER-DAY WORK—PREPARATION.

(From the *Star*.)

The glory of the Latter-day kingdom, the gathering together of the people of God, the building up of Zion, the restitution of all things, the second coming of Christ, and the Millennium, were themes on which the high-toned minds of the Prophets dwelt with fervid inspiration. These subjects lent them wings to soar in such lofty flights as would make the most eagle-eyed imagination of an uninspired mind grow dizzy. Borne higher, and higher, by the energy of the Holy Ghost, in the visions of the Almighty, they reached the celestial sphere of life and dipped themselves in that glory which they foretold should cover the earth, in the fullness of times, even as the waters cover the bosom of the mighty deep. As their prophetic souls grasped a few prominent points and generalities of these magnificent views, their descriptions were given with the most powerful eloquence. Indeed, on the above-named subjects, they spent the fullest vigor of inspired minds.

To follow them in their towering flights, to comprehend the grandeur of the scenes which they beheld, through the vista of the uncurtained future, and to look with confidence to the literal fulfillment of the prophetic visions, requires the mind to be enlightened by that Spirit which drew the curtain aside, and needs

[Price 1½c.

a faith as sublime as the Prophets themselves possessed. The things of God, to be understood and made lucid to the eye of faith, must be spiritually discerned. Viewed by the uncertain light of human wisdom, the obscurity will be heightened by the fantastic creations of the imagination, and misty, flickering conceits will be substituted for a clear and solid faith. Hence to those who are destitute of the gifts of the Spirit, the great events predicted to come to pass in the latter days will appear as mysterious, forgotten dreams, requiring a Daniel to narrate their substance, and interpret their meaning. Or, perchance, to distorted imaginations, they will seem like phantoms of the midnight watch, which strike terror to the soul, but elude the physical senses, which vanish at pursuit, but which all are careful to shun, and the most courageous are anxious to drive from their thoughts. It is thus that the promised glory and inheritance of the Saints, and the threatened judgments to be poured on the wicked, are generally viewed.

The Christian nations acknowledge the authority and inspiration of the sacred writers, and will not refuse to subscribe to the prophetic descriptions. Their priests make glowing discourses from those grand passages of scripture, relative to the subjects named. There are few who are altogether infidel regarding the great events foretold in the Bible.

But then, to the popular faith they are like fairy lands, and haunted castles, furnishing to ministers rare objects for description, imagination, and eloquence; but whose characters no one thinks of inviting to his fireside; no one expects the drama to become a part of everyday life.

Tens of thousands of sermons have been preached, and millions of pages written from the prophetic descriptions of the glory of the Latter-day Church, Zion, the Coming of Christ, and the Reign of Righteousness. There is hardly a man in Christendom who has not at some time prayed, "Thy kingdom come, thy will be done in earth, as it is in heaven;" nor a professor of religion who has not embodied in his supplication the sentiment—"Hasten the time, O Lord, when thy knowledge shall cover the earth, as the waters cover the bosom of the mighty deep, and a reign of righteousness dawn upon the world." But, then, one part of their faith is at war with the other. The flickering of their own conceits, in the spiritual darkness that covers them, dazzles their faith like a thousand Will-'o-the-wisps. They make no preparations for the great work of the last days; but all things move along with them as from the beginning. Their mystical interpretations of the Scriptures stand in the way of the literal fulfillment of the prophecies; and the glorious drama that fired the minds of the Prophets evaporate into airy nothings.

Being without the inspiration of the Holy Ghost—the spirit of revelation through which the events were seen—the vision is sealed to them, the substance is lost in shadowy dreams. Believing that the voice of prophecy is forever hushed, and the heavens closed against all communion between God and man, His kingdom coming, and His will being done on the earth as it is in heaven are little different to them, from fairy tales, and the knowledge of the Lord, covering the earth as the waters cover the deep, is to them nothing better than a myth. Thus is it with every other item of the Latter-day work to the foggy understanding of the popular mind.

We, however, look upon these glorious subjects precisely in the light in which the Prophets of old viewed them. To us they have a literal meaning; and we are ever looking forward to preparation and fulfillment. It is because the mission of the Prophet Joseph Smith fulfills the ancient prophecies, and every development of that mission prepares the way for a more complete revelation of the glory of the dispensation of the fullness of times, that we are bold to declare that all who have written upon the subject by the inspiration of God, testify to that which Joseph has done. When we listen to the proclamation from tens of thousands of voices that the kingdom spoken of by Daniel has been set up; when we hear the witnesses to the fact, that the Gospel which John said should be committed to the earth by the angel, has been restored, to be preached to every nation; when we see it winding its way to earth's remotest bounds, we say to ourselves the work is preparing; the prophecies are fulfilling—things move in the right direction. When we hear the voice thundering through the channel of the Priesthood, "Come out of her, my people;" and from lip to lip of God's servants the command passes along, "Gather together my Saints," we say the path is preparing; the glory of the latter days is dawning on the world. When we behold tens of thousands flocking to the chambers of the Lord, as doves to their windows, and busy hands building up Zion, that the Savior may suddenly appear in his glory; and when in answer to the cry, "Behold the Bridegroom cometh, go ye out to meet him," the Church of the Lamb puts on her beautiful garments of reformation, we are ready to shout Hosanna! God is preparing His people; the visions of the Prophets were not fables.

FAREWELL ADDRESS OF ELDER ISRAEL EVANS.

"Zion's Trumpet" Office,
Swansea March 3rd, 1857.

Kind Saints,

Since I have been released to go from your midst, and to return to the home of the Saints, I feel to tell you of my feelings about my labor among the Saints in Wales, and also about my return to Zion.

When I came to Wales, I was a stranger in a strange land, yet I was not a stranger to the majestic principle that caused the bosoms of the Saints to burn with gratitude to high Heaven for the blessings of light and truth that were poured out upon them in these latter days. When Elder Ashby and I arrived in your midst, the emigrating season was quickly drawing nigh. We endeavored to do what we could to assist in giving counsel and direction to the emigrants (for we had nothing else to give), and we accompanied them as far as Liverpool, and we gave the most energetic assistance we could in getting them on board the *S. Curling*, headed for Boston, which sailed April 17th, 1856. It is well known that it was a large group of emigrants that left Wales last spring, and, as is the case with every such group, there was a huge void left behind since all but two of the Conference Presidents and their families emigrated, which void also brought new hands to the field, most of which were not only strangers to their fields of labor, but also strangers to the situation they were called to. The emigration also took all the Traveling Elders, as well as those who could have gone into the ministry, so that no more than two or three traveling elders were left in the whole mission, and no one to be sent out. President Daniels was required to spend most of his time in the office, since he was called to assume the presidency of the mission, and the burden of publishing, &c., which drew his experienced labor away from the field.

Thus, brothers and sisters, was our condition at the beginning of the operations last spring, and had we looked at it with the eyes of the natural man, and considered what we had to do, we would have shied away from it. But, thanks be to God, we did not look at it that way, rather with the eye of that faith that enables the faithful Saint to overcome all things, and we were blessed and prospered accordingly. In this condition we began to build up a "shattered kingdom;" for, through God's blessing and the efforts of his faithful servants, there were not only branches but also conferences broken up by so many of the Saints leaving to go to America, and to the land of Zion. But it was necessary to do something, as none of the Saints wished to stop, rather they wished to rise up, and, in the name of the God of Israel, to go forth in the fulfillment of their duties; but as it appeared that the Lord was greater than them all, consequently there was some greater and stronger principle enabling us to more powerfully concentrate our energy, through which we received greater power to honorably bring forth the work that had fallen on us. What was the stronger principle? It was the law of tithing, which was presented in the first conference in Merthyr after the departure of the Saints last spring. And not only in Merthyr was it presented, but all the Saints in every conference throughout the Welsh Mission were called upon to pay their tithing. It is true that with grateful feelings to God and love for the Saints that we saw many answer the call, from the beginning. Gradually, several others have grasped the principle so they have been made more fully aware of it, and their faith has increased in the work of God. A few are still standing back, but the time of separation has come, and those who do not live their religion, and who do not obey the laws of God, will no longer be recognized as being among the people of God. The principle of tithing has power in itself that is equal to the task placed on it; for it has enabled us to pay our domestic expenses, to pay down much of the debt, and to raise about £300 for the temple fund, and it has become firmly established among the Saints, so that much more is being fulfilled this year than last. The sapling of last spring was very young and tender, but it has grown by now into a robust tree, bearing good fruit.

Therefore, dear Saints, take heart, and live up to these requirements as well as the other principles of salvation that will be made known to you, and they will bring the blessings of heaven down on your heads, and they will hasten your deliverance from the land of oppression to the land of freedom.

The signs before you are quite promising—the young plant is far beyond the reach of the "young Foxes," who long to hinder its growth. In the field you also have additional highly skilled Elders, some of them from Zion, who are "towers of strength" to you. Also, a series of the strongest pamphlets now promoting this work is coming to your hands, which are awakening many of the honest who, before now, had been kept completely unaware of the truth of the Gospel.

The coming *Reformation* will be a blessing to all of the faithful Saints, by cutting away all the dead branches, and separating the tin from them, bringing them closer to the Lord, uniting them more closely in the bonds of love, giving more power to them to bring the honest in heart from the errors of their ways to the glorious light of the truth.

When I begin to reflect on the condition and the signs of the mission, I feel truly grateful to the Lord, who has sustained us thus far, who we know will continue to sustain us for as long as we do His will.

I feel like I would like to remain with you, and I could assist you in rolling this great work forward.

During the past year that I have spent with you, I have labored with great joy and contentment, having assisted in presenting to you some of the laws of Zion, which until then you had not been called on to observe, and with which you have cheerfully complied. All we had to do was to lead forward, and point out the way, and you have followed bravely and faithfully hold up our hands, which have pulled down the blessings of heaven upon us, and proved a continual blessing to us all.

I have traveled twice around the mission thoroughly, and several times through the southern parts, and you have always been ready to bless me, and to minister to my needs, while I traveled like a stranger in your midst. If at times I failed to give such counsel and direction to you which would encourage and comfort you in time of need, and to strengthen you in the cause of truth, it was not because of lack of desire on my part, rather a lack of ability to do so.

I have labored in great pleasure with Presidents Daniels and Ashby; also with the Conference Presidents. Although unacquainted with their fields of labor, and with the condition to which they were called to act; yet they were men of integrity, with a constant wish to do good.

Elders Miller and Taylor are now here with you; I feel to thank you all for every manifestation of kindness to me, and to beseech you not to forget us in your prayers as we travel to Zion. Though we will be far from you, we will always remember the time we spent in the ministry in Wales, and our prayers will ascend on high for deliverance to come to the faithful of the people of the Lord.

May the blessings of Heaven continually follow us, so that we may meet again in Zion, is the prayer of

Your brother and friend,

ISRAEL EVANS.

ZION'S TRUMPET,

OR

Star of the Saints.

SATURDAY, MARCH 7, 1857.

REFORMATION.—A Reformation Meeting will be held in this Office, on the 12th day of this month, under the presidency of Apostle Benson. The various presidents have already been advised who are expected to be present, and we hope they will all be energetic in their efforts to be here promptly to meet with President Benson during his visit with us concerning a matter so important and serious as is the reformation of the Saints.

LETTERS, &c., FROM THE VALLEY.

Great Salt Lake City,

November 11, 1856.

My dear brother Daniels.—I am happy to inform you that I arrived here safely, with the Pantmawr family, who are all well. They went to Box Elder to their relatives. I am working in South Cottonwood, and when I come to the City, I take lodging in your house and with your family.

Your dear wife is well. Today your son Dafydd went out to meet with the immigrating Saints and assist them on the plains, and several others went with him.

One company came in last Sabbath day, and the rest are expected in within a week.

I am enjoying life to my heart's content, and thankful to God for the privilege of having arrived at this place. Here there are some of the best men I have ever seen, and also some wicked men.

My warm regards to all the Saints, but to no one more than to yourself.

Your humble brother,
RICHARD WILLIAMS.

Excerpts from the Letter of the above Richard Williams to his relatives.

Great Salt Lake City is a much more excellent place than I thought it would be, especially considering the short time its inhabitants have had to build it.

The time is getting closer when the wicked will not be permitted to stay here any longer. There is a call for every person to repent and do better from now on than they have ever done. Men have been appointed to visit every family of Saints throughout the Territory, and to inquire separately of every enlightened individual where he is guilty of any sins, such as stealing, lying, taking the name of God in vain, cheating any brother or sister, or any other sins. Each question will be asked individually, and every person is required to answer them. If he lies, the curse of God will be upon him: if he is found guilty, recompense will be required for the transgression. There is no place here for hypocrites. Hundreds of officers have been called to look into the condition of the people. Brother T. C. Martill is one of them in the area where he lives, and he is busily engaged in such work today. He sends his kind regards to you.

Sister Daniels sends her best to you, to the Cwmcoch family; remember me to my relatives, &c.

I have received sufficient work for eight shillings and fourpence per day plus my food. . . .

The time is getting close when the government of the United States will be in the hands of the Saints. President Brigham Young says that not many years will pass before the President of the Church of Jesus Christ of Latter-day Saints will have the right to place a President over the United States. The work is going forward very quickly. Let the Saints there wake up and prepare for the time that is at the door.

May the blessing of God be with you all. Amen.

RICHARD WILLIAMS.

(Ditto from the Letter for November 16, 1856, from the same place.)

Dear brother Daniels.—I am glad to hear through brother Captain Jones, of your faithfulness and your success in the work of our God. I pray constantly for you and your fellow laborers.

A thorough and general reformation is now underway throughout all the stakes of Zion, until the sinner in Zion is fearful, and the hypocrite flees from the questionnaire to the kingdom of the "yellow God," where they can satisfy their lusts in a way they cannot do here.

Brother Captain Jones received a great welcome from all on his return here. He was made a home missionary to preach the reformation in all places, but more particularly among the Welsh.

The immigration is unusually late this year. Those who arrived a week ago today suffered quite a lot in the snow; but they were delivered by about 250 teams that went from here to meet them, and about 100 wagons have gone to meet the last company. I expect them within 9 days. . . .

Tell the Hafod y Gofen people that I have sent two letters to them, and I have not had one answer, and I do not know who I should write to. . . .

My great desire is for your success in the work to which you were called, and my constant prayer is for God to watch over you that you may receive abundantly of His Spirit to enable you to yet do a great work in Wales.

Your dear Brother,
RICHARD WILLIAMS.

"THE MEASURE OF THE STATURE OF THE FULLNESS OF CHRIST."
By Elder Evan Rees.

(Continued from Number 2.)

After proving the origins of man, let us next observe his present condition and his future increase.

After *proving* that the Father of our Spirits is God, there is no cause more than the remembrance of our having sinned against

Him, and having gone back from his glory—having been born into this sinful world, in the midst of all kinds of trials and tribulations, so that the following words are borne out in us, namely, "Man that is born of woman is of few days and full of trouble." Nevertheless, all these things are for our good, for, without the bad, one cannot know and appreciate the good—without the bitter, the sweet cannot be so delicious.

I have already commented on man in his origins, and in his present sinful condition. Next, let us inquire as to whether it is possible for man to be raised up from this misery? Yes, it is possible to set the captive free, and bring the distant near; but it was not so before the coming of our Older Brother, Jesus Christ, our Savior, to this earth to put on flesh, and live and die to please his father—so that he opened the way for to save us, and exalt us for an habitation of God. (Ephes. ii, 22.) "In whom ye also are builded together for an habitation of God through the spirit." If God can dwell in us, we will be in possession of all things. Paul says boldly, that all things are ours. It is said also, "One God and Father of all, who is above all, and through all, and in you all." Here we see that the Father himself is to be in this body, after it is thoroughly cleansed and made fit, so there be in it neither spot nor wrinkle. I do not believe that these things can come to pass before this mortal puts on immortality, or before all the Saints receive clean and pure resurrected bodies, and are free from the present imperfection. Then the fullness of God will be in all the godly, and God will be all in all. That is the time that the prayer of our Savior will be answered, when he prayed to the Father like this, "O Father, I ask that they may be one in me, as I am in thee," &c. (See St. John.) Then we shall be in Christ, as Christ is in God.

I believe that I have showed quite clearly the possibility of the progress of man to the condition Paul mentions, and that all that is needed is an effort on our part for us to reach it. Our merciful Father has approved the way that was organized by the Son, and the Son says, "Come unto me, all ye that labor and are heavy laden, and I will give you rest," and His servants call and say, "We are missionaries for Christ to help you become reconciled with God."

My father, the Preachers of the Saints have the word of the covenant, and there are hosts of the Welsh like myself who know that. This plan is as effective today as it has ever been, and his work and its effects are seen on me myself, so that I can say in the words of the Psalmist in Psalm xl, 2, "He brought me up also out of an horrible pit, out of the miry clay, and set my feet upon a rock, and established my goings. And he hath put a new song in my mouth, even praise unto our God," and here it is:

"Praise for religion in its substance,
   I was in a very long shadow;
I was in darkness for a long time,
   With the Saints I received enlightenment,
Praise for it,
   I shall cling to the work forever."

Your dear son,
EVAN REES.

MY DREAM.

While I was in the area of Dyfed,
   I had a most enlightening dream,
Which contained revelations
   From my Heavenly Father.
In the dream I traveled for a time,
   Between very high mountains,
While gazing on their majesty,
   I saw on them perpetual snow.

I asked my fellow traveler
   "Tell me, my dear friend,
"What is all this I see here
   For the first time in my life;"
I heard a loud voice answer,
   That traveled from afar,
Its influence pierced my heart,
   I was mute, and filled with fear.

In a splendor that was unique,
   I saw a beautiful Heavenly being;
I felt the smallest,
   In His presence;

"This multitude you see,
    (He said,) are the Saints of our God;
They are gathering to their shelters,
    To them it is a true privilege."

"This is the great stewardship,
    Of the fullness of times;
Under it God's vials are poured
    Onto the inhabitants of Babylon.
All the false worshipers of the beast,
    Will feel in their woe, every plague
While the wrath passes by,
    The Saints will be safe!

"This is the reason why that crowd
    Is seen gathering together,
Before the wrath of God is poured out,
    The Saints will be home in time;"
There I felt for the first time
    The wondrous power of the Holy Ghost;
I saw light almost everywhere,
    And my whole heart was a fiery flame.

Quickly flew the piercing thought
    Like very quick and strong lightening,
And in the midst of the felicity,
    Morning and afternoon became one;
"What is the reason, (he asked me)
    That you spend your fleeting hours,
Groping in darkness
    You remain in a false college

"Come quickly to the true Church,
    Come inside, said the Spirit of God,
There you will gain eternal joy,
    Also peace while you dwell here;"
"I believed, (was the reply,)
    That I was now in Christ's kingdom;
But truly I do not have assurance,
    And for this I am feeling sad.

Tell me holy Teacher
    What religion is pure?
I am willing to consecrate my soul
    To possess this, truly."
"You shall receive a revelation from me,"
    (Was His cheerful reply;)
"Look up with sobriety
    And honesty toward heaven."

There I saw gentle Jesus,
    On his strong and solid throne;
Crowds were assembling together,
    To be judged by Him;
There I saw religionists
    Of this age, with sad countenances,
They hid their long faces,
    Without having a particle of faith.

Rotten rags were their raiment:
    All were weeping and wailing;
Jesus shouted with authority
    "The great host is lost;"
Then I saw the Mormons,
    White beings, clean beings.
In joy they appeared,
    Loud, loud was their song.

They surrounded the beautiful throne,
    Lifting up high praise,
They received respect from Jesus,
    To reach Him was their purpose,
These I recognized on earth
    In poverty, I found them,
Today all, they were Priests,
    And very high kings.

They received great kingdoms,
    Over which to rule forever,
Respect and honor they all gave,
    To their beloved Prophet Joseph Smith,

Soon I perceived that untrue,
    Was all my false religion:
There I wept in poverty
    While the world was ending.

I shouted in a deadly faint,
    "Angel, tell me what to do:
In poverty I grieve,
    The pleasant summer has passed."
"Take comfort, be brave;
    Exercise faith in thy God,
Thy life will again be extended,
    Thou shalt live for a long time."

May thy time be consecrated,
    To His splendid vineyard;
In the premortal life I say,
    Thou wert foreordained to heaven.
"Look up to the north country,
    Look, look in haste,
At that which I made in a short time;"
    A great sweat poured over me.

There I beheld an exquisite valley,
    A beautiful valley—the valley of God,
The valley of the dear mountains of Ephraim
    The valley where the Saints dwell together;
It was adorned with flowers,
    And with fruit of every kind;
They did not contain deadly seeds,
    They showed the love of God.

I saw there every delicacy,
    There were also grapes;
I saw there a host feasting,
    Their cups were all filled.
The perfume of the beautiful flowers
    Filled the air all around;
Jesus reigned there,
    With a beautiful crown on his head.

On the foreheads of the one hundred forty thousand,
   I saw a word inscribed;
In splendor it surpassed
   The gold a myriad times:
They were Gods to the highest,
   In them they had complete contentment.
They possessed other names—
   High Priests of the highest degree.
(To be continued.)

NEWS FROM UTAH.—(From the *Star*.)—Through the latest information received from Utah, containing a letter of President Young, for December 7, 1856, we are pleased that the last of the handcart companies has reached Great Salt Lake City. They had suffered quite a lot, but there were fewer deaths in their midst than usual among very well organized companies with oxen. There were still two independent companies with oxen behind the handcart companies, but they were expected to arrive within a few days. In our next issue we shall publish the letter in its entirety.

SAILING.—From the notification letters of some of the Saints we understand that the ship GEORGE WASHINGTON, registered at 1649 tons, is to sail from Liverpool for Boston. The passengers are required to be in Liverpool Saturday, the 21st of this month. The names of the emigrants will begin to be listed at the Liverpool Office the following Monday morning. Let no one go before receiving his notification letter, which should be read and understood in detail.

ADDRESS.—James J. Phillips, 7, Park-street, Swansea.

BOOK PAYMENTS, from February 6th to March 5th.—Isaac Jones, 10s; John Jones, 3s. 6c; Michael Vaughan, £1; A. L. Jones, £3; Joseph Griffiths, 6s. 8c.; David John, £1; John Treharne, 9s. 5c.

DITTO FOR PAMPHLETS.—John Treharne, 8s. 4c.; Michael Vaughan, £2 10s; John Jones, 11s. 6c; Isaac Jones, 10s, Charles Harman, 10s.; Wm. Ajax, Anglesey, 13s. 8c.

CONTENTS.

	PG.
The Latter-day Work—Preparation	65
Address of Elder Evans	68
Editorial:—The Reformation	72
Letters from the Valley	72
The Measure of the Stature of the Fullness of Christ	74
Poetry—My Dream	76

SWANSEA:

PRINTED AND PUBLISHED BY DANIEL DANIELS.

ZION'S TRUMPET,

OR

Star of the Saints.

No. 6.]　　　　MARCH 21, 1857.　　　　[Vol. X.

REPORT OF THE REFORMATION AND FASTING CONFERENCE, WHICH WAS HELD AT THE "ZION'S TRUMPET" OFFICE, SWANSEA, THURSDAY, MARCH 12, 1857.

OFFICERS PRESENT.

Ezra T. Benson, President; Elders Daniel Daniels, William Miller, and James Taylor, the Presidency, and Israel Evans and Benjamin Ashby, Former Counselors of the Welsh Mission; John E. Jones, Pastor over, and the representative in Council for the Conferences of the North; Presidents of the Conferences of East Glamorgan, West Glamorgan, Brecon, Llanelli, Carmarthen, Pembroke, and Cardigan, and several traveling and local Elders.

Not all the above Elders had arrived by 11:00 in the morning, when the Council was opened with singing and prayer.

The President.—Dear Brethren,—I feel happy to meet with you on this occasion; but since not all the brethren we are expecting have come, we shall not begin the task in a consistent and orderly format until they come. I think it will be good for us, since we have congregated together, to bow humbly before our God; to sing, talk, and instruct one another for a little while, and postpone until one o'clock, when it is expected the

[Price 1½c.

brethren will be here.

I feel it will be an important and interesting time for all these people, when they will have to either worship God or Mammon completely and undividedly. The scriptures say, "If the Lord be God, follow him: but if Baal, then follow him." However, since I understand the principles of the Gospel, I feel to serve the Lord. I believe that you wish to serve the same God, and to follow the same path that I do, to labor with all our might for Zion, while the day continues.

I do not intend to mention the past, rather that which is to come. I feel to give you perfect and equal freedom with myself in this meeting to pour out your souls—to speak your feelings boldly and freely. I shall remove every obstacle, and I shall give a full expanse to every one of you, from President Daniels on down, to give expression to all your feelings. If you have any complaints—any dissatisfaction, bitterness, or contention toward your presidents—if the bridle is being pulled too tightly, or not tightly enough (if the latter, we shall set it tight enough on you. There is no danger of the coach running away with the horses.) We cannot enjoy much of the Spirit of God, unless we feel free to express our feelings to one another; and unless we "counsel much together," as President Brigham instructs.

I felt that it was of great importance for me to visit this great field of labor, (not that I did not have many other places to go to) and to meet with the presiding authorities, in some advantageous place, so that we could achieve an understanding with one another about the important reformation that is required—to fast and pray, and to humble ourselves before the Lord, and to get you prepared and ready until you are suitable to repent for your sins, to go down into the waters of baptism, to renew your covenants.

I expect that an improvement will be made throughout the entire Mission—more will be accomplished by brothers Miller and Taylor than was accomplished by their predecessors, brothers Evans and Ashby; not that they were not faithful (for we know they were); but because of an increase of light, additional opportunities and further advantages, together with greater strength. From now on we shall have a grasp on the matter by its handle, and we can guide it as we wish, and, if necessary, we can use a club.

We (the British Presidency) were instructed to go out, and effect a reformation, by motivating the people to a consideration and fulfillment of their duties, by beginning in each place with the presiding authorities—to awaken them, to motivate them, and to shake them first, and, if required, to beat them and to club them until we are satisfied with the effect obtained. I am here with you ready to have at it in earnest, hoping that you are like unto soft and pliable clay, in this place, and that there is no brittle or split material in you, so that you can be formed into vessels for honor. After the earthen vessels go through the mill and the hand of the one who shapes them, they have to withstand the fire. Many split in the fire. There are many trials and tests to go through. There are some vessels present here, and more are expected; I hope that they will be worked to the proper form before I finish.

I wish to hear your feelings and your intentions—whether you intend to be obedient to those who preside over you. I have a President, namely brother Pratt. I am pliable in his hands. If he tells me to go, I go; if to return without delay, I return with the first carriage, and I say, "How can I serve you, brother Pratt? Can I clean your shoes, run an errand, or go to the sea brink to see if there is a ship there for hire?" I am always available, and ready for the call to go to any part of the earth I am sent, or to do anything that is required. I want to see a spirit of humility resting on all my brethren. Whenever there is a spirit of humility in you, at that time there is a spirit of exaltation in you. In some examples, instead of this humble spirit, there are arrogance and conceit. The Pastor and the Conference President have opposing opinions and are snarling at each other like two bears, afraid to collide with one another, lest there be a battle. Indeed, the humble Pastor considers the arrogant Conference President as greater and wiser than himself; or the self-elevating President believes that he is a greater man than his pastor, or at least he should get to be; and, in some cases, the great President was once a Pastor! I want for such a spirit, if it is here, to be stamped out of the mission, and I wish to see each one in his own place. The importance of this Mission rests on its President, brother Daniels, and not on his counselors. They are not responsible for any more than President Daniels puts on them.

This reformation in Wales needs to begin at the head, and go down to the feet and the toes.

Brother Miller has told me how the meetings where he was announced to preach have been spent in rehearsing and singing long hymns, which reached, (in a figurative sense) from here to Boston, before and after a similar prayer. Then, the President of the Branch, or the Conference, would arise and preach the introductions for the "stranger," and place him before the congregation, after praising him to high heaven, or calling on another brother to do the same thing again, until it would be nearly time to end before the distinguished man could begin. We wish to put an end to such things, and get men to actually put into practice their religion. It saddens the Spirit of the Lord. If any of us saddens the man who may be higher than we in the Lord, I tell you that it will be a great impediment on our way toward receiving abundantly of the Spirit of God. Such an impediment must be removed, if we have it here. We wish to be blessed and prospered—to see the Kingdom of God pushed forward, and if we do not do the work, we will be removed and others, who will do it, set in our place. All men do not always do things in the same way. If I have my faults, you must bear with me, and if my ways are different from those of other men, you can put up with them.

I was with brother Ross all over the London mission, where I spoke, worked, struggled, and scolded, as with a hammer and a club, until at last I got all things into the form I wanted them,— the brethren came to perceive things in the same light as I did in the end. Brother Ross said that he had labored under four ministries in the British mission, and had found all to differ in their organizations. It may be thus to some extent. Circumstances differ. We govern circumstances to some extent; but, some circumstances govern us; but it is we who should govern them as far as possible.

I wish to see your eyes opened, your understanding enlightened,—the veil of darkness and tradition torn from your eyes. You ought to keep the word of wisdom, and the words of wisdom, to contemplate how to be the most industrious and skilled. It is not proper for any Elders in this mission to run around, on horseback, or on foot, speaking wherever, whenever, and however they wish, without the instruction of their president who is higher than they. It does not look appropriate for anyone to go to some place he wishes to go, and send another Elder out in his place, while he remains to enjoy himself and be idle, and in the end, perhaps twenty miles from his proper field of labor. Will such a one win a single prize? Not a good one, at any rate. If I hire a man to plough my field, and he goes instead to his own house to sit, eat, drink, sleep, dress, and enjoy himself, let him expect no payment. We are Elders of Israel, and laborers in the vineyard of Christ. Even the Gentiles are considerate and careful, and interest themselves in the work of their master, although they receive oppression and hardships. When we consider the better work and wages of our kind and Great Master, and the freedom and the ease that we enjoy, in comparison to the gentiles, we ought to be more diligent, hardworking, careful and skilled with the work of our Father, in which all our future enjoyment is contained. I want you to ponder on these things, and see if you are pliable in the hands of the Lord; and if you are pliable in His hands, you are thus in the hand of your president. Our duty is to labor to the best advantage we can devise. Not one of us is obliged to believe and obey the gospel, or to take the priesthood and go out to labor; but we have done it all voluntarily. There are men who are excused from their duties when they are starving, naked, or ill; but when they are being well fed until they get fat, and are dressed splendidly; certainly, I think, they ought to go out and labor with all their might, and also accomplish something. There is nothing more needed than a complete reformation. We wish to start anew, and we may as well begin now.

The meeting is now at your service. I wish for the Lord to bless us, and allow us a time of rejoicing together, in the name of his son, Jesus Christ. Amen.

President Daniel Daniels rejoiced in the observations

already made, and in the thought of achieving improvement in the things of the mission. As for himself, he could say that his only reward and his principal objective were to build the kingdom of God. He knew that it was not designed for man to think of himself first. Whenever such a spirit tempted him, he would always resist it, seeking first the kingdom. That our President had come, and that he could judge where there is an obstacle that hinders the work. It is a fact that thousands in Wales believe the gospel, but they have not come to be baptized. He had preached faithfully and diligently through the entire mission; but he has baptized only a few. Personal invitations had been extended for getting a reformation with some success; he felt that he had received the true source of the reformation here in its full effect. He felt to say, that if his body and spirit were separated this day, no ill feeling toward any person on the face of creation would be found, though he felt sympathy for the work of his God. It is an intensive work. It is easy for us to destroy in one day what has taken years to restore. He felt the need of being renewed. He was satisfied to bow and kiss the rod and suffer to the extremes which he deserved. He wished for a good time in our conference, and an effective and thorough reformation, so that we might have an increase of the power of God. He did not know of any particular sin he had, except for faults and failings.

ELDER ISRAEL EVANS told how he had lived and behaved well according to his knowledge during the year he had been laboring in Wales. He felt well toward President Daniels, whose only objective was the success of this mission. The same for brother Ashby. He saw the same good signs which he related about President Daniels. He had preached outside last summer, and baptized a few. He believed that when we cleansed ourselves inside and out, together with the whole Church in the same way, the honest in heart would see some attractive and inviting virtues in us and would enter in. He had been around the entire mission twice, and several times through the southern part. He said about the Conference Presidents that they were faithful according to their limited experience and knowledge.

ELDER B. ASHBY made similar comments about the way he had labored, &c. He believed that the way to reform the people was to provide yet additional good instructions and examples to them, for them to follow. He had kept the word of wisdom, or he could not have lived in this *climate*, and he also kept some of the words of wisdom. He felt that the heart of President Daniels was pure and upright before the Lord, and if he had ever failed, he had done so with good feelings and intentions, and that he would sacrifice any personal comfort and enjoyment for whatever he thought he would be of benefit to God's work. About the Welsh Saints he said they were a people who stuck close to good doctrine and example; he had never seen a people more patient and precise in following counsel, and in obeying the priesthood which set good examples before them. There has never been a better and more tender-hearted people than the Welsh Saints to those who go from their midst with their hearts full of the holy Spirit. He mentioned the success of tithing.

Elder W. Miller commented on the preaching and success of tithing,—the diligence there had been in preaching, and the future signs,—his determination to live his religion, and to teach others to do likewise—on obedience to the priesthood, &c.

Elder Taylor expressed his love for the work,—his wish to see it succeed, and for the people to receive their reformation,— his determination to be obedient to President Daniels,—and agreement with Elder Ashby about the Welsh Saints.

Pastor John E. Jones said how the thoughts and circumstances of the people in the North had been prepared to receive the reformation—the privilege of being able to express his feelings of joy and those of the Northern people in preaching the gospel, and their diligence in doing so—his good feelings for his Presidents— how he had kept the word of wisdom, also fasting, praying, rejoicing, washing, anointing, and purifying himself before God, in order to receive his Spirit; and the other brethren with him—their wish for additional strength of the Priesthood—the poor circumstances of the people of the North in general—the frugality of the presiding brethren. For example, brother Wm. Ajax presides over the Conway Valley and Anglesey Conference, traveling throughout Anglesey and Arfon. He received only three shillings of church assistance during three months, by taking a bit of paper, &c., with him to sell, and by living frugally and sparingly. Elder Hugh Evans, who presides over the Denbighshire Conference, works at his craft, pays his tithing, and travels a lot. So did his predecessor, Elder G. Roberts, also. Elder David John, who presides over the Flintshire Conference, is faithful without relying much on the church. Elder John Treharne, president of the Merionethshire Conference, traveled a lot during last spring and summer, edifying the Saints under his care and preaching faithfully to the gentiles, and in the winter he went to work there and assisted his Conference in paying their temple fund and expenses, and in earning his own clothes, traveling on Sunday, and every opportunity he could. The debt of these four small Conferences to the two offices is about £100. The number of members of every kind is about 350. The number of faithful, hardworking, and supportive men and women in the cause is about 85. Three or four Elders are needed to travel through the North in the summer.

He indicated their conditions to assist brother Evans and Ashby to emigrate, in light of the fact that they had a duty to assist brother G. Roberts also, and their love for all of their presidents. The only objective of pastor Jones was the success of the Gospel. He trusted and rejoiced in the reformation. He was determined to be more sober, frugal and zealous than ever, in order to have greater strength. In order to visit the Saints of his Pastorate as often as he could, he had traveled about two thousand miles during the last eight months. He desired to renew his covenant and he was determined to continue to keep the word of wisdom.

PRESIDENT BENSON encouraged us not to follow the bad example of anyone, no matter how high he may be, contrary to the revelations given from heaven. Paul knew that if an angel from heaven preached contrary to them, that he would be an apostate angel, and the curse of God would be on him.

"O ye Mountains High" was sung sweetly and melodiously to the tune "Minnie Gray," and the meeting was adjourned until two in the afternoon.

We should have noted previously that President Benson, at the beginning of the meeting, called on the scribe to read the letter of President Brigham Young.

Two o'clock in the afternoon "Oh my father thou that dwellest," was sung, &c. President Benson prayed.

At the request of the President, the Scribe, Wm. Lewis, read the minutes of the reformation movement in Liverpool.

President Benson observed that those who were absent in the morning had assembled. He asked them to pour out all the contents of their souls—to give a detailed account of themselves if they were in favor of the reformation, which would sweep clean. He reminded them that the word of wisdom means what it says, and says what it means—that tea, coffee, hot or intoxicating drinks, &c., are bad and harmful, and prevent us from receiving sufficient of the Spirit of the Lord. He and President Pratt began the reformation in the Liverpool Office, and scrubbed and cleaned from the top of the garret to the bottom of the cellar, until a thorough reformation was effected. The same spirit must be carried through all the European missions. We have been trifling enough years with the revelations of God. The blessings of heaven follow the fulfillment of the revelations. He knew of one brother on a mission, Daniel Davies, who has been diligent in keeping the word and the words of wisdom, and he has been blessed. When he went to administer to the sick, they were made well; and the Spirit fell on him until he prophesied. He is not a man who by nature has a lot of mesmerizing power in him; but he does have a good heart and good feelings. There is not a Conference within the British Mission in better condition than his. Indeed, that is the only place where President Benson found that the spirit of Zion completely reigned. When he went to their meeting, he found them all to be in order: they did not turn to notice each one who came in, rather they paid strict attention to the speaker. Brother Davies said to him, "brother Benson, the meeting is in your hands, and it is time to begin." He wished for the presiding Elders of Wales to discipline their congregations the same way.

Let us concentrate the power of our Priesthood (he said) in this meeting. If you feel to prophesy, speak in tongues, express your feelings, or whatever you wish, be as free as the open air. If you do not feel free toward President Daniels, or any one of your presidents, express the feeling. If you do, go out according to his counsel, and be humble and obedient to him. It is he who is accountable for the things of this Mission, and we hold him accountable; but at the same time we do not expect that he will be insulted.

The first thing we request before us in this meeting, is concerning the reformation, and your determination to go out to work earnestly until you are called back. When brother Daniel Davies was asked when he intended to return to Zion, he said, "O, about the time the temple is finished, I shall see." If we are appointed to go out to work, let us work sincerely. If I hire a man to sow my wheat, and he sows tares instead, I shall turn him out, and I shall punish him. Thus the Lord will do. He does not ask us to sow death; rather the words of life and salvation. If we do not do that, our President will call us back, and he will excommunicate us; and he will set others in our places.

The Scribe read the minutes of the morning meeting.

All the elders expressed their feelings. They agreed in their determination to reform themselves, and to reform the Saints to live closer to God, in order to have his Spirit, and to cleanse the Church of those who will not live their religion, so the honest in heart may come into the Church, and so the work of the Lord may prosper anew. In the majority of the conferences it was found that not nearly all who should were paying their tithing.

President Benson showed that it was a duty of the Saints to pay their tithing, and leave the task of seeing how it is spent to whoever presides over the treasurer—the bare truth should not be uttered kindly; rather it should be delivered boldly, not worrying about hurting anyone's feelings; they should not be sympathized with, rather scourged, and scolded, beating the devil out of them, and then it would be possible to do some good with them—and those who do this will be more highly respected in the end. Let not the Elders give an account first; but let them get the people to pay their tithing, and then it is very easy to know what can be done.

Elder Henry Harries related his trials while testing the world.

Pastor J. E. Jones indicated the faithfulness of the Saints of the North in paying tithing—that some had office to pay it when they were without food, and how frugally and sparingly several live in order to pay it.

Other Elders spoke again on various topics.

The President commented on "Mormon sympathy," and the faults of people being expressed to them, and said that it is a poor substance for men to live on. A common fault in elders is to be carried along with a stream of pity for sin, instead of possessing the Spirit of the Lord, and teaching the principles as they stand.

He encouraged the Presidents not to permit any one of the Saints to go around speaking ill of their leaders, whether true or untrue; if the former, it must be said in the proper spirit and place.

"If you go (he said) among the people to tell them their duty impartially, powerfully, and throw words of truth like thunder, lightning, and hail into their midst, you will succeed in doing what you wish. I prophesy that a great work will again be done in Wales. The Welsh Saints are good people; and if a Presiding Elder approaches them in the right way to request that which is needed, and to bless the people, they will succeed. Let them declare the need definitely and clearly straightaway. This Mission will succeed.

Let brother Daniels go out of the Office as much as he can among the people, even if he is obliged to get someone else in his place with the printing, &c. Brother Daniels is a frugal man: he would wear his fingers and hands to the bone in working, and he would press himself for the benefit of the kingdom of God—to spare a shilling of the kingdom's money, he would walk twelve or fifteen miles, instead of riding. Oh, if only all presiding and traveling Elders would do the same. (President Daniels showed his willingness to do as requested.)

"It is a big loss to any presidency when they fail to counsel together.

"Let the Elders understand which spirit edifies, and which one pulls down the kingdom of God. I wish for the counselors of a president to live in his heart by willingly carrying out all his measures, and for the president to boldly ask them to do so. When men climb higher than their places, they are standing on slippery places.

"Recovenant to live by every word that proceedeth forth from the mouth of God, and, wherever it may be, do not bring up an old bad feeling a second time, rather bury it, the hatchet and its handle.

"Keep the word of wisdom, and do not break the new covenant made. Do not be too hard on the Saints, and do not let things fall behind either.

"Let every Elder increase his diligence, and let him go to the gentiles as much as he can to attract them a little instead of the Saints."

In the evening, all the brethren went down to the sea, where they renewed their covenants by Baptism.

At eight in the evening they met again, when they were confirmed and blessed.

Friday, the 13th:—

"Oh, say what is Truth" was sung. The President prayed. "The God that others worship" was sung.

President Benson.—When I decided to come to Wales I felt to get the presiding brethren together in a room for, at least, three days, to fast and pray without ceasing until we received an abundant pouring out of the Holy Ghost on us; for I know that the Lord is more ready and willing to impart it than are we to fit ourselves to receive it. Yet He will not force his Spirit on us: we are stewards unto ourselves, and at our liberty to serve the one we choose—God or the devil—to be a subject of the one kingdom or the other. We have chosen the former. We have proved that by our obedience to the gospel which He has sent to us with his servants, and through our covenants.

Each one here knows best his own heart, together with the path he has followed. There is no Elder in the room who does not reflect on his past behavior and see that hours, days, weeks have been spent in this Church that have been useless to them and the Church, rather an obstacle. You have now recovenanted for the last time, and, from now on, you are to live your religion, not by part of it, but by every word that proceedeth forth from the mouth of God. It is a great and important covenant, and the Lord will hold you to it. You were not forced to make it, but you have made it willingly. You knew that it was the proper, and the only, refuge for you, as you knew it when you obeyed the gospel. You know that you cannot live in this Church as you have been living; for you have trampled under foot the revelations of Jesus Christ, and have insulted the Almighty, and he has been angry with us—feasting, breaking the word of wisdom, and being idle, instead of going out to preach the gospel. Each one of you knows your fault in this. Now we are going to reform, and begin anew. You are asked to help us knock the scales from the eyes of the people; and to be as diligent and faithful as we are, and even more faithful if you can. No man is to be restricted— his privilege is to get all the light, wisdom, and power that he can achieve—to receive the revelations of Jesus Christ, and to be clothed with the holy Spirit as with a robe, from morning till night; and if you do according to your covenants, you shall be filled with it, and nothing will hinder your success. It is our privilege to receive it, and we shall receive it, if we are spiritually minded, and enjoy pondering and talking about the things of the kingdom. We must put aside light conversation of the fireside, and follow the path not to offend the Spirit of the Lord, or the feelings of our brethren. We should be as careful and appreciative of the feelings of our brethren as we are of the pupil of our eye.

The work of the Lord is to be fulfilled by us, his servants. He does not yet intend to come here personally to preach to and bless the people. He has done that once, and before he does so again, he will remove us, and place others in our places who will do it better.

Go out to your fields of labor with prayerful hearts, and instead of idleness, feasting, and playing, fill yourselves with the Holy Ghost, so that, whenever you go to an abode, you will recognize the spirit of the people. Wherever you go, teach them order and cleanliness, and to live their religion completely. We, the presiding and traveling Elders, have nothing else to do but to live our religion, and to teach others to do likewise. Instead of that, perhaps some will go to men's homes to engage in idle chatter. There are many honorable exceptions to this. Before leaving any family we have visited, we should, before teaching them, kneel down with them, and pray for them, and leave the peace of God on the home. This is better than jesting with the ladies. Instead of that, let us teach them virtue and holiness. Let us leave a good and indelible impression wherever we go, among the Saints or the Gentiles, so they will not find fault or evil in us; but that they may witness our godliness. It is better to preach by example than by words. We have practiced sufficiently long the doctrinal part of our religion—it is the practical part that is before us now. President Brigham says, "Work, labor for Zion." Our only work is the labor for Zion, and administering the ordinances in the house of the Lord. To what purpose is a man called to the Priesthood, if not to preach the Gospel? Men in these countries who hold the Priesthood work hard their whole time for the Gentiles for a few shillings each week, and, if they were brave and faithful, and full of the fire of the Lord, they could preach the Gospel, and carry the work forward, so there would be reason to send for elders from Salt Lake to do that. One reason why the work of the Lord does not prosper is because there are many old elders of that kind blocking the way. Whenever they are asked out to work, they hide themselves in their filthy shelters. They are lazy and rusty, and they grumble and bark at every course of action that others put at their feet, and they come out of their holes to oppose them and to go around to poison the Saints. Well, we intend to grapple them out of their shelters by the hair of their foreheads, and try the effect of soap and a scrubbing brush on them, and cleanse them and dress them to go out to preach the Gospel. If we do not, they will lie in their filthy holes and they will be damned.

Let brother Daniels and you see to it that every one who is able to go will go out to preach the Gospel. Let not soft soap and Mormon sympathy be used with them. It would not do for us in Salt Lake to bring some little excuses for not going. We could not expect to be excused for lack of fine cakes and sugar to take with us. A horse and a wagon, and things of comfort were secondary, and if we could not get all the comforts we wished, we just had to do without them. Occasionally one who is sent says, "If I were to go, my family would starve!" The teaching of President Brigham to me and to others of the Twelve was, not one of us was worthy of the apostleship if he did not go out to preach the Gospel, sustain his family, and dress himself smartly.

We want you Presidents of Conferences to see that these things are done, and if you do not do so, we will remove you out of the way, and get men who will. We do not want to hear the groaning and complaining of the people, rather we want for you to say to them definitely, and under the influence of the Spirit of the

Almighty what their duty is, and that it is proper for them to do it, and if they possess a grain of the Spirit of God they will do it.

God does not abandon those who go out to preach his Gospel faithfully, and who have his Glory in their sight. They shall have all they need. God has never sent mouths without food to fill them. Who is it that sustains us and feeds us if not God? and yet we complain, and fear that our family will starve!

Let President Daniels appoint the various fields for his counselors, so they do not come across each other, and so the labor of each one can be seen. Let him take the word of the Lord out among the people, as often as he is able. I would prefer for him to close up the office so he is not so enslaved.

After he understood from the Presidents of the Conferences that there are broad expanses with no Saints preaching in them, he said,—

"The responsibility of warning and baptizing the people is on you. To what purpose are many of the traveling elders kept? Frequently for nothing but to go from the house of one poor saint to the house of the other to get his food and clothing just to say a little of his good feelings about the work, &c., and to go around to the Saints in this manner like a wheel. One or two men in the conference will be sufficient, instead of all of them, if they take the thunder, the lightning, and the fire of the Lord with them. Let the others be sent among the gentiles to warn them, and if they do not go, let them go dig potatoes, if they wish.

"Let the elders go far into the midst of the gentiles, and let them get their sustenance from them, sparing the Saints. Alma and Nephi went into the midst of the Lamanites, their chief enemies, where threats were made to put the first Nephite who came there to death. They escaped day and night, and they succeeded through the power of God to convince and baptize thousands. What is the reason there is not more baptizing in our midst? Because of wickedness, and the lack of the power of God in us—because there are in our midst sluggish, wicked, dirty and impure men, who stink in the nostrils of good men; that is why; and they are in the way of the work.

"You must go to reform and cleanse the Saints—by fasting, prayer, work and discipline, or be damned, the whole pack of you. Go, as I have gone many times, with your bibles and blankets to the forest, to the mountains, to the rocks and caves to fast and pray until you are enshrouded with the fire of the Lord. Call all the officers together; let a sober fast be announced. Confess your faults to one another; repent and be baptized for the remission of sins, and may you fill them with the Holy Ghost. Then, do not rest until the Saints are filled with it also, and distinguish between those who serve God and those who do not. Baptize those who pay their tithing, and who covenant to live their religion. Do not baptize anyone on the promise of paying tithing, unless it is completely impossible for him to pay it. Let such a one alone where he is, without grafting him in, until he makes up his mind to cut himself out, or come in." "The Spirit of God like a fire is Burning" was sung.

After several elders had spoken again, President Benson said that he was satisfied at how much was said this time, hoping that we will go out to do according to our promise, so that, when we meet again we may be able to tell what we have done and not what we intend to do, and he blessed and dismissed the congregation.

W. LEWIS, Scribe.

☞ We intend to publish our next issue within a week, because of the importance of the news from the Valley, and the need for the rest of the account of the Liverpool Reformation Meeting. We remind our presiding brethren of our President's wish for them to organize their Reformation meetings in a similar way to the one at Swansea. Read the account that is in this issue, and the account of the Liverpool meeting deliberately and with understanding. There is plenty of time—24 hours in a day. We hope that you will be like giants after being renewed with new wine—full of the Spirit of the Lord, and determined to read the heart of every officer, and to completely uproot every wickedness, and to remove every obstacle that is in the way of the work, and to relight the fire of the Lord in the hearts of the Saints. Let every council you hold from now on be a reformation meeting increasing in the work of our God. May the contents of the "Trumpet" and the *Star* be your texts—your topics of sermons always, and do not sadden our heart any further by meeting with officers who do not know the content of the one or the other, nor caring much either. A needful and praiseworthy practice is to read some interesting part of them in the meetings, and make observations about them. That is the way to draw from the proper source, and to keep the spirit of Zion in our midst.

May your new brooms make a clean sweep.

ADDRESS.—Mr. John Davies, 7, Park Street, Swansea.

SWANSEA:

PRINTED AND PUBLISHED BY DANIEL DANIELS.

ZION'S TRUMPET,

OR

Star of the Saints.

No. 7.]   MARCH 28, 1857.   [Vol. X.

LIVERPOOL REFORMATION MEETINGS.
(Continued from page 63.)

President Pratt.—"I have rejoiced greatly in hearing you express your determinations, and desires to perform the good required of you. I feel the need of setting out anew, and trying to be more faithful. I have felt the importance and necessity of it for years. I have mourned in my feelings when I have seen my own apparent coldness. I have been habituated to reading in the Bible, Book of Mormon, and History of Joseph, accounts of the great manifestations of the power of God in past times, and then have compared myself and the little I have had, with them, my dullness has given rise to serious apprehensions. When I think of the little progress I have made I am ashamed of myself. I have greatly desired that I might purify myself, and attain to the blessings recorded as having been bestowed upon the servants of God in ancient times. I have mourned for weeks over my barrenness. What have any of us attained to? When I read what was done in ancient times, I oftentimes get alarmed. We find, in reading the Book of Mormon, that Nephi used to obtain the ministration of angels daily, and was blessed with revelations, visions, dreams, manifestations, and the voice of the Lord. And in the Bible we read of Elijah, Elisha, and

[Price 1½c.]

other prophets who were similarly blessed. One man of God could lead an army into the midst of their enemies by blinding them by the power of his faith. There is not anything but what we could do if we had the faith. We are dull, and almost dead. We must get the Spirit. Let us cry unto the Lord day and night to get the Holy Ghost. I hope we may all seek diligently, and fulfill our covenants. To be baptized will not benefit us unless we continue in diligence.

"I do not look for the elders to enjoy very remarkable external manifestations, until the times of the gentiles are fulfilled, and they turn to the House of Israel with the gospel. Notwithstanding I am confident it is our privilege to have more of the power of God than we have had. Each knows himself better than his neighbors know him. Notwithstanding the Lord has sent me here to preside, I feel weak, and entirely unable to perform my duties without the Holy Spirit. I feel thankful for the privilege of going out with brother Benson, after the hurry of the emigration is over. I hope the Lord will pour out his Spirit, and that we may get revived. It will be a relief to me to get freed a while from the business of the Office.

"With regard to the carrying out of the reformation, I feel to concur with the remarks of brother Benson. There is a degree of looseness with regard to temporal things that must be remedied. And this needs looking after under the present arrangement more than ever before. Money contributed as tithing should be regulated by some proper system, so that Presidents and officers may not dip in without consulting other authority. By the help of the Lord I will try to publish something in regard to this that will be beneficial, so that the tithing may be appropriated properly and economically.

"In regard to re-baptism—the Saints ought to be preached to first and stirred up. Baptism does not reform a person. It is a testimony of renewal. I think re-baptism throughout the Church will be the means of casting out many of the dead branches. The tree will be trimmed up—placed in a thriving condition—and will bring forth much good fruit. Brother Benson will go forth and knock the scales from the eyes of the people, and I hope I will follow soon and help him.

"I have reformed in some few things in my method of preaching since I have on this mission. I have seen the importance of doing so. Instead of long discourses, I have felt the necessity of bearing testimony. I think those who have heard me can bear record that I have endeavored to preach plain, simple principles, and have confined myself to the evidences of the truth of the work—the visions of Joseph, &c., without referring to all the Scriptures that could be brought to bear on the subjects. If the elders will bear their testimony, relate the visions of Joseph, and preach the Book of Mormon, this will do more good than long sermons."

Sung "O Zion, when I think on thee."

President Benson.—"I do not know but the brethren may think that I am very zealous. Well, I confess that I am in the cause of the Lord. It is as natural for me as it is for a child to love milk. When I get my mind bent on a thing, it is like steam in a *boiler*.

"In order to be renewed, I motion that we fast and pray one day, at least. I am sure it will have a good effect. In a good many places the wheels are clogged. The Elders and Saints indulge themselves with too much temporal food. They must have hearty meals on Sundays, if it takes all their week's wages. They would feel better if they would feed light on Sunday. They would have more of the Spirit if they would fast one day in a week, and live on spiritual food. Nearly every blessing that I have obtained out of the natural course has been by prayer and fasting. This eating hearty meals on Sundays makes us heavy, and we feel more like taking a nap than feasting on heavenly things.

"We should preach by the power of God, according to the talent that He has given us. We have to grapple with our weaknesses. When I feel that I preach by the Spirit of God, I am all right; I have nothing to mourn. When I cannot feel the Holy Spirit, I am dissatisfied and mourn. When I know I have the testimony of the Spirit I am satisfied—my heart is light—and my sleep sweet.

"Let us go ahead, preach the principles of the Gospel—and bear testimony of the work. The Saints are backward in attending the sacrament meetings as they ought. And many do not pay their tithing. We have now got the instructions that will enable us to find out who are faithful, and who are not. We shall cut the dead branches off. I would rather have half a dozen faithful Saints than a hundred hypocrites. We are called to hunt up the righteous. If we do not do it, we will come short of the blessing. We are looking for a blessing. If we do not go according to President Young's letter we cannot get it. The dead branches must go off, and then we will find out how many Saints we have got.

"I feel to uphold brother Pratt, and not be half-hearted. The Lord bless him (all—Amen) and brother Little! (all—Amen.) We will have a glorious time. We will be blessed and comforted.

"We ought to reverence each other in the Priesthood. If it were not my duty, I should not ask this of the brethren. I ask no more of them than I am willing to do myself. I do not ask them to be more pliable than I am. Do I open my mouth where brother Pratt is, without his consent? We should pattern after Zion. If we do not reverence the Priesthood, the Spirit of the Lord is grieved. I wish the brethren were here that we might preach to them."

Elder P. H. Young bore testimony to President Benson's remarks. Sung "Come, come ye Saints," &c.

Elder Truman O. Angell engaged in prayer.

President Pratt.—"The plan will be for the Presidents to call together the Priesthood, and point out to the officers their duties. When you have sufficiently preached reformation to the officers, and they have covenanted that they will keep the commandments of God, baptize them first. Then let them take hold and preach to the Saints the necessity of coming to meetings—all that can. I have made it a practice not to have any cooking done here on Sundays. This needs to be instilled into the minds of the Saints. Get them to covenant to do as they are told, then baptize them. A question has been put in regard to those who do not pay their tithing. We have not been cutting them off for neglecting to pay tithing, but we need not graft them in unless they agree to do so. We have felt that it was not really wisdom to cut people off for not paying tithing. But the time will come when it will be made a test of fellowship. It is wisdom if they will not covenant to pay tithing, not to graft them in. Thus they will cut themselves off.

"It has been proposed that we fast and pray tomorrow, that we meet here at seven o'clock in the evening, pray, and then go to the water for baptism."

Seconded, and unanimously carried.

President Benson closed the meeting by prayer.

Thursday, 5th of February, 7 in the evening.

The brethren all met according to arrangement.

Sung "The Spirit of God," &c. President Benson prayed. Sung "O, Zion, when I think on thee."

Elder Little exhorted the brethren to faithfulness, and especially the missionaries—to keep themselves pure, so that they might return home with upright hearts.

Sung "Come let us anew," &c.

All then repaired to the place of baptism. After an appropriate prayer at the water's edge by President Pratt, he and President Benson baptized each other. They then baptized the rest of the brethren.

The company then returned to 42, Islington.

Sung "How firm a foundation ye Saints of the Lord," &c. Prayer by President Pratt. Sung "Redeemer of Israel, our only delight," &c.

The brethren were then all confirmed, Presidents Benson and Pratt being the first. Many rich blessings were pronounced by the spirit of prophecy, and the hearts of all present were full of joy and of the Holy Ghost.

Elder W. G. Young prophesied that the work would roll on with greater rapidity and more power, after this, than ever before.

Sung "Praise to the man who communed with Jehovah."

President Pratt.—"I believe a work of great magnitude is about to be accomplished in this country. I consider it will be a great work if we get the Saints purified. If one-third should be cut off, and the rest remain united, it will be one of the greatest works that was ever accomplished in this land. We have all learned by experience that the more we are united, the more the Lord will bless us, whether we be few or many. I am impressed that the time is at hand when the Lord intends to accomplish something, not only here but in Zion.

I have not ascertained what it is—but I believe that the Spirit and power, resting on the Presidency, are preparatory to something of importance. It may be that the Lord intends this purification to prepare the Saints for entering into the Temple, in which we expect such manifestations, and blessings to be given as the Church has never had. We know this is a day of power, and that the time cannot be far distant. It seems as if it were near at hand. The Lord is preparing to bring us nearer to his presence. I do feel, and have felt, that something of importance is at hand. With regard to the work in this land, it is bound to go ahead. The Saints will require faith to stand up against opposition, and none but those having faith will be able to stand. The brethren here will go forth with greater power and energy, to administer, and heal the sick. They will have greater power than heretofore. I say, go forth, and the power of the Lord shall be upon you,—you shall feel it,—and the people shall know it, even if they fight against it the next minute."

After further spirited remarks from various brethren, the hymn, "Praise God from whom all blessings flow," was sung, and the meeting was dismissed with prayer by Elder James A. Little.

LETTER FROM THE STATES.

Pittston Ferry, February 4th, 1857.

Dear Brother Daniels,—By the goodness and mercy of our Heavenly Father, I have received the opportunity to write to you from this part of the earth. I hope these lines find you well and comfortable, and that you will continue so while you are in old Babel, fighting the enemy on the one hand, and building the kingdom of God on the other.

After my family and I sailed from Liverpool, the wind and weather continued fair for some time, when it changed into a storm. The impressive elements stirred themselves—the wind strong,—the sight and sound of lightning and thunder frightening,—the roar of the sea, which threatened to swallow us alive to its huge bowels,—and our safe landing in New York,—were all new signs to us of the power and mercy of our Heavenly Father.

After staying in New York for two nights and a day, we came here to Pittston Ferry, where I found my brother Rhys, my mother, and many of the brothers and sisters of the church. In this place there is a large branch of Saints, meeting to worship God. Some of them are Scots, others English, and many Welsh. Our entire number is about one hundred, and we have a good president, by the name of Benjamin Isaac, originally from Carmarthenshire, and Rhys E. Rees and Richard Dafydd, originally from Cwter Fawr, as his counselors. Richard Dafydd's wife has joined with the Saints, and rejoices in her testimony of the divinity of the church. I and some of the children found work here immediately, so that, by the time summer comes, we will be able to go further on toward Zion. The nearer we come to the Valley of the mountains, the greater is our desire to get there, as soon as we earn a way.

I have never been at such a loss having to be without the "Trumpet,"—I would give almost anything to get to hear its voice in America; we do not receive a single tract in Welsh. I would love to hear how the work of the Lord is prospering in Wales.

Remember me kindly to brother Dewi Elfed Jones.

With fondest regards of my mother, my brother Rhys, and myself and my family to you.

Your fellow servant in the Work of God,

JOHN E. REES,

(Formerly from Cwmamman.)

THE WAY TO KEEP PEACE IN A FAMILY.

1. Let us remember that our will is crossed every day, and let us prepare ourselves for that. 2. Everyone has a corrupt nature as do we; therefore, let us not expect too much. 3. Let us consider that different persons have different temperaments. 4. Let us look on every member of the family as one we should take care of. 5. Let us rejoice when something good happens to one of the family. 6. Let us overcome evil with goodness. 7. If we are sick or in pain, let us not grumble. 8. Noticing whenever others are suffering, let us show sympathy. 9. Let us take a loving look at everything. 10. Let us always give a "soft answer that turneth away wrath."

DEATH
OF PRESIDENT JEDEDIAH M. GRANT.
(From the *Star*.)

By the *Western Standard* of January 17th, we are informed of the death of Jedediah M. Grant, the Second Counselor to President Brigham Young. This sudden and unexpected event will produce feelings of sorrow and mourning among all the people of God, but more especially among those who were intimately acquainted with this great and good man. In early youth he connected himself with the Saints, and has been with them in all their tribulations. His faithfulness in adversity and prosperity—his untiring perseverance and energy of character, his unbounded love for the cause of truth, his warm attachment to the Saints, combined with a free, sociable disposition, have endeared him to the hearts of many thousands.

For many years he occupied the high and important position of one of the seven Presidents over all the Seventies, and was highly respected and beloved in that responsible station. In the capacity of a military officer, as Major General of the Militia of Utah Territory, he served with dignity and honor, and enjoyed the universal approbation and love of all. In the capacity of Mayor of Great Salt Lake City, he was wise, prompt, energetic, and indefatigable, in devising and executing plans for the peace and well being of the citizens. In the Legislative Assembly, during many sessions, he was unanimously elected Speaker of the House. In this honorable position, he exhibited, in a remarkable manner, those traits of character which so eminently qualified him to preside over that dignified body. As a *Statesman* he was surpassed by none. But in the high and holy calling of one of the three Presidents over the Church of God throughout the world, his wisdom and talents shone most conspicuously. The intelligence and power of the Holy Ghost were upon him mightily. His voice was like a thunderbolt, and his words like the vivid lightning to the hypocrite and transgressor. The words of burning truth flowed from his lips, piercing, penetrating, searching the inmost recesses of the heart. His unceasing labors, during the past year, in the great work of the reformation among the Saints, will never be forgotten in time nor eternity. Though we mourn his loss, yet we can but rejoice when we reflect how calm and sweet will be his rest for evermore. He has gone to the Paradise of our God,—to join the innumerable host of the redeemed. Farewell, dear brother Grant—farewell for a short season! Thou hast gone behind the veil; we soon shall follow, and with thee be forever blessed.

ZION'S TRUMPET,

OR

Star of the Saints.

SATURDAY, MARCH 28, 1857.

THE REFORMATION has begun in earnest in some places we are aware of, and we hope that it is thus in every place. We are confident that the Presidents will not rest until they have preached to the Saints, having them fast and pray, live better, and keep the Word of Wisdom, having family prayer in their home, following all the instructions, pondering about, talking about, and living their religion, warning their fellow men, and not wasting their money, but paying their tithing and preparing, by means of the Penny Fund, to gather home to Zion. Fast meetings are to be held often, in which all the Saints will gather that can come together, and the good Officers are to be sent forth to preach as much as they can. Remember that which our Apostle says, that our lack of the power of God is the reason we cannot baptize the honest in heart. In order to have the power of God we must get the Spirit of God, and in order to get that, we must be spiritually minded—read the history of Joseph and our well-known brethren and how they received revelations and the power of God; and the history of the old prophets of ancient times, how they prayed and fasted and received the Spirit or power of God to preach to the people. Let the elders and priests of Israel go forth full of the Holy Ghost to preach, not just verses, but a testimony of Jesus which they have, and they will bring down the walls of the Jericho where the honest in heart are held captive, and, if there are proper discipline and life in the branches, there is nothing that will prevent the success of the work of our God. We have lain in the same place long enough, until we have angered the Spirit of the Lord to the point that he has not cooperated so much with us. Who does not remember that men have failed to find comfort in their beds, and have been forced in the middle of the night to go and be baptized by a servant of God—when the spirit filled the meetings until it was like the day of Pentecost, and the Saints were prompted to speak great things of God? Why is it not so now?

Because of the increase of wickedness, negligence, and because the teaching of the Church of God has not been respected. How shall we have more of the power of God? By *reforming*—acknowledging our lukewarmness before him—having serious fasts—praying for his Spirit to fill us, and then receiving our baptism for the remission of our sins with a determination to respect the Priesthood, and help the work to move forward with our money and our possessions and all our efforts—to preach to the world and pray together until our prayers ascend like the smell of sweet mist before our God, for his Holy Spirit to enlighten and disturb the honest in heart; and to fill us. Our work is vain without the Spirit of God. The Saints are to be temples for the Spirit to dwell in. Let us keep our temples clean, then, inside and out. Keep the inside clean from hot drinks, intoxicating liquors, and all poisons and corrupt things forbidden in the word of Wisdom. O dear Saints, let us remember that our work is great and the time is short. The temple is coming forth and the Saints are being purified and cleansed before the Purifier and Cleanser of his people comes suddenly to his temple. It has to be one thing or the other—God or mammon—salvation or double damnation twice over because the light that was in us has gone out. This life is for a short time, and we cannot expect much enjoyment and rest in it. We can accomplish more in a year now toward our salvation than in a thousand years after going beyond the veil. Our objective is to be Kings and Priests and joint heirs of the majesty of the kingdom, and to have eternal lives. Who will heap damnation on his head by being an obstacle to the work of his God, when he knows that? Let us reform indeed, then, or the time is over, and God will surely move us aside, and woe unto us if that is the case. Just having your name in the Church of God will not be sufficient, but it is necessary to have the power of God. There needs to be a distinction between the Saints and the world. When pestilence and plague harvest countries—and when the destroying angel sweeps away loathsome, corrupt sinners, the Saints will have gathered "marrow to their bones, and strength to their navel," and they will have the power of God, so they can withstand it all, and prepare for the coming of their Older Brother, and to return to the presence and enter into the rest of their Father. If tomorrow were the day of judgment, how much faith do we have, and how much tribulation could we withstand? We fear it is too little! This is the time for us to awaken then, and ask ourselves what we believe? What condition do we intend to reach? How much have we increased, and how far have we reached? How close are we to having enough of the Holy Ghost in us to meet Jesus in his temple—to endure the presence of God, and there to give an accounting of our work? If we find ourselves near the pint of beer, puffing on the old stinky pipe—burning our entrails with corrupt rubbish, and stinking too much for even the angels of God to come near us, it is time for us to bestir ourselves from there, or to cease dreaming of salvation in the kingdom of God. We shall add nothing further at present, except to wish for an easy path for our presiding brethren to tear the veil from off the eyes of the people, so they may see their true condition.

We wish for the Branch presidents to read the editorials of the TRUMPET in the meetings and councils, whenever it is appropriate.

INSTRUCTIVE CHAPTER FOR THE CENSORS OF UTAH.
(From the *Western Standard*, January 24.)

An anonymous writer, in an article headed 'Utah,' published in the Chronicle of Tuesday, proposes a plan, which, if adopted, will in his opinion, effectually dispose of the difficulty attendant on the admittance of Utah into the Union. His suggestion is for Congress to partition Utah and apportion the different parts to California and the adjacent Territories. If this should be done, the deep disgrace which will be inflicted upon our country by the recognition of Utah as a sister State, will, he thinks, be avoided, and the holders of the Mormon doctrines will be subjected to the laws of the Territories into which they may be incorporated, and being likely to be but a small minority in each, all their peculiar institutions will, as a matter of course, be at once destroyed.

Were it not so serious a subject, it would be amusing to see the interest which writers manifest in regard to the "deep disgrace" likely to be brought upon them by the peculiar institutions of

"Mormonism." To read their writings, and not be acquainted with the people whence they emanate, it might be imagined that they were so very pure, upright and immaculate a community that they could not view the appearance of evil without horror. Those not posted up on the subject could not imagine that writers, who so hypocritically talk about the "revolting peculiar institutions" of the Mormons and the "deep disgrace" which association with them would entail, are themselves dwelling in the midst of a community where corruption, whoredom and abomination of every kind are glaringly exhibited on all hands. Yet such is the fact. These men who remonstrate with such affected indignation about the corruptions of the Mormons are themselves the daily spectators of the most disgusting and hideous vice and crime in their own streets. So notorious, and of so threatening a nature have these evils become, that they have forced themselves upon the attention of the late Grand Jury, who allude to them in the following language:—

"Here, [in the state of California] as elsewhere, [Utah must be excepted] it appears that a large part of our taxation is directly traceable to the existing vices in the community. The law should be strenuously enforced against the dens of infamy which are constantly filling our hospitals, courts and prisons, and causing a large share, not only of the misery, but of the taxation of this community."

On Chinese prostitution they say:—

"In this connection the Jury would call the attention of the Court, the Legislature and the public to an immense evil—an evil unmitigated by any, even the smallest shade of alloy—that of the importation of Chinese females for the purpose of prostitution. It was proven before the jury that those wretched creatures are slaves by law in China; that, as such, they are there purchased at from 25 to 75 dollars each; imported here and sold to the brothels or to the mines at from 300 to 800 dollars each, according to quality; that they are most brutally treated, flogged, &c., by those having the custody of them; and that when they become diseased they are always sent to the hospital to be supported at the public expense till they either die or are able to return to the service of their owners. Thus, not only incidently but directly, the community, every tax-paying citizen—is made to contribute to the support of a system not surpassed in abominable infamy by anything the history of the world has ever developed.

"It is in proof before the jury that from half to three-fourths of all the duty and expense of our police, criminal courts, prisons and hospitals is directly traceable to brothels. Would we diminish taxation, or make this city [Sacramento] a fit abode for the virtuous, or even preserve our boasted civilization, these prolific fountains of all corruptions must be dried up."

This is an official document, published in the public journals, and is intended, we presume, as a fair statement of the situation of affairs here. Can anything be conceived of more horribly disgusting, than is here represented? Dens of infamy filling the hospitals, courts and prisons with inmates? Three-fourths of all the expense of the police directly traceable to brothels! Women bought and imported from far-off China to supply the market with prostitutes for the gratification of the devilish and beastly appetites of wretches in human form! Could the records of Sodom and Gomorrah, were they spread out before our gaze, present anything more revolting than is here made public in the Grand Jury report of the Christian (heaven save the mark) city of San Francisco! Yet there are men found in this community—this brothel and hospital-taxed and supporting community—who will, with the most unblushing and brazen effrontery, hypocritically talk about being contaminated by contact with Utah! We can scarcely control our indignation and disgust when we read their cant, knowing as we do that their every breath is drawn in an atmosphere reeking with the most abandoned corruption.

Go to, gentlemen, and remove the offensive and heart-sickening spectacles and sounds that meet the eye and salute the ear of the stranger on every hand as he traverses your thoroughfares—utterly destroy the dens of infamy and schools of vice which are demoralizing your youth, and training your children in habits the most vicious and vices the most infamous—arrest the further progress of that disease, the virus of which is surely creeping into the veins, spreading through the systems, tainting the blood and destroying the constitutions of your people; and then, when you have done all this, you will have barely commenced to learn the lesson of virtue that Utah is teaching you and all the world. Until these results are brought about we would advise you, gentlemen, to confine your attention and the exercise of your abilities to the concerns that more immediately belong to you, and leave Utah to attend to her own matters, for the management of which she has ever been abundantly competent. Ridiculed as the idea may be, it is nevertheless true, that instead of a stain or a deep disgrace being inflicted on the national character by the admission of Utah into the Union, the Confederacy is actually honored by the association. So far as peace, morality, virtue, industry, good order, immunity from vice and crime of every description, are concerned, Utah is indisputably and incomparably superior to any of her sisters; and it is a great act of condescension on her part to consent to be associated with such a state as California confessedly is. Nothing but her love for the Constitution, for the perpetuity of this Republic, and for the freedom obtained by the blood and sufferings of the revolutionary fathers, would tempt her to such an act. Utah is assured that unless this nation repents and puts away the abomination and iniquity that are so rank in its midst, it must inevitably go down. If she should be admitted into the Union, the leaven of virtue and truth carefully preserved in her midst may be diffused throughout the whole nation, and be the means of saving it from the impending destruction; but if unable to save the nation, she may at least preserve the form of government, constitution, freedom and privileges handed down by the fathers of our country. This in inducement enough, and prospective reward sufficiently valuable to prompt her to ask for admittance.

MY DREAM.

(*Continued from Number* 5.)

I saw an exquisite construction—
    It is the house of the Holy One of Israel, I say;
There I drank from the life-giving,
    Holy, pure spring of my God.
I saw there one I recognized,
    Every sad thought flew away,
For he taught me much
    Of the secrets of the kingdom of Christ.

Behold part of the dream I had,
    For benefit, in time, from God,
True and correct is the testimony,
    Yes, it is uncomplicated truth.
Lord, open the doors of heaven,
    Make me brave in my journey;
The spirit of Jesus burns within me,
    To refine me for His work.

Make my heart a seat,
    For your Holy Spirit;
Make my voice as many waters,
    And my countenance as flame of fire,
So that I may glitter,
    In thy Church under heaven;
Behold, I am in thy service,
    Forever more. Amen.

          DAVID JOHN, Flint,
              Recently of Haverfordwest College.

DEPARTURE OF THE SAINTS FOR ZION.

Success to you, O brethren with happy hearts,
And to the dear sisters—praiseworthy Mormons,
When you are on this long journey,
That leads away towards the far west of the world.

You are now about to leave the land of the gentle Welsh,
And the land of your fathers and kind friends;
Where you spent your infancy without complaint
Without thought of enjoying a more pleasant land.

You are leaving the country of former delights,
By casting the mind over the watery ocean.
And in an instant it flies on a lovely journey,
And descends onto the plains at the end of the voyage.

May the Lord keep you as if in the palm of his hand,
While in the restless white crests of the waves—
While over the expanse of the faraway plains,
Or in the courts of the lofty mountains.

There a wonderful sight will be opened,
The green meadows a beautiful scene;
And breathing over them there will be peace,—
And salvation in your smiling faces.

Merthyr. ANEURIN L. JONES.

MISCELLANEOUS, &c.

ON page 74 of this volume, instead of Richard Williams, it should read Rice Williams.

WE WISH to know which distributor can supply us with the following number of volume IX of the "Trumpet":—3 of the 7th number, 53 of the 8th, 36 of the 9th, 2 of the 24th, and 2 of the 25th. We would like to get them as soon as it is possible.

BOOK PAYMENTS.—From March 6th to the 26th,—Charles Harman, £1; A. L. Jones, £3; James Phillips, £3.

AFFECTIONATE.—A lady said, in writing to her husband who was in California, that she knew that absence did not cause love to wane, because the longer he was away from home, all the more she loved him.

LET us take great care to watch out for two enemies in particular— the enemy that stands outside, and the traitor that opens the door from the inside.

CONTENTS.

	PG.
Liverpool Reformation Meetings	97
Letter from the States	102
The way to keep peace in a family	103
Death of President Grant	104
Editorial:—Reformation	105
Instructive Chapter for the Censors of Utah	107
Poetry—My Dream—Departure of the Saints for Zion	110

SWANSEA:
PRINTED AND PUBLISHED BY DANIEL DANIELS.

ZION'S TRUMPET,

OR

Star of the Saints.

No. 8.] APRIL 11, 1857. [Vol. X.

A LOOKING GLASS,
In which to examine ourselves, to see whether we be in the faith.
(From the *Mormon*)

Editor of the "Mormon,"

Dear Sir,—I find in my travels in the United States, many who profess to be brethren, or members of the Church of the Saints.

Among these there are a few who appear to me to deceive themselves, and think that they are in the faith when they are not.

If we inquire of a man whether he is in the faith, he will say, O yes, I am firm in the faith of "Mormonism;" I cannot consistently be anything else. I can see as clear as the noonday sun that the doctrine is scriptural, and that other modern systems are inconsistent with themselves, with each other, and with the Bible. Now this same man, who considers himself thus firm in the faith, being a man of means, will not lift a finger in the cause which he professes to believe. Or if he does, it is in a small way, and but very seldom—it is also done grudgingly—and in many cases because somebody urged, or teased him into the measure. He does nothing willingly or voluntarily, except, perhaps, the customary hospitality of lodging and of feeding the Elders.

[Price 1½c.

When it comes to clothing an Elder, or bearing his traveling expenses, or assisting to support his family, it is out of the question, the man never dreams of such a thing.

When tithing or donations are called for, or when he is required to sell out and gather with the Saints, he never makes a move. In short, he never thinks of cooperating with the Priesthood and Kingdom of God.

If he is questioned to the point, it will be found that he does not exactly believe in the *gathering*, or in tithing, or in some other peculiarities of the faith.

Well, brother, what is the peculiar system which you do believe? Or what is Mormonism as embraced by you?

Why, sir, I believe in the first principles,—the bible doctrines of faith, repentance, baptism for the remission of sins, and the laying on of hands for the gift of the Holy Ghost, &c. I also believe in praying, going to meetings, singing, preaching, &c., and in living a moral life. But all this has very little to do with money, or with gathering to some particular place, or cooperating with the body of the Saints in temporal affairs. If I sing and pray on, I shall inherit the kingdom of God at last.

Now it appears to me that such an one is deceiving himself, and that, in reality, he is not in the faith at all.

Let us look at this kind of faith in the mirror of another age, and see what it will amount to. Noah, for instance, was a Prophet—a preacher of righteousness. He, of course, taught first principles, as all God's messengers do. He required repentance, and the fruits of righteousness. He, no doubt, required the converts to obey the ordinances of God—to live morally, go to meeting, sing, pray, preach, &c. But he also foretold the destruction of the wicked, and the way of escape, or the means of temporal salvation for the righteous.

His followers must, there, not only believe and repent, and obey the ordinances, and live moral lives, and attend church, and pray, but they must close their business, gather up their means, withdraw from the fellowship of the world, and cease to intermarry with them, if they would save their children.

They must actually remove to the vicinity of the Ark with all their means, and there be dictated by the authority of Noah, his agents, and assistants, so as to cooperate with others in the same interests, in all their means and labors. Thus an ark could be prepared, with all its water, provisions, &c., for man and beast, and fowl and creeping thing. They must, perhaps, produce food to support the hands while they labored on the ark, or they must burn coal, or work in the smith's shop, to make and repair the tools, or to manufacture the nails, pins, and spikes; or they must make a road to the forest, or to assist in felling trees, and hewing and transporting timbers, or sawing plank; or perhaps it would fall to their lot to work on the body of the ark, inside or out; or in planning and fitting flooring, or decking, or partition ceilings, or stalls for animals, or storage rooms. Or they might perhaps work in the cooper's shop in preparing water casks, or in the meadows in cutting hay for the animals, or in gathering it and storing it away in the ark; or in drying meats and fruits, and gathering grains and other provisions. Or it is possible they might be appointed to travel and preach, and warn the world; or to select and purchase cattle or horses, sheep or swine, male and female, for the preservation of the best breeds of these animals. And finally they must put themselves and their families on board, with all the necessaries of life. And if they had any gold or silver or precious jewels left after all these outlays, they must, if they would preserve them, bring them on board, and treasure them up in the ark. Thus it is evident that they must be wholly dictated to by the leaders or Prophets, in their labors, and in all their temporal affairs and interests.

Now let us suppose, in the days of Noah some converts who received the first principles of Noah's preaching, who believed and repented and lived moral lives, and obeyed the ordinances; and who attended church, sang, prayed, preached, commented on the old prophecies of Enoch, and Seth, &c.

In process of time Noah, being too busy with the ark to go himself, sends out missionaries to these pious branches of the Church, or professed Noahites, to instruct them in their duty, and to inquire if they were firm in the faith of Noahism. O yes, says every one of them, we are firm Noahites. Well, then, says the messenger, God requires you to sell your possessions and gather up your means, and emigrate to the vicinity of the ark, and devote your money, your goods, your time, and your entire interests in furthering the Cause of the Ark, &c. But, as this will take some little time, you are invited in the meantime to furnish what ready means you can consistently spare, in pushing forward the great work of temporal salvation; that we, through faithfulness, may be heirs of the world when it is cleansed from the wicked by water.

O, say the professed Noahites, then it is our money and goods, and labors that you are after, is it? You wish to control our temporal interests! Well, sir, you can go home again and inform Mr. Noah, that it is only in spiritual things, or in matters of religion that we are willing to be dictated. We profess to be able to manage our own affairs, and no man shall dictate our financial matters nor teach us where to emigrate, or when or where to go or come. "*We are individual sovereigns*," and no man shall rule over us. Not but what we are firm believers in Noahism. That is, we believe in the first principles just as he has laid them down; we believe in faith, repentance, and obedience to the ordinances. We also believe in a moral life, and in going to church, singing, praying, preaching, &c., but nothing more.

But still, lest you might consider us indifferent or unfriendly, we will treat you with hospitality. But as to clothing, traveling expenses, and aid for your families while you are round warning the world, or teaching us, you must run in debt for it, or do without it, or get it where you can; we have no concern in that matter. But stop a moment, let me see, here is a dollar for you; we wish to be liberal—and finally, come to take second thought, we will donate a few dimes to the building of the ark; but you must consider it a mere charity on our part, and thank and bless us for it. We of course, have no personal interest in the matter, but we wish to be charitable to our brethren. O!—by the bye, we wish you to stay till tomorrow; a wedding comes off. Our daughter is going to be married to a rich gentleman; he is not exactly a Noahite, but he is a *very fine* man, a real gentleman; he thinks everything of our daughter, and will make a most excellent husband. Besides, this is the last single daughter we have. The others have all married well, and are very well situated in life, although none of them exactly believe Noahism, but they come to meeting once in a while just to please us—in short, they are very friendly.

The messenger sees how it is, stays to the wedding, pities all parties, but cannot enlighten them. He finally blesses them for their hospitality and charity, and returns to Noah to report progress.

Now query: What would Noah say of these Noahites?

He would doubtless say: Poor blind souls, they are to be pitied. They think they are Noahites, but alas, they deceive themselves. We will thank and bless them for their little kindnesses and charities, and will struggle on as well as we can in our duties of building the ark, and warning the world.

These professed Noahites have no real faith; they are not, in fact, Noahites at all. They are not fit for the kingdom of God, and to be joint heirs with us to a new world after the flood. They must, therefore, with all their prayers, religion, morality, and charity, perish with the disobedient, and miss salvation in the kingdom of God.

At length the ark is finished, furnished, and peopled. The obedient sail off in triumph over the fragments of a ruined world, and finally become heirs of a whole earth, when it is cleansed by water.

The professed Noahites lose their lives and all their property. Their sons and daughters, mixed up with the world, although they *married well*, raised up children and heaped up property to perish with them in the flood.

"And so," said Jesus, "shall it be in the days of the coming of the Son of Man."

"Mormonism" has come forth, not only to call people to believe in Jesus Christ, repent, live a moral life, obey the ordinances of God, go to church, sing, pray, and preach; but it has come forth to prepare the way for the coming of the Son of

Man. It has come to gather the Saints, and build up the kingdom of God as a stronghold, or refuge, in the day when the wicked are overthrown. If a person has any interest at all in the kingdom of God, all his interests are in it. He cannot consistently have any interests outside of it.

In short, if a man believes "Mormonism" at all, he must believe, not only in faith, repentance, and baptism, and the laying on of hands for the gift of the Holy Ghost, morality, prayer, and singing; but in the utter overthrow of the present political, religious, moral, and social institutions, and the building up of the kingdom of God, and its righteousness in their stead, to stand forever. Therefore, he can have no interests, motives, or affections aside from the same.

Such a man, as soon as he sees the light of the kingdom, will begin, with all his might, mind, and strength to shape his affairs, and to place himself, his family, his property, his labors, and all his interests, in a situation to be controlled, and properly directed by the Lord and his servants, in a way to cooperate with others who are interested in the same joint interests.

He will, in the meantime, if a man of means, in all wisdom and prudence, assist the Elders in their travels and missions, and bear their expenses and burdens. He will tithe himself, and also donate liberally from time to time, while he is getting ready to gather with the Saints. He will say to his son or daughter, do not marry out of the Church, and raise up children to perish with Great Babylon, for all corrupt institutions are about to be overthrown.

He will, in short, to use a figure, spend his treasures and his labors purely to build and provision the Ark, and warn the world; and then will get into it himself with his family, and all his remaining treasures. And thus he will lay the foundation of permanent riches, and become a joint heir with the Saints in the inheritance of a renovated world, when the wicked are cleared out of it by the judgments of the Almighty.

Yours, &c.,

Philadelphia, January 19, 1857. P. P. PRATT.

CREDIBILITY OF THE BOOK OF MORMON, AS COMPARED WITH THAT OF THE BIBLE.

BY C. W. WANDELL.

(From the *Western Standard*.)

Since the age of miracles and inspiration, the religious world, notwithstanding its multiplied divisions and contrariety of doctrines, has in one respect, at least, maintained a unity of faith; namely, "that the volume of God's word as contained in the Bible, is full, complete and perfect;" and, per consequence, the claims of the Book of Mormon to divine authenticity must be without foundation in truth.

If the Bible does indeed contain the whole of God's word, then we must admit that the Book of Mormon, as claiming to be a portion of His word, cannot be true. Therefore, our first inquiry necessarily relates to the former book; in which we propose, That if the Bible contains the whole of God's word, it contains, first, all that God ever has revealed. Second, all that He ever will reveal. Third, that which has been revealed must have remained pure, and been handed down to us, as God gave it to man.

1. *The Bible does not contain all that God has revealed to man.*

By referring to the Bible, we find the following sacred books mentioned as having once existed, and been reverenced as greatly by the people of God as those which have reached our times.

Solomon's three thousand Proverbs, (of which we have but a part) and one thousand and five Songs, (of which we have but one) 1 Kings iv, 32.

Book of the Acts of Solomon; 1 Kings xi, 41. Book of Nathan the prophet, and Book of Gad the seer; 1 Chron., xxix, 29. Prophecy of Ahijah the Shilonite, and the Visions of Iddo the seer, 2 Chron., ix, 29. Book of Jehu; 2 Chron. xx, 34. Prophecy of Urijah; Jer. xxvi. 20—23. Book of Wars of the Lord; Num. xxi, 14. Book of Jasher; Josh. x, 13. Apostolic Decrees; Acts xvi, 4, 5. Paul's first Epistle to the Corinthians; 1 Cor. v, 9. Paul's Epistle to the Laodiceans; Col. Iv, 16.

In addition to these, we have, in the 14th and 15th verses of

Jude, an extract from a Prophecy of Enoch, evidently referring to the second advent of the Savior. And

It is evident, that if Enoch could with the eye of prophecy pierce the future thousands of years, and predict the coming of the Son of God with power; it could by no possibility be otherwise, than that he also predicted many, if not all, the most remarkable events mentioned in Biblical history. And

It is evident from the quotation, that Enoch's Prophecy had been committed to writing. And

The records of antiquity give us no reason to doubt that the art of writing was known to the antediluvians. And

It is evident, that this record, or some part of it, was in existence in the days of the Apostles. And

It is evident, that without this sacred book and all the lost inspired writings, by whomsoever written, again restored and joined with the present Bible, the canon of Scripture cannot be full.

It is idle to contend that the lost sacred books were of but indifferent importance; and, indeed, it is to charge God foolishly to say, that he has made revelations of himself to mankind, which were not worth the keeping. We must admit, that a book containing a particular and full account of God's first dispensation of mercy to man, in which we find his adoration and worship established in the offerings of the children of Adam, and which must have been recorded in the Book of Enoch; would not only have been interesting beyond what any subsequent writing can be, but also important in clearly stating important matters, which the exceeding brevity of the Mosaic account leaves uncertain.

With regard to the Apostolic Decrees, before referred to, we know that the constituting of a new society is necessarily accompanied with important documents, in order to regulate its discipline, to set forth its principles, and to give it that consistency which will ensure its positive establishment and permanent prosperity. And

If we may judge of the importance of those Decrees by the one concerning circumcision, we must admit them to have been of the greatest consequence. And

This will more clearly appear, when we take into consideration the fact, that at that time no other Christian writings were in existence, so far as we know. And

When the Epistles and Evangelical books did appear, their slight allusions to church government and discipline seem to imply, that the Decrees were as nearly as possible all-sufficient in those respects. From these considerations we claim the Decrees to have been the word of God to his Church; and unless they be re-revealed, the sacred canon cannot be complete.

(To be continued at the end of the Editorial.)

ZION'S TRUMPET,

OR

Star of the Saints.

SATURDAY, APRIL 11, 1857.

GENERAL INSTRUCTIONS TO PASTORS, PRESIDENTS, AND ELDERS.—(From the *Star*).—In compliance with the instructions received from the first Presidency, we say to the Pastors and Presidents of Conferences throughout the European Mission send the elders forth among the gentiles, into the cities and villages throughout the land, and warn them to repent of their sins. Show them the necessity of entering into covenant with God, and of being gathered out of Babylon before the judgments of the Almighty shall sweep them from the earth. Let the Elders go forth without purse or scrip, as they did in the days of Jesus, and as they have done since the early rise of the Church. Go forth, brethren of the priesthood, having faith in the promises of Jesus Christ, and you shall prosper—your way shall be opened, none shall perish for want of food, or go naked for the lack of clothing, and you shall bring many souls to the knowledge of the truth. Fast and pray until the Holy Ghost rests upon you. Then preach to the people as you are led, and your words will have life and power in them—your words will be Gospel—the power of God unto salvation to all that believe. When you are rejected and persecuted in one place, go to another, leaving your testimony against them, according to the word of God. It will be more tolerable for Sodom and Gomorrah in the day of Judgment, than for those who reject your words. When you are turned away, and not fed for a day or two, do not despair, the Lord will provide for you in due time, if your faith fail not. You are called upon to do a great work; great will be your reward if you will do your duty; and glorious will be the result of the efforts that you are now called upon to make. God will not withhold any necessary blessing from those who will be firm in their determination to carry out this counsel.

Let wives and children fast and pray for their fathers and husbands who go forth into the vineyard of the Lord, and not hold them back through fear of want; and they will be blessed both spiritually and temporally, their lives preserved, and themselves gathered to Zion, as the result of the ministerial labors of the Elders.

There are now many elders located in the different branches throughout the European Mission whose talents are hid: they are lying dormant. We want all such to repent and arise from a state of lethargy and go among the gentiles, preaching to them the Gospel of the Kingdom. Let the Elders do something that will entitle them to a glorious resurrection at the coming of the Son of Man, which draweth nigh.

Traveling elders should give a report to the presidents of conferences every two weeks, or oftener if required, of their whereabouts, success, &c. Let the presiding elders of branches, through the aid of the teachers, collect the tithings, and the donations to the Penny Emigration Fund, weekly. And let the presidents of conferences, as much as possible, travel from branch to branch, stirring up the Saints to diligence in the discharge of all their duties, and receive from the hands of the presidents of branches the monies that they have collected.

Let there be no money disbursed by any president of a conference without the consent of his pastor. Presidents of conferences are to report to their pastors as often as required. Pastors are held responsible for all monies collected in their respective Pastorates, and they are hereby required to *make a semi-annual report to this office, of the amounts received and expended, and for what purpose.*

We require no more of you than is required of us. It is only the iniquitous that have cause to fear an investigation of their conduct.

We deem it wisdom to dispense with quarterly conferences, and to hold our conferences semi-annually, at such times and places as circumstances may indicate.

We want all unnecessary Conference house and hall rent dispensed with. Rent such halls for meeting rooms as the circumstances require, for the accommodation of the Saints and the strangers that visit your meetings. On special occasions when you anticipate a large congregation, rent a hall for the time, suitable for their accommodation.

We wish the presidents of conferences to spend as much of their time as their other duties will allow in preaching the Gospel to the unconverted. Woe unto them that are at ease in Zion.

We want the pastors and presidents of conferences to seek for the spirit of prophecy, and as directed by the Holy Ghost to call and send faithful Elders to preach the Gospel, as herein directed, also to ordain others that are worthy and send them forth. We want no drones in the hive.

Select as much as possible those who have no families; nevertheless, let those who have families, if they have faith, and can leave them in a situation to sustain themselves, be called to this ministry.

In conclusion, we say to the pastors, we enjoin it upon you to see that the instructions contained in this epistle, are carried into effect throughout the different conferences in your respective pastorates.

(Continuation of Credibility of the Book of Mormon.)

2. The Bible does not contain all that God promised to reveal. The general duties of the prophets seem to have been to reprove

the wicked—to comfort the righteous, and to predict prosperity or adversity, as the case might be; but the prophetic spirit has been chiefly directed to the great latter-day dispensation, in which it is announced, that so great will be the display of God's power, that the mighty wonders of former times will no more be remembered, or come into mind:

That in those days the nations shall say, "Come, ye and let us go up to the mountain of the Lord, to the house of the God of Jacob, and He will teach us of his ways, and we will walk in His paths; for out of Zion shall go forth the law, and the word of the Lord from Jerusalem." Isaiah ii, 3. And

That at his second advent, "He will reign in Mount Zion, and in Jerusalem, and before his ancients gloriously." Isiah xxiv, 23. And

That the going forth of this law for the government of the Millennial Kingdom, and the word of the Lord for the instruction of his people, is inseparably connected with this righteous and universal reign. And

The laws then promulgated, and the discourses then delivered, will be *bona fide* the word of God. And

As such, will be as sacred as, and of equal authority with, any revelation heretofore given. And

Will become an integral part of the great volume of God's word. And

There is no text in the Scriptures which in anywise militates against this happy result: that is, which seals up the mouth of God and interdicts revelation; though the prunings and interpolations of man are forbidden under the severest penalties.

3. That which has been revealed must have remained pure, and been handed down to us as God gave it to man.

There is, perhaps, nothing that gives the intelligent Christian greater pain than the reflection, that the New Testament has come down to us through the muddy channel of the Church of Rome. That a corrupt church, in order to make those writings tally more perfectly with its dogmas, ordered them to be *revised and corrected*! which order was given A. D. 506, by Anastasius, and was carried out at Constantinople. And that Jerome complained at that early day,

"That no one copy resembled another." And

That after such correction had been made, the Catholic monks, to exhibit their skill in iniquity, had so corrupted this corrected copy that there were, at the time of the printing of the Elzevir edition of Greek text, A. D. 1624, "upwards of 130,000 various readings."

In view of these facts, who can marvel that God should have provided a way to restore to man, in the latter-day dispensation of the *restitution of all things*, a pure copy of the Gospel history, either by causing a copy to be buried in the earth; or by revealing it anew from heaven; or both?

In order to clearly demonstrate the authenticity of any writing purporting to be of a sacred character, the following points are necessary to be established: namely: Who was the writer? What were the circumstances that called forth the production? These may be called the outward evidences; which having been established, we are at liberty to turn to the inner evidences, and judge from the intrinsic merits of its subject matter, whether it may or may not possess an excellence not inferior to those scriptures which we confess to have been written by divine inspiration.

The Book of Mormon, like the Bible, is a compilation of a number of books, written by men of different nations, and at different times. The first in order of time is the Book of Ether, which is a record of a colony which at the confusion of tongues and subsequent dispersion, left the plains of Shinar, and built ships in which they were driven across the Pacific ocean, and landing near what is now called Central America, established themselves there, and were the first founders of empire and civilization on the western Continent. They became a great people; but falling into great wickedness, which engendered strifes and civil wars, they were finally destroyed as a people. Ether abridged their history on gold tablets; which falling into the hands of one Moroni, of another nation, he further abridged it on gold tablets, and compiled it with the sacred books of his own people.

Moroni says: "He that wrote this record was Ether, and he was a descendant of Coriantor; Coriantor was the son of Moron; and Moron was the son of Ethem; and Ethem was the son of Ahah; and Ahah was the son of Seth; and Seth was the son of Shiblon; and

Shiblon was the son of Com; and Com was the son of Coriantum; and Coriantum was the son of Amnigaddah; and Amnigaddah was the son of Aaron; and Aaron was a descendant of Heth, who was the son of Hearthom; and Hearthom was the son of Lib; and Lib was the son of Kish; and Kish was the son of Corum; and Corum was the son of Levi; and Levi was the son of Kim; and Kim was the son of Morianton; and Morianton was a descendant of Riplakish; and Riplakish was the son of Shez; and Shez was the son of Heth; and Heth was the son of Com; and Com was the son of Coriantum; and Coriantum was the son of Emer; and Emer was the son of Omer; and Omer was the son of Shule; and Shule was the son of Kib; and Kib was the son of Orihah, who the son of Jared; which Jared came forth with his brother and their families, with some others and their families, from the great tower, at the time when the Lord confounded the language of the people, and sware in his wrath that they should be scattered upon all the face of the earth; and according to the word of the Lord the people were scattered. And the brother of Jared being a large and mighty man, and being a man highly favored of the Lord; for Jared his brother said unto him, cry unto the Lord, that he will not confound us that we may not understand our words. And it came to pass that the brother of Jared did cry unto the Lord, and the Lord had compassion upon Jared; therefore, he did not confound the language of Jared; and Jared and his brother were not confounded. Then Jared said unto his brother, "Cry again unto the Lord, and it may be that he will turn away his anger from them who are our friends, that he confound not their language." And it came to pass that the brother of Jared did cry unto the Lord, and the Lord had compassion upon their friends, and their families also, that they were not confounded. And it came to pass that Jared spake again unto his brother, saying, "Go and inquire of the Lord whether he will drive us out of the land, and if he will drive us out of the land, cry unto him whither we shall go. And who knoweth but the Lord will carry us forth into a land which is choice above all the earth. And if it so be, let us be faithful unto the Lord, that we may receive it for our inheritance."

The second book in the order of time, is the first book of Nephi.

Nephi was the son of Lehi, who was a descendant of Joseph the Israelite, who was sold into Egypt. Lehi possessed the spirit of prophecy, and dwelt in Jerusalem, at the commencement of the reign of Zedekiah, king of Judah, and previous to the Babylonian captivity. Being forewarned of God, of the captivity about to take place, he removed from Jerusalem, taking his family and the family of one Ishmael with him, he journeyed towards the Red Sea: after which they proceeded in an easterly, or southeasterly direction, till they came to the great waters, where, being again commanded, a ship was built in which they crossed the Pacific, landing on the western coast of South America. The exact spot of their first encampment is not known: but it is worthy of remark, that the ruins of an immense temple, situated a little southward of Valparaiso harbor, still serves as a landmark to mariners, to direct their course into that city, and it is not improbable that it was built to commemorate their first encampment in their "promised land." A sort of Plymouth *Rock* Monument.

Nephi was a good man. A bad heart never would have uttered the sentiments or cherished the principles which characterize his writings. He possessed the spirit of prophecy; and he wrote two books of prophecy, doctrine, and history.

At his father's death he succeeded to the Patriarchate; but his elder brother, Laman, to whom the office lineally belonged, but who had lost it by transgression, rebelled, and went to a distant part, taking with him as many as would follow him.

From this division arose two distinct nations, the Nephites and Lamanites. The former a civilized and pious people, who built cities, temples and towers, (or *pyramids*), who cultivated the arts—lived under the protected aegis of regular government, and were noted for their diligence in industrial pursuits. The latter degenerated into barbarism, and principally from whom are descended the Indians of the present day.

As the Nephites increased in numbers, they extended their boundaries northward, until in time they came to the Isthmus of Panama; which crossing, they came to the country of the Jaredites who had previously been destroyed.

The possessions of this people became the property of the

Nephites; and this section of the country, which they called "the land Bountiful," became the principal residence of their kings.

At Nephi's death, his brother Jacob assumed the reigns of government, and wrote a history of his reign.

After him, Enos became the Nephite historian—afterward Jarom, Omni, Amaron, Chemish, Abinadom, Amaleki, Mosiah, Alma, Helaman, Nephi son of Helaman, Nephi son of Nephi, Mormon, and Moroni. The writings of these persons forming a continuous history from the days of Nimrod down to the four hundred and twentieth year of the Christian era.

These writings are contained in the Book of Mormon, and are not *in extenso*, but are abridgements made by Mormon and his son Moroni, and engraved by them on gold plates, and by God's command were buried in the earth, with a promise, that they should be discovered and published in the last days. At the time of this occurrence the Nephites and Lamanites were at war, in which the latter were victorious, and the burial of the archives was the only sure method of their preservation.

Most of the Nephite writers were good men and possessed the spirit of prophecy. And hence the Book of Mormon is made up of much the same materials as is the Bible. It also contains an account of the visit of the Savior to the Nephites, after his resurrection.

The Egyptian was adopted as the basis of their written language, though it was materially altered and improved.

Having given the reader a general idea of the Book of Mormon, I will now proceed to relate the manner of its discovery and translation; which having done, I will proceed to compare the evidences of its credibility with those of the Bible.

CONTENTS.

	PG.
Looking Glass, &c.	113
Credibility of the Book of Mormon	119
Editorial:—General Instructions, &c.	121

SWANSEA:
PRINTED AND PUBLISHED BY DANIEL DANIELS.

ZION'S TRUMPET,

OR

Star of the Saints.

No. 9.] APRIL 25, 1857. [Vol. X.

A LOOKING GLASS, OF LOCAL MANUFACTURE,
For the use of the Welsh Saints and others.

———

Merthyr Tydfil, April 8, 1857.

Esteemed President Daniels.—My reason for sending this to you personally you will see in the content of my writing. And by the way, I can report to you that there is preaching of the Reformation, and reforming, by many, through the length and breadth of these regions. The first love is enjoyed—one feels a more abundant life—the spirit of their offices rests on, and, works powerfully in the various officers, so that they determine to labor more diligently to preach, to testify, and to encourage everyone to obey the gospel, which was presented to Joseph Smith, the great Prophet of the Latter Days. Several have already accepted the testimony, and have joined with the Saints, which you probably know through brother A. S. Williams, whom I have determined to be a straightforward man, considering himself along with his brothers, as fellow workers in Christ's vineyard.

Quite a number of the Saints still have not committed themselves to a renewed effort on behalf of their faith.

These may be divided into three or four classes, which serves as a reason for their postponing covenanting themselves anew to do the will of God.

First. Those who for a long time have been slow, lazy, and idle in the Church; who seem to be alive, and they are dead.

These are the ones who meddle with things which do not belong to them, but which belong wholly to others who are of proven virtue, and goodness, and are accountable for their behavior only to the chief authorities of the Church. They poison themselves

[Price 1½c.

internally, poisoning whoever comes into contact with them. They are the ones who jeer, mock, and despise the faithful brothers who visit them, urging them to repent and turn from the error of their ways to a covenant with God, and walk in the ways of wisdom. They have never paid the Lord his due—they refuse the law of Tithing—they entered into gross darkness, attributing indifference, violence and oppression, even to the Prophets and Apostles of the living God, in these last days.

Secondly. Those who have lost the Spirit of God through meddling in the affairs of others; having forgotten the Prophet Brigham's advice, which says to everyone, *"Mind your own business."* These people do not see their own faults, but they see faults in others where they do not exist. The failings and weaknesses of the faithful Saints are like a feast to them. They do not believe that "in many things we are *all* backsliding." "Although the righteous man slips seven times, the Lord will raise him up," which is completely contrary to their wishes.

They are remarkably sharp-eyed. They claim to be able to see through the *rafter* or the *great beam* in their own eyes, the *mote* or the tiny *speck* in the eyes of their most righteous brothers! A kite's eye is said to be more piercing than the eye of an eagle. But the eyes of these people are more piercing than both of them: they can see the speck in the eyes of their brothers through the post, rafter or the beam in their own eyes. Be careful of the eyelids. It would be a great blessing for them to cast the rafter out of their own eyes first, and then they will see clearly to cast the mote out of their brothers' eyes, and not be offended because of the mote in another's eye, to point it out to another in order to be hurtful, trying to increase it. For he alone feels the pain which even the smallest mote causes even in his own eye, and he tries to get it out for his own sake and get eye ointment and the light of the Holy Ghost to guide him and keep his eye only for the glory of God in everything he does, so that he may not suffer from motes as he looks and "reaches for the goal of exalted achievement of God's calling in Christ Jesus."

Thirdly. Those who have not practiced keeping the "Word of Wisdom" completely in all its parts. I know several brothers, and especially sisters, whose heart's wish is to serve God and live by every word which proceeds out of God's mouth through his servants. Yet, because of their familiarity with the usual way of life since their birth, they feel that changing some of the foods they are used to would be harmful to their constitutions. These, most of them, are weak, unhealthy, feeble, old and infirm. Such people were counseled according to the instruction of Apostle Benson and your own in *"Zion's Trumpet,"* namely, "Do not be too hard on the Saints, and do not let things lag either." They were urged to repent—to covenant—and pray after that for the Holy Ghost to guide them and to instruct them in wisdom to know that which is beneficial and to refuse that which is harmful—to strive with their whole heart to build the Church—to practice thrift in everything, and to prepare wisely in order to receive their deliverance to the "Valley of the Mountains."

Fourthly. Those who consider the "Covenant" to be too important to have anything to do with it in almost any way. They are content to tithe to the Lord; and several of them have done so almost since the beginning: they feel an urge to go out and preach the Gospel, &c. But they consider the "Covenant," particularly the "Word of Wisdom," as if, were they to transgress one part of it on any occasion, that would be an unforgivable sin for them; and if they were to disobey it in the slightest degree during their lifetime, it would be enough of a sin to damn them forever.

The devil is cunning in this business.

First of all, in trying to convince them that Christ's Gospel contains nothing but "teetotalism." He does not want the main things related to the Covenant ever to enter their minds. Preaching about Joseph Smith, the great Prophet of the latter days, the gathering of the Saints, &c., is one of the most abhorrent things in the whole world to the devil.

Secondly: To hide this as far as he can, he creates every scheme to frighten some of the Saints, and show them that entering into a covenant is a danger to temporal and spiritual life until they have first of all conquered every desire: and that it is outside of the Church of Jesus Christ that they will find strength to live, and overcome every evil, and lust and desire, and corrupt affections, &c., until they become sufficiently righteous, pure, and undefiled to be taken in, so that neither God's mercy, Christ's intercession, nor the gift of the Holy Ghost might have anything to do with them in the Church.

The evil one is so cunning, that through this he entices some people further and further, without making a covenant, and yielding further to his own corrupt will; and in the end after their tithing debt to the Lord accumulates, he shows them that after delaying so long without covenanting, they have gone too far for them ever to be able to do so and move forward with a clear conscience. A great deal of effort has been made to teach them differently. They have also been shown that God calls not "righteous people but sinners to repentance," and that it is not outside of the Church of Jesus Christ that one finds strength to conquer Satan's temptations, but by coming forward and covenanting, and being baptized for the remission of their sins, and receiving the laying on of hands in order to reconfirm them, that they may again receive the Holy Ghost, striving with all their might to do the will of God—to pay their tithes to the Lord—to live by every word of God—to go forward in faith, to witness, preach, and warn the nations about the swift destruction which will come upon the unrepentant and the disobedient to the Gospel of our Lord Jesus Christ.

There is also something else that has appeared in the *Trumpet*, and of which some wish to take advantage in order to stop paying their tithing, i.e., that there is a clear suggestion there that "it is impossible" for some to pay it. Some people in that circumstance have been found, such as old people unable to earn anything, being wholly supported by others—women and children who are entirely under the supervision of others not in the Church, and who are unwilling on any account to give them the smallest mite toward building the kingdom of God.

Yet another thing that is a great obstacle to many of the Saints' committing themselves is, those Saints who are like a will-o'-the-wisp. Moving from place to place, from job to job and from one Conference to another, until finally becoming completely heedless of their faith in all its parts and totally drowning in the spirit of the world and causing harm to others, and corrupting and poisoning the minds and spirits of many. I think that the Aberdare and Merthyr regions suffer more from these characters than anywhere else in Wales. They come here steeped in poison; they poison others, and then they return after a while to their old location, to sow seeds of rebellion again in the minds of others; and they do so almost entirely unbeknown to the presidents of branches and conferences; but by now they have been stopped, unless they repent, which, let us hope, will take place soon. Yet, "Respect where respect is due." Many brothers and sisters have moved from one Conference to another because of compelling circumstances, and God's blessing follows them and makes their move a blessing to others, and the blessing of their presidents is with them always.

The state of things is something similar to the above description, as far as I can tell, as I strive to do my best to preach to the world, visit the Saints, teach them, and train them, and build the Church in every way in my power. I am determined to preach and bear witness in every town, village, nook and corner, where I have been preaching, and where I have not, if I come to know about it somewhere in my field of labor.

Praying to our Heavenly Father to bless my efforts and the efforts of his faithful servants throughout the world, to find many souls for his Son, Jesus Christ, and to bless you in all of your works, I remain,

Your brother in the Gospel,

DEWI ELFED JONES.

FOURTEENTH GENERAL EPISTLE

Of the Presidency of the Church of Jesus Christ of Latter-day Saints, to the Saints in the Valleys of the Mountains and those scattered abroad through the earth, greeting:

Beloved Brethren: Feeling impelled by the Spirit of our God to write unto you concerning the things of the kingdom, and having greater boldness therein by reason of the faith and testimony of the Lord Jesus and the Holy Ghost of which we have received and bear record unto the whole world, we proceed to manifest unto you such intimations of the Spirit pertaining unto the Church and kingdom of God as are or may be presented unto us, trusting that they may prove instructive and beneficial unto the Saints.

To those who read our publications we need not minutely recapitulate the operations and success attending the labors of our missionaries, as all such information is promptly and fully laid before the people through those channels. Suffice it to say, uniform success has attended the efforts of our Elders, and thousands are now rejoicing in the light of truth, having renounced their traditional errors, obeyed the ordinances of the House of the Lord and received with gladness, praise and thanksgiving the pure principles of the gospel of Christ. They are now anxiously looking for deliverance, to unite and cast their lot with us in these peaceful vales.

The missionaries who have been absent in Europe two years and more, have mostly returned this season, having been relieved by others appointed at our last April Conference. Notwithstanding thousands from Europe annually find their homes in Utah, still the numbers are increasing abroad.

The interest excited in favor of and to learn the truth and hatred of its opposers were never greater than at the present time. The power of Almighty God is made manifest in the administration of his servants, and is plainly discernible in his hand dealings with the nations of the earth, as well as with his people, making the assurance doubly sure that his word will not return unto him void, nor his promises be made in vain. He will sustain the righteous, the ungodly will he cut off.

In California the *Western Standard* is faithfully warning the people, under the able care and guidance of brother George Q. Cannon, who has also published the Book of Mormon in the Hawaiian language. The publication of that paper has proved very useful and beneficial in correcting public opinion, and in exercising a salutary influence over the few to be found in that land who are seekers after truth. Gold is the shrine at which they bow, and the truth emanating from High Heaven's King has but few admirers. The Standard, however, will be able to sustain itself, mostly through the aid of the Saints, and will continue to be issued so long as it shall be considered beneficial in aiding the cause of truth in that region.

The Sandwich Islands and Australian missions are in a healthy and prosperous condition. We learn by late advices from Silas Smith, who is at present presiding over the Sandwich Islands' mission, that the crops on Lanai are much better this season than usual, which will greatly facilitate the gathering of the native Saints upon that island, the appointed place. The repeated failure and destruction of their crops has involved the mission somewhat in debt, and partially frustrated the design in gathering the Saints to that place, where they could be measurably protected from the hireling missionary operations and other contaminating influences of licentious civilization. But, through the present prosperity, the aid of the faithful Elders, and continual blessings of the Almighty, who is every mindful of His faithful Saints, we hope and expect that the mission will soon rise above its present embarrassments. There was represented at a Conference held on Lanai, on the 24th of July, 1855, 90 organized branches, 4,220 members, 723 of whom had been baptized within that year—25 American and 118 native Elders then laboring on the islands, besides native priests, teachers and deacons.

From the Society Islands we have no very satisfactory accounts. Owing to the difficulties with the French government, the Elders were compelled, some two years ago, to leave those islands. Brothers Addison Pratt and Ambrose Alexander were appointed to that mission from San Bernardino, at their last April Conference, and sailed for those islands on the 24th day of the same month, but were soon obliged to leave, and have since returned.

Elder Farnham, from the Australian Mission, arrived in this city on the 21st of November, leaving a shipload of Saints at San Bernardino, the most of whom, it is expected, will come on during the ensuing season.

Brothers John S. Eldredge and James Graham, with 28 Saints from Australia, on board, were wrecked near the Society Isles on the 4th day of October, 1855. We regret to add that five persons, two women and three children, were lost, the remainder barely escaped with their lives upon a barren and uninhabited island, where they remained, subsisting upon turtle, for six weeks. They were finally relieved from their perilous situation by the captain of the *Julia Ann*, who had sailed over three hundred miles in an open boat to an inhabited island and procured another vessel, but were left upon that group and the Sandwich Islands, with no means to further prosecute their journey; though they have since arrived on the western coast, on their way to Zion.

Without reflecting upon the officers of the *Julia Ann*, all of whom are well spoken of by our brethren, or even upon the strength and sea worthiness of the vessel, which we understand was good and new, still we wish to caution our Elders, not only those in Australia, but all in foreign countries, not to permit an over anxiety to emigrate and gather with the Saints to make them careless or indifferent to the kind and condition of the vessel in which they embark, nor to the character of the officers and crew on board. This is the second instance of vessels, sailing from that mission with Saints on board, not reaching their destination. In the other case no lives were lost, though the vessel had to put into port where she was condemned, and the Saints, after having paid their passage to the western coast, were left on the Sandwich Islands. It is a matter worthy of record, and a source of great joy and satisfaction to us, that in all our foreign emigration those are the only losses by sea, of that character, that have occurred.

From the Cape of Good Hope, South Africa, there is a company of Saints en route for this place, the first fruits of the labors of brothers Jesse Haven, William Walker, and Leonard I. Smith, who have been manifestly blessed of the Lord in planting the work in that distant part of the Lord's vineyard. At a Conference held at Port Elizabeth in the month of August, 1855, three conferences and six branches, comprising 126 members, were represented. The brethren of the mission, having awakened the various branches, and ordained faithful Elders to prosecute the work, are, together with a small company, on their way home, except brother Leonard I. Smith, who arrived in this city on the 31st of last May.

The East India missionaries have now all returned, having effected but little in the redemption of that benighted people. How truly have they become "joined unto their idols" and left of the Lord, even like unto the aborigines of America, a law unto themselves, until the Lord shall again visit them with salvation in great power and glory.

From the report of the conference held at Copenhagen we learn, through brother John Van Cott, that over two thousand Saints have emigrated from that mission; and there still remained over twenty-four hundred anxiously looking for deliverance. Although the Elders in the Scandinavian mission and in various places in Germany, Italy, Switzerland, and France, owing to the suspicions and intolerance of those governments, have been thrown into prison and banished from place to place, still the work of the Lord has gained a foothold in those countries which cannot now be eradicated. When our Elders are banished from one kingdom they go to another, still teaching the people the way of life and salvation. Thus the enemies of the truth, by their over anxiety to suppress, have unwittingly been the means of spreading the gospel and causing the bread of life to be cast upon the waters, which will be gathered after many days.

From the British Isles we have the most cheering accounts of the progress of the work. We learn, by brothers F. D. Richards, Daniel Spencer, Cyrus H. Wheelock, and others lately returned, having been succeeded in the presidency of that mission by brothers Orson Pratt, Ezra T. Benson, and James A. Little, that notwithstanding the great annual emigration from Britain's shores, it does not keep pace with the annual increase and onward progress of the work in those lands.

In the United States and the British Provinces we also hear of an increased interest springing up in behalf of the truth, and of the work of God now fully established upon the earth.

It is the testimony of all the elders that, while signal success attends their labors in all of these lands, being attended by the Spirit and power of the Lord in all of their ministrations, the opposition also increases in equal proportion. In truth it is stated that the deep-rooted hatred of the wicked toward the work of God was never so great as now, and appears to steadily increase with the increase of the work. But their opposition cannot hinder this work, for it is from heaven; and if the Saints of the Most High God will be faithful, diligent and united, they will always be able to wield an influence and power which none shall be able to gainsay or withstand.

In consequence of the temporary absence of brother Erastus Snow, and the subsequent death of our beloved brother Orson Spencer, who was left in charge, the *Luminary* published in St. Louis, was discontinued; and, although brother Snow has since returned to the field of his labors, it has been as yet deemed wisdom not to resume that publication.

It is considered that the *Mormon*, having the increased patronage which the aid and influence of the patrons of the *Luminary* would give it, might become as useful to the Saints as the publication of both papers, and be much better sustained.

In the death of brother Spencer we sustained a loss which, though lamentable to us, our faith compels us to admit is to his superior gain and happiness. He fell asleep in the faith of Jesus on the 15th day of October, 1855, in the city of St. Louis, being absent from home in the performance of the mission which had been appointed him at the April Conference of 1854. Our beloved brother has gone to try the realities of the spirit world, in the full faith of our holy religions and confidence of the people; and though our words of commendation may not extend to cheer and encourage him in his onward and progressive labors, yet we cannot refrain from bearing our testimony to his unwavering fidelity and integrity, his useful but arduous labors, always evincing great firmness of character, and to his unyielding and uncompromising integrity to Joseph and his brethren.

We deplore his loss for our own and his friends' sake, and who was not his friend that knew him? But we rejoice that another faithful and able champion of the truth has gone to assist in the labors of Jesus and Joseph behind the veil.

It has also become our painful duty to record the death of our beloved brother Jedediah M. Grant, whose obituary and funeral proceedings are published in this day's paper. In this afflicting dispensation of providence we feel that the Lord hath touched us "in a tender spot;" but we realize that in his unabounded goodness He is able and willing to make good our loss, yea, more abundantly as we draw nigh unto Him and live our holy religion.

Although he is gone to another and more extended field of labor, having ripened in the knowledge of God and efficiently and faithfully performed his work upon the earth, still his frequent admonitions, his burning eloquence, his zeal and anxiety, which he manifested for the salvation of Israel, are too indelibly impressed upon our minds to be easily forgotten. Let us, therefore, exhibit our respect to the memory of our departed but beloved friend and brother, by remembering and practicing his precepts and emulating, so far as is in our power, his virtues.

Owing to the illiberality, bigotry, and intolerance of so many of this priest-ridden generation, every obstacle and hindrance that can be is thrown in the way, with a view to obstruct the progress of the work and hedge up the way of those whose most earnest desire is to leave their parting testimony with old neighbors and associates in life and come home to Zion. The gospel of salvation now as anciently finds more ready access to the poor than the rich, forcibly illustrating and confirming the truthfulness of the remark of our Savior, "how hardly shall they that have riches enter into the kingdom of God." The poor, downtrodden oppressed of ages, whom the aristocratical lordlings have for centuries continually crushed with the iron heel of despotism, feel, when the light of truth and salvation penetrates their minds, a new impulse to try again to redeem themselves and their posterity from the thralldom of ignorance, wickedness, error, superstition and tyranny which so long enchained them and their fathers. They are inspired by an all-absorbing desire to rise above and throw off the filth and abominations, mystery, corruption, and worse than Egyptian darkness of wicked Babylon, and bask in the sunlight of pure principles emanating from Heaven's King; to rejoice with the Saints in Zion, and become coworkers in that cause which, having redeemed them, may enable them to contribute a share in the redemption of others who are still in the bonds of iniquity and gall of bitterness.

This ever rising, ever increasing desire for the gathering of the remnants of Israel pertains unto all the Saints of God, who live their religion and enjoy the rich blessings of the Holy Ghost. It is in the heart of every faithful Saint, their constant prayer to the Almighty Father to enable them, not only to promulgate the Gospel of Christ to those who sit in darkness, but to gather out the honest in heart, even the Israel of God, from their long dispersion and to aid them in returning to a knowledge of the Lord God of their Fathers, that they may participate in the society of the Saints and a peaceful inheritance in these sequestered vales. To this end, and the further accomplishment of this object, are continually directed the efforts of the Perpetual Emigrating Fund Company for the emigration of the honest and worthy poor, those who desire to serve God and keep His commandments, being full of virtue and integrity toward God and their brethren. These are those we wish to deliver from the oppression of wicked Babylon, whose vital energies the proud and powerful are crushing out; upon whom the despotism, bigotry, ignorance and superstition of the world hang like an incubus, and to bring them to a land where manhood though found in poverty is respected, and where the God of Heaven can receive the homage due from man to his Maker; where freedom and liberty of conscience can enjoy protection, honest and faithful labor meet a just equivalent, and where the light of revelation and power of the Holy and Eternal Priesthood hold the adversary of truth in abeyance and roll back the curtains of error and darkness, sin, and death which have so long enveloped the earth.

This season's operations have demonstrated that the Saints, being filled with faith and the Holy Ghost, can walk across the plains, drawing their provisions and clothing on handcarts. The experience of this season will of course help us to improve in future operations; but the plan has been fairly tested and proved entirely successful. The entire trip from Iowa city, a distance of over thirteen hundred miles, to this city has been thus accomplished in less traveling days than it has ever been by an ox train of wagons, and with far greater ease to the travelers. These companies, with the exception of the two last, which started too late in the season, have made their trip from the Missouri river in a little over two months, and could have made it in less time, had they not been hindered by the few ox teams which accompanied them. Herein have our expectations been realized, and the usual vast expense and trouble attending this branch of business been in a good degree avoided.

The account of this year's operations not yet being completed, we are at present unable to state the precise amount of expenditure incurred per passenger; but we know that it must be far less than heretofore, and may still be lessened in the future.

The Saints who have come in this way have been healthier, more contented and happier, and have encountered less trouble and vexation than those with teams; and have, moreover, manifested to the world their faith, perseverance and good works.

They have shown a willingness to have others as well as themselves assisted, by using as little as possible of the Company's means for their own emigration. They have manifested a disposition to accede to any terms, so that their emigration might be accomplished without impeding that of anxious thousands looking to the same source for relief.

Although, in the first instance, drawing laden handcarts so long a distance appeared to some difficult to be accomplished by the brethren, and especially by the sisters, yet the result has proved that it is fully as easy as and indeed easier than the method hitherto practiced; and the women endured the trip quite as well, in comparison, as the men.

We have taken pains to collect facts upon this subject, as it was an experiment this season. The enterprise, having proved so eminently successful, will in future enter largely into all our emigrating operations.

Let the Saints take courage and avail themselves of the privilege of gathering to this place while the way is open before them, for the time will come when whoso would gather to Zion must needs flee with his budget upon his shoulder, or under his arm. Verily, they will come like flocks of doves to the windows, comparatively bare and naked, without food or clothing, escaping, as it were by the skin of their teeth, from the righteous indignation of an offended Deity poured out upon and passing over a wicked and adulterous generation.

While we, therefore, feel to congratulate ourselves and our brethren and sisters upon the happy issue of this experiment, we wish to direct our agents and others concerned to a few suggestions, drawn from this season's experience, by way of improvement.

In the first place, our emigration MUST start earlier in the season, and the necessary arrangements MUST be made and completed by the time they arrive on the western frontier, and no company must be permitted to leave the Missouri river later than the first day of July.

They must be provided with stronger handcarts, and endeavor to arrange so as to have the burden upon each cart vary as little as possible during the journey. Than starting with such heavy loads and lightening them up so soon, it would be better to start with lighter loads and gradually increase them, as the brethren become more accustomed to the labor. This might be accomplished by sending our a few teams with provisions a few days in advance of the companies, to be taken on the handcarts as they come up, when the teams could return.

All emigrants should provide themselves with an extra supply of good shoes.

The hub or nave of the cart wheels should be eight inches long and seven inches through the center. The boxes at the shoulder should be 2¼ inches, and the point boxes 1½ inches in diameter.

If it should be considered best to have cast iron arms, they should be 1¼ inches thick at the shoulder and ¾ inch at the point. The wooden axles should have iron or steel skeins, and track four feet apart. The timber must be of the best quality for toughness, and be well seasoned. In other respects they may be constructed as heretofore.

The very aged and infirm should be brought in wagons, in a separate train.

On account of their greater experience, let good, faithful Elders from this territory have charge of the companies. By observing these suggestions it is believed that, with one four- or six-mule team to each two hundred persons, the emigration will be much facilitated at a still lessened expense.

We had the pleasure, at our October Conference, of meeting with our brethren Franklin D. Richards, Daniel Spencer, John Van Cott, George D. Grant, and others of the returned missionaries who had been long absent, from whom we learned the condition and situation of our immigrating companies still upon the plains.

We immediately took effective measures for sending them such aid and assistance as, owing to the lateness of the season, they should require to enable them to reach these valleys, before the snow of winter should block their way and render their progress impossible. This was the first business which engrossed the attention of the Conference, and has since absorbed almost the entire attention of many of our citizens. But little has been done except to forward teams and assistance to their relief, and yet they have not all arrived, though the remainder are expected in a few days.

To companies immigrating to this place we wish to say a word, by way of counsel. Move every day, even if it is but a few miles; that is far better than tarrying in one camping place. On the Sabbath, after meeting and resting during a portion of the day, it will generally be better to make a short march. Move on every day, if you wish to accomplish your journey in due season.

Absolute necessity may justify stopping a few days in a place, but that will but rarely occur, and should be avoided so far as possible. It is far better, for both the teams and people, to keep traveling, until the journey is fully accomplished.

The through emigration will be conducted by our traveling agents, under the general direction of the agents presiding in Liverpool, from which place it starts, but will receive the aid and cooperation of our agents presiding in New York and St. Louis. All other emigration will be received and disposed of by our agents in the United States.

It is desirable to make a few locations along the line of travel, and our agents at Florence and St. Louis have been instructed in relation thereto.

We trust, therefore, that the brethren and sisters will be sufficiently mindful of the general interests of the cause of Zion to readily respond to our wishes and the requirements of our agents, who are entrusted with these matters. Any material departure from the spirit of these instructions will be considered cause for disfellowshipment from the Church, or suspension from office.

Elder Orson Hyde is still presiding at Carson county, Utah, and Elders Amasa Lyman and Charles C. Rich at San Bernardino, California.

Elders Orson Pratt and Ezra T. Benson are presiding over the European mission, and publishing the Millennial Star in Liverpool, England.

Elder John Taylor is presiding in the United States, and publishing the Mormon, in New York City. That publication commends itself to the favorable consideration and patronage of the Saints, being ably conducted and exercising a very salutary influence in correcting public opinion and defending our people and the principles of our holy religion from the calumny, abuse, and misrepresentations of the world.

Elder Erastus Snow is also in the United States, presiding at St. Louis, assisting in the emigration, &c. Elder George A. Smith, being one of the delegates elected by the Convention and people to present our Constitution and application for admission as a State into the Union, has gone to Washington to perform that mission.

Elder Parley P. Pratt is also in the United States on a temporary visit, intending to return in the spring.

Elder Wilford Woodruff is in this city, engaged in the historian's office.

Elder Lorenzo Snow is presiding at Box Elder, in this territory; and Elder Franklin D. Richards is at his home in this city, having recently returned from his mission to Europe.

(Continued on page 145.)

LETTER FROM CAPTAIN JONES.

Salt Lake City, October 31, 1856.

President D. Daniels,

My dear Brother—I write these lines in your house, with your dear wife at my elbow; imagine my feelings! I arrived here alive, of course, or, at least, half alive, a week ago today, and I found myself immediately surrounded by my dear family, with a host of close friends to welcome me home in many a language more kindly than I deserved or expected.

Again imagine our chats: all I will say is, that the name and memory of Bro. Daniels are held in high, frequent, and respectful regard by all, yet no one is more filled with yearning than myself, believe me!

With the friendly chit chats over, Sunday morning arrived, and imagine again how small I felt when the walls of the magnificent Tabernacle echoed to these words—"Elder Dan Jones is requested to come to the stand and to preach." At this you could have seen five or six thousand eyes following a little man who was humbly making his way from their midst to answer the unexpected call until he pushed forward and found himself treading where the feet of more holy prophets, apostles, and the best of the world had trodden—he felt he should take off not only his shoes, but also his socks in the midst of such men treading on such a place, with heaven open above his head, whose tongue would not speak? What heart would not melt under such heavenly heat? But it is pointless to try to say more than this, All right, all went well. Everyone is pleased to see me here, but I am more pleased than anybody to see myself in this heavenly place, in the midst of these virtuous, incomparable people.

But enough of my own story; perhaps less would serve the same purpose; perhaps you would prefer to hear the story of the companies of Saints, &c. I understand now that Sister Daniels has written to you with this mail, and it is almost the last hour for us before it closes, and I shall not go into detail about them.

I wrote many letters back to you, yes, at every opportunity, from the Plains, informing you of the remarkable events of our crossing. Briefly, in case they did not arrive, I will say that I labored for three months in the camp, Iowa, with my brethren, until all the companies were sent before us, and lastly of all it fell to me to supervise two companies of wagons, that is one hundred, and when after teaching, yes teaching, as well as training wild animals to travel twenty miles per day, I was called to leave them and come with F. D. Richards and twelve other missionaries at 50 or 60 miles a day, until we passed all the companies, apart from the first three handcart companies, which arrived here before us, the Welsh third, and in less time than anybody.

The handcart plan answers the purpose better than expected, and many say that they would prefer to come that way again than with wagons. They had better health than usual on the way; but it is a pity that several, through eating too many vegetables, delicacies, fruits, and rich and unfamiliar foods which were brought to them free by the wagonload, by the Saints in the City, have mortally affected their constitutions Among others, I heard of bro. and sister Brookes, from the North; Owen Jones Towyn; John Roberts, Ffestiniog; Wm Jenkins, Cardiff; Edward Phillips, Twynyrodyn; Henry Jenkins, Merthyr; and a few others that I do not know now. The Bishops cared for everybody, so that no one is without a comfortable home. About two thousand more are expected soon who are on the way in companies—some are near at hand. Say from Dan to Beersheba that over fifty teams of horses have left here to meet the Saints within three days of the news of their need arriving, with over 12 tons of flour apart from other things in proportionate amounts.

Last Sunday there was another call for oxen to go, and within a few minutes about fifty yoked teams were promised to go the next morning for that purpose. That is life in Mormonism here for you!

The weather is quite cold here, and there is snow from there to Green River, whatever it is like further on; yet these thousands of Saints have enough faith and actions to save every last one from being overcome by the snow.

My brethren and I who have returned from our missions have been appointed to preach and hold assemblies throughout all the settlements, beginning with this city, and not to stop until every settlement, city, town, family and person is full of the heavenly fire flaming powerfully or withdrawing from those who will be so.

Some incomparable spirit of revival has grasped the Saints—the Presidents first; and the decision is that he whose profession is not alive in everything will be excommunicated. Woe betide those who live a comfortable life and the wicked in Zion, says everyone now; for there is no longer any room for them. The Spirit of God is like a fire purifying and consuming all refuges of oppression, and I believe that soon purer wheat will be seen on the threshing floor of pure-hearted Zion than was ever seen before. May the God of Israel help us to bring it about quickly and thoroughly is my prayer.

This city has increased in the number and size of its buildings, so that I barely recognized it when I returned. The largest dwellings that you knew are hidden in the shadow of larger ones until you go up close to them.

I hope from the answer I received from President Young when talking about you and the Welsh Mission, that you will have reinforcement from these mountaineers full of the mountain fire to help you to fire and light up Wales. He asks to be remembered to you and a host of others too numerous to name now, but you will see as many of them there as I can help to set on their way.

Remember me and my family kindly to all my fellow workers who are with you, as well as all the Saints who love you and your work. My wish is that God shall bless those who bless you, and that he shall wither the arm which is raised against you; and may he give to you and your dear Counselors, with my remembrance, ever greater grace, and save us all, with the fruit of our labor, in his heavenly kingdom. . . .

My regards to everyone who asks about me. . .

The prayers of the faithful Saints which I merit and which you and I receive, my gracious Brother, will ever be my prayer. Amen.

And I shall always remain your sincere friend,

D. Jones.

[We presented the above long-awaited letter to the typesetter as soon as we received it. The Saints will surely rejoice, as we do, to hear from our old Captain, and understand that wherever he may be, he is still involved in the same important task, namely doing his energetic part in pushing forward the work of our God. May he have long life and health to continue thus. We wish his welcome letter had arrived sooner.—Ed.]

ANNOUNCEMENTS, &c.

Let The Presidents Take Note that it is not wise to sell the new series of pamphlets, because of their infrequency and the connection they have with one another. Do not sell them to the world except on the condition that they receive the whole series, but you may sell the pamphlets of D. Jones and J. Davies as you wish. Do not keep any pamphlets on hand, rather keep them in constant circulation as previously directed.

We are keeping a sufficient number of the new pamphlets on hand, until the series is completed, to be bound in order to supply the libraries of the Saints.

The Letter of brother D. E. Jones at the beginning of this issue is a complete answer to a variety of questions and complaints we have received—it is an accurate looking glass; look closely into it lest some have done as that miner who washed himself thoroughly right up to his face, which he forgot to wash; he put on his best clothes, and he went to see himself in the looking glass—imagine his surprise!

The Epistle of the First Presidency has obliged us to make a supplement to this issue, so that it may be read deliberately, accurately, and thoroughly in the meetings.

CONTENTS.

	PG.
A Looking Glass, &c.	129
Epistle of the First Presidency.	132
Letter of Captain Jones.	142
Announcements.	144

SWANSEA:
PRINTED AND PUBLISHED BY DANIEL DANIELS.

ZION'S TRUMPET,

OR

Star of the Saints.

No. 10.] MAY 2, 1857. [Vol. X.

HOME CHURCH ACCOUNTS.

Due to lack of space in the Trumpet, our readers have been deprived of the interesting contents of letters from our diligent and faithful brethren who are full of the fire of the Lord, thundering the reformation wherever they walk.

We provide a few excerpts:—

From the Brecon Conference Elder James Taylor writes "that he has gone through the Branches in the company of Elder J. Thomas, and the majority of the houses of the Saints, succeeding in every attempt to get the Saints to obey the conditions of the Reformation with considerable trouble in some cases, and a few new members have been baptized. He went from there to the Monmouthshire Conference to deal with the same pleasant task obtaining success, and great manifestations of the spirit of prophecy, and various gifts of the Holy Ghost. The Abertillery Branch was sluggish. Preaching out has begun in earnest." Some letters of Elder Benjamin Evans give the same good account, that eight new members have been baptized, and more are on their way. The Tithing is not as much this month because some works are on *stop*."

We are glad that the account from everywhere is of so many who are good, but we pity the others who are slumbering and not obeying the call of God to awaken to reform. They will be divided and re-divided and will be separated until only the faithful few will stand pure like the army of Gideon, and we believe that they shall fight and win the battle and bring souls to the Church of the Lamb.

[Price 1½c.

Elder Abednego Williams reports "that there is more life among the Saints of the East Glamorgan Conference: that between 500 and 600 have been baptized, and at least 20 of those are new. We have had the old customary worry with a few who have become unfaithful. Preaching out has been going forward for some time. There are about 70 villages in the Conference that have no Saints living in them, to which several young men are preparing to go to preach." May the wisdom, power, and blessing of God be on them.

Make sure that all who covenant are paying tithing, for that is one of the conditions of the reformation.

Elders W. Miller and S. Roskelley are very diligent in the Cardiff area. The officers are preaching out of doors in four places in the town, and *Camp Meetings* are being held in the environs. Very nearly everyone has covenanted and several new members have been baptized.

Elder J. Davies gives an engaging account of all who are desirous in the West Glamorgan Conference. About one-third have covenanted. There is preaching out in old and new places, and a determination to warn the world. We understand the same is true of every other place.

The brethren of the North are turning out Presidents and Officers to preach long and loud to the world the Eternal Gospel, and bro. Jones has sore feet from galloping from Anglesey to Montgomery to awaken and direct the Saints. May the omnipresent God who knows of his efforts keep good track of his faithful deeds until the day of recompense, together with those of the other diligent brethren.

Continue on brethren, and let us unite from now on that neither negligence, sluggishness, idleness nor wickedness nor rebellion may raise their monstrous heads in the Church. Let us work, as the Prophet says, for Zion, and we shall see that great success will follow our present labor.

Send an account of the number who have re-covenanted, &c., so that we may know for certain the measure of our success.

We call particular attention to the list of debts in this issue.

CONTINUATION OF THE EPISTLE.

Owing to the almost total loss of crops last season, loss of stock during the past winter, and heavy indebtedness occasioned by the last year's immigration, we were compelled to suspend operations upon the Public Works, until we could pay our debts and somewhat replenish our means. Since harvest we have partially resumed, but will not commence laying stone upon the Temple until next Spring, when we hope to prosecute that work with much vigor. We are collecting and preparing materials, and it is our wish and intention, in the meantime, to finish the canal for boating the rock for the Temple.

The wheat crop of this season was good, but corn was rather light and potatoes were almost an entire failure, though, by a very prudent course, we trust there will be sufficient provisions to last until another harvest.

In pursuance of an act passed at the last session of the Legislative Assembly, a Convention of Delegates met in this city on the 17th day of last March, and closed their labors on the 27th of the same month; having, in a session of ten days, formed a constitution, elected delegates, and adopted a memorial to Congress making application for admission into the Union as a sovereign State. Their proceedings, subsequently submitted to the people, were unanimously sustained.

We learn, by recent advices from our Delegates to Washington, that in consequence of the exceeding great opposition and prejudice against us as a people, they have not deemed it wisdom to present our application, although no fault has been found either with our constitution or our ability to sustain and administer a State Government. The opposition seems to be arrayed against us rather on account of our religious faith and Church ordinances, as though they were a legitimate subject for congress to canvass. What course may be taken is to us unknown, for our memorial has not yet been presented. When the excitements of the presidential election are past, it is hoped more favorable indications, foreshadowing a candid and honest action upon its merits, may warrant its presentation. If this can be accomplished, and the claims of our application for admission into the Union as a State be fairly and honorably canvassed upon every point legitimate to the issue, we have not a doubt as to its successful termination.

We are more indifferent in regard to this subject in a religious than in a political sense, for, whether we are organized in a Territorial or State capacity, Government is bound to protect us in the rights of conscience, or override plain Constitutional guarantees. And no intelligent person holds in very high estimation that union which is hourly endangered by the frenzied zeal of rampant, misguided, and fanatical demagogues, who trample that heaven-inspired instrument, the Constitution, into the dust, and regard neither their fathers' legacy nor their children's inheritance.

It is not our purpose in this Epistle to discuss political questions, but we cannot refrain from honestly and sincerely invoking the power of Him who sits enthroned in the heavens, to behold those who are distracting the Councils of our nation and hastening the destruction of this great Confederacy of sovereign States, and to thwart their wicked and nefarious purposes, to restrain their iniquity and cause others to arise in their places who will rule in righteousness and save our distracted but beloved country from its impending ruin.

At the April Conference some three hundred and fifty Elders were called to go on missions, all of whom promptly responded and departed to their various fields of labor. The Conference was blessed with rich, seasonable and interesting instructions, and a general good spirit seemed to pervade every bosom. It was numerously attended, and the brethren rejoiced in the unity of the most holy faith, in praise, thanksgiving and worship unto our Father and our God.

Before harvest much destitution was experienced by the masses of the people through the want of provisions, but the commendable liberality exercised by those who were fortunate enough to possess a supply, and the energy of the Bishops in enforcing a rigid economy and distribution to the destitute, prevented any great amount of suffering. We trust that the same generous disposition will always be manifested, in sharing even scanty supplies with the really destitute, so generally practiced among this people during the past season. Still we prefer that all should practice that diligence, economy, and obedience so often urged upon them, that the blessings of heaven be not withheld, and that the elements and the labors of the husbandman may be blessed of the Lord, and the earth bring forth in its strength the grain and the rich fruits thereof for the sustenance of man.

Notwithstanding these and many other good qualities which characterize this people, still we find too prevalent a disposition to murmur, find fault and complain at the dispensations of an All-wise Providence; a disposition of careless indifference to His counsels, and a dull lethargy which lulls the people into a false security; all of which gives Satan the advantage, darkens counsel, and leads many into a spirit of apostasy. We must remember that we live in a world of sin, wickedness and sorrow, and that the enemy of all righteousness is ever on the alert to destroy the Saints and lead them into temptation, darkness, sin and transgression.

Brethren, we exhort you to awake from this lethargy, to put on the armor of righteousness, of the Gospel of Jesus, and rebuke the adversary and the power of Satan and drive them far from you;

to hold frequent converse and communion with your God, that the power of the Highest may rest down upon you, burn in your bosoms, in your families, in your neighborhoods, cities, counties, and wherever there are Saints of the Most High God; that fearfulness may seize the hypocrite in Zion, and the fire of the Almighty consume the wicked and ungodly from the whole earth. Thus, while the indignation of the Lord is passing over the nations, and we also receive a portion of the chastisement, let us be wise and properly receive the correction, as coming from the hand of a kind Father who seeks the best interests of his Children. Let us, hereafter, more fully appreciate our blessings, and now, when a plentiful harvest has again crowned our labors, be wise and practice economy in using and preserving our grain, that no waste nor unwise disposal thereof shall characterize our acts.

We are happy in being able to say that the Indians are peaceful in all our settlements. We have abundantly proven that a friendly interest for their welfare, and a pacific policy are much the most successful in preserving their good feelings, in promoting and preserving peace, and are gradually leading them to an understanding of the benefits derived from a civilized existence. To reflect their angry words and acts, and kill them for every trivial offense, as is the usual course pursued toward them by the whites, is condescending to their savage and barbarous customs, thus reciprocating their evil deeds. Such a course will never cause them to appreciate the blessings of civilized society, nor influence them to seek its benefits, but will, as all past experience proves, drive them to the opposite extreme, and, in addition to their own, cause them to imbibe the vices, without the virtues of civilization. Therefore, let us, in all our intercourse with them, exhibit a superior understanding, a larger comprehension of right, forbearance and honor.

Be just, brethren, in your dealings with them; no matter what course they may pursue towards you, never retaliate a wrong, but always exhibit a firm determination to do right, and seek to palliate their conduct and conciliate their feelings.

This course steadily pursued must, in due time, induce them to yield their savage barbarity, wild customs and vicious course of life, to the dictates of superior wisdom, and raise them to a higher degree in the scale of human existence. It has already had an effect in this direction, sufficient to encourage us in our efforts to bring them to a civilized, not to say a Christianized, life. They must be civilized; must learn to plough, sow, plant, harvest, build houses, and make fences; must learn mechanism as well as agriculture; their minds will then become sufficiently expanded to receive Gospel light, and the principles pertaining to their salvation and exaltation in the kingdom of our God.

Remember, brethren, that they are the remnants of Israel, and, although they may apparently continue for a time to waste away and sink deeper and deeper into the depths of sin, misery, and woe, that unto them pertain the promises made to faithful Abraham, and they will be fulfilled. Be diligent, therefore, to do them good, and seek in all of your intercourse with them to bring them back to a knowledge of the Lord God of their fathers. Preserve yourselves from their savage ferocity; never condescend to their level, but always seek to elevate them to a higher, purer, and, consequently, a more useful and intelligent existence.

In our intercourse with the world we find that we have more to do with the poor and those of low estate, and we might say of low worldly esteem, than those of any other class. This only affords another of those strong testimonies of the Lord Jesus in behalf of this being his people, his Church, his kingdom. Truly, "the poor ye have always with you," and it behooveth us to teach them how to live, how to combine their elements, that they also by their own exertions may draw support from Nature's great storehouse, which is ample for all. Yes, teach them to live, and place them, by your intelligence and charity, in a position to earn or in some laudable manner obtain a living by their own exertions. Calculate and contrive for them, and encourage them by leading on and exhibiting objects ahead.

We direct the attention of the bishops and their assistants more particularly to this subject, as it devolves upon them to minister in temporal things. In Israel, as in the world, there are many rulers, but few with the feeling of fathers to the people. Be fathers to the people, ye bishops, and lead them on, step by step, until they shall wax strong in the knowledge of things, both temporal and spiritual, pertaining to the kingdom of our God.

This is a peculiar people; they have already become very great, with all the elements for prosperity and rapid advancement. We have before us the examples of the nations of the world; we witness their prosperity, their pride and arrogance; are made sensible of their power and their oppression, and know their foul corruption, profane pretensions, and hypocrisy; are acquainted with their systems of poorhouses, poor farms, prisons, houses of correction, asylums and hospitals, and with their misery and degradation.

In the heterogeneous mass of a population hastily thrown together from every nation, kindred, tongue, and people, let us pursue that course which comprises the elements of a nation's prosperity, greatness, and glory, and spurn the course which engenders the above disastrous results. Avoiding the track which grinds the face of the poor to elevate the rich, let us bestow our charity not so much to feed the hungry and clothe the naked, as to cause them to feed and clothe themselves, and lead the people to practice virtue, to walk in the paths of honest and truth, not so much by the fear of punishment, prisons, and penalties, as by implanting in their bosoms an abiding and ever increasing love for those pure principles which induce to honor, prosperity, salvation, and exaltation in this life, and which will clothe them with the riches of eternity in the life to come.

Build schoolhouses instead of jails, and make our religion effective in dispensing with the use of courts and jurors, prisoners and prisons; have no lawyers, because there is no litigation; no doctors, because there are no sick; no hospitals or asylums, because there are no invalids. The Saints of the Most High God should sustain themselves by their industry, economy, and sobriety; their health by their virtue, prudence, cleanliness, faith and observances of the holy ordinances; and their morals by the love they bear to their God and their holy religion. They should be united that they may be powerful, and enjoy the blessings of peace and quietness at home and abroad.

Notwithstanding the efforts that have been made to manufacture iron and to make sugar from the beet, as yet no available results have been realized; yet we expect to continue our efforts until these objects are fully accomplished. It is believed that every obstacle in the way of making iron will be removed, when steam can be brought to supply the place of the water power which frequently fails in the time of need. We have an engine here now that is of sufficient size to furnish the requisite power; if the Company make use of this, through its aid we hope to be sully supplied with that useful and indispensable article, iron.

We have been delayed in making sugar mainly through the failure of the beet crop for the last two seasons, the grasshoppers destroying the seed last year to such a degree that sufficient seed could not be raised for this year's sowing. We trust, through the blessing of the Lord, that no failure of the kind will again thwart our wishes, and that we shall soon be able to furnish, from the beet, sugar sufficient for home consumption; we are sanguine that this can be done, and it is our purpose to continue our labors in this enterprise until it is fully accomplished.

Considerable quantities of leather are now manufactured in this Territory, though not quite sufficient to supply the wants of the people; the same may be said in relation to the manufacture of many other articles, such as hats, *jeans*, linsey, flannel, blankets, *shawls*, &c.; but we are mainly deficient in supplying ourselves with cotton and linen goods, and are quite negligent in raising cotton and flax.

The Territory furnishes localities suitable for raising both those commodities in great abundance, and it is our earnest desire that those acquainted with their culture should make it their business, until our markets are fully supplied therewith. Also raise indigo, hemp, make ropes, cords and thread, and extract oil from the seed of the flax and cotton, and from the *castor oil bean*. And let our brethren who have the means, bring on cotton and woolen machinery, that we may be enabled to manufacture our own goods, as fast as we shall be able to supply ourselves with the raw material; also bring the best selections of horses, cattle and sheep.

Cultivate the thorn, *osage, orange*, and *meskete*, for hedges, the *cottonwood* and the *locust*, for ornament, and, in suitable locations, for wood and timber, which they make rapidly, and the mulberry for silk. Be forward and cultivate all kinds of fruit and other seeds and grafts; plant trees, shrubbery, vines, &c., for ornament and use; cultivate the best varieties, including grapes, currants, gooseberries, strawberries, the various kinds of grasses, indigo, madder, and everything calculated to cheer and gladden the heart, delight the eye, and make pleasant and agreeable the homes of the Saints.

In the vicinity of Las Vegas a very extensive and rich vein of lead ore has been discovered, and is now being successfully worked by our enterprising citizens. Judging from the description, it is the most extensive vein of galena ever discovered, and specimens of the portions being mined for smelting yield a large percent of lead. From this prolific source we shall soon be abundantly supplied with lead, and we wish our manufacturers of lead pipe, sheeting, white and red lead, and other useful articles made from that metal, to prepare themselves, as soon as practicable, to supply all such articles from our own resources.

Let those report themselves to us in person, or by letter, who are acquainted with working in lead, iron, coal, or boring therefore; who are acquainted with raising or manufacturing cotton, flax, and hemp, and with making oil, nails, steel, glass, &c., that we may classify our labor and bring forth from the native elements those things which contribute to the benefit of man.

We say unto all our mechanics, press onward in your labors; be not disheartened, but continue to supply the community with your wares and fabrics, with leather, boots, shoes, hats, caps, muffs, robes, soap, candles, glue, shoe pegs, saleratus, alum, saltpeter, pitch tar, turpentine, oil, furniture, and labor-saving machinery. Let the farmers encourage the mechanics with their best patronage, and let each promote their own by seeking their brother's interest.

Fathers, teach your children to practice industry; teach your sons agriculture or some useful mechanical trade.

Mothers in Israel, you are also called upon to bring up your daughters to pursue some useful avocation for a sustenance, that when they shall become the wives of the Elders of Israel, who are frequently called upon missions, or to devote their time and attention to the things of the kingdom, they may be able to sustain themselves and their offspring. Teach them to sew, spin, and weave; to cultivate vegetables, as well as flowers; to make soap, as well as cakes and preserves; to spin, color, weave, and knit, as well as work embroidery; to milk, make butter and cheese, and work in the kitchen, as well as in the parlor. Thus will you and your daughters show yourselves approved, and prove helpmeets in very deed, not only in the domestic relations but in building up the kingdom.

Very creditable was the exhibition of home productions at the Annual State Fair, which came off on the 1st, 2nd, and 3rd of October, but we trust it will be far exceeded another year. It encourages a commendable rivalry, and excites an emulation for the general good.

Owing to the irregularities of the eastern mail, our agents and correspondents will duplicate their letters by way of San Pedro, California, each winter. And we caution one and all that, unless they personally attend to the mailing of their letters and documents, the duplicates, as was the case last season, though plainly directed, will not be forwarded as ordered. We gave our eastern agents the same instructions last year, and they complied therewith, so far as mailing duplicates with the proper directions, but originals and duplicates came in the same mail sacks in the spring, evidencing that some postmasters are as indifferent in regard to the performance of their duties as some mail contractors are of theirs.

We cannot close this Epistle without congratulating ourselves, the Saints and the inhabitants of this widespread Territory, with the general health of the people, the prosperity which attends our efforts, the quietness and peace everywhere predominant. No record of crime enlivens the courtyards and jails; no convictions and sentences of court send to desolate home, anguish and despair; nor yet do unblushing offenders walk our streets unpunished, requiring the aid of a Vigilance Committee to rid our Territory of their unwelcome presence.

Fortune, or rather Providence, has indeed favored us by spreading before the eager gaze of the world's cupidity the talisman of wealth, the hope of earthly riches, at a distance from these sequestered vales, and placed mighty barriers between—though we inherit the most uninviting portion of the earth, we feel happy that the temptations of gold and this world's power beckon their votaries and seekers to another bourne, from whence no such travelers find inducements to return, leaving us to enjoy in these peaceful retreats that quiet and freedom from the wicked and ungodly, which we have so earnestly sought.

When such characters find themselves in our midst, the barren prospects for any considerable degree of success, and the glitter of gold a little farther on, soon relieve us, our courts, and criminal calendar, of their hated and unwelcome presence. Never before were the Saints so favorably situated to cleanse the flock from the half-hearted and apostate spirits and the imps of Satan, who follow after us only to destroy. One or two seasons, and they begin to feel their way out, rightly judging that this is no place for them. Their corrupt desires, intentions, and acts are soon made manifest and the inducements to remain with a righteous people are too few.

Therefore, while we gather, like the net which was cast into the sea, from every nation, kindred, tongue, and people, of every kind, we also sift them out like the winnowing of wheat upon the summer's threshing floor. We have sought peace and freedom from the power of wicked and designing men, and measurable have found it.

We have put forth our hand to gather out the honest in heart from among the nations, and are rapidly accomplishing our object. We are attempting to build up cities, towns and villages unto the most high God, pure and holy in His sight, and surely expect, through His aid and blessing, to be successful.

When we look upon the advancing hosts of Israel, and consider their rapid improvement in faith, knowledge, good works, influence, power, and constantly accumulating numbers, we feel to thank the Lord for His goodness, even Him who hath brought forth salvation and caused light to spring up upon the earth. We feel grateful that we have been permitted to live in this day and generation, in which the Great Jehovah has seen proper to re-establish his authority upon the earth, and to reconfer the holy and eternal Priesthood upon the children of men.

We feel grateful that we have the privilege of witnessing the stately steppings of the Almighty among the nations, the goings forth of his word with power, the fulfillment of the words given by inspiration in ancient times, and the fulfillment of the words given by the living Oracles in our midst; that He has spoken from the heavens; that messengers, angels and legates from his throne have broken the silence that has intervened since the mission and dispensation of the only begotten Son of God, Jesus of Nazareth, and reopened a communication with his children upon this his earth, organized again his Church and Kingdom, and endowed it with all the authorities, ordinances, Gifts, sacraments, blessings, privileges, power, and glory pertaining thereunto.

We rejoice that the words which have gone forth from the ancient Prophets, and from Jesus, Joseph, and the Apostles, and do not return void, neither are like sounding brass or tinkling cymbals; for behold, the Lord of hosts, through the faithfulness, energy, and perseverance of his servants, has faithfully warned and is warning the people. In the spirit of meekness and humility have they declared the Gospel unto them, wherefore are their skirts clear of their blood, and they are left without excuse before the Lord, to reap the reward of their iniquity, to experience the calamities which are abroad in the earth, to feel the wrath, the withering, bitter anguish which the justice of a justly incensed and offended Creator will pour out upon them. They have set at naught the words of his servants, scoffed at and held them in derision; have trodden upon the young and tender plant which the Lord Almighty has planted, and done despite unto the words of life and salvation which He has caused to be proclaimed in their ears. They have ignominiously slain His Prophets and wasted away His people, His faithful Saints, whose blood cries unto him from the ground for vengeance.

Their long, hypocritical prayers, lip service, pretended piety and idolatrous worship, have become an abomination before Him; wherefore will He proceed to bring upon them the judgments which have been foretold by His servants the Prophets, and great will be the desolation thereof. Their great and mighty nations, empires, and kingdoms, with all the pride, pomp and power thereof, will be broken and crumbled in pieces, and come to naught. Their cities will become a howling waste, a solitary place, wherein shall be found the wolf and the vulture, and no man shall be found an inhabitant therein. Yea, verily, He will empty the earth of the wicked, and those who work abominations in His sight, so shall the kingdoms of this world become the kingdoms of our Lord and His Christ, so shall the Lord prepare the way for his coming, and reign upon the earth.

Let the Church, therefore, prepare as a bride to receive her bridegroom; let the Saints have on their wedding garments, and have their lamps well supplied with oil, trimmed and burning; let all things be made ready for the reception of our Savior and Redeemer, even our Lord the Christ. Let all the Saints throughout the world live their religion, that they may be worthy to enjoy his presence, and have converse with the angels of our God; let them gird up their loins and step forth in the power and might of Elijah's God to do battle in this great cause, and armed with High Heaven's panoply, even the armor of salvation and the helmet of righteousness, go forth conquering and to conquer, until the gospel shall be sounded to every nation, kindred, tongue, and people, and the pure in heart, the meek of the earth, the Israel of our God, be gathered out from the wicked nations and brought to inherit and worship under their own vines and fig trees, and learn of Him whose glory will rest upon his Temple as a cloud by day and a pillar of fire by night.

BRIGHAM YOUNG,
HEBER C. KIMBALL,

G. S. L. City, Dec. 10, 1856.   [Trans. Dewi Elfed.

REPENTANCE AMONG THE SAINTS.

(From the *Star*.)

The Latter-day Saints in Great Britain are called upon to repent. But why is this call? Are they not already a good people? Did they not repent when they came forward and received the Gospel, and were baptized for the remission of their sins? Yes, they are, by far, the best people in England; and they have repented of many sins, such as have been made manifest to them from time to time; but they are not yet perfect; neither will they be, while surrounded by the corrupt influences of Babylonish Christianity. So long as they are not perfect in keeping the law of God, so long they have need to repent.

Then we say to all the Saints, that repentance and a thorough reform among yourselves are greatly needed. Do you wish to know what sins you are guilty of? Your own consciences will point out many of them. The strict law of God, if you will read it, will convict you of many evils. If you will go and hear the faithful servants of God preach, they will show you many of your transgressions. If you will read the Church publications, they will be an assistance to you in discovering your sins. The Holy Ghost, if you will let it dwell in your hearts, will convince you of sin, and show you many imperfections which you would not otherwise discover.

When you discover anything in your practices which is not conformable to the word of God, you should immediately repent, by making an humble confession of the same to God, and by a reformation of conduct in that particular. Or if your sin is against man, to man you should make confession and restitution. He that sins in secret, should confess in secret; he that sins openly, should confess openly. He that trespasses before many, should confess before many: and in all cases, let your confessions be to God, and to as many as you have unjustly offended, whether they be in the Church or out of it.

If a Saint has committed any sin against God, and that sin has not injured any other person but himself, he should only make his confession before God: he should not reveal such sin to others, for in so doing, he would give occasion for them to reproach him, or such transgression might have a tendency to destroy their confidence in him, and thus he would fall into the snare of the devil. When our sins are not against others, then they have no business to know them, unless we remain in impenitence, then their exposure is necessary, that the same may be rooted out. But when they are against others, then a confession to God is not sufficient: God will not accept our confession, nor hear our prayers, when we neglect to be reconciled to our brother, or sister, or neighbor whom we have offended.

We shall now proceed to point out some sins that the Saints frequently indulge in, and of which they must repent.

SLANDER.—There are those among you who do not cease to slander their brethren and sisters. This is a great evil, and may be indulged in different degrees of excess. You may slander persons who are entirely innocent, merely because you imagine they are guilty; you may have seen some circumstances which caused you to have suspicions; and instead of burying those suspicions in your own breasts, you give publicity to them, and, perhaps, with an additional coloring: your own suspicions produce a dislike to them, and you seek to create these disagreeable feelings against them in others. You do not speak directly against them, for this would expose you as an open slanderer, and would measurably destroy your influence. In order that your slanders may have the greatest possible effect, and obtain a degree of credibility, and produce more serious injury, you clothe them with piety. You hypocritically pretend that you very much dislike to speak of their faults; but you are very careful to insinuate, in a guarded and blind manner, some great evil, leaving the impression that there is something very serious, about which you do not like to speak. And thus you endeavor to instill bitterness of feeling and prejudice into the minds of your listeners. Woe unto you! for it would be better for you to be cast into the depths of the ocean, than to unjustly offend those who are innocent before God. Woe unto you! for your hypocrisy and deceit shall fall with pain upon your own heads.

Again, you may slander persons who are not altogether innocent. You may expose them to others, who should be kept in ignorance concerning their faults, until the proper steps can be taken with them, according to the law of God. You seek to make their sins public, and to create a prejudice among the Saints against them. You do not seek to save them, but to destroy. You place yourself in the attitude of a destroyer. Such a spirit is of the devil, for he also seeks to destroy, and to accuse the Saints, and to stir up wrath against them. Will you follow in his footsteps? Will you slander and speak evil of your brother or sister who has sinned? Will you seek to trample the weak Saint down to hell, because he has been overtaken in a fault? Remember, that if you do this, you are no longer the Saviors of men, but their destroyers. Cease, therefore, your slanders against the transgressor. Cease to spread forth his evil deeds upon the housetops. Cease to make public that which will injure and destroy. Cease your back-bitings, and all your evil speakings one against another. Cease your tattlings about your own family affairs, or those of your neighbor.

> Let every man mind his own business,
> And take from his eye the grievous heavy beam;
> And let him keep it out so he can see clearly,
> By purifying his heart to receive the truth.
>
> If he feels the desire to slander some man,
> Let him do so faithfully about himself,
> May his scandalous behavior be a pain to him,
> And shame, until he becomes as innocent as a lamb.
>
> Let us benefit a neighbor, or let us not chide him,
> Let REFORM be carved on the heart of each one.
> Let our motto from this day on be,
> Let Eternal Life spread abroad.

It is the duty of the teachers who visit from house to house, to search diligently after the spirit and feelings of the Saints. Search out the slanderer—the backbiter—the evil-speaker. Exhort them to repent quickly. Make them ashamed of their hard speeches. Teach them that no person, held in fellowship by the Saints, can be evil spoken of without sin. Teach them the law of God, and how to deal with transgressors in order to save them. Teach them that neither the innocent nor guilty among the Saints can be slandered without bringing condemnation upon the slanderers. Teach them that if they do not reform in these things, they themselves will wither away, and be cast out from among the people of God.

THE SIN OF LIGHT-MINDEDNESS.—There are some among the Saints whose minds are lighter than chaff. One would think from their everlasting ding dong of *jokes* and light speeches, that their heads were destitute of brains, being either empty, or at most filled with some kind of worthless gas. Common sense or sober thinking is as rare with them as figs on a thorn bush. How the Gospel ever made any impressions upon such craniums is among the incomprehensibles. It must be that they considered the plan of salvation a joke, and concluded to receive it for fun. If such characters speak of God, it is to tell some funny anecdote; if they quote Scripture if it to help them out with a ridiculous story; if they refer to sacred ordinances, some ludicrous saying must be incorporated in the sentence. To speak a sober sentence or think a sober thought, would almost make their heads ache. In fine, they think gas; they talk gas; they sleep in gas; they live in gas; and gas seems to be the only element entering into their constitutions.

Go into some of the houses of the Saints, and listen to the conversation of the young brethren and sisters, and instead of hearing sound common sense in relation to the beauty and glory of the religion which they have embraced, you will hear a *joke* about this young man or that young woman, or some marriage which is about to take place, or some courtship that is going on, or such a one's sweetheart. Such conversation is well enough at times, and under certain circumstances innocent; but when such things are constantly indulged in, there is no room left for the more important things of the kingdom of God; the Spirit is grieved away, and the vacancy left in the heart is filled up with trash, which manifests its worthlessness in light speeches; "for out of the abundance of the heart the mouth speaketh."

A Saint of God cannot indulge in light speeches to excess without feeling a corresponding barrenness of soul. Of such things we say unto the Saints, Repent. Cease from foolish joking, from light and vain speeches, from all wicked, corrupting anecdotes, from all unprofitable conversation; henceforth let your speech, and your anecdotes, and your proverbs, and all your wise sayings, be dictated by the Spirit of truth to edification, and instruction, and reproof, being fitly chosen and fitly timed, that good, and not evil, may be the result; for to this end is man endowed with the gift of speech. Shall we abuse the gift of God? Shall we make the gift of God scatter the seeds of death instead of life? Remember, that by thy words thou shalt be justified, and by thy words thou shalt be condemned.

BOOK DEBTS, MARCH 31, 1857.

Conference			
Brecon	7	12	7
Monmouth	55	18	5
East Glamorgan	105	3	11
West "	126	1	6½
Llanelli	56	12	0
Carmarthen	24	16	0
Pembrokeshire	8	2	7½
Cardiganshire	16	11	7
Merionethshire	10	17	3
Flintshire	17	17	11½
Denbighshire	15	9	8½
Anglesey and Conway Valley	11	13	3
	£456	16	10

PAYMENTS from March 6 until April 29.—C. Harman, £4; A. L. Jones, £3; J. J. Phillips, £2; M. Vaughan, £2 10s; Wm. Ajax, Anglesey, £2; Dd. John, £3.

Ditto, for Pamphlets.—A. L. Jones, £9; M. Vaughan, £2 10s; C. Harman, £1 10s; David John, £1 15s; W. Ajax, Anglesey, £3.

VOLUNTEERS for the Mormon Army! Your time for starting for the battlefield has come—Captain Jones is blowing his horn loudly in the North-land—the enemy is active—but you have the victory, and you will win the honest in heart for the kingdom of Jesus. God himself is looking over you! Who, who is not ready?

CONTENTS.

	PG.
Home Church Accounts	145
Epistle of the First Presidency	146
Repentance among the Saints	156

SWANSEA:
PRINTED AND PUBLISHED BY DANIEL DANIELS.

ZION'S TRUMPET,

OR

𝔖tar of the 𝔖aints.

| No. 11.] | MAY 16, 1857. | [Vol. X. |

LETTER FROM ELDER HENRY HARRIES.

Carmarthen, April 22, 1857.

Dear Brother Daniels,

Many are the questions asked to me relative to the Indians killing the companies on the Plains, &c. I know of no better way than this to answer all of them at the same time, if you see fit to sound them through your "Trumpet," so that all will hear how it happened, as far as I understand concerning them.

The Indians called the Cheyenne [not Chinese] were camped on the bank of the *Little Blue* river, a little this side of Fort Kearney, when the mail happened to come by; their chief sent two of his sons on horseback to meet the mail, asking for tobacco, for they were accustomed to getting some from the men of the mail, every time they saw one coming that way, but when the two Indians came to meet them, they did not stop to talk with them. At that the Indians, since they were on horses, rushed ahead of the mail, trying to stop it, for the purpose of getting tobacco for their master, but the men of the mail did not pay any attention to them. When the Indians saw this, they tried their best to stop it, by shouting in such a fearsome way that they frightened the mule that carried the mail, until they went off the usual track, and when that happened the *guard* pulled out his pistol and shot at one of the Indians, but he failed to hit him in the head, rather the bullet went through his hair without harming him. At that, the Indian turned, drawing up his bow, and shot the *driver* in his wrist, which prevented them from going any further, and after they stopped, they gave them all the tobacco, with Indian corn and clothes, and it was good that they saw their way clear to

[Price 1½c.

do that, for the entire camp was coming up. Then the Indians helped them, pulling out the arrow and binding the wrist, and putting them back on the usual track, considering that everything had taken place because of impulsiveness and misunderstanding, and there was no bad intention on the part of the one or the other. So they left in peace, the Indians to their camp, and the mail toward Fort Kearney, and it is likely the men of the mail said at Fort Kearney that the Indians had been after them, trying to catch them, but that they had delayed them by throwing their clothes along the way, as Captain Jones says in his letter, and when chief officer in Kearney heard that, he sent the Cavalry out to avenge them for that, and when they reached the camp, they found the Indians happily by their fires roasting the *corn* they had received from the men of the mail, together with the clothes and the tobacco they had gotten, not thinking that any harm would follow, but before they could speak the soldiers shot them. They killed from ten to twenty of them, and the others escaped with their lives.

This was the thing that first angered the Indians, and they have a law that if white men kill any one of them, there is to be no peace until justice is done, and nothing will suffice as justice but the blood of some white men, no matter who they may be; it makes no difference who—the first ones that come into view, no matter who they are. Thus they met up with Babbitt's camp, containing 5 wagons; they killed four people, and the fifth escaped, namely the only Mormon that was there, and there was the woman that Captain Jones mentioned; she and her baby were killed; she did not have a bad character as did the others, although she was not in the church, but she had been, and was intending to again be after arriving in the Valley, but it was not wise for her to be traveling with such ungodly people, and it was they who were killed. The second company the Indians met were Californians; I do not have their number, or many details about them, but I do remember seeing a company passing by the Valley last Summer, when I was coming to the bottom of Box Elder. I traveled with them for a time, but I do not recall their number, but that some were riding mules, and one man and a woman were in a wagon. After a long conversation, I found out that the man who was conversing with me was a *Dutchman*, and that he come to the Valley as a Mormon years before, and that he had gone from there to California, and had made his fortune there, and that he was going back to the States to make his home, and he told me that I was a fool if I stayed in a filthy "hell hole" like the Valley, and I let him go his way; since he had once been a Saint, he did not speak in ignorance, but from the wicked intent of his heart, and there were very strange yellow letters on the side of the wagon, which I recognized immediately when I saw it coming in a line of Bishop Smoot's wagons on the bank of the Platte river, which they had found on the way with no man close to it, where the assumption was made that all had been killed. Although that man had intended to make his home in the States, and had made his fortune, that, in the end, was insufficient to keep his life on the Plains.

The third company was that of T. Margetts and Cowdy, with their wives and children. The story of those persons is already well known.

The fourth company was that of Col. Babbitt himself. Because of his foolishness and that of the two who were with him, namely getting drunk, and going right up to the Indians of their own free will, despite all the persuading to the contrary in Kearney.

These are all who were killed as far as I know, but I do know this, or at least it's what I believe, that the white men were more to blame than were the Indians in the first place, and the Indians knew that quite well, for one day they, before we went past Fort Laramie, had sent a messenger there to offer peace, because they had increased in their numbers, and considered themselves as free as they, and also they had one white woman with them in the mountains, and they would give her up if they could have one of their own in return, namely the one who had been taken about two years before that and imprisoned in Fort Laramie for some transgression.

You see now that the Indians were not at fault, and it is much easier for me to believe the Indians than to believe the wicked white people. I would much prefer to entrust my life in the hands of the Indians, than with many of the white people of America. But no matter who our enemies are, if we keep God's commandments, it is certain that there will be more on our side than can be against us. Living our religion is all that is required of us, in order for us to enjoy every gift and comfort and success in every way in the present world, and eternal life in the world to come.

Now I shall report some of the names of the Saints I saw on my way here, since I shall not have the chance to have a chit-chat by the fire, as noted previously. First, in Florence, I saw brothers Lewis J. Davies, Cefnmawr; Phillip Vaughan, Mountain Ash; D. Evans, Cardiff; William Hughes, from the North; John Richards from Cardigan; and Isaac Green from Monmouth; all healthy and doing well.

Again in Gravois, near St. Louis, I met up with John Powell, William Rees from Georgetown; William Roderick, Hannah Watkin from Llanarth, Cardigan; the sister of Hughes from the North; Thomas Roderick, Pembroke; John Roberts, Glamorgan; Margaret Davies, the daughter of Thomas Jones, Gellideg, near Merthyr; Jane Jones, the daughter of Jennet Davies, near Merthyr; David Joseph, Penydarren; and John his brother, together with others.

In Caseville, I saw Walter Roach, Llanelli; David S. Jones, Merthyr; William Lewis, earlier from Carmarthen; and several others whose names I do not recall now.

In Ferry Hut I met up with William Jones, David Giles, and David James.

In Minersville there were John Pheanix from the North; Thomas Matthias, near Brymbo; Thomas Jones, Llanbrymbo; David Hopkins, Merthyr; Lewis M. Rees, Cwmtileri; David Davies, Aberdare; Jonathan Ellis Green, Brymbo; John James, Tredegar; Richard Call, Rhymney; William Williams, Tredegar; Joseph Joseph, from the same place; Thomas, David, and Catherine Morgans, Cefn-coed-y-cymmer; and John B. Jones near Brymbo.

In Pottsville I met up with Daniel Davies, Llansawel; sister Edwards from Swansea; Thomas Jones, Liverpool; and Thomas Thomas, Georgetown.

Also, in Williamsburg, I met up with John Edmunds, from Llandeilo.

All these were in perfect health, happy, and doing well, continuing firm in the faith, and wishing to be remembered to their relatives and friends, who are too numerous to mention, and also to all the Saints, and wishing to see the Saints come to those places where they are, before they are ready to leave them, for there are better places there to obtain a way of going further than there are in this country. Therefore, dear Saints, be earnest and diligent, in season and out of season, not only to chastise, warn, and persuade, but also to redeem yourselves out of Babylon, before it falls like dust to the ground, is the wish of

Your Brother in Christ,
HENRY HARRIES.

THE "DAILY TELEGRAPH'S" SLANDERS AGAINST "MORMONISM."

(From the *Star*.)

JOSEPH ELLIS, the publisher of a London paper, called the "Daily Telegraph," in an editorial of the 22nd ultimo, has exhibited his holy delight for slander and falsehood against the "Mormons" of Utah Territory, by representing them as "a disgrace to civilization," accusing them of "desperate profligacy;" declaring that they are in rebellion against the laws and authority of the United States; calling their religion an "imposture," a "delusion," and stating that "moral degradation universally prevails among them."

The editor has made these wholesale denunciations without referring his readers to any reliable evidence of their truthfulness. Did it never occur to the editor that his readers are capable of making their own denunciations? Any person who has access to an English dictionary can select, without the assistance of an editor, an abundance of suitable words, to denounce any system, whether true or false, which he may feel disposed to condemn. To denounce is one thing; to substantiate by evidence is another. The denunciations against "Mormonism" lack one very essential ingredient, namely, *truth*.

We must, however, give the gentleman credit for having occasionally inserted a truth among his mass of falsehoods. For instance, he acknowledges that the Saints are unchangeable in their faith and doctrine. Hear his testimony:—

"What they were previous to their expulsion from Nauvoo, they now are; the spirit of JOE SMITH survives in BRIGHAM YOUNG; the new Mormon Bible is still the accepted rule of faith and practice; and polygamy, it is clear, has not yet lost its attraction as a distinguishing doctrine of their creed."

How this London Publisher could have uttered so much truth in this short paragraph, we are almost at a loss to determine. Why, Mr. Ellis, every word of this sentence is true! excepting where you have altered the name of Joseph to JOE; but, then, we must suppose that this slight alteration was merely made as being more poetic or euphonic— less harsh to the ear than that of JOSEPH. If this name has become particularly offensive and repulsive to your refined taste, we have no objections whatever to adopt your appellation as an amendment of the name, and henceforth out of respect for your vanity, we will adopt for you the distinguished title of "JOE ELLIS."

In speaking of that great philanthropist and eminent statesman, Governor Young, "Joe" Ellis further remarks:—

"Every account from Utah shows that the sway of the arch-impostor is as undisputed as ever."

Will "Joe" please point out to his readers one act or word of Governor Young, or one doctrine which he teaches, or one practice in his religion or politics that is an imposition? But, continues he,

"The Saints and Elders submissively acknowledge his authority, and bow to his mandates."

Why did the United States appoint Brigham Young Governor, if they did not desire the Saints and Elders, and all other citizens of that territory, to submissively acknowledge his authority and bow to his mandates?

"The murmurs and complaints," says the Editor, "that occasionally arise, seem to emanate chiefly from newcomers, unused to the iron rule that awaits them; but they soon find that they have no choice but submission or flight; and they are lucky if, at the cost of being despoiled of their property, they are able to emerge from the meshes of the Mormon net."

The laws and authorities of Utah do not prohibit "newcomers" nor oldcomers, from murmuring and complaining just as much as they please. They have the most perfect freedom in this respect; there is no more restraint upon grumbling in Utah than there is here in England. What the editor means by "the iron rule that awaits" the newcomers we cannot imagine. Does he mean that the laws of the territory, submitted to the United States Congress, and sanctioned and approved by that illustrious body, are an "iron rule?" Does he mean that the Governor, and Judges, and other authorities appointed by Congress are an "iron rule?" Does he mean that the execution of these just and wholesome laws is an "iron rule?" "But," says Joe Ellis, in speaking of these newcomers, "they soon find that they have no choice but submission or flight." Not exactly correct, Mr. Editor, the laws of Utah require submission or punishment, according to the nature of the crime. Flight or banishment is no part of the penalty of Utah's laws. If a man murders, commits adultery, or any other capital crime, he has not the choice of "flight." If a man forfeits his property by fines, or by debts, he will be "despoiled" of a sufficient amount to satisfy the demands of the law, and no more. "The meshes of the Mormon net" are just strong enough, and broad enough, to catch both persons and property, where either is legally forfeited. If this is what the editor means by iron rule, we feel proud to acknowledge such a wholesome government.

In speaking of Governor Young, the Editor remarks,

"Not being able to tolerate any authority but his own, he is continually embroiled with that of the United States."

Will the *Telegraph* point out one single act of Governor Young, either in his private or official capacity, in which he has violated the laws or Constitution of the United States, or rebelled in the least particular against that government? We defy the whole world to bring the least particle of evidence against him or against the Church over which he so ably presides, to substantiate these false, though often reiterated charges. But listen! let us hear what the famed Editor JOE further says,

"One of the latest exploits of Brigham Young and his associates is the burning of the records of the Supreme Court of Utah, together with about nine hundred volumes of law, belonging to the offices of the district judge."

This is a grave charge, indeed, were it true, but it lacks that very essential element called truth. But Joe must not be charged with the fabrication of this falsehood; it originated in San Francisco, California, about eight hundred miles from Salt Lake. Its author was the notorious Judge Drummond, who, upon his appointment as a district Judge for Utah, left his amiable wife in Illinois, and took with him a picked-up lady, with whom he criminally lived, and whom he called Mrs. Drummond.

Upon his arrival, it so happened that some of his wife's relations living in the territory, discovered his crime and made it public; and the righteous, pious judge, no doubt, thought it prudent to make tracks for California. It was he who forged the ridiculous story about the members of the Legislature of Utah, being crippled and near-sighted. But "Joe" of the *Telegraph* very candidly acknowledges that he can "learn but little that is reliable," from Utah, and we are inclined to believe that his stock of information must be very small, indeed, when he resorts to such base calumnies and vulgar denunciations.

Says the *Telegraph*, Judge Drummond

"Refers to a charge delivered by him on a statute enacted by the Legislature of Utah Territory, providing for the punishment of Polygamous intercourse."

The statutes of Utah are published, and we beg to inform the *Telegraph* that no such law can be found in the volume, and no act has ever been passed, condemning the divine institution of polygamy in that territory. The Legislature of that territory have too much good sense to pass such an infamous, unjust, and anti-scriptural law.

But we will let Joe continue his story; he says,

"By the Mormons, Brigham Young is held as a better authority than Judge Drummond, [quite true, Mr. Editor, you can tell the truth now and then.] and as the latter frankly confesses, the only law that can be enforced in Utah territory is the law of the Church, of which, by the way, the former is the supreme interpreter."

This is a most glaring falsehood. The civil laws of Utah are just as independent of ecclesiastical or Church laws as in any territory of the Union. Each religious denomination in Utah regulates its own members by its own discipline; while the civil laws give to each equal protection. The Latter-day Saints have no more rights or religious privileges guaranteed to them by the civil laws of Utah than the Methodists, Baptists, Quakers, or any other denomination.

The *Telegraph* further asserts that Brigham Young

"Now aims at temporal as well as spiritual ascendency—a dangerous assumption, as he is situated, since of necessity it compels the American government, unwilling as it may be to interfere, to put down so daring a rival to its own rightful authority."

Will the *Telegraph* inform its readers what temporal ascendency the Governor now aims at? The United States have appointed him to the highest post of honor in the territory. Does he aim at some office still higher? Or has he assumed any temporal powers which the American Government has not vested in the office of Governor? In what respect is Governor Young considered a "daring rival" to the United States? Has he waged war, either in word or deed, upon the Constitution, laws, or authority of that government? Has he ever manifested the least desire to throw off a Republican form of government, and establish something else in its stead? The answer of the *Telegraph* to these reasonable questions, will impart some light to its readers, and will reflect far greater honor upon the talents of JOE than abusive epithets and wholesale slanders against an innocent and persecuted people.

"We cannot doubt," (continues he,) "that it will be viewed as an imperative duty, on the part of the United States, to subvert the whole system of Mormon government."

Now the Mormons have two kinds of government: one is their ecclesiastical or Church government, with which the United States have no right to interfere; the other is a Republican form of government, established by the United States, themselves, for the benefit, not only of Mormons, but of all other people who become citizens of Utah. This latter form of government, Congress has no power to subvert or alter without destroying its own Constitutional fabric. The confident expectations of JOE, therefore, have a very slight chance of being realized, while the American nation remains a Republic.

"Joe" says, that he

"Shall rejoice heartily at any steps that may be taken by the American Government to break up this gigantic imposture, which is a festering sore upon society, and cries aloud for a cure."

To hasten the consummation of his joys, would it not be magnanimous for Joe to recommend the re-establishment of the "Holy Inquisition?" Don't you think, sir, that a few hundred thousand "Mormons" put to death by pious editors would reflect great honor upon your profession? Perhaps your fertile imagination will be able to suggest to the United States, some feasible plan of destroying the eight thousand men, women, and children who inhabit Utah. Could not JOE leave the editorial chair, for a short season, and offer his services as commander-in-chief of a mob to march against the unoffending Mormons?

BRECON CONFERENCE.

Black Rock, Llanelly, Brecon, May 8, 1857.

Dear Brother Daniels,

I write this letter to you for the purpose of reporting the condition of things here. The Officers and Saints feel well with the work of the Lord. Presently they are diligently distributing tracts from house to house, and also testifying and preaching out on Sundays, and during the week as well. This is the condition of the brothers and sisters who have renewed their covenants, and are living their religion. The number of those who are in conformity with the Reformation, as far as I have determined, is 60.

The Tithing that was paid in last month is £5 4s. 7c.

Our present Debt is £1 12 s. 9c.

I am, your brother in the Lord,

JOHN THOMAS.

ZION'S TRUMPET,

OR

Star of the Saints.

SATURDAY, MAY 16, 1857.

DEPARTURE.—The ship "Westmoreland," Captain R. R. Decan, bound for Philadelphia, cleared on the 24th of April, and sailed on the 25th, having on board 540 souls of Saints from the Scandinavian mission, besides four returning missionaries from England.

May the blessings of heaven attend these Saints, and deliver them from the dangers of the sea, and give them a safe arrival at their place of destination.—*Star.*

The East Glamorgan Conference is hereby divided into two; one of which is to be called the Cardiff Conference; the other to retain the original name. The division to be made under the counsel and direction of President Daniel Daniels.

Elder Samuel Roskelly is appointed to preside over the Cardiff Conference, and is required to make the necessary organization, by appointing a General Book Agent, selecting Traveling Elders, &c.—*Star.*

CONFERENCES of the Welsh conferences will be held at the following times in the places indicated:—

May 17, Pembrokeshire, West Glamorgan, and Merioneth.

May 24, East Glamorgan, Llanelli, and Anglesey.

May 31, Monmouth, Carmarthen, and Denbigh.

June 7, Cardiff, Cardigan, and Flintshire.

President Daniel Daniels intends to be present at the conferences of West Glamorgan, Llanelli, Carmarthen, and Cardigan; President Taylor at those in the North, and President Miller at the rest.

THE SUCCESS of the work of the Lord in the Scandinavian Mission reminds us of the establishment of the Church in Wales, the persecutions and the lovely times we had. During the last half of last year, 575 persons were baptized, despite the exertions of the priests of Baal, and the civil authorities. The work prospers and spreads, and the Lord truly blesses the efforts of the Elders and the Saints, who are generally faithful in testifying and tracting. A total of £919 16s. 2c., for the half year, was sent to the Liverpool Office, in addition to what was used to sustain the work at home. A total of £788 will provide for the emigration this Spring. The tithing is at work in force.

May our faithfulness in Wales in tracting and preaching, and sustaining the work, and our fasts and earnest prayers for the success of the work of our God ascend like sweet incense before Him, so that we may be worthy of the success we long for.

We are glad to see the beneficent effects of the reformation. Let us continue to reform, for a critical time is at the door, and God is preparing his people. Important matters are underway in Zion, to prepare for the future, and, perhaps it will not be long before accommodations will be opened in the everlasting hills, for the faithful to hide in from the wrath of men and devils, as well as from the judgments of God.

THE GOVERNORSHIP of Utah Territory, as we understand from the *Mormon* for March 28th, was offered lately to the Honorable Fayette McMullen from Virginia, by President Buchanan, by means of five members of Congress, but they have not received a definite response. The honorable gentleman asked for time to think about it. The observations of the "*Mormon*" on the topic are as follows:—

"Elsewhere we have expressed our views of appointments in the Federal Offices of Utah; we shall therefore only add that if President Buchanan thinks of his own election being the expression of the popular will, he will think of the popular will in Utah. His Excellency Governor Young is the choice of that people; but should rotation be the order, and *must be the order*, there is not necessity to run to Virginia or elsewhere out of Utah to find the right man for the right place The Honorable F. McMullen does well to reflect—and so will around. The wish of the citizens of Utah ought to be as much respected as that of any other Territory."

In the *Mormon* for April 25 we read the following quotation from the *New York Herald*:—

"No decisive steps have been taken relative to Utah. There is difficulty in finding a proper man for Governor, although there are half a dozen applicants for the office."

The *Mormon* comments abundantly on the commotion that the publication and circulation of the office-resigning letter of Judge Drummond has caused. It re-publishes the old stories of J. C. Bennett, Tom Sharp, Van Dusen, &c., together with the existence of the "danite band," or the secret murderers to kill as many of the enemies of the Mormon authorities as they had opportunity to do, and the other things that begin this issue. But the trouble concerning the "new woman," &c., has done harm to the poor Judge, so that the gentlemanly editors of the States have not made any mention of that. To give his story we quote from a letter sent by a gentleman from Utah, (who was not a Mormon) to one of the editors of the *Mormon*:—

"When first I came here, I had a strong prejudice against the people and feared them much. An intimate acquaintance with many of my "gentile" brethren, [i.e., officers of the United States, &c., who were not Saints] did not lessen my prejudice and fears, but to the contrary, increased them. From them I learned that their lives were in danger in consequence of "hard speeches" delivered against them by the "heads" of the Church, at their religious meetings; and that the "powers that be" were bitterly opposed to the Federal Government, traitors to their country.   *   *   *

"After five months residence here, I have discovered the real cause for the "hard speeches" of the elders, and, to some extent, I can account for the spirit of the articles on Mormonism which have appeared from time to time in the newspapers."

"I have found that a number of the Gentiles and the Mormons here are guilty of gross licentiousness. Judge S—, (United States Official and Quarter Mormon,) was last week found guilty before the Church court of adultery, and excommunicated from the Church, and published throughout the territory.

"I know that P—, D—, C—, (United States Officers) and other leading "Gentiles" have been guilty of the same crime, and have hired an old *hag* to aid them in their hellish designs; and also that Gen. B—, Dr. H—, (United States Officers) J—, and others have joined them in gambling, drinking, and misrepresenting the acts and policy of the leaders of this community to the Departments at Washington, (I have read the documents,) and to the press in New York. As for myself, I confess that I have kept their company to some extent, and plead guilty to the crime of drinking with them, and thereby incurred the displeasure of the Mormons, but thank God I have never in my life been guilty of fornication and *gambling*, and I hope I never will.

"The [Mormon] authorities are well posted in all these movements, and I am positively astonished that they have done nothing but deliver a few "hard speeches" against such conduct, when it is well understood both by Mormons and Gentiles that the "Mountain law" is *death to the adulterer*. But I presume that the Mormons are afraid to put the law in force, believing that if they killed any United States official, or banished them and their associates from the Territory, that it would be construed into rebellion against the Government, while Mormonism is already so unpopular in the States, that all the country would rise up for revenge, not on the avenger, but on all the 70,000 Mormons in the Territory."

He goes on to argue in favor of the Saints in Utah being able to have Officers of their own choosing, and to show the difference between polygamy and immorality. He says there is no tavern, nor *gambling house*, or brothel in the Territory, and he asks what village, town, or city in the United States could compare to Utah.

Lack of space prevents us from giving all the details, but we counsel every Conference President and Pastor to try to obtain a copy of the *Mormon* early through the *post*, so in his conference he may defend our holy religion from being maligned by the children of the lie. Send the prepayment for it to Liverpool, as previously instructed, or you will have to wait for it longer through the order it comes to the branches.

LETTER FROM ELDER ISRAEL EVANS.

The ship "*George Washington*," April 16, 1857.

President Daniels,

Dear Brother,—

Having a little time to spare, as we near Boston, I shall use such to write a few lines to you, for I know that you are desirous of hearing from us.

We sailed within the *Channel* on Saturday, the 28th of March. On Sunday, the wind arose, and the sea became very rough, and consequently some of our people became sick, until there were but few of us left to watch over those who were sick. The wind continued strong for several days, which left our people down longer than they would have been otherwise. But about the end of the week the majority of them were quite well.

We had two deaths here, an elderly man from England, and a child from the Southampton conference. We also had one birth. The mother of the child has been very sick, but she is improving gradually.

The count of emigrants on board the ship is 816, and, considering our circumstances, we have moved forward quite well. Elder James Park is our president, and Elders J. B. Martin and Dana are his counselors. We are divided into wards, of which there are five. The first is under my care as bishop; Elder J. C. Hall is bishop of the second; Elder Ashby of the third, Elder Carrigan of the fourth, Elder Dille of the fifth, and Elder A. M. Musser as scribe. With this organization, and with the rules of the company being kept regularly, we are going forward very well.

The ovens of the ship are intended to cook for no more than 400 emigrants, but with the rules we have adopted, we can easily manage for more than twice that number. All the Saints are enjoying good health, and they are in happy spirits, for soon we shall be on land now. We have been on the sea for 22 days, and on the whole we had quite a comfortable voyage, and the blessings of heaven have followed us, and our prayers have been answered immediately. The winds were caused to blow, the sick were healed, devils were cast out, and the Spirit of the Lord has watched over us all during the time.

The Saints from Wales have gone along extremely well. Some of them were sick, but now all are healthy, or at least close to being thus, and a few days on dry land will be enough to set everything in its place.

Since I started writing this letter, the woman who had given birth died, and she was buried in the depths of the ocean. There are yet one or two elderly women who are not entirely well. All others are enjoying robust health, and are feeling happy.

The feelings of my heart are indescribable, as the beautiful view of the land of my birth rises before me, for I feel as if once again I am within my cozy home, and when I say that about myself, I believe I speak the feelings of all on board.

I know of nothing else I can say, for each one is quite happy, and we pray without ceasing evening and morning, for all of you our brothers and sisters in Babylon, that you might be comforted and blessed, for as long as the will of the Lord keeps you there, and that soon you will have the privilege of following after us, and being blessed as have we.

Remember me kindly to brothers Miller and Taylor, and all who are there with you.

May numerous blessings of heaven follow you forever and each day, perfecting you for every good deed, is the earnest and constant wish of

Yours, as ever,
ISRAEL EVANS.

Rhosllanerchrugog, May 8th, 1857.

President Daniels,

Dear Brother,—

The reason I have not written to you more frequently, is that I know Pastor Jones has supplied this need in his epistles to you from time to time.

With respect to the Reformation, it has been and continues to be of remarkable worth here, as in other places. I rejoiced when I first heard of it, inasmuch as we had laid the foundation for repentance and the "doctrine of baptisms," &c. I had known for several months that I had great need to reform in many things; but I had a completely different look at myself through the teachings of our Pastor, the Trumpets, *Stars*, and brother Benson, &c. In short, I believe that I have had a very correct look at myself, through the aforementioned means, and in this looking glass I have seen where I need to reform, in thought, in conversation, and in deed. On the 23rd of March, in Liverpool, I covenanted in the name of the Trinity again, to live my religion, to purify, and to sanctify myself before my Father, which he has commanded me to do. The covenant was sealed, and a more abundant outpouring of the spirit of God than ever before came over me, according to the promise. And until now a fire, as it were, is going through my whole constitution, yea, it is increasing, and through its strength I have preached on the same topic for seven weeks, namely the "Reformation," in the morning, the afternoon, and in the evening. And as men are separate in their bodies and their spirits, thus also does the effect of preaching the reformation separate. Some of the chief leaders and the *lords* believed that the reformation was the death blow to Mormonism, originating from a lack of love, self-interest, and violence. Others thought differently, knowing that it was a blessing originating from God's love and mercy; and in this light about fifty percent have re-covenanted through baptism to live better, and I can say that they have, as their works testify of that. I expect to baptize more soon, but I believe that it will be from forty to fifty short of the previous number, which proves that they were moribund before. But this is a fact, there will be greater success in their midst from now on, and that is natural and spiritual, because there is more of the spirit of God in their midst, and as a result more work will be done. We have begun to preach with a greater fervor in the open air, and there are large crowds who hear us, attentively and seriously, but one must allow that the occasional Saul will be in every meeting. Many of our listeners exhibit a smile of honesty that plays on their faces, which proves to a great extent that it is in their hearts. Many of these smiles have been created through the effect of the faithful distribution of pamphlets over the past five months; there is no doubt that these have done much good. When preaching out of doors, if troubles arise in the midst of the people, these are most often caused by the ministers and the preachers, as they call themselves. They are known in the congregations, not by their virtue and their goodness, but rather by their *Babylonish Flags*, namely their white handkerchiefs, their long faces, and their works of the evil one. By now they carry their newspapers and their almanacs to strive to prove us wrong. But the sharp-eyed see through this that they fail to have anything against us in the written word of God, so it is obvious that all things work to the good of the children of God, and the spreading of the kingdom of God on the earth, and the time will soon dawn when the kingdom, and the greatness of the kingdom, will be in the possession of the Saints of the Most High.

This is how we are going forth here, wishing for an interest in your prayers, knowing that our labor will not be in vain in the Lord. My warmest love to you and to all the faithful brethren with you.

I am, yours obediently and faithfully in the Lord,

DAVID JOHN.

LETTER FROM PASTOR JONES.

Alongside the road between Caernarvon and Cricieth,
As happy as can be,
May 11th, 1857.

Dear Brother Daniels,

Last week I was in Llandudno, Eglwysfach, Bethesda, Amlwch, and Holyhead, and Brother William Ajax was with me, and we had many hundreds listen to us, especially in Bethesda and Amlwch, and they frequently asked us when we would come again. O, if only some good man, some craftsman could come to this place. There is only one sister here. They were like a great Assembly, each one sitting on the ground, and listening for life. There is no doubt that Saints will come here. The traveling brethren are here once in awhile, but not half often enough. We came to Caernarvon Saturday night, and we preached out-of-doors twice, and held a Saints meeting. The Saints here are quite dead. Brother T. Jones has not found work, and he is traveling around until he finds it. I received your letter and brother Taylor's letter. Had you not sent them to me, I would have gone on my way to Machynlleth, but not to have a conference; but *all right*, brother Daniels, tonight I will be in Cricieth, preaching on my own, tomorrow night in Porthmadog, from there to Harlech, Barmouth, Tywyn, and to Machynlleth Saturday night, to meet brother Taylor, and preaching every night, if I can. Last week I walked about a hundred miles. Brother Ajax was with me from Bethesda until today; he is as good as I could wish him to be. O yes, remember, remember to send a Collier who is good at his work as well as in the Church, to brother Thomas Jones, Brymbo. He will receive 3s. per day for his work. I am not requesting him to preach, but to assist with the little that is here in connection with distributing books. Also remember about Llanidloes. If Benjamin Davies is not coming perhaps someone else will come, John Morgans in his place to Brymbo, or the boy who lives near Bryn from Pembrokeshire.

Brother Taylor and I will go back this way next week, and to preach in Caernarvon, Bangor, and Bethesda, &c. Remember me to everyone. I am very happy, and O if only we could have from four to ten good lads up here.

My love to you from the base of the hedge.

Your fellow servant,

J. E. JONES.

[Who will consent to brother Jones's call? Let him send his name here without delay, with notice that he is a ready Mormon, and he shall be blessed and strengthened, and may he succeed to his heart's content. Again we ask, *who?*]

"My fellow sinners," said a preacher, "if you were told that by going to the top of those stairs over there, (pointing to the stairs at the far end of the church) you could secure your eternal salvation, I fully believe that not one of you would try to reach it. But if somebody proclaimed that there was a hundred dollars up there for you, may I be bound if there were not there *"such a getting up stairs as you never did see."*

CONTENTS.

	PG.
Letter of Henry Harries	161
The "Daily Telegraph" and Mormonism	164
Brecon Conference	168
Editorial	169
Letter of Israel Evans	172
Letters, &c.	174

SWANSEA:

PRINTED AND PUBLISHED BY DANIEL DANIELS.

ZION'S TRUMPET,

OR

Star of the Saints.

No. 12.] MAY 30, 1857. [Vol. X.

THE PUBLIC SHAME OF JUDGE DRUMMOND.

(Translated from the Millennial Star, by Dewi Elfed.)

This infamous scoundrel and dastardly wretch, having escaped from the just penalty of the law, is still running at large, endeavoring to hide his own filthy, and most heart-sickening crimes, by abusing and slandering the "Mormons." Our readers will recollect that this man, though an ignorant, backwoods, pettifogger, was appointed by President Pierce to fill the honorable office of one of the associate justices for the territory of Utah, which had been rendered vacant by the death of the honorable Leonidas Shaver. After DRUMMOND had secured his appointment, he left his wife in the State of Illinois, and started for Utah. On his way, he picked up a woman, slept with her during the whole journey, boarded and bedded with here while in the territory, calling her Mrs. DRUMMOND. It so happened that the real wife of this beastly criminal had some relations living in Utah; and thus the crime of the degraded judge was discovered; prosecutions were about to commence against him, and the majesty of the law to be enforced; but the horrible monster escaped to California.

While in the city of Fillmore, capital of Utah, he sent Cato, his negro slave, to murder Levi Abrahams, a Jewish Merchant; but the negro was foiled in the brutal attempt, and the black-hearted judge was apprehended for the crime; and would, without doubt, if he had been brought to trial, have been sent to the Penitentiary; but out of respect for his official dignity, it was concluded to drop proceedings, and save the poor wretch from the punishment of the law, which his crimes so richly deserved.

12 [Price 1½c.

This lying, adulterous, murderous fiend, having escaped from the punishment of his execrable crimes, has pretended to make a report to the Attorney-General of the United States, giving his reasons why he resigns his office as associate judge in Utah. That anyone in the civilized world could be found silly enough to be duped with such barefaced, monstrous lies, related, too, by such a notorious criminal, whose black deeds were publicly exposed many months ago, is a strange anomaly, and exhibits the weakness and gullibility of the human mind. But stranger still, to see popular editors, who professedly have some respect for their own characters, pretending to give credence to such absurd, most improbable, Don Quixote falsehoods. We would not disgrace our columns by noticing such a loathsome specimen of humanity as that scapegrace, were it not that gentlemen of the press are trying to impose these known absurdities and slanders upon their readers, as the veritable truth. But now for the lies contained in DRUMMOND'S report.

Lie 1. "Brigham Young, the Governor of Utah Territory, is the acknowledged head of the Church of Jesus Christ of Latter-day Saints, commonly called Mormons, and as such head the Mormons look to him, and to him alone, for the law by which they are to be governed; therefore, no law of Congress is by them considered binding in any manner."

There is no man in America or England, in the least acquainted with the views or practices of Governor Young and the "Mormons" who does not know the above statement to be a willful, infamous lie, without the most distant shadow of a foundation. When and where did Governor Young or the Church ever violate even the least of the laws of the United States? When and where did he or the Church ever violate one of the civil laws of Utah? When or where did he or the Church ever believe or teach, either in public or private, verbally or in writing, that the laws of Congress, or the Constitution of the United States, or the civil laws of the Territory, were not binding upon him or the "Mormons?" Such an instance cannot be pointed out, since the existence of the Church either in Utah or in the States. There is not a people upon the face of the whole earth more devoted and loyal to their government, than are the peaceable, industrious, unoffending citizens of Utah. They are wedded to the Constitution and laws of the American Republic. Indeed, they go further than other citizens; for it is incorporated in their articles of faith, that the form and Constitution of the American Government were the products of the inspiration of the Almighty. To deny its authority and laws would be a direct denial of the divinity of the revelations which God gave through Joseph Smith; it would be a denial of "Mormonism." It would be a flat denial of the constant teachings, counsels, and practices of Governor Young. It would be a denial of the patriotic examples and practices that have conspicuously characterized the Saints in all the horrid persecutions they have suffered.

What! Does this infernal liar, Drummond, suppose that he can make any sensible man believe that Governor Young and the "Mormons" have concluded to deny "Mormonism?" to deny the revelations given through their martyred Prophet; to deny their own teachings; to deny their own articles of faith; to deny the whole platform of their religion, for the sake of turning rebels to the great Central Government of the American Union, a government, too, which they believe God himself established through their illustrious fathers? As well might he tell us, that the "Mormons" had formed or created the Great Salt Lake; erected the Rocky Mountains to prevent an invasion of their territory, and sent an earthquake upon California to frighten the inhabitants.

Lie 2. "I know that there is a secret oath-bound organization among all the male members of the Church, to acknowledge no law save the law of the Holy Priesthood, which comes to the people through Brigham Young, direct from God, he, Young, being the vice regent of God, and the prophetic successor of Joseph Smith, who was the founder of this blind and treasonable organization."

This is only a repetition of the absurd and ridiculous lie, invented by the Missouri murderers in the year 1838, pretending that the "Mormons" had an "oath-bound organization" among them, called "DANITES," or "DESTROYING ANGELS," whose business it was to destroy the Gentiles. There were some poor, silly people then who actually pretended to believe this malicious slander; never once thinking that those who were base enough to murder defenseless women and children, were also wicked enough to slander their murdered victims, in order to justify themselves in their horrible butcheries. This same lie is now renewed by this pious whoremonger of a judge, who fled from the territory to escape the penalty of the civil law. If he ever returns to that territory, he will be able to learn very effectively whether the civil law is respected in Utah or not. He will then learn, to his deep sorrow, that the Mormons acknowledge the civil and criminal laws, without requiring, in his case, the aid of the "Law of the Holy Priesthood," as he calls it.

Lie 3. "I am fully aware that these are a set of men set apart by special order of the Church, to take both the lives and property of persons who may question the authority of the Church, (the names of whom I will promptly make known at a future time.")

This is only an enlargement of the 2nd lie, and a mere repetition of the absurd stories introduced in such novels as "Female Life among the Mormons." It is very curious, indeed, that such a band of murderers and robbers should exist among fifty thousand or a hundred thousand inhabitants, and no one detect it, until discovered by this beastly adulterer. But, then the "names" are to be made "known at a future time." Why not make them known now? Why not give an instance of some murder committed by them? Why not substantiate some of these charges with some little evidence? If such a band exists, whose business it is to rob and murder "persons who may question the authority of the Church," how is it that the property and life of Drummond escaped? How did the lying Secretary Ferris and his wife escape? How have the hundreds of Gentiles, who have resided in Utah for years, escaped? How have the hundreds of dissenting "Mormons" who have inhabited the territory year after year, escaped? How do hundreds of others who leave the Church and return to the States, or emigrate to California, escape? These robbers and murderers must be very dilatory, indeed, in carrying out their hellish object, "by special order of the Church," if they have robbed and murdered no one. Strange that one hundred thousand people could live in a territory year after year, and not even an average of one murder annually happen among them. Strange, that an organized band "*set apart by special order of the Church*" to the high calling of murder and robbery, should not be able to compete with the unorganized murderers among the civilized and pious Christian nations. Nay; not even to kill one-fiftieth part as many as are murdered in civilized California? One would naturally suppose that there would be somebody, every now and then, mysteriously disappearing; that the property robbed would be discovered. But here we have the wonderful anomaly of a band of robbers and murderers, but no one murdered or missing; no plundered property found or identified.

Lie 4. "That the records, papers, &c., of the Supreme Court have been destroyed by order of the Church, with direct knowledge and approbation of Governor B. Young, and the federal officers grossly insulted for presuming to raise a single question about the treasonable act."

In other communications said to have originated with this slanderer, it is stated that about 900 volumes of the laws of the United States were burnt. Though we have had no information in relation to this accusation, only what originated with Drummond, yet we do not hesitate to pronounce this, also, a wicked, malicious falsehood. We are too well acquainted with the good people of Utah, and with the frank, open-hearted, liberal principles of Governor Young, to believe, for one moment, that either his Excellency or the Church would be guilty of such a low, mean, contemptible act, as the one laid to their charge in this statement. The very acts of the Governor and Legislative Assembly of the territory, during the past winter, prove the falsehood of this charge. The principal business of the Assembly, during the late session, has been to select and compile from the Acts of Congress all laws or parts of laws, in the least degree applicable to Utah, or other American Territories, so that the same might be condensed into one volume, that the citizens of the territory might the more readily learn the United States' laws governing them. Does this look like wishing to burn and destroy the laws of Congress? Does this appear like acknowledging *"no law save the law of the Holy Priesthood?"* As well might Drummond have accused the Mormons of burning the Congressional Library in the Capitol at Washington City, as to have charged them with this dastardly lie. But it is of a similar character to his other absurd slanders.

Lie 5. "That the Federal officers of the territory are constantly insulted, harassed, and annoyed by the Mormons, and for those insults there is no redress."

That Drummond might have been "insulted, harassed, and annoyed," scorned, derided, and hated, for his criminal connections with his picked-up harlot, we do not feel disposed to doubt. But that any decent, half respectable Federal officer was ever "insulted, harassed, and annoyed by the Mormons," is entirely false. Indeed, Chief Justice L. H. Reed, and his successor Chief Justice J. T. Kinney, both speak in the highest terms of praise of their cordial reception among the Mormons. Associate Justice Z. Snow received such a cordial welcome that he fell in love with the people and their doctrines and joined the Church of the Saints, and is now an able missionary of our doctrine in South Australia. Associate Justices George P. Stiles and Leonidas Shaver were received with the greatest marks of respect, and highly honored by the Governor and all the inhabitants. All these Federal Officers, with many others, have given the most unequivocal testimony directly in opposition to the slanderous absurdities of Drummond.

Lie 6. "That the Federal Officers are daily compelled to hear the form of the American Government traduced, the chief executives of the nation, both living and dead, slandered and abused from the masses, as well as from all the leading members of the Church, in the most vulgar, loathsome, and wicked manner that the evil passions of man can possible conceive."

The annual enthusiasm of one hundred thousand Mormons in celebrating the 4th of July—the day of the American Independence—gives the lie to this 6th charge of Drummond. If "the masses," and all the leading members of the Church slander and abuse "the chief executives of the nation," how did it happen that they named two or three of their counties in honor of these distinguished men? or that they named the capital city of Utah—FILLMORE, in honor of that illustrious President? That there may have been individuals in Utah who have been displeased with some of the acts of the American Presidents, and who have freely expressed their opinions in relation to the same, we do not doubt. But are the Mormons in Utah the only ones in the American nation that exercise the freedom of speech? Do all the States and Territories speak in the highest terms of respect of their "chief executives?" or do the different political parties traduce and abuse them, both verbally and in their periodicals? We do not hesitate to say, that there is not a State or Territory in the American Union, but what abuses, vilifies, and reproaches the chief Magistrate more in one week, than the citizens of Utah would do during the whole term of his administration.

The next accusation is that Governor Young exercised the legal authority vested in him by the United States, in pardoning two criminals sentenced to the Penitentiary. Is this the first case that has happened, where Governors of States and Territories have exercised their executive authority in the pardon of criminals? Who does not know that this is of very frequent occurrence throughout the whole Union?

The next charge is that the civil and legal Courts of Utah have sentenced five or six young men, who were guilty of no crime, to the Penitentiary. If Drummond had been tried for his notable crimes, and by the law sentenced to imprisonment, we have no doubt that he would have pleaded not guilty. The Courts of Utah have too much respect for the law to imprison any person not guilty of crime. The court records will show the crimes for which all convicts are sentenced. Moreover, the United States Supreme Court for that territory has power to reverse or confirm the decisions of the lower courts; this is a thorough preventative against unjust, illegal imprisonments.

The next lie Drummond has worded as follows:—"I also charge Governor Young with constantly interfering with the federal courts, directing the grand jury whom to indict and whom not, and, after the judge's charge to the grand juries as to their duties, that this man Young invariably has some member of the grand jury advised in advance as to his will in relation to their labors, and that his charge thus given is the only charge known, obeyed, or received by all the grand juries of the federal courts of Utah Territory."

The following facts will show the utter impossibility of this malicious lie having even the semblance of truth. In the first place the territory of Utah embraces a large tract of country some six hundred miles in length, and three hundred and fifty in breadth, including an area of about two hundred and twenty-five thousand square miles. Many large settlements of towns, villages, and cities have been promiscuously formed throughout this large domain. This whole territory has been divided into three judicial districts; and the United States Judges are each assigned to a district, in which he holds his federal courts at different times and places. Grand juries are appointed in about twenty counties. Now, we ask, how would it be possible for Governor Young to communicate with all these grand juries, dispersed through so large a territory, frequently sitting simultaneously at the distance of four, five, and six hundred miles from each other? It must be recollected that there are no railroads or *telegraphic wires* in the territory, and frequently whole months pass away without any news or communication between the distant settlements, where grand juries are sitting. And yet, in the face of all these impossibilities, Governor Young is represented as controlling the decisions of "*all the grand juries of the Federal Courts of Utah Territory!*"

Wonderful man, this Governor Young! to have such extraordinary powers! Only think of the marvelous wonder of being in twenty counties at the same time, prying into all the intricate cases of each of the grand juries, and controlling their decisions! But, then, all this must be true, say popular editors, for the great, the immaculate judge Drummond says so!

The next charge is penned as follows:—

"Again, sir, after a careful and mature investigation, I have been compelled to come to the conclusion, heart-rending and sickening as it may be, that Captain John W. Gunnison and his party of eight others, were murdered by the Indians in 1853, under the order, advice, and direction of the Mormons; that my illustrious and distinguished predecessor, the Honorable Leonidas Shaver, came to his death by drinking poisonous liquors, given him under the order of the leading men of the Mormon Church in Great Salt Lake City; that the late Secretary, A. W. Babbitt, was murdered on the plains, by a band of Mormon marauders, under the particular and special order of Brigham Young, Heber C. Kimball, and J. M. Grant, and not by the Indians, as reported by the Mormons themselves, and that they were sent from Salt Lake City for that purpose, and that only; and as members of the Danite band, they were bound to do the will of Brigham Young, as the head of the Church, or forfeit their lives."

The causes which led the Indians to murder Captain Gunnison and his party, including *some Mormons*, are too well known to need any comments from us. We merely state that some wicked "Gentile" California emigrants wantonly murdered some one or more of the Indians, and the latter in revenge murdered some of the Mormons, together with Captain Gunnison, and some of his party. It is very strange, indeed, that Chief Justice Kinney, and other Federal Officers who have diligently inquired into these Indian murders, have never made the heart-rending discovery, that they were all perpetrated "under the order, advice, and direction of the Mormons." About what time did this runaway criminal form his "heart-rending conclusions?" Was it while he was in the territory, or after he had fled from justice? In regard to the highly respected, Honorable Leonidas Shaver, we take pleasure in saying, that the Governor, and all the inhabitants of the territory who were acquainted with his sterling integrity and upright course in his official capacity, considered him as an ornament to society, and an honor to the Federal Government who had appointed him to that distinguished position. His death, though long expected from his excessive, constant, and long-habituated use of opium, caused the tear of mourning to fall from many an eye. His loss was deeply deplored by the whole community, and his funeral was attended by the highest honors. We, ourselves, were solicited by the Honorable Chief Justice Kinney to preach the funeral sermon of this distinguished federal officer. His loss was still more keenly felt, when contrasted with the heart-sickening, beastly conduct of his successor, who has the unblushing impudence to state that his "predecessor came to his death by drinking poisonous liquors, given him under the order of the leading men of the Mormon Church. Drummond has not told us how he himself was murdered by the Mormons. If he had reported his own death to the Attorney General, we presume that there would have been editors wicked enough to have pronounced it all truth. Next, we are gravely told that "the late Secretary of the Territory, A. W. Babbitt, was murdered on the plains by a band of Mormon marauders, under the particular and especial order of Brigham Young, Heber C. Kimball, and J. M. Grant, and not by the Indians."

Now, where did this murder happen! Answer: some seven hundred miles from Salt Lake City. Who committed this murder?

Answer: the same persons who fell upon several trains of emigrants, and indiscriminately butchered men, women, children, and infants. But who were they? The Cheyenne Indians have confessed that they themselves were the murderers; and that they did it in retaliation for the lives of those whom the United States troops had shot down. These same Indians state that Babbitt fought for his life, like a grizzly bear; but that they *tomahawked* him; and that they shot Sutherland (a Mormon), who was with Babbitt; and that having killed the same number of whites that the troops had killed of Indians, they were satisfied to make peace, which they did with the United States officers at Fort Laramie. With all this contradictory evidence, public and before the world, this Don Quixote of a judge pretends to report that Danite Mormons came seven hundred miles, being sent *"by the particular and special order"* of Governor Young and others, "for that purpose and that only." Why did not Drummond tell us that the Mormons, and not the negroes, last winter, murdered the southern slaveholders in the United States? that the Mormons poisoned Bonaparte on the Island of St. Helena? and that the Mormons, and not the English, destroyed the Russian armies, during the late war with the Western Powers? Such assertions could not have failed in finding believers, especially if backed up by the denunciations of popular newspapers, such as the *London Times*, *London Illustrated News*, *&c*. "But," says Drummond, "I could, sir, *if necessary*, refer to a cloud of witnesses to attest the reasons I have given, and the charges, bold as they are, against those despots who rule with an iron hand their hundred thousand souls in Utah, and their two hundred thousand souls out of that notable territory."

O don't, Judge Drummond, "refer to a cloud of witnesses;" it's not *"necessary."* Your word alone is abundantly sufficient! and then only think—the "lives" of these witnesses would be in such imminent danger! O, spare them! their lives *"would not be safe for a single day!"* especially the witnesses in California, where they have only a single state to protect them! O, don't betray their innocent blood! for who can doubt your word? it's so reasonable—so consistent—so very probable—so agreeable to priests and editors! it would be such a pity to spoil it with *unnecessary witnesses!*

MR. THOMAS BULLOCK, IN REPLY TO JUDGE DRUMMOND'S CHARGES.

London, May 3, 1857.

Elder Orson Pratt,—Dear Brother,—

Having read in the *Times* a long letter from Judge Drummond on the subject of "burning the laws of Utah Territory," &c., I feel to write a few of my ideas, and, perhaps they may be of benefit.

When the Pioneers went to the great basin of the Rocky Mountains, in 1847, it belonged to the Government of Mexico, and as Mexican land we entered it, and took possession.

In the spring of 1848, a treaty of peace was made at the close of the war, which ceded the land to the United States.

When the emigration from the United States arrived there in 1848, the people in solemn assembly made a Constitution, organizing that land into "The State of Deseret;" they sent a delegate to Congress, and made laws to govern the people; among those laws was one, incorporating the Church of Jesus Christ of Latter-day Saints, with all their religious forms and ceremonies; and granting equal protection to all other religious denominations.

The Congress of the United States afterwards granted a constitution, organizing the same boundaries into the territory of Utah, and empowered the Governor of that territory to order a census to be taken, on which, to apportion the members of the legislature.

The Legislature of Utah was organized according to the Organic Act, and they reconfirmed all the laws of the State of Deseret, which were applicable to Utah Territory.

At the close of the session of 1855, a feast was given by the Honorable Secretary, A. W. Babbitt, when Chief Justice Kinney, the Assistant Judges and Attorney General, bore testimony to the good and wise laws, enacted for the government of Utah. And they also bore testimony to the loyalty of her people as American citizens, and of their integrity and morality, socially, politically, and religiously.

The Utah laws, as published to the world, were sent to the Congress of the United States, (who had the repealing power,) and were approved. * * * *

I have no knowledge of any books or laws having been burned in Utah, either with or without Governor Young's knowledge or consent, and such a thing could not have transpired without my knowledge, up to the time of my leaving there last fall, which was after Drummond left for California.

In the session of '55–6, which sat at Fillmore City, a few amendments were found necessary, and made. Judge Drummond frequently sat within the bar, and made suggestions to the members; those suggestions were discussed, and adopted when found necessary; thus, I consider, that Utah Territory had as concise, and perfect a set of laws to govern the people, as their situation required.

In regard to the charge of murder of Mr. Secretary Babbitt, Mr. Margetts and others, the company of men who crossed the plains with me last fall, first heard of the massacre on the 24th of September, at *Independence Rock*. On the 3rd of October we passed the Indian agency a few miles east of fort Laramie, where eighteen lodges of the Indians were camped, and who wanted to be at peace. We were told at fort Laramie, and also by the Indian agent, that they were the men who had killed the whites, and that they acknowledged to having done it, in retaliation for a number of Indians who had been killed near Fort Kearney by the United States troops. They warned us, fearing that we were too few in number to pass through the Indian country in safety. Thus do I know that Drummond published an abominable falsehood. As to the charge of the Mormons having given the lamented Honorable Judge Leonidas Shaver "poisonous liquors which caused his death," is known to be a deliberate, wicked lie. As I was the Inspector of liquors for the Territory of Utah, I am knowing of the fact that he bought the greater portion of the liquors that he drank from Mssrs. Livingston and Kinkead, merchants in Great Salt Lake City, since 1849; and who are not members of the Mormon Church; and it is well known by the people in Utah, both Saints and sinners, that Judge Shaver did not, at the time of his decease, lodge with Mormons, neither was his doctor a Mormon; he got his drugs from the United States; the person who opened the window and found him dead, the greater of the witnesses and the jury on the coroner's inquest, were not Mormons; but the Mormons universally lamented his death; and now we see, that if it had pleased Almighty God, that his life had been spared, Utah Territory would not have been cursed with such a despicable, immoral, lewd man as Drummond has proved himself to be.

I indignantly deny the unblushing falsehoods made in the letter of Judge Drummond, and declare to all who read this letter, that the day will come, when in the presence of assembled millions, his lies will be made manifest, and then will also be manifest whether this letter be true or not. Governor Young's conduct will then be known to all the world, and the lies of his traducers manifestly revealed, when they are sent to receive their reward.

O Lord, enable me to do my duty, as faithfully as Governor Young has done his.

I have been as brief as the subject will allow me, therefore please excuse.

I remain, dear brother Pratt,
Yours, very obediently,
THOMAS BULLOCK.

Formerly Clerk of the House of Representatives of Utah Territory. [We have been personally acquainted with Elder Thomas Bullock for many years, and know him to be a man of truth and veracity, and we recommend all candid inquirers after information from Utah, to peruse his letter. Elder Bullock is an Englishman by birth, who embraced the Gospel, and emigrated to America, his adopted country, some twelve or fourteen years ago. He is lately from Utah, on a mission to his native land.—ED. *Star.*]

TO PRESIDENTS OF CONFERENCES.

Presidents of Conferences will please to use their influence in sending our answer to Judge Drummond's Report, or any other articles of interest in any of our other periodicals, to editors of papers, respectfully requesting them to publish them. Editors are complaining that it is very difficult to obtain anything reliable about Mormonism. Give them every opportunity which they desire. The excitement is so great that any reliable information on this subject gives increased sale to their respective papers.—ED. *Star.*

NEWS FROM UTAH.

The latest mail brought a variety of news, letters, &c., too large to include in this issue. The letter from President Young, &c., will appear in our next. We quote a little from the *Mormon:*—

We have this week another mail from Utah giving accounts until February 25. The most stirring and refreshing intelligence is the Reformation, and its good effects upon the community. Arrangements on a grand scale are entered into for the successful prosecution of the public works. About 300 men have engaged to labor on the Big Cottonwood canal to bring the block to the temple and water for city use.

The Deseret Agricultural and Manufacturing Society have already published the list of premiums to be awarded at the second annual exhibition—to take place in October next—for *stock*—field crops—vegetables—fruits and flowers—farming implements—agricultural machines and machinery.

The Utahns had only learned of the election of President James Buchanan, and, of course, are still in glorious ignorance of their extensive preparations for war, their awful outrages upon five or six American citizens from Missouri and Iowa, their tortures of the dumb boy, and their profanation and sacrilege (isn't it?) in burning 700 volumes of law. What wicked folks these Utahns must be, to do all that and never know anything of it till that slush-pot and "slanderer," the N. Y. *Tribune,* gets to their Territory—the echo of the "horse-trader judge," Drummond. We may as well add here that the poor "horse-trader" has got out another letter. He has addressed the widow of Captain Gunnison, and adds to his former charges, the names of the persons who he believes accomplished the bloody deed under the guise of Indians. A person so charged, now in this state, (New York,) informed us the other day of his intention to prosecute Drummond, as he can prove that he was in California at the time of Gunnison's murder. If the others charged thought him worth notice and any chance of getting at him, the "horse-trader judge" would cut another figure in the courts here than when the Washington lady sat by his side with him on the bench in the Fillmore Court.

Won't some of the pious get up special prayers for poor Drummond? Poor man, he ought to be an object of commiseration. He has got himself into a tight spot worse than that of Peck, and he knows it; and what is worse for his peace of mind, he knows that we know it, and are likely to give, one of these first days, the advantage of our knowledge, as widely as he has spread his fulsome calumnies.

TO DRUMMOND AND HIS COMPANY.

Arch-blasphemer—squanderer of the truth—is Drummond
    His look in every lie;
  This hellhound, before long,
  With vengeance will be paid.

His own remarkable stench—without slander!
    Has become painful to Satan;
  Every devil calls him unclean—
  His character is black—and his fate is the blackest.

Hark! The shout of the editors,—Priests,
    And the fairground of Reverends!
  Their dull words—rough wave—
  Carnage of angry enemies!

The prop of the "Mormons" of Utah,—is their God,
    He will hold them in contempt,
  The song of Zion is this,—ha, ha,
  O happy Hallelujah.

DEWI ELFED.

LETTERS FROM THE VALLEY.

Great Salt Lake City,
February 5th, 1857.

Dear Brother Daniels,

I am ashamed that I have not written to you more often, but the irregularity of the mail is enough to discourage anyone from taking pen in hand to write. My family and I are well, as is your family also: I see sister Daniels every week, since I am preaching the reformation among the Welsh in this neighborhood. Capt. Jones and Jeremy are my fellow missionaries. We are teaching the Welsh to purge out all wickedness, and determine to serve God from now on. We are encouraging them to learn English, and not to keep speaking Welsh, since that is an obstacle for persons learning another language. I would be glad to hear that the Welsh in the old country are following this practice as well.

Presently we are having a lovely time here while all are striving to serve God, and keep his commandments. The first love we had for the Gospel is returning, and the kingdom of God is foremost in the minds of the people. The ungodly are shaking, and inventing a way they can escape from our midst.

The entire Church throughout this Territory is determining to purify and cleanse themselves, so they may receive abundantly the blessings of the Lord. My heart is full, and I would love to write more to you, and to my brothers, the Welsh Saints; but time does not permit at present. Nevertheless, I will say this: to all who wish to come here, do not come in order to get rich, or to better themselves, but only for the sake of the truth. Love for the truth ought to be our principle objective; and let other things come as they may.

> "Seek ye first the kingdom of God,
>   Seek not the wealth of the world;
> Seek ye the greater treasure,
>   The rest will still be found."

It is quite likely that many will leave in the spring, for it is getting too hot for them to remain among those who are determined to serve God. My family and I are determined to stick with the Church, come what may; and I know that we will be blessed if we do that. Let the world mock as they wish, and let them rage as they will, God is with us, and the victory is ours.

Remember me kindly to all the Saints, and especially to yourself; and don't fail to write back.

Yours in the truth,
JOHN S. DAVIS.

Ogden City, October 20, 1856.

My dear Brother and Sister, and your families,—

I am happy to be able to inform you that my family and I arrived safely at the end of our journey on the second of this month, at which time we were welcomed with a sumptuous meal prepared for us, which contained a variety of delicious fruits of the Valley.

We started on the 30th of July from Florence, with our handcarts, as many faithful as there were, leaving the faithless and weak-hearted to face the consequences of their slothful ways.   *   *   *   *   *

Those of our company who died were Sister Brookes, from the North; Henry Jenkins, Merthyr; Abraham Evans, and one from Pembrokeshire, together with one from Scotland, and a child of Anne Williams, Llanelli. With the exception of the first, they all died after reaching the Great Salt Lake Valley. Henry Jenkins and Edward Phillips, Cardiff, also died.

We had an unusually successful journey across the plains and through the mountains, and the weather was splendid. We did not have snow along the way, but a snowstorm hit the wagon companies which were ahead of us. The storm kept up for 24 hours and 18 of their animals died. By the time we reached the mountains the winter had turned into cheerful spring for us; consequently, we overtook the wagons and left them behind. They were six months, and we only two on the same journey: all of which makes manifest the watchful care of the Lord over his poor Saints with handcarts. Alma and Joan were with me and my dear wife to pull the entire way: Elisabeth, Mari, and Margaret walked the entire way. Sometimes we traveled 30 miles per day.

The necessary clothing in order to come with the handcarts is one warm suit and one light one. The *luggage* allowed for adults is 17 pounds each, and 10 for those under 14 years of age. The wagons carry *extra luggage* across for 6¼c. per pound.

We are living in Ogden City, 40 miles from Great Salt Lake City; I have worked gathering potatoes for a week, and have earned from 11 to 12 dollars, (£2 5 10 to £2 10,). John Edwards, earlier from Cwmbach, has been very kind to me.   *   *   *   *   *

There is an abundant harvest of wheat, corn, potatoes, &c., together with all kinds of fruits. [What does the *Gwron* say now about the grasshoppers, I wonder.—ED.]

The price of wheat is two dollars a bushel; flour, three cents a pound; potatoes, a dollar a bushel.   *   *   *   *   *

Hoping that this information will be useful to you, and hoping that you are living united with your religion, I close with fond regards from all of us,

Your dear Brother,
HOPKIN MATTHEWS.

P. S.—The Welsh who came across the plains with the handcarts this year received the highest praise from the Prophet Brigham Young at the Conference.—H. M.

Payments for Publications from April 30 to May 29.—Isaac Jones, £1 2s. 7c.; John Jones, Brecon, 10s.; E. D. Miles, £2 0s. 3c.; John Davies, £4; John Treharne, £1 4s. 1c.; David John, £5; Michael Vaughan, £5; W. Ajax, Denbigh, £1. Total, £19 16s. 11c.

We intend to publish the Articles that are in this issue about Drummond in the form of a *pamphlet*, so the Saints may distribute them as widely, if they can, as the circulation achieved by the disgraceful publications in opposition, without selling their Trumpets, and breaking their volumes, &c., and let every President visit as many editors who may be in his area, acting as President Pratt instructs.—Ed. of the *Trumpet*.

CONTENTS.

	PG.
Judge Drummond, &c.	177
Letter on the same topic	185
News from Utah	188
Verses to Drummond	188
Letters from the Valley	192

SWANSEA:
PRINTED AND PUBLISHED BY DANIEL DANIELS.

ZION'S TRUMPET,

OR

Star of the Saints.

No. 13.]　　　　JUNE 13, 1857.　　　　[Vol. X.

LETTER FROM PRESIDENT B. YOUNG

President's Office,
Great S. L. City.
March 1, 1857.

President Orson Pratt,

Dear Brother,—Since we last wrote to you, but little of public note has occurred. The contract for carrying the *mail* from here to Independence, United States, has fallen to Hiram Kimball and others, of this city, at 23,000 dollars per annum, for four years; and these gentlemen have so arranged this matter, that it is expected it will be subject to our direction. On the 8th of last month we sent out the first mail eastward, in charge of eight men, W. H. Hickman, conductor; they had much snow to pass over, but we doubt not they have overcome these difficulties, and are now near the States.

O. P. Rockwell, with a full complement of men, will carry out this mail, and commence operations for establishing an "Express and Carrying Company," for the transportation of goods and passengers—building stations on the way; and by having a change of mules at these stations, we purpose making the trip across the Plains regularly in twenty days.

Thus our merchants, and those who can advance the means, can have their goods in large or smaller quantities, as they may order. Eventually this may destroy the merchants' trade, for who

[Price 1½c.

will give 40 cents per pound for sugar and coffee, when they can send on their means and orders, and have it delivered here for 25 or 26 cents, and other things in proportion. And as our *passenger* and goods *trains* will all be mule teams, traveling 50 miles per day, who that has means in England, or in the States, will now be at the trouble of buying wagons and ox teams, and be three months on the Plains, wearied in body and harassed in mind; when he can take his passage and that of his family by these *express mail trains*, accompanying which he may have any amount of freight conveyed, at a lower rate, more speedily, and with far less trouble, than he could by any other means transport his family and goods? No one.

I call your attention to this subject, that you may counsel those who have means to come by these *cars, via* Independence, Missouri.

Can you inform us what has become of the Saints who were engaged as soldiers in the Crimean war?

The spring opens with more favorable prospects for abundance than we have witnessed for some years, and we think the people are in a better state to receive, appreciate, and enjoy heaven's blessings.

My own health is good, and improves as the season opens, so also is it with brothers Heber C. Kimball, Daniel H. Wells, and Joseph Young, senior.

Brother Horace S. Eldridge goes on to St. Louis, and will relieve brother Erastus Snow. Brother Eldridge will continue to act as our agent there.

I do not recommend any more emigration by New Orleans, St. Louis, and the southern route. I recommend the Boston route, Chicago, and Iowa, since the northern route is the most healthy. At any time when you have *passengers* or freight, or are likely to have, notify us through our agents at St. Louis and Florence, and we can inform the conductors, so you can have the passengers intersect our cars at some convenient point, to be named hereafter. Our *mail agent* will generally reside at Independence. The railway through to Council Bluffs will be completed this year, and then we hope they can have a speedy through *passage* from the east.

Ultimately, we calculate on having stations every 50 miles, and provisions, feed, &c., there. We shall establish a few of such this year. Thus you will perceive a man and his family with small means can walk from station to station, and have his supplies renewed at every such place, without encumbering himself with very heavy loads at the first, the time when he is least accustomed to such travel, nor so well able to endure as he afterwards can.

May an additional portion of intelligence and the spirit of truth, excelling the wisdom of man, and the blessings of peace, health, and prosperity, be and abide with you.

BRIGHAM YOUNG.

CONFERENCE ACCOUNTS, &c.

The West Glamorgan Conference was held at the Saints Hall, Orange Street, Swansea.

President D. Daniels and the Conference Presidency were present.

In the morning meeting it was unanimously covenanted to acknowledge and obey all the authorities of the Church, from the Prophet Brigham down to the Presidents of Conferences.

President Davies commented about the beneficent effects of the Reformation, and the necessity of continuing to preach the Reformation and reforming. He was strengthened in this by numbers of the different presidents who reported the condition of their Branches.

At two in the afternoon, President Davies taught in detail on the word of Wisdom, and on the necessity of adding workers to the field of the world in this Conference—that the field was great and the workers were few—dozens of villages containing hosts of inhabitants, starving for the word of God, and he encouraged the Elders and Priests to shout long and loud until the people hear the sound of the Gospel of Christ.

President Daniels followed him, earnestly expounding on the same topic, and commenting on the blessings and the lovely place of rest that will be enjoyed after completing the journey, and the shortness of time to work, for it is God's hour of judgment.

At six in the evening Elders D. Davies, Llanelli, and W. Powell,

Llwyni, preached plainly and clearly on the first principles—the former in Welsh, and the latter in English.

The number of members of the Conference [according to the rules of the Reformation] is 148.

JOHN DAVIES, *President.*
WM. RICHARDS, *Scribe.*

The East Glamorgan Conference, was held at the Cymreigyddion Hall, White Lion, Merthyr Tydfil, May 24, 1857.

At half past ten o'clock, after opening the Conference with singing and prayer, President A. S. Williams said:—Beloved brothers and sisters: we have met together again in a conference. It is a time of building in this work, and, as we know, logically, there is no value on a building without taking the trouble to build it; there must be work, or the building will never be finished. The Kingdom of God is on the earth, and it will never again be taken from the earth. It is now being built for the last time; and there is plenty of space in it for each one to do his best, as much as he can, and to increase in ability continually—in preaching out of doors on the streets to those who have not perceived anything of the excellence of this work; but we who have understood a little of the Kingdom of *God* have the power to put them on the way. He encouraged the Saints to pray for a great portion of the Spirit of God, so that we could be in a good place throughout the day; and for all to feel edified as we leave."

President William Miller—A Saint is known by the look on his face, and I feel happy in the belief that you are happy as well. We are inquiring to know your feelings in connection with the authorities of the Church, which are directly before you. The great purpose to which we have to reach out is, to live up to our religion—Saints, live your religion, or you will fall by the wayside; keep the Word of Wisdom. Some complain that I have been quite strict in the Conference before; I do not seek to flatter anyone, but to put the truth before them in its proper color, as pure as it is; that is the way, and if some do not accept it after that, where are they going? To Heaven? No; but on the path that pertains to disobedience. But as for me, I seek to live with the faithful—die with the faithful— and be resurrected with those, and be glorified with them. Inasmuch as the *Reformation* has begun, Saints, let us strive, and live our religion.

The authorities of the Church were put before the congregation, and all covenanted unanimously to pray for them, and give them complete obedience.

Then the report of the Conference was read by the Scribe as follows:—Elders 157, Priests 40, Teachers 22, Deacons 29, Baptized 35, Received 44, Transferred 12, Cut off 3, Died 2, Emigrated 3, Total 607.

Some very lively and beneficial teachings were presented by Eld. Dd. Rees, Aberaman, who rejoiced in the Reformation, exhorting us to live according to it as well.

Eld. S. Roskelley:—There have been happy feelings inside me throughout the day, especially in this meeting, and whenever a man speaks under the influences of the Holy Ghost, he is bound to speak good and solid doctrine, the same as that given by President Miller today, though rather rough and rugged to the view, yet true. God's way is rough, and not like the ways of the world generally, to please and tickle the fancy or the imagination. You cannot have this in an Elder of Israel. Like President Miller, I do not feel inclined to engage in much flattering of men, but when a man comes into this Church I expect him to come completely in, and love the plain truth for what it is, and not in order to get some name, or profit and a living by that.

He exhorted the Saints to keep up side by side with the increase of the Church, in knowledge and understanding, knowing that if we are negligent, and turn aside to have a rest, that it will be hard work to come up and catch up with it again. He showed the necessity of keeping the word of Wisdom, and giving obedience to our Presidents, and governing our thoughts, our hearts, and our lusts, then we will be about right, and the Lord will bless us.

Eld. Dewi E. Jones, felt to be obedient to the priesthood

constantly, and for each one who sees a brother or sister down, to give help for them to get up, and if there is a spark of life in them, make it even brighter, so that we will emulate our Father whose bowels are filled with mercy.

President Miller:—I feel well here: it is Reformation time; and as I go about, I find that reforming is taking place, yet there is room to reform in many things. This is as scriptural as anything, namely, that he who helps himself is helped by God, and I ask who is willing to do according to the best of his ability? That is the one who is helped by God. Further, will he who makes no effort for the Penny Fund be saved? I answer, no; for it is on the principle I mentioned that God works, even though someone slips through, yet he will not stand. It is the clear and plain principles that we wish to set before you. No, he will not stand, for the hypocrite will fear and tremble in Zion. They are like that now; that place is too warm for anyone who does not serve God with his whole heart.

Many around here complain about things that do not pertain to them. If the path from here to Zion were closed, and if no one came to you from there to here, you would be as dead as a doornail; for the way would be closed between you and life; for it is in that place, among Prophets and Apostles, that life is to be obtained. I wish to impress on your minds the Word of Wisdom; the specific blessings in connection with keeping that, are the same as in the time of Israel, when sprinkling blood on the doorposts caused the destroying angel to pass by. And what are the promises in this age? Has not the Lord promised the same thing for those who keep the Word of Wisdom? Obey it; for *as the Lord liveth* if you do not, you will suffer from your disobedience.

With regard to keeping the Word of Wisdom, it is, in part, the power to rule: plagues and pestilences will visit the earth, as some have already done. The devil will have the freedom to test us, as he tested Job. Yes, he will; for it is the same Lord who lives and reigns, and He will grant permission to the evil one. Therefore, we ought to prepare, lest we fall under the tribulations, and so that we may remain unscathed while the wrath of Jehovah goes by.

Let us reform in all things—in carrying forth meetings and

many other things. One thing in particular I shall note: in some places I visit, I am requested to lay hands on the sick, bless children, set apart some to offices, or confirm some. I place my hands on the head of the brother or the sister, and other brethren place their hands with mine; then, after practically every word I say, my two ears ring with the heavy breathings of the brethren whispering their sealing amens. Reform in this matter: when I am praying, I wish for all to pray with me in their hearts, and keep all their amens to say together at the end of the prayer, instead of disturbing a man when speaking with his God.

We are to live our religion, and keep it up as noted—not falling to one side, and, after having a short rest, rising up, running and puffing to try to catch up, and perhaps, despite all our effort, being behind eternally.

Be in agreement with the principles of the kingdom as they come out, and enjoy the Spirit of the Lord: I feel it, and I know when I am feeling it.

Even though, in the present days, some men around us turn into apostates, and try to oppose this work, what can they do? If they only knew that God is at the helm, and that their frail arms cannot forestall his work, they would turn from their ways. The Lord pays no heed to them or to the devil; and if such characters do not turn from their ways, they will be trampled underfoot; for the power does not exist that can forestall this work. I know this: God is at the head, and were all the powers of the earth and hell gathered together to oppose it, they would all be a *blank*, yes, a *blank!* and God is certain to visit such men with vengeance, but not before His children are safe. Only the wicked will suffer; yes, the way is to be prepared for our deliverance. Then God will pour out his wrath and his anger on the wicked, the same as in Sodom; that time the Lord sent his angel down to proclaim his purposes, and through that Lot escaped; so it is again; do we not have Prophets? and when everything is ready will not the Lord proclaim to them his purposes, so that we may escape?

Keep the commandments of God, and live your religion, and I feel to say, May the Lord bless you, in the name of Jesus Christ. Amen.

Eld. Benjamin Evans spoke on the necessity of keeping, consecrated and unbroken, our covenants with God.

It was agreed that Elder Evan Richards be released as Traveling Elder in this Conference, so that he may go to travel through the Cardiff Conference.

In the evening meeting a good time was had, and strong and important sermons were preached by brothers Dewi E. Jones, S. Roskelley, Wm. Miller, Evan Richards, and President Williams, and then the Saints happily went their way, saying that this was the best Conference yet.

ABEDNEGO S. WILLIAMS, *President.*

ANEURIN L. JONES, *Scribe.*

ZION'S TRUMPET,
OR
Star of the Saints.

SATURDAY, JUNE 13, 1857.

NEWS FROM THE VALLEY.—We received the *Deseret News* up to April 1, and several letters to ourselves and others. We wish for all who received news of interest to the *public*, to send them to the *Trumpet*.

We quote from the letter of brother F. D. Richards:—

"After seeing our worthy brother D. Jones, I received proper understanding about the gift of the Welsh Saints to me and brothers D. Spencer and C. H. Wheelock. Therefore, I take this opportunity to present to you and the Saints in Wales grateful recognition from each of us, for the same, and to assure you and them that we are fully appreciative of the good feelings that prompted the deed. We feel to bless them, and say, that they will be blessed for single-minded generosity toward the welfare of the Kingdom of God, and for his servants, that that they will not be without their reward.

"Certainly it will be interesting for you to understand that the great work of God is increasing powerfully in this territory, and the dividing line is becoming more obvious daily. During the past winter, people have been striving to live more closely to God than they have perhaps since the rise of this Church in the latter days. They have done good wherever there was need; they have repented of all their sins, and have been re-baptized with great frequency. The result is that the meetings are overflowing; trust in the one and in the other, in the Priesthood, and in God, has greatly spread, and a visible foundation has been laid as a swift disclosure of the purposes of the Most High in relation to his kingdom on the earth. In Zion, sinners cannot exist much longer; rather everyone who lives on this sacred and favored land must adhere to the heavenly law.

"The influence which has been created here, will no doubt be felt to the extreme ends of the world where the Church has been established, and where the principles of salvation are being taught, adding more convincing proof to the fact that God surely has established his Kingdom among men, and that soon his Son Jesus will take the reins of government, until the exclusion of every earthly kingdom, and the complete terror and confusion of the ungodly. In view of these things the Saints have great pure and virtuous joy at the dawning of that day when he will reveal himself from Heaven to set his people free, and when he will be proclaimed king over the whole of it.

"I am glad to say, despite the scarcity of crops last year, and the one before, that there is a good base to believe that there is an abundance of wheat and some other kinds of produce for all the people until the next harvest. The storehouses of the Lord in this city are groaning under the weight of the tithes of this people, and yet the wheat, the corn, &c., are still coming in.

"Our dear Prophet, bro. Brigham, bro. Heber, and others, have testified that God has multiplied the fruits of the labor after they were gathered into the storehouses of the Saints; for after the last harvest, and before any flour was sent out to the emigrants on the Plains, it was thought by many that there would not be sufficient to continue any longer than April of this year. Why not increase the stores of the Saints? Were not the cruse of oil and the handful of meal of the widow in ancient times increased when God had a prophet on the earth to do his will? Yes, certainly; and will He be less mindful of his Saints in these days, when far more important things are coming to an end, than have ever been known since the creation of the world?

"In closing, I pray that God will bless you abundantly for the task that has been given you to facilitate his work, and over which he has made you steward. I hope that your health is good, as is mine and that of bro. Spencer; bro. Wheelock's health is a bit poor. They join with me in fond memories of you and your fellow laborers.

Yours faithfully,
F. D. RICHARDS."

AFTER looking carefully through the *Deseret News*, we failed to catch a glimpse of the least bit of news about the "*Mormon rebellion!*" "*Brigham Young has fled!*" killing or burning or anything of the kind, only talk of building the Kingdom of God in an orderly fashion. We see an invitation for 300 cultivators and stone masons to begin working, last April, on the public works,—an account of the hosts of workers on the Big Cottonwood canal—preparations for the "Freight Companies" to be established along the Plains, with every branch of commerce lively and full of work, and the sweetest of all is the variety of sermons of the Prophets and Apostles of Jesus, some of which we will quote as space permits. Concerning the religious condition of the people we shall not add to the account of brother F. D. Richards.

The following was *telegraphed* from Saint Louis to New York:—

"*News from G. S. Lake City*,
"St. Louis, May 18, 1857.

"The Utah overland letter-carrier arrived here with dates of Salt Lake from April 2.

"The Territory was peaceful. Preparations are being made to

send a considerable number of missionaries to all parts of the world.

"The accounts of the movements of Brigham Young do not agree with those received via California. It appears that he has the complete trust of the people, and was planning a pleasure excursion to the Mormon settlements along the Salmon River.

"For some reason the Mormons in San Bernardino are unaware of the surrounding settlements that have been erected around Great S. L. City.

"The Cheyenne (on the Plains) were becoming bold and defiant. A merchant who arrived from Fort Laramie reported that the Indians have acknowledged the loss of 60 warriors who were sent to carry out a slaughter on the California trail, because they have made prisoners of 16 merchants, and have sent 100 warriors to the trail noted to avenge the loss."

FAMINE.—*Detroit, May* 15, 1857.—An account was received here of the great destruction in Gratiot County, and other neighborhoods in the northern part of the State of Michigan. Several persons died of hunger, and the animals were perishing from need.—*Mormon.*

EARTHQUAKES.—Mention was made in our previous number of the California earthquake; we give, now, the following details from the *Deseret News:*—"Light earthquake tremors shook San Francisco on the 8th and 9th, and Sacramento on the 16th of January.

"An earthquake happened at Fort Tejon on the morning of the 8th of January. The shaking continued from three to five minutes, and it shook adobe walls and chimneys down. One woman (Mexican) was killed.

"EFFECT OF THE EARTHQUAKE.—Below Benson's Ferry, waters of the Mokelumne river, which was greatly swollen by the late floods, were thrown over the banks, leaving the stream bed nearly bare. Houses were severely shaken, glass things were destroyed, and furniture was thrown down. Branches were broken from trees; the trees in some instances were rooted down two or three feet in the ground. The inhabitants of the area were terror-stricken, while the dumb animals appeared to be paralyzed.—*Sacramento Age.*"

In January, and near the San Joaquin Ranch Mountains, California, a Sheriff by the name of Barton, and three of his company, were killed by highway robbers. The people of Los Angeles and the surrounding settlements had formed search parties, caught about 40 persons, and hanged 4.—*Los Angeles Star.*—[Strange that not one small fact of this kind ever came to light about the "secret oath-bound body" said to exist in Utah, is it not?—ED.]

CAPTAIN DAN JONES (says the *Deseret News*) has told us that he has begun to sail across our (Salt) lake in the 'Timely Gull,' built and owned by President Young, and that he anchored at the Black Rock dock, on the 13th [of March] with a "common shipload," which, for the most part, contained cedar wood, fine salt, and gravel for pathways, cellar floors, &c., which things he has for sale at Black Rock, also at his residence in the 14th Ward, for reasonable prices.

"Captain Jones informs us also that he has made arrangements to quarry an abundance of roof slates, which he thinks will compete with the price of currently used shingles. [A pleasant voyage to the old captain, may the breezes of heaven fill his sails, and may the God of Israel guide him and his ship along the way of success. We cannot give more about him in this issue.]

PAMPHLETS.—We are sending the 7th and 8th treatise of the new series with this issue. Although the series is not ending at this point, the author intended to take a break after the publication of the eighth number.

Through our previous trust and knowledge of the frugality and good organization of the presidents, the faithfulness of the Saints in paying their tithing to the Lord, we expect the Conferences to be close, if not completely free of this Office, although they are now in deep debt, so that we may pay the debt of the Office to the Church of God, *owner of all that we publish*, Orson Pratt, supervisor, while there is such a need and call for the money. The task will be far easier when there will be only the *Trumpet* every week, as far as we know at present.

We would like to have still more of those issues of the *Trumpet* of the previous volume about which we published some time ago, and it will be a kindness to us.

ACCOUNTS OF CONFERENCES, &c.
(*Continued from Page* 200.)

4, East Lane, Tredegar,
June 4, 1857.

President D. Daniels—Dear Brother,

We would have written to you sooner, but we were waiting for the Conference to be over, so that we could have the number of those baptized since the beginning of the Reformation. We had baptized thirteen new ones since the Reformation began. We had a very good conference this time. There was a very good influence throughout the day.

In the morning, we presented the authorities of the Church in the usual manner, and they were sustained unanimously. It was covenanted to contribute to the work according to their counsels.

In the morning bro. S. Roskelly taught that it was not wise for any of the Saints to beg any man to come forward. If men do not have the love for the work after once being in the Church, and receiving a witness of the truth, it would be better to let them go to hell to teach obedience. The meeting was closed under the blessing of Pres. Miller.

At two, bro. Harris taught, and showed that the Valley of the Mountains excels over this country in a great many things, like its airs, and its waters, and that it is much healthier. He also said that he is well acquainted with those who are the leaders of the people in that place—that they are good and godly men, and that they are the best men he has ever seen.

Then President Miller taught the Saints and the sinners that it was necessary for them to keep the law of God if they intend to have eternal life. He proved that from the Bible, with a powerful influence.

The number in this Conference is 190. I know of many others who are determined to come, and renew their covenant. At the end of this quarter I shall have brother Vaughan make a *list* of tithing money—how much has come in during the last six months, and that which has been spent, and for what I have paid, so that you will be able to see how we are going forward here. You shall also know how much debt we have, and whose it is.

Brother Miller has gone away to Cardiff. Francis is here with me at present.

BENJAMIN EVANS.

CONFERENCES OF THE NORTH.
(From the *Weekly Gazette* of Pastor Jones.)

Denbigh, June 1, 1857.

Last week Bro. Taylor and I were around here, preaching when time and place permitted. We had a very good conference yesterday; several of the brothers and sisters came together, and the Spirit of God was in our midst in great abundance, and all were very content—Bro. Taylor as happy as any of us. We had two meetings indoors, and two out in the middle of town; one at half past four in the afternoon, and the other at half past seven; and we had hundreds listening to us, some believing a little, and several greatly in doubt. The animosity is increasing daily, everywhere we go. Babylon is filling its cup every day; yet I think that when the day comes that the Saints will leave this land unexpectedly, they will open their eyes in surprise, saying, "Wait a little while, we are coming now." This is the story that I expect; after that they will have a greater desire to have servants of God in their midst than we had, perhaps to go to them.

It is quite likely that were the men to know of the blessings available to them they would be good now, but they are not. We are working out our salvation, and doing so by faith. I frequently tell the Saints that God deals with his children as an earthly father does. Sometimes he persuades his son to go to school; his son refuses, although he says to him, "If you go to school, and be a good boy, you shall have currant cake, and a penny when you come home." "No, I won't do it," says the little man. The father or the mother persuades him gently now; but upon seeing the child refusing to go through fairness, he then gets an angry look, grabbing the switch, and says sharply, "You must go, little man, and go now, without the cake or the penny either." So it is also with the gospel; its invitations now are gentle, and it is better to kiss the boy lest he get angry, and cause us and everyone else to shake against our will.

This Conference is a bit smaller than it was, as you see in Ajax's letter. The entire count throughout the Conference is 55. Last quarter many of the Brethren were out of work. All the collections from the last Conference until this one were only £6 9s. This has thrown us in arrears with your office and the Liverpool office. * * *

I can say that bro. Taylor is one of the best yet from among the English—happy with everything. We are like two oxen raised together from birth: all the Saints have great love for him. This week we shall be preaching throughout Flint as we can. The brethren we have out in the world are like giants; I shall be with them, and throughout the whole country as they, after the Conference of Bro. John. All the Saints are doing their duties, and all the officers are preaching everywhere. I am determined to complete my work this summer in this country.

J. E. Jones.

Denbigh, June 1, 1857.

Dear Brothers Daniels and Miller,—

I am managing splendidly among my adopted compatriots; for I feel myself as much a Welshman as anyone in the kingdom of God; for in it we are neither bond nor free, Jew nor Greek, English nor Welsh, but one in Christ Jesus through his gospel.

Well, I hope you are enjoying the best health as we *boys* in the North are at present.

We had an excellent Conference yesterday, and we preached out of doors in the town in the afternoon and evening, and we had hundreds listening to us. We have traveled through, and preached in several places this week. Generally, the people listen very attentively; but a rather wicked spirit appears in the young people, backed by the older people.

I don't believe the people of these areas have much need for much additional preaching to them; for I think that they feel as if they refuse us and the gospel we offer them: they feel very wicked toward us as a people.

The Saints up here are good people, and worthy of every blessing, and I feel more and more attachment to them every day. They work sincerely for their salvation, and they have a number of brave men out testing the world, and they are working in earnest like men of God.

When I observe how much the Saints do up here, with the little means and opportunity they have, I feel to say, may God bless them; for if ever there were a worthy people, they deserve to receive your blessing. They have been blessed with good men to preside over them—some of the grand men of the Lord, such as John E. Jones, J. Treharne, W. Ajax, David John, Hugh Evans, and others in whom I take delight.

We will begin traveling today to the Flint Conference, visiting the branches as we go along.

The overseas letter I received was from Iowa Camp, from Bro. Ashby. Everything is fine, and almost ready to start. Bro. Israel Evans was to lead the first handcart company to the Valley. Hurrah for Wales—all the people are well.   *   *   *

My regards to you and your counselors in the Office.

That you may have health, strength, wisdom, and power from on high, is the prayer of

Yours,
JAMES TAYLOR.

☞ THE verses of Dewi Elfed, and the letter from the Valley to Llanybydder, were too late for this issue. They will be just as interesting and welcome for us in our next.

CONTENTS.

	PG.
Letter of President Brigham Young	193
Conference Accounts	195, 205
Editorial—News from the Valley—Famine—Earthquakes—Murder—Condition of Captain Jones—Pamphlets	200

SWANSEA:
PRINTED AND PUBLISHED BY DANIEL DANIELS.

ZION'S TRUMPET,

OR

Star of the Saints.

No. 14.]   JUNE 27, 1857.   [Vol. X.

LETTERS FROM THE VALLEY.

Great Salt Lake City,
March 30, 1857.

My dear husband—I was thinking you would be released to return to the bosom of the Church, and to your dear family, this year; but by now I have been brought to understand through the *Mormon* that you have been appointed to stay in Wales another year. Although my fondest wish is to get to see you, yet, through the power of the Holy Ghost, I shall be content, and I pray daily for the will of God to be done in relation to your important mission.

    I hope that brother Henry Harris has arrived there safely by now: he will give a more complete account of things than I can do in writing in a letter. But there are some things that have happened after his departure from the Valley—there is constant work on the temple at present, and a call for all stonemasons within the Territory who can to make it expedient to come to work on it.

    Even more intensive are the teachings given by the teachers, day after day, and the pourings out of the Holy Ghost on the obedient are more abundant than ever before felt.

    The Lamanites are increasing in knowledge: some of them are having heavenly visions. The divine work is going forward remarkably well in every sense. Several have been

[Price 1½c.

called and are being called to go on a mission to England: there are two of the Welsh, Wm. P. Thomas, Box Elder, and Wm. Jenkins, formerly from Cardiff; and it is said that some others of the Welsh are to be called before the Conference is over. Dafydd and I are well, and everything is fine. Thomas and his wife are well and prospering: they have a daughter and two sons.

All the Welsh here without exception send their regards, and feel that your mission in Wales is a very long one. They join with me in praying for you to receive strength to be faithful in your mission, and for the time to come when we will have your pleasant association in the Valley of Salt Lake.

Presidents Young and Kimball, together with a large company of Saints, intend to go on an *exploring expedition* to the north. The home manufactories receive great support—woolen work is undertaken throughout the entire Territory, and all are encouraged to sow flax. The gentiles are generally leaving, and many of the unbelieving apostates are going with them. The time has come when the idler cannot eat the bread of the worker. The wicked and the hypocrite in Zion fear as they hear the law of God being taught. Purity and holiness are increasing, and unrighteousness and wickedness must vanish from the land.

It is intended to have an *express* to run back and forth from here to the States, beginning during this season. Several are being sent to settle in different places across the Plains for the task.

It is thought that the missionaries will travel with handcarts across the Plains from now on, and not with horses and mules.

Bounteous crops of wheat were obtained throughout the Territory last season, and there are good signs for a similar blessing this coming season. The grazing is excellent already, and there are signs of plenty of water to irrigate the lands. * * *

Yesterday brothers W. P. Thomas and Benjamin Thomas returned from here to Box Elder: they send their kind regards to you; so do bro. Capt. Jones, John Davis, T. C. Martill, Thomas and David Jeremy, Wm. Lewis, Thos. James, Owen Roberts, John Evans, and the rest of the Welsh who usually visit us. Remember me and Dafydd kindly to my sisters and their husbands and their families, to your brothers and sisters, and the aged woman, your mother, if she is still alive. Remember me to the Cwmcoch family, and Hannah Williams of the 'Masons': her son Richard sends his regards to them. Give my greetings to the family at Crybynau, Llawrbarth, &c. Brothers Jeremy and Martill send their regards to all the Saints with whom they are acquainted. Bro. J. Lewis, Sadler, formerly from Llanelli, is in the house at present, and wishes to be remembered to you. Brother Sam Thomas wishes for you to remember him and his family to his father, his brothers, and his sisters. He hopes to see Hannah his sister come across to the Valley. Remember him and his wife to Evan Jones: they hope they will see him in the Valley.

I wish for you to write as soon as you can,

Your obedient Wife,
MARY DANIELS.

Brigham City, Box Elder County,
February 15, 1857.

To Mrs. Mary Thomas, near Llanybydder.

My dear Mother, Sisters, &c.—Once again I and my family take pleasure in writing to you, hoping that you are healthy and happy as we are and have been ever since we came to this lovely place, thanks to Him who called me out of oppressive Babylon.

I received your kind letter for September 20, '56 within four months: the snow obstructed the mail carrier.   *   *

Although there is a lot of snow on the mountains, as usual, winter is lovely in the Valleys, where the Mormons are. The animals are fat, and play as I saw them do there in the summer.

I am obliged to always keep one mule in the stable for Evan to bring the cows home by nightfall, so the wolves will not devour them. They kill animals sometimes, if we are not careful: they killed two of my calves last year because of my carelessness, in part, and I said, Never again! Benjamin Thomas, formerly of Gelly Green, and I went to begin killing them, and we killed 30 of them in less than a month.

We had good crops last summer: I planted about half my wheat last fall; I intended to plant it all, but I took Margaret, Daniel and Mary Anne to S. L. City to meet the last company of immigrants who arrived, in which was our brother Dan Jones, who brought our money safely. * * *

I do not yet know for certain whether I will come back to Wales on a mission or not: I shall know before long. *All is right with me, as I am a Mormon.* If I do come, I am glad that my family is in a comfortable condition for support while I am there. Although I have cattle, oxen, mules, horses, &c., yet when I start off, I shall leave it all to my family, except for a few provisions, and a handcart to carry them across the vast expanse of the plains, where is practically no house or dwelling place except for the Indians. I shall start off in the strength of my God, having confidence that He will speak through me salvation to all that will accept it.

Since I have said so much about the plan of salvation, even if I do not have another chance, I am free, God is witness! Beloved mother! dear sisters! brother or brothers-in-law! Do not turn a deaf ear to the invitations of heaven while they are in your midst! Do not wait for me to come back; the invitations of heaven are the same through those who are there in your midst: go to hear them despite all the persecutions of the merchants of souls; yes, world, flesh, and devil. Go to wherever you can hear that the Latter-day Saints are preaching, for the sake of your eternal salvation. Go to listen to them; indeed they proclaim life or death to whoever hears them. * * *

When I received the money from brother Dan Jones, the rest of which I gave to brother Daniels to assist the poor Saints to come here, I felt sad that the part I received would not be assisting you, my dear mother or sisters, to come to the place where your well wisher is. I have sufficient for your transportation; it's just a matter of receiving the news that you have obeyed the Gospel of Christ, as I said before. I was believed in this by six persons from the Llanelli area, although they had never seen me before, and they are here presently blessing me for their deliverance. * * *

This briefly and disorganized from
    Your faithful son, and his family,
          WILLIAM THOMAS.

AMBUSH—MURDER
OF THE APOSTLE PARLEY P. PRATT.
(From the Star.)

ANOTHER Martyr has fallen—another faithful servant of God has sealed his pure and heavenly testimony to the truth of the Book of Mormon, with his blood. Though our own dear brother according to the flesh, yet we weep not. He fell in a righteous cause—he fell in the defense of suffering innocence, while endeavoring to aid by his letters a helpless female with her little children, to escape the fury of her savage persecutors. He had been made acquainted, from the most respectable and reliable sources, with the sad and most heart-rending description of her sufferings. Years ago, the poor woman had been turned into the streets of San Francisco, in a dark, dismal night, houseless and unprotected, by an unfeeling, brutal monster of a husband. For years her life had been threatened, and deadly weapons brandished about her head; and to cap the climax of brutality, he tore the children from their fond mother's embrace, stealing them, without her knowledge, and smuggled them on board a Pacific steamer, to traverse thousands of miles of water and land, unpitied and uncared for, to the distant port of New Orleans. This inhuman fiendish act, added to the long catalogue of her sufferings, made her resolve to renounce forever the society of one whom she could no longer look upon as a husband, but as a tyrannical, unfeeling, inhuman monster. The final separation took place at San Francisco about two years ago.

Learning that her children had been sent to her parents, near New Orleans, she set sail, friendless and unprotected, for that port. Upon her arrival, what was her surprise to find that her parents were in the dark plot, and that she could have no freedom with her own children. And, at length, becoming wearied with the persecutions which she endured, she started without any acquaintance to accompany her, for Utah Territory—a journey of about three thousand miles, from New Orleans. After incredible hardships she arrived in Great Salt Lake City, in the autumn of 1855. In the autumn of 1856, she again returned to her parents in New Orleans, and sometime about the close of last year, she succeeded in rescuing the children from their unnatural and tyrannical bondage, and fled with her own little family to Texas. But the hellish brute in California, from whom she had been separated about two years, came in pursuit; and having employed some of the old "Mormon" persecutors to join him in his bloodthirsty expedition, he, at last, discovered the object of his former abuse, and again tore from her embrace her lovely little children.

The sympathies of thousands who have been made acquainted with the unparalleled sufferings of this lady, have been aroused in her behalf. Among these, we are proud to say, was that great philanthropist, and good man, Parley P. Pratt, who, on learning the facts of her escape with her children, sought to advise her, by letters through the post, of the pursuit of her old enemy. While engaged in this work of humanity, this monster from California, swore out a writ against him and several others, under a false charge of larceny. They were tried before the United States Commissioner, at Van Buren, Arkansas, and found not guilty, and discharged. The murderer then, in a cowardly manner, waited for him to leave; and in about ten minutes after, in company with two other murderers, started in pursuit, immediately followed by others; all thirsting for the blood of innocence. About twelve miles from Van Buren on the road leading northward, they came up with their victim—fired seven shots, and then stabbed him several times in his left side, one of the cuts piercing his heart. After this he lived about two hours and a half.

And thus he fell the victim of his bigoted enemies, but the friend of suffering humanity.

The following correspondence, dated Cincinnati, Ohio, February 20th, 1857, taken from a New York paper, will give further particulars concerning—

THE MOTHER AND CHILDREN.—During my late missions to California, I became acquainted with the following train of lamentable and heart-rending circumstances, growing out of the spirit of intolerance, which, alas, still characterizes some of the more popular sects of the age.

A certain family had emigrated from the South a few years since, and were then residing in San Francisco; consisting of a man, his wife, and three children, and a young man who was a brother of the wife and a boarder in the family.

The whole were a branch of an old and somewhat noted Presbyterian stock, which still resided in the vicinity of New Orleans.

The lady was an accomplished and educated person, given to reading and intellectual pursuits; and was withal, a woman of sound judgment, and of an independent turn of mind.

As is generally the case with such minds, this lady had only to investigate Mormonism in order to become most firmly convinced of its truths.

She therefore wished to embrace them. On learning these facts, the husband and brother manifested a most violent and tyrannical opposition. They raged, foamed, cursed, railed, stormed, and called hard names, &c., but all to no purpose. The lady was still of the same mind, and wished to obey the Gospel.

The husband finally purchased a large *sword cane* with which he entered the parlor one day; and, turning pale with rage, he unsheathed the same in the presence of his wife, and menacing her and brandishing the naked steel over her head, swore with an awful oath, that that weapon had been purchased expressly for her, and the minister who dare baptize her, and should penetrate both their vitals the day she should be baptized.

Her brother, in turn, brandished the same weapon over her in the same angry manner, with the same threats.

These, and many other threats, railings, and abuses repeated from time to time, by both husband and brother, served to deter the lady's baptism for some two years—the Elders there making it a point not to baptize a woman without her husband's consent.

After many long, painful and prayerful struggles, she at length obtained a written consent of her husband and was baptized, and duly confirmed as a member of the Church of the Saints. She still remained a faithful and obedient wife and mother. She served her husband, looked after his interests, kept his house, continued to board her brother, and trained her children in the ways of obedience, morality, and truth. She took great pains in their education, and taught them to believe in Jesus Christ, to read the Bible, and to sing and pray.

Her husband was still harsh and tyrannical in the highest degree, and her brother also. Her life was often threatened, and she was utterly forbidden to mention any point in her religion in presence of her husband, or to intrude any sentence on his notice from any of the books of the Church. She had not even the privilege of singing a single line of her hymn book in his hearing. Having lived in this unnatural bondage for a few years, and having borne with meekness and submission every railing, insult, and abuse which a tyrant could heap upon her, she finally ventured, on one quiet Sunday evening, to sing in his presence two lines of one of her favorite hymns. [See Saints English Hymn Book, page 201.]

Behold the great Redeemer comes,
To bring his ransomed people home!

Her husband on hearing this, flew into a violent rage; he snatched the book out of her hand, tore it up, and threw it in the fire. He then laid violent hands on her, and forced her into the street and locked the door on her. It was a dark evening, and in one of the back dark streets of San Francisco where an unprotected female would hardly be considered safe for a moment. She, however, entered a neighboring house, and immediately sent a message to Dr.———, an old family physician, who was the mutual friend of both herself and husband. She threw herself upon his protection, and he conducted her to a respectable hotel, where she took lodgings and board at the husband's expense. Next day she called on the city recorder and made oath of the assault and battery and other outrages of her husband, demanding his arrest, and that she might be secured in her life and peace in the future. But through the influence of Dr.———, and other parties in high places, the matter was finally dropped, and the parties seemed reconciled so far, that she returned to her house, and again took charge of her children, and of her husband's housekeeping.

For a few weeks, all seemed to go on as usual. The husband and brother went to their daily business—returned at the proper hours, found their meals in order, and the usual economy, industry and taste which she had ever displayed in trying to render home agreeable.

On a certain day—breakfast being over and the husband and brother gone to business at an early hour, as usual, she assembled her children, as her manner was, for family devotion.

These consisted of two boys, between eight and ten years of age, and a girl of seven. The mother and children mingled their glad voices in the morning hymn, and bowed the knee together in solemn prayer—when, rising from their knees, the children gave their dear mother the usual parting kiss, and cheerfully hasted away to the city school.

O! how little did that tender mother and those innocent babes then realize the awful trial which immediately awaited them; or, that two oceans and a continent would separate them ere they should meet again.

Talk not of Rome, of Nero, of the dark ages, or of the Spanish Inquisition. All these combined could scarce form a parallel worthy to compare with the heartless, unfeeling, inhuman, savage, and worse than fiendish tyranny of the nineteenth century. And all this enacted by Protestants in a land of freedom! Nay, rather by the nearest kindred, and on a helpless woman and children!

Evening came—the husband and brother returned from the business of the day—but no children came to gladden the heart of a fond mother! Where are our children? exclaimed the anxious mother in alarm.

The brutish husband, and unfeeling brother answered, with a fiendish grin, or a taunt of triumph—They are on the bosom of the Pacific, you will never see them again—they will be brought up Presbyterians—not Mormons!

The only answer to this was a wild shriek and a sudden fall.— The mother had fainted! Her heart, as it were, had died within her. She remained through that dreadful night, in alternate spasms, fainting fits—occasionally awaking to a realizing sense of her desolation: "Rachel weeping for her children, and could not be comforted, because they were not." She would sometimes so far awake from her swooning fits as to rave, and wander, and call loudly for her little ones by name, and then she would burst into tears—groan and lament, and finally, again drop away and become insensible.

The brutal husband and brother stood over her through the entire night, somewhat troubled and alarmed, but durst not call a physician or any assistance, lest their fiendish cruelty should be detected in all its horrors. In the morning, being compelled to go to business at an early hour, they left her alone in the house, locking her in as a prisoner, in solitude and helplessness.

She, however, sufficiently recovered in the course of the morning, to open a window and raise the alarm. The neighbors soon learned the true circumstances and sympathized deeply in her bereavement. Some of the merchants best acquainted with the family, offered to raise a subscription and send her to her children, it being soon ascertained that they had been sent to her parents in New Orleans.

Public odium soon wrought upon the obdurate husband and brother that change which human sympathy had failed to accomplish. They saw that the matter must be ameliorated, and hushed up as far as possible by compromise.

They had been plotting for weeks, and, by the assistance of other bigots of their sect, had prepared trunks of clothing for the children, and had procured through tickets for them on the transit route between the Pacific and Atlantic. All things being in readiness, they had watched an opportunity to snatch them from school, and thrust them on board of a steamer, without so much as a farewell look or word from their mother, and had committed them to the care of strangers to pass two oceans and a continent, with no kindred or acquaintance to love or care for them.

This done, the inhuman bigots had resisted all the eloquent and heart-rending appeals of a mother, and nothing but the fear of disgrace, or the vengeance of an excited and indignant populace constrained them to compromise, and hush up any further excitement, by agreeing to send the mother to the children.

She was finally soothed and comforted with the hope of following them in two weeks, on the next steamer; she went quietly and diligently to work to prepare for the journey. Her house was now desolate and lonely beyond endurance. She, therefore, by consent of her husband, spent the time with some friends in the country, till near the time of her embarkation.

But alas! her trials had but just begun. She had a prosperous passage to New Orleans, found her parents, and with them her two youngest children—but alas! the other she was never permitted to see. He is concealed from her in some distant part of the country. She found her bigoted and hard-hearted Presbyterian parents and brothers and sisters in the same plot. Her children were held by them in bondage, under a strict watch as prisoners. She must not associate with them, even in her own father's house, except in presence of others—she must not sleep in the same room, nor even to retire to a private room, to bow the knee with them at the hour of prayer, as she had always been in the habit of doing. In short, she was in bondage intolerable, and was daily abused, insulted, mocked, ridiculed and railed at in every possible manner. She endured these things for months, and finding herself sinking under the accumulated wrongs and oppressions of those who should have been her friends; as well as under the effects of the pestilential climate of the advancing summer of New Orleans; she, by the consent of her children, left them for a season for the north, promising to return to them in due time.

She, at length, after incredible hardships and toils, made her way to Great Salt Lake City, where she arrived in safety in the autumn of 1855. She had, by this long journey, somewhat recovered her health, and, true to the instincts of a mother, she immediately commenced, and constantly persevered in a most rigid course of economy and industry, in order to redeem her pledge to her children.

She taught school in that city almost constantly for one year. She then made her way over the dreary plains, for some fifteen hundred miles to the frontiers of the States, and thence down the rivers to the children.

The account which appeared in the New Orleans *Bulletin*, some time near the close of the past year, may possibly refer to her.

If so, making due allowance for its numerous falsehoods and misrepresentations it opens another chapter in her somewhat romantic and heroic life.

Had the lady in question had a kind and dutiful husband, instead of an unfeeling tyrant, religious differences would not have separated the family to this day; but, on the contrary, the father, mother, and children might still have been living in San Francisco in peace.

It was not Mormonism, [as the Bulletin says] but *Presbyterianism*, that broke up the family.

A FRIEND OF THE OPPRESSED.

Cincinatti, Ohio, February 20, 1857.

FURTHER PARTICULARS OF THE MURDER.

Arkansas, Americia, on board the Steamer *H. Tucker*,
Arkansas River, May 22, 1857.

Dear Brother Orson,—It has become my painful duty to send abroad the news of the imprisonment and murder of your beloved brother Parley. I know it will be painful to you to learn that his body was mangled, and that he lay fully an hour without anyone coming even to raise his head or give him a drink of water, though he was in full view of a house where a family lived, by the name of Winn.

I was journeying quietly along in a wagon, in an Indian nation, with my children, on the frontiers of Arkansas, when McLean, the demon of my life, met me. He tore the children away, and then had me arrested upon a charge of stealing clothes belonging to and worn by my children—Albert and Annie McLean. There were also named in the charge, P. P. Pratt, James Gamwell, and Elias Gamwell, all sought as engaged in this larceny of $10 worth of clothes, on my children's backs.

The following day, after I was arrested, I heard that your brother was also arrested, the greatest excitement prevailed, and when we rode in sight of where they had Parley, I saw him lying on the ground like a man who had stopped to let his horse graze. He was surrounded by twelve or fourteen armed men— military officers and soldiers. I alighted, with the permission of the marshal, who rode with me, and advanced to brother Parley, and extended my hand saying, "Brother Parley, we have it, it seems, as prisoners." He said, "How is your health, Madam? have you been well?" I then said, "We have one thing to thank God for; we have learned how to live and how to die." And then looking around upon the soldiers, I said in a loud tone of voice, "*All these armed men and soldiers* can only kill the body, and I am as ready to die as to live." He only answered, "It is all in one little life, and this is only a speck of eternity."

We were then put upon a forced ride of twenty-five miles, he being bound by a rope around his ankle, which was held by an officer who rode near him. They also arrested another young man, Elder Higinson, who was found preaching to the Creed Nation; and when we left Fort Gibson, he and Parley were in chains, and I in a carriage—because I was so wounded that I could not ride on horseback. Soldiers drove the carriage, and the Marshal rode with the two who were in chains.

We rode from Fort Gibson, Saturday, Sunday, and half of Monday, which brought us to the town of Van Buren, on the Arkansas river, State of Arkansas. We were then taken before the Court, only to be told that we might depart—"FOR WE FIND NOTHING AGAINST YOU."

I have written a full account to the *Mormon*, which I hope you will see, but lest it should be intercepted, I will briefly state, that when Parley was liberated from the jail, McLean followed him about ten minutes, with two men, citizens of Van Buren, close behind him, and then soon afterwards numbers of other men. Twelve miles from the town, on the road leading north, they overtook your beloved brother, fired seven shots, and then stabbed him in his left side—one of the cuts piercing his heart. The first six balls only made holes in the skirt of his coat; he was then headed by one of the men, which threw him in close contact with McLean, *and that fiend himself gave him the deadly wound*; and after leaving him for dead, came back, and fired at him where he lay upon the ground, dropped the pistol by his side, and left! I went to see him, under the protection of the "real Marshal," the following day, the details of which I have sent to Brother Taylor, New York.

Brother Higinson and myself rolled his dead body in fine linen, and Brother Higinson stayed to see him put in the ground, about a mile from the place where he was murdered. He lived two-and-a-half hours, and answered a number of questions asked him by the neighbors near the spot.

The citizens of Van Buren furnished me with means to leave in four days after this bloody scene, and I am now alone on my way I know not whither; but I know that the Spirit of God is with me, and I have nothing to fear.

I am very lonely—pray for me, thou man of God, that I may stand firm to the end, and be saved with Jesus, Joseph, and Parley, in the Celestial Kingdom of God. Amen.

Your Sister,
ELEANOR J. MCLEAN.

THE ORPHANS' LAMENTATION, ON HEARING OF THE MARTYRDOM OF THEIR FATHER.

I heard a grievous lament from a far mountainous town;
The rocky heights above were penetrated by the sound,
The sound ran over hill, and stream, and meadow,
To the grave of the one who was martyred in innocent blood.

It was the voice of wives and children in awful wild sorrow,
Their voice to heaven, in tears, for comfort now;
Because they knew, from the land of a far country,
The news that they no more could see a father's happy face.

That in a land of *lust*, *profanity*, and *wine*,
Where once they dwelt beneath a sweet, virtuous vine;
The gentle father and husband had met a Martyr's fate,
By the hands of *fiends*, surcharged with black wrath and anger.

That when his heart was pierced, he fell upon the wet ground,
Where there was none to raise his head, or bind his wound;
Though he lived for some hours, he saw no dear friend,
Who could send word of his fate when he died.

The wail increased until it reached the throne of heaven,
And *Eloheim Himself* did take His rod,
And said, "I'll cut *them* down, I'll destroy *them* every one,
"For killing holy Prophets on the soil of their own land.

"I'll send upon them *famine, pestilence*, and war will come,
"I'll call my legions from the northern land afar,
"And they *shall hunt them* down in every land, every living soul,
"Where the blood of every one of Joseph's race was trampled—listen!

"The blood of Parley shall not long before me plead,
"For wrath on those who did this hellish deed;
"And e'er it cease to cry, that nation *shall atone*
"For every orphan's moan, and the widow filled with tears.

"Every drop of guiltless blood ever shed in the world,
"Shall quickly come upon the heads of all of these;
"For once I have sworn, *to myself and to my fine throne*,
"*That in the Book of Life their names shall ne'er be known!*"

[By the persecuted Lady, E. J. McLean.—Ed. the *Star*.]
Trans. Dewi Elfed Jones.

CONFERENCE ACCOUNTS, &C.

The Llanelli Conference was held May 24—President D. Daniels and the Presidency of the Conference were present.

In the morning meeting all the authorities of the Church on the earth were sustained, from the Prophet Brigham down to the Presidents of Branches.

The presiding elders presented accounts of the effects of the *Reformation* on the branches and on the world—that some were greatly improved, and others were much worse, from among the Saints and from among the world, and that the devil is stirring things up.

Pres. Davies remarked that the Gospel is prospering in this Conference, and surely affecting the one side or the other, much like the sun that melts the wax and hardens the clay—even though a few of the world are being saved by it, yet it condemns every soul of the rest. Almost all the Saints in this Conference are being purified except for those whose light has turned into thick darkness.

In the following meetings several local and neighboring elders preached on the beneficent principles to the Saints and the world.

President Daniels earnestly exhorted the listeners to hear and obey the solid words of God through his authorized servants, for the sake of the salvation of their precious souls, during the approved time in which such priceless blessings await the obedient and the faithful. He said that the hour of judgment of God is on the earth, and that His Great Work will be cut short in righteousness. Happiness will be the end of the journey, after finishing the work, and going in to the rest of Christ escaping the plagues of Babylon.

He encouraged the officers and the Saints to be diligent and faithful in preaching the Gospel, distributing tracts, and testifying of the great and present message of heaven, so they may merit a part in the blessed inheritance of the Saints.

Our current number is 84.

DAVID DAVIES, *President.*

The Cardiganshire Conference was held at Cwrt Newydd—Pres. Daniels was present.

The Pres. of the Conference and Elder John Evans, Penywern, took an active part in the work of the day.

All the authorities of the Church were sustained unanimously.

The Reformation was preached effectively to the Saints, and some were greatly enlivened, and were made happy.

All the officers and Saints expressed their feelings of determination to be more diligent along the path of the reformation, while others who had not renewed their covenants promised to do so right away.

After two o'clock, there was preaching out of doors to the people coming from the chapels, who listened very attentively and politely, and the same thing in the evening meeting. The wisdom and power of the Holy Ghost was received to enlighten and revive the Saints, and to cause an unusual excitement throughout the neighborhood. Members, 29.

JOSEPH GRIFFITHS, *President.*

☞ We do not have space in this issue, or time to make editorial observations. Nevertheless, the heart-rending accounts speak very clearly for themselves. Further details of the horrible murder will be available in two or three days. Saints, be diligent in defending this innocent and blameless victim of murder from the false accusations of the host of his malicious enemies.—Ed. of the *Trumpet.*

VERSES.

Death of David John Griffiths, infant of Daniel and Anna Griffiths, Capcoch, Aberdare, and grandson of the Poet. Died April 29, 1857.

Dearest little Dafydd—thou are fairer—and more joyful
    In the light of the stars;
    From the time of thy trials—
    The end of thy pain has come.

Paradise is more pure—and a dwelling place
    More deserving of such as thee;
    A sweet son to live in joy—
    It is a resting place for the worthy.

He saw the dear face of the Prophet—the great, Joseph,
    And Jesus who was slain;
    And the host of the splendor, in a heavenly feeling,
    And the misery from which he was delivered.

The little one, and the sinless pure one—today
    Is free from all affliction;
    He is living where there are,
    Faces who recognize him.

He is well among his ancestors—he has the enjoyment
    Of righteous relatives,
    And a happy throng of the purest dwelling place,
    And the divine communication of the beautiful surroundings.

His pavilion is far better—from the earth
    He will come when it is purified;
    On this he will dwell before long—
    And then it will be complete.

May 31, '57,   DEWI ELFED.

CONTENTS.

	PG.
Letters from the Valley	209
Ambush-murder of the Apostle P. P. Pratt	213
The Orphans' Lamentation	221
Conference Accounts	222
Verses	224

SWANSEA:
PRINTED AND PUBLISHED BY DANIEL DANIELS.

ZION'S TRUMPET,

OR

Star of the Saints.

No. 15.] JULY 4, 1857. [Vol. X.

WAR AND THE MORMONS.

MENTION has been made of the rebellion and carnage of the Eastern Indians—the general massacre of European men, women and children by these hot-headed, zealous, ugly, black-skinned pagans, and the sharp penalty visited upon them by the British government, and the host of soldiers that are on their way towards the East Indies! This is not enough to draw attention away from the Mormons in Utah and their camps.

It is a compulsory fact that editors must have something interesting or disturbing always at hand, or they will not satisfy the corrupt appetite of their numerous readers. The leading editors of the day are followed by their followers in truth or lies. It does not matter which—the small dogs are ready to bark when hearing the large ones. Therefore, we take less notice of them than we do of the thousand and one voices of the other species of creatures. It can be imagined by grimacing mouths, ruddy chests, rising wings, and the unpleasant, strange screech of the creature that is given the flattering title of *Hero* that *turkey cock* is the best comparison we can make of him—that the sound of all the rest with the breeze has reached him first, on top of his pile paper rubbish, at last, *via London, of course,* and that he too desires to test his voice.

Well, surely, then, something is afoot over there! What if we were to turn our sights away from the curs of Wales, to

15 [PRICE 1½c.

see what the matter is. Hush! here she is! *hurrah! bow, wow, wow!* Now little curs, reach out your mouth, lift your wings, and you also screech from the top of your pile of rubbish, you turkey cock! Lies fly like electricity—Brigham Young has retreated! *Hip, hip, hurrah!* Another governor is going to Utah! *glory!* An army of soldiers is going to kill the Mormons! *hush too, tiger!* A Mormon Apostle has been killed for taking another man's wife! *Well done, ruffians.* The Mormons have become disunited and are rising in revolt against their church leaders! *Strike fire!* The women have risen in unison against plural marriage! *Well done the Scotch Petticoats!* Hayoohoo! "Wash on her, boys!" and, to tie together this constant news, "Brigham Young carries on everything with a high hand, by chasing away all the officers of the Chief Government, together with all the judgmental 'gentiles!' Oh, hunting curs, gather together for the *crusade* against the Mormons; for it is remarkably virtuous, and the celebrated Judge Drummond has exposed the Saints! *Success to progress!* There is no need for the *turkey cock* to have his distributors send oats to him for a while yet, after such a tuneful melody, at least that is our opinion.

True is the proverb that says, "A lie flies to the ends of the earth before truth can put on her shoes." "Do you know what, (says the Northerner) things are very amusing here, friends." It was no less amusing for the Utahns, poor things, when they received coach loads of papers giving them *news* of their supposed tricks. One wonders whether Brigham Young is sure that he is *he himself*, and that he has not retreated? It is "very amusing" for the Mormons themselves to see such an ugly, jagged, bony, and false idol that the editors place and name in the place of Mormonism! Yes, flights of fantasy in the watery brain of the editors who are of the same character as Macbeth and are being hunted wantonly through the air, and just when they imagine they have caught them, behold there is not one substance to be had! There are others who always walk like the man who tried to catch his shadow! All of this is Mormonism, of course. Who would dare to doubt the truthfulness of a newspaper? Not the Mormons themselves, at the peril of their peace. Believe us, friends, it is extremely "amusing" the whole time! With a closer look there was no cause for the Mormons to doubt the dreaming, Macbethian editors, for they are now laughing in their sleeve as they see some of the *leading actors* trying to convince the others of their mistake.

Our story gets even more amusing. It has gotten considerably clearer by now. We heard of a man who imagined seeing a magic bier "between the two lights," with its four posts visibly sticking out in front and in back. A closer look revealed that the magic was nothing but two donkeys with their tails entwined, their long ears appearing to be the posts of a bier! A closer look, friends, revealed that it was Brigham Young, in the company of hundreds of his brethren, going on a pleasure and research expedition to the Salmon river. It is his practice to search for places to establish new settlements. The Mormons had *not* rebelled against him, and there was *not* any dissention among them, rather it was the editor of the *New York Herald* who had suggested a plan to bring that about—and Johnny the son of Jane had *not* vomited from his innards *three* crows, rather it was something as *black* as a crow. The Reverends and the Editors have preached the funeral sermon of Mormonism so many times since the time the Prophet Joseph proclaimed his mission until today, that the Saints have become accustomed to living next to the forest and hearing the sounds of owls without being afraid.

Colonel Steptoe and his government and his soldiers went past without having so much as even one small skirmish! The grasshoppers have failed to scatter or starve the Saints as prophesied, and at last Drummond the donkey has been kicked for making such a stir. His true character was published to the world by the Saints, but that was not sufficient—editors prefer for things to be as they portray. By now most of the newspapers have changed their opinion, condemning Drummond, and doubting the news from Utah. A pity, indeed! What will be next, I wonder?

The May 28th *Chicago Weekly Tribune* (one of the chief enemies of the Saints), said that an article in the Oquawka *Plaindealer*, published in the city where the *true* wife and family were living, and where he himself had lived earlier, proved that the Judge was in no position to say anything about immorality in Utah, or in any other place. The newspaper *Plaindealer* says:—

"And if his secret history were to be written, it would reveal a career of so cruel and inhuman treatment to his family as can be had in annals of human shame. The local press well understood his deceit, but it remained silent out of respect for his family's feelings. After resigning his office, and after Drummond's return [with *Ada*, his whore] to the States, he showed no desire to see his family, [no, to his shame, so we believe.] When it was disclosed in the press that Drummond was in Chicago, Mrs. Drummond [the *real* Mrs. Drummond, understand] went there to try to converse with him, but although she stayed in the same hotel, and stayed one night while he was there, he managed to hide from her sight, and the next morning he went clandestinely to the train, and he came to this place, and then he took two of his children away with him. His wife stayed for a week in Chicago, looking in vain for her deceitful husband; and then she returned home only to find another pain added to her heart that was already broken, when she learned that her children had been taken away, she knew not where." In the next issue the *Plaindealer* reports,—

"Drummond is a man whose word is not considered of the least importance by those who know him here [in the city where he lived earlier, remember], no, not even if he repeated it under oath, since our citizens have received some examples of his harsh oaths. We do not believe that the stories of the evils of the Mormons while relying to one degree on the testimony of Drummond." In another article the *Plaindealer* deals even more plainly:—

"It has been proved beyond argument that Drummond gave up his judgeship for the purpose of being appointed Governor of Utah, so that he could return there wealthy with sufficient power to exact revenge on the Mormons for the insult his "Ada" received, the mad-faced lady whom *he saw in a dream!* The Mormons are bad enough according to every conscience, but Drummond's shameful behavior makes them appear respectable in comparison, and since the mask has been torn from his face, we trust that not one respectable publication will support him by so much as publishing one of his letters again."

The *New York Tribune* was so foolish as to publish another accusation by Drummond against the authorities of Utah whom he accused of asking a man by the name of Davenport, who was about to start for the States, to pay taxes two years in advance, and that he was forced to pay them or be in danger of losing his possessions, and one day after he departed, he was caught, and his goods were stolen, and he was forced to return to "Salt Lake."

Instead of being in Salt Lake, Mr. Davenport was in Nebraska, from where he wrote to the *Tribune* that it was a lie, but that he was participating with President Kimball in an assignment; that the tax collector, by mistake, had asked for the payment of taxes on all that he had with him, that he had paid them, and that President Kimball, as a gentleman, had reimbursed him, as soon as he had knowledge of the mistake, and that his safe arrival in Nebraska with his goods was sufficient evidence to disprove the last lie of the impudent scoundrel.

We trust that this is enough about Drummond, and we will but one quotation from the *Quincy Whig:*—

"It is known that Drummond took with him to Utah a woman who appeared to be his wife—leaving his wedded partner, the mother of his children, in Oquawka. Mrs. Drummond wrote to her husband in Utah, and in answer she received a foolish epistle from this woman [Ada], which was published in the *Plaindealer*, telling her that she must not write to *her* husband again.

We are not proponents of the Lynch law; but if any human being ever deserved a heavy club, and to be tarred and feathered, this *ex* Judge from Utah is he."

Concerning the new Governor to Utah. Every other day the daily American newspapers have been publishing different names, and casting doubt on the reports of the previous day. By the time the news arrived here, it was affirmed—the Saints did not close their mouths—this one or the other was the man, and he was to set out with numerous soldiers immediately. All the following names, &c., were published on different days, as governors to Utah, and that each one was going without fail! March 15th, Benjamin McCulloch; 18th, "not to be appointed;" 26th, Fayette McMullen, "who refused the offer with distaste." April 2, Geary; 24, B. McCulloch, "with peaceful intent;" 25, "wanting to send ten thousand volunteers, as well as the support that can be raised from the army, as war is inevitable, to attempt to take the strong Sevastopol of the Saints, and after that it is possible for the charmed Mormons to sweep away from ten to twenty thousand men before them like chaff." May 18th, "Drummond, with an army to support him. The most knowledgeable here do not believe the story about the fleeing of Brigham Young." May 19, Culloch has refused. The 20th, one has been selected, but not named. Good news from Utah, everything is quiet. The 21st, 2000 soldiers *on their way* to Utah—the Mormons to be swept for the least opposition. The 22nd, Mr. Wright from Indiana, but "it is a lie, and no one else is going!" May 22, Col. Cummings again, but "he refused." The 24th, Major Heiss, "if the talk on the street is true." The 29th, "the President has been appointed, and has accepted the office; his name will be made known within a few days," and 2000 soldiers *will* be sent to Utah." June 2, the new governor *to be* selected before long! June 20th, F. F. Thomas, but he has refused.

Let our readers judge from the above what trust can be put in the newspapers of our day. The truth is that editors who are enemies of the Saints invent hateful lies, and publish them as correspondence from Utah from their own reporters, so they say, to stir up the mindless public against thousands of men, women, and innocent children who are dealing diligently with their daily tasks without interfering with anyone else's work, while the best peace thrives in Utah. Several of the chief American newspapers have seen their mistake and have admitted it fairly. The *New York Herald* says that not one American newspaper has reporters in Utah, and that all the bad news about Utah is being made this side of the Mississippi by penny-a-line scribblers.

With regard to the accusation against Apostle Pratt, we direct our readers to the treatise that disproves it.

One fact is obvious to the Saints, that the Kingdom of God is becoming great in the eyes of the world, and a topic of horror and fear to the wicked and the faithless, those who agitate to break out such storms of slander with nothing but their own guilty consciences. Quickly we leave them with the blind idol of Mormonism building castles in the air, and hunting ugly fantasy.

COUNSEL TO ELDERS.

(From the *Millennial Star*.)

THERE is, at the present time, considerable excitement in the public mind, relative to what the world is pleased to call "Mormonism." The object of this editorial is to give the Elders a little advice, as to the best course to be pursued to allay excitement as much as possible. We know that it must needs be that offences will come, but, as Jesus said, "Woe unto those by whom they come."

You are called of God through his Prophets, and sent forth into the world to tell the people on what terms their sins may be remitted, and they put in possession of the Holy Ghost, which will guide them in the ways of truth, according to the promises of the Son of God. You are not sent to dispute or wrangle with them, but to preach the Gospel of peace and salvation to all who will listen to, believe, and obey the instructions of the Holy Spirit given through you. We therefore say go forth in the spirit of Christ, which is characterized by meekness, gentleness, longsuffering, and kindness. Honor your high and holy callings by a dignified demeanor in all your associations, both in public and in private life. Refrain from all untimely jesting, a thing which is beneath the position of one holding the office of an Elder in the Church of Jesus Christ of Latter-day Saints. Many Elders imagine that they have not preached a good sermon unless they have said something that is calculated to excite laughter, which amuses or disgusts rather than edify their hearers. Some again manifest a disposition to boast, by challenging, and bidding defiance to opposition, and seem rather to court it than otherwise. They speak of powder and ball as playthings. Lay aside such trifling and low-mindedness, and preach the Gospel of Christ. Reason with the people from the Scriptures, the Book of Mormon, and the Book of Doctrine and Covenants. Show them that such a work, as the one in which we are engaged, has to be performed prior to the second advent of the Savior, and you will meet with less opposition. Many who oppose your efforts to do them good, believe that they are doing God service, as did Saul of Tarsus. You should, therefore, rather pity and commiserate than indulge a spirit of anger towards them, for they know not what they are doing.

As ministers of the Gospel, you need not violate any law of the land, but be subject to the powers that be. When you are maltreated and persecuted by the wicked, seek redress through the legitimate channel; honor the government, and the officers of its appointment, by appealing to them to redress your wrongs, by punishing the guilty. The laws of England are good, and guarantee to all the right to worship God according to the dictates of their own consciences. We therefore say, instead of disputing with the rabble, claim at the hands of the government that protection which her gracious Majesty is pleased to allow to all her law-abiding subjects. When the legal authorities of the land cease to suppress disturbances, and give you a chance to deliver the message of Heaven to the people, that all may have an opportunity of judging for themselves, and believing or rejecting upon their own agency; then the responsibility will rest upon them, and your garments will be clear of the blood of all men. It will be required at the hands of those whose duty it was to protect you, while in the discharge of the duties enjoined upon you by the God of Israel.

Do right, and when you are persecuted let it be for righteousness sake, that you may claim the promises of Jesus, for he said, "Blessed are they which are persecuted for righteousness sake: for theirs is the kingdom of heaven. Blessed are ye when men shall revile you, and persecute you, and shall say all manner of evil against you falsely for my sake. Rejoice and be exceeding glad; for so persecuted they the Prophets which were before you. * * * * Let your light so shine before men, that they may see your good works, and glorify your Father which is in heaven."

☞ Even though it will be in our next issue that the book debts appear, we will send information soon through the post to the different distributors.

ZION'S TRUMPET,

OR

Star of the Saints.

SATURDAY, JULY 4, 1857.

EXHORTATION—The progress of the Kingdom of God, the influence of Zion and the opposition of the enemies require progress in us too, so that when conflict takes place, we will be on safe ground.

The call of God has long urged the Saints not to lose one opportunity to preach the Gospel faithfully to the Gentiles, purifying themselves from day to day, and striving to free themselves from the chains of Babylon.

A host of Welsh Saints have succeeded in reaching the land of Joseph, or America, although not all of them have gone on to Zion; but they can work their way to the end of their journey more easily than those who remain here groaning under the yoke of oppression, and longing for deliverance, with faint hope because of their poverty or the large size of their various families.

In the face of all the faint hopes we know of families who were among the poorest and the largest in number; nevertheless, they were among the foremost in faithfulness—preaching the Gospel, tracting, living righteously, and contributing generously to the work. During hard and unpromising years they strove patiently, earnestly pleading with the Lord and trusting in Him for assistance in his good time. Behold! they have pounds aside in the Office now, and more still rolling in.

How did the blessing come? Did the Lord reveal some treasures, or send money in the beaks of ravens? No; but He blessed them in their temporal labor and their daily diligence. The blessings of God are like a rope thrown into the water to someone who may be about to drown—it is extended to him, but he must take hold of it.

The unwise do not perceive the blessings of God when they are within his reach. No matter how much he earns—he spends the last penny, his harvest goes past, and the winter catches him unprepared.

There have been high expectations for assistance from Zion to emigrate the poor Saints out of Babylon, and some have received it; but it is not wise, at present, to depend on such hope.

With respect to money, Zion will not be very rich for a while yet, until important preparations are made, for when her King suddenly comes to his temple, and the wealth of the Gentiles is brought in. They deal mainly in goods there now. Instead of taking the way of the Gentiles to get rich—each one for himself heedless of everyone and everything else, the Saints join together in going out to preach the Gospel and warn the Gentiles—raising and establishing a powerful nation of hosts of the Lord—building cities and temples—breaking trails through the forests and wilderness lands—putting into practice the principles of life, rearing our children in the ways of purity, so that they may achieve the great, intended works of God in this age.

The ways to Zion are opening. We have seen the effort of Zion's people in sending generously what they had to meet the emigrants on the Plains; carriages loaded with gold and silver would not have served the purpose out there!

We see the settlements beginning across the plains, and it is intended to have one every 50 miles, and the emigrating Saints are to fill them as they come along, and at the end of another emigration they go on their way, yielding their place to others who may come. Thus the poor of our God can walk from station to station at a deliberate pace, taking the summer before them to do so, leaving whatever luggage they have to the *Express and Carrying Company* to transport for them. They can sleep, without fear of catching cold, a night or two if they wish between each station, and thus having less trouble in the end than the men of the ox teams! while there will be preparations to carry the weak and the sick.

You see that the only obstacle to the Salt Lake over there is the salt lake that borders us, and that the biggest thing is to get to go from here across to the land of Joseph somewhere. Let the wise, then, look for a way in which God will open the way; for He is sure to do so. He opened the heart of Pharaoh of old, and he raised Joseph from the prison to the side of the throne, and Daniel the servant to be head of an empire.

The same God is the one we have; therefore, dear Saints, gird up your loins, and gather up your faith. Be ye diligent, faithful, honest, and sober, and, like several of the other brethren, you will be chosen by your master for responsible places before those who are less prudent; and earthly blessings will roll into your hands. Then, if you are frugal, wise, and organized, you will at least have a way to reach the land of Joseph, or America, and soon you will see Zion. Put your faith into action and be watchful and diligent with your religion and your stewardships, although religion is all inclusive, and look for the salvation of the Lord. Lively and patient faith and energy are what attract blessings. Brothers and Sisters, organize yourselves to live more frugally, so that you can spare a little for the Penny Emigrating Fund. Remember that two shillings per week for a year will make up more than enough to emigrate one adult to the United States.

Instead of wasting your money on some little, useless and short-lasting baubles, dress in serviceable, simple, and clean clothes, and deny yourselves unnecessary, luxuriant food to eat, then, even if you have not saved enough yourself, the help you need will be the less for it, and it will be even easier to obtain it.

Do not be inconsistent in your families. May your family prayers be as regular as the meals you eat. Do not waste all your leisure time in jesting, but ponder the principles of the kingdom so that you may grow with it, remember the saying "Zeal without knowledge is not good."

It is obvious to all who have the light of the Spirit that false religion, tradition, wickedness and animosity, like the powerful boa constrictor, wrap themselves around mankind, and soon they will be overpowered. The tares are bound together in sheaves so compactly, in whole congregations, very, very tight, so that it will be practically impossible to pull out the grain of wheat that may be mixed in with them.

Elders and Priests of Israel! do not focus so much on preaching scripture and the "milk" of the word that you do not give your testimony. Also give it with power and enthusiastic zeal. If you do not feel you have sufficient power of the Spirit, withdraw, fast, and pray without ceasing until it comes on you, and then preach powerfully, and tell the people clearly about the judgments that are coming after you expose the abomination of Babylon and the deceit of human religions, and the only way for deliverance, and if you do not convince them, make them *feel the power* of your testimony.

The Prophets and Apostles of God jointly testify that the small stone is about to shift and smash the toes of the old idol, but that our remaining here is the cause of tolerating the Saints in Zion so that things can be as they are. That the storm is gathering and the atmosphere is obviously darkening, and God expects for his Saints in Babylon to flee promptly before the way is closed by the bloodthirsty enemies. Nevertheless, let the faithful poor take comfort, for they will see the salvation of the Lord if they strive their utmost for themselves first.

Work exists in every place from where letters are written to us—preaching, tracting, and faithful testifying, and the honest payment of tithing. Do you not suppose that this will draw the attention of heaven on us, and that we shall soon see the intervening hand of the Lord to a greater extent? And is it likely that the Lord will not favor those Presidents who have saved, sacrificed, and been out helping their weak and small conferences to preach the Gospel and clear their debts?

Where the first pamphlets of the series have been sold, &c., it is appropriate to sell as many as you like of those that follow, of course; we say to all who have requested counsel in this regard, and it would be good to sell all they can of the account of the Martyrdom of Parley, since the profit is for his diligent and orphaned family.

By a letter from the Valley from brother Isaac Rees, late of Blaenau Gwent, we understand that he and some of the Welsh are living in Ogden city and environs—Thomas Giles, James, G. W. Davies, M. Dudley, Mesech Williams, W. Williams, J. Thomas, W. Lewis, John Price, &c. That brother Giles is great in the sight of the authorities, and has been ordained a High Priest, and has been called to travel throughout the outlying areas. He said that sister Margaret Giles died in childbirth on the Plains.

The latest *Mormon* we have seen says that the murderer McLean has searched St. Louis and environs for the woman who was once his wife, and that her sectarian family was helping him to catch her and put her in an insane asylum on the excuse that she was crazy; but she escaped to the Plains. They feared her, for she knew more than a few things.

The *Bulletin*, a New Orleans newspaper, asked the Saints to turn away and give a wide swath to McLean. The *Mormon* says that if he goes to the Plains he will have whichever one he wants, a "wide swath" or a narrow one.

TEACHINGS,

THE Kingdom of God is to be built, and it appears to some that that will come about through three grand principles that are in our midst; first, the increase of its subjects in number and virtue. Second, the gathering of those from among every nation, tribe, and language, to Zion.

First, increase of the subjects—to multiply numbers of the subjects we must convey to others the better knowledge or the understanding that we have. A person cannot have knowledge of the kingdom of God but by one of three ways—seeing, hearing, or feeling. Consequently, brethren, if we leave the world alone until they see, hear, or feel something about the kingdom, we have determined the end of any increase in our numbers. We prove also that we do not have the necessary and required virtue or diligence; for those are the old and also the latest commandments—"Be instant in season and out of season." "Cry aloud and spare not," &c. Also we should do to others as we would have them do to us. Let everyone ask himself and consider how he would like for someone to behave toward him if he were outside the Kingdom of God—without knowing him—bound by the traditional fetters of the world, and having not the least spark of light of the Holy Ghost, his conscience answers, "You should put off the vain ways of the world, and go from house to house with the printed word, so that your contemporaries can *see*, and you should cry out so they may *hear*, having the Spirit of God to make them *feel*, and you should be obedient and ready to do the will of God, always, as Jesus cried out from the dwelling place of his holiness, "Here am I, send me."

In this way the subjects of the kingdom would increase in number and virtue.

Second, *the collection*. All know that money is required to transport men across oceans and continents, and to free the Church here from debt, &c. Our all wise Father has instructed that the most efficient way to accomplish this is for each one to consecrate to His name a tenth part of his possessions, and their daily increase, and to act faithfully according to his direction. He promises in return to bless us with blessings that there will not be room enough to receive them. We have enough room for what we have at present; therefore, it must be that we will get richer as we pay our tithing faithfully. Therefore, brethren, let us devote ourselves to doing the will of our Father, lest He keep us in Babylon, as he kept the ancient children of Israel in the desert to wander for forty years, dying in the end, for their disobedience and their unbelief.

Fasting is a duty that is pressed upon us for two reasons.

First, because fasting, like prayer, is effective in bringing power over the spirits of darkness, as can be proved from the account of the ancient disciples in failing to cast out that devil, because, as Jesus says, this kind goeth not out but by prayer and fasting.

If a man were to throw a stone with the intention of killing one bird but manages to kill two, he would consider himself fortunate. In the same way, brethren, fasting brings strength to us that we could not do without, and it also saves our money, so that we can put it in the Penny Fund, and so much, in time, toward our emigration.

Third, *the preparation in Zion*.—When the Son of Man comes He will come to his temple; thus, the Temple will need to have been built and dedicated to his name. Everyone knows that there must be stone, mortar, wood, iron, brass, copper, silver, gold, and many other precious things to build a temple, and such things do not come on their own—there must be craftsmen and workers to prepare them and set them in place, and they must have food and clothing: it is obvious that some must labor to feed and clothe them.

Furthermore, it would be strange to see only a temple there to welcome the King of Kings; for He will come to be glorified in his Saints, and, of course, the Saints will be expected to be there around their King. They will be many thousands in number, and, to be like the King, they will have to have splendid houses to live in. The houses will form grand and splendid cities, which will have been built by then, the government strengthened, and the Saints perfected, to a great degree, through the principles of the Gospel: for all that, there must be much labor and money.

Let us take heart—the majestic work is going forward as quickly as we are able to follow it. It is not a bit of talk over the pulpit and in the *Society* from false believers, but rather it has claimed its place in the thoughts of the crowned heads of the earth, and asserted itself as the chief topic of debate in the main parliaments of the world. The Almighty God is on our side, and who *can* be against us?

An Elder in Israel.

MARTYRDOM OF PARLEY P. PRATT.

(To the tune "*Minnie Gray.*")

THE blood of God's servants is now a sign to the living
    That the destruction of old Babylon is at hand;
The martyrs of our age, tortured by pain—
    To the world will be death in fear.
O! Parley, dear Parley! a martyr for God.
    Night and day thy blood calls from the earth,
"Vengeance" among mankind.

The world is in turmoil, all an outrage,
    Soon it will be completely perceived as such;
It is America, for a season,
    That will be the focus of Babylon's wrath—
Dear Parley! dear Parley, he has been martyred;
    But still he lives, beneath the smiles of his God,
In the midst of those who dwell in Heaven.

All through us is great grief, piercing like an arrow,
    At the thought that Parley is in a grave!
A true martyr now is he,—my soul was bruised,—
    His side was pierced by the sword;
Brother Parley! brother Parley, thou sawest our Leader,
    When thou wast killed, thy spirit received
Heavenly strength to tear the veil.

Alas! in this age, woe to thee Babylon,
    Says the spirit of revelation of our God;
For we find your cup almost full,
    Nearly, it is nearly to the brim now;
O! Babel, O! Babel, thou hast offended our Father,
    For this, before long, true destruction, indeed,
Will be seen ravaging every land.

Before long we shall rejoice, our Parley we shall have,
    Soon he will rise again from his grave;
It will never again be possible to give him a single injury,
    With a handgun or by the edge of the sword;
Our Parley! our Parley! a martyr for Christ:—
    Soon he will come to Zion, with no fear,
To cheer us, without a single feeling of sadness.

Our Brigham is alive, glory be to God,
    "A Lion" is he, from yonder tribe of Ephraim;
When he roars, everyone beneath the Heavens
    Is filled with dread and fright;—
O Brigham! Dear Brigham, the seer of our God,
    Long mayest thou live, for shortly
Will the world and the "kingdom" be ours, indeed.
Flint.   David John.

☞ We have had considerable trouble in getting the semi-annual numbers in the proper form, but we must consider that it is the first attempt on the part of our hard-working brethren. To such we say that we need the names of the branches and their amounts of tithing for the six months, instead of the total for the Conference. Remember, from now on, to keep track of the details, such as the names of things, persons, dates, &c., with regard to the expenses. Where the account of sums paid from the tithing for books was given, we expect from each one, without exception, proof that his Conference has received credit for that: where the sum was divided for several branches, we wish to have their names, and the amount credited to each one. Not all the book distributors have sent their semi-annual 'Balance Sheets' in. Let it be understood that it is either the distributor's acknowledgment of the tithing sum received for his Conference, or the names of Branches as noted that provides the aforementioned that is required. Let every Branch President have the tithing account, &c., of his Branch on hand for when ——— calls by to compare things.

CONTENTS.

	PG.
War and the Mormons	225
Counsel to Elders	231
Editorial	233
Teachings	237
Song—Martyrdom of P. P. Pratt	239

PRINTED AND PUBLISHED BY D. DANIELS, SWANSEA.

ZION'S TRUMPET,

OR

Star of the Saints.

No. 16.]   AUGUST 1, 1857.   [Vol. X.

TEACHINGS.

By President Heber C. Kimball, *Bowery, April* 6, 1857.

You have heard what brother Wells has said in reference to the Temple, the canal, &c. The Temple is designed for many purposes, and there are many things that God will reveal and many blessings that he will confer upon this people in that building, if they will use due diligence in forwarding its completion.

Some may think that the erection of the Temple more particularly devolves upon bro. Brigham, bro. Heber, bro. Daniel, the Twelve, and a few of the Seventies, High Priests and Bishops, and when it is finished they may imagine that they will receive their blessings therein, but that work is designed to be general. There must needs be a universal exertion, not only by the leading official members of this Church, but by every member, male and female, for the Temple is not for us alone, it is also for our sons and daughters and succeeding generations. They will receive blessings in it, and therefore it concerns them as well as us.

If I obtain all the blessings of the priesthood, all the endowments, all the blessings that God has to confer upon us in this probation, and keep those things sacred while I live, I am then as pure and holy as it is possible for a man to be while in the flesh. Then if my wives are one with me my children and their posterity will partake of those blessings which have been placed upon me. Every blessing conferred upon me tends to benefit my posterity. Those blessings are for every righteous man, and the blessings that are conferred upon faithful men and women in their holy anointings and sealings will rest upon their posterity after them forever and ever, through their faithfulness, and there is no end to it.

It is a strong additional inducement for you to live your religion, in view of the benefits that will be continued to your posterity. If you can only bear this in mind, I think it will serve to keep you steadfast in the line of your duties. Will our posterity partake of the blessings we will receive in the Temple which we are building? They will, forever and forever. Our blessings are to continue always, if we live so as to attain to the principles and fullness of perfection and to secure the promises of eternal lives, then those blessings will rest upon us and our children.

How long will it take this people to build the Temple on this Block, supposing that every man and woman, and every child that has arrived to the years of accountability, will unitedly strive for its completion? Not very many years. Were I laboring on that Temple I would constantly endeavor to work upon it with an eye single to pushing it forward, and to the blessings I expected to receive therein. But supposing that you do not all live, will you not be benefited by it? Yes, you will.

We are now attending to matters that will answer every purpose, until that Temple is completed. Those who go through their endowments now and are sealed up unto eternal lives, those blessings will stick to them if they will stick to the blessings and promises that are made over unto them, and step forward with one heart and one mind to do the will of God as made known to them from time to time from this stand.

Is it requisite that every member of my family should feel the same interest that I do in my welfare and prosperity? Yes, every woman and child from the oldest to the youngest. They should be just like a tree that has many branches to it. The extremity of the longest limb is dependent upon the tree from which it grows. We should become one tree, and be like the "tree of life, which bare twelve manner of fruits," all connected to one stalk. I presume that those fruits came from grafts, else the tree probably would not have borne so many kinds. We must be grafted into the true vine and continue to partake of its fatness, and then we shall go back to our Father and God who is connected to one who is still farther back, and this Father and God who is connected to one who is still farther back, and this Father is connected to still farther back, and so on; and just so far as we respect our superiors and try to save our children, so shall we receive blessings from this time forth and forever, and shall become as numerous as the sands upon the sea shore. What is there to hinder us from obtaining these blessings? Nothing, except it be our own want of faithfulness, for by diligence, integrity and perseverance we can accomplish all we desire and help to move forward the great work of God.

I have heard a whispering that some who work on the Temple at dressing rock, and in the machine and blacksmith shops, having nothing but bread to eat. It seems as though this could not be so, for I have seen the public hands packing home carrots, parsnips, potatoes, &c, and it is not so very bad while there is plenty of them; and every man gets a pound of flour a day, and I think there should not be any grunting. It will not be a month before we shall have lettuce, radishes, &c., and there now is a plenty of greens; and onions are plenty in the tithing Office, and we will be very glad to have you come and get them at your leisure.

I have just touched upon these things in connection with bro. Wells's remarks concerning the Public Works, for I am one with him and he is one with me, and we are one with bro. Brigham. We have not set our feet to the race for any other purpose than to follow him and run through, for he is our leader and will be our leader, temporally and spiritually, from this time forth. When Joseph comes again, will bro. Brigham be removed? No, never. Brother Joseph is ahead, bro. Brigham is after him, I am after bro. Brigham, and you are after me, are you not? and we will not flinch, and God will bless and prosper every man that will help himself, and he will bless, prosper and sustain this people and they will never fall as a people, though we expect that many will apostatize, pitch over the dam and go to wreck.

If we sin and do not repent, God will chastise us until we do repent of and forsake all sin, but he never will scourge us so long as we do right. I have said a hundred times that we never will want for bread, meat and the comforts of life, worlds without end, if we will only do right. That is my prophecy, and always was, and it is true. I agree with Daniel, with Joseph, with Brigham, with Jesus and the Apostles, and all the holy Prophets, and I have spoken as I have to arouse your feelings, to waken you up and comfort your hearts and cheer your minds, for I have no other feeling than to do you good.

When the Big Cottonwood canal is finished, aside from its being of material benefit in our operations for building the Temple, it will be of great worth for irrigating lots in this city, especially in the east part of it; and you will soon be able to raise enough more than heretofore to pay you for your labor upon that work, yes, tenfold more. You may think that extravagant, but I say it is not. Reckon it up yourselves, and see how much more you could raise if you had plenty of water. You could raise as much corn fodder as would keep your cows through the winter, and I believe more than you have cows to eat it, besides the large extra amount of vegetables you could raise.

I will now make a few remarks in relation to building storehouses; not particularly in regard to building tithing storehouses here, for there are enough at present to hold all the grain we have; though I believe that by another year this people will fill our tithing houses until they overflow, for a great many of them are going to continue to do right and live their religion; and if they do that you will see the wheat, the corn, the oats, the barley, and all our stock and possessions increase. If we increase it will increase; our wealth will grow and increase with us, and there will be no end to it. But in order to lay up grain you must prepare storehouses. Every man who has a farm needs a storehouse, one made of rock and lime that will guard your grain against the mice, rats and all other four-legged vermin, also against the two-legged ones. I have more fears of the two-legged ones than I have of the four-legged ones.

Plan to build a good storehouse, every man who has a farm, and never cease until you have accomplished it. And do not forget to pay your tithing before you put the grain into the storehouse. Lay up enough for seven years, at a calculation for from five to ten in each family; and then calculate that there will be in your families from five to ten persons to where you now have one, because you are on the increase.

It now takes about one thousand bushels of wheat to bread my family one year, and I want to lay up six thousand for each year of the seven for which I calculate to store it up.

Reflect upon the probable increase of my family within seven years, they alone will be almost numerous enough to people a small city. Where a family now requires only a hundred bushels a year, let the head of that family lay up a hundred bushels the first year, two hundred the next, and increase the amount every year in proportion to their probable requirements.

When we have stored away our grain we are safe, independent of the world, in case of famine, are we not? Yes, we are, for in that case we will have the means for subsistence in our own hands. When the famines begin upon the earth, we shall be very apt to feed them first.

If judgments must needs begin at the house of God, and if the righteous scarcely are saved, how will it be with the wicked? Am I looking for famines? Yes, the most terrible and severe that have ever come upon the nations of the earth. These things are right before us, and some of this people are not thinking anything about them; they do not enter their hearts. Still there is not an Elder here who has read the revelation which says go forth and warn the inhabitants of this land of the wickedness, the death and disasters that are coming upon this nation, but what must be satisfied of the truth of what I am saying. You have done according to the instruction given in that revelation, and now reflect upon the things that I am declaring in your hearing, and lift up your voices unitedly as a people to the God of Heaven that he will be merciful unto us and favor Zion.

Be wise, listen to counsel, and obey the voice of the head and you will prosper and never want for bread, *but as the Lord liveth you will feel it, if you do not continue in the line of duty.* [President B. Young: *That is true.*] Yes, it is as true as it is that God ever spake to this generation. I consider that carefully storing our surplus grain against a time of need is of the greatest importance to this people, in connection with building the Temple. You may build that Temple, and at the same time neglect those things that I am speaking of, and you will perish temporally.

Now go to and raise grain, for I feel satisfied that the Lord will give us two, three, or four years of good times, and will hold the enemies of the upright by the bit, if we will do right. I will have the 'if' in every time, for in such case I tell you that God will hold our enemies and they cannot have any power, until he has a mind to permit them; and then he will only permit them for a time, in order to manifest his Almighty power and to qualify and prepare them for a time to come. I mean just what I say.

I have talked here year after year, and told you that I was going to work to build a good storehouse, and I now have a good one, though it is not yet quite finished. I have five or six hundred bushels of wheat in it, and I am going to make a tight floor of rock by grouting it with lime and sand and plaster the walls on both sides so that it will be proof against mice and all other kinds of vermin.

As I have said, I know that we will see those things of which I have spoken, such famines as this world never beheld. Yes, we have got to see those scenes, but if we will keep our vows and covenants the Lord will hold them off until we can prepare ourselves; and if you will wake up and do as you are told you will escape.

I will advise every man in every settlement to build a storehouse; and if one cannot do so alone, let two or three build one between them. Store up and preserve your grain, and then you will be safe. But if the famine should come upon us in our present condition, what could we do? If we do not do as we are told in this thing, the displeasure of the Lord will be upon us and he will not continue to bless us as he is now doing.

I know that he is able to suffer famines to come upon us, and then to rain manna down from heaven to sustain us. I also know that he could increase our grain in the granaries and our flour in the bins, and make one small loaf of bread suffice for many persons, by exerting his creative power. I do not know how he does that, but I know that he can do it just as easily as he could bring me into existence upon this earth.

There are a great many things we can save and take care of, as well as we can, wheat, barley and oats. We can dry pumpkins, squashes, currants, apples, peaches, &c., and save them; we can also save beans, peas and like articles and keep them for seven years. And if you take the right care of your wheat you can save it just as long as you may wish to, but in the usual mode of storing it you have got to stir it, move it, remove it and turn it over, or it will spoil. It is just so with this people, they have had to be moved and removed from place to place, to prevent them from getting into dotage.

I would not be afraid to promise a man who is sixty years of age, if he will take the counsel of bro. Brigham and his brethren, that he will renew his age. I have noticed that a man who has but one wife, and is inclined to that doctrine, soon begins to wither and dry up, while a man who goes into plurality looks fresh, young and sprightly. Why is this? Because God loves that man, and because he honors his work and word. Some of you may not believe this, but I not only believe it but I also know it. For a man of God to be confined to one woman is small business, for it is as much as we can do now to keep up under the burdens we have to carry, and I do not know what we should do if we had only one wife apiece.

Let us go to work and cultivate the earth, and go into the fields and bless the land and dedicate and consecrate it to God; and then dedicate the seed, the implements and the horses and oxen. Do you suppose that that will have any effect? I know that it will.

Nearly twenty years ago I was in a place in England in which

I felt very curious, but I did not know at the time what it meant. I went through a town called Chadburn, beyond Clitheroe. Before I went there, some persons told me that there was no use in my going, and asked me what I wanted to go to Chadburn for, saying it was the worst place in the country, for the sectarian priests had preached there faithfully for thirty years without making any impression.

Notwithstanding that, I went and preached once and baptized twenty-five persons, where the priests had not been able to do a thing.

(Continued on page 252.)

ZION'S TRUMPET,

OR

Star of the Saints.

SATURDAY, AUGUST 1, 1857.

THE wise perceives evil from afar, but the fool loiters next to destruction. Our appeal is to all who feel the least interest in this magnificent and wondrous work of the latter days and the most important and prophetic.

Is it not obvious to you that the hour of the judgment of God has begun, and the prophecies of the martyred Seer, JOSEPH SMITH, are being literally fulfilled? Who would believe a simple, uneducated, (with respect to the teaching of the world,) and beardless young boy who meekly declared that he had received the eternal Gospel, to preach to the whole world—to Protestants and Catholics, Muslims and Pagans—to every intelligent being, and that the hour of the judgment of God had come? Who would believe him when he spoke of a Church that contained only six members would increase to become a strong nation, when he spoke of the truthfulness of the Book of Mormon, the gathering of Israel—the building of Zion—the judgments of God and the fall of Babylon? Despite all the doubt and the opposition of the wise and strong ones of the world, the attraction of Mormonism continues to go forward, and every one of its movements is like the irresistible tide of the sea that sweeps away the sand embankments of slander and negative predictions against it! Is it possible for anyone not to understand the predictions of the prophets of God, even in this issue of our TRUMPET, about the severe famines that are *at our doors*? Can the sight of the warring, bloody, and corrupt world be improved?

It is true that the messengers of God must wash their hands completely from the blood of this generation, or woe betide them the next morning. If the mild voice of the humble servant of God is weak and despised as he kindly invites sinners to covenant with their God, and it is all in vain, a stronger voice will come. "And after your testimony (says God) cometh wrath and indignation upon the people; for after your testimony cometh the testimony of earthquakes, that shall cause groanings in the midst of her, (namely Babylon) and men shall fall upon the ground and shall not be able to stand. And also cometh the testimony of the voice of thunderings, and the voice of lightnings, and the voice of tempests, and the voice of the waves of the sea heaving themselves beyond their bounds. And all things shall be in commotion; and, surely, men's hearts shall fail them; for fear shall come upon all people; and angels shall fly through the midst of heaven, crying with a loud voice, sounding the trump of God, saying, "Prepare ye, prepare ye, O inhabitants of the earth; for the judgment of our God is come."

Since the judgment begins in the house of God, the Saints are to listen to the voice of their pastors, and prepare themselves so they will not be swept away with the chaff of the threshing floor, namely Zion. We call the attention of the Saints to the prophecies of Pres. Kimball in this issue about the severe famines that are at our doors! Truly, the present is not the time to idle and waste!

When the grasshoppers, crickets, and locusts, &c., visited the Saints, it was a topic of mocking for the Gentiles—They joyfully spread abroad their papers containing the news, and they rejoiced at the idea of the starvation of the Saints in Utah, but by today the tables have turned, as shown by the account of

THE GRASSHOPPERS IN MINNESOTA, U. S. A.

(From the *Saint Anthony (Minn.) Express.*)

"THE region around Monticello is literally alive with grasshoppers. Never in our life did we see so many of these troublesome and destructive insects. They crackled under one's feet like brittle shells. There was no such thing as avoiding them: whichever way one looked or went, they were manifesting themselves. Though not yet half grown, they are already doing immense damage, and unless they speedily emigrate, must devour every green thing in Wright county.

"Well-informed men who have watched the grasshoppers, and who know something of their instincts and habits, assert that they are already preparing to take up their line of march for the southern country, and that the region of the upper Mississippi will soon be delivered from them. [Time will tell that best.]

"Mr. Ferguson, who cultivates a farm on Minnetonka Lake, informs us this week that he had twelve acres of wheat which, ten days ago, looked in excellent condition. Four or five days since the grasshoppers commenced on it, and not a single blade can be seen on the whole field. Several acres of corn which had come up in fine order, had been destroyed in like manner.

"J. F. Bradley, Esq., of Monticello, informed us that on Saturday evening last he passed a wheat field of about twenty acres, near Monticello, which was in excellent condition, the wheat standing four to six and seven inches high, and very thick. On passing the same field on Monday morning last, some thirty-six hours later, the field looked as if it had never had a crop on it; not a blade of wheat was to be seen. The cold rains do not seem to have destroyed any, at least not to any appreciable extent."

If the righteous will *hardly* be saved, where do the ungodly and the sinner stand? If people hardly keep from freezing after preparing a house and warm clothes, what will become of the naked in the field? If the Saints hardly escape after saving and storing sufficient wheat and food for seven years, where do the wasteful Gentiles stand when the black famine comes?

The war dogs are to be released to the field, together with pestilence and destruction; for the Lord Jesus is about to come, and the fate of those who refuse his Gospel is sealed.

EMIGRATION.—Because numbers of the Saints have emigrated to the United States through the Emigrating Agents of the world, President Pratt wishes to notify the Welsh Saints that he will transport the least number as well as the greatest number of emigrants when necessary, even if it is only one family. Instead of going mixed in with the evil and unclean gentiles, the Saints should cross the sea in the company of as many of their brethren as they can.

Brother Pratt sends some out practically every month of the year.

Besides being a definite commandment for the Saints not to go in other ways, it is necessary to keep a record of their names. It is understood that all who go against the rules after this notice will forfeit their membership in the Church. The names of those who have prepaid are to be sent through this Office. Also, let the presidents send the names of all who have emigrated after the departure of the S. CURLING whose names have not been sent here.

To Presidents, &c.—We are sorry that we could not give a literal translation of the article that is in the "Star," issue 32, for lack of space. We shall give the essence of it.

He says that it is the duty of a Conference President to visit the branches and the homes as often as he can, feeding the Saints under his care, and informing them of every new movement of the work of God, and of the opposition of its enemies, and not to leave them in ignorance of everything that is going on and every teaching that is coming out, and keeping everything in order and in good form. If a President is full of life and diligence, the Saints under his care will be the same way, and if otherwise, it is easy to perceive the bad effects. Many are too inclined to stay in the finest and most luxurious places to feed their bellies instead of taking care of their Saints.

This is not a day to feast, to ride horses, and take delight; rather it is a day of hard labor, a day of sacrifice—a day in which all faculties of the body and the Spirit are to be put into action to save men, and to bring forth Zion on the earth. They are to hear your voices, and follow your light day and night, until the vineyard is cleansed; then will the Lord of the vineyard say to his servants, "Rest with me in my kingdom, and rejoice in the fruits of your labors."

The next article is on

LIBERALITY.—He says that the payment of tithing is not sufficient to do away with this heavenly principle. If the Saints keep their homes and their hearts open as they usually do they shall enjoy the blessings of the Lord on their food, and all they have.

What is a greater privilege than having the honor of lodging, feeding, and washing the feet of a servant of the Lord, and receiving his teaching and blessing? And what better opportunity will the servants of God have to come to know and benefit the Saints than in their homes and their family circle?

Next he comments about the

CONFERENCE Houses.—Besides the heavy expenses for these houses, and besides a president who is going around to the homes of his Saints not having time to be in one, they tend to nurture idleness and laziness, depriving the Saints of their blessings, in the loss of the visit of their Presidents. The fewer of them, then, the better.

BOOK DEBTS are increasing by now! With nothing but the *Trumpet* every fortnight, frugality and order, we are confident that we will be enabled to close our accounts without any loss when we have the privilege of going home.

(Continued from page 248.)

I went through the streets of that town feeling as I never before felt in my life. My hair would rise on my head as I walked through the streets, and I did not then know what was the matter with me. I pulled off my hat, and felt that I wanted to pull off my shoes, and I did not know what to think of it.

When I returned I mentioned the circumstance to bro. Joseph who said, "Did you not understand it? That is a place where some of the old prophets traveled and dedicated that land, and their blessing fell upon you." Then try it, and see if it will not leave a blessing for us to dedicate our lands. If you think that it will not, never bring another bottle of oil and ask us to dedicate and consecrate it for the benefit of the sick. I know that we can bless the land, and that through our blessing it will be filled with the Spirit and power of God, and that too in great profusion, especially if we are filled with the Spirit ourselves. Some may call me enthusiastic, but I am no more so that the old prophets were when they had the Spirit of God upon them.

Let us bless the land we cultivate and the fountains of water and they will be blest; and then men may drink of those waters and they will fill them with the Spirit and power of God. Let us bless and dedicate the fountains of life that are in us, in our wives and children and in everything else around us. Can the Spirit of God enter a stone, or one of those posts? Yes, and it can fill every pore as well as it can every pore in my body. Can it enter into my pores? Yes, even into my hair; and it can also enter my bones and quicken every limb, joint and fiber.

Let us not dispose of any grain, only what is actually necessary. When it is actually necessary to part with any grain, let us put it into the right hands. If I have any to part with, I will put it into the hands of those that will make good use of it. We have got to become one in our financial matters in the church and kingdom of God. How can you become one tree, with limbs and branches all pertaining to the selfsame tree, when there is disunion among you?

Then go to work and build up this kingdom, establish righteousness and prepare yourselves for the famines that are coming upon the earth, for I tell you that they are coming.

Do you suppose that God would give revelations and tell us to warn the inhabitants of the earth of things which were coming speedily upon them, if he did not intend that those things should come? He said that they should feel them, and I know that they are bound to feel them, for they will not repent. Let us go to work and prepare for the thousands upon thousands who will come unto us.

Our Carrying Company is only in its infancy, but it will prepare the way, and the day will come when people will gather here by hundreds and by thousands; yea, fifty thousand in a year, and very many will come trudging along with their bundles under their arms. I have heard bro. Joseph, bro. Brigham and several other men say that it will be, and I know it will, because they have said it. Many of you will venture to say that you believe it, but I know that it is true, and it will surely come to pass.

Brethren and sisters, these are some of my feelings; and I hope and pray that those whom we have warned will go home and warn their neighbors and tell them to be up and doing, and then we shall not have to tell you these things again. It is no time for grunting, it is no time for having the *blues*, it is not time for sugar tits, for dancing and amusing ourselves. Amusements are stopped for the present, but when bro. Brigham says dance, then dance; but when he says stop, then stop; and when he says prophesy, then prophesy, but be sure to prophesy right.

I have said nothing but what the Spirit has dictated, and all the principles that I have touched upon are contained in the Bible; if you don't believe it, take that Book and look for yourselves; and then take the Book of Mormon and see what the Lord said to the Nephites. He said, "The nation or people that will not serve me on this land, I will cut off from the face of the earth," and I know that he will do it. And bro. Brigham, the Twelve Apostles, and Patriarchs John Young and Isaac Morley will all declare that it is true. May God bless you: Amen.

THE TEMPLE BLOCK.

*(*From the *Deseret News.)*

One day last week according to our expressed intentions we took a walk inside the wall that surrounds the temple block, to see what was passing there and what so many men were employed at, that had been seen going and coming in the direction of the east gate, the only one kept open for the ingress and egress of the workmen, and for the teams hauling stone, lime, sand, coal, lumber and other materials necessary for carrying the various kinds of work and mechanism, the men are engaged in on and about the foundation of the Temple, in the Public Shops and other places on the block.

As was expected from the noise heard for many weeks, the first thing seen on passing through the gate was a large company of stone cutters busily engaged in hewing the huge rocks that had been hauled there from the quarry four or five miles distant, and fitting them for the place they are to occupy in the basement of the Temple.

We saw there, cheerfully at work, men whose hairs were white with age, middle aged and young men, with many boys just commencing to use the chisel, and the noise they made was nearly deafening as we are unaccustomed to noise of that kind. We did not count the men, but the stone cutters with the laborers engaged in placing the stones ready for the masons when they get to work would make a small army, and so soon as the Cottonwood Canal is completed, and the facilities for delivering rock faster are increased, the number of stone squarers and laborers will be augmented in a corresponding degree.

After spending a short time looking on the busy scenes without, we passed through the public shops, taking a cursory view of what was going on there, and found them alive with workmen. The stone shop, where stones are hewn in better style and greater variety than those for the basement of the Temple; the blacksmiths' shop, the carpenters' shop, the paint shop, the gunsmiths' shop, the machine and other shops all presented scenes of industry, ingenuity and skill worthy looking at.

Among other things the fire engine, which the city council are getting made, attracted our attention, as it has been thought by some that a good one could not be made here. The workmen are progressing with it slowly, but when done if it is not as good as any that could be imported we shall be mistaken. At all events it will be of valley manufacture, and another can be made, if it fails to work well, that will do better, in accordance with the spirit of the age.

Having but little time to spend in feasting our mind in examining the various kinds of work done and in the progress of completion in the various departments through which we passed, and seeing an imitation of our patent notice to loafers posted up at every angle, we did not stay long in any one place, and returned with as little delay as our own curiosity would admit to attend to our own business, much pleased with the excursion and with what we had seen.—*Deseret News.*

BOOK DEBTS, JUNE 30, 1857.

CONFERENCE.	£	s.	c.
Brecon.	10	2	10
Monmouth	61	0	0
East Glamorgan	112	18	11½
Cardiff	56	9	6
West Glamorgan	130	10	6½
Llanelli	63	8	7
Carmarthen	24	10	5½
Pembrokeshire.	10	1	11½
Cardiganshire..	18	13	7
Merionethshire	12	0	5½
Flintshire...	14	1	4
Denbighshire...	18	2	1½
Anglesey	12	13	1½
	£544	13	5½

BOOK PAYMENTS FROM MAY 28 TO JULY 31.—A. L. Jones, £7; J. Thomas, £1 8s.; J. Davies, £11; J. Griffiths, 12s.; J. Treharne, £1 2s.; I. Jones, £4; E. D. Miles, 10s; W. Ajax, Denbigh, £1 18s.; W. Ajax, Anglesely, £3 11s 8c.; M. Vaughan, £5.

☞ Do not forget the requests in our previous issue, together with the accounts for the previous year, as was requested by letter.

WE EXPECT the missionaries from Utah any day now.

Addresses—Rev. David Davies, Cil Heol, Llanelli, Carmarthenshire.

Mr. Levi James, 7, Park St., Swansea.

CONTENTS.

	PG.
Teachings of Pres. Kimball	241, 252
Editorial—Appeal—Grasshoppers—Emigrating—To the Presidents, &c.	248
The Temple Block	254

PRINTED AND PUBLISHED BY D. DANIELS, SWANSEA.

ZION'S TRUMPET,

OR

Star of the Saints.

No. 17.] AUGUST 15, 1857. [Vol. X.

A NUT OR TWO FOR THE "LEADER" TO CHEW ON.

LET our readers understand that the *Leader* is a newspaper published in Pwllheli, North Wales.

This strange *Leader* is himself so blind with respect to "Mormonism," that he is led by some of his correspondents who are even more blind, truly fulfilling the scripture, 'If the blind lead the blind, both shall fall into the ditch:"—the ditch of lies and contradiction in this example.

He gives some savory accusations against the Saints, mocking their God in a very unusual way.

With regard to his first accusation, namely, "that 'Mormonism' does not have established beliefs, but that its principles and its doctrines are open to being changed according to whim, and according to the special purposes of church leaders," we say that this is a baseless and lying assertion, and we ask for the proof! Accusing, maligning, and condemning are an easy task—it is not as easy to prove the subject that establishes the fact—*the proof* Mr. *Leader*.

Accusation 2.—"At present it is a mixture of paganism, Judaism, Christianity, Mohammedanism, idol worship, and atheism."

Extremely witty and clever; but again where is the *proof,* Mr. Editor? Only one thing is lacking in your 'mixture,' namely, *truth*: if you had that, two other things would follow—consistency and proof. You did not say *which* part of the above 'isms' are within Mormonism. Perhaps even the pagans

17 [PRICE 1½*c.*

have some correct ideas, yes, better than those of the so called Christians of our age. Even the idol worshippers and atheists of our age have better ideas than some who call themselves Christians.

We shall not imitate or follow the *Leader* in assertions without proving them with undeniable facts.

1. The 'Christians' of our day believe in a God without body, parts, or passions—present everywhere, or filling all space, heaven, earth and hell although he is immaterial, yet the creator of all matter. The poem of brother John Richards says that

> The sectarians' God, up in the third heaven,
> And here on the earth, fills every spot and place;
> He fills hell below, and the sun and the moon on high,
> And does so every second, though 'tis a great surprise to me!

> There is no picture or image that can be made to this being,
> He has no head nor eyes, nor hand, nor leg, nor foot;
> He is a God of no substance, and Father of the substances of the world,
> Author and Keeper of all the great *chaos*!

> He is greater in size than the earth, and all the great seas,
> Sun, moon, stars, and the planets, were they all put together;
> Neither has he boundaries—his center is in the heavens,
> And his center is here also—a very strange being is he!

> Good and bad are indifferent, making tremendous nonsense,
> And worlds without number, all in his huge belly!
> A variety of elements, and a myriad of beings without number,
> Dwelling in their emptiness, which is a great surprise to me!

> Where does God dwell? Oh, in the third heaven,
> We are there also, if we are in his belly;
> If so it is to believe, hideous foolishness for a people,
> To say that the family of death goes to him.

> If the worlds are in him, we are there in them,
> And thus in him as well, and what more do we need?
> 'Tis foolishness to talk of heavens, on high far away,
> Or any blessed places—there is no need for anything better.

> Everyone is in God already, according to their creed,
> 'Tis great foolishness to preach of Christ and his fatal wound;
> Despite this we need preachers, paying them a big wage,
> And we need to bow our heads, and kneel down to them.

> And also they pray, each one beneath his burden,
> "O Lord God of hosts, reveal thy arm;
> "And come here thyself to fully bless us;
> "We are poor, thou hast plenty."

'Tis foolishness to say *Reveal* that which has never existed,
And invite an object to them that *more than fills the house;*
And who can be *poor* and *dwell in him?*
When he is *all wealthy*, and in the third heaven!

O Lord God of hosts, everyone, white and black,
Will soon come to recognize thee by way of the blessed atonement;
Lest they in the end suffer his terrible wrath,
When the day comes to judge and prove us each one.

The meaning of a god without a body, &c., is an immaterial god, *or a god of nothing!* If he were matter, that matter would have to fill a part of space, and then it would be a *body*, for a body *is the size of any matter that fills space*. Who can perceive or describe *nothing?* What hold or power does 'nothing' have over matter? Were we to fear or love the 'god of the sectarians,' what would we fear or love? *Nothing!*

2. They believe that this non-existent shadow has brought all the elements of existence out of nothingness! "Out of what did the *great* God create this world, my dear children?" says the teacher to the Sabbath school children. "From *nothing*," is the ready answer after 'learning the subject.' This is how more repugnant ideas are rooted in the minds of the children of 'Christians' of our age even than in the children of idolators! The idol worshipers have some objects to worship—the elements of fire, water, and air, or the sun, the moon, a river, a creature, or a human being that has a body, parts, and passions. These can be understood; but who can conceive of an immaterial god who has a person, but no body, and that person is three persons, and the three persons are one person? The sectarians blame the idol worshipers for not going according to the light of their understanding and reason, instead of traditions and fanciful ideas, while they themselves are a hundred times more foolish!

Atheism, is it, Mr. Editor? Is not the above sufficient to nauseate any thinking man, and make him a callous atheist if he does not *know the true God?*

While absurd notions are taught that the elements of our earth were brought out of nothingness into existence, about six thousand years ago, geology teaches the atheist otherwise. Obvious impressions are left on substances by the effect of time as consistently as the rising of the sun or the change of the seasons which prove their existence for more than six thousand years back. It is easier for the atheist to believe that which he can see for himself than the old fanciful nonsense of superstitious and selfish fanatics.

Who can understand the bringing of substance into existence out of nothingness? No one. What man in his right mind will believe that which cannot be understood, and which is absurd in the face of his reason? What just being will hold him responsible for not believing? How are your teeth as they crack the nuts, Mr. Editor?

The Bible is not the standard of the nonsense noted. The account of the creation of the elements out of nothing cannot be found in it. Nor can one find an account in the Bible of a god without body, parts, or passions; but to the contrary, it gives an account of a God who has body, parts, and passions, who has walked with, eaten with, striven with, and associated *face to face* with man—a God who can love or be jealous, which proves his passions.

Accusation III. You say that our "ideas have changed considerably with respect to the Godhood from the *beginning* of our organization." We ask in what instance, together with what meaning of the *beginning* of our organization? Another nut that Mr. Editor has to crack is that the God the Saints worship is no more than "some notion to tickle their curiosity." We believe that we have enough friends who have a worse ticklish itch, from the facts we have noted.

IV. He asserts that the Saints are reaching to obtain in the end the crown of Godhood for their own heads. Quite right for once, accidentally. Paul was also "tickling the curiosity" of the Philippians in the same way, when he said, "Let this mind be in you, which was also in Christ Jesus, who, being in the form of God, thought it not robbery to be equal with God."

In order to prove and establish these topics, we are sending a copy of "Who is the God of the Saints" to you, Mr. Editor, so that we will not take up too much of our space in answering you, since the treatise explains its topic, and disproves your false accusations.

We will answer for any doctrine you see in our books, which contain every principle of our religion that has ever been preached in this country; but we will pay no attention to the lying and baseless repetitions of malicious slanderers, such as the reference to the declarations of brothers Wheelock, Kaye, &c. We will give what the South Waleans call a hop, skip, and a jump over the pack of baseless lies invented by a malicious enemy.

The correct translation of the quotation of the revelation noted is as follows:—[from the "Millennial Star," number 48, vol. 15.]

"Now hear it, O inhabitants of the earth, Jew and gentile, Saint and sinner! When our father Adam came into the garden of Eden, he came into it with a celestial body, and brought Eve, one of his wives, with him. He helped to make and organize this world. He is Michael, the Archangel, the Ancient of Days, about whom holy men have written and spoken. He is our Father and our God, and the only God with whom *we* have to do. Every man upon the earth, professing Christians or non-professing, must hear it, and will know it sooner or later."

There are gods many and lords many, but to *us* there is but *one* God, says Paul, and for our reasons for worshiping that *one* God, we direct you to the treatise, "Who is the God of the Saints," trusting that you will see that we have a better God than one who is without body, parts, or passions.

We also direct you to 1 Cor., chapter 2, where you will learn a mystery, i.e., that the natural man cannot know and understand the things of God without having the Spirit of God, and if you cannot believe the lads of the Saints who preach Christ and belief in him, professing that they have authority to administer the ordinances of the Gospel, and that the gift of the Holy Ghost is to be obtained through that, we do not expect that you will be able to believe or discern the deep things of the Spirit.

The old, well-known tale of Elin Dafydd shows that your paper is years behind the times. The same thing with the great, wise man of Llŷn, who makes the remarkable discovery that the Saints in Utah believe in and practice polygamy, and challenges anyone of the Saints to prove otherwise, while their publications have proclaimed the doctrine for years, and no one has yet refuted it! The "lads of Llŷn" are way ahead of you, dear Jones; hasten to the *patent office* with your remarkable discovery, and stop saying what you do not know. We suggest, then, that you get a new name for the *Leader*, namely the *Follower*, and we expect to hear before long that it has no name in the world!

A FEW MORE QUESTIONS FOR MINISTERS TO ANSWER.

(From the *Western Standard*.)

The Bible calls Abraham the friend of God; and states, that it was because of his obedience and faithfulness that God entered into a covenant with him. His readiness to offer up his son Isaac is proof that God could give him no commandment that he would not unhesitatingly and with all his heart obey. If this be so, and if plural marriages are sinful, impure, and improper in the sight of God, how is it possible that He did not make Abraham acquainted with the sinful nature of such marriages, when he promised that kings should come out of him, and that in his offspring the world should be blessed, seeing, that at that very time he was a polygamist?

When Israel made a war of extermination upon the Midianites, God commanded them to spare the young women for wives for the Israelites. They captured thirty-two thousand young ladies; and by God's command they were apportioned among the army, the congregation, and to the Lord. By this apportionment, the army drew sixteen thousand, the congregation 15,968, and the Lord 32. Now as the Mosaic ritual required no Vestal virgins nor consecrated maids, to minister in the offices of religion, and as Moses, in Exodus vii. 1, is said to be God, were not those 32 maids given to Moses, and if given to him, were they not intended to be his wives? If not, what were they intended for? Consult chapter 31 of Numbers.

When God, in Numbers xiv. 12, threatened to destroy the men of Israel for their wickedness, and told Moses that He would make a great nation of him, upon what principle did He promise that, if not upon the principle of polygamy?

Hannah was the second living wife of Elkanah; Samuel therefore was the offspring of a polygamic marriage. Now polygamy is either pure and holy before God, and its children legitimate; or it is impure and unholy, and its offspring are bastards, and by the law of Moses were not permitted to enter into the congregation of the Lord. If, therefore, Samuel was not born in lawful wedlock, how was it possible for him to minister at the altar, as the chosen Prophet, Seer, and Revelator of the Most High God?

By consulting 2 Samuel xii. 8, we find that God himself gave unto David, Saul's wives, and if they had not been enough, he would have given him more: How could that be, according to the uninspired ideas of monogamists?

Isaiah prophesies that at the building up and glorifying of Zion in the last days, seven women shall offer themselves as wives of one man: do monogamic Christians believe that this prediction of the "Evangelical Prophet" will be fulfilled? And if this passage is to be spiritualized, what kind of wives will those spiritual wives be?

Christ promised them who forsook wives, &c., for His sake, to reward them an hundredfold in this world. Does not the fulfillment of that involve the principle of polygamy?

Where in the Bible is polygamy forbidden, and declared to be unlawful?

What passage in the Bible says that it is unlawful for a Christian man to have more than one wife?

Is not Paul's expression in 1 Timothy iii. 2, 12, equivalent to saying that Bishops and Deacons must be married men, having at least one wife?

Which system is better calculated to produce a healthy and vigorous posterity; the polygamy of the "Mormons" which entirely separates a woman from her husband during pregnancy and the nursing period, or the monogamy of Christians which wantonly violates those laws of life and health which even brutes respect?

In Utah, even upon the testimony of apostates, there are but two classes of women: viz., wives and daughters. Which is the better, the condition of things in Utah, or the society in California [yes, and in Britain also], where in addition to wives and daughters, a third and very numerous class of females is added?

[Come, Mr. 'Leader,' since you are so annoyed by the 'hallowed nest,' and compare the nest to which such a bird as yourself belongs with those of the 'hallowed nest.'—Editor.]

☞ Whenever our readers see some piece in any publication touching on 'Mormonism,' do us the kindness of sending it here. Our thanks to bro. Evans, Tredegar.—Editor.

ZION'S TRUMPET,

OR

𝔖tar of t𝔥e 𝔖aints.

SATURDAY, AUGUST 15, 1857.

TROOPS FOR UTAH.—After the American newspapers speaking so much for months about sending soldiers and a new governor to Utah, they have set out at last, when it was suspected that they might be caught by the winter before they arrived; but what do the *Leader* and Mr. "Jones of Llŷn" say now, I wonder? The *St. Joseph* Journal, for August 2, says that a company of 100 soldiers and 50 teamsters were all killed on the *plains* by the Indians. Colonel Summers was their commander. This happened about 200 miles from Fort Kearney. The Indians had told our missionaries that they were preparing for them.

How far did the Troops go?—The *New York Herald* informs us that another insurrection has broken out in Kansas, because a city committee had prepared a city charter different from that granted by the territorial legislature. The governor rose up against it, and was forced to send for General Kearney and the troops who were on their way to Utah to have them return at once to Kansas to keep the peace. Several armed men gathered to the field, and an unavoidable battle was expected. Perhaps we will have some news before we go to press.

EMIGRATION AGAIN.—We trust that attention has been given to our notice on this topic in the previous issue. We publish now the names we received of those who have left, some of them against the rules, and without being in their place as members of the church, and others through President Orson Pratt, without informing us:— From the East Glamorgan Conference, Thomas Evans, Cefn, and his family, M. Powell, Robert Evans, Jno. Ventries, Cardiff, and his family, W. Vaughan, "a number from Georgetown;" seek to know their names, and send them here; Dd. Jones, Dd. Thomas, Henry, Phillips; Jane Williams, Edward Lewis and his wife, the three from Dowlais; David Thomas, and his family, James Keate and his sister,

John Harris, John Morgan and Elisabeth Moslin, all from Cardiff; T. Stephens, Hopkin Hopkins, Cwmbach; Albion Jenkins, Llanfabon, and his wife; John Edwards, Aberdare; Wm. Powell, Merthyr, and his wife; and Wm. Thomas, from the same place; "one from Rhymney and one from Cwmbach." Can their names be obtained? &c. From Brecon—J. Jones and Robert James. From Monmouthshire—Maria Bath, Elizabeth Talbot, and her family, David Rees, Griffith George, John Price, Rees Rees, John Masters, his wife, and two children. If there are more, send all their names, &c., here without delay, since President Pratt is calling on us for them, and says "that it is *necessary to present* such a procedure from now on, and go according to the rules."

INSTRUCTIONS.—All the Conference Presidents by now understand how we wish to receive their semi-annual 'Bal. Sheets.' Besides the semi-annual reports, we wish for the presidents to send a more frequent accounting in their correspondence how they have used the tithing, let us say monthly; nevertheless, the 'Bal. Sheet' still needs to be sent. We request that a letter be sent for the "balance sheet" of all money the treasurer received from the beginning of the presidency of the current presidents beginning in 1856 until the 31 of last December; except, of course, for the book money, which the Distributors received, and the money for the Penny Fund. Neither of the last two accounts are to be on the *Bal. Sheet* we noted. Opposite the total received we request an accounting of the expenses during the same time. We request, also, the names of the branches who received credit from the Book distributors for book money they received from the tithing. For example let's say that A. B., the distributor, received £5 (five pounds) from the tithing to pay the Office for books. He thus gives credit to branch A for £1, to B for £2, to C for £1, and to D for £1; then, at the top of the semi-annual report, he sends a *list* here with the names of the branches and the totals in it; after that, we will publish them in the Trumpet, so the branch distributors can see there is no mistake. Therefore, we request this *list* for the last six months, from January 1 to June 30, and another from the beginning of the Tithing to December 31.

For the Penny Fund we request an account of the totals and names of the Branches and their contributions from the establishment of the Fund to June 30, 1857, on the debit side, and on the payment side put the totals paid in here, and the balance on hand, if there was one.

Chief book distributors, who have not sent them, will send their Bal. sheets by June 30. We do not request a *list* of the branches who owe money, or the books on hand—only the *totals* of these two things, and the money on hand to answer the requests of the offices.

We hope that at the end of this half year that each will understand his work, sending these required things: namely, the *Annual* Report, the Tithing Bal. Sheet from July 1 to December 31; the Names of Branches and the totals of Tithing credited to them for books; and the Bal. Sheets of the chief Distributors. Our patience will not endure much longer for those who delay in sending some of the things noted. Take warning.

———

LETTERS FROM THE VALLEY as late as June 27 confirm the news that the crops are remarkably abundant, and that the farmers, in obedience to the counsel of our Prophet, are preparing storehouses to keep the wheat, &c., over a seven-year period, while the soil may rest, and all the Saints are awakening to prepare themselves to be able to await the grievous day that is *at the door!* Brothers D. Jones and T. Jeremy send their fondest regards to the Welsh Saints. The news their letters contain have already been published.

ELDERS Enoch Reese, (Welsh, by blood—American by birth), Wm. P. Thomas, (formerly from Llanybydder,) and Richard G. Evans, formerly from Pembrey, arrived at this office, on a mission from Utah to Wales—the first two on the 5th, and the last on the 12th of this month, healthy and active. They found the Indians to be friendly and brotherly along the way; but they were harshly threatened by the Government troops. The States were boiling with strife and disputes, as the American newspapers show, which shows clearly that the prediction of the Prophet Joseph is rapidly being fulfilled. Our brethren are full of the godly fire, and their eyes are open to see the atmosphere blackening, and the storm gathering—men becoming more and more bloodthirsty, and war breaking out on every side, and many of the Saints sleeping!

POEM.

A greeting of the Poet to his gifted Brother, &c., Nathan Ddu of Llywel.

Nathan Ddu is beloved for his poetry,
Can it be that his kindly, sweet voice is stilled?
The bard and his text are silent
Pining after not having one.
From thy room, oh, arise at last,
Give us part of a small verse;
From thy happy muse send a sample,
Obligingly from Defynnog:
Thy muse's smile is honey—
Even excellent says Dewi's muse.

The 'Song of Winter' was not received,
Weaving a portrayal of gray frost.
And the 'Spring' with its beautiful emergence—
The undergrowth making our land green;
And a host of primroses before us—
The beautiful rising of their mantle.
And the sweet song of a bird,
In praise above the luxuriant growth of the dale
And she, the proud blackbird
Bringing praise to our lovely head.
And the thrush traveling quickly,
With its sermon on the twig.

The cuckoo came to travel the branches—
To sing a hymn to the small trees.

Summer, languishing, in splendor also—
All nature sings together!
The cuckoo has retreated again,
Her fair song was not a long one;
For our part despite the rejection,
Serve us readily in the 'Song of Summer;'
Thy song to us, now,
Will turn more treasure.
The garden and the field are in beauty,
Beneath the sight of a carpet of flowers!
Sweet melodies weave through the woods,

And leaves dress the meadows.
Honey has come on every twig;
And dew on the grass of the glen.
The myriad of trees are green—
A feast from the bounty of the Lord—
The provision of the creator of worlds,
We receive abundantly and openly.

The Summer with its order is fleeing—
Instead of Summer—a pleasant Harvest.
Behold, Autumn has arrived!
To draw the produce home:
The vast crop is reaped,
Covering the entire face of our land;
The curved and sharp sickle,
And the scythe with its blade on fire!
Glistening in bright color,
Shining beneath the rays of the sun!
The grain from the ears of corn,
Behold, are gathered quickly.

Doubtless—a strange season,
Is this, it is the day of the Lord God!
The day of black vengeance will come—
The day of cleaning the threshing floor,
The wheat will be winnowed,
To be treated carefully there—
The will of God is such—
And will bear the *wheat* to his house;
And all the *chaff* that will remain out—
Will be seen thrown into the fire.
Altogether correctly—a privilege—
To live godly lives as cheerful Saints.

Swansea, Dewi Elfed.

In response to the above poem behold the following

SUMMER SONG,

(By Nathan Ddu from Llywel, now from Defynnog, Breconshire.)

The Summer season has approached
More clearly above the glen;

Great rejoicing I shall have,
    For this visitation;
Such an amazing and beautiful sight,
    The whole earth is like a garden!
And a gentle breeze flies through the sky
    Above the playing table of the world!

The rich abundant hills,
    I now see in dignity,
And the branches heavily laden with fruit,
    Bending their load to the ground.
And every hill and meadow appear
    To be covered with an abundant crop;
Asserting the sward's transformation
    Under gentle summer breezes.

The morning stroll is so precious,
    In the midst of a merry glade;
One can listen to the summer *anthem*,
    Of the lovely birds at will.
In a fanfare in the wood,
    The blackbird is without pain;
Giving forth the loudest sound amidst the branches,
    Charming the day with its tune.

When the little birds sleep,
    After singing all day long;
Some charming sweet sound,
    That the fair nightingale gives forth.
One of the messengers of summer,
    Is the bird, finest of its kind;
The fairest songster we have,
    And its gift is to worship God.

The old man from his cottage takes,
    A walk in the garden;
And he receives a free promise,
    And its unforbidden fruits;
Although his mien is gray,
    Bowed down under many infirmities;
The delicacies of summer on the branches,
    Give him a new lease of life.

To Thee, kindest Father
>   Of life, be the praise;
Throughout all existence,
>   Let every voice be constant,
May every living thing
>   Join in the song,
Throughout all the borders of the round earth,
>   And man with his heart on fire.

NEWS FROM UTAH.

President's Office: Great Salt Lake City.
May 29, 1857.

Brother Orson Pratt, Liverpool.—We are yet without a mail from the east, since the November mail was brought in, and I have nothing from you by the last South mail. We left this city on Friday, April 24, for the north, and returned on Tuesday, May 26, all well, and no accidents, having traveled nearly 800 miles. We saw much land, some little of it good soil, much good grazing land. But the best soil we were told "lies still ahead," in Bitterroot Valley, and in the valleys still further east, and on the headwaters of the Missouri. We saw enough to satisfy us, had we hitherto been ignorant of the fact, that the world is not yet over-peopled. There are thousands of acres of good arable and pasture land, where thousands of the honest and industrious poor, who are now immured in factories, and other civilized prison, could sustain themselves, and thrive as industrious bees of the Deseret hive, breathing a pure and wholesome air, free to do all the good they can to the human family and to themselves.

One word more on the reformation begun among the Saints in Europe. Obedience to the Gospel at first brings peace and joy. By and by, all becomes with some as an old song. Local Elders have nothing new or exciting in their addresses; soon they know a little more than they did in the sectarian churches; they are tempted to think they know all, lose the Spirit, become indolent in their attendance at meetings, formal and dull in their prayers, frequently forgetting entirely to acknowledge the goodness and power of God in thanksgiving and praise. By and by they lose the spirit of gathering, if ever they had it, and finally fall asleep in infidelity. Hence the necessity of a sudden pause—"Where am I? What am I? What am I doing? Am I living my religion? Are the good angels ever near me ministering to me? Have I wronged my brother in anything? Am I believing in, and obedient to every legally constituted authority in the kingdom of God? Have I increased faith and power in God, His ordinances, and increasing confidence in myself, my brethren, and my God? Have I nothing to repent of, nothing to amend, reform or improve? Have I become perfect, or is my course eternally progressive?" These and a hundred similar queries put by the Saint to himself have awakened many, and will, no doubt, continue to arouse the watchful, while humanity has its frailties, and the enemies of the kingdom seen and unseen, live and have power to oppose. All hell lies now awake to destroy the work and kingdom of God here, and may become more so in foreign countries, ere long. And just as we begin to arouse ourselves to live and build up another house to our God, the enemies of His work stir themselves up and are more active to our injury and destruction than ever. But we feel to joy in the God of our salvation. We know this work is His, and that we are his, and he will turn and overturn till his purposes are accomplished, and his kingdom established that shall never be thrown down. Even so. Amen.

There are settlements at Beaver creek, nine miles east of the old Pawnee village. Also at different points on the Platte river which will accommodate the emigrants from northern Europe, who necessarily start late. We are planting stations on the line from here to the East for the mail, and the 'Express Carrying Company.'

Your sincere friend and
Brother in the Everlasting Covenant,
BRIGHAM YOUNG.

SABBATH SCHOOL OF UTAH.

Last Friday morning, several companies of Foot Soldiers were seen traveling out of this City with benches toward the north and east of the city up to City Creek Canyon, and upon inquiring as to the purpose for such an unusual turnout, and the appearance of the young portion of the people, we were informed that it was the First of May, and that the Sunday School Teachers in the various Wards, together with their students, according to previous arrangements, had turned out for a procession, on a day in May, after which they were to meet in the Tabernacle, at 2 p.m., and were to be addressed by Elder Woodruff and others. Everyone looked happy and lively as they passed by, and during the early part of the day crowds of them could be seen on the slopes above the city, traveling and coming back in every direction, enjoying themselves in youthful games and amusement.

At 2 p.m. they returned toward the city and repaired to the Music Hall, where they were formed into a line by the Marshall of the day, R. A. Allred, and his assistants, and being led by the Brass Band, they traveled up past the Governor's home, and from there down to the Tabernacle.

The spectacle created by their passing through the streets was entirely fitting—many of the young women were dressed in white and attractively adorned in a variety of modes with wreaths of flowers and green leaves; and the boys had not neglected to adorn their person in the most pleasing manner for themselves, which, with the banners carried by each one, bearing many appropriate mottoes added greatly to that which was most certainly a fitting exhibition of youthful and innocent enjoyment.

CONTENTS.

	PG.
A nut or two for the 'Leader' to chew on	257
Questions for Ministers	262
Editorial—Troops for Utah—Emigration—Instructions—Letters from the Valley—Arrivals	264
A Poem of Greeting to Nathan Ddu—the Close of Summer	267
Sabbath School of Utah	272

PRINTED AND PUBLISHED BY DANIEL DANIELS, SWANSEA.

ZION'S TRUMPET,

OR

𝕾tar of the 𝕾aints.

| No. 18.] | AUGUST 29, 1857. | [Vol. X. |

NEWS FROM THE VALLEY.

(From the *Millennial Star*.)

President's Office: Great S. L. City,
June 30, 1857.

Elders Orson Pratt and Ezra T. Benson.

Dear Brothers.—On the 24th of April I departed on my contemplated journey north to Salmon River. I returned to this place May 26, after an absence of 32 days. We had a large company of 56 wagons and carriages, and 142 persons, but during the whole trip, I did not hear an angry word, or observe a malicious feeling.

On the 29th of last month, Elders G. A. Smith, J. M. Bernhisel, and T. O. Angel arrived in good health and spirits.

There are many improvements being made in the city, streets, sidewalks, fences, buildings, &c. There are between three and four hundred men upon the public works, and 30 teams rolling in the stone for the Temple. Although money is scarce, business is lively, and everything is flourishing with this people, because of their renewed diligence and faithfulness.

Our city looks as though it had taken an emetic, and vomited forth apostates, officials, and in fact all the filth which was weighing us down. The prospects were never better for a bountiful harvest than at present. There is now more grain,

18   [Price 1½c.

and food is cheaper than has ever been the case previously at this season of the year.

The *Express Company* is prospering finely. I have dispatched A. O. Smoot and N. V. Jones to locate permanent stations in the black hills; they have 80 men with them, and it is my intention to furnish them with sufficient provision to enable several hundred persons to winter there, in case of such emergency as occurred last fall. I learn from brother Haight, of Iron County, that the cotton and indigo crops are looking well on the Rio Virgin.

The mail, conducted by F. Little, arrived at three o'clock, the 23rd, 22 days and 3 hours from Independence.

By the *St. Louis Republican*, I regret very much to learn of the assassination of brother Parley by the villain McLean; one more good man has gone to assist brothers Joseph, Hyrum, and Jedediah in another sphere. May God comfort and strengthen you in your afflictions, brother Orson.

The prejudice against us, which you have to meet, brethren, is nothing more than we may expect; it is the devil against Christ; and be assured that the devil will always howl when the Saints are faithful.

I sent a good many missionaries to the States and Europe; they left this place April 23rd with handcarts, and from latest accounts they were making better time than any company on the road.

Brethren, may the blessings of Christ abide with you continually.

BRIGHAM YOUNG.

HISTORIAN'S OFFICE,
Great Salt Lake City,
July 1, 1857.

Editor of the "Millennial Star."

Dear Brother.—The eastern mail from the United States arrived on the 23rd *ultimo*, in charge of brother Ephraim K. Hanks, 23 days from Independence, one of the shortest trips on record.

Elders Amasa Lyman and Charles C. Rich have arrived from San Bernardino, the former with the California mail, June 3, the latter on the 8th, with a small company of

Saints; subsequently, another small company arrived from San Bernardino, who brought along a *seven stopped organ*, donated to the Church by the Australian Saints; which is being fitted up in the Tabernacle, in the north end, by brother Joseph Ridges, who built it in Australia. Presidents Young, Kimball, and Wells; and Elders George A. Smith, A. Lyman, and others stepped in on Sabbath last, and heard brothers Ridges, and Orson Pratt, Jr., play upon the organ, with which they expressed themselves much gratified. It is a valuable acquisition to our choir.

Elder George A. Smith has visited Utah County since his arrival, found the people of Provo in good health and spirits; with excellent prospects for grain this season. Attended a Sabbath School meeting with 300 scholars, and preached to a congregation of about three thousand Saints in the Bowery.

By the arrival of the May mail, we learned of the agitation of the public press in the United States, pertaining to Utah, her Governor, and the Saints. Never at any former time have we witnessed a more universal, bitter feeling against "Mormonism" than at present. Governor Young, thinking the working bees of Utah would not take time to read what the public press says in relation to them and himself, set apart Sabbath, June 14, at 8 a.m., to have some of the most rabid articles read to the Saints in this city and vicinity, and had two of our best readers employed for the occasion, who read alternately from 8 till nearly noon, the loathsome trash which the corrupt press of the United States had given birth to. It was, indeed, novel, however, to hear the Governor propose such articles to be read, seeing they were mostly aimed at his private and public character; this, however, only shows the consciousness he possesses of the rectitude of the path which he treads, and the confidence he has in the people whom he leads.

June 16th—Teams recommenced hauling rock for the Temple, operations having been suspended in that department for a few days, in consequence of the Church selling many of their cattle to cancel Church obligations, but the Saints, having the privilege of turning in stock to help to defray these liabilities, contributed so liberally that but a few days elapsed before the Church had as many cattle as before; and not any who donated have been hindered in their business, nor have felt any the poorer in consequence of their liberality; and thus the Saints have witnessed to God and His servants that the spirit of the Reformation lives in their hearts, and brings forth fruit in their lives, and therefore, President Young frequently of late has said this is a "God blessed people."

It is a general time of health, peace, and plenty throughout this territory.

Love to brother Benson, and all the elders of my acquaintance associated with you.

Yours truly,
Wilford Woodruff.

SLAVERY PROSPECTS IN THE UNITED STATES.

The *Rising Sun* of Newburg, South Carolina, says in regard to the signs of the times in the political horizon:—"Clouds and darkness, threatening clouds, ominous darkness, gather around our political future. A night gloomy and terrible sets in upon us. We are drifting slowly, silently into an ocean of storms, furious whirlwinds, quicksands, and fearful whirlpools. A solemn silence prevails—'tis the precursor of a horrible tempest. Hark! the muttering rumbling of distant thunder breaks upon the stillness. Fitful flashes reveal the sullen gloom. The lurid air is heavy and chilly. The storm approached—nearer and nearer it comes—louder and more loud it howls. Man the sails—all hands to their posts. The South expects every man to do his duty. Life and duty, honor and liberty are involved. Let each heart be firm—each nerve be steady. The conflict will be fierce as hate and malice can make it. Stand firm. Hark! what crash was that?

Kansas is gone! List! a triumphant shout from the spirits of the storm. Missouri is yielding. How fierce the blasts, how lurid the lightning! Howls horrible, yells terrific, tear our ears. Virginia is assailed. Gloomy, dark, terrible howls the tempest! Watchman, what of the night? All is dark—no dawn appears.

The *New York Herald* reports that the troops were stopped on their way, to repair to Fort Leavenworth or Laramie preparatory to their march for Utah.

It quotes from the account of the surveyor-general Burr, who was sent by the Government to fill that office in Utah, where he was criminal in his accounting. He was exposed by some of the Saints who were working for him. Men like Burr and Drummond are trying to harm the innocent, and hide their own crimes and evil deeds.

The *Herald* also acknowledges the statement of Mrs. Babbitt that it was the Indians, and not the Saints who murdered her husband.

———

Kansas is still in the same condition of collision. The government has endorsed the action of Governor Walker, and has directed him to administer the laws and keep the peace at the point of bayonet if necessary.

———

Governor Cummings is uncertain as to when he will leave for Utah. He may be detained yet for some time. It appears that neither the Governor nor the troops have considered that the winter will come on them.

———

Minnesota is fearful of the threats of the Indians, and is increasing the troops.

A railroad riot occurred near Baltimore, in the early part of May. The militia was called out, and several of the rioters were killed and many wounded.

———

Spring Freshets did much damage in portions of the Eastern, Middle, and Southern States.

EMIGRATION.

(From the *Star.*)

THERE are, occasionally, Saints emigrating singly or by families on ships with emigrants who do not profess the faith of the Gospel, but are opposed to it in spirit and in practice. We have applications from such parties from time to time requesting us to obtain passages for them from this port; we also learn of others who go off without apprising us at all; and some, we are led to believe, emigrate from other ports without consulting with anyone as to the step they are about to take.

The Saints have been repeatedly counseled not to emigrate singly or in small companies, among Gentiles. But it seems to be again necessary to draw attention to the subject, and we wish Pastors, Presidents of Conferences, Presidents of Branches, and all Elders, to remind the Saints from time to time of their duty in relation to this matter.

It is impossible for us to enumerate all the advantages that accrue from the Saints going together, or all the disadvantages of their going in detached companies, but we will name a few of the most prominent. Each company of Saints on board a ship is fully organized for the performance of the duties devolving upon them as Saints and fellow passengers, and they are presided over by an experienced Elder of Israel, with two counselors, appointed by us. Under this arrangement prayers are held in the different sections of the ship morning and night, fellowship meetings are held three or four times a week, and the regular services on the Sabbath day. A constant watch is kept up by brethren appointed to be watchmen, to prevent iniquity among the evil-disposed, if there be such; and to prevent, what is too common upon other ships, namely, the encroachments of the sailors in places where they have no business. Arrangements are also instituted under this organization for the daily cleaning of the passengers' deck— by which health is promoted, and disease arising from dirt prevented. The cooking arrangements, an important affair in a large company of passengers, and about which so much dissatisfaction exists on all other ships, are made so as to place all on equal terms, and secure general satisfaction.

How different are all these things on other ships. The result of this state of things is—the captains who have carried companies of Saints across the sea say they would rather carry them than any other passengers. Captains, surgeons, and other officers on board of our ships have given testimonial after testimonial of the superiority of our passengers over any others that they have ever crossed the sea with. Newspaper reporters who have visited companies of Saints on their arrival at New York, Philadelphia, and Boston, have been unable to withhold their expressions of surprise and admiration at the cleanliness, comfort, order, and peace exhibited among our passengers—drawing contrasts between them and others that were highly favorable to our people.

On other ships no such organization exists—no prayers are unitedly offered for the peace, blessings, and protection of Him who controls the winds and the waves—no faith is exercised in Him. The spirit of prayer is not there. He who would call on his God, Daniel-like, two or three times a day, there, would be scorned, persecuted, and scoffed at. But he who would swear, blaspheme, and utter the language of vice the loudest, would be accounted the "biggest" man on board. How much of the blessing of God can be realized under such circumstances? How much faith can any Saint be expected to exercise on such a ship? There are no Sabbath services, no worship there. No watch is instituted there to suppress immoral conduct, or prevent the intrusion of sailors, who, in the North American line, are notorious for their immorality. A large proportion of the passengers are often too much on a par with the crew. No arrangements are made among the passengers to promote general cleanliness, or even to manage the cooking department so as to give all equal privileges, but at the *cooking galley* the strongest and most boisterous get the first and best served, while the weak and the quiet seldom get their cooking attended to.

These are but a very few of the advantages to be secured by the Saints going in companies. Emigrants generally are imposed upon both before starting and after their arrival, but more especially after their arrival, where *sharpers* in abundance, aware that the people are landing in a strange country and that they are mostly inexperienced, use their most subtle arts to deceive, impose upon, and rob them.

But both in leaving and landing, the Saints have those attending to their business who feel an interest in their welfare, and who will direct them for their best good. A reporter, who attended at the arrival of our last ship, the "Tuscarora," observes the fact that the Mormons have an agent awaiting their arrival to preserve them from the 'sharpers,' whose chagrin when they see their prey passing by them is given vent to by scoffs at their religious profession.

While, during the period since the commencement of the Saints' emigration till now, many accidents, shipwrecks, and much loss of life have taken place on other ships; the Lord has so far acknowledged His people as to altogether preserve them from any of those disasters; the consideration of which ought to be another stimulus to the Saints to go home in that way which HE has pointed out, acknowledged, and blessed. In view of all these and other weighty considerations, we again counsel the Saints not to emigrate by any ship but those chartered by us, which carry only our own passengers. Let those who feel themselves in so great a hurry to get off that they think they cannot wait for our next ship, ask themselves if the Lord requires them to exercise so much haste, and whether they can depend upon His blessing to accompany them while they go out of the proper channel, and subject themselves to so many evils and temptations. If they still think they must go, let them counsel with their Pastor, or President, upon the subject, make known to him their circumstances, and follow his counsel. To all such as it may thus be deemed necessary to emigrate, we have to say that we can make arrangements here for their passage better than they can do through any other Liverpool house, and if they will communicate to us through their President, we will secure passage for them.

We keep a list of the names of all the Saints who leave the British Isles within our knowledge, and desire to have the names of all. No one therefore should emigrate by any other means without informing us of the date of their departure, by what ship, and from what port. And again we say, no one should emigrate otherwise than by the regular channel of the Saints' emigration without the counsel or approbation of the President of his Conference.

A ship will be dispatched as soon as we have a sufficient number of applications. Those desirous to emigrate will please send their names and deposits as soon as possible. Those who have the means of emigrating should not delay sending them until they know we have a ship on hand, but they should forward, at least, their names and deposits, as soon as they know they are able to emigrate. Should circumstances present them going, and require a return of their deposit—they can have it at any time, by writing to us. In chartering a ship we are guided by the number of applications on our books. We cannot exactly tell when a ship will sail until one is chartered, or there are a sufficient number of applications to warrant us in chartering one. We send out notifications as soon as the charter is made, which is about three weeks, generally, before the ship sails. This gives everyone ample time to complete their arrangements.

As there are many parties obliged, contrary to their own desires, to emigrate by other ships, through their friends in the United States making arrangements with other houses for their passage, we would advise all who have friends in the States upon whom they depend to send for them, to request them to do so through the *Mormon* office in New York. Elder Appleby will receive passage money on account of parties to emigrate from this country, and his advices in their favor will receive immediate attention.

ZION'S TRUMPET,

OR

Star of the Saints.

SATURDAY, AUGUST 29, 1857.

DIRECTIONS.—President Orson Pratt gives the following important instructions concerning

"TITHING.—On examination of the financial reports from several of the Conferences for the last half year, we observe that there is very little order, and manifestly a great want of economy and prudence displayed in the expenditure of the tithing money;

and we are pained to learn, that in too many instances, there evidently has been a careless squandering or misapplication of it. This is an evil which must be corrected, or the object for which the tithing was instituted will be not attained.

Tithing is designed for the building of the Temple, and for the spreading of the Gospel, and not for the personal benefit of individuals.

There are large amounts now due from many of the Conferences to the Temple, and the Perpetual Emigrating Fund accounts, which should have been paid long since. Large portions of those amounts have been swallowed up in the extravagant expenses of 'Conference Houses,' 'Visiting Elders,' and 'Relief of the Poor,' and, as we are informed, in some instances, in the emigration of individuals from this country to America.

We have, already, in a former number, called the attention of Pastors and Presidents to the subject of Conference houses, and instructed them to be given up as far as practicable.

We deem it wisdom, also, in some measure, to restrict the expenses of visiting elders, and that all those elders who have particular fields of labor assigned them, such as Pastors, Presidents, and Traveling Elders, should pay their own expenses, whenever they leave their fields of labor and visit other places, the same as if they were traveling at home, with certain exceptions, which have been and will be made known to Pastors and Presidents as occasion may require. This, we think, will greatly lessen this item of expense and, perhaps, remove one inducement to the frequency of such visits.

The Pastors and Presidents should be particularly careful that they are not imposed upon by individuals who join the Church, more for the sake of obtaining pecuniary relief than from a pure love of the truth, as has been the case in some instances.

We have never given anyone the right or authority to use or dictate the use of any tithing or other Church fund for the emigration of any person from this land.

No person has a right to order or direct the disposal of tithing money in the European mission, except the President of that mission, only as they derive the right and authority from him. Pastors and Presidents are authorized to pay certain necessary and unavoidable expenses, such as chapel rents, lights, &c., and in all this, the most rigid economy should be used, and a careful watch kept over those expenses, that no unnecessary extravagance creeps in. In order more effectually to secure this end, the FINANCIAL REPORTS are required henceforth to be sent to us *Quarterly*, on the first of January, April, July, October, and December.

In handling this fund, it should constantly be borne in mind, that it is tithing, and that the Lord has commanded it to be paid into His Treasury, for the furtherance of his work, and that whoever squanders it, or diverts it from its legitimate channel, robs HIM."

We shall not add to, explain, or offer any remarks on the foregoing by our President; rather this is the teaching as it is in the *Star*. Lest there be further misunderstanding, we say in agreement with the instructions of President Pratt in a letter to us, that no tithe-payer, from now on, should obtain a single book from the tithing; but that the books are to be *purchased*.

We earnestly wish for Presidents to understand every jot of the foregoing directions, and use the utmost wisdom, under the influence of the Holy Spirit, to put them into action soon and effectively—*to the letter*.

At the beginning of the present volume of the *Trumpet*, we gave them the freedom to order the number that was required of it, so the Conferences would not be burdened; at the same time, we asked them to encourage everyone to receive it, so that no place where it could go would be neglected. Since that time the Reformation and the emigrations have had an effect; therefore, we wish for you to use your influence to get all who can to receive it, for their benefit, and not because there is a bit of difference as far as we are concerned with regard to profit, rather so it will nurture the spirit of Zion in their bosoms.

Let those who have requested a change in the numbers of the next bundle, send new orders by the second of September at the latest, or we will not be able to fulfill the orders until Number 20 comes out.

Remember that it will not be possible to allow persons

to receive their books on credit, and if assistant distributors wish to extend credit until payday, &c., it will be on their own responsibility. We call on Conference Presidents to take a count when the payment is less than the worth of the books, and they can make further inquiries.

The payment for the new series of the Pratt pamphlets is to come out of the tithing. We shall yet have more to say on that.

Because of frequent complaints from some parts that "the *Trumpet* does not arrive promptly," we offer to do a kindness for the distributors, i.e., if they will send us enough *stamps*, we will address their books from here by *post* to all the branches, according to the addresses they write. Nine or ten copies of the *Trumpet* can be sent for a penny.

INDIVIDUAL OR PENNY EMIGRATION FUND.—President Pratt says the following:—

"A misapprehension has existed with some in relation to this fund. They seem to have considered it as being on the same footing with, and liable to be used as, Church funds or tithing. Others we learn have used or squandered it, intending to replace it out of tithing. This is an error. No person has any right to use one penny of this fund for any purpose or under any circumstances whatever. It is an individual fund, created for a specific purpose, and for the special benefit of the contributors, and paid over by them to treasurers, or agents, of their own choosing, and may be withdrawn at any time.

We have not counseled, nor do we either directly or indirectly counsel, or countenance the using of this money, in any manner whatever; and if those funds are used or squandered by such treasurers, or agents, they cannot be made up out of tithing.

Inasmuch as we have never, through the *Star*, counseled the Saints at all in relation to this matter; we wish it distinctly understood that neither the Office here, nor the tithing, will be held responsible for any defalcations of those treasurers or agents. The Office will be responsible for whatever is deposited here, and for that only. The people themselves must take the responsibility and sustain all losses which may arise from the carelessness or dishonesty of their agents.

Nevertheless, we feel constrained to say, that we believe the principle is a good one, and if honestly carried out would result in much good to those who are engaged in it. But the Saints have been so often wronged and swindled by unprincipled and designing men, through various schemes, such as the "Joint Stock" concern, and others, that we are fearful that they may again be plundered through this fund operation by some of their agents, unless the utmost caution is observed in securing the safe custody and faithful application of the money.

Unless the Saints feel perfectly safe in placing their penny deposits in the hands of their own agents, it would be far better for them to retain them in their own hands; and then, if these funds are unwisely squandered, they have no one to blame but themselves. We wish it distinctly understood that we do not counsel anyone in the British mission to deposit his small Emigration Fund with any person in the land, without a full and sufficient guarantee of its safety. It is proper and right for every person who has the least doubt as to the safe keeping of his fund in the hands of an agent, to retain it, until he shall have accumulated £1; then if he feels disposed, he can forward it directly to this Office, and a receipt of deposit will be returned to him.

Perhaps some of the Saints will say, that if they undertake to keep the Fund in their own possession, they will be very likely to squander it away. To such we would reply, that if they have not sufficient stability to keep a Fund of so much importance, it is very probable that they have not sufficient stability to keep the faith in case their agents should squander the Fund. Suppose some of your agents should prove to be dishonest men: how are you to be remunerated for your losses? Would you not be tried? Would you not condemn yourselves for having more confidence in an irresponsible agent than in your own stability? We have just learned that scores of pounds sterling, of this Fund, have already been dishonestly used. Ought you not to look after these things? Or will you lie down and sleep and let your own agents cheat you out of your hard earnings? Well did the Savior say, that 'the children of this world are wiser in their generation than the children of light.' The children of light ought to be wiser in all things than the world; but it seems that the Saints are often too careless in their business transactions. Because they themselves are honest, they imagine that all who bear the name of Saints are also honest; this is far from being the case. Therefore, your property or funds should be entrusted only where you have undoubted confidence. Rather than be plundered of the little means which you have so laboriously obtained, it would be better to abolish all the agents which you have appointed in connection with this Fund, and only make the deposits at this Office."

MISSIONARY—Elder Wm. Jenkins sailed from New York about a month ago.

THE belligerent world and the Press still continue in their downward path. The most toothsome preparations on the table of the newspapers of our day are the accounts of the spilling of blood, robberies, and every evil and pain. Terrible assassinations of Europeans by the agitated Hindus, and like revenge on the rebels; threats of the Kafirs to rise in rebellion. Persia has not completely complied with the peace treaty; China still continues obstinate, and the English Government has a number of irons in the fire, so that it is likely it will lose some of them, and burn their fingers in the bargain.

Closer to home—in the 'garden of Christianity' we have columns filled with accounts of prostitution, poverty, lying, deception, treason, fraud, robbery, fights, murder, suicide, infanticide, and every other wicked thing with the exception of Mormonism. The cup of Babel is rapidly filling.

Among the other ugly pictures, the editors have to insert a false image of Mormonism, else the *grand show* will not be complete.

Until last week we could not believe that Welsh Editors could be so obtuse in their anti-Mormon zeal as to put the blatant and contradictory lies which they claim have all come from one John Davies. We would not try to refute them in order to convince any sensible person; rather we would hold the noses of the editorial *scavengers* for a moment near the stinking filth they have scraped so laboriously and willingly to smear their betters.

Said John Davies was the son of brother David Davies, formerly from Newton, Glamorgan, who, with his family, emigrated in April, 1856. He died on the way, and his widow and children continued on, and reached the Valley in the fall.

J. Davies returned to the States—he started on about April 17, and arrived on June 13. The missionaries who are here now from the Valley came a few days after him. They testify that the Saints had not turned into *blacks* when they left them, and they themselves are white men! They also say that the approved laws and officers sent by the *Congress* are what governs there, and they have not heard of the diabolic cruelty that our hero mentions. In the hundreds of letters sent to Wales by the Welsh, we have no example of any such thing. Scores of them have appeared through the *Trumpet*, but they do not suffice for the men of the solid error.

Although we have been in the Salt Lake Valley ourselves, and although our beloved family is there, we did not learn about the walls, the narrow gates, or the moat around Salt Lake City before reading this 'interesting' account, as it is called by the *Welsh Herald*, which smacks its lips after consuming the carcass.

We shall put gloves on our hands while we hold a *specimen* to the nose of Dr. 'Herald,' and we shall ask him the following questions:—

I. How could men leave, on foot, from the Valley, in December, when snow covered the Mountains and the desolate Plains for hundreds of miles away?

II. For what purpose would the females and the males exchange clothes with one another?

III. Why were the males so foolish as to give all the scraps of provisions to the females, and live entirely on the milk; would it not have been wiser for them to share the provisions, milk the females and share the milk? What ever happened to the infants? We suggest the following plan, i.e., that the wise Editor of the 'Herald' purchase the *waxwork exhibition of the Grecian Daughter*, and add to it this strange *group*; for we think that he would make a better *showman* or a *cheap Jack* than a newspaper editor.

IV. Where did the poor lad get the means to purchase "six revolvers and one rifle?" What kind of boots did he have to hold two revolvers, and to enable him to be so nimble? How did his sneaky friends escape on foot from men on horseback? What trees were they in? We do not know about them. Surprising that three armed men failed to kill one. Even more surprising, the one of the three, after getting J. Davies on the ground, did nothing but cut his belt with a knife, taking four revolvers, instead of cutting his throat and taking everything!

We suggest that the translation in the 'Welsh Herald' be compared with the original in the English Herald which was published in Swansea, about three weeks ago.

V. Where else can one find the story that Mrs. Babbit's company defeated a thousand Indian warriors? A thousand!!

VI. Where did the poor one get the 500 dollars to leave to his mother? If he got them, what wonder that he was pursued?

He was a cunning lad, wasn't he, Mr. Herald? But, despite that, his English was not as good as it is in this contrived 'interesting' tale.

———

BROTHER John Bowen.—Although it filled our heart with gladness to hear from you that you have renewed yourself with the work of the Lord, and that such an excellent letter has come from your brother, from the Valley, yet, we do not feel that it is sufficiently free of subjectivity to appear before the public. We can quote abundantly from it. May the Almighty strengthen you to fulfill your promise.

CONTENTS.

	PG.
News from the Valley	273
" from the United States	276
Emigration	278
Editorial—Tithing—The 'Trumpet'—Penny Fund—The World, and the Press—The 'Welsh Herald'	281

PRINTED AND PUBLISHED BY D. DANIELS, SWANSEA.

ZION'S TRUMPET,

OR

𝔖𝔱𝔞𝔯 𝔬𝔣 𝔱𝔥𝔢 𝔖𝔞𝔦𝔫𝔱𝔰.

No. 19.]   SEPTEMBER 12, 1857.   [Vol. X.

SETTLEMENT OF THE SAINTS IN NEBRASKA.

Our readers will remember our statement, some time ago, concerning the decision of the Presidency of the Church and the Saints in the United States to make new settlements along the broad Plains and the desert that lie between the States and Utah. The first ones were to begin in the Kansas and Nebraska Territories, in the far west, and the next one further along, as quickly as the emigrants settled in them. At the same time Utah was stretching out its boundaries toward the east, to the point that the desert journey is hundreds of miles shorter. The following letter gives an account of the settlement of the Saints in—

Genoa City, Monroe County,
Nebraska Territory, July 1, 1857.

Editor of the Mormon—*Dear Sir*—According to the instructions of Presidents J. Taylor and E. Snow, (as Historian of the Nebraska Mission,) I take up my pen to inform you of our progress and prospects.

We left for this place, from Florence, May 11, and reached our destination after a tedious travel of 5 days. In consequence of the lateness of the season, the feed was poor, scarcely a blade of grass a finger long was to be seen; nevertheless, all arrived in safety, and commenced putting in the plough.

We have very little wheat, but intend to sow liberally in the fall. Our farm lies south and southeast of the city. It contains about 750 acres, bounded on the south by the Beaver River, southeast by the Loup Fork, and north and west by a sod fence. This farm is occupied chiefly by the Florence and St. Louis companies; the Alton company are not included in the above, but are located 14 miles north, in a bend of the Beaver river, containing 800 acres.

Our crops are of the most flattering character; corn, potatoes, buckwheat, and garden stuffs are looking finely, and if our corn escapes the early frosts that are peculiar to this latitude, it is the opinion of some of our best judges that the yield of corn will be from 50 to 70 bushels per acre.

We have our sawmill in operation, and expect enough lumber will be got out this season to help us to put up houses sufficient for our present population. We have a brickyard in full blast, and expect soon to be able from such auxiliaries as sawmills, brickyards, and willing hands to build a city not a whit behind any other in Nebraska.

The city of Genoa is about 102 miles from Florence, contains about 400 acres, 10 acres in a block, from center to center of streets, 8 lots in a block, 18 rods long, 9 rods wide; the streets cross at right angles, 4 rods wide. It is laid off on a beautiful eminence near the bluffs on the north, gradually descending to the east, south, and west. As the ground is a little the highest in the center, standing on the *public square*, you have a fine view to the east, some 20 miles. Looking to the south, the Loup Fork (river) presents itself with its ever shifting sand bars, and zigzag course, spotted with islands of cottonwood, Box Elder, Willow, and some Cedar; still farther in the distance you see the bluffs rising, the dividing ridge between the Loup Fork and the Great Platte rivers. Strain your vision a little more, and a dark blue line presents itself; that is the bluffs. Beyond the Platte, some 30 miles off, southwest, groves of timber, the Loup Bluffs, and a sea of grass meet your eye. At every turn west, bluffs in majestic grandeur, covered with ancient ruins, telling us plainly, without any translation, that their occupants understood the arts and sciences; for we have found specimens of both copper and earthenware, being another *link* in the great chain of testimony of the authenticity of the Book of Mormon.

I will now give you a statistical item about us.—Our number is 97 men, 25 women, 40 children, 42 yoke of oxen, 20 cows, 6 horses, and some two dozen chickens, 20 hogs, 2 cats, and dogs aplenty.

We are expecting plenty of *sport* in the fall, for we are surrounded with all kinds of *game*. Our streams are teeming with fine fish, and we hope soon to have both time and inclination to indulge.

Yours truly, &c.,
HENRY J. HUDSON.

[Such a wonderful contrast to the wickedness, deceit, oppression, and misery and distress of old Babylon are the virtue, sincerity, freedom and pleasure of the Saints in the promised land of Joseph! Yonder is a spacious land—plenty of space for every family to dig their provisions out of the earth—a healthful, beautiful, and pleasant land; free people, religious freedom, common state rights. No oppressive kingdom, heavy burdensome taxes, low wages, harsh masters, unusually hard work, or the thousand and one other complaints we hear in this land.

Here, in the 'land of the gospel light,' we have over-populated towns, men without work, poverty, misery, robbery and deceit of every kind, oppression of the poor, neglect of the widows and the orphans, taverns, prisons, insane asylums, and houses of prostitution full of inhabitants. Here war breaks out, the men are being swept away; pestilence and famine come to perform their own massacre, while squalor, prostitution, and the resulting illnesses of this generation assist in emptying the earth, and but few men are left, so that the word of the Lord is fulfilled.

Protestantism and its monogamy and its resulting harlotry: Catholicism and its doctrine of a celibate life, separation, &c., and the natural result of hindering the objective of the first great commandment; and the path of decline of society—all this shows that the cup of old Babel is rapidly filling.

In contrast to this, behold the redeemed of the Lord

hiding for a small moment in the chambers of the far west, while the wrath goes by, and at the same time being fruitful and multiplying, and filling the place with a strong, healthy, and pure progeny; going therefrom and possessing the land, increasing like a fatted calf, according to the prediction of the old prophet. The order of the old and godly Patriarchs is in their midst, and the blessings of old Father Abraham follow them, according to the promise of the New Testament.

In what period of time does one family populate a city, and the land surrounding it? We declare that it is by the head of a family of several wives, keeping the rules given by the great Creator, which are respected by even the animals of the field, namely, by not mating except in the proper season and time. It would be so foolish for a farmer after plowing and planting his land, seeing it sprouting, were he to go back and put seeds in the same land before harvesting the crop. Would that not be wasting valuable seed instead of using it properly? How much more valuable is that of the few righteous whom the Lord expects to raise unto Him subjects fit for his kingdom, while he destroys the wicked.

Besides that, that is where the word of wisdom is respected, and health and strength have a stronghold in every constitution. By careful observation of the rules of nature, by living their religion, and by having an abundance of the Spirit of the Lord, the Saints in Zion will be fruitful and gigantic like the nation of Israel of old; and by practicing the Patriarchal order, their numbers will increase on a principle so extensive that when the Patriarch reaches what is considered an old age, he will be the head of a city populated entirely by thousands of his own posterity.

The wicked and adulterous Gentiles shout so hypocritically against polygamy and the moral law of the 'Mormons,' while the latter punish with death for that which their accusers tolerate, namely, adultery and prostitution. Only one Christian group knows the meaning of the ancient Apostle's saying about the destruction of the body so that the spirit will be saved in the day of the Lord Jesus. And only those can inherit the earth.

The Lord says about the land of Joseph, or America, that

whatever nation may dwell on it and does not keep his laws, He will wipe from the face of the earth.

It will not be long, therefore, that the prophecy of Joseph Smith will be completely fulfilled—the North and South of America will rise in war against each other, and war, famine, pestilence, and the plagues of our God will be poured out upon the whole world, except for Zion and Jerusalem only, where there will be redemption.

Let the wicked go to the States to meet the storm, or they can remain here until it comes, and they are caught, while God favors his chosen people.

The Saints will fill not just one or two settlements, rather the whole earth, inasmuch as they continue to keep the commandments of their God—*Editor of the* TRUMPET.]

WHY ARE THE APOSTATES FLYING FROM UTAH?

THE MORMON answers as follows:—

"We rarely take up a paper that speaks of Utah without being told that seceders from Mormonism who leave that Territory for the States do so with great difficulty and at the imminent peril of their lives. We do not expect that our denial of all grounds of apprehension will meet with as wide a circulation as the charge—in fact we are so accustomed to be calumniated, and see so seldom the least evidence on the part of the conductors of the Public Press to do us justice by publishing our replies to the hosts against us, that we have long since concluded ours is a *lying generation*.

The people, evidently, take so much pleasure in reading of the horrible and extravagant that the professional quill driver speculates quite as much on what he can the most profitably produce to nourish the vitiated and depraved tastes of his customers, and for which he shall receive the best remuneration, as does the fancy dry goods merchant in his selections, to please the tastes and whims of the fair sex, with everything in his line for any color desired.

It would be time badly spent and space in our paper as ill occupied to take notice of what everybody has said who has come from Utah this season; but it is worthy of remark that all the people who were afraid of being killed were neither killed nor molested! We confess that we are astonished at the shallow pates of many of our contemporaries; they seem to be too dull to perceive the contradiction of their statement about the almost impossibility of leaving Utah but by flight, and their recording the arrival of scores and hundreds by slow ox teams. There is doubtless fear in the bosoms of many. Some nervous folks will sit by the fireside in a long winter's eve, listening to tales of ghosts and hobgoblins, till they are almost riveted to their seats with fright, and for their soul's salvation would not go through their own familiar homestead without a light to convince them that all of the murdered, poisoned, and hanged of ten generations were not dancing in their bedrooms. If they be so very fortunate as to get into their sheets without fainting and an hour afterwards dare to save themselves from suffocation by uncovering their frenzied brains, they may see poor harmless pussy, half dozing in a corner, and she suddenly is transmogrified into Auld Sootie, trying to seduce them by cunning winks and nods of friendship—daylight, however, dissipates the reign of terror.

Editors in the States have published so much about 'Danites,' and 'Destroying Angels' cutting off seceders on the Plains that many a person, starting from Utah, has doubtless dreamt of troops of Danites or Destroying Angels buckling them on their swords, dreadful *revolvers* and the still reeking knife that had dispatched some unfortunate, and nothing, we presume, but their safe arrival on the Frontiers has convinced them that these dreadful folks and dreadful instruments only had existence in their weak and frenzied brains.

But who are these who are flying from Utah? Are they so much purer, so much more virtuous, so much more honest than the Utahns whom they have left in the mountains, that they have hastened from their society to mingle with a better people and to breathe a more heavenly atmosphere—something more congenial and consonant with their refined tastes and high moral qualities? We certainly cannot answer for all who have hastily tripped back to the States recently; but we do know that the Reformation Catechism made many dance about, and make preparations for departure, without the assistance of either music, Danites, or Destroying Angels. We now republish the remarkable Catechism—the axe laid at the root of the tree, that made the chips fly! 'Read slowly, think deeply, and act wisely' all who read the following Utah Catechism:—

'Have you committed murder, by shedding innocent blood or consenting thereto?

Have you betrayed your brother or sister in anything?

Have you committed adultery by having any connection with a woman that was not your wife (or man that was not your husband?)

Have you cut hay where you have no right to, or turned animals into another person's fields without his consent?

Have you lied about or maliciously misrepresented any person?

Have you borne false witness against your neighbor?

Have you taken the name of the Deity in vain?

Have you coveted anything not your own?

Have you been intoxicated with strong drinks?

Have you found lost property, and not returned it to the owner or used all diligence to do so?

Have you fulfilled your promises in paying your debts, or run into debt without the intention of paying the same?

Do you pay your tithing promptly?

Do you teach your family the gospel of salvation?

Do you speak against your superiors in the Church or against any principle taught in the Book of Mormon, Book of Doctrine and Covenants, or against the revelations given through Joseph Smith the Prophet and the Presidency of the Church as now organized?

Do you pray in your family, night and morning, and attend to secret prayer?

Do you labor six days, and rest or go to work on the Sabbath?

Do you and your family attend the ward meetings?

Do you preside over your household as a servant of God? and is your family subject to you?

Have you labored diligently and earned faithfully the wages paid you by your employers?

Do you oppress the hireling in his wages?'

"We should think that after reading the foregoing, everyone will understand why at least many left Utah, and that will be particularly understood when it is known the penalties of ancient Israel in restoring fourfold were exacted in Utah from the unfortunate transgressor. For the present, enough."

ZION'S TRUMPET,

OR

Star of the Saints.

SATURDAY, SEPTEMBER 12, 1857.

THE KINGDOM OF GOD.—After all the gibberish of the Priests, Sabbath after Sabbath, and their repetitions of the Lord's prayer, in which it is said, 'Thy kingdom come, thy will be done on earth as it is in heaven,' &c., we are not, as far as they are concerned, a bit closer to having one or the other.

Jesus says accurately that men draw near to the Lord with their lips, and their hearts are far from him. In our enlightened age, when our country is ablaze with the 'gospel,' and speckled with 'reverends,' despite all their prayers for the coming of the kingdom of Jesus, &c., they say that the country is sufficiently enlightened, with no need for additional revelation, &c., as if the pinnacle of perfection had already been reached.

Instead of having Jesus as the King of the earth, and men doing the will of God on the earth as the holy angels do in heaven, we have kings and emperors, not ordained by God, claiming the right and the power, independent of any direction from heaven, to rule this planet according to their own whim, heedless of a supreme Being who, in ancient times, would raise up and bring down crowned heads according to his will, and direct armies to war or not according to His justice.

Is that how things are now? All are aware that the answer to this question is that it is simply the prerogative of kingdoms and parliaments to proclaim war, to rob countries of their freedom and their comfort—to sacrifice hundreds of thousands of lives on the altar of pride and greed—to stain the land with the blood of humanity for the most worthless baubles, out of a lack of sense and discretion. Such horrible things have become so common in our boastful Christian world, that it is not considered that an accounting of them will have to be given in the world to come. Indeed, the hireling bishops and Priests of Belial go so far as to pray for the King of Kings to look with favor on such murderous carnage and bless the objects of their interest.

Despite all this, as long as the pay continues, the priests continue to pray that 'thy will be done, that thy kingdom may come.'

The earth is the Lord's and the fullness thereof; the world, and they that dwell therein, he says again, by reading the Psalm. To priests and others who pray and read in this manner we ask

1. When you pray 'thy will be done, and thy kingdom come,' are you aware that the will of God is not being done, and that his kingdom will literally come?

2. If you are not aware, why do you practice hypocrisy, and speak nonsense?

3. If you believe what you pray, how do you expect the kingdom of Christ to come, and how are men made aware of the order of heaven, so they can behave like the clean, loving, and kind beings who are there?

It is a self-evident fact that the various sects who call themselves Christians are far from being in conformity with the part quoted from the prayer; but one Christian sect would join with un-Christian Muslims to kill the other Christians. In short, self-interest, personal gain, wealth, power and avarice are the chief aims of the countries, and it is through this human power *(might is right)* that the kingdom of heaven was taken by force, according to the words of Jesus. It was on the blood-covered ruins of the Apostolic Church that the Pope built his throne, and several subsequent centuries were characterized by his oppression, his violence, his murders, his bonds on the conscience, and his support, under the façade of religion, for the most repugnant things.

Protestantism was established by a war of blood, and the highly vaunted Reformation is nothing more than human plans and deeds. What the highest court of Heaven wants has nothing to do with all these behaviors. If others happened to prevail by the force of arms, they would be the founders of the kingdoms and Churches, and the objects of the hireling priests' prayers, even though they had swum in innocent blood.

But the most remarkable happening in the accounts of the apostate world is the restoration of the kingdom of heaven by an Angel from on high to the Prophet Joseph Smith; his lowliness as a man—an uneducated and poor boy following the plow—the persecution he and his followers received from the world and the church—his incomparable success, and the current civil condition of the Saints, are facts that satisify the Saints that God planted in the forecourt of the rocky mountains this kingdom, which, as Daniel says, will crush all the kingdoms of the earth.

Just a glance by the unbiased and wise will show that the fruits of the order of heaven and the will of God are obvious in the society of the Saints of Utah, especially when compared with the rest of the world. Laziness and poverty, hatred and war, robbery, adultery, and the other evils of Great Babylon have no place there. There are no hireling priests there to plant absurd traditions in the mind, and 'care for the soul,' as it is said, paying no heed to what men do in their daily business and societal condition. There are hard workers as civic leaders there, and bishops in every ward of every city who go from house to house seeing to it that the widows and the orphans are not suffering and that the lazy are not idle, and making right all the inequalities without receiving any pay for their work. The land is fruitful, the people are diligent and free in the full meaning of the word. The voice of the people confirms the state laws, and chooses officers to serve them. And all these beneficent things are taught in the order of the salvation that was restored to the Prophet Joseph Smith. It contains principles that are adaptable to all circumstances, having been proved perfect throughout eternity—in worlds upon worlds exalted from a fallen condition to heavenly glory, a full understanding and implementation of which clothe the Gods with immortality and omnipotence—to be able to gather the chaotic elements in the endless space and form them into worlds—to be able to multiply their species, namely to generate the spirits of men, clothe them with flesh, and place them on new planets as a school of experience, namely the bitterness of death, and to present to them the principles which will sustain life and continue forever in their midst, and progress toward immortality.

According to this grand design our Heavenly Father came into existence, and gave us this earth to dwell on. Who, then, dares to oppose HIS right to govern this world as he may wish. A general revolution has begun, and it will not end until all the kingdoms of the world belong to our Lord and His Christ.

The order we noted is to extend to eternity, forming worlds, governing them, and placing their inhabitants in a condition of happiness, progress and continuity. O, the incalculable amount contained in these words! O, if only the Saints who have had a glance at the order of heaven, and a small bit of the spirit of the gods, could clothe with words the ideas they perceived like breadth itself, and could open the eyes of the natural children of the world! They have the attributes of the gods, so that the attributes of the father are in the children; but they are not cultivated; and we see, even in the worldly teaching the difference between learned and unlearned men. Only the reception of the gift of the Holy Ghost will bring the light that is required, and will set the people to govern themselves, and seek to act for the greatest benefit, and the deprivation of that is the cause of misery, woe, and the shedding of blood.

The period that began with the fulfillment of Joseph's mission was foretold by the Prophet Joel—'And it shall come to pass in the last days, says God, that I will pour out my Spirit upon all flesh—your sons and your daughters shall prophesy, your young men shall see visions, and your old men shall dream dreams, and upon my servants and my handmaids will I pour out my spirit,' &c. This Spirit and power was possessed by Daniel of old, and by John on the Isle of Patmos. It enlightens and expands the mind, and fills a man with grand ideas to reach for lofty things, to the point of forgetting about worldly baubles, and present crosses, which are swallowed up in the preparations for ETERNITY, like a child having a look at human life. That is a broad portrayal of what is 'Mormonism,' which is to bring about the blessed Millennium, or the general reign of Christ.

Mormonism is the law, rule, or settled principle of perfect beings or gods—the law or order of the kingdom of God on this earth, and the Saints are the subjects. Its objective at every attempt at all times is to bring progress, life, and happiness—an increase in numbers, in fruits and produce of the earth, in handmade things, and in everything in which creatures have interest, with the least amount of waste.

Some think that progress of the kingdom of God depends on the additions made by baptism, and since the Saints in Wales are not baptizing many at present, that the kingdom is diminishing. Mormonism does not depend on congregations and chapels in Wales for progress. In another part of this issue we point out a better way to increase our numbers, namely through our children—our future hopes.

The Saints are called to emigrate from Wales to the land of freedom, where they will be allowed to practice the principles of life, and observe the appropriate familial government. Families make tribes, and tribes make nations, and nations populate the world. How is the will of God done on earth as it is in heaven? By beginning in each family.

Brethren in Israel, what rule do you have in your families? Do you teach your children in the order of salvation? Has the Reformation reached every member of your family? Have as many of your children who have reached the age of eight been baptized? Do they have the gifts of the Holy Ghost, have heavenly dreams and visions, and keep themselves from the corruptions of the age? Do you appoint times in your families for teaching, counseling, disciplining, praying, or whatever may be necessary? Do your wives and children recognize their place and acknowledge yours? If you do not strive for your best in these matters, you will not have part in the heavenly glory of the kingdom with Abraham, Isaac, and Jacob, and all the other patriarchs, and you will not be worthy of being conveyed into Zion, where only those who sanctify the name of God, and do his will on the earth as the blessed inhabitants of heaven do in their families and their dwellings, will live.

Do not pray any longer, "Thy kingdom come," for it has come, together with a revelation of the will of God.

HOME CHURCH ACCOUNTS.

WEST GLAMORGAN CONFERENCE.

Swansea, August 8, 1857.

President Daniels.—When the season for preaching out of doors is as if closed to us, I consider it my duty to write a few lines to inform you concerning our activities in the past, and also of our present condition.

We have had a busy time from the beginning of the "Reformation" until now, preaching, teaching, counseling, encouraging, baptizing and establishing in the minds of our brothers and sisters that the intention of all the conditions of the Reformation were for their benefit and their salvation. Through the assistance of the Spirit of God, and the counsels we received from you from time to time, we succeeded in getting nearly everyone to covenant with their God, to serve Him with greater energy and faithfulness than ever before: and by now their former anxious hopes, through their actions, have turned into proven facts for them that God in Israel blesses those who trust in him and who do his will.

Having gotten things into the order we wanted, we set about to preach the gospel to the world, at the cost of sacrificing everything, as if they had never been preached to before; and by so doing we got the brothers and sisters to be especially faithful. We divided the various towns, villages, and the country, insofar as possible, into areas; and we assigned to every Officer and Saint their area to take pamphlets from house to house by testifying of the goodness of God.

Public preaching was done faithfully and diligently by the brothers indoors and out of doors, town and country, as much as they could; and just as faithfully, the sisters followed them from place to place, through scowl and scorn, hot and cold, fat and thin, to stand in living columns before the public side-by-side with their brethren to witness in deed that this grand work is of God. By continuing our efforts in this manner all during the summer, we succeeded in winning several for the Church who knew little or nothing about it before; and as far as we can tell many have been called, if not pricked in their hearts with respect to the kingdom of God. On the other hand, we have succeeded in pulling all the liars, drunkards, adulterers, sorcerers, believers, preachers, priests, and all the fiends of hell into one pile. The generation of vipers sometimes comes together in numerous multitudes to persecute the Saints, and to break up the meetings. While the undeclared cursed frightfully, those who were too religious to curse (only in the body) devoted themselves to mocking, and throwing the first thing that came to their hands; but, poo! what of it? if there is a frown from hell, there is a smile from heaven, and if there are rocks, mortar, clay, and *cabbage* stumps from below, there are all the blessings of the Eternal Covenant from above. We feel *first rate* through it all, although we were forced to join with common sense to come to the unavoidable decision that the Saints have their own kingdom, whether it is God's or Satan's. Since there are but two of those in existence, and since in the kingdom of the devil there are cursing persecutors and maligners, the Saints must be of God's kingdom; and although these *imps* are divided among themselves, they join unanimously to persecute the kingdom of God. If we were to take for granted that the 'Christian' sects of our age are in the kingdom of God and that the Saints belong to the devil, would it not be illogical for one part of the kingdom of the devil to join with the kingdom of God to persecute the other part? What connection is between light and darkness—Christ and Belial?

Furthermore, the fact that they are destitute of the gifts of the Spirit of God—the promises of the New Testament, which are enjoyed by the Saints, shows that the former are like wild, barren trees of the forest compared to the fruitful tree of the Saints in the orchard—that we are of God, and the whole world lies in darkness and wickedness.

With joy I report to you that there are unity, charity, and

cooperation in our midst, with few exceptions, and God, in return, loves us until we feel to increase in goodness, so that we may have

>More, until we are rewarded—with select
>>Family blessings;
>Gone home, above the cry of the crowd,
>>Entirely healthy in great power.

Affectionately yours,
JOHN DAVIES.

CARDIGANSHIRE CONFERENCE.

Aberystwyth, August 3, 1857.

President Daniels.

Dear Brother.—My health is not as good as it was; I have a heavy cold. Having just arrived I am in favor of proclaiming 'Mormonism' loud and clear this time without resting for three weeks.

Sunday, three weeks ago yesterday, I and brother Joseph W. Tuckfield preached out of doors in Goginan. We preached twice to crowds of attentive listeners.

The following Tuesday we went to Llanrhystud. After baptizing one sister, I proclaimed throughout the place that I intended to preach there in the evening. I was passionately opposed by two of the Priests of the church of Henry the eighth. They called me a servant of the devil, commanding me to go from there, 'since this is a Christian land, and if I dared to preach there that I would certainly be mobbed—and a shower of rocks would be hurled at me,' and one said further that 'he would cast the first stone!' [*College education!*] You be the judge as to the kind of 'Christian land' this would be under their government!

In any event, I did in fact preach after having additional trouble in getting a place, preparations, &c. I asked the tavern keeper of the *Black Lion* if I could stand on top of his *horse-block* to preach? He refused the favor because the priests drank there! [a proper excuse, I must admit.] After showing my license to the constable and receiving his protection, I preached, to the great disappointment of the infuriated priests, to a large crowd of polite listeners. I received an abundance of the spirit of my Father; I preached like a giant, and the constable stood there until the last.

Wednesday, July 15, I went through the land selling tracts and testifying of the Gospel of Christ until I came to the Ystwyth Hospital, where I preached out of doors, after walking about twenty miles, and I had several who listened to me.

I shouted out 'Mormonism' also in Aberaeron, where several came to listen; but I had much persecution there.

I preached also in Tregaron, and Waun Llanfer, Clydoge,

and through the lower parts of the Conference; twice also in this neighbornood—in Llanbadarn and Penparce.

I feel well; thanks to God for Mormonism. . .

Your dear brother,
JOSEPH GRIFFITHS.

The above is worthy of emulation by numbers of our brethren who are like brother Griffiths, young, and chronicled in our volume though it is small. The above examples show how the work is to be performed, not only in a few weeks, but during the season. Although the names of all the diligent brethren there are not listed, they will not be forgotten by the Master of the Vineyard on the day of recompense.—EDITOR.

BRECON CONFERENCE.

Llanelly, (Brecon) September 8, 1857.

Dear Brother Daniels—We are here going forward with the work of God minding our own business. The majority of us agree with all the measures formed for us to carry out, while others, I am sad to say, are contrary and lazy, having lost the Spirit of the Gospel almost completely, and if they do not repent and reform soon, it appears that their end will be worse than their beginning.

We continue to preach out of doors, and are having a good hearing, especially in Brynmawr. We intend to preach at Llangatwg and Cerrighywel: we would love to have the assistance of brother Taylor on the occasion.

The tithing for last month was not as much as usual because of a happening in the works.

Yours in the Gospel,
JOHN THOMAS.

PAYMENTS from August 1 to September 11.—John Davies, £10; Evan Richards, £5; A. L. Jones, £5; John Thomas, 13s; J. Griffiths, 13s; David John, £3 5s; W. Ajax, Denbigh, £1 6s 4c; S. Roskelley, £5.

☞ The Indians have begun to war against the soldiers, taking 800 of their animals to kill. Blood was spilled on every side. There are preparations for war in Kansas.

CONTENTS.

	PG.
Settlements in Nebraska	289
Apostates from Utah	293
Editorial—Kingdom of God	296
Home Church Accounts	301

PRINTED AND PUBLISHED BY D. DANIELS, SWANSEA.

ZION'S TRUMPET,

OR

Star of the Saints.

No. 20.] SEPTEMBER 26, 1857. [Vol. X.

HOME CHURCH ACCOUNTS.

CONFERENCES OF THE NORTH.

Llandudno, September 16, 1857.

Dear Brother Daniels—On the first of last May we called together several faithful brethren, according to the counsel we received to test the world, that is, to go out without purse, &c., among the unbelieving gentiles, preaching the Gospel to them, and seeing whether they would accept, respect, and feed the servants of Jesus, or seal their damnation by refusing them.

There were at the time hundreds and thousands of the works of D. Jones and J. Davies decaying by the boxful here and there throughout the Conferences like a burden—like a debt to the crown, with no hope of it ever being paid. Considering that they were the words of life, and that men were dying in the six counties of the North from want of knowing their contents, we decided to distribute them.

Eight elders who had their hearts in the work, were selected to go out, and a good bag full of books was given to every two elders, and they were instructed to take them to the whole country, tracting every house, and preaching in the evening.

Brothers Thomas Jones, (formerly from Aberystwyth,) and Edward Parry, Jr., from Tanygraig, Llandudno, went throughout the entire counties of Caernarvon and Anglesey, distributing tracts intensively in town and country throughout. Sometimes they received food and a hearty welcome; at other times, quite a surly look. One time they would receive good food, and plenty of it; other times, poor food and only a little of it, and many times they received nothing. Sometimes they would be in a bed, other times at the base of a hedge, in a haystack, in a barn, in a sheepfold, or in the middle of a field. Sometimes with a full stomach, other times without anything from the morning or the previous night. Sometimes the people would receive them kindly, with hundreds listening to their sermons: other times the people would swear at them and curse them, and send the dogs after them, threatening to shoot them or come after them with their sickles as if cutting straw—or as our meek brethren were preaching the people would mock them and shout *hurrah!* and drive them from the place like thieves, chasing after them for a mile, and leaving them to go hungry and soaked to the skin to sleep on the field. All the commotion was created by some old Pharisaic Methodist with his heavy head, deadly groan, long prayer, light weight, and short stature, with his old pitiful, choppy voice, devilishly sanctimonious, saying, "This age is too enlightened and civilized for that kind of heresy to be received in our Christian land! We have known of the work of grace on our conditions through the Atonement of the Cross for a long time by now; and we are too well informed of the story of the fraud Joe Smith and the Mormons to be deceived; but if you work one little miracle we will believe!" At the same time he was filled with lies and dishonesty, deceit and harlotry. I am prepared to believe that the devil brought the old murderer, John Calvin, to the top of one of the highest hills of Caernarvon, and got him to fall down before him and worship him, for that which Calvin received as an inheritance, Anglesey, and Arfon, and a corner of Bala.

David Jones, Denbigh, and Daniel Lewis went over toward Bala, tracting the entire country, and they received the same treatment as already described.

Edwin Price, Trefor, (the husband of one who is worthy of the name wife, who with all her heart is in favor of her husband's having every opportunity to do the will of God, that's the *quality* that is in the women of the Saints in the north,) and Robert Williams, (Priest,) Cefn Mawr, went to the border of Llangollen, and along the border of Cheshire down to Montgomeryshire, tracting and preaching in Welsh and English throughout the entire country. They had the same treatment as our other brethren: I believe that these two suffered the most by sleeping out of doors and having a scarcity of food.

Elder John Treharne and I traveled together for about 6 weeks, through parts of Merionethshire, Montgomeryshire, Cardiganshire, and Radnorshire, preaching more than tracting; but after I left him, he continued by himself, throughout the summer, to preach and tract for his livelihood. Contained in him are the qualities of the lion and the stag combined, and these are required to enable him to travel the barren, jagged, and everlasting hills of Merionethshire.

Elder Hugh Evans, and the other brethren who are working, are around laboring for the cause every Sunday. Brother Hugh Evans proves in his behavior that his heart is burning with zeal for the success of the work of God—he works hard every day, supporting a family of 6 in number, pays his tithing, presides over the Conference regularly, and feeds the elders, and gives them lodging.

Brothers Wm. Ajax and David John have taken good care of their conferences and have preached around in the neighboring villages where it was inconvenient for those who were working during the week to get to, leaving tracts at every house that would receive them. Other times they would go far into the country to prove the world and themselves, without purse or scrip. Your humble brother did the same way, preaching and tracting everywhere I could.

It is easy to know us by our work, our circumstances, and our spirit—the highest in his office, the foremost in the most unpleasant part of the work—saying Come, and not Go, and Do as I do, and not sit on the *sofa* and give orders like a *Lord*. We are all one—one heart and one work, and no one sees the work of his brother as being less than his own.

Now all the boxes of books are empty—thousands of tracts are in possession of the people, and all the brethren have been called back, from the first of this month, and released to go to work; this includes conference presidents and all except myself, (and I would go as well if that were wiser,) and their mission is to earn money to emigrate next time: they have six months' time to fulfill that and pay whatever they can of the debt for the books that have been distributed. We shall pay the entire amount if we can, and if we fail, others will have it to do, or it will be had as a debt of the crown—unpaid forever.

We are in unity and love, and content in our hearts. We are baptizing some, and there are scores preparing to emigrate to Zion next time. Amen.

Yours, J. E. JONES.

REVIEW,

Of the Treatise, *Heresies and Deceptions of the Latter-day Saints, and the Book of Mormon, Exposed, by the Reverend W. J. Morrish, translated from the English by David Roberts, from Caernarvon.*

At the request of several of the Saints of the North, who have informed us that there is renewed commotion because of the above treatise, we shall endeavor to show as much of its inconsistency as our limited space will allow us to provide.

The author, Mr. Morrish, is a Priest of the Church of England, if we understand properly his *First Warning* to his flock.

Upon beginning his Warning, he refers to the obligations of his important office—that he is to put down all heresies contrary to the Word of God, through his 'ordination as a Minister of God, by the laying on of hands of a *Christian Bishop.*'

Who, pray tell, ordained the Bishop? or who ordained the first Priest of the Church of England? The Church of England was disassociated with anathemas pronounced on its head by Catholicism, and no divine emissary came from above to ordain or authorize one of its apostate ministers; for our author and his hired brethren oppose the doctrine of the ministering of angels in these days, because it is 'strange and contrary to the Word of God.' From whence, then, did the authority of this Reverend come for him to be a minister of God? If a priest of the Church of England is under such obligations to uphold the doctrine of the Word of God, why was not Henry the Eighth excommunicated for his devilishness, as the Catholic church excommunicated him? and where in the Word of God were Henry's tricks authorized?

The author complains bitterly that the 'Mormons' are especially successful in 'unsettling the minds of several pious Christians, and in teaching them doctrines contrary to the Gospel of our Lord Jesus Christ,' and he pretends to have 'researched their origins,' so that there can be no mistake, we would suppose.

The result of this detailed research is that it was *God himself* who hid the plates of the Book of Mormon in mount Cumorah. Where in the books of the Saints did this careful researcher find such a story? We have understood that Mormon, in the year 384, after

Christ, hid them all, except for some he left to his son, Moroni, who completed the story of his nation, and sealed up the written records in the year 421, A. D.

'Now God in his mercy has allowed the untruthfulness of the assertion to be proven,' says the researcher. Amen, we say; and we exhort the flock to do their own research from now on.

Next, the *researcher* got hold of an old tale which has been refuted over and over again for many years, namely the Spaulding tale. We direct our readers to read the Book of Mormon, and the pamphlet that refutes the Spaulding tale, and we assure them that they will have complete satisfaction.

Upon concluding his first Warning, this godly (?) Minister asserts that the 'Mormons' claim that God himself wrote the Book of Mormon *with his finger!* while the Book itself, together with the publications of the Saints, show that inspired men, in different ages, wrote it on plates, and that the Seer Joseph Smith translated it into English. Do not the atrocious and barefaced lies of the *researcher* whirl his judgments back on his own head? and truth thunders the answer of the Prophet to the King of Israel— THOU *art the man!*—thou who dost 'pretend to be a Minister of God'—his speech is based on a lie—he knows about the deceit he practices—the people should separate themselves from him and his avaricious, hired, and boastful brethren—and he and his kind are those who mix some degrees of the truth with the *Common Prayer*, wages, and selling *livings*. It is he who condemns dreams, revelations, and visions of angels in this age while Joel says that such things will be in the last days, beginning with the Jews, and their children, and everyone, finally, whom the Lord our God may call to him. Joel taught this foolish doctrine, and Mr. Morrish, the 'Christian Bishop,' and all the church of Henry the Eighth doubted him. They, then, are teaching strange doctrines that are contrary to the word of God, and doctrines that are contrary to the Gospel of our Lord Jesus Christ. That will come in power, and in the Holy Ghost, and in much assurance, says Paul. Listen you, O, Churchmen; If your Priests are Ministers of God, they will say to you, 'Receive ye the Holy Ghost'—a promise of Joel— dreams and visions as the Prophet Joseph Smith and the Saints have received—a confirmation of the word through various gifts of the Holy Ghost and signs will follow the true believers. As many as the Lord our God may call will receive them, if we believe the unchanging word of God. But the Ministers must be called by God as was Aaron, and not as Mr. Morrish and the 'Christian Bishop.'

Something very foolish in the view of the author is the doctrine of the gathering. This is not strange, since he has closed his heart against everything 'strange and new.' No doubt he and the other Priests and Christian Bishops see the world as going forward splendidly, as it is, without a single one of the prophecies that are the word of God ever being fulfilled. Since our pamphlets explain the doctrine of the gathering we shall not add anything else except to direct the author and his flock to read them, and to stop measuring the Saints by his own measuring stick. Good heavens! The priests of the Church of England talking so shamelessly about worldly profit! Let them read the article of Reynolds in this issue, and let the Priests shut their mouths in shame.

As for the land the Saints possess in America, it is to be had practically for free, and they are independent *freeholders*, without any Priests or a Bishop to swallow their tithing, or great taxes or rents to keep them in bondage to the idle great men.

Upon concluding his First Warning, he wishes for it to have the proper effect on his flock. We shall see if it did. He refers also to the warnings of Paul and Peter. We say again, Thou art the man! Thou and thy brethren are selling *livings*, namely the Ministry of parishes, containing thousands of men's souls, for hundred or thousands of pounds, making merchandise of the souls of thy flock—thou and thy Church fail to endure sound doctrine—the fulfillment of the definite promises of the Word of God, and heaping to themselves hired, lazy, proud, boastful, avaricious, and greedy, and lustful teachers.

We join the author with all our heart in warning the flock with the verses he quotes; for *he is the man.*

WARNING 2,—The proper effect the first Warning had on the flock is perceived in the following quotation,—

'My dear Friends—I sent a letter to you some time ago, to warn you about the deceit that is practiced toward you by a number of men who call themselves "Latter-day Saints;" and with PROFOUND SORROW [we sympathize and feel pity for the reverend when we consider his wage!] I perceive that MANY of you are being led astray by these false teachers; and the only reason I can give for this is that you do not understand *in truth* the teachings they teach you.' He could add 'without my doing additional *research* for you, so that if you do not understand in truth, you may understand in one of my *lies*!'

The pastor complains that his flock does not have a sure enough foundation in the faith of the *Common Prayer*, that they are fickle and unstable, and desirous of hearing something new besides 'as it was in the beginning so it is now, &c., and because they believe the elders of the Saints when they prove their subjects from the Bible, while they should take not of his research into the origin of the Book of Mormon, and believe his assertions in the second Warning.

Next we have a poor translation from the first page of the Book of Mormon—what history it is—the testimony of witnesses, &c., and that the Doctrine and Covenants teaches that 'principles of the Gospel of Jesus Christ are in the Bible and the Book of Mormon, in which there is a fullness of the Gospel.' This is the only church of God on the earth, and that God continues to reveal his will. After that he addresses his flock as follows:—

'You perceive that these people pretend to be apostles and prophets from the Church of the Latter-day Saints—the only true and living church on the face of the earth: and as such they tell you that God has not revealed in the Bible all that is sufficient for salvation, but that they have been sent to proclaim to you a new revelation, in which is the fullness of the Gospel.'

They can perceive the above without the assistance of his Warning; for that is what they were hearing from the preachers of the Saints. We take note again of the following feeble attempts to refute the doctrine of continuing revelation:—

'Now, the question is, Is this assertion in harmony with the Scriptures?' You are told (Romans xvi. 25,) that 'the Gospel and the preaching of Jesus Christ, according to the revelation of the mystery, which was kept secret since the world began,' &c. He refers also to Col. 1. 25, John xv. 15, and 1 John ii. 20. From these verses he concludes that all the counsel of God and all He ever intended to reveal is contained in the Bible! This is an example of the college teaching of the nineteenth century! We consider such rubbish hardly worth noting!

That the early Saints had the fullness of the Gospel and had received a transfer of all the counsel of God that pertained to them is no proof that it was all written in the few epistles of the Apostles to them, which were written when the writer was unable to be present, and there is only a piece here and a piece there of the teaching of Christ, while John says 'the world could not contain the books,' &c. Besides that there are some books that are lost, and despite all that our reverend author asserts that *all the counsel and will of God is contained in the Bible!* Scattered books of the Bible were gathered together and were made into a volume by a throng of corrupt priests, who took upon themselves the right of closing the heavens against presenting additional revelations, and to select the books they considered inspired, and making them into a *Bible*, throwing aside whatever did not agree with their taste: and after that the *Common Prayer* was added. Our author acknowledges that it was necessary for the early disciples to have the Holy Ghost to guide them to the divine truths of the Gospel: why, then, does he deny it while the Bible promises it to every believer who calls upon God? (Acts ii.)

The next accusation against the Saints is that they 'deny that the Bible is the pure word of God, and put it aside entirely.' The author tries to deceive his flock into believing that by citing the following segment which he plucked from the revelation in section 47 of the Doctrine and Covenants. (The translation of D. Roberts differs from the translation of the Doc. and Cov.)

'Behold, I say unto you that all old covenants have I caused to be done away in this thing, and this is a new and an everlasting covenant.'

Through deceptive reasoning and cutting away as much of the revelation as served his crafty purpose, he asserts that the covenant of the New Testament and the virtue of the Atonement are the things the revelation did away with, a revelation which he abbreviates and colors so disgracefully!

The same Covenant, and the same divine Church are what have been presented anew to the Saints in this age which existed in the ancient days, and the revelation under scrutiny says that! but the cunning author took care to leave that out. The revelation refers to people who believed that the first baptism they received was sufficient without getting baptized again. This is how this hired pastor keeps his charmed flock from being 'unsettled in their thoughts!'

The remainder of the Warning treats in the same way several other revelations, &c., to try to prove the accusations of denying the virtue of the Atonement, the power of God, and preaching high treason. In order to understand otherwise we direct our readers to read the Doctrine and Covenants for themselves.

ZION'S TRUMPET,

OR

Star of the Saints.

SATURDAY, SEPTEMBER 26, 1857.

OUR JOURNEY to the Brecon conference and through parts of Monmouthshire and East Glamorgan, in the company of our worthy counselors and Elder A. Calkins, from the Liverpool Office, was of great benefit to us, and, we trust, a blessing to the Saints. We found all true Saints in the condition we expected they would be—full of the light of the Holy Ghost, busily anticipating the bad time that is at the door, and preparing for it. Going about properly—warning the world in soberness and unmistakable words, by preaching and tracting—keeping heavenly order at home—being frugal, paying an honest tithe, considering that God has his eye on them, and saving every penny they can to emigrate as soon as possible. O! how wonderful the way has opened. Several brethren who had families testified that they were poor, and some in debt, before they complied with the separation and began to render unto God the things which be God's. Soon after that they became able to render unto Caesar the things which be Caesar's, and they increased in their wages and their earnings, and God, after being proved good, poured out blessings, until there was not room to receive them without sending them to the Office for their emigration. We could fill an issue of the Trumpet with testimonies of this kind. But we are sorry to have to cast a dark shadow over this lovely picture! Some do not pay an honest tithing—they are afraid to prove God whether He will pour out to them a blessing, until they do not have room to receive it. (Malachi iii. 10.) This chapter, besides referring to the children of ancient Judah, also refers to the last days, when Israel would gather to Zion and Jerusalem, and they would build a Temple. Those who are half-hearted and untrue in the payment of tithing are no doubt guilty of the reputation of 'robbing the Lord;' and of drawing his 'curse,' as verse 9 of the aforementioned verse shows. Let everyone read this verse, and let the Saints rejoice for being born in this blessed age (for them) in which a Temple of God will come forth, and for the privilege of assisting, through their tithing, to build it. Let the disobedient and the wicked fear those who say, 'It is vain to serve God: and what profit is it that we have kept His commandments?' for in the day of tribulation, *which is at the door*, 'His,' only those who have 'thought upon his name,' will 'He spare, as a man spareth his own son that serveth him.' Those who are lazy, apathetic, and unrighteous who are called Saints will soon WEEP in bitterness of soul for not having magnified the opportunities they received. Saints, do you not know the steadfastness and certainty of the word of God through his inspired servants, and that they are in Zion preparing for something that is close to arriving, and should we not do our part?

RELIGIOUS PERSECUTION—"*The Mormons*—Lately this deluded sect has been continuing out in several places that neighbor our town, (Swansea,) and it appears that they have reached something of a 'stronghold' in Llansamlet. Last Sunday, (the 13th) however, they upset their listeners so much with their corrupt and bizarre sermons, and their assertions relating to the deceiver Joe Smith, that they were assaulted with cabbages, potatoes, apples, &c., and they were forced to retreat quickly with the scorn and rebukes of 200 or 300 people."—*Cambrian.*

[Here is another example of the boastful 'Christianity' of the nineteenth century! Can the slanderous asp, the *Cambrian*, show where his Bible supports and praises persecutors and maligners, and we ask from which sections are the persecutors and the persecuted—the one who strikes and the one who turns the other cheek? Stronger preachers than the Saints will come, soon, when perhaps the *cabbage*, the potato, or any other bits and pieces will not be so plentiful!]

NOTICE.—Lately several locusts have paid a visit to various parts of the British Isles, and one that was tested was in excellent health and appetite. We read that a few spies have gone before the army to the land of Caanan: that situation is not impossible yet.

FROM THE PLAINS.—What with losing animals to the Indians, poor arrangements, fear of having to live in tents next winter, and the flight of such numbers of the soldiers as a consequence, the military expedition to Utah has turned out to be a disgrace and a shame on the American government!

The Express Company is provisioning their stations along the Plains splendidly. This will be a priceless blessing for emigrants.

REYNOLDS NEWSPAPER, SECTARIANISM, AND MORMONISM.

The above newspaper for September 13 contains an interesting article on the "*Mormons and the Priests*."

It observes that Nana Sahib and Brigham Young have destroyed the peace, the appetite and senses of the religious *Times* forever. While one kills our fellow nation by the thousands in the East, the other attracts them by the thousands to his paradise in the far west. The *Times* wonders where the Priests are, and what they are doing by letting their parishes be emptied of thousands of people under their noses!

To the question, What are the priests doing; the 'Reynolds' gives the answer, and that is "they are doing what they usually do—they are defending the evils that exist, which tends to add to Brigham Young's numbers. They are driving the poor who are in hopeless destitution to seek refuge from their ecclesiastical robbers, in the distant territory of the Mormons. The priests, with few honorable exceptions, are engaged in their old task of smiling at the wealthy, and frowning at the poor—flattering and bowing to kings, the powerful and the wealthy, and chastising in the severest way the minor faults of the working people. This is part, but not all of that which they do; they are also striving to increase their worldly treasure, and many of them have succeeded in accomplishing that which the great Master proclaimed as impossible. They are serving God and Mammon—or as worded by one of them, 'making the best of the two worlds.' Several priests are recognized among the cleverest of our businessmen. Some of them are large shareholders in the tasks of *Stock Jobbing* and *Swindling*. They are large-scale dealers in railroad and other stock; they are honored in Chapel Court, and they are recognized on the 'Stock Exchange;' they have purchased landed estates, they acquire house after house, they have purchased commissions for their sons in the army, &c.; they plot to obtain lordly men for their daughters, and they go down on their bellies before any nobleman, or government officer, for the sake of worldly profit. The Bishop of London left only £50,000 to his children, while it was considered that he could have accumulated much more besides the enormous yearly wage he pocketed for a number of years. It is said that that was nothing in comparison to the possessions of other bishops, and, if so, what in the name of Heaven is the general and usual accumulation of a 'Very Reverend Father in God'? We know that it is double and quadruple £50,000, and not infrequently more than that. We know not what the tentmaker Paul, and the fisherman Peter, would say to such successors, although we believe that those forebears would not acknowledge such avaricious Christians, and that another Apostle who used to deal in money and carry the bag is more likely to be the spiritual forebear of our ecclesiastical financiers than the poor and hard-working Apostles, to whom the proclamation of the first simple and plain truths of the Christian religion was entrusted. To roll around in velvet-cushioned carriages—to be waited on by a pack of powdered and plush servants—to live in splendid furnished palaces with luxurious food—to drink the best wines—to keep the fairest concubines—to die in the aroma of sanctification, and to leave to their heirs £50,000, £100,000, or even £1,000,000—it is quite likely that they are making the best of this world, but whether it is the safest way to make the best of the next is not as certain."

Then he goes on to encourage the priests to deny themselves and respect the poor, as do the Mormon elders, so as not to force people to flee to Utah to save themselves from the *work-house*, their sons from prison, and their daughters from the streets. Although he does not praise Mormonism, he says that it is "something substantial in exchange for the false sympathy, the forms devoid of passion, the religious husks, and the disheartening, powerless Christianity of those who, in the present day, are the commodities of the pulpit in the British Isles."

A "LIVING" FOR SALE.

Punch has derived considerable enjoyment concerning an impudent statement in the *Times* and says there is a convenient opening for a lazy Priest—an inactive ministry that reaches to about £370 per year, and the seller is 58 years old. *Money* will buy the care of the souls and access to the salary all together without attracting the condemnation of Simon Magus, says *Punch*. The seller has another *living*, worth £700 per year, in Essex, and preaches the Gospel (?) in Chelmsford for £800 per year, besides traveling the highways and the fields to steal souls in the area from the rural Dean of Rochester. Since his Reverend is 58 years old, and has so many places, it is feared that he will work himself to death!

CHASTITY OF A PRIEST OF THE CHURCH OF ENGLAND.

The Reverend Wm. B. Sutherland, of the city of Burlington, at last has been exposed in his custom of seeking and ruining young women. About a month before being caught, he had invited his maid, Teressa Gilbert, age 23, on the first day of her service, to sit by his side on the *sofa*, and read a chapter to him, which she did. Then he took the Bible from her hand, and he began to handle her body, whereupon she arose and went out, saying that she was going away; he urged her to stay by offering her a silk dress and gold rings, which she refused. Another time he went to her while she was in her bed, asking her to stay. But she threatened to make noise, which infuriated him, and after she informed his wife, he kicked her out of the house. Although she swore this before the magistrate, the church did not believe her testimony.

Within a month after that, a short time ago, the Priest succeeded in raping a young girl, about 15 years of age. The scoundrel just barely escaped from the enraged and armed father of the girl, or he would have had to make amends for his shameless sins. He has fled to no one knows where, say the newspapers.

SUCCESS OF THE KINGDOM OF CHRIST.

>The gospel of the kingdom is succeeding,
>   Through our Lord's infinite power;
>Soon it will fill the whole earth,
>   As the waters cover the sea.
>It will, it will, as the waters cover the sea.

>The old traditions are uprooted,
>   And all the empty ceremonies;
>Deep darkness is exiled,
>   This is the light of righteousness.
>Listen, listen, this is the light of righteousness.

>Kingdoms and their greatness are shaken.
>   All evil laws are destroyed;
>And then the laws of the Spirit of life
>   Will be the ruling standard of our world,
>It will, it will, it will be the ruling standard of our world.

>The 'stone' will powerfully defeat—
>   And fragment the kingdoms of the world;
>The parts of the idol previously seen,
>   Will be shattered—they will all fall.
>Rank and status will be shattered—they will all fall.

>Onward like an adamantine stone,
>   And quick as lightning it will go;
>Kings and great statesmen
>   Will faint in fear before it,
>Listen, listen, they will faint in great fear before it.

How small it was when cut,
    But thanks be, it increases every hour,
Soon it will be called a mountain,
    Without measure or weight—a great one,
Praise, praise, without measure or weight—a great one.

The kingship of our Father pre-existed,
    Swiftly it will be seen under heaven;
Its heavenly laws will be restored
    To bring to pass his purposes
Beloved, beloved, to bring to pass his purposes.

The King and the laws will be heavenly.
    And the officers of this great kingdom;
They magnify all their excellent environs,
    Splendidly, on the dust of Babylon.
Listen, listen, splendidly, on the dust of Babylon.

We shall harvest our fields in peace,
    Those that were sown through the sword and blood;
We shall see our Jesus in person,
    In the pure image of his Father.
True, true, in the pure image of his Father.

Devilish curses will flee,
    Before the holy strength of our God;
The true characteristic of the ages to come,
    Will be peace and love, it is true,
Beloved, beloved, will be peace and love, it is true.

The avowal of infinite Elohim,
    Myriads of the Saints will receive;
And our earth will be connected to Kolob,
    This will be a privilege for the natives.
Beloved, beloved, this will be a privilege for the natives.

Yonder, yonder, I see it too confined,
    To hold all its subjects;
Some thousands repeat the news,
    Make another new world, and a new man.
Listen, listen, make another new world, and a new man.

Creators will create anew,
 New Saviors will come;
And beings will be filled with Deity,
 I expect to see this without fear.
I do, I do, I expect to see this without fear.

The sublime Gods will visit
 Our earth sometime without wrath;
And all its heavenly inhabitants,
 Will dance in praise together.
Listen, listen, they will dance in praise together.

Pure beings, eternal myriads,
 Will produce spirits like God;
Those will at a future time,
 All receive tabernacles in which to live.
Beloved, beloved, all will receive tabernacles in which to live.

For an end to the increase of the kingdom,
 In vain would it be expected forever,
An exceptional soldier who has fought,
 Not in vain, is our dear Prophet Smith.
Listen, listen, not in vain, is our dear Prophet Smith.

Flint, September 20, 1857. DAVID JOHN.

☞ Let the Conference Presidents continue to pay the tithing totals to this office until the debt of their Conferences comes down to the figure that existed June 30, 1856; by doing this the pamphlets will be paid for, &c., which were to come from the tithing. We trust that the pamphlets are still being kept in circulation insofar as possible, so the purpose for their publication will be fulfilled, and the gentiles will be warned.

LATEST NEWS.—Taylor has reached the Valley—peace, prosperity, and abundance there—remarkably abundant crops. The new Governor and the troops have started for the second time. The accusations against President Young have been refuted to the satisfaction of the President of the United States.

MONMOUTHSHIRE Conference will be held September 27; East Glamorgan, October, 4; Cardiff, 11th; West Glamorgan, 18th. Presidents Pratt and Benson will be present at the latter. Information will be forthcoming later on.

CONTENTS.

	PG.
Home Church Accounts	305
Review	308
Editorial—Condition of the Saints—Religious Persecution	313
Reynolds Newspaper, Sectarianism, and Mormonism	315
A "Living" for sale—Chastity of a Priest	317
Poem—Success of the Kingdom of Christ	318

PRINTED AND PUBLISHED BY D. DANIELS, SWANSEA.

ZION'S TRUMPET,

OR

𝔖𝔱𝔞𝔯 𝔬𝔣 𝔱𝔥𝔢 𝔖𝔞𝔦𝔫𝔱𝔰.

No. 21.]　　　OCTOBER 10, 1857.　　　[VOL. X.

TEACHING OF PRESIDENT BRIGHAM YOUNG.
Bowery, Great S. L. City, July 26, 1857.

I will read a portion of the writings of the prophet Daniel, commencing at verse 27 of the second chapter.

27. Daniel answered in the presence of the king, and said, The secret which the king hath demanded cannot the wise men, the astrologers, the magicians, the soothsayers, shew unto the king;

28. But there is a God in heaven that revealeth secrets, and maketh known to the king Nebuchadnezzar what shall be in the latter days Thy dream, and the visions of thy head upon thy bed, are these;

29. As for thee, O king, thy thoughts came into thy mind upon thy bed, what should come to pass hereafter: and he that revealeth secrets maketh known to thee what shall come to pass.

30. But as for me, this secret is not revealed to me for any wisdom that I have more than any living, but for their sakes that shall make known the interpretation to the king, and that thou mightest know the thouths of thy heart.

31. Thou, O king, sawest, and behold a great image: this great image, whose brightness was excellent, stood before thee; and the form thereof was terrible.

32. This image's head was of fine gold, his breast and his arms of silver, his belly and his thighs of brass,

33. His legs of iron, his feet part of iron and part of clay.

34. Thou sawest till that a stone was cut out without hands, which smote the image upon his feet that were of iron and clay, and brake them to pieces.

35. Then was the iron, the clay, the brass, the silver, and the gold, broken to pieces together, and became like the chaff of

the summer threshingfloors; and the wind carried them away, that no place was found for them: and the stone that smote the image became a great mountain, and filled the whole earth.

36. This is the dream: and we will tell the interpretation thereof before the king.

37. Thou, O king, art a king of kings: for the God of heaven hath given thee a kingdom, power, and strength, and glory.

38. And wheresoever the children of men dwell, the beasts of the field and the fowls of the heaven hath he given into thine hand, and hath made thee ruler over them all. Thou art this head of gold.

39. And after thee shall arise another kingdom inferior to thee, and another third kingdom of brass, which shall bear rule over all the earth.

40. And the fourth kingdom shall be strong as iron: forasmuch as iron breaketh in pieces and subdueth all things: and as iron that breaketh all these, shall it break in pieces and bruise.

41. And whereas thou sawest the feet and toes, part of potter's clay, and part of iron, the kingdom shall be divided; but there shall be in it of the strength of the iron, forasmuch as thou sawest the iron mixed with miry clay.

42. And as the toes of the feet were part of iron, and part of clay, so the kingdom shall be partly strong, and partly broken.

43. And whereas thou sawest iron mixed with miry clay, they shall mingle themselves with the seed of men; but they shall not cleave one to another, even as iron is not mixed with clay.

44. And in the days of these kings shall the God of heaven set up a kingdom, which shall never be destroyed: and the kingdom shall not be left to other people, but it shall break in pieces and consume all these kingdoms, and it shall stand forever.

45. Forasmuch as thou sawest that the stone was cut out of the mountain without hands, and that it brake in pieces the iron, the brass, the clay, the silver and the gold; the great God hath made known to the king what shall come to pass hereafter: and the dream is certain, and the interpretation thereof sure.

46. Then the king Nebuchadnezzar fell upon his face, and worshipped Daniel, and commanded that they should offer an oblation and sweet odors unto him.

47. The king answered unto Daniel, and said, Of a truth it is, that your God is a God of gods, and a Lord of kings, and a revealer of secrets, seeing thou couldst reveal this secret.

48. Then the king made Daniel a great man, and gave him many great gifts, and made him ruler over the whole province of Babylon, and chief of the governors over all the wise men of Babylon.

49. Then Daniel requested of the king, and he set Shadrach, Meshach, and Abednego over the affairs of the province of Babylon: but Daniel sat in the gate of the king.

These verses are of themselves a text and texts—a sermon and sermons.

We have a great deal of talking, preaching, exhorting, counseling, giving advice, &c., from this stand in many other places where the Saints assemble, but perhaps it may be the case with many, as it is somewhat with me, that they in a measure neglect to read the Bible and forget many things which are written therein. Perhaps there are many who have not read much in the Bible since they came into this Church, not having had much time to do so.

I was a Bible reader before I came into this Church, and so far as the letter of the book was concerned I understood it. I professed to be a Believer in the Bible so far as I knew how; but as for understanding by the Spirit of the Lord, I never did, until I became a Latter-day Saint. I had many a time read Daniel's interpretation of Nebuchadnezzar's dream, but it was always a dark subject to me. I was well acquainted with many of the priests of the day, and I would frequently think to myself that I would get some knowledge from them. And as I became acquainted with smart, intelligent, literary priests and professors of religion, I thought, now I can obtain some intelligence from this or from that man, and I would begin to ask questions on certain texts of scripture, but they would always leave me as they found me—in the dark. They were there themselves, and I knew of a surety, before I heard the Gospel, that the priests were blind guides leading the blind, and that there was nothing left for them only to stumble here and there and perhaps fall into a ditch. That much knowledge I had, previous to my becoming acquainted with what is called 'Mormonism.'

It would be very profitable to the inhabitants of the earth to learn one face, which a very few in the world have learned, that they are ignorant—that they have not the wisdom, the knowledge, and the intelligence outside of the circle of what is called the wisdom of man. For persons to know and understand their own talent, their own strength, their own ability, their own influence, would be very profitable to the inhabitants of the earth, though but very few learn it.

I do not know that I feel particularly thankful that I learned what I did with regard to the lack of intelligence and knowledge professed by Christians to be in their possession, but I have been thankful that my lot and fortune were such that my God gave me good, sound sense; I am thankful for that. When the gospel came to me, surely, within me and all around me, I could see very plainly what the Apostle meant in the words, 'when the commandment came, sin revived, and I died.'

I could see clearly where the inhabitants of the earth were in their position before their God. The whole world, everything upon this globe, was veiled in darkness. There was a mist, a fog, a veil or covering over the minds of the whole of the people on this earth, and what they understood was nothing more than a faint glimmering of light that would dazzle before their eyes for a minute, and they would see it no more. They were like a ship befogged on the ocean and depending for guidance upon a lighthouse, whose glimmering rays could only be discerned at long intervals, when the ship could again be put upon a safe course. But the wind has shifted, and without light or compass they do not know whether it is blowing east, west, north or south, and then how could they tell whether they were directing their course aright? The Christian world, I discovered, was like the captain and crew of a vessel on the ocean without a compass and tossed to and fro whithersoever the wind listed to blow them. When the light came to me I saw that all the so called Christian world was groveling in darkness.

We profess to have the light, intelligence and knowledge with which to understand the things of God. The dream of king Nebuchadnezzar and its interpretation by Daniel are as plain to the man and woman filled with the power of the Holy Ghost as are the most common lessons to the school children; they most clearly understand the interpretation. Daniel saw that in the latter days the God of heaven was going to set up his kingdom upon this his earth. He has set that kingdom up, as you who are here this day are witnesses.

What brought you from the States and other regions to these mountains? What caused the men and women before me to leave their good farms, their good houses, their merchandise, and all the luxuries and comforts of life so dear to the natural man? What caused many women to leave their husbands, their children, their parents? What caused all this? What is the reason of such conduct? Can any man tell? The world is trying to; but they are even more ignorant about it than they are of the present movements and designs of the President of the United States. They know not the reason why the people are assembled here, for they cannot and will not see and understand anything except as they discern it by the powers of the natural man.

I have told them many times, and I can now tell them again, if the whole world could hear my voice, they are to be pitied, and I pray for them. We have traversed the earth to preach the Gospel to them. We have often started upon our missions almost destitute, without hats, nearly without shoes and any of the comforts of life, to travel thousands and thousands of miles to preach the Gospel to the people. If they will not be benefited, our skirts are clear of their blood, and they must bear the blame.

Can they tell the cause of this people's being here today? Can they give the cause for the influence I have over the Latter-day

Saints? They cannot. If this was not the kingdom of God upon the earth, do you suppose that the world would be arrayed against it? No. There is not a sound, well-informed mind in the world but what would decide at once that there is no cause of enmity against the people, and that all hostility toward us arises from the fact that we have the eternal priesthood and the influence thereof. The kingdom of heaven is here, and we are in it, and they are angry at us solely for that.

There is not a king, governor, or ruler but what desires and is endeavoring to obtain the influence that I and my brethren possess and are lawfully striving to obtain. Do you suppose that there was ever a President of the United States but what desired the confidence of his constituents? No, never. Was there ever a senator, a representative, a governor of a State, a politician or a priest, but what desired the same power in his sphere that I have in mine? They cannot get it because they do not know how. What is the reason? They have not got the kingdom of God, which binds the people together. They are ignorant of it, though we have traveled barefooted and almost naked to preach it to them, and I say that they are to be pitied.

How many times I have gone to preach to them, and with all the kindness and calmness I was capable of, told them that I had something to cheer and comfort them, if they would hear it with good honest hearts. How often I have asked, Can I have your meeting house or your schoolhouse to preach in; can I have the privilege of preaching to the people? 'No, you cannot, if I can prevent it.' That is the spirit of the priests.

It is the priests and elders of Christendom who have the power of hell in them which causes the trouble that you see, and that you have seen and borne for many years. They are like that unruly member—the tongue, which sets on fire the course of nature and is lit with the fire of hell.

The priests have this fire, and who fans the flame? brother Smoot has told you who blows the bellows. It is the politician, the drunkard, and the filth and offscouring of the earth who run at the beck and call of those who have a dollar or sixpence for them—of those who will treat them and give them an oyster supper and a good lodging.

There is another class—the speculators, who endeavor to get up some plan or other by which to make money. Bro. Smoot has given you a few items concerning their present movements in the east. Through their whining, bickering, howling, groveling, squalling and scratching, and in a political and speculative point of view, many are striving to most egregiously befool our government and squander its revenue. And the priests are also at the bottom of this movement; for they have the power that is of hell, and others blow the flame and furnish the fuel to persecute the Latter-day Saints, because they are in the kingdom that the God of heaven has set up in the last days, and that shall never be destroyed.

It is a little more than 27 years since I commenced reading the book of Mormon and defending the cause we are engaged in. My mind was open to conviction, and I knew that the Christian world had not the religion that Jesus and his Apostles taught. I knew that there was not a Christian Bible on the earth within my knowledge. A few years previous to that time, Joseph had obtained the plates and began translating the Book of Mormon, and from the time he found those plates in the Hill Cumorah, there has been that same tirade of abuse, lying, slandering, and defaming the name and character of the Prophet and his associates, as there is at this day. It is no hotter a time now than it was then, and there is no more persecution now than there was then.

God has commenced to set up his kingdom on the earth, and all hell and its devils are moving against it. Hell is yawning and sending forth its devils and their imps, what for? To destroy the kingdom of God from the earth; but they cannot do it.

The God of heaven showed Nebuchadnezzar that this kingdom would never be destroyed, and that is my testimony.

(To be continued.)

NEWS FROM UTAH.

We received the *Deseret News* up to August 12. On August 13 the mail started off and with it Elder S. W. Richards, and four other elders on a mission. They crossed the Plains in 19 days, and to New York in 28 days.

There was as plentiful a harvest as has not been had since the settlement of the Saints in the valleys! Health abounded, all were diligent and remarkably successful, and thankful for getting rid of so many corrupt apostates and enemies, longing to be rid of yet a few more. The temple was being built energetically.

Despite the depth of the treacherous wiles of some of the officers of the American government who influenced president Buchanan to hold back the mail and to send 2500 soldiers there, some elders went in with the news. Let our readers judge what effect it had on the peaceful people of Utah. They remembered their cruel persecution from Missouri and Illinois—all the killing and burning that were suffered, and the hunger and hard times that were experienced until they went far enough into the wilderness among the savages to till the earth which did not produce fruit except by considerable labor and the blessing of the Lord. As soon as they came and the wasteland became as if a garden, and the desert blossomed as a rose, there was the avaricious and corrupt officialdom seeking state offices and pestering them and testing the limits of a man's patience. It brings to mind also the tricks of the Steptoe troops, and the frequent troubles of the diligent Saints. It appears now that Zion, instead of suffering more, has decided to rise up and fight if need be. All the printed lies about the destroying angels, the cruelties of Brigham, the narrow escapes of deserters and more who wish to leave after arriving, are burdening and causing the Presidents and the Saints to grow weary. The Prophet Brigham says—

"The time must come when there will be a separation between this kingdom and the kingdoms of this world, even in every point of view. The time must come when this kingdom must be free and independent from all other kingdoms. Are you prepared to have the thread cut?

"It would be hard for the people to explain away the idea that the government of the United States is shutting down the gate upon us, for it is too visible; and this is what hastens the work of the Lord, which you are praying for every day. . . . Now, take care, for if the Lord does, maybe you will not be prepared to meet it. . . .

"Now let me tell you one thing; I shall take it as a witness that God designs to cut the thread between us and the world, when an army undertakes to make their appearance in this Territory to chastise me or to destroy my life from the earth. I lay it down that right is, or at least should be, might with Heaven, with its servants, and with all its people on the earth. As for the rest, we will wait a little while to see; but I shall take a hostile movement by our enemies as evidence that it is time for the thread to be cut. I think that we will find three hundred who will lap water, and we can whip out the Midianites. Brother Heber said that he could turn out his women, and they would whip them. I ask no odds of the wicked, the best way they can fix it."

Old brother Heber C. Kimball says that the world must acknowledge Joseph, Brigham, and all the prophets of God before they will receive salvation. He said, "you may kill Brigham, and his brother Heber, if you can, which you will not be able to do until the time comes. If you kill Brigham, there would be a thousand Brighams that would rise through him, for his posterity would be prophets. . . . Can the world obliterate Mormonism, this Church—the kingdom of God? You might just as well go to obliterate the stars of the firmament.

"There is no man except for brother Brigham, or his successor in the priesthood, that will ever rule over me as a governor. (Voices all over the congregation, 'Amen.') A man not holding the priesthood may come here in the capacity of a governor, if he pleases, and will act properly in the line of his office; but if he does not magnify wholesome laws, we will teach him his duty.

"Sending a man here with 2500 troops!—they have no design in God Almighty's world only to raise a rookery with this people, and bring us into collision with the United States, and when they come here, the first dab will be to take brother Brigham Young and Heber C. Kimball, and others, and they will slay us; that is their design, and if we will not yield to their meanness, they will say we have mutinized against the President of the United States, and then they will put us under martial law, and they will begin to massacre this people. That has been the design of the men that have been here. [Voice in the stand, 'They can't do it.'] No, they *can't* do it.

"Drummond and those miserable scoundrels and some that are now in our midst, how do I feel towards them?—pray for them? Yes, I pray that God Almighty would send them to hell, some say the shortest way, but I would like to have them take a round about road, and be as long as they can be in going there. How do you suppose I feel?

"I have been driven five times—been broken up and my goods robbed from me, and I have been afflicted almost to death."

He shows further that the Government of the United States has treated the saints as the sons of Jacob treated their brother Joseph, and they have come again to Zion with a more humble attitude than troops to bow down to prophets and Saints of God and to request nourishment to save their lives; is the President of the United States asking the authorities of this Church what will be the best to do for its people? He says to those who do not believe to stay and see for themselves, and that when the authorities of the States suppose that they have the Saints in the snare, at that time, the Lord and they themselves will be bound. He also said,—

"Will this land be a land of milk and honey? Yes. Missouri is considered to be the greatest honey country that there is on the earth; but it will not be many years before they cannot raise a spoonful in that land, nor in Illinois, or in any other land where they fight against God. Mildew shall come upon their honey, their bees, and their crops, and desolation shall come upon the nation like a whirlwind. . . . We have felt the rod. The judgment is to commence at the House of God, and then it will go on the rebellious and the wicked, the Apostates especially, and they shall suffer: they have got to pay all the debt of the trouble that have brought upon the innocent from the days of Joseph to this day. . . .

"Shall we have manna? Yes. The United States have 700 Wagons loaded with about two tons to each wagon with all kinds of things; and then 700 head of cattle, and it is said that 2500 troops are coming here with this and that and the other: that is all right. Suppose the troops don't get here; but all these goods and cattle come; well, that would be a mighty help to us: That would clothe up the boys and the girls and make them comfortable, and then remember, there are 15 months provisions besides. I am only talking about this. Suppose it extends on for 4 or 5 years and they send 100,000 troops, and provisions and goods in proportion, and everything else got here, except for the troops. I am talking by comparison to the Saints, and you that are without do not understand it. [There were some there who did not like that.] I am a kind of funny fellow, I always was. . . .

"May the Almighty bless you; may the peace of God be with you and upon your children and your children's children forever and ever; and may God Almighty curse our enemies. [Voices, 'Amen.'] I feel to curse my enemies, and when God won't bless them, I do not think he will ask me to bless them; if I did, it would be to put the poor curses to death who have brought death and destruction on me and my brethren, upon my wives and my children that I buried on the road between the States and this place.

"Did I ever wrong them, a man or woman of them, out of a halfpenny? Poor rotten curses! and the President of the United States, inasmuch as he has turned against us, and will take a course to persist in pleasing the ungodly curses that are howling around him for the destruction of this people, he shall be cursed, in the name of Israel's God, and he shall not rule over this nation, because they are my brethren, but they have cast me out and cast you out, and I curse him and all his coadjutors in his cursed deeds, in the name of Jesus Christ and by the authority of the Holy Priesthood, and all Israel shall say Amen.

"Send 2500 troops here, our brethren, to make a desolation of this people! God Almighty helping me, I will fight until there is not a drop of blood in my veins. Good God! I have wives enough to whip out the United States, for they will whip themselves."

In an editorial in the *Deseret News* the American Government is addressed as follows:—

"If you intend to continue the appointment of certain officers, we respectfully suggest that you appoint actually intelligent and honorable men who will wisely attend to their own duties, and send them unaccompanied by troops, which you yourselves well know are of no lawful use here, and your officers will be respected and treated strictly according to their acts and merits, as you also well know has always been the case, except that we did not hang up some of the infernal scoundrels you have heretofore sent, as they most richly deserved. And if you will not receive this fair counsel, but persist in sending us officials from the *tag, rag and bobtail* of whore houses, grog shops and gambling hells, we shall take the liberty of guessing your kind (?) intentions towards us, and shall also take the liberty, for the first time, of using that class of officials strictly in accordance with their deserts.

"Should you elect to send the last named class, and should they venture to come and act out their devilish natures, they will really need a far larger bodyguard than 2500 soldiers."

All the stories, as we said, are about the tricks of Brigham, the increase in apostates, &c., after reaching the Valley, and, in answer to the assertion that hosts in Utah wish to escape if they could, and that troops are needed there so they can flee safely, &c., President Brigham Young offered to outfit every such family with horses, carriages, provisions, and all their needs, on the condition that "Uncle Sam" (the government) do the same thing with all those who wish to go from the States to Utah. The Prophet considers this a fair offer, especially if it is to free and take out the weary and fearsome apostates that the soldiers are sent, and if Utah is such an unpleasant place.

The above is but a small part of much that was said of the behavior of the American government, the truth of which is confirmed in the account of the evils of the troops, &c., together with later accounts from the States.

All this shows that the devil is enraged, and heaping up to his old walls of defense and refuge—the lie, which in every age has been set against the kingdom of God. But despite the envy of the powers of this world, and all the opposition of the false priests, the Kingdom of God will come up victorious over all enemies, and soon, for this is the kingdom that Daniel saw, and its progress will not be hindered.

ZION'S TRUMPET,

OR

Star of the Saints.

SATURDAY, OCTOBER 10, 1857.

THE SOUND OF THE TRUMPET this time is a weak echo of the roar of the 'Lion of the Lord' and his brethren in the strongholds of the Everlasting Hills. Whether we are ready or not, the small stone will roll at a gallop, and like a snowball it will increase in its size with every turn. The Saints in times past are as if they had been rolling the Stone up to the highland, and now are increasing its size along the tops of the mountains, where it is dangerous for their enemies to attack it lest it slip from its high place onto their heads and shatter them to pieces.

Zion is about to be delivered, and the connecting thread, as the Prophet says, is about to be cut; who is ready for the consequence? We shall not add to all that is already before the eyes of the Saints. He who has ears, let him hear; and he who has eyes, which are not shut in apostate slumber, apathy, laziness, and darkness, let him perceive the remarkable and grand signs of the times.

———

EMIGRATION *to the States stopped for the present.*—To the Saints who are making preparations to emigrate to the States and to Utah during the ensuing season, we say, for the efforts you have made you will be blessed. Our salvation, as a people, depends upon the obedience which we yield to the counsels of the Lord, given us from time to time through his servants. You have been told to save means to pay your way from here to Zion, and you will be rewarded according to the effort that you have made.

In view of the difficulties which are now threatening the Saints, we deem it wisdom to stop all emigration to the States and Utah for the present. We anticipate that it will not be long until the way will again be opened so that you can go home. As the morning mist is dispelled by the glory of the rising sun, so will the present intervening difficulties be banished by the glory of God, when he shall make bare his arm of power, in defense of his people, as he did in the days when he led them out of the land of Egypt.

It will not be long until the way will again be opened, so that the Saints can gather to Zion according to the desires of their hearts. Continue to treasure up means, and add to what you already have, so that you may not be delayed when the way opens [in some other direction].—*Star.*

———

THE MORMON—which is published in New York City, is discontinued.

Pamphleting.—While the Saints are in Wales saving and preparing a way to emigrate when the door opens for more of the sheaves to go to the threshing floor, as if between showers, when the time of the harvest is far past, do not forget the lesson of cleansing completely our skirts from the blood of this generation, by not leaving a man or woman who will give their attention without teaching them about the grand kingdom of God and its destiny, and the consequence of not coming into it.

Let it be definitely understood that all the Welsh pamphlets by Pratt that have been sent to the conferences belong to the tithing money and are to be kept in circulation out in the world. Not one

Saint is to receive a volume of these which have been covered, stitched, and cut for the purpose of circulation until further notice.

We understand that some have slackened their pace with this indispensable work, but when they are not received to any special place in Zion, because their hands are not free from the blood of this generation, perhaps they will remember their negligence. Concerning the Conference or branch President who gives little importance to the *Star* and the *Trumpet*, &c., and to distributing tracts, we say without hesitation that he will lose the Spirit of Zion, and sluggishness will creep in among the Saints under his care.

Every important and interesting editorial of the publications should be read in public in the meetings, and the officers ought to learn from that; for therein is the voice of the presidency; and those who give little importance to them will wither in their conceit, and their thoughts and their understanding will be unfruitful and deceitful.

While we recognized everyone's free agency to receive the number they wished of the *Trumpet*, we were not encouraging the Saints who could understand Welsh to disregard them and set them aside, nor were we encouraging the presidents to be lazy and apathetic as to who should receive it and who should not; rather, as we noted, the loss will be theirs.

Certainly there will be in the bosom of the wise and principled a desire to have a bound volume of the enlightening, explicit, and splendid treatises of Apostle Orson Pratt, in which there is such an excellent display of the first principles of the Gospel, an account of the general apostasy, and a superb description of the kingdom of God.

We have a few volumes on hand, which have not been stitched or cut. The first to order them shall have them, and we believe that some will be disappointed. The price of a cloth-bound volume with *gilt edges* will be two shillings each to the public. Trustworthy brethren will be given from now till the end of the year to pay for them.

For all who wish to secure a volume, prepayment is requested of eight pence for binding so that we may bind all that are ordered together more cheaply. The price per volume with the finest binding—2s 3c.

We wish for the presidents to hasten in gathering the prepayments so the volumes can be bound promptly, since the worthy author wishes for them to be sold this year.

LATEST FROM UTAH.

ARRIVAL OF ELDER S. W. RICHARDS.

Liverpool, October 4, 1857.

Elder O. Pratt.

Dear Editor,—I take pleasure in informing you of my arrival

here yesterday, in company with Elder George G. Snyder, per steamship "Europa."

We left Great Salt Lake City on the 13 of August, with the express for the States; our mission extending to the Churches in the States, Canadas, and Europe. George W. Knowlton, and a passenger per the express, accompanied us over the Plains, and Elder Bryant Stringham as far as Horseshoe Creek with the instructions to the several stations on the line. We spent the night of the 14th at Bridger. Brother Lewis Robinson, in charge of this station, had just completed the walls of the new Fort, built of rock laid in mortar. Some 40 lodges of the Snake Indians were making a friendly visit at the Fort, and Wash-a-kete, the Chief, seemed much pleased in being made acquainted with us, and interested in the answers made to his inquiries. About 18 miles west of this post we met Levi Stewart, Isaac Bowman, Mrs. McMinn, and others returning from the States. The night of the 16th we spent at Markham's station, upper crossing the Sweet Water.

Morning of the 18th, we left Devil's Gate, and about 5 miles east of Independence Rock met the two first handcart companies, in charge of Elders Israel Evans and J. B. Martin. Elders Dana, Ashby, Walker, and Workman were in company. These companies were in excellent health and spirits, traveling, when we met them, at the rate of 4 miles per hour. Our short interview with them was indeed cheering. The next we met was Elder Moody, with a part of the Texan company, about ten miles east of Willow springs, and but a few miles further we met the first Government train with stores for the troops of the Utah Expedition, consisting of 26 wagons, each drawn by six yokes of oxen. Evening, we reached the upper crossing of the Platte, where one or more Government trains were encamped, and three companies of our emigration, including the Danish and all the remaining handcart emigration. It being in the night, we did not make a general acquaintance with the Saints, but learned from Elders Cowley and Parkes that they were unusually prosperous, and the general condition of the companies improving. These handcart companies contained many aged, sickly, and infirm persons, when leaving the frontiers.

Wednesday, 19th, forded the Platte, and 3 miles down met Homer Duncan, with a part of the Texan brethren, who had with them a very large herd of cattle. At 10 o'clock in the morning we reached Deer Creek where we found Elders Hoffheins and Hart with their companies from the States; they had been traveling together and lost 46 head of cattle in a *stampede*, which weakened their teams, but had not essentially detained them. They obtained some cattle from the Deer Creek station, and moved on with a good degree of ease. Elder N. V. Jones and the boys with him at this station, merit much praise, as their works there abundantly testified. We tarried here near 24 hours, and then passed on to Horseshoe Creek station, Elder Jones accompanying us.

Here we learned that Elder W. G. Young had passed in advance of Elder J. A. Little's company, and that one or two Government trains of stores had passed up the north side of the Platte, which we had not observed. After making some little necessary preparations at this place to enable us to complete our journey to the frontiers, we took two of the brethren from here with us for a return express, and reluctantly parting with Elders Stringham and Jones, we proceeded on. At evening we camped with Elder Little and company, being the last of this year's emigration, 11 miles above Laramie. This company appeared to be in an excellent condition for rapid traveling, and were expecting to make good time from there in.

Thursday morning, the 20th, at daybreak, we crossed the Platte opposite Laramie, and passed down the north side of the river. From this point to Kearney it was a frequent occurrence to see large trains, both in motion and in camp, with enormous herds of cattle, horses and mules. Seventy-eight wagons moving in one train, with about 1000 head of cattle, were as many as we saw together. They generall moved and camped in companies of about 26 wagons.

Monday, 24th. The first company of troops that we discovered were in camp 118 miles below Laramie. We camped on the opposite side of the river, in view of some 200 tents or upwards, and 5 or 6 trains of Government equipage. The Government has designed to make the Utah Expedition a magnificent affair.

On the 28th we called at Kearney, where we were informed that most of the troops for Utah had passed that point, and many heavy trains of merchandise, in view of a rare chance for speculation, purchasing wheat, grain, forage, &c., for the troops in Utah. Poor creatures; what a pity they should be disappointed!

At Fort Kearney we learned that many were deserting from the expedition, both troops and teamsters, and the officers had been obliged to hold out inducements, and adopt rigid regulations, withholding pay for one year, &c., to suppress, as far as possible, the spirit of desertion. It was thought this spirit would greatly increase as they advanced toward the mountains and encountered the severity of the mountain storms, which must necessarily overtake them. Even at Kearney the soldiers were in very high glee at the idea of wintering sumptuously in Utah, where, as the Paddy said, "the women are as thick as blackberries," and it was a great wonder to them what Brigham Young would say to see them with his wives parading the streets of Great Salt Lake City. Every dirty, foul-mouthed Dutchman and Irishman, of which many of the troops were composed, fully expected some "Mormon" woman would jump into his arms upon his arrival in Utah, and hail him as a heavenly messenger sent to bring deliverance from "Mormon degradation, wretchedness, and despair." Who doesn't wait with almost breathless suspense for the issue? Suffice it to say, the information we received at this point was of the most interesting character to such as have families in Utah, and afforded us considerable amusement.

[The other stations and branches where they called were Genoa, Florence, Crescent City, Bluff City, Keokuk, St. Louis, and New York.]

After consulting with brothers Appleby, Clinton, and Stenhouse, in New York, upon the general condition of the Saints in the Eastern States, some changes in the affairs of the Church were deemed expedient, and the publication of the "Mormon" was discontinued. [A great sign for those who can see.]

On the 23rd we took passage on the "Europa," and had a very favorable voyage of ten days to this port.

The blessing of our Heavenly Father has truly been with us upon this mission, fully equal to the importance of the duties we have had to perform. We passed several bands of Indians upon the Plains, together with the principal body of the Sioux nation, but were not molested by any, further than the little annoyance of their wish to trade, or 'swap,' for tobacco, matches, bread, &c. Every evil eye towards us has seemingly been blind, and no angry heart has been suffered to do us any harm, and we have been made as swift messengers that go forth from Zion, bearing glad tidings of great joy to all Saints; for our message has been received with gladness and great joy by the faithful elders, who, as watchmen upon the walls, can behold the dawning of the day that brings with it the redemption of Zion from all her enemies. . . .

Having performed a journey of 5800 miles in 33½ traveling days, and near 1400 of this with animals, as you may naturally expect, we are wearied somewhat in body, though we are continually refreshed in spirit and in the knowledge of the work of our God.

In conclusion permit me to extend a hearty greeting in the name of the Lord to the Saints under your administration, in which Elder Snyder joins me. In landing once more upon these shores, I am reminded of many days that have in years past been devoted by me to the welfare of the faithful in these lands, and am constrained to rejoice in the integrity of the faithful. To all such I would say, Rejoice ye, for our God reigneth in Zion, and his Prophets declare his will.

The day of Zion's redemption is at hand, and her children shall speedily behold the salvation of our God; and in that day the nations shall know that Zion is established, and that she is a place of safety for those that flee thither from the wrath and anger of the ungodly, who shall seek each one to destroy his neighbor and his brother from off the earth. Know ye, dear Saints, that faithfulness to your covenants, and endurance to the end in the way that God through his servants shall direct, are the terms of your exaltation to mansions of eternal glory.

Praying that success and honor may continue to crown your efforts for the salvation of Israel, I am

Your Fellow-servant,
S. W. Richards.

MISCELLANEOUS, &c.

The *scurvy* has broken out among the troops of the Utah Expedition following their filthy treatment of the Indian women in Fort Kearney! That is the kind of civilization that pious (?) Christians want to plant in Utah! They had better take care.

☛ We lament to announce that important and unavoidable tasks prevent Presidents Pratt and Benson from visiting Wales.

Llanelli Conference will be held October 25; Camarthen, Nov. 1; Pembrokeshire, 8th, and Cardiganshire the 15th.

The Conferences of the North will be held, in Merioneth, October 18; Anglesey, the 25th; Denbigh, November 1, and Flint on the 8th.

Payments, from September 12 to October 9.—J. Treharne, £2; E. D. Miles, 10s.; J. Davies, £5 5s.; T. Rees, £2 2s. 7c.; J. Griffiths, £1; W. Ajax, Anglesey, £1.

CONTENTS.

	PG.
Teachings of President B. Young	321
News from Utah	326
Editorial	330
Latest from Utah	332
Miscellaneous	336

PRINTED AND PUBLISHED BY D. DANIELS, SWANSEA.

ZION'S TRUMPET,

OR

Star of the Saints.

No. 22.] OCTOBER 24, 1857. [Vol. X.

TEACHING OF PRESIDENT BRIGHAM YOUNG.
Bowery, Great S. L. City, July 26, 1857.

(Continued from Page 326.)

THIS is the kingdom of heaven—the kingdom of God, which Daniel saw—the kingdom that was revealed to king Nebuchadnezzar and interpreted to him by the Prophet Daniel. This is the kingdom that was to be set up in the last days. It is like a stone taken from the mountain without hands, with all its roughness, with all its disfigured appearance, uncomely, even a stumbling block and a stone of offense to the nations of the earth. This is the kingdom that is set up, and the history of the kingdoms of this world all understand, or can read and understand it.

Some may cry out, 'your saying that this is the kingdom of God does not make it so.' No, not by any means. 'Your testimony,' Mr. Young, 'is that this is the kingdom of God on the earth, that which was shown to Daniel the prophet centuries ago?' Yes, that is my testimony. 'Does this make it so?' No, it does not, but let me tell you that it is true; consequently, I bear my testimony of its truth, although my testimony does not change that truth in the least, one way or the other, neither does any other man's. That is my testimony, and has been all the time.

Why I testify of these things is because they are revealed to me, and not to another for me. They were not revealed to Joseph Smith for me. He had the keys to get visions and revelations, dreams and manifestations, and the Holy Ghost for the people. Those keys were committed to him, and through that administration he blessed the name of God. I have received the Spirit of Christ Jesus, which is the Spirit of prophecy. Our testimony does not make this true, and the

22 [PRICE 1½c.

testimony of our enemies that it is not the kingdom of God does not make that true or false. The fact stands upon its own basis and will continue so to stand, without any of the efforts of the children of men.

I have told you the cause of all the bustle and stir against us. The blind are leading the blind, and if their hearts were honest, if they would throw off the mask of prejudice and erroneous parental education, they could receive the truth as well as you and I have. Once in a while one says 'farewell' to the traditions of the fathers. A few will cast off those prejudices that surround the people, and say, 'we will read, pray, think, and meditate, and we will ask God for ourselves.' That is the reason why you and I are here today. We asked God for a testimony, and he witnesses to us from the heavens that this is the kingdom which Daniel saw, and we have embraced it and it is dearer than everything else upon the face of this earth.

Do we expect that the devils will howl? Yes. When has this Church had the peace that we have had since we have been in the 'mountains'? Never. Where is there peace now upon the face of the earth like the peace we enjoy here? Nowhere. Bro. Smoot said that he had been in the lower regions. He could say that with propriety, for in face we are all in the lower regions. Where do you think the devils live?

Do you suppose that there is any such thing as a devil? Yes, a great many believe that there is. Where does he live? The answer comes very readily; he lives in hell, of course. Then if there are devils here, we must also be in hell. Do you not think that the devil is in pain? I should think he was, by the groanings that are uttered from the east. You see that with propriety, brother Smoot could say that he has been to the lower regions, but when he arrives here, although the altitude is much greater, he still is in the same world. We are all here, and we are surrounded by the devils.

Men rage and boil with wrath and indignation, and they do not know the cause of it. If they think, 'what injury have the Mormons done to me?' The response from their own minds will be, 'not any.' What can the men truthfully say, who have civilly passed through here to the west to make their fortunes? That here is a place of peace and contentment; and though a thousand miles from civilization and from all the luxuries and many of the comforts of life, yet here is a people satisfied, contented, and happy. Did they injure you? 'No.' Did they treat you kindly? 'Yes.' Ask the people in the east what is the matter? 'We cannot tell you, only that somebody has said something.' What have they said? 'We do not know; we only heard a rumor, that is all.'

The people abroad are just as foolish, unwise, and short-sighted as they can possibly be, represented by the best learned men in the world. What are they doing? What they have done all the time. Have they been trying to destroy Mormonism? Yes. Did they destroy it when they took the life of Joseph? No, 'Mormonism' is here, the priesthood is here, the keys of the kingdom are here on the earth, and when Joseph went they did not go. And if the wicked should succeed in taking my life, the keys of the kingdom will remain with the Church. But my faith is that they will not succeed in taking my life just yet. They have not as good a man to deal with as they had when they had Joseph Smith. I do not profess to be very good; I will try to take care of *number one*, and if it is wicked for me to try to preserve myself, I shall persist in it, for I am intending to take care of myself.

When they killed Joseph, they were talking about killing a great many others. Would you believe that the apostates say that I was the instigator of the death of Joseph and Hyrum? And William Smith has asserted that I was the cause of the death of his brother Samuel, when brother Woodruff, who is here today, knows that we were waiting at the *depot* in Boston to take passage east, at the very time when Joseph and Hyrum were killed. Brother Taylor was nearly killed at that time, and Dr. Richards had his whiskers nearly singed off by the blaze from the guns. In a few weeks after, Samuel Smith died, and I am blamed as the cause of his death. We did not hear of the death of Joseph until some three or four weeks after he was basely martyred.

What is now the news circulated throughout the United States? That Captain Gunnison was killed by Brigham Young, and that Babbitt was killed on the Plains by Brigham Young and his Danite band. What more? That Brigham Young has killed all the men who have died between the Missouri river and California. I do not say that President Buchanan has any such idea, or the officers of the troops, who are reported to be on their way here, but such are the newspaper stories. Such reports are in the bellows, and editors and politicians are blowing them out.

According to their version I am guilty of the death of every man, woman and child that has died between the Missouri river and the California gold mines, and they (the soldiers) are coming here to chastise me. The idea makes me laugh, and when do you think they will get a chance? Catching is always before hanging. They understand, you know, that I had gone north and intended to leave this place with such as would follow me, and they are coming to declare a jubilee. It is their desire to say to the people, 'you are free, you are not under the bondage of Brigham Young; you need wear his yoke no longer; now let us get drunk, fight, play at cards and race horses; and every one of you women turn to be whores and become associated with the civilization of Christendom.' That is the freedom they are endeavoring to declare here.

I will make this proposition to Uncle Sam [the Government]. I will furnish carriages, horses, the best of drivers and the best food I have to transport to the States every man, woman, and child that wishes to leave this place, if he [our Uncle Sam] will send on at his own expense all those who want to come to Utah, and we will gain a thousand to their one, as all who understand the matter very well know. It would have been much better to have loaded the wagons reported to be on the way here with men, women and children, than with provisions to sustain soldiers, for they will never get here without our helping them; neither do I think that it is the design of President Buchanan that they should come here.

I am not going to interpret dreams, for I don't profess to be such a prophet as were Joseph Smith and Daniel, but I am a *Yankee Guesser*, and I guess that James Buchanan has ordered this expedition to appease the wrath of the angry hounds who are howling around him. He did not design to start men on the 15th of July to cross these plains to this point on foot. Russell & Co. will probably make from eight to ten hundred thousand dollars by freighting the baggage of the expedition. What would induce the Government to expend that amount of money for this Territory? Three years ago they appropriated 45,000 dollars for the purpose of making treaties with the Utah Indians. Has even that diminutively small sum ever been sent here? It is in the coffers of the government to this day, unless they have stolen it out, or improperly paid it out for some other purpose.

Have they ever paid their debts due to Utah? No; and now they have capped their meanness by taking the mail out of the hands of Hiram Kimball, simply because they knew that he was a member of this Church. If he had only have apostatized in season, and written lies about us, it is not probable that his mail contract would have been taken from him without the least shadow of right, as has now been done. He was to have 23,000 dollars for carrying the mail from Independence to this city once a month, which was the lowest bid; but because he is a 'Mormon,' the contract must be disannulled, and that too after he had put by far the most faithful and efficient service on the route that there ever has been, as is most well known at Washington. If I thought that my prayer might be answered, I would pray that not another United States mail may come to this city; for until Mr. Kimball began his service, it has been a constant source of annoyance and disappointment, and, to us, a loss. We can carry our own mails, raise our own dust, and sustain ourselves.

Woe, woe to those men who come here to unlawfully meddle with me and this people. I swore in Nauvoo, when my enemies were looking for me in the face, that I would send them to hell across lots, if they meddled with me, and I ask no more odds of all hell today. If they kill me, it is all right; but they will not until the time comes, and I think that I shall die a natural death, at least I expect to.

Would it not make any man or community angry to endure and reflect upon the abuse our enemies have heaped upon us, and are still striving to pour out upon God's people? . . .

Our mail rights and other rights and privileges are most unjustly trampled underfoot; but they can spend millions to raise a hubbub and make out that something wrong is being done in Utah.

Let me be the President of the United States a little while, and I would say to the Senators, Representatives, and other officers of Government, Gentlemen, you must act the part of men and statesmen, or I will reprove you. What are they angry at me for? Because I will reprove men for their iniquity, and because I have such influence here, the very thing they are all after. They think that they are going to obtain it with money, but they cannot do it.

There is no influence, truth, or righteousness in the world that does not flow from God our Father in the heavens. We have that power, that influence; we also have such love and submission that we submit ourselves to our Father and God, as a child does to a kind parent.

May God bless you, brethren and sisters. Amen.

A PROPHETIC WARNING TO THE INHABITANTS OF GREAT BRITAIN.

(By Apostle Orson Pratt.)

Expecting to leave Great Britain, and return to our mountain home in the Territory of Utah, we feel it a duty to leave with the inhabitants of these countries a solemn warning concerning those things which will soon befall them; and to point out their only way of escape.

Being called and sent of God, we humbly, and in a most respectful manner, say to Her Most Gracious Majesty the Queen, and to all the Lords, Nobles, Rulers, Authorities, and Inhabitants in the United Kingdom of Great Britain, that God Almighty, in this nineteenth century, has set up his Latter-day Kingdom upon the earth, as predicted by his ancient Prophets and Apostles. Angels have been sent forth from heaven, by whom power and authority have been conferred upon many, not only to set up and organize the Kingdom, but to minister in all things pertaining to the same. These inspired messengers have been sent, by the commandment of God, to nearly every nation under heaven, and have testified in humility and meekness, but, yet, with great boldness, that the great and terrible day of the Lord is at hand, and that the preparatory kingdom is established in the heights of the mountains on the great western hemisphere.

The kingdoms of the world have waxed old; and, because of wickedness, they are destined to be speedily broken to pieces; but the kingdom of God will endure forever. It is destined to increase in strength, power, and dominion, and to bear rule over all the earth. Those nations and kingdoms which will not unite themselves with the kingdom of God, and become one with it, honoring its laws and institutions, will utterly perish, and no place will be found for them.

In view of these things, we humbly, as a servant of the Most High God, entreat all the people of these countries to repent; and in the name of the Lord we exhort you to put away the evils and abominations in your midst, and seek the Lord and his kingdom, and you shall be forgiven, and your great transgressions shall be blotted out, and you shall become a great and mighty branch of that universal theocracy which is to fill the whole earth, and thenceforth be governed by its laws.

But if you will not, as a nation, repent, and unite yourselves with God's kingdom, then the days are near at hand when the righteous shall be gathered out of your midst; and woe unto you when that day shall come! for it shall be a day of vengeance upon the British nation; and your armies shall perish; your maritime forces shall cease; your cities shall be ravaged, burned, and made desolate, and your strongholds shall be thrown down; the poor shall rise against the rich, and their storehouses and their fine mansions shall be pillaged, their merchandise, and their gold, and their silver, and their rich treasures shall be plundered; then shall the Lords, and the Nobles, and the merchants of the land, and all in high places, be brought down, and shall sit in the dust, and howl for the miseries that shall be upon them; and they that trade by sea shall lament and mourn; for their traffic shall cease.

And thus shall the Lord Almighty visit you, because of your great wickedness in rejecting his servants and his Kingdom; and if you continue to harden your hearts, your remnants which shall be left shall be consumed as the dry stubble before the devouring flame, and all the land shall be cleansed by the fire of the Lord, that the filthiness thereof may no more come up before Him.

Your armies in India have already been smitten with a sore judgment, because they cast out the Lord's servants who were sent to warn them and to prophesy to them; they were rejected by your missionaries and your officers; and being without purse or scrip, they "had not where to lay their heads." But they were faithful in delivering their warning message until the Lord called them out of their midst, that He might execute speedy judgment, and show to all nations that His servants cannot be rejected with impunity. Let Great Britain take warning! and not follow the wicked examples of the Europeans in India. Your fastings and your prayers will be a solemn mockery before God, if you receive not the message He has sent. Though you appoint days of fasting and humiliation before the Lord, yet He will not hear you, nor answer your petitions, so long as you receive not his kingdom, and treat his servants with scorn. He will mock at your calamities and multiply them upon you, until you are wasted away, as chaff by the whirlwind of the mountains.

PREACHING TO THE WORLD.

Cwmhen, Llangunllo,
October 2, 1857.

Dear President Daniels,—

I am glad at last to have the chance to write to you a little of my activities. I would have done this earlier had I had some spare time and a chance to get to a *Post Office* to put the letter in. I have been here and there for many miles in places quite unknown to me previously in Cardigan.

I have preached and testified back and forth in several places where they have never before listened to a Saint. This came about mainly because some of my unknown relatives live in areas I have never before been. And I made it a point to warn all I met and saw.

You would be surprised if you were in these environs, to come to understand just how deep the false and zealous believers have sunk in old customs, and become rooted in old traditions—I can hardly believe that they, thousands of them, have come to this, a law unto themselves.

By now I have, without purse or scrip, tested the world, and the world and its inhabitants—the devil and his servants are trying to test me.

I thank my Heavenly Father for the strength that I receive from him to overcome until now, and that he gives to me a witness that my testimony is rooted deep in the hearts of many of the honest in heart.

I have traveled much of Carmarthenshire where there is not one Saint, and much more of Cardiganshire. I have seen only one brother, a Saint, since about a fortnight ago. It is a very *nice* thing to breathe in an atmosphere where some Saints of God dwell, better than dwelling on the move among traditional Christians who are opposed to the truth. Nevertheless, it is more blessed to have the privilege of being free and unsoiled by the blood of the men among whom one toils. I am striving toward that. I also pray frequently for the old inhabitants of the land of my birth. The greater part of them are too religious to believe the truth!

Yesterday I preached out of doors to a large crowd near the Chapel of the Baptists in Llandysul, where I am presently finishing the writing of this letter to you. I was announced in the meeting, and a host of members came to hear me, in addition to scores of others. They behaved very politely, and I received food at the home of a neighbor, and I am requested to preach here again, and, if I have a chance, I intend to do that.

I intend to start off to the neighborhood of Cwrtnewydd, and do my best there for several days. Then I will need to travel through the country between that place and the sea, through Llanarth, Llandysul and Penrhyn. . .

My faith continues until now to have lodging and food, apart from a few times, and a few nights I have paid for a place to lie down. I do not see the color of a penny in practically any place; but the bread and cheese, the milk, and soup all together agree with me extremely well.

> Land of oats, and yellow white barley,
> Land of the red-coated wheat,
> Land of the healthiest food for me,
> Is the district of old Glan Teifi.

It would be bliss had I any tracts, but there is no remedy for it now . . .

Your brother,
D. E. Jones.

ZION'S TRUMPET,

OR

Star of the Saints.

SATURDAY, OCTOBER 24, 1857.

The Farewell Address of President Pratt in the 'Star' is as follows:—

Having permission from President Young to close our labors in this mission, and return to our home in the mountains, we already anticipate that day with much satisfaction. Preparatory thereto, we close our labors in connection with the *Star*, and have called Elder Samuel Whitney Richards to succeed us in the Presidency of the European Mission.

Elder Richards has just arrived from the Presidency in Zion, by whom he has been sent out to counsel and instruct the Elders and Saints scattered abroad, in those things that more immediately concern them; and the spirit of his mission is richly with him. We have been much refreshed, and our joy greatly increased, by his arrival on these shores, and the glad news we have received of the rapidly increasing interests and welfare of the kingdom of God, and the rolling forth of his purposes. To many, Elder Richards is well known from his former efficient labors as President of the Church in these lands; and we would only say to the Saints, Give him your faith and prayers, and give diligent heed to his instructions and counsels, and he will be an instrument in the hands of God, through which much blessing and salvation shall come unto you. To this end he has our fullest blessing, and the blessing of the Presidency in Zion.

In closing our editorial labors, we most heartily reiterate to the Saints and the world all our former testimonies of the truth of this Latter-day work. The Saints who receive the Gospel, and enjoy the Spirit of it, *know* its truth for themselves, for the Spirit beareth record; and in that great day when the Judge of all the earth shall call the Spirits of all flesh before him, they who obey not the Gospel, and receive not the Holy Ghost, shall know that our record is true.

As we wish to be released from the care and anxiety that necessarily attend so important a calling, all communications pertaining to the Presidency of the European Mission must be addressed to Samuel W. Richards, instead of
ORSON PRATT.

INTRODUCTORY.—In commencing our editorial labors of the *Star*, we expect to be excused from making the many *apologies* customary by learned men, as we should be fearful of manifesting our ignorance too much in the attempt. Very unexpectedly to us, our name is presented to its readers as the one on whom those labors rest, and we shall endeavor to perform them to the best of our ability. Should we succeed in edifying and instructing our readers, we shall feel very thankful in being the honored instrument in doing a little good on the earth, while so very much is needed.

So far as we can learn the wants and necessities of the Saints, we shall endeavor to supply them. Our present mission is more immediately to benefit the Saints than to preach repentance to the ungodly; yet, as a servant of God, we are ever ready to bear our testimony to the truth of the Everlasting Gospel as revealed to the prophet Joseph Smith, the keys and power of which are now held by, and are in full force under, the administration of President Brigham Young; and no power can take them from the earth until the government of God, under the administration of a Prophet, becomes universal in its dominion over all creatures upon the earth.

To care for and administer to the Saints will be our first consideration; and we can assure them God is mindful of them, and his servants in Zion are also mindful of them, or we might have been now otherwise engaged than in writing for the *Star*. The world cares not for the Saints but to trample them under their feet and destroy them; consequently, the Lord has said it is His business to provide for his Saints; and it was said a long time ago that He 'will do nothing but he revealeth his secret unto his servants the prophets.' Therefore, if we ever learn what the Lord provides for his Saints, we know just where to look for the information—it will come through his Prophet. Ready obedience to the Prophet will secure every blessing that we are capable of receiving for our present and future salvation, in a general application to the Church; but much individual blessing comes through individual exertion, connected with obedience. All in the kingdom of God will receive the reward their exertions merit.

Let every Saint be assured that whatever changes be made either in administration or policy, affecting their wishes or expectations, they will all be for the best, and prove the very source through which salvation is to be obtained. The Prophet's eye is an eye of vision; it beholds the future, and enables him to provide for its evils; but the days have come in which, where there is no vision, the people must perish. The way of the Lord—which may not be our way—is not less the way of peace and life. Let us, therefore, walk faithfully in it. If we are told that the Lord's way to Zion is not through the United States, let us not go that way; if we are told by the Prophet that it is some other way, let us be ready to go in it, and we shall find deliverance, peace, and salvation.

During our absence from this country, of a little more than three years, we have enjoyed much our labors and associations with the people of God in Zion. They are a people blessed above all other people, and God is indeed their friend. Murder, seduction, infanticides, crime in every form, and the innumerable train of evils so rife in all Christian societies, are almost unheard of there. No angry feuds, arising from civil or political causes, disturb the quiet of a people who are one in faith, one in works, and one in Him—the Son of Peace. But now the scene is changed to us—a change which none can appreciate but those who have experienced it. Every tie that binds man to his fellow man, whether of consanguinity, marriage, or other social obligation, is violated by deeds of murder, rapine, and prostitution, while the spirit of profanity, drunkenness, and every species of vice and immorality is rampant in every grade of society. Virtue, as a thing that was, and shame, her offspring, have retired to holier spheres, to blush unseen over the deeds of those in whom they have no place. Both the tongue of eloquence and the pen of the able writer have been employed in vain to stay the tide of iniquity that is destined to speedily make desolate the earth. Every day's experience proves that *few there be that will be saved*, and to search out, watch over, gather up, and deliver those few becomes the most prominent duty of the Priesthood. Under these circumstances, with little room to hope for the accomplishment of much good to the world, other than to develop truth, that they may be without excuse, we commence the important labors of our calling, earnestly invoking the blessing of Heaven upon our efforts, and desiring the prayers of the faithful in our behalf.

Elder Henry Whittall, whose name is already well known to our readers, has been called to assist us in connection with the *Star*. He is one whose ability will aid us much in the discharge of our labors, and whose pen will often strengthen and comfort the Saints.

Communications from the Elders, or others, for the *Star*, either in prose or verse, will receive our attention,

S. W. RICHARDS.

EMIGRATION.—Inquiries are already being made relative to the probability of any emigration from this country next season. We are somewhat aware of the great anxiety prevailing in the minds of the Saints concerning emigration; and we take this early opportunity of saying that it is possible some few may have an opportunity of emigrating to Utah next spring. Should such be the case, it will be only those who have sufficient means to take them directly through, without detention by the way. If the Saints will possess their souls in patience for a short time, they will find the way open again for them to go out from Babylon. In the meantime, let those who have deposits in this Office continue to add to them as much as possible, inasmuch as the time of your emigration may depend upon the amount of means at your command. Be faithful and industrious in your labors, saving and frugal with your money, so that when the door opens, you may be ready to go. Do not be over-anxious concerning the future. Any instructions we may have to give will in due time be imparted to those who preside over you, or through the *Star* to the Saints. The signs of the times indicate much to the careful observer. Watch ye! Foresee the evil, and keep out of the enemy's path.

NOTICE.—All payments and financial and business matters pertaining to the Office of the *Star* are to be sent in the name of Asa Calkin, and those pertaining to leadership, doctrine, &c., are to be sent to S. W. Richards.

President Richards has called Elder Calkin as his First Counselor, and George G. Snyder as his Second Counselor, in the Presidency of the European Mission.

AN ERROR that needs to be corrected is requesting the transport of books in the tithing account. That was permitted for the Pratt pamphlets, since there was no profit in them; but not for any other books.

THE PRESENT and troublesome signs of the times are predictive of the fulfillment of the grandest prophecies of all the prophets who have ever been on this earth. To the ungodly are promised wars and rumors of wars, famine, pestilence—the pouring out of the judgment vials that are mentioned in the revelations of John: to the Saints redemption and government.

The Gospel of *the kingdom* has been faithfully preached, with a promise of its blessings to the obedient, and a threat of rejection to the disobedient. Disobedience to and deprivation of the Gospel is the cause of the corrupt, polluted, contemptible, and loathsome condition of our world. The gospels originating from man have failed to stem the overflowing tide of sin that has flooded our fallen world; and, like the man who tried to lift himself by the handle of the basket he stood in, or the teacher who tried to teach his scholar who was more able than he, the organizations of men have failed to provide divine teaching and heavenly laws to mankind, rather to the contrary. They have filled the "garden of Christianity" with deadly and poisonous weeds, so that only the "fire of the Lord" will uproot them.

The antediluvian world, Sodom and Gomorrah, or ancient Babylon, are nothing compared to the extremes of abomination of the nineteenth century. What wonder that God has, and continues to gather his people out? Despite all the predictions of the Bible of the destruction of Babylon of the latter days, and the gathering of

Israel, the Bible worshipping sectarians of our age neither can nor will see them, and they persecute those who show them.

For many years the meek servants of the Lord have graciously invited men to covenant with their God—to leave their harlotry, and all their deadly and wicked deeds, and practice the principles of salvation; but, with a few exceptions, it has been in vain, as in the days of Noah. Men have refused the message of heaven, killed its prophets and its Apostles, and have been obstinate in their wickedness until God himself earnestly urges his Saints to flee from their midst so that He may pour out his judgment.

Saints of Wales! Are you ready were the call to come suddenly as it came to the Israelites in Egypt? Are you poorer in your circumstances than they were? Is it not the same God who now reigns? Is He not baring his arm in the gathering of his people in the last days, and working more wondrous things than before?

But remember that 'many are called, but few are chosen.' The Reformation that has taken place, and the more severe tests that have come, have separated, and will continue to separate the servants of God and mammon. Do not forget the parable of the virgins.

The Saints are not required to bother with stiff-necked, derisive, and disdainful men to preach the Gospel to them without being asked to do so; rather they are to warn everyone of the frightful judgments at the door and point out the way to escape, so that not one will be ignorant.

Let prayer meetings be held constantly, and let the faithful Saints edify and comfort one another, sending up their sorrows to the throne of their Father for the success and exaltation of Zion over all enemies, and for their own redemption; for, verily, verily, there is need for their prayers these days, and not a hundredth part of what can be said has been said, but let the wise be the ones to judge. Let us draw near to, and cleave to one another; let us be silent and humble; evil is near, and the opportunity to flee is *at the door*. Who is ready?

REASONS

Why Elder John E. Jones is in favor of gathering to Zion.

THE glory of every man is his life, and since eternal life is longer and happier than the present short, sorrowful, and temporal one, he strives so much to obtain it, and by doing so, his zeal and determination are the strongest of anything under the sun. Oppressing and enslaving a man, because of his religion, is connected to taking this life, and is the heaviest oppression and enslavement that a man can ever endure. And since I am in this condition, in the land of my birth, I wish to 'go out of her.'

I. I am, because of what I love best (namely my religion), in this land 'hated by all.'

They prove this by mocking me, maligning me, persecuting, smiting, swearing, cursing, and stoning me, and at times I have to escape somewhere for my life for refuge from persecutors of my blood, and, despite it all, I am often met with misfortune, and my place of refuge is nothing better than a den of thieves, and I am in their midst like a lamb among wolves.

Those who hate me are priests, preachers, editors, religious people, drunkards, thieves, whoremongers, and murderers. The chief believer is the foremost among the persecutors, and the first, and the most strident voice in crying, "Away with him, throw him out and drive him from the place, he no more deserves his life than a murderer." Then the religious and the irreligious in one choir are chiming together for the tune, with a *"hurrah!"* to start them in a *bedlam chord, bass, tenor, treble,* and *counter,* and the most dignified of them makes new tunes, (a newspaper tale) and assists them with the infernal and *bagpipe-like hoo hoo* "polygamy," 'troops going to kill the Saints,' &c. They all agree in one brotherhood to try to badger me to death.

I am a man, with human feeling in me. Neither my mother nor nature taught me to be willing to stay in such circumstances; therefore, I shall go, if I can, out of her, namely Babylon.

II. In this country the things that reign on a personal, family, societal, and national level are lies, jealously, iniquity, deceit, hatred, violence, oppression, treachery, contention, war, and destruction, both temporal and spiritual. Here there are misers, thieves, whoremongers, and every other class that serves to bring destruction. Here there are sicknesses of every kind—fevers, scores of kinds that each day are generated by intemperance and wicked behavior. Here there are thousands of angels of our earth—purposefully helpful and comforting for the life of man, and participants in his good times and his bad times, and smoothers of the roughness of his forehead from the adversities of life—some who were nurtured warmly on the breasts of the most tender and merciful mothers—decaying on their feet, and with death hiding their shame, and that year after year. Poxes, consumption, scrofula, cancer, and every destroyer of life are devouring their thousands continually, while awaiting a reinforcement of new illnesses and plagues to swell their destructive ranks, when God pours out his terrible judgments on loathsome Babylon. There are wars and rumors of wars constantly increasing. The sound of a severe beating is heard, swords are heard eating the flesh of men, and the neighing of the red horse is heard on the battlefield galloping over the bloodthirsty throngs, and with his iron hooves trampling his thousands like the primitive ox threshing the corn. The flowers, the glory, and the strength of our country—its strongest men are, and will be, whirled around in their unready condition to the spirit world, while others who were prepared will step forward to fill the gap, and meet with the same destructive fate! Every rank and condition are wallowing in their debauchery and their sin—the higher the rank, the greater the depravity, and it is all one great Babylon—in muddled piles all topsy-turvy, while the earth groans and moans under the burden of sin that is on it, considering that it must burn before it is cleansed from the frightful and monstrous abomination that is taking place on its face.

I am like a castling lingering and moving about in the middle of the place of abomination that is becoming practically a dwelling place for no one but devils and every unclean bird, failing to see, feel, smell, or taste anything but that which tends to pollute and destroy, and to disturb the peace and kill each one who tries to live godly in Christ Jesus, myself among a few others. And a great part of all this is in the land of my birth.

My grief and pain here are greater than my pleasure; therefore, at the first opportunity I shall go out of her.

III. In this land the government gives licenses to sell intoxicating liquors, and the consequence is—*drunkenness* and its resulting evils, and women and children growing pale from the lack of nourishment—their feet bare, their clothes tattered—they themselves shivery, and falling to fevers and dying because of them. Other poor creatures are forced to go to the poorhouses to be fed by the community with hardly enough to keep body and soul together, in shame because of drunken fathers or husbands, who would be sober were it not for licensed taverns.

Whorehouses knowingly licensed by civil authorities are an even blacker class of the infernos described above. There, not only are health, sense, love, and prudence sacrificed on the altar of drunkenness in exchange for devilish monstrosity and poverty and misery, but the vessels of the respect of the Almighty are shattered on the firewater rocks of filthy and corrupt lust of beings who are half man and half devil.—*To be continued.*

BOOK DEBTS, SEPTEMBER 31ST, 1857.

CONFERENCE	£	s.	c.
East Glamorgan	156	18	5½
West ”	123	18	0½
Monmouthshire	61	18	2
Breconshire	10	10	9
Cardiff	22	9	0½
Llanelli	65	2	11
Carmarthen	25	19	7½
Pembrokeshire	10	11	0½
Cardiganshire	18	1	3
Merionethshire	10	11	2½
Anglesey and Conway	10	7	6½
Denbighshire	18	6	9½
Flintshire	13	5	4
Total,	£548	0	2

CONTENTS.

	PG.
Teaching of President B. Young	337
Prophetic Warning	341
Preaching to the world	343
Editorial—Address of Orson Pratt—Introductory—Emigration—Notice—Signs of the times	344
Reasons for Emigrating	350

PRINTED AND PUBLISHED BY D. DANIELS, SWANSEA.

ZION'S TRUMPET,

OR

Star of the Saints.

No. 23.] NOVEMBER 7, 2857. [Vol. X.

REASONS
Why Elder John E. Jones Is in Favor of Gathering to Zion.

(Continued from page 352.)

FROM drunkenness rise transgressions of every kind; Peacekeepers, Lawyers, Judges, imprisonment and prisons, and from 6 to 9 of every 10, together with 70,000 every year die directly or indirectly because of *drunkenness*. Without mentioning the Sodom-like sins that are committed every day, sufficient to bring the judgment on our country, the hardworking and sober innocent forced to suffer because of it. And since I see and feel this as a malady too deadly to mend in the land of my birth, I shall go out of her, and to the land where neither a tavern nor drunkenness exist.

IV. In this country, fields come together—in every corner the weakest shout and the strongest oppress—the entire country is possessed by a few *statesmen*—*private property* is a qualification for parliament. Therefore, the poor man, no matter what his knowledge and experience may be, can never be in parliament. To make his oppression even heavier, his circumstances force him to give his *vote* many times against his will, and if he does not, he is turned away from his work, business, or farm, and by doing so he jumps to meet poverty, and on the other hand, by doing so, he empowers a wicked, inexperienced and ignorant man, very often, to make and pass laws to answer his own purpose, and bring much heavier poverty and oppression on the poor man and his family. O! the enslavement of the land of my

23 [PRICE 1½c.

fathers; how long I have groaned and wished to go out of her; for it is still getting worse and worse.

V. In this country we are obliged each year to pay for the support of its potbellied idlers, the 'cream' of the parishes, namely the hired Priests, from £50 to £70,000 yearly, who are like the body of death on society, making commerce of the Word of God, and merchandizing the souls of men, and bringing them captive to everlasting destruction. Thanks be for the light of the everlasting Gospel: through such I see who I am, and where I am, namely in great Babylon, and I shall go out of her.

VI. In this country a man has the freedom to deceive whomever he wishes from among the best women, those who think that a man is the strongest sanctuary of their trust and their respect, and he, after it all, turns into the greatest and worst traitor and enemy under the sun. After a man wins the love of a woman, deceives her, becomes the father of her child, and at the same time two or three others likewise, their characters shattered, their relatives turning their backs on them, enshrouded in shame, need and poverty staring them in the face, the doors of the workhouses forced to open to receive them in dishonor and disrepute, their hearts about to be shattered by shame and grief, their friends having left them, their lives sick, trouble generating sickness too heavy for their bodies to withstand, and obliged to die under the shame and scorn of their relatives and country! O *pity! pity!* and the one responsible for it all a haughty, free, and creditable man, if he has paid a few shillings at a particular time, and, according to his situation, after that, a shilling and sixpence or half a crown per week to rear the child or the children, the law considering him a *respectable* man, and woe to anyone who says a word to the contrary, when at the same time having perhaps been the means of destruction of peace, character, health, and temporal and spiritual life. And then in his ostentation and licentiousness, like a wild horse, his intent on trampling and destroying the peace and life of his better, generating illegitimate children as a burden on society, dressed with the shame of their mothers on them as long as they live, and the three and a half quarters and a quarter murderer—their father, a free man according to the law.

A poor woman is punished with three months of hard labor, if in her need she steals as little as ten pounds of coal from a strong and prosperous company; for catching a rabbit, or stealing a sheep, not worth more than seven shillings, with *penal servitude* for a period of time.

Despite it all, a man is free to fornicate as much as he wishes, and by so doing waste as much as would sustain three or four women and their children, and he is set free to destroy the bodies and spirits of the best women of our country, the character, the virtue, and the lives of whom are worth more than all the coal, rabbits and sheep in the world.

For stealing a sheep one can be exiled; for depriving a woman of her comfort, her circumstances, her virtue and her life, one can be set free for a few shillings. Let a man fornicate with a thousand, if he wishes, by committing every evil and sin in one appetite, which is enough to draw down plague and judgment on the world, and he shall have the law to back him; but if one man is heard of marrying two wives, giving them his name, and supporting them comfortably, and teaching their children according to the law and the will of the Lord, 'O, atrocious sin! to think of such a thing in a Christian country!' say the religious arch-fornicators of our age. O! the inequality of punishments and the Sodomite abomination of the land of my birth! How much longer shall my soul be vexed within thee? O! that I might go out of her.

VII. I shall go out of this country because Zion is better—there I shall be greeted as a friend and brother, and I shall be respected as a member of society; there I shall have land for practically next to nothing, rich land that produces every kind of healthful fruits. Yonder is fresh and pestilence-free air—a land free from illnesses and the old abominable sins of a malodorous Babylon; clear water, and the freedom to fish from it; a fair wage for one's labor, every man happily living on the fruit of his own labor; no heavy taxes to support idlers—every able-bodied person to work for his food: building and planning, and each one living under his own vine and his own fig tree; O, that I were there!

VIII. I shall go to Zion, for there I shall hear Apostles, Prophets, &c., teaching and administering the ordinances of the Gospel, marrying, washing, anointing, and baptizing for the dead. There we shall have the ministering of angels, and be sealed up to eternal lives—we shall be able to live by celestial laws, bring up and train children lawfully and according to the will of heaven, to be children of the faith and deeds of our Father Abraham, and his blessings that are promised to all his followers who fill our land.

IX. I shall go there, for righteousness abides there, and the servants of God will govern me, temporally and spiritually—I shall go there, for Christ is coming to HIS Zion, and the plagues are coming on Babylon, and God says, Come out of her.

After tiring completely of Babylon and the portrayal of it, I feel to sing with J. R., (hymn 482.):—

> I am completely tired
>   Of the great and abominable Babel;
> My prayer, my God knows,
>   Is to go out of her:
> I'm almost asking from my Father,
>   The loan of two great wings,
> So that I may fly toward my country,
>   Now to fair Zion.

Trusting that the foregoing reasons are sufficient for the Editor and the respectable readers of the TRUMPET, I conclude.

Yours, from the heart,

JOHN E. JONES.

TEACHING OF APOSTLE ORSON HYDE,

(The Tabernacle, Great Salt Lake City, March 8, 1857.)

WHILE sitting here and reflecting upon our condition, this morning, the words of our Savior came to my mind with peculiar force, which say, 'Strive to enter in at the strait gate: for I say unto you that many shall seek to enter in, and shall not be able!'

These words, in and of themselves, cannot fail to awaken and alarm every reflecting mind—that many will seek to enter in, and not be able! Is this thy state and condition? Let each one answer the question. It is like the awakening peals of Mount Sinai's thunders. It is a summon of itself—a volume. It should serve to us all as the warning cry to be up and doing, and to seek in the right way to enter in.

If we were to seek for a lost treasure in places where it was not, we might seek as diligently, and even more so, than the person who sought where it was and found it. How necessary, then, that truth and wisdom guide our steps! To this point I wish to call your attention today.

We have had a good season during the past winter, and a precious opportunity to improve our minds, and to gain knowledge and information preparatory to our assuming those responsibilities, and to act that part in the great drama of God's eternal kingdom which our profession, office, and calling imperatively demand at our hand. But if the season had been open and mild as it sometimes is in this country, we might, perhaps, through a great desire to accumulate comforts around us, have been led away by our worldly interests to the great neglect of the 'one thing needful.' If, therefore, an overruling Providence has mercifully laid an embargo upon our temporal pursuits by the pitiless storms of a long and dreary winter, and poured out his Holy Spirit upon us to awaken us to reformation, we have double reason to acknowledge His hand, and to praise him forever for the good and benevolent designs he has manifested toward us.

It now behooves us, in this time of prosperity when Zion shines under the smiling face of her God, to lay by in store a good foundation against the time to come. To the faithful Saints, it matters not whether the seasons are mild and pacific, or boisterous and severe. If we do right, we shall all have abundant reason to say, 'True and righteous are thy ways, Thou King of Saints.'

You were taught, brethren and sisters, before my arrival from Carson, (which was on the 9th of December last,) to awake from your sleep—to repent of your sins, and then to restore to the injured according to the wrongs you may have done them.

Next you were taught in doctrine and in principle—reproved, admonished, comforted and guided in the path wherein you might seek, and seek not in vain.

Truths of almost every character and kind have been declared and dealt out to you with a profuse and a liberal hand. Day after day, and night after night, the voice of inspiration has been heard in your midst. Truths adapted to every character, every state, and every condition in life have been faithfully portrayed unto you in letters of living light, and in words of most burning and soul stirring eloquence, even such as the Holy Ghost inspired; from the simple to the sublime, and from the tone of the harp to the voice of thunder.'

Have you performed the tasks given you? Have you done the work and kept abreast with your instructions? Or have you indulged a wish to get some new thing—something far-fetched which can have no effect other than to allure your minds from the truths that worthily demand your sincere attention and observance? It sometimes happens that a scholar at school, anxious to advance, takes a lesson today in one branch of science, and tomorrow in another, and the third day in another, and so on, until, in his own estimation, he comes out a polished and refined student, a professor and a sage; when, in fact, he understands nothing that he has read, and is only cherishing a deception that he has practiced upon himself.

Is this the case with us? Have we thoroughly learned the lessons that have been given us, and reduced them to practice? There is nothing better calculated to imprint upon the mind any science or theory than to reduce it to practice it—and really act upon it. Then we see its force and bearing; and while engaged in the practical part, it stamps indelibly upon our minds, never to be forgotten, the principles we have imbibed.

If we have practiced upon the lessons and teachings we have received, we know that they will stand by us; but if we have merely heard them, and not entered into the practical duties thereof, they will die in our memory, never having been incorporated in our organization, and we become like the man beholding his natural face in the glass, and straightway goes away and forgets what manner of man he is.

I might explain to you all about the art of printing; yet, with all the knowledge that my explanation could give you respecting this important art, who of you, that is not a compositor, can take my sermon and go into an office and set it up? 'Practice makes perfect.' If we learn righteous principles, and practice them, they have power to change our natures in conformity with themselves.

They become a part and parcel of ourselves, bringing us into an alliance with them that knows no separation. Hence we become a righteous people, and if we continue, we not only strive, but shall be able to enter in.

Each of you can recollect acting upon certain things taught you in the days of your childhood. They are as fresh in your recollection now as they were in the day you acted upon them. Therefore, let us ever act upon true and righteous principles, and they will remain with us, and we shall become righteous in our natures; and if we never act upon an evil principle, we shall forget all the evil we ever knew, and God will forget it also, and our natures will never be evil inclined.

If we have reduced to practice all the teachings and instructions given us from this stand and from other places, we are a blessed and happy people. If we have not, we have not done justice to ourselves. Let us honor the teachings we have received, and we shall find ample ground to occupy without anything far-fetched and dearly bought.

We are a congregation of Latter-day Saints, (so called) assembled to hear the words of life or edification concerning the kingdom of God. This question arises in my mind—Are we all Saints of the Most High God? Or, are we composed of individuals bearing that name when, indeed, we all may not merit it?

I will present to you a figure to illustrate my idea; for I wish to make plain to your understanding the thoughts of my own heart, and if I can transmit them to you as they exist in my bosom, they may operate on your minds as they do upon mine.—

It is now the time of seeding. Our farmers are sowing at the north and in the south:—a matter of great satisfaction to me. And here allow me to express a wish, that while they sow in faith, they may reap with joy! By and by, when this wheat grows up, you may see it waving in the wind, and you will say, Here is a beautiful field of wheat. It is fine and healthy, and it presages a bountiful harvest. It gradually matures in the sun's scorching rays, and you see the field white, already to harvest. You call it all wheat. Now the question is: Is it all wheat? Is not the greater portion of it straw? Though you call it all wheat, even as you call this congregation all Saints, may not a portion of the products of that field be chaff likewise? Certainly! Then, again, is there not often considerable smut in that which you call wheat? Yes, and a great many shrunken kernels that will yield no flour, but will be blown away! In bulk, you call it all wheat; yet come to analyze and separate its different properties and qualities, you find, from the bulk of the growth of that field which you called all wheat, but a small portion that is really genuine wheat. Then after the plump berry is separated from the straw, chaff, smut, &c., there remains yet a finer quality of chaff which you call bran. Then there are different qualities of flour. No. 1, or superfine, No. 2 and 3, or *shorts*. But a small portion of the produce of that field, we discover, is really fit for the Master's table.

Now then, here is a thing which I wish you to consider, which is this: the chaff, straw, &c., produced in that field draw their nourishment from the very same source that the berry does— from the moisture and fatness of the soil! They all feed upon the very same food! Not only so, but we perceive that by ligaments and fibers, the chaff, the straw, and the berry are all connected together; and in view of a similar principle, our Savior said, 'Root not up the tares until the time of harvest, lest by rooting up the tares, ye root up the wheat also.'

(Continued on page 364.)

ZION'S TRUMPET,

OR

Star of the Saints.

SATURDAY, NOVEMBER 7, 1857.

PRESIDENTS Pratt and Benson, together with Elders John A. Bay, John Scott, John Kaye, and William Miller, sailed from Liverpool, October 14th, on board the *Baltic*, for New York, on the way to their homes in Utah.

The mission of President Pratt was distinguished by his effort to thoroughly warn the British through his treatises, and that of President Benson in the same way by his several pledges. In addition to that, the Church received priceless nurture, strength, and growth under their effective ministry.

THE TROOPS AND UTAH.—President S. W. Richards encourages the Saints not to worry their minds with this matter; but instead to rejoice and redouble their diligence and their trust in God, so they might be able to see His Salvation.

APPOINTMENTS.—President S. W. Richards has appointed Elders George G. Snyder and John L. Smith to travel under his direction, and to communicate with Pastors and Conference Presidents upon matters relative to their respective callings and duties, and impart such instruction as may be deemed necessary.

THE TOTAL NEWS of the day, as usual, with a few exceptions to the worst side, contains various murders, whoredoms, the lying of a Priest with his *footman*, stealing, violence, oppression, poor people dying from hunger begging to be accepted into the workhouses, infanticide, war, pestilence, and a host of evils and judgments, all ever increasing. In short, the world is going to hell at a gallop.

FAREWELL ADDRESS OF APOSTLE EZRA T. BENSON.

To the Saints scattered throughout the European Mission, greetings.

Beloved Brethren and Sisters—In the mysterious revolutions of God's providence, by which all things are moved according to his pleasure and purposes, my labors in these lands have been brought to a termination.

The history of the Church, the signs of the times, and our own individual experience point distinctly to one great fact—that

God is cutting his work short in righteousness, and rolling along his strange designs with increasing velocity. He has risen up in power, and put on his strength as in days of old. The nations are being moved to the accomplishment of the purposes of Jehovah. Unwittingly they are verifying the words of the Prophets, and fast filling up the destiny of the world. The God of our Fathers is remembering his covenants unto his people Israel. The Spirit of the Lord moves upon their hearts—his power invigorates their souls. They trust in Him with great faith, and the still small voice whispers to them, that Jacob shall not wax pale, nor the children of Zion be put to shame. The designs of the wicked, as well as the works of the righteous, tend to one end—the establishment of the latter-day kingdom, and the development of its glory.

I am about, dear Saints, to return to my mountain home. But before leaving these lands, I have felt moved upon to address to you a few words of comfort and counsel, as well also as to return you my grateful acknowledgments for your many acts of kindness to me, as a servant of the Lord Jesus. Those acts are engraven on my heart. They will be to my remembrance sweeter than honey, and will be dwelt upon as precious manifestations of the love and faith of the Saints in Europe towards the cause of God and his servants. You shall not be forgotten by me; and our Father in heaven will also have your works in remembrance. I bless you in the name of the Lord; and you shall be blessed, if you continue in well-doing.

Be not cast down, dear brethren and sisters, nor let your faith waver. If a cloud gathers for a moment, be assured that behind every frown of Providence, God hides for you a "smiling face." There is no cloud in your future so thick that will not soon pass away and reveal to you a brighter sun.

Though, for the time being, the emigration is closed, think not that your deliverance is afar off, nor imagine that God has forgotten the gathering of his Saints. In a moment, peradventure, he will open the door again, and lead his people to Zion with an outstretched arm and power, such as heretofore he has not manifested in their behalf. Perchance it will be found that hardly a break will be made in the great chain of gathering. In any case, know that all is well! Fear not;

sleep not; but be courageous and awake, O Israel, and behold the salvation of your God!

Let every branch of the Church keep its organization compact, and its members full of faith. Let all be diligent; cease not your labors, nor fall into lethargy. Go on as heretofore, and let your course be unbroken. Increase, and not decrease. Multiply your works, add to your faith, gather fresh energy and determination, cement your union, and cultivate a double portion of wisdom and prudence. When the Lord again opens the way for your deliverance, brethren, *be you prepared*. In your connections with the world, return not railing for railing, but seek to conquer by love and kindness, and avoid aggravating the feelings of any. Be not aggressors, but act on the defensive. If you are persecuted, let it be for righteousness' sake, and not the result of unwise conduct on your part.

No weapon formed against Zion shall prosper, nor device against the people of God flourish. I feel to bless all Israel. All who bless them shall be blessed, and they who prophesy good concerning God's people shall have good multiplied unto themselves, and the spirit of their words shall not fail. But he who predicts evil against Israel shall be among false prophets; and they who rise up against the work of our God shall wither, and their influence depart. Those who fight against Zion shall be as a dream of a night vision. It shall even be as when an hungry man dreameth, and behold he eateth; but he awaketh, and his soul is empty; or as when a thirsty man dreameth, and behold he drinketh; but he awaketh, and behold, he is faint. In the name of the Lord Jesus Christ, I curse, by the authority of the holy Priesthood, every anti-Mormon association, movement, member, and leader, throughout the world; and let all Israel say, Amen.

Before leaving this land, I feel once more to bear my testimony, through the medium of the *Star*, to the British Saints, and to all who shall peruse this communication. I *know* that God has again established his kingdom on the earth, and that it will never be overcome, but it shall ultimately hold universal dominion, and Jesus shall reign as its King forever. I *know* that Joseph Smith was called of God to establish that kingdom, and that he accomplished the work given him—even the beginning of the restitution of all things; and that he committed unto the Church the keys and power to continue what he had begun. He was one of the greatest of Prophets, and died a holy martyr of Jesus, sealing his testimony with his blood. I *know* that Brigham Young is his successor, and that he is a man of God, and a Seer and Revelator to the Church of Christ. I *know* that the general authorities [of the Church] have for their object the glory of God and the salvation of man. Finally, I *know* that no one who does not receive this work can be saved in the celestial kingdom, and escape the condemnation of the Lord, the Judge of all. In the day of judgment this testimony shall be remembered, to the confusion of those who reject it.

I will now close this communication by requesting an interest in your faith and prayers, and invoking the choicest blessings of heaven to be multiplied unto you.

I am, your servant and brother in Christ,

Ezra T. Benson.

TEACHING OF APOSTLE ORSON HYDE.

Continued from page 360.

It is necessary that the straw exist to sustain the wheat, the chaff to protect the berry, by serving as an overcoat and shield from the various and varied influences of the weather—from insects, and to keep it warm. The same nourishment that supports the berry, and keeps it alive, also sustains and keeps alive the chaff as its cloak or mantle. There is not a sparrow that flies in the air that partakes not of the goodness of our God. He maketh his sun to rise on the evil and on the good, and sendeth rain on the just and on the unjust.

All the tribes of men, the swarms of insects, the herds of animals, the flocks of the feathered millions that fly over our heads, are all sustained by the same liberal hand of our Heavenly Father. His Providence provides for all, even for the wolf and the poisonous rattlesnake.

Now, in the midst of all this, who among us are prepared to say whether we are straw, chaff, smut, or wheat? Bran, shorts, or flour? Many shall seek to enter in and shall not be able!

Perhaps I may be able, ere I close my remarks, to give you some key to this matter, which, if it shall not enable you fully to determine, may, at least, materially aid you in your inferences in relation to yourselves. But of this one thing, rest perfectly assured: the way to life is straight and very narrow. The straw and the chaff are growing up, and striving to enter the granary; but they will be hardly able.

As I look about upon this congregation, and as I mingle with the Saints at large, I discover that there are different spirits. Every organization has a spirit peculiar to itself. I do not say that there is any fatality in this. Do not understand me to convey that idea. But I do say this, that every spirit connected with an earthly organization may be tempered by the Spirit of God according to its fidelity, intelligence, and faith, so that there is no excuse. If I point you to the horse, you find a peculiar spirit attending the organization of that animal. When he is fine, and in good condition, there is something stately and grand about him.

When we see the beautiful dove flying through the air, a pleasing sensation is produced in us by its graceful movements, because the Holy Spirit was once sent in that form. Again we look at the serpent, and another feeling is produced—a fear—a chill—a horror. So every creature, beast and bird, man and woman, has a spirit peculiar to its own organization; and no organization is entirely independent of the Spirit of God; for all have some intelligence. Were the spirits and temperaments all alike, the same instructions would serve for all. But as it is, every man must receive his portion of meat in due season. And the word must be rightly divided—giving to every man his portion that is adapted to his organization and temperament, that he may thereby be saved.

Man is composed of matter and spirit; and the Spirit of God operates upon and tempers man's organization according to his faith and good works. Some are tempered very highly.

Such not only carry a keen edge, but are susceptible of a high polish. Others are of low temper, because of a low, dull, and sluggish disposition and character which they have indulged and consequently formed. They are not a very smooth or sweet cutting tool. They have not sought to cultivate their temperament by seeking and courting the Spirit of God as they should.

Yet, these may be guilty of no outbreaking sin. They keep within the pale of the law—pay their tithing, and keep along; and are considered good, peaceable, and honorable citizens. They despise to steal—are willing to labor, and pursue an even, straight forward course. Still, we cannot look upon them as being tempered by the Holy Spirit to the extent of their privilege. Yet they work righteousness so far as they work at all. These persons are fond of going to meeting, and are often heard to say, What a good sermon we have had!

This is all right, if you did have a good sermon. They will ask you a thousand and one questions in order to draw out something to satisfy their eager desire for knowledge and understanding, hardly recollecting their privilege to ask of God and receive for themselves. But there is no crime in this; still, one can hardly refrain from thinking, when he sees his neighbor begging and borrowing bread, how much more commendable it would be in him to apply himself to labor and produce, thereby, bread from the soil by his own exertion.

And inasmuch as our Heavenly Father is accessible to all, it is far better to store our minds with the treasures of wisdom and knowledge, by our own spiritual labors and toil, direct from the great fountain of celestial light and love, than to trust wholly to the testimony and teachings of others.

Obtain the testimony of Jesus which is the spirit of Prophecy. Startle not at the idea of prophecy and prophets; for I would to God that all the Lord's people were prophets. There is no professing Christian in the world who does not possess the Spirit of prophecy, that can tell whether he is wheat, straw, chaff, smut or tares. And no person can have the spirit of prophecy, who declares that the days of prophets are gone by, and are not needed now, unless that spirit should be given to seal condemnation upon the narrow minded bigot who will not confess it and give God the glory, after it may have fallen upon him: for he loves the praise of men more than the praise of God.

The sun, moon, and stars are the representatives of the final homes of the departed dead, if not their real homes. The sun is said to shine by its own light, inherent in itself. I might not admit this, under some circumstances, but the popular thing will here answer my purpose. The moon and stars shine by borrowed light. These stars or plants vary in their size, motion, distance from the earth and intensity of heat, cold, &c. Some of them may revolve in eternal day, while others roll in endless night; and still others, like our earth, may have alternate day and night.

Here are homes for all grades of spirits; from the faithful martyr to Christ's kingdom and gospel, whose glory is represented by the sun in the firmament, to the wicked tare who will be sent away into outer darkness, upon some planet destined to roll in endless night. 'In my father's house are many mansions. There is one glory of the sun, another glory of the moon, and another glory of the stars.' One star differs from another star in glory; so also is the resurrection of the dead.

The children of this world who love darkness rather than light will find themselves, finally, to be inhabitants of those planets that move in outer darkness; having a home adapted to their disposition and character.

The inspired Apostles and Prophets, together with the martyrs of Jesus, and all the pure and sanctified ones will inherit a glory like the sun, while the hypocritical professor, the liar, the adulterer, the profane swearer, with all who hold to a religion without prophets and Apostles—without inspiration and miracles—without revelation, prophecy, keys and powers to bind on Earth and in Heaven, after the call is made upon them by the messengers of the true religion, will be damned, and sent away into outer darkness, even into prison, where they will gnaw their tongues for pain.—*To be continued*.

MISCELLANEOUS, &c.

THE WORD OF WISDOM.—We wish to say to our brothers and sisters that the Word of Wisdom is no less important now than it was a few months ago. We have not intended the few *tolerances* made here and there to be a general law for everyone; but we trust that the general body of the Saints have understood by now that the Word of Wisdom was revealed for the purpose of being *observed*.

RETURN OF BOOKS.—We request the best effort of our kind distributors to supply us with the following numbers of the present volume of the Trumpet:—9 of number **20**, and 3 of **21**. Also, from volume IX, 47 of number **8**, 28 of **9**, 1 of **24**, and 1 of **25**. Do your best, brethren.

THE TIMES.—It is obvious to all who read the newspapers that destructive and unfortunate happenings are increasing frightfully. Besides that, the run on the banks of America has thrown thousands of poor workers out of work, and has given a heavy blow to commerce. Ships full of goods were sent back to their manufacturers in England, and the consequence will be obvious to every attentive person.

All this is but a fulfillment of prophecies known to the Saints for a long time: it is but the first drops of the heavy showers that will come. But let not the Saints be saddened as long as they conduct themselves honestly before their God. He will provide for them, and he will bless even the unthankful Gentiles in order to take care of his Saints. They know where the best *Insuring Office* in the world is!

CONTENTS.

	PG.
Reasons for emigrating	353
Teaching of Apostle O. Hyde	356
Editorial—Departures—The Troops—Appointments—Total News	360
Miscellaneous, &c.	368

PRINTED AND PUBLISHED BY D. DANIELS, SWANSEA.

ZION'S TRUMPET,

OR

Star of the Saints.

No. 24.] NOVEMBER 21, 1857. [Vol. X.

SIGNS OF THE TIMES.

CONVERSATION BETWEEN TWO WORKERS.

Thomas.—Good morning to you, Rhys; how are you feeling?

Rhys.—Middling, thank you, Thomas; but not too well.

T.—I'm no better off, indeed, Rhys. This fall of two shillings in the value of the pound is sad news, isn't it?

R.—And they're saying that we haven't yet seen the worst, Thomas.

T.—Rhys, since you read the newspapers and the publications, perhaps you can tell me how it is over in America, and what will become of us here in this country. What do you Saints think of it now? Rhys, you have told me so much for years that the judgments are coming on the countries, that I am really frightened.

R.—True, Thomas, I have testified many times that Zion has been established, and that it is only there that deliverance will be had when God pours out his wrath on the disobedient nations who have killed his servants, refused his gospel, and who have become obstinate in their violence, oppression, deception, whoremongering, and every evil.

T.—Who thinks such a thing, when the preachers have been shouting Peace, health, abundance, and success all the time.

R.—Well, listen to me, what is more obvious than the fact that the judgments of God have already begun, and that the earthly

24 [Price 1½c.

governments are being found to be too incapable of satisfying the needs of the people, and taking things in hand, and setting them to work properly, until everyone has enough work and food?

T.—It is an incomparable turn of events that the banks are failing, and the Americans are sending goods as you said, back to England, and workers are going idle, and hunger is staring them in the face this winter.

R.—Yes, Thomas, in Macclesfield, for example; they had a big meeting there of men out of work, and it has already become known that there is bitter suffering for lack of food, and they *must* have assistance from somewhere, or starve. It is the same thing in other places—thousands out of work—far worse than the fall of prices, Thomas. Besides that, there are thousands upon thousands the same way in America, and they are grumbling and threatening, and the newspapers are urging them to become *filibusters* and things like that, you see.

T.—Well, what's the cause of such a state of affairs. Listen to me; is there famine in the land, and no food to be had, or has the world stopped using iron, instruments, cloths, fabrics of all kinds, and all the things that are made in Great Britain? What do the newspapers say?

R.—God, until now, has been merciful enough not to send all kinds of judgments at once. He gave a good harvest, and the storehouses of America and this country are full of mercies, and there was more call than ever for the goods you noted when this thing happened.

T.—Listen to me, what *sense* is there in that sort of thing? The storehouses full, and need for goods, and yet the workers are suffering want and famine! What order is there in things like this? Where is the government, and what good is it, if it doesn't set things right immediately? But what is the meaning of banks failing here, Rhys; why would the thieves not put the money back like honest men?

R.—Listen, Thomas, and I will show you the way things are. Now you know that, the masters and the workers compose every part of the market. The masters of the ironworks, for example, handle the money for the work of thousands of workers; the same way for masters of factories, and other works, and they deal with the banks.

T.—The d—l may take the banks!

R.—But be patient, Thomas, to hear the *rest*. Now let us say that a hundred of the masters and others put a thousand pounds each in a bank, and the bank gives their loans to other men at great interest on *securities*, such as houses, estates, or any possessions, on the condition that they receive them back in such and such time. Well, then the rumor gets out that the bank has gone bad by giving so much in loans, without good *security*; or that there is no good account to be given of the money. Then the payers and those who possess *notes* run to the bank for their money, without caring what will become of the others, and there is not half enough money at the time in the bank, or from its direct petitioner, to pay everyone that is pressing on it at the same time, and then it goes into collapse, you see, just as the *balance* of the mountain *pit* went crazy, and workers of the mountain pit were out of work, and there was a great call for coal at the same time—that is what a bank failure is to a tee.

T.—I see it exactly. Now, when the mountain pit collapsed, Dai Shams the banksman was drunk and deranged—he thought a full tram was coming up when Beni the hitcher had shouted *Empty carriage*, and Dai had filled the bucket with water, when the old pit blazed alight, without setting the brake or anything, and the place was wrecked to pieces!

Well, they had to extinguish a furnace for want of coal, when there was plenty in the bowels of the mountain, hundreds of men idle for want of cutting it, and no orders for them in the company shop, and all that because of drunk old Dai Shams just as the old *Balance Pit* went crazy.

R.—But there are many Dai Shams in this business, Thomas, and the consequences are much bigger; but to return to the story—

That is the same sound for other banks, besides their having perhaps lost money through those that have already failed, and they are all swept off one after the other, and the whole country is in commotion.

Then after that, the masters fail to pay the workers, and the works come to a stop. Then the merchants of America send shiploads of goods back to England, for lack of a market for them, and they fail to pay for them. There are already thousands of workers out of work in America, the same as in this country.

After that the storm comes over here. The great masters and merchants of this country deal so much with America, and lose so much, and know that the banks in this country are losing in the same way, and then they receive the effect to the point of collapse—many of the banks and merchants of this country have failed, and others are about to.

And now, while the assets of the bankers are being sold, and those of the ones who are in their debt, a period of time will pass before a few shillings on the pound perhaps will be extracted from their claws, and in the meantime—during a cold winter, the poor workers will have to suffer miserably, while those who were so lucky as to get their money will feast, fearing to trust it to venture to benefit their fellow men!

T.—May a curse follow them, and every hard-hearted miser of their kind, say I. Now I see what kind of greedy pack are the gold merchants who do not use their gold to benefit the poor—may the miserly scamps be hanged with the lawyers, the bum-bailiffs, and the rest of the hornets of the parish. In my blindness I was nearly blaming the master of our mine; but I see now that his main concern, poor thing, is to feed the thousands of his workers.

Well indeed, it's strange how this money works! In the old times the people starved because there was no food in the land, but in our enlightened and wealthy Christian age, there are famine and abundance in the land at the same time! Listen to me, what is a Government good for, if not to defend and provide for its subjects, search out ways to go forth with business, and feed the workers? They are *handy* enough to collect taxes, and take care of themselves; but where are they now? I would like to know.

R.—My dear Thomas, the Government is in as bad a pickle or

worse than the merchants. It has two wars to handle in India and China. Paper money will not do the trick in India, at the present time; therefore, this country is being scoured for as much gold as the Government can scrape to pay the soldiers in India, and we are left to the mercy of a bunch of gold merchants!

T.—Do you know what, Rhys, it's getting heavy for us, isn't it? What do you think will become of India? You have Delhi taken, and the *sepoys* squeezed out of there, in any event.

R.—The tree of rebellion has been shaken, and many of the deadly seeds have been scattered. Perhaps some kind of peace will be established for a while, while the deeper and more treacherous plans are quietly at work. But no matter what, war and rumors of war will be the chief characteristics of the age, until God avenges the blood of his Saints, and punishes the rejecters of his kingdom.

The storm of bank failures, and the stoppage of commerce, may blow by, and the stream will run normally; but what do you say, Thomas, about the Saints in Utah storing the output of their crops for the day when a general famine will be on the earth, and gold will be as worthless as dirt on the street because of it?

T.—That is quite plain speaking, Rhys; I don't know how to doubt you, for you said a long time ago that judgments will come on the land; but, good heavens, I hope not!

R.—It is God who has proclaimed that, through his prophets and Apostles, in this age; and I know that his words will come to pass. Thomas, did you read the prophetic warning of Apostle Orson Pratt to the inhabitants of the British Isles?

T.—No, indeed; what does he say?

R.—He says that if the government does not put a *stop* to all the evils it is licensing, God will soon visit the country in judgment.

T.—The government licensing evils, you say? Goodness gracious! What evils?

R.—Drunkenness and prostitution, for example, the evils that lead to practically all other evil. The authorities are licensing taverns, and renewing the licenses of taverns which they know perfectly well are also houses of prostitution.

T.—Indeed, Rhys, it must be as bad here as it was in ancient Sodom and Gomorrah.

R.—It would take too much time for me to point out to you the various abominable evils that are calling for judgment. The cry of the poor, the widow, and the orphan, the waste and oppression of the nobles, together with all the killing, stealing, and adultery that fill the country with misery and woe, are enough to bring down the fire from heaven to destroy the evildoers. Apostle Pratt warns this nation if they do not repent and reform, by accepting the kingdom of God, their navies and armies will be destroyed, and their strong places will be brought down: the poor will rise against the noblemen and rob them, and all this because of their shameful sins, and their refusal of the kingdom of God.

T.—Well, that says it quite clearly; but I can hardly believe that things will be that bad in Great Britain—the bully of the world! but time will tell, Rhys, and time will tell concerning the famine the Saints are preparing for.

What are your views about the kingdom of God? Last Sunday I was in a Methodist meeting, and I heard the minister say that the kingdom of God is in the belly of the Methodist. Indeed, Rhys, I could hardly keep from laughing when I thought about his paunch, for it would hold a good share of it! I have no idea if there will be a fall in price for the preachers here? I heard in reading the newspapers that a priest in America preached splendidly about frugality during the bad times, and that the members held a *society* and brought his wages down from a thousand, to five hundred dollars. Never mind about that; what are your views about the condition of the world and the kingdom of God?

R.—When Jesus Christ says to the old hypocritical and long-faced Pharisees of His age, the Kingdom of God is within you, reason shows that it is was not in their devilish bosoms, but in their midst or among them as a nation. The King of the Kingdom was there, and he would deliver them from their enemies, if only they would accept Him as the King of the Jews; but they did not want Him, for which destruction came upon them.

Now, you well know that the Saints preach and prove in accordance with the prophecies of the Bible that the Kingdom of God, or the Apostolic Church, was taken from the earth.—Look at the condition of the world when the Prophet Joseph Smith came forth to proclaim his message!—the pope in one place—the head of the Greek Church in another—the Muslims, and the Protestants all claiming that the kingdom of God was with them. Fie on such a kingdom! The Protestants had separated from the Church of Rome, because, they say, it had deteriorated a long time ago. And where say you, Thomas, did they get the authority to establish the kingdom of God, and that with no head or tail to it? It was called the Church of England, quite appropriately, and not the Church of Christ.

Well, now you see, Thomas, that these reformers grew tired of the Church of England; and no wonder! They saw the bishops and the chief priests receiving their thousands of pounds every year—living in splendid palaces—riding in their carriages—keeping servants and maids, bowing before kings and high authorities, and scowling at the poor. They engaged in a form of prayer, or something to please the king, the same way they offered a prayer of thanks on behalf of Henry the Eighth, for his having married a handsome woman, after butchering his other wives. It made no difference to them what they prayed, as long as they received the salary, the tithing, and the tax of the Church.

Well, if you are over there, the reformers broke away, and a frightful commotion was made as these different religions were established. But, in the end, where was their authority? Each one of them considered that he had as much right as anyone else to establish a religion, until the countries are full of them. One sect pulls this way, and the other that way, and each one of them going to heaven, they say.

In spite of all the religions, the country is full of dishonesty and prostitution, oppression and violence, and the oppressors are as religious as the victims, and no sign of a millennium, and the reign of Christ; but wickedness increasing constantly.

That's not the sort of kingdom of God the Israelites had in the ancient days. In it there were temporal and spiritual blessings for them, and prophets to foresee every evil, and to lead them along the path of prosperity.—In the Apostolic Church there were prophets and apostles, together with blessings of the Gospel. The poor were cared for and fed, and men who had gold laid it at the feet of the Apostles; but it was not like putting tithing at the feet of paid and wealthy bishops. The ministers of the ancient Church were poor fishermen, and hardworking men: not so of the churches of the sects when Joseph Smith came.

Well, to cut the story short, indeed, Thomas, the kingdom of God was restored through the Prophet Joseph Smith. In it there are prophets and Apostles, gifts of the Holy Ghost, knowledge, revelations, and temporal and spiritual assurance and blessings. Jesus Christ is its King; therefore, it is to rule the world, although the preachers have long proclaimed the funeral sermon of "Mormonism."

Zion is now being built. Israel has begun to gather, and make great preparations for the King of the Earth to come to dwell among his people, the Latter-day Saints.

Mormonism will increase, while the world called Christian will become smaller and smaller under the destructive judgments of God, for refusing his kingdom, and from today forth, Thomas, look for wars and rumors of wars, earthquakes in places of famine, pestilence and plagues, and no deliverance, except in Zion and in Jerusalem. Let the preachers shout what they may about peace and prosperity; they will be proved false prophets, when the true servants of the Lord are recognized, who, like their brethren of old, will receive every bad word from the world, while the false, fat-bellied, lying, hireling priests will be revered as were the ancient Pharisees; but woe unto them, said Jesus, when men speak well of them; for so did they say of the false prophets.

T.—Well, truly, Rhys, the world is as you say, regardless of what Mormonism is. If I cannot believe you, I have had enough of sectarianism. I don't know where in the great world to go for rest for the old body, as well as for the soul. The preachers take good care, they say, to feed the soul; but if famine or pestilence come, woe unto the old body. Let them say whatever they want about Brigham Young, I read that he receives no salary from the Church, and that he tends to things for the temporal comfort of the Mormons, as well as preaching for the soul. And if he now sets the Saints to storing their wheat against the coming of famine, I suppose that the worth of such a man will be seen when his word is fulfilled.

R.—My dear Thomas, had not the Lord revealed to the Prophet Brigham, and to Joseph before him, many other things to lead the Church, before now, the Saints would have been finished a long time ago. That is the difference between the servants of God and the servants of Baal, for it is true what the proverb says. Where there is no vision the people perish.

T.—Well, indeed, I will try with a sincere heart to see if what you say is true, and to obtain the knowledge from God which you have so assuredly promised.

R.—You could do no better, Thomas, if you wish to save your body and soul from temporal and spiritual destruction, and if you obey that which you have heard many times before, you will KNOW of the teaching, as Christ has promised.

Thomas.—Well, I will come to the meeting tonight, and I will be baptized, and if I understand that things are as you say, you can bet your life that I will not be long before gathering my things together, and hoofing it toward the Valley over there, for my life, as soon as the way opens up. Good day to you now.

Rhys.—Good day to you, Thomas. I'll see you tonight, remember.—*W. L.*

ZION'S TRUMPET,

OR

Star of the Saints.

SATURDAY, NOVEMBER 21, 1857.

FINANCIAL.—President Richards says, in the 'Star,' as follows:—

From the reports lately received at this Office, we discover that the financial condition of the Conferences generally requires the particular attention of both Presidents and Pastors. We expect wthat all on whom any degree of responsibility rests in this matter will give the subject their immediate attention, that the end of the present quarter may not find them deficient in their amount of Temple Fund, and other requirements. It is supposed that all Pastors and Presidents know what is expected from their respective jurisdictions; and we sincerely hope no one will have occasion to plead lack of attention or inability by way of excuse.

Some Conferences and Elders we find much too free in the use of tithing money. Retrenchment in many respects is indispensible; and even then, we fear there are those who will find themselves unable, at the close of the year, to meet the demands upon them.

Economy will be regarded by every wise steward; and he that is not faithful over the earthly mammon cannot expect to have stewardship over the welfare of souls.

A Branch President, when asked why he employed such an expensive Hall for meetings, when the few that attended it would be even more comfortable in a much smaller room, replied that the tithing collected in the Branch nearly paid for the Hall. The answer was conclusive. Anything in the world that the Tithing would nearly pay for, though actually disadvantageous, seemed to justify the expense. This illustrates the spirit too much indulged in. A spirit of extravagance and prodigality, which leads to an excessive and unreasonable squandering of money, is the reigning spirit of the age; and some Elders and Saints are not as clear from it as we wish they were. This is a mighty evil. It is breaking up and bringing ruin upon the haughty and proud nations that have been led by it to indulge their lustful pride. The wise will observe the command, "Shun even the appearance of evil."

When Hall Rents are reduced one half, Elders travel and labor in the ministry, instead of paying weekly board, and as many excuses sought for to save the Tithing funds as there are now to expend them, it will place something to the account of the REFORMATION.

It should not be left optional with Branch and Conference Presidents to appropriate funds at the mere diction of circumstances; but there should be a definite understanding with the Pastor for what purposes alone they can apply them, and in no case should they exceed those limits without special authority.

Money, to a considerable amount, which is now reported at the end of the quarter as being in hand, should be forwarded to this Office.

Neglect, inattention, and indifference often become a crime, and incur lasting responsibilities. Some appear to make it an object to consume the tithing money, so that it shall not reach this Office; but all are not so. When important Pastorates have been long punctual in forwarding regularly their full amounts to the various funds, and, upon change of ministerial functions, there is a serious falling off, amounting to almost a total failure, the delinquency is very likely to be attributed to those in charge. From these smaller circumstances, an Elder's ability to manage the affairs of those committed to his care is often judged.

All true and worthy Saints will take pleasure in paying their Tithing, knowing it to be a requirement of the Lord; and as a law of the Gospel which we have embraced, it must be observed, or we do not live our religion.

NEWS FROM UTAH.—*(*From the *Star.)* We have received letters from our friends in Utah, with dates to September 14th, among which are communications from President Young, Elders W. Woodruff, and F. D. Richards, and from our family [S. W. R.], all which afford us the most cheering intelligence. In addition to Elder Woodruff's letter, which appears in another column, we extract the following from President Young's letter of September 12th.

"Since the departure of brother Samuel W. Richards, events of some moment have transpired in relation to the future of 'Mormonism.' My last to you supposed General Harney on his way to this Valley with a command of 2,500 soldiers. More recent advices state that he is detained in Kansas; and one Colonel Johnson, of Texas, is appointed in his stead. In place of three full regiments, about 1,400 men only were collected; of those, although they reached Laramie about the 31st of August, nearly one half had deserted. By express this morning, we learned that 700 men left Laramie on the 3rd of this month, for Salt Lake. Captain Van Vliet, of Harney's 'Staff,' arrived here on the 8th. He left his escort on Ham's Fork, and came in with Elders Bryant, Stringham, and N. V. Jones. We have decided to send Dr. J. M. Bernhisel down this fall. He leaves here on Monday, the 14th, with Captain Van Vliet, and, by special invitation, will accompany him directly through to Washington. . . .

"All is well with us in the Valley. We have an abundance of grain, vegetables, and fruit. Health, peace, and faithfulness are universal; and at no period of our Church history have the Saints had so much occasion for rejoicing as at present. The Temple and other public improvements are progressing finely. In fact, the brethren throughout the Territory continue to build and improve with the same degree of interest that would be manifested, were there no prospect of trouble in the future."

By letter from brother Franklin, we learn that the object of *Quartermaster* Van Vliet's visit to Salt Lake was to ascertain if forage, lumber, and fuel could be obtained for the troops ordered by the Government to Utah, and report to the Department at Washington thereon; also to learn the facilities for a proper cantonment of the troops sufficiently near the City to efficiently aid the new Governor in executing the civil law, and in extending the laws of the United States over the Territory.

Elders Little, Dana, Martin, Evans, and all forward of the St. Louis Company had arrived September 14th. Elder G. A. Smith had returned from a tour through the southern settlements, and brought a very flattering report of their condition and prospects. Brother Franklin says—"I wish to be remembered with much love to the brethren in the ministry, as well as to all the faithful Saints; for the memory and prayers of the just are precious, after having labored so long in those islands."

From the information before us, it is evident that Governor Young fully intends to pursue that policy in the present crisis with the United States which will make the General Government show their true colors in reference to their designs with Utah.

A system of double-dealing and disgraceful partiality has so long characterized the conduct of the general Government toward the Saints, that it is quite time the mask was torn off, and the grim visage of a shame-faced monster made to appear, if there is one. From the settlement of the Saints in a town, city, or county capacity, they have grudgingly permitted to enjoy the common rights and privileges of citizens; and, in almost every instance where any chartered rights have been given, they have been soon repealed, because of that fear and jealousy toward the Saints which have actuated the authorities of the land. Utah cannot now be admitted to the Union, for fear she would have too much power. The General Government must fill every office in the Territory, which from usage, they can claim any right to fill, so as to keep the "Mormons" under, or they will soon usurp powers and prerogatives as monstrous as themselves. Consequently, civil officers must be sent, sworn to suppress "Mormon" institutions, and troops must go to help to do it. That the "Mormons" may be kept ignorant of their intentions, until perfectly in their power, troops must march under *sealed orders*, lest the Saints should get wind of the determination to make them like their civilized (?) neighbors and plant a force strong enough to keep them so. This kind of conduct implies a belief that such intentions might be objected to on the part of the people of Utah, as unreasonable and unjust, and a little stratagem must be used to avoid a formidable opposition. This *modus operandi* may be necessary where there is a want of strength, or a want of justice in the cause; but as there is no lack of strength, we necessarily conclude that a want of justice demands this hitherto hypocritical policy (so far) to accomplish certain unjustifiable ends.

An almost utter disregard has been shown by the General Government to the petitions of the people of Utah for seven years past, in relation to their rights and interest in that Territory; and it is a source of untold satisfaction to us to see a disposition on the part of Governor Young to make the Parent Government declare her intentions toward the people which he has for so many years faithfully and wisely presided over. When those intentions are understood, and are before the world, they will receive that response which will show to the world that the spirit and blood of '76 are as warm today as then, and that constitutional liberty is worth maintaining.

When *Uncle Sam* wants troops in Utah to protect the country, and defend constitutional liberty, he can find them right on the ground, ready at a moment's warning; and he would do better to bless the country at home with the money expended in such expeditions than to spend his millions to curse the country and people who are so far away. No one can reasonably expect the people of Utah to be satisfied with anything less than their constitutional rights, so long as they are a part and portion of the great political structure built upon that basis.

TEACHING OF APOSTLE ORSON HYDE.

(Continued from Page 367.)

IN this prison they must remain until they have paid the utmost farthing. The Antediluvians were in this prison for a long time; until, at length Christ preached the gospel to their spirits, that they might be judged according to men in the flesh. He opened the prison doors to them that were bound and proclaimed a release to the captive sons and daughters of Earth, enslaved by sin in the days of Noah.

While the Savior's body lay entombed in the sepulcher, his spirit was not inactive. He was preaching the gospel to the spirits in prison. But after they have suffered in prison, and are finally released, after many a thousand years' servitude in pain and darkness, their glory cannot be like that of the sun, neither like that of the moon; nor yet like the stars of the first magnitude; but perhaps like the faint glimmer of a distant star—so distant from the sun that a ray from that brilliant orb can hardly reach it.

The foolish virgins, not having the means of light in themselves, could never enter a mansion or world that shines by its own light; but as they had no oil in their vessels, they were compelled to borrow, and hence, they must go to a world or mansion that shines by borrowed light. Have light in yourselves! You may borrow all you can of me, and I will cheerfully lend all in my power, but have, at least, some light in yourselves, and salt likewise.

Oh, that the testimony of Christ, which is the spirit of prophecy, were freely shed upon all this people! It would be if we were all pure and worthy. Then one need no longer say to another, Know ye the Lord; for they would all know him from the least unto the greatest. Then we should know that we were neither straw, chaff, smut, bran, nor tares; but pure and genuine, superfine, No. 1, and labeled for the celestial Kingdom—"right side up, with care."

With the light and knowledge which we through the grace of God have obtained, let us press forward with boldness, and a laudable ambition, to secure the prize bought by a Savior's blood, and freely offered unto us in the full blaze of inspiration, which light is despised by the world, scoffed at by religionists, and hated of all nations. God grant to establish this light in the earth, and us in this light, and this light in us, and the love thereof forever and ever:—Amen.

TEACHING OF PRESIDENT HEBER C. KIMBALL.

(July 5, 1857.)

I CAN say one thing in regard to preaching before this congregation: it is a great deal harder to speak to the people in the afternoon than it is in the forenoon, because they generally come together after partaking of a hearty dinner, and that in connection with the word they receive in the forenoon fills them up, and they are somewhat like a barn that is nearly full of hay; for you know it is a great deal harder to put in the last load of hay than it is the first.

I speak of these things because the circumstances that surround us call them forth.

This is the work of God, and all the world cannot stay its progress. They have given me the character in the world of calling things by their right names. It is a good deal with them as it was with the old Dutchman, who said, "it is not the thing itself, but it is the name of the damned thing," that is it exactly.

They can talk and hint about everything, but never call them by their names. I call that hypocrisy, and there never was a nation that lived upon the earth that was fuller of it than this nation.

As to what they call 'Mormonism,' properly speaking, the Church of Jesus Christ of Latter-day Saints, I say it is true, and Joseph Smith the Prophet, who was killed in Illinois, in Carthage jail, is the author of it, or, in other words, he was the instrument in the hands of God of bringing it forth. Peter, James and John, three of the ancient Apostles, came and ordained him and set him apart for the work of the ministry of this last dispensation.

I am bearing testimony of those things that are true—things that I know and understand. And I also testify that Hyrum Smith was a Patriarch of God, and just as much so as Abraham, Isaac, or Jacob ever were. Joseph Smith the Prophet ordained his father a patriarch and he ordained Hyrum.

MISCELLANEOUS, &c.

A riot has just happened in Nottingham. After thousands of workers, who were without work and suffering from hunger, held a meeting in the market place, they assaulted a jewelry shop and stole jewelry worth hundreds of pounds.

WE ARE INFORMED that disease and death are very heavy in North Wales.

☞ The Saints are aware of the great changes that are now being made, and their powerful impact on the kingdom of God. One of these is the call home of the elders that are here on a mission. This will greatly affect the emigration of the poor Saints from this country. In the face of this, and other important requirements that have come so suddenly, the Saints are called on to show, according to their circumstances, who of their poor will be worthy, when the time comes, of being *chosen* out of MANY who have been called, by striving greatly to make a generous contribution, to assist in accomplishing these feats, by which they will secure their own deliverance earlier than they think. A word to the wise is sufficient. We shall publish the names and the contributions together with the pledges in the TRUMPET, so they may be judged out of the books. It is requested that the final pledge be paid before the end of January, and the contributions as they are collected.

PAYMENTS from October 10 to November 20.—D. Davis, £1; H. Harris, £1, I. Jones, 10s.; J. Davis, 10s.; M. Vaughan, £1 10s.

CONTENTS.

	PG.
Signs of the Times	369
Editorial—Financial—News from Utah	377
Teaching of O. Hyde	382
" H. C. Kimball	383
Miscellaneous, &c.	384

PRINTED AND PUBLISHED BY D. DANIELS, SWANSEA.

ZION'S TRUMPET,

OR

Star of the Saints.

No. 25.]　　　　　DECEMBER 5, 1857.　　　　　[Vol. X.

THE SPIRIT OF THE TIMES.

(From the *Star*.)

WE have again received letters from our brethren in the Mountains, and also numbers 24, 25, 26, and 27 of the *Deseret News*. The latest date of the news received by us is September 9th. We have also received a variety of American papers. From these sources we gather the "spirit of the times" relative to the great latter-day work as illustrated by the people of the United States on the one hand, and our brethren at home on the other. We hardly need inform the Saints that there is a vast difference between the feelings and intentions of the two parties. On the one hand the United States manifest a disposition to continue in their course of injustice and oppression toward the people of God. Instead of redressing our wrongs and giving us our constitutional rights, after having endured so much from the hands of our enemies, and with the extraordinary history of our settlement in the wilderness to prove how nobly the Saints have won their claims to self government, they are determined still to add insult to insult, injury to injury, and oppression to oppression. Instead of letting us alone to develop the kingdom of God and the vitality of its institutions, they are determined, if possible, to crush the Saints and everything of "Mormon" origin. Be it so! It is the greatest compliment that our enemies can pay us and our holy religion. If it is a fact that this kingdom is filled with the seeds of dissolution, so that, untouched,

[PRICE 1½c.

it would dwindle to decay,—if its inherent strength will not bear up its body, and its light is so flickering that it would soon expire of its own accord, why is there such an effort made to destroy us, such gigantic arms put forth to grapple with us, and such a whirlwind blown up to put out that light? All this is an acknowledgment of the stability of the work, a proof of the vigor of young Israel, and a glorious omen of his rising star.

On the other hand, the authorities in Zion are determined to be no longer oppressed, insulted, and trodden under foot by those who hate the Saints. They will no longer see the spirit of republican government violated, which says that the people shall choose their own rulers, and that a community capable of self government shall have that privilege. This is obviously the tenor of a republican spirit. We defy the world to show a community which has such claims on self government as that of the Saints. Their history—more especially since their exile to the Mountains—is full of evidence of this fact. They are evidently no longer inclined to receive every rascal that Government is pleased to send to pick quarrels with the Church; neither to have an armed force in the territory to worry the people and embarrass the men of their choice in the discharge of their callings. Neither will they allow the community to be subdued and exterminated, without giving strong evidence that the fire of '76 burns in the heroes of '57. In this the Saints nobly second their leaders, and the whole Territory is unanimous in the heroic demonstration.

A PROPHET IN ISRAEL.

EVERY one of our readers who is at all conversant with the Bible must often have been struck with the peculiar and extraordinary history of Israel under the Prophets. They were then, indeed, a peculiar people. A common standard would not measure them, nor was their history to be understood by ordinary minds; for Israel revolved in a higher sphere than that in which the other nations were accustomed to travel. Many extraordinary events in their experience will rush to the memory—many examples of the superior wisdom and deep insight of the Prophets could be cited. But just now we have in our mind's eye one particular case.

The king of Syria was troubled because the king of Israel knew of his stratagems, and by some means discovered, and was thus enabled to escape the traps laid to ensnare him. And the Syrian king called together his servants, "and said unto them, Will ye not shew me which of us is for the king of Israel? And one of his servants said, None, my lord, O king: but Elisha the Prophet, that is in Israel, telleth the king of Israel the words that thou speakest in thy bedchamber."

Latter-day Israel, like Israel of former days, are also a peculiar people. Neither they nor their institutions are to be measured by a common standard. This all the world who are brought into contact with the Saints realize, and they are continually acknowledging the fact. They feel that "Mormonism" is altogether an innovation, and that the movements and developments of this Church are as novel and strange to their everyday experience as though beings from another world had come to take part in the great drama of this earth. Notwithstanding the enmity that exists in the hearts of the Gentiles against the Saints, one fact they all seem to realize—namely, that this Church and the world are revolving in two diffcrent spheres.

There are Prophets also in Latter-day Israel, even as there were Prophets in Israel of old. It will yet become a matter of trouble to the rulers of the earth—as a nightmare to oppress them in their sleep—that those Prophets will know the words which they shall give utterance to in their "bedchamber" and secret councils. The following testimony from the *New York Herald* is full of significance:—

"Major Van Vliet held a long interview with the President last evening. He says Young is as well informed in relation to the government as any man in Washington."

We will reveal the secret. The fact is, *an Elisha, and more than an Elisha, is again in Israel.*—STAR.

AMERICAN NEWS.

UTAH EXPEDITION.—Captain Van Vliet, Assistant *Quartermaster,* United States army, arrived in this city last evening, direct from the Territory of Utah, having left Great Salt Lake City on the 14th *ult.*

We understand that the Mormons are determined not to allow the United States troops to enter Salt Lake Valley, and will use force to prevent them, if necessary. They look upon the present movement of the Government as only the renewal of the persecutions which they complain of having endured in this State, and Illinois, and are determined to resist it at the outset.

Captain Van Vliet met the troops on the 22nd of September, on the Sweet Water, some 230 miles beyond Fort Laramie. They were all well and in good spirits. Some of the supply trains were at Harris Fork, 143 miles this side of the Valley, while others were far behind; and it is very doubtful if they can enter Salt Lake Valley this season.

Colonel Johnston, with his escort, was met on the 1st of October, 90 miles this side of Fort Laramie, and determined to enter the Valley of Salt Lake this fall. Governor Cumming and Secretary Hartnett were met on the 8th of this month 90 miles beyond Fort Kearney, all well. A heavy snow fell at Fort Bridger on the 15th of September.

Captain Van Vliet has made an extraordinary trip—over 2,400 miles by land, since the 1st of August. He leaves for Washington today.

We hear that Captain Van Vliet passed a week in Great Salt Lake City. He was treated with much consideration, and invited to partake of the hospitalities of the leading men of the city. But on all occasions, and from every quarter, he heard only one expression of opinion—and that was, that they would never permit United States troops or the officers appointed by the United States Government to get a foothold in their dominions. In all their public declarations, and in their private conversations, this sentiment is boldly avowed—they will never suffer the troops to enter the city!

And if they do, it will be after the city has been committed to the flames, the territory around it has been laid waste, and all the inhabitants have fled to the mountains. They believe Brigham Young to be the appointed agent of the Lord, and whatever he commands them to do, they will perform with alacrity. They say that they have provisions sufficient to last them for three or four years; and that, persecuted as they have been, and are, by the Americans, they will resist to the last extremity.

These statements being true, as they undoubtedly are, the Government will have to make levies of new men, and to dispatch heavy reinforcements to the army in Utah next spring.

Dr. Bernhisel, Delegate from Congress to Utah, arrived in company with Captain Van Vliet.—From the *Saint Louis Republican*.

TROUBLES OF THE EXPEDITION.

THERE is no grass at all between Fort Laramie and Green River, a distance of *four hundred miles*. The contractors for delivering the Commissary and Quartermaster's supplies, (Messrs. Russell and Wadell,) are losing large numbers of their cattle; and the trains accompanying the different commands that have gone by Fort Laramie could make only twelve miles a day.

We look for the six companies ordered out as an escort to the Governor and suite tomorrow. They cannot make over 18 miles a day, and will be until December making the trip. I do not believe that they can get their horses through at all this winter; and perhaps A GREAT MANY OF THE MEN WILL PERISH FOR THE WANT OF PROTECTION. I know that there will be AN ABUNDANCE OF SNOW by the middle of this month in the passes through which they have to go. From the *Buffalo Commercial Advertiser*.

STILL MORE.

THE cattle of the Government trains, on the Plains, were DYING FAST; and it is believed the trains will encounter GREAT

SUFFERING through the winter.

Colonel Johnston, head officer of the transport service, with 19 light wagons, was met. He was traveling rapidly, at the rate of 60 miles per day. The mules were breaking down. Numbers of them were dropping on the way, worn down and rendered useless by the extraordinary labor they had been compelled to undergo.—From the *Saint Louis Democrat*.

PATRIOTIC DEMONSTRATION OF UTAH.

THEIR expressed determination, from first to last, was this: to resist at all hazards the ingress of the troops this autumn. When they were reminded of the certainty that, in case their resistance one year should be effectual, a force would be dispatched to Utah the next, against which twice their population in arms would strive in vain to close the passes; they replied that they had considered all that, and that when such a force had stormed those passes, they would enter a valley in which not one shrub would be green, nor one stone remain upon another. They took pains to show him their gardens and vineyards, their harvest, barns, houses, and *livestock*, and to contrast their present prosperity with such a scene of desolation.

Their object now, they said, was to gain time to enable the National Government to retrace its steps; and they intend to present their case to Congress through their Delegate Dr. Bernhisel, who accompanied Captain Van Vliet on his departure, and is now in his camp. It was at one period his determination not to proceed to Washington this winter; but that was reconsidered.

They said that they would regard the entrance of the troops as the beginning of a repetition of their sufferings at Kirtland, Independence, and Nauvoo; that they had learned a lesson from experience, and would now meet aggression at the start, and would resist the wedge before it should enter the wood.

If they could not keep the troops out this year, they would sacrifice all for their religion, take to the mountains, and fight a war of glory and extermination. Brigham Young remarked repeatedly that this was the most glorious era of his faith, and that a happier day never dawned on Mormonism than that on which the advance of the troops was ordered; for the more his Church was persecuted, the more it would thrive.

At the close [of his discourse] Mr. Taylor called the attention of the people to the Captain, and alluded to his business in the city, recounted the substance of his conversations, and said that he would make a request, in order that Captain Van Vliet might learn that he had been made acquainted with the determination of the whole people. He would ask that all those present who were willing to raze their houses, burn their crops, pull down what they had passed ten years in building up—make their beautiful valley a desert—and retreat to the mountains, in case the troops should force an entrance, would rise; and the audience, without exception, rose to their feet, and remained standing long enough to enable him to see that they were absolutely unanimous.—The *New York Daily Tribune.*

ALARMING EARTHQUAKE IN BUFFALO.

THE entire city was startled and alarmed yesterday afternoon, about ten minutes past three o'clock, by a shock which agitated the most solid buildings, and set household utensils and furniture dancing in a most unaccountable manner.

So severe was the shock, which lasted about thirty seconds, that people ran out of their houses in wild dismay.

In many instances walls were cracked and chimneys thrown down, and we hear of one gentleman having his arm injured by a falling brick. Bells were rung, and a variety of strange incidents occurred otherwise. In the neighborhood of our office, the impression was obtained that our steam boiler had exploded, but that is more stable than the foundations of the town appear to be.

We were in the midst of a sentence, when the low, deep rumbling of subterranean thunders startled us, and shook the building as with a palsy.—*Buffalo Express.*

THE GRASSHOPPERS.

Two gentlemen are in this city, soliciting subscriptions for the relief of the sufferers by the grasshopper plague, which desolated many of the settlements in Northern Minnesota last summer. They represent that many families there are in a suffering condition, and ill prepared to stand the winter. They appeal to the charitable for relief.—*Galena Advertiser.*

ZION'S TRUMPET,

OR

Star of the Saints.

SATURDAY, DECEMBER 5, 1857.

EVEN though thousands in our country are suffering from lack of food because of the accursed business arrangements of the Gentiles, and although the sound of pestilence and war is thundering in our ears, and black clouds heavy with the coming judgments are about to burst above us, the complete hope of the Saints is the deliverance of that God who was in ancient Israel. His hand is working, the destruction of the gentiles on the one hand, and the prompt deliverance of his Saints on the other.

While the world around us is in tumult and confusion, tranquility and trust are the chief characteristics of the Saints; for Jesus says, When you see these things, lift up your heads and rejoice.

This is not the time for multiplying words, and let not the Saints expect to receive all the details through the press—they can understand the mind of God, through the Holy Ghost, from suggestions and *hints*. The wise show their understanding through their works—their prompt obedience to the requirements of God, without explanation, &c.

We are publishing a few names and pledges of contributions, some from memory, and others that were sent to us. We wish for the names of all to be transferred. Let some of the brethren of the Swansea Council forgive us if we forgot them, and send them again.

CONTRIBUTIONS TOWARD EMIGRATING AND OUTFITTING THE MISSIONARIES.

PLEDGES.

	£	s	c
David Davies, Swansea,	1	0	0
William Richards, "	1	0	0
George Cutliffe, "	1	0	0
Henry Matthews, "	1	0	0
John Evans, Treboth,	1	0	0
Thomas Lewis, Morriston,	1	0	0
Hopkin Jones, "	1	0	0
William Richards, Cilha,	1	0	0
Levi James, "	1	0	0
Thomas Evans, Cyfing,	1	0	0
John Hill, "	1	0	0
Thomas Harris, earlier from Georgetown,	1	0	0
Benjamin Jones, Skewen,	0	10	0
From Pembrokeshire Conference:—			
John Gibbs, Haverfordwest	1	0	0
David Harries	0	12	6
Mrs. M. White	0	11	0
Miss M. White	0	6	0
Jane White	0	6	6
Mary White	1	2	6
Ellen Gibbs	0	5	0
Mary Phillips	0	5	0
Jane Lalliss	0	6	0
Elizabeth Lalliss	0	11	0
Elizabeth Rogers	0	3	0
John Lallice	0	1	0
Charles Lallice	0	0	6
Rosanna Griffiths	0	1	0
Carried over	£17	11	0

	£	s	c
Carried forward	17	11	0
Susan Williams	0	0	6
Pembroke Branch:—			
William Thomas	1	0	0
Richard Jones	0	10	0
Thomas Hitchings	0	7	6
Charlotte Davis	0	1	0
Eliza Jones	0	5	0
Francess Purcer	0	11	6
Francis Purcer	0	1	0
Lydstep Branch:—			
John Davies	0	12	0
Francis Davies	0	1	0
Milford Branch:—Wm White	1	5	0
John White	0	2	6
William Adams	0	7	0
Cuffern Branch: Jas. Thomas	0	10	0
Thomas John	0	10	0
Phillip Dell	0	10	0
Fishguard—Jno. Morris	0	5	0
Cathrine Jenkins	0	4	0
Mary Anne Jenkins	0	1	0
Elizabeth Williams	0	3	0
Pater.—Jenkin Edwards	0	5	0
Sutton,—George Gibbs	0	5	6
William Howells	1	2	6
George Roberts	0	11	6
Martha Roberts	0	1	0
William Hughes	0	10	0
Thos. Dee, Swansea	1	0	0
TOTAL	£ 28	13	6

☞ Let the Presidents of Branches of West Glamorgan send the names, &c., directly to this Office.

Sixpence is the lowest contribution that will be published.

TEACHING OF H. C. KIMBALL.

(Continued from page 384.)

The same gospel which was preached by Jesus and by his Apostles has been delivered unto us through Joseph Smith the Prophet of the living God, and the keys and powers pertaining to that gospel and priesthood are now resting upon brother Brigham Young, for he is Joseph's legal successor.

All the prophets from the days of Adam, and from the creation of the world, have conferred their priesthood and keys in this dispensation, and brother Brigham holds them in connection with the old Prophets and Apostles, and in connection with our Father and God pertaining to this Earth.

I am telling you the truth, and testifying to that which God has made manifest unto me. Well, the world wants that we should lay aside that which God has revealed, and not speak of Joseph Smith, nor of the revelations which he gave.

When I was abroad preaching, some said to me we would be popular if we would say nothing about the Book of Mormon, Joseph Smith, baptism for the remission of sins, or the laying on of hands for the Gift of the Holy Ghost; they said if we would let these things alone we would be popular.

Good heavens! We are now more popular than any other religious community upon the earth; we extend, as some would call it, from Dan to Beersheba—we extend to every nation, continent, and country, and almost to every island of the sea. The gospel has been carried to almost every people; we have offered them the principles of life and salvation, and we shall continue to do so while there is any hope for them.

I expect, like us, the inhabitants of the earth will have their ups and downs, their troubles and afflictions. There has been a great chill among them; they had one when we had one, and now the fever has begun to increase with us, it has begun to increase upon them, and by and by there will be another *chill*, and it will keep doubling and redoubling, till the whole world is in motion. Will it overthrow this work? No, never.

I want the gentlemen that are here today, and who are going east, to tell the people of the United States that they need not trouble themselves, for 'Mormonism' will increase and triumph until every king will be cast down from his throne and the President of the United States, unless he and the people repent; and what they call 'Mormonism' will continue to increase henceforth and forever.

When they killed Joseph Smith and Hyrum, David Patten and many others, they supposed that was the end of 'Mormonism,'—that it was annihilated. Bless your souls, instead of its being annihilated it has increased a hundred fold, and we have now more elders preaching the Gospel; yes, about ten times more than there are people in this vast congregation this afternoon, and I presume there are some seven or eight thousand here today.

You may think this rather extravagant, but there are more elders in England than there are people here today, and England is not as big as the State of New York, where I lived. They will spread and increase from this time on, and this work is bound to increase and spread abroad, and all hell cannot pull it down.

Suppose the Gentiles were to try to put it down, and to kill brother Brigham, and me, and brother Daniel, and the Twelve Apostles, still there are some 50 or 60 Quorums of Seventies that are capable of spreading abroad this Kingdom. Why, bless you, it is like the mustard seed; you know it is the most troublesome to get out of the garden. You get vexed with it, and go and kick it about, and by that means you make ten thousand more little mustard trees.

We want you to tell this, gentlemen, when you get down to the States, for we don't have a mail very often, and therefore we drop a word here and there, and we want everybody to carry the tidings. It is not only me, but the Prophet Brigham talks just so. I suppose you will think 'what a monstrous fellow he is.'

I have been afflicted with colds ever since I came from the

North, but I all the time grow fat. I do not drink ale, whisky, rum, nor any kind of liquor, but I seek to drink largely of the peaceable Spirit of God, that I may be strengthening to my brethren and sisters.

As for the world, and the United States, and their opposition, which they call outside pressure, we care very, very little. We have some big mountains between us and them, and they cannot remove them, because they have not faith.

Such a row as there is in the States at the present time I never before heard of; it is 'Mormonism,' down with 'Mormonism.' Mr. President, send up the troops, and set those 'Mormons' in order!

Gentlemen, [he said to the strangers] did you ever see anybody out of order here? Have you seen anybody drunk? You have not, unless it was yourselves. I have not seen anybody drunk, no, not on the Fourth of July. I have not seen a drunken man in the streets, much less a woman. One reason is, perhaps, that we have not got any liquor, and God grant that we may not have much.

You do not see many people about our streets idling away their time. Tomorrow morning, you may see a few persons who have come from the country to get a little counsel, but after that you won't see a man in the street excepting those who are going to or coming from their work, for they are all hard at work hoeing their corn, watering their wheat, and getting their wood from the canyons.

God Almighty bless this people, I say, and increase their faith and their strength, that they may increase and multiply. And may God increase the 'mustard seed' and cause it soon to fill the earth.

May the Lord our God bless the bees in the hive of Deseret, and root out the drones, for they only eat out the honey, while the bees go out and gather it in.

Well, gentlemen, we are calculating that we have got the best crops that we have ever had, and the best that are in the world, and the Lord our God has blessed the land for our sake.

We had a famine last year, but we lived through it, and we are now going to work to lay up our grain, and we are building storehouses to store it away in; and we shall not only store away grain, but other things that will keep; and the day will come that you (strangers) will have to come to us for bread to eat; and we will be your saviors, here, upon Mount Zion. You don't believe it now, but wait a little while, and you will see that it will come to pass.

Many of the people of the United States exulted over us when we were brought down to a morsel of bread, and had to deal out one to another in order to subsist. I put my family on short rations in order to have some to deal out to others, and so did brother Brigham and many others, and at the same time our enemies and the priests in their pulpits were praising God that we had hard times, with trouble and perplexity.

We were never more happy in our lives than we were at that time, and we did not have the belly ache through eating too much; but we were lively and diligent in serving God, and that is the reason we are becoming so corpulent this year. Last year we had not enough, but this year we have plenty, and we are going to lay it up in store; wheat and everything that will keep.

I am telling these gentlemen what we are going to do so that they can carry the news to the States.

Ladies, we do not want you to tease your husbands for silks and satins and fine bonnets, but go to work and manufacture your own clothing, and if you will do that you will do the best that you ever did in your lives; this is as true as that the Lord ever spoke by his prophets; the time has come for us to lay up our stores.

Will the world follow our example? No, they will not; and if we do our duty, who cares whether they do or not. They will come with their bonnets, their fine clothing, and their jewelry, and be glad to work for us to get their bread.

You tell that in the States, gentlemen, won't you? Whether you do or not, they will learn of it; they publish nearly everything that we say, and this will be published.

We are a people, here in the valleys of the Mountains, who are hated, and have been broken up, and driven for our religion, till we have got used to it. Brother Brigham told you he had been driven five times, and so have I, and I have had everything taken from me that I had; but yet, I have got enough to eat and drink, and enough of everything, and so have you, and my prayer is all the while, God bless you.

Lay up your stores, and take your silks and fine things, and exchange them for grain and such things as you need, and the time will come when we will be obliged to depend upon our own resources; for the time is not far distant when the curtain will be dropped between us and the United States.

When that time comes, brethren and sisters, you will wish you had commenced sooner to make your own clothing. I tell you, God requires us to go into home manufacture, and prolong it as much as you like; you have got to do it.

You will also see the day that you will wish you had laid up your grain, if you do not do it now; for you will see the day, if you do not take care of the blessings God has given to you, that you will become servants, the same as the world will.

We have told you this before; you have been exhorted year after year to prepare for hard times; you have been told of this often enough. We have told you that when hard times come again you won't have the privilege that you had last time, of having food dealt out to you gratuitously, but you will have to pay for all you get; this will come to pass.

I suppose there are many who don't believe it: to such it is like a tune that strikes upon the drum of the ear, passes off and is forgotten.

I will prove to you that I will put my faith with my works and lay up stores for my family and for my friends that are in the United States, and I will be to them as Joseph was to the people in the land of Egypt. Every man and woman will be a savior if they will do as I say. You may write this down and send it to the States, for it will be published.

Let repentance take place amongst you, where it is necessary, and let confidence, diligence in the performance of duty, and humility be manifest in your lives; keep the commandments of God, be subject to God's authority, and save yourselves all the time, and the Lord our God will have pleasure in making you like Joseph of old.

Now, if persons were coming from the old country, from far distant lands, would you not feel comfortable if you had plenty to feed them with when they come? These things bear heavily upon my mind, and they have done so for some time. There are very few who have got any surplus grain on hand. There is considerable in the Tithing store, and there are a few individuals who have some on hand, but there is not a great deal in the country, excepting our present crop. It behooves us to be saving and preparing for the time to come.

The day will come when the people of the United States will come lugging their bundles under their arms, coming to us for bread to eat.

Every Prophet has spoken of this from the early ages of the world. Already we begin to see sickness, trouble, death, famine, and pestilence, and more yet awaits the nations of the wicked.

Jesus said, When you hear of these things in foreign nations—destruction and desolation—you may then look forth for my coming, and know that it is nigh at hand. In relation to the world, our enemies, their soldiery, and their governors, I do not fear them, and I never did.

If you will do right, keep the commandments of God; I can say with all the propriety that any man, prophet, or apostle ever did, you shall never want for food, nor raiment, nor houses, nor lands, and no power on the earth can harm you. No power shall prevent our prosperity, for we shall increase while every other power upon the earth that is opposed to this work and our God will go down. I just know it. Amen.

MORE PLEDGES, &c.

As we were going to Press we received the few following names, from Cardiff, which, so far, are first in line.

	£	s	c		£	s	c
Brought forward (from p. 394)	28	13	6	Brought forward	42	17	0
Samuel Shepton	5	0	0	Evan A. Lewis	2	4	0
Samuel Evans	2	0	0	Thomas Rees	2	0	0
Alfred Edwards	3	0	0	Samuel Seviors	2	0	0
John Evans	2	0	0	Rees Jenkins	1	12	6
John A. Lewis	2	3	6	Jacob Thomas	1	10	0
Carried over	42	17	0	Total	£52	3	6

CONTENTS.

	PG.
The Spirit of the Times	385
A Prophet in Israel	386
American News	388
Editorial—Contributions, &c.	392
Names, Pledges, &c.	393
Teaching of H.C. Kimball	395

PRINTED AND PUBLISHED BY D. DANIELS, SWANSEA.

ZION'S TRUMPET,

OR

Star of the Saints.

| No. 26.] | DECEMBER 26, 1857. | [Vol. X. |

PROCLAMATION OF PRESIDENT BRIGHAM YOUNG.

(From the *New York Weekly Herald*.)

CITIZENS OF UTAH.—We are invaded by a hostile force, who are evidently assailing us to accomplish our overthrow and destruction. For the last twenty-five years we have trusted officials of the Government, from constables and justices to judges, Governors and Presidents, only to be scorned, held in derision, insulted and betrayed. Our houses have been plundered and then burned, our fields laid waste, our principal men butchered while under the pledged faith of the Government for their safety, and our families driven from their homes to find that shelter in the barren wilderness and that protection among hostile savages which were denied them in the boasted abodes of Christianity and civilization.

The constitution of our common country guarantees unto us all that we do now or have ever claimed. If the constitutional rights which pertain unto us as American citizens were extended to Utah, according to the spirit and meaning thereof, and fairly and impartially administered, it is all that we could ask—all that we have ever asked.

Our opponents have availed themselves of prejudice existing against us, because of our religious faith, to send out a formidable host to accomplish our destruction. We have had no privilege or opportunity of defending ourselves from the false, foul, and unjust aspersions against us before the nation. The Government has not

26 [PRICE 1½c.

condescended to cause an investigating committee or other person to be sent to inquire into and ascertain the truth, as is customary in such cases. We know those aspersions to be false; but that avails us nothing. We are condemned unheard, and forced to an issue with an armed mercenary mob, which has been sent against us at the instigation of anonymous letter writers, ashamed to father the base, slanderous falsehoods which they have given to the public—of corrupt officials, who have brought false accusations against us to screen themselves in their own infamy, and of hireling priests and howling editors, who prostitute the truth for filthy lucre's sake.

The issue which has thus been forced upon us compels us to resort to the great first law of self preservation, and stand in our own defense—a right guaranteed unto us by the genius of the institutions of our country, and upon which the Government is based. Our duty to ourselves, to our families, requires us not to tamely submit to be driven and slain without an attempt to preserve ourselves. Our duty to our country, our holy religion, our God, to freedom and liberty, requires that we should not quietly stand still and see those fetters forging around us which are calculated to an unlawful military despotism, such as can only emanate, in a country or constitutional law, from usurpation, tyranny, and oppression.

Therefore, I, Brigham Young, Governor and Superintendent of Indian Affairs for the Territory of Utah, in the name of the people of the United States, in the Territory of Utah, forbid,

First—All armed forces of every description from coming into this Territory, under any pretense whatever.

Second—That all the forces in said Territory hold themselves in readiness to march at a moment's notice to repel any and all such invasion.

Third—Marshal law is hereby declared to exist in this Territory, from and after the publication of this proclamation; and no person shall be allowed to pass or repass into, or through, or from this Territory, without a permit from the proper officer.

Given under my hand and seal, at Great Salt lake City, Territory of Utah, this fifteenth day of September, A. D., eighteen hundred and fifty-seven, and of the Independence of the United States of America the eighty-second.

BRIGHAM YOUNG.

PLEDGES.

Brought from p. 400	£52	3	6	Brought forward	£64	11	0
Llanelli Branch:—				David Williams	0	2	6
Hugh John	0	10	0	Jane Amos	0	2	0
William Treharn	0	5	0	Susana Lewis	0	2	0
William Williams	0	5	0	*Pontnewydd:*—			
John Morgans	1	0	0	David Hughes	0	2	0
Thomas D.	0	10	0	David Evans	0	15	0
John Thomas	0	10	0	Joseph Treharn	0	10	0
John John	0	10	0	Richard Jones	0	5	0
Henry Williams	0	10	0	John Evans	0	2	6
John Wilkins	0	7	0	*Vangalch:*—			
John Harri	0	10	0	William Williams	0	5	0
William Lewis	0	10	0	David Owens	0	10	0
Richard Treharn	0	2	6	Mary Hughes	0	7	0
David Treharn (son)	0	2	6	*Pontyberem:*—			
William Treharn "	0	2	6	David Williams	0	5	0
Hugh Dafydd	0	5	0	Thomas Williams	0	10	0
Thomas Morris	0	5	0	Margaret Williams	0	10	0
William Bowen	0	2	0	*Cwmaman:*—			
David Roberts	0	3	0	John Evans	0	2	6
John Longhurst	0	5	0	Edward Jones	0	2	6
John Thomas	0	2	0	Jane Jones	0	1	6
John John, jun.	0	1	0	Thomas Bowen	0	5	0
Morgan William	0	5	0	James Phillips	0	1	0
Morgan John	0	5	0	*Llandybie:*—			
Ann Coclough	1	0	0	Thomas Thomas	0	5	0
Ann Harris	0	5	0	Elizabeth Williams	0	2	0
R— W—	0	10	0	Jemima Davies	0	2	0
A— W—	0	5	0	Jane Davies	0	2	0
Mary Michael	0	5	0	*Cyfing Branch:*—			
Mary Davies	0	10	0	Esther Williams	0	10	0
L— M—	0	10	0	George Morgan	0	10	0
Ann Evans	0	5	0	Alfred Thomas	0	2	6
Martha Thomas	0	2	6	Griffith Williams	0	5	0
Elizabeth Evans	0	1	0	Lewis Lewis	1	0	0
Rachel Hughes	0	2	6	*Swansea Branch:*—			
Ann Hughes	0	1	0	Francis Williams	0	10	0
Sarah Hughes	0	1	0	David Lewis	1	0	0
A— J—	0	5	0	John Lewis	0	5	0
Ann Longhurst	0	1	0	David Jones	1	0	0
Waunbaglam:—				Jane Lloyd	0	2	6
Thomas Morgans	0	6	0	Henry Allen	0	2	6
Elizabeth Morgans	0	6	0	Susan Allen	0	2	6
William Rees	0	2	0	Richard Brooks	0	5	0
Thomas Griffiths	0	2	0	William Brooks	0	1	6
Carried over	£64	11	0	Carried over	£75	19	0

Brought forward	£75	19	0	Brought forward	£95	18	6
Henrietta Dyer	0	2	0	Henry Parry	0	2	6
Ann Cutcliff	0	0	6	Samuel Stenbridge	0	5	0
Agnes Cutcliff	0	0	6	T. R. W——.	0	10	0
Mary Dyer	0	1	0	J. D——.	0	10	0
John Davies	0	3	0	Ruth Bayliss	0	5	0
Cathrine Davies	0	2	6	Thomas Mason	0	5	0
Elizabeth Dee	0	2	6	J. W——.	0	10	0
Emma Hughes	0	2	0	David Morgan	0	10	0
Ystradgynlais:—				Mary Morgan	0	10	0
Anne Jones	1	0	0	Leah Thomas	0	5	0
William Davies	0	5	0	Sarah Vaughan	0	1	0
Morgan Davies	0	5	0	Isaiah Thomas	1	0	0
William Thomas	0	2	0	*Rhymney:*—			
David Jones, Sr.	0	4	0	George P. Adams	1	0	0
Roderick Williams	0	2	0	John Price	1	0	0
David Jones	0	1	6	Edward Humphreys	1	0	0
Alltwen: Jas. Davies	0	1	0	Evan Phillips	1	0	0
John H. Davies	0	10	0	William Lewis	1	0	0
David Morgan	0	2	0	David Owen	1	0	0
John S. Morgans	0	5	0	James Edwards	1	0	0
David S. Morgans	0	10	0	Rees Price	0	12	0
Daniel Williams	0	1	0	Thomas Rees	0	2	6
Tredegar:—				John Rees	0	2	6
Joseph Colledge	1	0	0	E. Morgan	0	5	0
Elizabeth Colledge	0	2	6	H. Richard	0	5	0
Benjamin Evans	1	0	0	Elizabeth Sansom	0	2	6
Michael Vaughan	0	10	0	John N. Evans	0	1	0
Thomas Williams 1st	2	0	0	John D. Evans	0	1	0
James Abrams	1	0	0	Wm. Powell, Cwmbach	1	0	0
Martha Abrams	1	0	0	Morgan Vaughan	0	5	0
John Griffiths	1	0	0	John Davies	0	5	0
James Carter	0	10	0	David Vaughan	0	5	0
John Goold	1	10	0	Wm. Thomas	0	5	0
Dan Nicholas	1	0	0	Thomas Davies	0	2	0
Mary Nicholas	0	1	0	Wm. Williams	0	2	6
Margaret Ward	0	10	0	David M. Jones	0	10	0
William Brittain	0	5	0	John T. Llewelyn	1	0	0
John Mears	0	5	0	Mariah Vaughan	0	1	0
Joel Mears	0	1	0	Margaret Llewelyn	0	0	6
Martha Davies	0	5	0	Sarah Rees	0	0	6
Joshua Corsey	1	0	0	Harriet Lewis	0	1	0
Thomas Jones	1	0	0	Eleanor Jones	0	1	0
Anne Jones	0	5	0	John Pritchard	0	2	0
Isaac Humphrey	1	0	0	*Aberaman:*—			
Sarah Humphrey	0	5	0	Lewis Lewis	0	10	0
Sarah A. Humphrey	0	2	6	James Grear	0	10	0
William Parry	0	5	0	Jenkin Williams	1	0	0
Carried over	£95	18	6	Carried over	£115	4	0

	£	s	d		£	s	d
Brought forward	115	4	0	Brought forward	133	8	6
Richard Price	0	5	0	David John	0	1	0
David D. Jones	0	5	0	Dinah James	0	2	0
David Rees	0	10	0	Mary Richards	0	0	6
Thomas Rees	0	10	0	Elizabeth Harries	0	2	0
William Leyshon	0	4	0	William Richards, Jr.	0	1	0
Wm. Williams	0	5	0	*Caernarvon:—*			
Jenkin Edwards	0	5	0	John Davies	0	2	6
John James	0	2	6	John Thomas	0	0	6
Daniel Griffiths	0	5	0	Mrs. Jane Thomas	0	1	0
David Llywelyn	0	5	0	William Thomas	0	0	6
John Jones	0	10	0	Miss Jane Thomas	0	0	6
John Davies	0	2	0	Evan Jones	0	2	6
John Davies	0	10	0	Ellis Owen	0	1	0
Charlotte Jones	0	1	0	Sarah Thomas	0	0	6
Ann Leigh	0	2	6	Jane Jones	0	0	6
Mountain Ash:—				Catherine Jones	0	1	0
John Morley	1	0	0	Anne Lloyd	0	1	0
Thomas Bullock	1	0	0	Mary Williams	0	0	6
Thomas Burchell	0	10	0	Jane Roberts	0	0	6
Morgan Williams	0	10	0	*Llandudno:—*			
James Peard	0	5	0	William Ajax	0	10	0
George Sheppard	0	10	0	John Roberts	0	5	0
John Jenkin	0	10	0	Edward Parry, Sr.	0	2	0
William Edwards	0	5	0	Edward Parry, Jr.	1	10	0
Thomas Eynon	0	10	0	Peter Hughes	0	5	0
Aberdare:— J. Boden	0	10	0	Thomas Jones	0	5	0
Thomas Llewellyn	0	5	0	John Jones	0	5	0
William Williams	0	5	0	Jane Parry	0	2	0
John Floyd	0	5	0	Anne Jones	0	2	0
William Samuel	1	0	0	Mary Davies	0	0	6
William Griffiths	1	0	0	Margaret Evans	0	3	0
Walter Bowen	1	0	0	*Tenby:—*			
Timothy Crawley	1	0	0	William Griffiths	0	8	0
Lewis A.	1	0	0	Elizabeth Griffith	0	2	0
David Davies	0	5	0	Joshua Richards	0	10	0
John Williams	0	10	0	Sarah Richards	0	5	0
David Williams	0	10	0	Thomas Noot	0	2	6
William Sims	0	3	0	Mary Williams	1	0	0
Sarah Sims	0	3	0	Mary Ann Morgans	0	11	0
Lewis Jones	0	0	6	Eliza Griffiths	0	5	0
Sarah Jane Sims	0	2	0	Harriet Clark	0	2	6
Alfred Sims	0	2	0	Mary Morgans	0	3	0
Margaret Powell	0	1	0	Hannah Davis	0	1	0
Elizabeth Reese	0	0	6	*Stepaside:—*			
'Lofince' Reese	0	0	6	Charles Rees	0	12	0
Cilha:—				Thomas Phillips	0	12	0
Thomas Phillips	1	0	0	William Griffiths	0	5	0
Carried over	£133	8	6	Carried over	£142	16	0

Brought forward	£142	16	0	Brought forward	£144	19	0
Haverfordwest:—				*Abergele:*—			
John Griffith	0	5	0	Evan Jones	0	5	0
Neyland:—				Rice Williams	0	5	0
George Hewlett	0	1	0	Michael Parry	0	5	0
Fishguard:—				William Conway	0	10	0
Martha Jenkins	0	1	6	Robert Conway	0	2	6
Sutton:—				Joseph Parry	0	2	6
Abigail Roberts	0	1	0	Leah Williams	0	1	0
George Twiggs	0	2	6	Eleanor C. Edwards	0	2	6
Margaret Howells	0	2	6	Edward Williams	0	1	0
John Summers	0	1	0	*Newmarket:*—			
Denbigh:—				Hugh Evans	0	5	0
Edward Lloyd	0	5	0	Phebi Evans	0	1	0
Margaret Lloyd	0	1	0	Robert Parry	0	2	0
Anne Williams	0	2	0	David Jones	0	10	0
Ruthin:—				Thomas Williams	0	10	0
Elizabeth Williams	0	3	0	Elizabeth Williams	0	10	0
Elis Williams	0	2	6	Joseph Evans	0	1	0
Jane Williams	0	1	0	Robert Parry	0	1	0
One who is for the work	0	14	0	One who loves the work	1	5	0
Carried over	£144	19	0	Total	£149	18	6

ZION'S TRUMPET,

OR

Star of the Saints.

SATURDAY, DECEMBER 26, 1857.

CONCLUSION.—Our editorial work concludes with this issue, and our presidency with the end of this unforgettable year, in which the direct works began for the independence of the Kingdom of God on the earth.

After five years of heartfelt enjoyable labor with the Saints and our fellow nation, we have been granted the wish of our heart, namely the privilege of returning home to the servants and Saints of God, and our dear family in Zion. We trust that the Saints have been satisfied with and blessed through our labor, and that we shall receive the benefit of their fervent prayers to be able to return safely home. The work of God does not depend on human power for success—it is God who prospers it in a wondrous manner. It matters not how inadequate the instruments, if they are humble, obedient, and teachable. Some suppose that because of the departure of the American Elders from here, the Saints will suffer for want of pastors to instruct them and to feed them: not so. Here there are local brethren who have been proved through many difficult circumstances, and who have always been faithful. They have faith, wisdom, experience, and ability; the fire of the Spirit of God burns within them, and their breasts swell with the desire to prosper the kingdom of God. Some of these will be chosen to lead the Welsh Conferences the coming year. They possess the same Priesthood, the same Holy Ghost, and the same truths as their predecessors. As men, they have the same qualities, which are just as strong, as far as we know, and we cannot see what the Saints will lack, if they are obedient and teachable in the hands of these brethren.

Inasmuch as the presiding local brethren look carefully at the light and movements of the STAR in Liverpool, and spread the same, together with every ray from the Sun of Righteousness in the west, having the sound of Zion's Trumpet weekly, they will prosper the kingdom of God to their hearts' content.

With these considerations, we feel safe to close our labor, and present to your attention our worthy successor and his counselors, Benjamin Evans, John Davies, and David John, together with the various Presidents, wishing for the blessing of God to follow them, and the Saints under their care, who wish a speedy deliverance to Israel. We expect to yet give a brief word of farewell, before we take our leave.—ED.

CONTRIBUTIONS—The pledges show for themselves how much each one, in his own circumstances, is striving: compare the names, and if some who did not pledge as much as the rest, who were no better off than they, are repentant, let them send a new pledge, and we shall republish the name, &c. Some believing gentiles have contributed and have pledged to contribute: let the gifts of all alike be received, and may the contributors be blessed, whoever they may be.

CHRISTMAS BOX—The yearly Report, the quarterly *Financial Report*, the total tithing on hand, and the *Balance Sheet* for the books, the 31st of this month.

NEW YEAR'S GIFT—The TRUMPET weekly for the Welsh Saints, with the 'new old hands' to bring it forth!

APPOINTMENTS
OF ELDERS TO PRESIDE OVER THE WELSH CONFERENCES, FROM JANUARY 1, 1858.

OVER THE MISSION,
President—Benjamin Evans.

John Davies.]　　　Counselors,　　　[David John.

CONFERENCES.	PRESIDENT.
East Glamorgan	John Davies.
Monmouth	William Ajax.
Cardiff	Edward D. Miles.
West Glamorgan	Thomas Rees.
Llanelli	David Davies.
Pembrokeshire	Edward Burgwyne.
Cardiganshire	John Treharn.
Caernarvonshire	Thomas Jones.
Denbighshire	Hugh Evans.
Flintshire	Edwin Price.

PASTOR over the Northern Conferences—Thomas Jones.

The Monmouthshire and Brecon Conferences will be joined under the name of the former.

The Carmarthen and Merioneth Conferences will be dissolved, and their branches will be aligned as follows:—Carmarthen and Saint Clears in the Llanelli Conference, and Brechfa, Pencader, Llansawel, Dinas Mawddwy and Machynlleth in the Cardiganshire Conference: Harlech and Ffestiniog in the Caernarfon Conference, which from now on will be known by the name of Conway Valley and Anglesey Conference.

We are deprived of the labor of our faithful brother, Joseph Griffiths, in the presiding circle, because of his illness.

The diligent and tireless labors of Pastor J. E. Jones are known to God and his children. More will yet be said about him.

CONTENTS.

	PG.
Proclamation of President Brigham Young	401
Pledges	403
Editorial—Conclusion—Christmas Box—New Year's Gift	406
Appointments	408

PRINTED AND PUBLISHED BY D. DANIELS, SWANSEA.

INDEX

A

Aaronic Priesthood, 34
Abraham, 262
Abrahams, Levi, 177
absence, and affection, 112
Adam and Eve, 261
adversity, 75, 338
affection, 112
agriculture
    in Nebraska settlement, 289–90
    in Salt Lake City, 243, 266, 397–98
Ajax, William, 87–88, 175–76, 307
Alexander, Ambrose, 134
angel, in vision of John, 2
Angell, Truman O., 42, 52
apostasy, 323–24
apostates, 199, 293–96
Apostolic Decrees, 120–21
Ashby, Benjamin, 42, 86–87
Atonement, 75
Australia, 133–34

B

Babbitt, Almon W., 18–19, 162–63, 183–85, 186–87
balance sheets, 265–66
Baltic, 360
banks, run on American, 368, 370–73
baptism(s)
    in East Glamorgan Conference, 205
    rebaptism, 98, 101
    and reformation, 106

baptism(s) (*continued*)
    and tithing, 96, 100–101
Bay, John A., 360
beets, 151
Benson, Ezra T.
    calling of, 141
    farewell address of, 361–64
    leaves Great Britain, 360–61
    rebaptism of, 101
    and reformation, 61–62, 72, 81–85, 88–96, 99–100
    summary of teaching in Swansea Saints' Hall, 1–9, 27–30, 45–46
Bernhisel, John M., 379, 389–90
Bible
    Brigham Young on studying, 323
    credibility of Book of Mormon versus, 119–21, 123–28
    Ezra T. Benson on, 6
    LDS belief in, 312
    plural marriage in, 262–63
    tithing in, 33–34
biblical corruption, 124–25
Big Cottonwood Canal, 244
blessings
    of tithing, 37–39
    of Word of Wisdom, 198
body, of God, 259–60
book of Ether, 125–26
Book of Mormon, the
    credibility of Bible versus, 119–21, 123–28

INDEX

Book of Mormon, the (*continued*)
  Heresies and Deceptions of the Latter-day Saints, and the Book of Mormon, Exposed, 308–9, 311
Book of Nephi, 126–27
books, payments for, 283–84
Bowen, John, 288
Brecon Conference, 145, 168–69, 304, 313–14, 408
brother of Jared, 126
Buchanan, James, 188, 340
Buffalo, earthquake in, 391
Bulletin, 237
Bullock, Thomas, 185–88

C

California, 108–9, 203–4
Calkin, Asa, 348
Cannon, George Q., 133
Cape of Good Hope, South Africa, 135
Cardiff Conference, 169
Cardiganshire Conference, 223, 303–4, 408
Carmarthen Conference, 408
Carrying Company, 253
Catechism, Reformation, 295–96
Catholic Church, and biblical corruption, 124–25
Chadburn, England, 248, 252–53
chaff, 43, 359–60, 364–65
Cheyennes, 18, 161–63, 184–85, 203
children
  illegitimate, 354
  raising, 153, 234
children of God, 20–22
Chinese prostitution, 108–9
Christians, and will of God, 297–98
Church of England, 308, 375
Church of Jesus Christ of Latter-day Saints, The. *See also* gospel
  false news regarding, 164–68, 225–30, 257–61, 286–88
  growth of, 29, 248–49, 395–96
  Heresies and Deceptions of the Latter-day Saints, and the Book of Mormon, Exposed, 308–13

Church of Jesus Christ of Latter-day Saints, The (*continued*)
  and kingdom of God, 300
  leadership of, 243
  lies regarding, 56–57
  membership in, 113–18
  opposition to, 338
Civil War, 14, 276–77, 293
clothing, 398–99
Columbia, 48
commandment, tithing as, 35
conference houses, 252, 282
conference presidents
  appointments of, 408
  balance sheet instructions for, 265–66
  counsel for, 44–45
  duties of, 251
  general instructions to, 121–23
  and payment of tithing, 320
  to relay information to newspaper editors, 188
conferences
  appointments to, 408
  financial condition of, 377–79
conferences of the North, 206–8, 305–7, 336
confessing sins, 157
consecration, 2, 30
continuing revelation, 67, 123–24, 311–12
Conway Valley and Anglesey Conference, 408
Copenhagen conference, 135
cotton, 152
courts, federal, 182–83
Creation, 259–60
criminals, imprisonment of, 182
Cummings, Alfred, Governor, 277

D

Dafydd, Richard, 103
Daily Telegraph, 164–68
Daniel, 5, 321–24, 337
Daniels, Dafydd, 72
Daniels, Daniel, 69, 85–86, 91, 195, 223

Daniels, Mary, 209–11
Danites, 179–80, 294
Davenport, Mr., 228–29
Davies, Benjamin, 176, 222–23
Davies, Daniel, 89–90
Davies, John, 146, 195, 287, 301–3
Davis, John S., 190–91
Ddu, Nathan, 268–70
dedication of lands, 252–53
Defense pamphlet, 10
degrees of glory, 367, 382
"Departure of the Saints for Zion" (Jones), 111–12
Deseret Agricultural and Manufacturing Society, 188
Detroit, Michigan, 203
Drummond, William, Judge, 166–67, 177–89, 192, 227–29
drunkenness, 353, 373, 397

E

earthquake(s), 203, 391
Eastern Indians, 225
East Glamorgan Conference, 146, 169, 196–200, 205–6
East India, 135
economic crisis, 368–73
Edwards, John, 192
elders, general instructions to, 121–23
Eldredge, Horace S., 194
Eldredge, John S., 134
Elisha, 387
Ellis, Joseph, 164–68
emigration
    and building kingdom of God, 238
    counsel regarding, 49–50, 52–54, 134–35, 139–41, 278–81
    Dan Jones's letter detailing, 17–19, 142–43
    from Denmark, 135
    "Departure of the Saints for Zion," 111–12
    departures, 169, 264–65
    exhortation regarding, 233–36
    Ezra T. Benson on, 29–30, 362–63
    First Presidency's report on, 138–39

emigration *(continued)*
    Henry Harries on, 23, 163–64
    Hopkin Matthews's letter detailing, 191–92
    information regarding, 10–13, 250–51
    Israel Evans and, 68–69, 172–74
    John E. Jones on, 350–56
    and learning English, 190
    motivation for, 324
    news regarding, 42, 48, 54–58, 74, 80, 102–3
    pledges toward, 392–94, 400, 403–6, 407
    of poor, 384
    possibility of, 347–48
    route for, 194
    stations for, 194–95
    temporarily stopped, 331
emperors, 296–97
English language, 190
Enoch, 120
Ether, Book of, 125–26
Evans, Abraham, 191
Evans, Benjamin, 145, 200, 205–6
Evans, Hugh, 88, 307
Evans, Israel, 42, 68–71, 86, 172–74
Evans, Richard G., 266
Express Company, 271, 274, 315

F

faith, 7–8
family
    Ezra T. Benson on, 27
    keeping peace in, 103
    and temple blessings, 241–43
    and will of God, 300–301
famine, 203, 245–47, 370
Farnham, Elder, 134
fasting, 99, 238
fast meetings, 105
fault-finding, 130
federal courts, 182–83
"Few More Questions for Ministers to Answer, A," 262–63
financial crisis, 368–73

fire engine, 255
First Presidency, Fourteenth General
    Epistle of, 132–41, 146–56
first principles and ordinances of gospel,
    114–16
food, 38
fornication, 354–55
Fort Kearney, 18–19, 334–35, 336
Fourteenth General Epistle of the First
    Presidency, 132–41, 146–56

G

Gamwell, Elias, 219
Gamwell, James, 219
gathering of Israel, 138, 310. *See also*
    emigration
General Epistle of the First Presidency,
    Fourteenth, 132–41, 146–56
"General Instructions to Pastors,
    Presidents, and Elders," 121–23
Genoa City, Nebraska, 289–93
George Washington, 80, 172–74
Gilbert, Teressa, 317–18
Giles, Margaret, 236
Giles, Thomas, 236
glory, degrees of, 367, 382
God
    body of, 259–60
    children of, 20–22
    of Latter-day Saints, 261
    trust in, 7–8
    will of, 296–301
    worshipping, 2
Godhood, 260, 299
gospel. *See also* Church of Jesus Christ of
    Latter-day Saints, The
    constancy of, 395
    continuing in, 6–7
    first principles and ordinances of,
        114–16
    light-handedness in, 206–7
    living, 4–5
    receiving, 3–4
governments, worldly, 296–98
Graham, James, 134

grain, storing, 244–47, 397–400
grand juries, 182–83
Grant, George D., 53
Grant, Jedediah M., 104, 137
grasshoppers, 151, 249–50, 392
Great Britain
    judgment upon, 369–70, 373–74
    missionary work in, 136
    moral conditions in, 350–51, 353
    prophetic warning to inhabitants of,
        341–43
Great Salt Lake, 204
Griffiths, David John, 224
Griffiths, Joseph, 303–4, 408
Gunnison, John W., 183–84
Guy Manwaring, 24

H

hall rental, 123, 378
handcart companies
    counsel regarding, 49–50, 140
    met by S. W. Richards, 333–34
    news regarding, 48, 54–56, 57–58
    trials of, 53
handcarts, 139–40
Harries, Henry, 13, 22–24, 25, 161–64
Haven, Jesse, 135
Hawaii (Sandwich Islands), 133–34
Henry VIII, 308
*Heresies and Deceptions of the Latter-day Saints,
    and the Book of Mormon, Exposed*
    (Morrish), 308–13
Hickman, W. H., 193
Higinson, Elder, 220, 221
Holy Ghost
    and continuing revelation, 67
    Ezra T. Benson on, 3
    gift of, 261
    influence on man, 365–66
    and power of God, 105–6
    tithing and, 38–39
"Home Church Accounts," 145–56,
    301–4, 305–7
honesty, tithing and, 36–37
Hudson, Henry J., 289–91

humility, Saints called to, 50–51
Hyde, Orson, 141, 356–60, 364–67, 382–83

I

imprisonment, unjust, 182
Independence Day, 182
Independence Rock massacre, 186–87
India, 342–43, 373
Indians
    begin war against soldiers, 304
    kill troops sent to Utah, 264
    missionary work among, 209
    misunderstanding with, 161–62
    murders committed by, 183–87
    pioneers killed by, 162–63
    relations with, 18–19, 23, 149–50, 203
    S. W. Richards's dealings with, 335
"Invitation of a Saint to His Relations" (Thomas), 46–47
iron, 151
Isaac, Benjamin, 103
Israel
    gathering of, 138, 310
    and plural marriage, 262
    under prophets, 386–87

J

Jared, brother of, 126
Jenkins, Henry, 191
Jenkins, William, 210, 286
Jesus Christ
    "measure of the stature of the fullness of," 19–22, 64, 74–76
    premortal existence of, 21
    second coming of, 238–39
    teaches gospel in spirit prison, 382
    worshipping, 2
Job, 21–22
John, 2
John, David
    as leader, 88
    letter from, 174–75

John, David (*continued*)
    "Martyrdom of Parley P. Pratt," 239–40
    missionary efforts of, 307
    "My Dream," 76–80, 110–11
    "Success of the Kingdom of Christ," 318–20
Jones, Aneurin L., 111–12
Jones, Dan, 17–19, 74, 142–44, 204
Jones, David, 306
Jones, Dewi Elfed, 25, 129–32, 189, 197–98, 224, 267–68, 343–44
Jones, Edward, 19
Jones, John E.
    on Conferences of the North, 206–7, 305–7
    labors of, 408
    letter from, 175–76
    "Paying Tithing," 33–40
    reasons to support emigration, 350–56
    and reformation, 87–88, 90
Jones, Thomas, 175–76, 305–6
judging others, 130
judgment, 248–49, 369–70, 373–74
Julia Ann, 134–35
juries, 182–83

K

Kansas, 277
Kaye, John, 42, 360
keys, priesthood, 338–39
Kimball, Heber C.
    exploring expedition of, 210
    false news regarding, 229
    and Fourteenth General Epistle of the First Presidency, 132–41, 146–56
    teachings of, 241–48, 252–54, 383–84, 395–400
Kimball, Hiram, 193, 340–41
kingdom of God
    Brigham Young on, 337
    building, 196, 237–39

kingdom of God (*continued*)
   compared to fish net, 43
   progress of, 296–301
   restoration of, 374–76
   seeking, 3–4, 356–57
kings, 296–97
Kinney, J. T., 181, 184, 186
Knowlton, George W., 333

L

Lamanites, 127
land(s)
   dedicating, 252–53
   ownership as qualification for parliament, 353–54
latter days, 348–49, 369–77
Latter-Day Saint Psalmody, 64
latter-day work, 65–68
lazy priest, 317
Leader, 257–61
lead ore, 152
leather, 152
Lewis, Daniel, 306
liberality, 252
light-mindedness, 159
liquor, 16, 397. See also drunkenness
Little, James A., 52, 62–63, 101
Liverpool reformation meeting, 81–96, 97–102
Llanelli Conference, 222–23, 336, 408
locusts, 315
"Looking Glass, A" (Pratt), 113–18
Luminary, 136
Lunt, Henry, 42
Lyman, Amasa, 141, 274–75

M

mail
   contract for carrying, 193–94, 340–41
   duplication of, 153
   misunderstanding with Indians regarding, 161–62
   from Utah, 54
Margetts, Thomas, 18

Martill, T. C., 73
Martin handcart company, 53
"Martyrdom of Parley P. Pratt" (John), 239–40
materialism, 28
Matthews, Hopkin, 191–92
McLean, Eleanor J., 213–22, 236–37
McMullen, Fayette, 170
"Measure of the Stature of the Fulness of Christ, The" (Rees), 19–22, 64, 74–76
meddling, 130
Merioneth Conference, 408
Midianites, 262
military expedition, to Utah, 264, 315, 326–29, 334–36, 340, 361, 379, 388–91, 401–2
Millennial Star, 345–48
Miller, William, 13, 87, 146, 196–99, 205, 360
Minnesota, grasshoppers in, 249–50
missionaries and missionary work
   among Conferences of the North, 305–7
   arrival of, 25
   Brigham Young on, 51–52, 324
   calling of, 148, 209–10
   in Cardiganshire Conference, 303–4
   counsel to, 231–32
   of Dewi Elfed Jones, 343–44
   Ezra T. Benson on, 29
   First Presidency's report on, 133–36
   instructions regarding, 121–22
   pledges toward, 392–94, 400, 403–7
   and reformation, 94–95
   in spirit world, 382
   success of, 133
   in Wales, 170
   in West Glamorgan Conference, 301–2
money, spending, 28. See also economic crisis
Monmouthshire Conference, 145, 320, 408
moon, and degrees of glory, 367

Morgans, John, 176
Mormon, 136, 141, 171–72, 236–37, 331
Mormon army, volunteers for, 160
"Mormons and the Priests," 315–17
"Mormon sympathy," 91
Morrish, W. J., 308–13
Moses, 8
moving, 132
Musser, A. M., 42
"My Dream" (John), 76–80, 110–11

N

Nebraska, settlement of Saints in, 289–93
Nebuchadnezzar, 321–24, 337
Nephi, first book of, 126–27
Nephites, 127–28
New Orleans, 194
New Year, 14–15
New-York Tribune, 228–29
Noah, 114–17
Northern Conferences, 206–8, 305–7, 336
Nottingham, riot in, 384

O

obedience, 357–58
Ogden, Utah, 236
opposition, 75, 338
organ, 275

P

pamphlets
    circulation of, 331–32
    included with *Zion's Trumpet*, 204
    information regarding, 9–10, 40–42
    on Judge Drummond, 192
    sale of new, 144
    selling, 236
parliament, qualifications for, 353–54
Parry, Edward, Jr., 305–6
pastors, general instructions to, 121–23
peace, in family, 103
Penny Fund, 28, 30, 45–46, 122, 198, 265–66, 284–86
perfection, in living religion, 7

Perpetual Emigrating Fund Company, 10–11
persecution, 232, 302, 314–15, 324–26, 350, 398, 401
Phillips, Edward, 191
Plaindealer, 227–28
plural marriage, 247, 262–63, 292, 355
"Poem" (Jones), 267–68
poor, 30, 36, 137–38, 150, 353–54
Pope, 297–98
power of God, 105–6
Pratt, Addison, 134
Pratt, Orson
    calling of, 141
    Ezra T. Benson's obedience to, 83
    farewell address of, 344–45
    leaves Great Britain, 360–61
    on Penny Fund, 284–86
    "A Prophetic Warning to the Inhabitants of Great Britain," 341–43
    rebaptism of, 101
    and reformation, 59–61, 97–99, 100–102
    teachings of, 281–83
Pratt, Parley P.
    "A Looking Glass," 113–18
    calling of, 141
    death of, 213–24, 239–40, 274
premortal existence, 21
preparedness, 245–47, 376, 397–400
President of the United States, slander of, 182
Price, Edwin, 306
priesthood, 34, 45, 100, 338–39
priests, 315–18, 325–26, 354
progression, 7–8, 75, 299
prophecy, spirit of, 366–67
"Prophetic Warning to the Inhabitants of Great Britain, A" (Pratt), 341–43
prophets, 2–3, 249, 386–87, 395
prostitution, 108–9, 352, 373
Protestantism, 298
Punch, 317

Q

Quincy Whig, 229

R

Ray, John A., 63
rebaptism, 98, 101
Reed, L. H., 181
Rees, Dd., 197
Rees, Evan, 19–22, 64, 74–76
Rees, John E., 102–3
Rees, Rhys E., 103
Rees, Ruth, 13
Reese, Enoch, 266
reformation
    announcement for conference regarding, 72
    call for, 50–52
    Dan Jones on, 143
    David John reports on, 174–75
    Dewi Elfed Jones on, 129–32
    effects of, 170
    information regarding, 105–7
    Israel Evans on, 70
    minutes of meeting regarding, 58–63
    news regarding, 42–45, 47, 57, 188
    repentance and, 156–59
    report of conference regarding, 81–96, 97–102
    Richard Williams on, 74
    taught in Cardiganshire Conference, 223
    and tithing, 146
    William Miller on, 198–99
Reformation Catechism, 295–96
repentance, 131, 156–59, 342
resurrection, 75
revelation
    and biblical corruption, 124–25
    continuing, 67, 123–24, 311–12
    keys of, 337
Rich, Charles C., 141, 274–75
Richards, Evan, 200
Richards, Franklin D., 141, 200–202
Richards, Samuel Whitney, 326, 332–36, 345–47
right, doing, 244
righteous principles, practicing, 357–59
riot, in Nottingham, 384
Robinson, Lewis, 333
Rockwell, Orrin Porter, 193
Roskelley, Samuel, 13, 25, 146, 169, 197, 205

S

Sabbath School, 272
St. Louis, 194
St. Louis Company, 380
Salt Lake City. *See also* Utah
    conditions in, 397–98
    false news regarding, 287–88
    letters from, 72–74, 142–44, 190–92, 209–12
    news from, 47–48, 146–47, 200–203, 266, 273–74, 320
    progress in, 254–55
Salt Lake Temple, 241, 242, 254–55, 275–76
salvation, 41–42, 176
Samuel, 262–63
San Bernardino, California, 203, 274–75
Sandwich Islands, 133–34
Satan, 131
Saunders Curling, 68–69
Scandinavian Mission, 170
Scott, John, 360
scurvy, 336
Second Coming, 238–39
settlements, 42, 234
Shaver, Leonidas, 181, 183–84, 187
signs of the times, 348–49, 369–77
sin, 156–59
slander, 157–59
Smith, George A., 141, 275, 380
Smith, Hyrum, 384
Smith, John L., 361
Smith, Joseph
    Daily Telegraph on, 165
    death of, 339
    Ezra T. Benson's testimony of, 363–64

Smith, Joseph (*continued*)
    foresees Civil War, 14
    Heber C. Kimball's testimony of, 383–84
    influence of, 248
    keys held by, 337
    mission of, as fulfillment of ancient prophecies, 67
    prophecy regarding, 299–300
Smith, Leonard I., 135
Smith, Samuel, 339
Snow, Erastus, 136, 141
Snow, Lorenzo, 141
Snow, Z., 181
Snyder, George G., 333, 348, 361
Society Islands, 134
"Song of Noah," 15–16
South Africa, 135
Spaulding tale, 309
speculators, 325–26
Spencer, Orson, 136–37
spirit of the times, 385–86
spirits
    of organizations, 365–66
    premortal existence of, 21–22
spiritual progression, 7–8, 75, 299
spirit world, 367, 382
stars
    beings compared to, 21–22
    and degrees of glory, 367
State Fair, 153
statistical report(s), 31
Stiles, George P., 181
storehouses, 244–47, 397–98
straw, 359–60, 364–65
Stringham, Bryant, 333
"Success of the Kingdom of Christ" (John), 318–20
sugar, 151
"Summer Song" (Ddu), 268–70
sun, and degrees of glory, 367
Sunday School, 272
Sutherland, William B., 317–18
Syrians, 387

T

Taylor, James, 13, 87, 141, 145, 206–8
temperance, 27–28
temples
    blessings of, 241–43
    Ezra T. Benson on, 28–29
    and Second Coming, 238–39
    tithing and, 314
temporal matters, receiving guidance in, 116–18
Thomas, Benjamin, 211
Thomas, John, 145, 168–69, 304
Thomas, Mary, 211–12
Thomas, Thomas F., 46–47
Thomas, William P., 210–12, 266
tithing
    and baptism, 96, 100–101
    and building kingdom of God, 238
    Ezra T. Benson on, 28–29, 90
    instructions regarding, 320
    Israel Evans on, 69–70
    liberality and, 252
    nonpayment of, 44, 314
    Orson Pratt on, 281–83
    paying, 33–40
    and reformation, 132, 146
    regulation of, 98, 377–79
    requirements beyond, 26–27
"To Drummond and His Company" (Jones), 189
Treharne, John, 88, 307
trials, 75, 338
True Repentance, 10
Tuckfield, Joseph W., 303

U

United States
    admission of Utah into, 107–10, 147
    agitation against Utah, 275, 326–30, 380–81, 385–86, 397
    civil war in, 14, 276–77, 293
    and government of Utah, 186
    John E. Rees's letter from, 102–3
    judgment upon, 369–70
    president of, 73, 182
    run on banks in, 368, 370–73

Utah. *See also* Salt Lake City
  apostates flying from, 293–96
  conditions in, 153–54
  Daily Telegraph on, 165–67
  exhortation regarding, 233–36
  false news regarding, 225–30
  government of, 186
  governorship of, 170–72
  Judge Drummond on, 177–85
  mail from, 54
  manufacturing and advancements in, 151–53
  military expedition to, 264, 315, 334–36, 340, 361, 379, 388–91, 401–2
  news from, 42, 47–48, 80, 146–47, 188–89, 270–71, 326–30, 379–81
  order of heaven and will of God in, 298–99
  positive aspects of, 355–56
  Rice Williams's letter from, 72–74
  Sabbath School of, 272
  statehood of, 107–10, 147
  US agitation against, 275, 326–30, 380–81, 385–86, 397

V

Van Vliet, Stewart, Captain, 379–80, 387–88, 391
"Verses" (Jones), 224

W

Walker, William, 135
Wandell, C. W., 119–21
war, 14
waste, 35
Water Baptism pamphlet, 9
Welsh Herald, 286–88
Western Standard, 133
West Glamorgan Conference, 146, 195–96, 301–3
Westmoreland, 169
wheat
  Church members compared to, 359–60, 364–65
  separation of chaff and, 43

Whittall, Henry, 347
whorehouses, 352
Williams, Abednego, 146, 196
Williams, Anne, 191
Williams, Rice, 72–74
Williams, Robert, 306
Willie handcart company, 53
will of God, 296–301
wolves, 211
Woodruff, Wilford, 141, 274–76
Word of Wisdom
  blessings of, 198
  Ezra T. Benson on, 27–28, 89
  kept by Daniel, 5
  observance of, 368
  and reformation, 106–7, 130–31
work, 37, 94, 236
works, 41–42
world news, 286

Y

Young, Brigham
  accounts of movements of, 203
  accusations against, 315, 339–40
  Daily Telegraph on, 165–68
  exploring expedition of, 210, 227
  false news regarding, 226
  and Fourteenth General Epistle of the First Presidency, 132–41, 146–56
  gives instructions regarding emigration, 11–12
  Heber C. Kimball on, 327–28
  Judge Drummond on, 178–83
  as leader, 376
  letters from, 49–54, 193–95, 270–71, 273–74, 379–80
  proclamation of, 401–2
  teaching of, 321–26, 337–41
Young, W. G., 101

Z

zeal, 6–7
Zion's Trumpet, 284, 332, 406–7